PROCESS MAP SYMBOLS

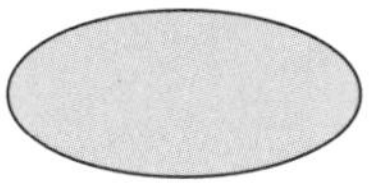

An oval is used to show the start and/or finish of a process. The start is usually the input of the business process, and the finish is the output. The input and output may be materials, activities, or information.

A rectangle shows a task or activity in the process. Typically, only one arrow comes out of a rectangle (one output). However, many arrows can come into a rectangle (inputs).

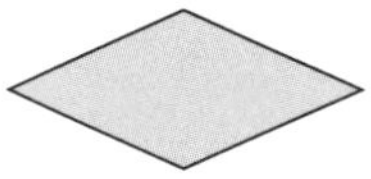

A diamond represents a point in the process when a decision must be made. In many cases the decision is a yes/no decision, but not always.

An arrow shows the direction of flow within the process.

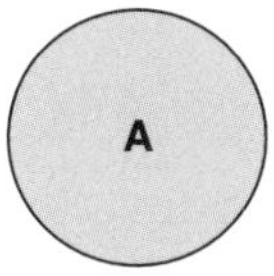

A circle with a letter or number inside is used as a connector. A connector is used when there is a break in the process. The connector is used at the beginning of the break in the process, and again where the process resumes.

DATA FLOW DIAGRAM SYMBOLS

A square is a terminator. It represents both sources and destinations of data.

A rectangle with rounded corners represents a process. Any tasks or functions performed are depicted by this rectangle.

An open-ended rectangle is a data store or the storage of data. Storage could be in manual records or computer files.

An arrow shows the direction of flow of data.

ACCOUNTING INFORMATION SYSTEMS

Controls and Processes

LESLIE TURNER

ANDREA WEICKGENANNT

WILEY

John Wiley & Sons, Inc.

Leslie Turner—
To my parents and the many students who have inspired and motivated my work.

Andrea Weickgenannt
To Les for the stimulus to this project. To my family for their support.

PUBLISHER	Don Fowley
ASSOCIATE PUBLISHER	Christopher DeJohn
PROJECT EDITOR	Ed Brislin
SENIOR MARKETING MANAGER	Julia Flohr
EXECUTIVE MARKETING MANAGER	Amy Scholz
CREATIVE DIRECTOR	Harry Nolan
DESIGNER	Hope Miller
SENIOR PRODUCTION EDITOR	Trish McFadden
EDITORIAL ASSISTANT	Kathryn Fraser
MARKETING ASSISTANT	Carly DeCardia
SENIOR MEDIA EDITOR	Allison Morris

This book was set in 10/12 by Aptara, Inc. and printed and bound by Quebecor World Versailles. The cover was printed by Quebecor World Versailles.

This book is printed on acid-free paper. ∞

To order books or for customer service, please call 1-800-CALL WILEY (225-5945).

ISBN-13 9780471479512

Printed in the United States of America

10 9 8 7 6 5 4 3 2 1

About the Authors

Leslie D. Turner is a Professor and the Chair of the Department of Accountancy at Northern Kentucky University. He has taught at Northern Kentucky University since 1988. He earned a DBA in Accounting from the University of Kentucky, an MBA from Wheeling Jesuit University, and a BBA in Accounting from Ohio University. Dr. Turner is a Certified Management Accountant (CMA) and a Certified Financial Manager (CFM).

Professor Turner's research interests are in internal controls and Sarbanes-Oxley compliance, educational pedagogy, and ethics. His research has been published in *Accounting Horizons*, *Journal of Accounting and Public Policy*, *Journal of Internet Commerce*, *Journal of Information Systems*, *Management Accounting*, *The Review of Accounting Information Systems*, *The Journal of Management Accounting Research*, *Strategic Finance*, The *CPCU Journal*, *National Accounting Journal*, The *Oil and Gas Tax Quarterly*, *Accounting Systems Journal*, and the *Journal of Accounting Case Research*.

Professor Turner is a member of the American Accounting Association, the Institute of Management Accountants, and the Information Systems Audit and Control Association.

Andrea B. Weickgenannt is an Assistant Professor of Accountancy at Northern Kentucky University. She holds an MBA from the University of Maryland and a BBA from the University of Cincinnati. She is a Certified Public Accountant (CPA) and has over 13 years of experience with Ernst & Young LLP (Cincinnati and Baltimore).

Professor Weickgenannt's research interests are in the areas of accounting information systems, financial accounting, auditing, and ethics. Her research has been published in the *National Accounting Journal, Journal of Accounting Case Research, Critical Perspectives on Accounting,* and the *Journal of College Teaching & Learning.*

Professor Weickgenannt is a member of the American Accounting Association, American Institute of Certified Public Accountants, and the Ohio Society of Certified Public Accountants.

Preface

INSTRUCTOR

OVERVIEW

Each of us who teaches Accounting Information Systems faces the problem of providing students a comprehensive, but interesting knowledge base of AIS. However, we all know that it is difficult to find the right balance of coverage of technical concepts and student comprehension. When addressing this issue of balance, we began to see clearly that a better, more comprehensible approach was needed. With this book, we have achieved a good balance of covering technical concepts while still making the text easy to read and understand. Our textbook also reinforces AIS concepts with relevant, real-world examples and reasonable end-of-chapter materials.

This text incorporates the important content found in a typical Accounting Information System course, but has four distinguishing characteristics. Four characteristics we focus on throughout the text are simplicity and understandability of the writing, business processes, accounting and IT controls, and ethics as it relates to accounting systems.

We place extra emphasis on the students' understanding. We explain AIS in the context of business processes and incorporate many real-world examples. The richness of these examples improves the text, the discussion questions, and end-of-chapter exercises and cases. We explain IT controls by employing the framework in the AICPA Trust Services Principles. This is an encompassing, but easy to understand, framework of IT controls. Finally, we believe that ethics continues to increase in importance as a topic to be included in accounting texts. We have included an ethics section in each chapter.

We think that including all these characteristics in a single text has resulted in an extremely user-friendly product: one that will help your students achieve a better foundation in accounting information systems.

FEATURES

The book is designed to enhance student learning with a focus on ease of use, business processes and the related controls, and ethics and corporate governance as they relate to accounting information systems.

EASE OF USE

This AIS textbook will allow students to easily read and comprehend the material, understand the charts and graphs and successfully answer questions and cases at the end of the chapters. To accomplish ease of use, we included several features, including the following:

- **An approach to technical topics with a writing style that is easy to understand.**
- **Process maps and document flowcharts that provide a picture of business processes and are easy to understand.** While there are several approaches to charts that depict systems, we have used the types of charts that illustrate business processes in the simplest, yet complete manner. Especially in the chapters focused on business processes, we use matched process maps, document flowcharts, and data flow diagrams to illustrate the processes that occur, and the related flow of information and documents. These charts are easy to follow and they will enhance understanding of the business processes.
- **AICPA Trust Services Principles framework for IT controls.** Controls within Information Technology can be a very difficult subject to comprehend because of the underlying complexity of the technology. While COBIT is the most comprehensive source of IT control information, it is not typically easy for students to understand. This is especially true for students who have not had the opportunity to gain work experience with IT systems and business processes. We use the simplest framework available for the explanation of IT controls: the AICPA Trust Services Principles. The Trust Services Principles categorize IT Controls into five areas: security, availability, processing integrity, online privacy, and confidentiality.
- **Control and risk tables that summarize internal controls and the related risks.** Internal controls are easier to understand when students can see the corresponding types of risks that the controls are intended to lessen. We use control/risk exhibits to present risks that are reduced when controls are used.
- **Real-world examples to illustrate important concepts.** Concepts are often easier to comprehend when presented in a real-world scenario. Each chapter includes examples of issues faced by actual business organizations that help illustrate the nature and importance of concepts in the chapter. Real world discussions are boxed in a feature titled "The Real World."
- **Microsoft Dynamics GP® screen shots to present topics in the context of a real computer system.** New concepts are often easier for students to understand while presented within a real-life application. We use screen shots from Microsoft Dynamics GP® software to show how various aspects of business processes would appear in this computer system.
- **End-of-chapter questions, problems, and cases that match well with the chapter content.** It is important to provide material at the end of each chapter that helps students reinforce the topics presented. It is equally important that this material be relevant and understandable. We have devoted our attention to providing a variety of end-of-chapter activities that are meaningful and manageable, including a concept check, discussion questions,

brief exercises, web exercises, problems, cases, and a continuing case. Topics are also reinforced with a continuing case that runs throughout all chapters, **Spatelli's Pizzeria.** In addition, most chapters include activities adapted from professional (CPA, CMA, and CIA) examinations.

BUSINESS PROCESSES, ACCOUNTING CONTROLS, AND IT CONTROLS

Business transactions are portrayed within the text in terms of business processes, which are widely recognized throughout the accounting profession. These business processes are described in a manner that is applicable to many different business environments.

We incorporate the COSO framework and integrate discussions of risks and controls in all business process chapters. These discussions are also carried out in as many of the other chapters as possible. The COSO framework, especially the control procedure component, is used as a framework to describe accounting controls. This continued use of the framework across several chapters is intended to increase student understanding and retention of risk and control concepts.

In addition, we place a strong emphasis on IT controls. We accomplish this by using the guidance provided by the AICPA in the revised (2006) Trust Services Principles for WebTrust® and SysTrust® assurance engagements. The Trust Services Principles are the AICPA's guidance that is closely related to COBIT.

The Trust Services Principles risk and control procedures are incorporated into the chapters covering business processes and controls. These controls are also discussed in chapters on databases, ERP systems, auditing IT systems, and the system development life cycle.

ETHICS AND CORPORATE GOVERNANCE

It is indisputable within the business world that honest, consistent reporting and management of information has never been more important. Considering the increased responsibility on corporate managers for the overall financial reporting of the company, the study and use of accounting information systems is critical. Accordingly, business ethics and corporate governance continue to increase in focus and we made them a focus of this textbook. An ethics discussion is also found at the end of each chapter and an ethics icon highlights applicable end-of-chapter material.

In order to place emphasis on business ethics in many chapters, it is important to establish a foundation of ethics to build upon. Chapter 3 includes a significant section on ethics in the current environment and the relation of ethical problems to the need for internal controls and ethics codes. We establish Chapter 3 as the foundation for the chapters that follow. The ethics and control concepts in Chapter 3 are reinforced as themes throughout the text. We also include ethics-related questions or cases in the end-of-chapter materials.

In addition to business ethics, corporate governance is a related topic that has received much attention in the business world without a corresponding increase in focus by AIS texts. Chapter 5 in this text is devoted to corporate governance topics and the Sarbanes–Oxley Act of 2002 as they relate to accounting information systems. In addition, each process chapter in Module 3 discusses corporate governance in its application to the various business processes. Sarbanes–Oxley discussions are highlighted in the textbook margins with the letters "SOX."

SUPPLEMENTS

A **solutions manual, solutions to Spatelli's Pizzeria continuing case, test bank, computerized test bank, instructor outlines,** and **PowerPoint** presentations accompany this textbook. They are available on the instructor companion site available with this textbook. The authors would like to thank Patricia Fedje, Minot State University, Yvonne Phang, Borough of Manhattan Community College, and Coby Harmon, University of California–Santa Barbara for their help in developing the test bank and PowerPoint presentations.

Modeling and Designing Accounting Systems, Using Access to Build a Database, by C. Janie Chang and Laura R. Ingraham. This supplement helps students understand data modeling from an **REA** perspective, as well as its application and ultimate implementation in database design.

Acknowledgments

We would like to thank every instructor whose feedback helped us in all stages of the writing, editing, and production of this textbook. In particular, we thank Amelia Baldwin, University of Alabama; Somnath Bhattacharya, Florida Atlantic University; Pascal A. Bizzaro, University of Mississippi; Richard Dull, Clemson University; John Butler, Ohio State University; Stephanie Farewell, University of Arkansas—Little Rock; Lawrence Grasso, Central Connecticut State University; Neal Hannon, University of Hartford; Michael Harkness, University of Michigan—Dearborn; Kenneth Henry, Florida International University; Frank Ilett, Boise State University; Jack Kissinger, Saint Louis University; David Knight, Borough of Manhattan Community College; Antoinette Lynch, Miami University; Dorothy McMullen, Rider University; Johna Murray, University of Missouri—St. Louis; Michael Palley, Baruch College; Karen Otto, University of Arizona; Tom Oxner, University of Central Arkansas; Jeffery Payne, University of Kentucky; Georgia Smedley, University of Nevada—Las Vegas; George Schmelzle, Indiana University—Purdue University Fort Wayne; Wallace Wood, University of Cincinnati; Curt Westbook, California State University—San Bernadino; and Yan Xiong, California State University—Sacramento.

Student

Businesses, and the products and services they provide, are unquestionably a critically important part of our society. We would not have food, shelter, cars, computers, iPods, or the other things we need and use every day without smoothly functioning businesses to provide those goods and services. Likewise, individual businesses could not operate at a level to sustain our society without accounting information. Accounting information is the lifeblood of business. Without the regular flow of accurate accounting information to managers and investors, businesses would collapse. Operating a business or investing in businesses without accounting information would be as difficult as driving with a covered windshield. You would have no feedback information about where you are going and what corrections you must make to get there. Just as your view through the windshield tells you when to make steering, braking, and accelerating corrections, accounting information allows managers and investors to determine how to make corrections that will allow them to achieve business objectives.

Accountants generate, evaluate, summarize, report, and confirm the information that managers and investors need to make good choices in their operations or objectives. The system that allows accountants to accomplish this is the accounting information system.

The study of AIS provides a very important set of concepts to prepare you for an accounting and business career. We hope the features of this book make your study of AIS a little more pleasant, interesting, and understandable. Now, go forward and learn more about AIS and its role in providing critical information to managers and investors!

A List of Real World Examples in This Textbook

Chapter	Company Example	Subject
1	Hardee's and McDonald's remote order taking at drive-throughs	Business processes
1	McDonald's and a dedicated supplier of buns, East Balt	Supply chain
1	Ford and its reengineered vendor payment system	Business process reengineering
1	Anonymous company that inflated revenues	Ethics
2	Medieval Times updated drink ordering system	Business processes
2	Bowen Workforce Solutions and implementing a new system	Legacy systems
2	Cole Haan, a subsidiary of Nike and system integration	Legacy systems
2	Hobie Cat Company and the purchase of an e-commerce module	Accounting software
3	Phar-Mor fraud	Top management ethics
3	Association of Certified Fraud Examiners and fraud statistics	Fraud
3	Enron and its demise	Fraud
3	Xerox GAAP violations	Fraud
3	Dow Chemical's warning signs of fraud	Fraud
3	Data Processors International and access to its database	Hackers
3	Denial of service attacks at Yahoo, eBay, Amazon.com	Hackers
3	Ethical conduct in corporations	Code of ethics
4	ShadowCrew hacker gang's illegal activities	Hackers
4	2003 North American power blackout	Disaster recovery
4	Martha Stewart Living Omnimedia	Business continuity
4	Microsoft Windows operating system	Hackers
4	Pornography on State of Kentucky Transportation Cabinet computers	Fraud
5	Procter & Gamble awarded "Best Corporate Citizen"	Corporate governance
5	EMC Corporation's corporate governance guidelines	Corporate governance
5	Poor corporate governance at Enron and WorldCom	Corporate governance
5	Sarbanes Oxley compliance and Guidant Corporation	Sarbanes–Oxley
5	Web delivery of ethics training at Dow and BASF	Ethics
5	Downsizing and ethics at Motorola	Ethics
6	Information and technology strategy committee at UPS	IT governance
6	Prioritizing IT projects at Allstate	IT governance
6	Anheuser Busch's use of IT to improve beer sales	IT governance
7	Aurafin Corporation, a jewelry supplier to JCPenney and Walmart	IT audit benefits
7	Use of CAATs at Ernst & Young LLP	IT audit
7	Audit mistakes at Phar-Mor	Auditor independence
7	Crazy Eddie's fraud	Auditor independence
7	Enron, WorldCom, and Xerox and the need to test balances	Substantive testing
8	Sales processes performance measures at Staples	Sales processes
8	Internet sales processes at Staples	Sales processes

8	Internet EDI at Nortel	Internet EDI
8	Advantages of a POS system at Pizza Hut	POS systems
8	Fraud at MiniScribe	Fraud
8	Sales misstatements at Sunbeam	Fraud
8	Sales misstatements at HealthSouth	Fraud
9	General Electric's electronic invoice presentment system	IT enablement of purchasing
9	Frymaster's automated invoice matching system	IT enablement of purchasing
9	Evaluated receipt settlement system at an anonymous company	IT enablement of purchasing
9	General Electric's procurement card use	Business process reengineering
9	Special checking account used at Phar-Mor	Fraud
9	Multiple instances of fraud by Paul Pigeon	Fraud
9	Wal-Mart's ethics guidelines for employees in purchasing	Ethics
10	Prince George's County payroll problems with ERP	Payroll processes
10	Automated payroll system at Scott Paper Company	IT enablement of payroll
10	WorldCom's misclassification of fixed asset purchases	Fraud
10	Adelphia's poor corporate governance related to fixed assets	Corporate governance
11	Nissan's robotic plant	IT enablement of manufacturing
11	CAD in the manufacturing process at Jean Larrivée Guitars	IT enablement of manufacturing
11	CAD/CAM at Wild West Motorcycle Company	IT enablement of manufacturing
11	Wal-Mart's sophisticated database	IT enablement of logistics
11	Fraud in conversion processes at F&C Flavors	Fraud
12	Typical timing of month-end closing processes	Administrative processes
12	Integration of systems into general ledger at Toyota	Administrative processes
12	Fraud in administrative processes at echapman.com	Fraud
12	Automated authorization at Wal-Mart	Administrative processes
12	Authorization from vendors at Wal-Mart	Administrative processes
12	Automatic triggering in ERP systems	Administrative processes
12	Misleading data for investors at Krispy Kreme	Ethics
13	Large database at Wal-Mart	Databases
13	High impact processes at Anheuser-Busch and Hewlett Packard	High impact processes
13	Data mining at Anheuser-Busch	Data mining
13	Distributed databases at McDonald's	Distributed data
13	Theft of data at Bloodstock	Ethics
14	Wal-Mart's change to Internet EDI	Internet EDI
14	E-business at General Electric	E-business
14	E-business at General Motors	E-business
14	E-business at Komatsu	E-business
14	E-business at Kenworth Truck Company	E-business
14	E-business at Staples	E-business
14	Extranet use at Staples	Extranet
14	Abuse of private information at Gateway Learning Corporation	Ethics
15	Advantages of an ERP system at Agri-Beef Company	ERP
15	Advantages of an ERP system at Viper Motorcycle Company	ERP
15	Failed ERP implementation at the city of Tacoma, Washington	ERP implementation
15	Successful ERP implementation at Marathon	ERP implementation

Brief Contents

MODULE 1 INTRODUCTION

CHAPTER 1 Introduction to AIS 1

CHAPTER 2 Foundational Concepts of the AIS (Including an REA Appendix) 39

MODULE 2 CONTROL ENVIRONMENT

CHAPTER 3 Fraud, Ethics, and Internal Control 77

CHAPTER 4 Internal Controls and Risks in IT Systems 119

CHAPTER 5 Corporate Governance and the Sarbanes-Oxley Act 169

CHAPTER 6 IT Governance 201

CHAPTER 7 Auditing Information Technology-Based Processes 241

MODULE 3 BUSINESS PROCESSES

CHAPTER 8 Revenue and Cash Collection Processes and Controls 283

CHAPTER 9 Expenditures Processes and Controls—Purchases 347

CHAPTER 10 Expenditures Processes and Controls—Payroll and Fixed Assets 409

CHAPTER 11 Conversion Processes and Controls 457

CHAPTER 12 Administrative Processes and Controls 493

MODULE 4 IT INFRASTRUCTURE TO ENABLE PROCESSES

CHAPTER 13 Data and Databases 525

CHAPTER 14 E-Commerce and E-Business 559

CHAPTER 15 IT Infrastructure for E-Business 597

Index 629

Contents

MODULE 1 **INTRODUCTION** Defines business processes, AIS, and all foundational concepts. This module provides the knowledge building blocks to support the remaining chapters.

CHAPTER 1

Introduction to AIS 1

Overview of Business Processes 2
Overview of an Accounting Information System 4
Business Process Linkage Throughout the Supply Chain 6
IT Enablement of Business Processes 8
Basic Computer and IT Concepts 10
- BASIC COMPUTER DATA STRUCTURES 11
- FILE ACCESS AND PROCESSING MODES 12
- DATA WAREHOUSE AND DATA MINING 13
- NETWORKS AND THE INTERNET 14

Examples of IT Enablement 15
- E-BUSINESS 15
- ELECTRONIC DATA INTERCHANGE 15
- POINT OF SALE SYSTEM 15
- AUTOMATED MATCHING 16
- EVALUATED RECEIPT SETTLEMENT 16
- E-PAYABLES AND ELECTRONIC INVOICE PRESENTMENT AND PAYMENT 16
- ENTERPRISE RESOURCE PLANNING SYSTEMS 16

The Internal Control Structure of Organizations 17
- ENTERPRISE RISK MANAGEMENT 18
- A CODE OF ETHICS 20
- COSO ACCOUNTING INTERNAL CONTROL STRUCTURE 20
- IT CONTROLS 20
- CORPORATE GOVERNANCE 20
- IT GOVERNANCE 21

The Importance of Accounting Information Systems to Accountants 22
- USERS OF THE AIS 22
- DESIGN OR IMPLEMENTATION TEAM 22
- AN AUDITOR OF THE AIS 22

The Relation of Ethics to Accounting Information Systems 22
Summary of Study Objectives 24
Key Terms 25
End of Chapter Material 26
- CONCEPT CHECK 26
- DISCUSSION QUESTIONS 27
- BRIEF EXERCISES 28
- PROBLEMS 29
- CASES 31
- CONTINUING CASE: SPATELLI'S PIZZERIA 32
- SOLUTIONS TO CONCEPT CHECK 37

CHAPTER 2

Foundational Concepts of the AIS 39

Interrelationships of Business Processes and the AIS 41
Types of Accounting Information Systems 43
- MANUAL SYSTEMS 43
- LEGACY SYSTEMS 44
- MODERN, INTEGRATED SYSTEMS 47

Accounting Software Market Segments 48
Input Methods Used in Business Processes 50
- SOURCE DOCUMENTS AND KEYING 50
- BAR CODES 50
- POINT OF SALE SYSTEMS 51
- ELECTRONIC DATA INTERCHANGE 52
- E-BUSINESS AND E-COMMERCE 52

Processing Accounting Data 52
BATCH PROCESSING 53
ONLINE AND REAL-TIME PROCESSING 54
Outputs from the AIS Related to Business Processes 55
Documenting Processes and Systems 55
PROCESS MAPS 56
SYSTEM FLOWCHARTS 57
DOCUMENT FLOWCHARTS 59
DATA FLOW DIAGRAMS 60
ENTITY RELATIONSHIP DIAGRAMS 62
Client-Server Computing 63
Ethical Considerations at the Foundation of Accounting Information Systems 65
Summary of Study Objectives 66
Key Terms 67
Appendix: Resources Events Agents (REA) in Accounting Information Systems 67
End of Chapter Material 69
CONCEPT CHECK 69
DISCUSSION QUESTIONS 71
BRIEF EXERCISES 72
PROBLEMS 73
CASES 74
CONTINUING CASE: SPATELLI'S PIZZERIA 75
SOLUTIONS TO CONCEPT CHECK 75

MODULE 2 CONTROL ENVIRONMENT Describes the proper control environment to oversee and control processes.

CHAPTER 3
Fraud, Ethics, and Internal Control 77

Introduction to the Need for a Code of Ethics and Internal Controls 78
Accounting Related Fraud 80
CATEGORIES OF ACCOUNTING-RELATED FRAUD 82
The Nature of Management Fraud 82
The Nature of Employee Fraud 84
The Nature of Customer Fraud 86
The Nature of Vendor Fraud 86
The Nature of Computer Fraud 86
INTERNAL SOURCES OF COMPUTER FRAUD 87
EXTERNAL SOURCES OF COMPUTER FRAUD 87
Policies to Assist in the Avoidance of Fraud and Errors 89
Maintenance of a Code Of Ethics 89
Maintenance of Accounting Internal Controls 90
THE DETAILS OF THE COSO REPORT 92
REASONABLE ASSURANCE OF INTERNAL CONTROLS 100
Maintenance of Information Technology Controls 101
Summary of Study Objectives 103
Key Terms 105
Appendix A: Recent History of Internal Control Standards 105
Appendix B: Control Objectives for Information Technology (COBIT) 106
End of Chapter Material 108
CONCEPT CHECK 108
DISCUSSION QUESTIONS 110
BRIEF EXERCISES 111
PROBLEMS 111
CASES 113
CONTINUING CASE: SPATELLI'S PIZZERIA 116
SOLUTIONS TO CONCEPT CHECK 116

CHAPTER 4
Internal Controls and Risks in IT Systems 119

An Overview of Internal Controls for IT Systems 120
General Controls for IT Systems 122
AUTHENTICATION OF USERS AND LIMITING UNAUTHORIZED USERS 123
HACKING AND OTHER NETWORK BREAK-INS 125
ORGANIZATIONAL STRUCTURE 128
PHYSICAL ENVIRONMENT AND SECURITY 129
BUSINESS CONTINUITY 131
General Controls from an AICPA Trust Services Principles Perspective 132
RISKS IN NOT LIMITING UNAUTHORIZED USERS 133
RISKS FROM HACKING OR OTHER NETWORK BREAK-INS 136
RISKS FROM ENVIRONMENTAL FACTORS 136
PHYSICAL ACCESS RISKS 137
BUSINESS CONTINUITY RISKS 137
Hardware and Software Exposures in IT Systems 137
THE OPERATING SYSTEM 139
THE DATABASE 141
THE DATABASE MANAGEMENT SYSTEM 142
LANS AND WANS 143
WIRELESS NETWORKS 143

THE INTERNET AND WORLD WIDE WEB 144
TELECOMMUTING WORKERS 144
ELECTRONIC DATA INTERCHANGE 145

Application Software and Application Controls 145
INPUT CONTROLS 146
PROCESSING CONTROLS 152
OUTPUT CONTROLS 153

Ethical Issues in IT Systems 154

Summary of Study Objectives 155

Key Terms 156

End of Chapter Material 157
CONCEPT CHECK 157
DISCUSSION QUESTIONS 159
BRIEF EXERCISES 160
PROBLEMS 161
CASES 163
CONTINUING CASE: SPATELLI'S PIZZERIA 164
SOLUTIONS TO CONCEPT CHECK 164

CHAPTER 5

Corporate Governance and the Sarbanes-Oxley Act 169

An Overview of Corporate Governance 170

Participants in the Corporate Governance Process 171

Functions within the Corporate Governance Process 175
MANAGEMENT OVERSIGHT 175
INTERNAL CONTROLS AND COMPLIANCE 176
FINANCIAL STEWARDSHIP 178
ETHICAL CONDUCT 179

The History of Corporate Governance 179

The Sarbanes–Oxley Act of 2002 180

The Impact of the Sarbanes–Oxley Act on Corporate Governance 186

The Importance of Corporate Governance in the Study of Accounting Information Systems 189

Ethics and Corporate Governance 190

Summary of Study Objectives 192

Key Terms 193

End of Chapter Material 194
CONCEPT CHECK 194
DISCUSSION QUESTIONS 196
BRIEF EXERCISES 197
PROBLEMS 197
CASES 198
CONTINUING CASE: SPATELLI'S PIZZERIA 198
SOLUTIONS TO CONCEPT CHECK 198

CHAPTER 6

IT Governance 201

Introduction to IT Governance 202

An Overview of the SDLC 206

Elements of the Systems Planning Phase of the SDLC 209
THE MATCH OF IT SYSTEMS TO STRATEGIC OBJECTIVES 210
FEASIBILITY STUDY 211
PLANNING AND OVERSIGHT OF THE PROPOSED CHANGES 212

Elements of the Systems Analysis Phase of the SDLC 212
SYSTEM SURVEY: THE STUDY OF THE CURRENT SYSTEM 213
DETERMINATION OF USER REQUIREMENTS 214
ANALYSIS OF THE SYSTEM SURVEY 215

Elements of the Systems Design Phase of the SDLC 216
IN-HOUSE DESIGN 218
CONCEPTUAL DESIGN 219
EVALUATION AND SELECTION 220
DETAILED DESIGN 222

Elements of the Systems Implementation Phase of the SDLC 224
SOFTWARE PROGRAMMING 224
TRAINING EMPLOYEES 224
SOFTWARE TESTING 224
DOCUMENTING THE SYSTEM 225
DATA CONVERSION 226
SYSTEM CONVERSION 226
USER ACCEPTANCE 227
POST-IMPLEMENTATION REVIEW 227

Elements of the Operation and Maintenance Phase of the SDLC 227

The Critical Importance of IT Governance in an Organization 228
SDLC AS PART OF STRATEGIC MANAGEMENT 228
SDLC AS AN INTERNAL CONTROL 228

Ethical Considerations Related to IT Governance 230
ETHICAL CONSIDERATIONS FOR MANAGEMENT 230
ETHICAL CONSIDERATIONS FOR EMPLOYEES 230
ETHICAL CONSIDERATIONS FOR CONSULTANTS 231

Summary of Study Objectives 232
Key Terms 233
End of Chapter Material 234
CONCEPT CHECK 234
DISCUSSION QUESTIONS 236
BRIEF EXERCISES 236
PROBLEMS 237
CASES 238
CONTINUING CASE: SPATELLI'S PIZZERIA 239
SOLUTIONS TO CONCEPT CHECK 239

CHAPTER 7
Auditing Information Technology-Based Processes 241

Introduction to Auditing IT Processes 242
Types of Audits and Auditors 242
Information Risk and IT-Enhanced Internal Control 244
Authoritative Literature Used in Auditing 245
Management Assertions and Audit Objectives 246
Phases of an IT Audit 248
Audit Planning 249
Use of Computers in Audits 251
Tests of Controls 252
General Controls 253
Application Controls 256
Tests of Transactions and Tests of Balances 260
Audit Completion/Reporting 262
Other Audit Considerations 263
DIFFERENT IT ENVIRONMENTS 263
CHANGES IN A CLIENT'S IT ENVIRONMENT 265
SAMPLING 266
Ethical Issues Related to Auditing 266
Summary of Study Objectives 270
Key Terms 271
End of Chapter Material 272
CONCEPT CHECK 272
DISCUSSION QUESTIONS 275
BRIEF EXERCISES 276
PROBLEMS 277
CASES 278
CONTINUING CASE: SPATELLI'S PIZZERIA 279
SOLUTIONS TO CONCEPT CHECK 279

MODULE 3 **BUSINESS PROCESSES** The sets of business processes and the internal controls in organizations. With process maps, document flowcharts, and data flow diagrams, the core business processes are described and the necessary controls to manage risk are discussed.

CHAPTER 8
Revenue and Cash Collection Processes and Controls 283

Introduction to Revenue Processes 284
Sales Processes 287
Risks and Controls in Sales Processes 292
AUTHORIZATION OF TRANSACTIONS 293
SEGREGATION OF DUTIES 293
ADEQUATE RECORDS AND DOCUMENTS 293
SECURITY OF ASSETS AND DOCUMENTS 294
INDEPENDENT CHECKS AND RECONCILIATIONS 294
COST-BENEFIT CONSIDERATIONS 294
Sales Return Processes 296
Risks and Controls in Sales Return Processes 296
AUTHORIZATION OF TRANSACTIONS 296
SEGREGATION OF DUTIES 296
ADEQUATE RECORDS AND DOCUMENTS 299
SECURITY OF ASSETS AND DOCUMENTS 300
INDEPENDENT CHECKS AND RECONCILIATION 300
COST-BENEFIT CONSIDERATIONS 300
Cash Collection Processes 302
Risks and Controls in Cash Collection Processes 302
AUTHORIZATION OF TRANSACTIONS 302
SEGREGATION OF DUTIES 305
ADEQUATE RECORDS AND DOCUMENTS 306
SECURITY OF ASSETS AND DOCUMENTS 306
INDEPENDENT CHECKS AND RECONCILIATIONS 307
COST-BENEFIT CONSIDERATIONS 307
IT Enabled Systems of Revenue and Cash Collection Processes 309
E-Business Systems and the Related Risks and Controls 311
SECURITY AND CONFIDENTIALITY RISKS 313
PROCESSING INTEGRITY RISKS 313
AVAILABILITY RISKS 314

Electronic Data Interchange (EDI) Systems and the Risks and Controls 315
Point of Sale (POS) Systems and the Related Risks and Controls 319
Ethical Issues Related to Revenue Processes 320
Corporate Governance in Revenue Processes 323
Summary of Study Objectives 324
Key Terms 325
End of Chapter Material 326
CONCEPT CHECK 326
DISCUSSION QUESTIONS 329
BRIEF EXERCISES 329
PROBLEMS 330
CASES 337
CONTINUING CASE: SPATELLI'S PIZZERIA 343
SOLUTIONS TO CONCEPT CHECK 344

CHAPTER 9
Expenditures Processes and Controls—Purchases 347

Introduction to Expenditures Processes 348
Purchasing Processes 351
Risks and Controls in the Purchasing Process 357
AUTHORIZATION OF TRANSACTIONS 357
SEGREGATION OF DUTIES 357
ADEQUATE RECORDS AND DOCUMENTS 358
SECURITY OF ASSETS AND DOCUMENTS 358
INDEPENDENT CHECKS AND RECONCILIATION 358
COST-BENEFIT CONSIDERATIONS 359
Purchase Return Process 360
Risks and Controls in the Purchase Return Processes 365
AUTHORIZATION OF TRANSACTIONS 365
SEGREGATION OF DUTIES 365
ADEQUATE RECORDS AND DOCUMENTS 365
SECURITY OF ASSETS AND DOCUMENTS 365
INDEPENDENT CHECKS AND RECONCILIATION 365
COST-BENEFIT CONSIDERATIONS 366
Cash Disbursement Processes 367
Risks and Controls in the Cash Disbursement Processes 372
AUTHORIZATION OF TRANSACTIONS 372
SEGREGATION OF DUTIES 373
ADEQUATE RECORDS AND DOCUMENTS 373
SECURITY OF ASSETS AND DOCUMENTS 373
INDEPENDENT CHECKS AND RECONCILIATIONS 374
COST-BENEFIT CONSIDERATIONS 374
IT Systems of Expenditures and Cash Disbursement Processes 375
Computer-Based Matching 377
Risks and Controls in Computer-Based Matching 379
SECURITY AND CONFIDENTIALITY RISKS 379
PROCESSING INTEGRITY RISKS 379
Evaluated Receipt Settlement 380
Risks and Controls in Evaluated Receipt Settlement 381
SECURITY AND CONFIDENTIALITY 382
PROCESSING INTEGRITY 382
AVAILABILITY 382
E-Business and Electronic Data Interchange (EDI) 382
Risks and Controls in E-Business and EDI 383
SECURITY AND CONFIDENTIALITY 383
PROCESSING INTEGRITY 384
AVAILABILITY 384
E-Payables 385
Procurement Cards 386
Ethical Issues Related to Expenditures Processes 386
Corporate Governance in Expenditure Processes 388
Summary of Study Objectives 389
Key Terms 391
End of Chapter Material 391
CONCEPT CHECK 391
DISCUSSION QUESTIONS 394
BRIEF EXERCISES 395
PROBLEMS 396
CASES 399
CONTINUING CASE: SPATELLI'S PIZZERIA 404
SOLUTIONS TO CONCEPT CHECK 405

CHAPTER 10
Expenditures Processes and Controls—Payroll and Fixed Assets 409

Introduction to Payroll and Fixed Asset Processes 410
Payroll Processes 412
Risks and Controls in the Payroll Processes 420
AUTHORIZATION OF TRANSACTIONS 421
SEGREGATION OF DUTIES 421
ADEQUATE RECORDS AND DOCUMENTS 422

SECURITY OF ASSETS AND DOCUMENTS 422
INDEPENDENT CHECKS AND RECONCILIATIONS 422
COST–BENEFIT CONSIDERATIONS 423

IT Systems of Payroll Processes 424

Fixed Asset Processes 426
FIXED ASSETS ACQUISITION 426
FIXED ASSETS CONTINUANCE 430
FIXED ASSETS DISPOSALS 431

Risks and Controls in Fixed Asset Processes 434
AUTHORIZATION OF TRANSACTIONS 434
SEGREGATION OF DUTIES 435
ADEQUATE RECORDS AND DOCUMENTS 435
SECURITY OF ASSETS AND DOCUMENTS 435
INDEPENDENT CHECKS AND RECONCILIATIONS 435
COST–BENEFIT CONSIDERATIONS 437

IT Systems of Fixed Asset Processes 437

Ethical Issues Related to Payroll and Fixed Assets Processes 438

Corporate Governance in Payroll and Fixed Assets Processes 441

Summary of Study Objectives 442

Key Terms 444

End of Chapter Material 444
CONCEPT CHECK 444
DISCUSSION QUESTIONS 447
BRIEF EXERCISES 448
PROBLEMS 448
CASES 450
CONTINUING CASE: SPATELLI'S PIZZERIA 453
SOLUTIONS TO CONCEPT CHECK 455

CHAPTER 11

Conversion Processes and Controls 457

Basic Features of Conversion Processes 458

Components of the Logistics Function 460
PLANNING 460
RESOURCE MANAGEMENT 463
OPERATIONS 465

Cost Accounting Reports Generated by Conversion Processes 469

Risks and Controls in Conversion Processes 470
AUTHORIZATION OF TRANSACTIONS 470
SEGREGATION OF DUTIES 470
ADEQUATE RECORDS AND DOCUMENTS 471
SECURITY OF ASSETS AND DOCUMENTS 471
INDEPENDENT CHECKS AND RECONCILIATIONS 471
COST–BENEFIT CONSIDERATIONS 472

IT Systems of Conversion Processes 473

Ethical Issues Related to Conversion Processes 476

Corporate Governance in Conversion Processes 477

Summary of Study Objectives 478

Key Terms 479

End of Chapter Material 480
CONCEPT CHECK 480
DISCUSSION QUESTIONS 482
BRIEF EXERCISES 483
PROBLEMS 484
CASES 485
CONTINUING CASE: SPATELLI'S PIZZERIA 489
SOLUTIONS TO CONCEPT CHECK 490

CHAPTER 12

Administrative Processes and Controls 493

Introduction to Administrative Processes 495

Source of Capital Processes 497

Investment Processes 498

Risks and Controls in Capital and Investment Processes 500

General Ledger Processes 501

Risks and Controls in General Ledger Processes 504
AUTHORIZATION OF TRANSACTIONS 504
SEGREGATION OF DUTIES 506
ADEQUATE RECORDS AND DOCUMENTS 509
SECURITY OF THE GENERAL LEDGER AND DOCUMENTS 509
INDEPENDENT CHECKS AND RECONCILIATIONS 509

Reporting as an Output of the General Ledger Processes 510
EXTERNAL REPORTING 511
INTERNAL REPORTING 511

Ethical Issues Related to Administrative Processes and Reporting 513
UNETHICAL MANAGEMENT BEHAVIOR IN CAPITAL SOURCES AND INVESTING 513
INTERNAL REPORTING ETHICAL ISSUES 514

Corporate Governance in Administrative Processes and Reporting 515
Summary of Study Objectives 516
Key Terms 517
End of Chapter Material 517
CONCEPT CHECK 517
DISCUSSION QUESTIONS 519
BRIEF EXERCISES 520
PROBLEMS 521
CASE 522
CONTINUING CASE: SPATELLI'S PIZZERIA 522
SOLUTIONS TO CONCEPT CHECK 522

MODULE 4 IT INFRASTRUCTURE TO ENABLE PROCESSES The hardware, software, and systems that support business processes.

CHAPTER 13
Data and Databases 525

The Need for Data Collection and Storage 526
Storing and Accessing Data 527
DATA STORAGE TERMINOLOGY 528
DATA STORAGE MEDIA 529
Data Processing Techniques 529
Databases 531
THE HISTORY OF DATABASES 532
The Need for Normalized Data 535
TRADE-OFFS IN DATABASE STORAGE 537
Use of a Data Warehouse to Analyze Data 538
BUILD THE DATA WAREHOUSE 539
IDENTIFY THE DATA 539
STANDARDIZE THE DATA 539
CLEANSE, OR SCRUB, THE DATA 540
UPLOAD THE DATA 540
Data Analysis Tools 540
DATA MINING 541
OLAP 542
Distributed Data Processing 542
DDP AND DDB 543
CLIENT/SERVER SYSTEMS 544
IT Controls for Data and Databases 545
Ethical Issues Related to Data Collection and Storage 546
ETHICAL RESPONSIBILITIES OF THE COMPANY 546
ETHICAL RESPONSIBILITIES OF EMPLOYEES 548
ETHICAL RESPONSIBILITIES OF CUSTOMERS 548
Summary of Study Objectives 549
Key Terms 551
End of Chapter Material 551
CONCEPT CHECK 551
DISCUSSION QUESTIONS 553
BRIEF EXERCISES 554
PROBLEMS 555
CASES 556
CONTINUING CASE: SPATELLI'S PIZZERIA 557
SOLUTIONS TO CONCEPT CHECK 557

CHAPTER 14
E-Commerce and E-Business 559

Introduction to E-Commerce and E-Business 560
The History of the Internet 562
The Physical Structure and Standards of the Internet 565
THE NETWORK 565
THE COMMON STANDARDS OF THE INTERNET 566
E-Commerce and Its Benefits 569
BENEFITS AND DISADVANTAGES OF E-COMMERCE FOR THE CUSTOMER 569
BENEFITS AND DISADVANTAGES OF E-COMMERCE FOR THE BUSINESS 570
THE COMBINATION OF E-COMMERCE AND TRADITIONAL COMMERCE 571
Privacy Expectations in E-Commerce 572
E-Business and IT Enablement 574
B2B: A PART OF E-BUSINESS 576
E-BUSINESS ENABLEMENT EXAMPLES 578
Intranets and Extranets to Enable E-Business 580
Internal Controls for the Internet, Intranets, and Extranets 581
XML and XBRL as Tools to Enable E-Business 583
XML IN INTERNET EDI 583
XBRL FOR FINANCIAL STATEMENT REPORTING 585
Ethical Issues Related to E-Business and E-Commerce 586
Summary of Study Objectives 588
Key Terms 589
End of Chapter Material 590
CONCEPT CHECK 590
DISCUSSION QUESTIONS 591

BRIEF EXERCISES 593
PROBLEMS 593
CASES 594
CONTINUING CASE: SPATELLI'S PIZZERIA 595
SOLUTIONS TO CONCEPT CHECK 595

CHAPTER 15

IT Infrastructure for E-Business 597

Overview of ERP Systems 598
History of ERP Systems 601
Current ERP System Characteristics 603
ERP Modules 605
FINANCIALS 605
HUMAN RESOURCES 606
PROCUREMENT AND LOGISTICS 606
PRODUCT DEVELOPMENT AND MANUFACTURING 606
SALES AND SERVICES 606
ANALYTICS 606
SUPPLY CHAIN MANAGEMENT 607
CUSTOMER RELATIONSHIP MANAGEMENT 607
Market Segments of ERP Systems 607
TIER ONE SOFTWARE 608
TIER TWO SOFTWARE 609
Implementation of ERP Systems 609
HIRING A CONSULTING FIRM 609
THE BEST FIT ERP SYSTEM 610
WHICH MODULES TO IMPLEMENT 610
BEST OF BREED VERSUS ERP MODULES 610
BUSINESS PROCESS REENGINEERING 611
CUSTOMIZATION OF THE ERP SYSTEM 612
THE COSTS OF HARDWARE AND SOFTWARE 612
TESTING OF THE ERP SYSTEM 612
DATA CONVERSION 612
TRAINING OF EMPLOYEES 613
THE METHODS OF CONVERSION TO THE ERP SYSTEM 613
Benefits and Risks of ERP Systems 615
BENEFITS OF ERP SYSTEMS 615
RISKS OF ERP SYSTEMS 617
ERP Systems and the Sarbanes-Oxley Act 618
Summary of Study Objectives 619
Key Terms 621
End of Chapter Material 621
CONCEPT CHECK 621
DISCUSSION QUESTIONS 623
BRIEF EXERCISES 624
PROBLEMS 624
CASES 625
CONTINUING CASE: SPATELLI'S PIZZERIA 626
SOLUTIONS TO CONCEPT CHECK 626
Index 629

CHAPTER 1

Introduction to AIS

STUDY OBJECTIVES

This chapter will help you gain an understanding of the following concepts:

1. An overview of business processes
2. An overview of an accounting information system
3. The business process linkage throughout the supply chain
4. The IT enablement of business processes
5. Basic computer and IT concepts
6. Examples of IT enablement
7. The internal control structure of organizations
8. The importance of accounting information systems to accountants
9. The relation of ethics to accounting information systems

THE REAL WORLD

Cristian Ardelean/iStockphoto

A new trend in the fast food restaurant industry is remote order-taking at the drive-through. Hardee's and McDonald's are both experimenting with remote order-taking at their drive-through windows. In the case of McDonald's, the experimental order-taking center takes drive-through orders for 15 different McDonald's locations. A recent article described the process as follows:[1]

> The center uses voice over Internet protocol, or VoIP technology, a T1 phone line and instant photographs to process the orders. A car pulling up to the menu board trips a magnetic loop that alerts the call center. There, the agent takes and confirms the order and shoots it instantly to the restaurant. In-store employees focus on taking the cash and delivering the food. Using photos of diners allows stores to install multiple drive-through lanes, which can boost car counts.

OVERVIEW OF BUSINESS PROCESSES (STUDY OBJECTIVE 1)

You might wonder how the preceding example relates to accounting information systems. An accounting information system must capture, record, and process all financial transactions. Prior to the implemention of the experimental drive-through order system, all in-store and drive-through orders were processed through the cash registers at each local McDonald's. When the new, experimental system was implemented, consider the effects on the system that recorded sales. The new technology had to be configured in such a way that

1. order details were taken accurately;
2. those details were forwarded to the correct McDonald's location so that the order could be handed to the customer at the drive-through;
3. the order data had to be included with McDonald's sales and cash received for the day; and
4. the correct McDonald's location had to be properly credited with the sale so that the franchise and managers would be given credit for sales they generate.

The point of this example is that there are many different ways that sales transactions can be conducted. No matter the form of those business transactions, the accounting information system must identify the transactions to record, capture all the important details of the transaction, properly process the transaction details into the correct accounts, and provide reports externally and internally. Many types of transactions that result from business processes must be captured, recorded, and reported.

A **business process** is a prescribed sequence of work steps performed in order to produce a desired result for the organization. A business process is initiated by a particular kind of event, has a well-defined beginning and end, and is usually completed in a relatively short period. In the previous example, the business process is the taking and filling of a drive-through order. Organizations

[1]Karen Robinson-Jacobs, "At the drive-through, you may be ordering long-distance," *Dallas Morning News* January 26, 2005.

have many different business processes, such as completing a sale, purchasing raw materials, paying employees, and paying vendors. Each business process has either a direct or an indirect effect on the financial status of the organization. For example, completing a sale directly increases cash or other assets, while paying employees directly reduces cash or increases liabilities. Purchasing new, efficient equipment also directly affects assets and/or liability accounts; yet this transaction is also expected to indirectly increase sales and assets, as it provides for increased productivity and an expanded customer base. Therefore, we can see why, as business processes occur, the accounting information system must capture and record the related accounting information.

The names of all possible business processes would be too numerous to list. However, the four general types of business processes typical in organizations, which will be described in later chapters of this book, are as follows:

1. Revenue processes (Chapter 8)
   a. Sales processes
   b. Sales return processes
   c. Cash collection processes
2. Expenditure processes (Chapters 9 and 10)
   a. Purchasing processes
   b. Purchase return processes
   c. Cash disbursement processes
   d. Payroll processes
   e. Fixed asset processes
3. Conversion processes (Chapter 11)
   a. Planning processes
   b. Resource management processes
   c. Logistics processes
4. Administrative processes (Chapter 12)
   a. Capital processes
   b. Investment processes
   c. General ledger processes

In the example at the beginning of this chapter, the remote drive-though processing is part of the revenue processes. The order-taking combines the sales process and the cash collection process. For a fast food franchise such as McDonald's, these processes are the most visible and obvious to customers. However, there are many other business processes that occur that may not be as obvious to customers.

In addition to revenue processes to sell food to customers and collect the cash, McDonald's must implement some or all of the remaining processes in the preceding list. That is, to sell a Big Mac Extra Value Meal® to a customer, McDonald's must first engage in purchase processes to buy meat, vegetables, buns, soft drinks, and other food items, as well as operating supplies. In addition, it must have payroll processes to pay employees, and fixed asset processes to buy and maintain equipment and other fixed assets. McDonald's must have conversion processes to convert the raw meat, vegetables, and buns into customer products that can be sold.

Also, McDonald's must have capital processes that raise funds to buy capital assets, and investment processes to manage and invest any extra cash flow.

Finally, McDonald's needs general ledger processes to ensure that all transactions are recorded into the appropriate general ledger accounts and that financial information is reported to external and internal users. For example, each sale to a customer must be recorded as a sale, and the results of the sale must eventually be posted to the general ledger accounts of cash and sales.

The purpose here of reviewing these processes is not to cover the entire set of details, but to emphasize that there must be prescribed work steps in every area. Employees, work steps, and transaction recording systems must be established in any organization to ensure that business processes occur and that any accounting effects of those processes are captured and recorded. For example, employees who work the cash register must be trained to apply company policies for customer payment (such as cash and credit cards accepted, but no personal checks). As these employees perform their work steps, the system in place should be capturing the relevant accounting information. In the case of McDonald's, the cash register captures the in-store sales data including the items sold, price paid, sales tax, and date of sale. The cash registers are connected to a computer system that feeds the sales and cash data to corporate headquarters so that management reports can be created and external financial statements prepared at the end of the period.

In addition, organizations implement internal control processes into their work steps to prevent errors and fraud. **Internal controls** are the set of procedures and policies adopted within an organization to safeguard its assets, check the accuracy and reliability of its data, promote operational efficiency, and encourage adherence to prescribed managerial practices. For example, McDonald's probably requires that at the end of every day, a manager close each cash register and reconcile the cash in the register to the recorded total sold at that register. This is an internal control process to prevent and detect errors in cash amounts and to discourage employees from stealing cash. Reconciliation of cash to cash register records is a business process designed to control other processes. Thus, we begin to see that the accounting information system has many components, as explained further in the next section.

OVERVIEW OF AN ACCOUNTING INFORMATION SYSTEM (STUDY OBJECTIVE 2)

The **accounting information system** comprises the processes, procedures, and systems that capture accounting data from business processes; record the accounting data in the appropriate records; process the detailed accounting data by classifying, summarizing, and consolidating; and report the summarized accounting data to internal and external users. Many years ago, accounting information systems were paper-based journals and ledgers that were recorded manually by employees. Today, nearly every organization uses computer systems for maintaining records in its accounting information system. The accounting information system has several important components, listed next. An example from McDonald's is used to describe each component.

1. *Work steps within a business process intended to capture accounting data* as that business process occurs. When McDonald's employees greet a customer at the cash register, they have several work steps to complete a sale, some of which are accounting related and some of which are not. Greeting the

customer with a smile may be an important step, but it has no impact on accounting records. However, using the touch screen at the cash register to conduct the sale does have an accounting effect. That accounting effect is that sales amounts in the sales records should be increased and cash amounts in cash records should be increased.

2. *The manual or computer-based records to record the accounting data* from business processes. As is true of most companies, McDonald's has a system of computers and computer processes to record the appropriate data from the sale process. These systems usually have a combination of manual and computerized steps. For McDonald's, the manual process is that a person must operate the cash register. The remainder of the McDonald's system is computer based, and the computer records the sale and all related data.
3. *Work steps that are internal controls* within the business process to safeguard assets and to ensure accuracy and completeness of the data. As mentioned before, the requirement that a manager close and reconcile the cash register at the end of the day is an example of an internal control within the sales processes.
4. *Work steps to process, classify, summarize, and consolidate the raw accounting data*. For example, sales at each McDonald's franchise must be summarized and consolidated into a single total of sales revenue to be reported on the income statement. At McDonald's, these steps are accomplished by the computer system and the accounting software. In some companies, there may be manual or handwritten accounting records, although currently most organizations use IT systems to conduct some or all of the accounting recording and summarizing processes.
5. *Work steps that generate both internal and external reports*. McDonald's needs many types of internal reports to monitor the performance of individual franchise locations and of regions. In addition, year-end external financial statements such as the income statement, balance sheet, and statement of cash flows must be prepared for external users.

These five components are part of any accounting information system. All business processes have either a direct or indirect effect on the accounting records and must therefore be recorded in the accounting information system. For each business process that affects accounting records, the accounting information system must capture any resulting accounting data; record the data; process it through classification, summarization, and consolidation; and generate appropriate reports. Exhibit 1-1 shows an overview of an accounting information system.

The circles represent the many business processes that occur in the organization—revenue, expenditure, conversion, and administrative processes. As those processes occur, data are captured and become input into the accounting information system. The accounting information system classifies, summarizes, and consolidates the data. As input and processing occur, data must be stored to or retrieved from data storage. From this stored data and processing, several types of output are prepared. Some of the output would be documents such as purchase orders, invoices, and customer statements; other output would be checks to vendors and employees. The output reports are feedback that managers within the organization use to monitor and control the

Exhibit 1-1
Overview of an Accounting Information System

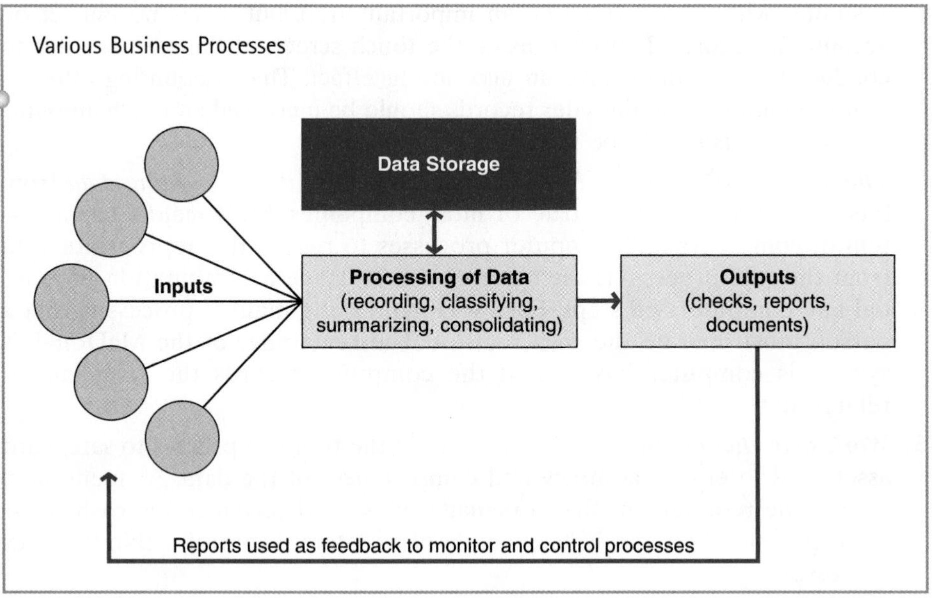

business processes. The number of computerized versus manual work steps may vary across organizations, but every organization should have each of these component pieces. In some organizations, the processes may be manual steps performed by employees, and the accounting records may be paper journals and ledgers. At the other extreme are companies where many or all of these work steps are performed by computers, and the accounting records are in computer disk files. In most cases, there is a combination of manual and computerized work steps.

The accounting system internal controls are not pictured in Exhibit 1-1, but there should be internal controls throughout the accounting information system. As defined earlier, internal controls are the set of procedures and policies adopted within an organization to safeguard its assets, check the accuracy and reliability of its data, promote operational efficiency, and encourage adherence to prescribed managerial practices. Internal controls are described later in this chapter and covered in detail in the Control Environment section (Chapters 3 through 7) of this book.

BUSINESS PROCESS LINKAGE THROUGHOUT THE SUPPLY CHAIN (STUDY OBJECTIVE 3)

The accounting information system and the reports generated by the system are intended to help management monitor and control the organization. However, any organization operates in an environment in which it has many interactive relationships with other organizations and entities. For example, McDonald's could not operate without its relationships with the many suppliers that provide the meat, cheese, vegetables, buns, and other ingredients that go into its menu selections. There is an entire set of activities (business processes) that culminate when McDonald's sells a Big Mac® to a customer. Consider the road that leads to this culminating sale—it stretches far back into many other organizations. To illustrate these activities, let's trace just a small part of that Big Mac sale back as far as we can reasonably go. In order to sell a Big Mac, McDonald's had to purchase and keep an inventory of hamburger meat. McDonald's would have purchased this meat from a meat supplier called a vendor. A **vendor** provides materials or operating supplies to an organization. The terms "vendor" and "supplier" are usually used interchangeably.

However, for the McDonald's meat vendor to supply meat, that vendor had to buy cattle to process into raw meat. Therefore, McDonald's meat supplier must have relationships with vendors that sell cattle. The cattle seller can be called a secondary supplier to McDonald's. To trace back one step farther, we could say that the cattle seller had to buy cattle from a rancher who raised cattle.

Likewise, the bun on the Big Mac can be traced back to a bakery, which had to purchase flour from another company, and that flour producer needed wheat to produce flour. Tracing back one step farther, we find that the wheat was sold by a wheat farmer. You might wonder what the purpose is of this exercise to trace a Big Mac back to the rancher who raised cattle and the farmer who grew wheat. The point is that for McDonald's to operate efficiently, each of these interactive relationships between buyer and seller must operate efficiently. For example, a labor union strike at a bakery that provides buns to McDonald's could interrupt the supply of buns for McDonald's. Therefore, the top management at McDonald's must ensure that it properly manages, monitors, and controls the internal processes, as well as those processes that are linked to outside parties such as vendors. McDonald's may not be able to directly control all of these interrelated activities that stretch back through the many suppliers, but McDonald's may be able to influence those activities by the suppliers they choose and the expectations they place on those suppliers in terms of price, quality, and delivery timing. This set of linked activities is called the supply chain. The **supply chain** is the entities, processes, and information flows that involve the movement of materials, funds, and related information through the full logistics process, from the acquisition of raw materials to the delivery of finished products to the end user. The supply chain includes all vendors, service providers, customers, and intermediaries.

THE REAL WORLD

An organization such as McDonald's must have many different suppliers of the same product because of the need for fresh ingredients. For example, the regional bakery in the next example provides buns for McDonald's in a five-state area.

As you have traveled, you may have noticed that your Big Mac is always the same, no matter where you go. Even the buns are exactly the same in each town and city. McDonald's plans for this uniformity in buns and must have many suppliers throughout the world that can make and deliver a consistent quality bun.

East Balt Inc. is one of the large bakeries that supplies McDonald's with buns. East Balt bakeries make these buns according to strict standards of size, shape, color, height, and seed coverage. To maintain freshness, the buns have to be baked in regional locations. It would be much too difficult to have one central location bake all buns for McDonald's. Therefore, McDonald's must have many different suppliers of buns throughout the world.

Exhibit 1-2
A Simplified Supply Chain for McDonald's

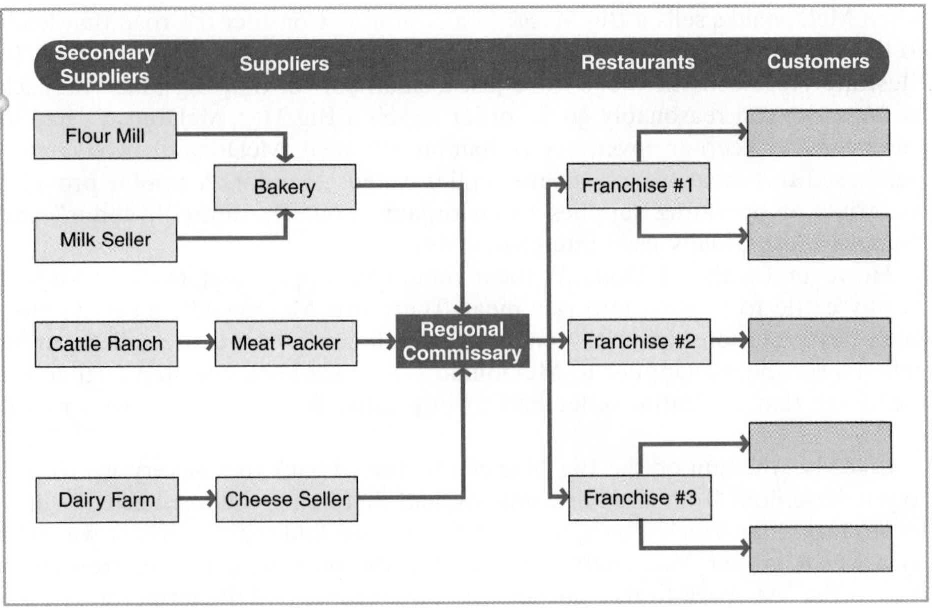

The concept of monitoring and controlling the linked set of activities in the supply chain is called supply chain management. **Supply chain management** is the management and control of all materials, funds, and related information in the logistics process, from the acquisition of raw materials to the delivery of finished products to the end user (customer). A simplified view of a supply chain for McDonald's is shown in Exhibit 1-2.

The management at McDonald's would find it in the best interest of its company to manage, monitor, and control the processes within the supply chain to the extent possible. For example, a large organization such as McDonald's can demand certain levels of quality from the bakery that supplies buns. In addition, McDonald's can apply pressure to make sure that the bakery has reliable suppliers of high-quality flour. To the extent that McDonald's can influence primary and secondary suppliers to maintain quality of supplies and efficiency of operations, the business processes within McDonald's will operate more smoothly. As an example, the corporation's processes to purchase buns operate more efficiently when the bakery's selling processes run efficiently. This connection between the purchasing processes used by McDonald's and the supplier's selling processes represents a supply chain linkage. In order to increase the efficiency and effectiveness of these supply chain linkages, many organizations employ IT systems. Using IT systems to enhance efficiency and effectiveness of internal or supply chain processes is called **IT enablement.**

IT ENABLEMENT OF BUSINESS PROCESSES (STUDY OBJECTIVE 4)

Generally, information technology (IT) comprises all forms of technology used to create, store, exchange, and utilize information in its various forms, including business data, conversations, still images, motion pictures, and multimedia presentations. For the purposes of this book, **information technology** is defined as the computers, ancillary equipment, software, services, and related resources as applied to support business processes. IT usage to support business processes accomplishes one or more of the following objectives:

1. Increased efficiency of business processes
2. Reduced cost of business processes
3. Increased accuracy of the data related to business processes

Any of the processes within an organization, including the linkages within the supply chain, are processes that may benefit by IT enablement. The touch-screen cash register at a McDonald's is an example of IT that increases the efficiency of the sales process. Another popular example of IT enablement of processes is e-commerce sales such those in place at Amazon.com, Inc. Amazon.com uses complex IT systems to present a sales model that allows customers to place orders on its website.

These two examples only scratch the surface of the types of processes that can be IT enabled. Any business process has the potential to be improved by IT enablement. In many cases, using IT to enable processes leads to a completely different approach to those processes. For example, the remote order-taking system described at the beginning of this chapter is a completely different order-taking process from the usual drive-through system. Using more complex IT such as voice over IP and digital photos, McDonald's is experimenting with improving the efficiency of drive-through order taking. Applying IT to business processes is an opportunity to "think outside the box" and consider completely different methods for business processes. This concept of revising processes as IT enabling occurs is called business process reengineering.

Business process reengineering (BPR) is the purposeful and organized changing of business processes to make them more efficient. BPR not only aligns business processes with the IT systems used to record processes; it also improves efficiency and effectiveness of these processes. Thus, the use of these sophisticated IT systems usually leads to two kinds of efficiency improvements. First, the underlying processes are reengineered so as to be conducted more efficiently. Second, the IT systems improve the efficiency of the underlying processes. Through rethinking and redesigning a process, the organization may be able to improve, and thereby enhance, the process. This rethinking and redesign is especially aided by the use of IT. When technology or computers are introduced into processes, the processes can be radically redesigned to take advantage of the speed and efficiency of computers to improve processing efficiency. IT and BPR have a mutually enhancing relationship. IT capabilities should support the business processes, and any business process should be designed to match the capabilities that the IT system can provide. BPR should leverage the capabilities of IT to improve the efficiency of processes. This is exactly what McDonald's has done in the remote drive-through example; it has taken advantage of the capabilities offered by technology to improve the process and match it to the capability of the IT.

THE REAL WORLD

A well-known example of business process reengineering with IT enablement occurred at Ford Motor Company a few years ago. Ford used a purchasing process to order parts that required a three-part purchase order. One copy was sent to the vendor, one was kept by the purchasing department, and one was forwarded to the accounts payable department. When those purchased goods were received, the receiving department prepared a two-part receiving report. The receiving department kept a copy, and the other copy was forwarded to accounts payable. The vendor mailed an invoice to Ford's accounts payable department. Matching the purchase order, receiving report, and invoice required more than 500 people. These employees spent a great deal of their time trying to investigate mismatched documents. For example, the quantity on the purchase order might not have agreed with the quantity on the invoice. These time-consuming steps of document matching and reconciling mismatches led to late payments to vendors and, therefore, unhappy vendors.

Using IT and business process reengineering, Ford changed the purchase and payment processes. After BPR, the process occurred as follows:

> A purchasing agent entered purchase orders into an online database. No copies were forwarded internally. When receiving received an order, the receiving employee checked to make sure the goods received matched to an outstanding purchase order in the online database. The computer system checks to make sure that the part number, unit of measure, and supplier code match between the purchase order and receiving report. When the computer matches the receiving order and purchase order, the computer system prepares a check for the vendor. This reengineered process allowed Ford to reduce the number of employees in accounts payable by 75%.[2]

Each of the business process categories described in the early part of this chapter (revenue, expenditure, conversion, and administrative) has been affected by business process reengineering and IT enablement. In this book, the chapters in the section entitled "Business Processes" provide more detail about those categories of common business processes. Parts of those chapters also provide details of IT enablement that allowed BPR to occur in organizations. The next section of this chapter briefly describes basic IT concepts, and the section after that describes IT enabling systems. Each of these IT enabling systems is covered in yet more detail in the chapters in the "Business Processes" section of this book.

BASIC COMPUTER AND IT CONCEPTS (STUDY OBJECTIVE 5)

Nearly all accounting information systems rely on computer hardware and software to track business processes and to record accounting data. Therefore, it is important for you to have some understanding of basic computer terminology and concepts. Many details about IT systems are described in later chapters of this book, but some of the basic concepts are included in this chapter.

[2]Michael Hammer, "Reengineering Work: Don't Automate, Obliterate," *Harvard Business Review*, July–August, 1990, vol. 68, issue 4 p. 104–112.

BASIC COMPUTER DATA STRUCTURES

Accounting data is stored in computer files, and an accountant should have some understanding of data structures in IT systems. Data are organized in a data hierarchy in computer systems, as follows:

1. Bit, or binary digit
2. Byte
3. Field
4. Record
5. File
6. Database

The term "bit" is a shortened reference to **b**inary dig**it**. The **bit** is the smallest unit of information in a computer system. A bit can have only one of two values: zero or one. All data in a computer system are reduced to a set of bits, or zeros and ones. A **byte** is a unit of storage that represents one character. In most computer systems, a byte is made up of eight bits. For example, the character "A" would be represented in a computer system by a set of eight bits. Every character, including letters, numbers, and symbols, are represented by a byte.

A **field** is one item within a record. For example, *last name* is a field in a payroll record, and *description* is a field in an inventory record. A **record** is a set of related fields for the same entity. All fields for a given employee form a payroll record. Such fields would be employee number, last name, first name, Social Security number, pay rate, and year-to-date gross. The entire set of related records form a **file**. The set of all employee records forms a payroll file.

Thus, the data structure hierarchy is as follows: Eight bits are a byte, a collection of related bytes is a field, a set of related fields is a record, and a set of related records is a file. The entire collection of files is called a database. A **database** is a collection of data stored on the computer in a form that allows the data to be easily accessed, retrieved, manipulated, and stored. The term "database" usually implies a shared database within the organization. Rather than each computer application having its own files, a database implies a single set of files that is shared by each application that uses the data. A **relational database** stores data in several small two-dimensional tables that can be joined together in many varying ways to represent many different kinds of relationships among the data. An example of a relationship in data is a single customer having more than one order. A relational database is intended to allow flexibility in queries. This means that managers or users can query the database for information or reports as needed.

The computer files of traditional accounting software systems use master files and transaction files. The **master files** are the relatively permanent files that maintain the detailed data for each major process. For example, a payroll master file maintains the relatively permanent data necessary to process payroll transactions. The payroll master file contains a record for each employee. Details such as name, address, pay rate, and year-to-date amounts are in the master file. Thus, the master file is much like the subsidiary ledger. The **transaction file** is the set of relatively temporary records that will be processed to update the master file. A payroll transaction file would contain the set of hours worked by each employee for a particular pay period. The transaction file is processed against the master file, and employee year-to-date balances are updated in the master file.

Not all modern IT systems and accounting software implemented within the last decade use master files and transaction files. Some systems use a database approach to processing and storing accounting data, storing the many details of financial transactions in huge databases. These systems do not necessarily maintain computerized ledgers and journals. Because all transaction data are stored in databases, when needed, the transactions can be organized or summarized by the important dimension requested. For example, the sales transactions that meet certain criteria can be extracted from the database—it is not necessary to construct or review a sales ledger.

FILE ACCESS AND PROCESSING MODES

In computer systems, files are organized either as sequential access or random access. **Sequential access** files store records in sequence, with one record stored immediately after another. The sequence is usually based on a key field such as employee number or customer number. Sequential files are read and written in sequence. This means that for the user to access record number 500, the previous 499 records must first be read by the computer. Sequential access is faster when the records are always accessed and used in sequential order.

Random access files (sometimes called direct access files) are not written or read in sequential order. The records are stored in random order on a disk media. Since records are distributed randomly on the disk surface, an underlying system enables the computer to find a record among the random records, using either a randomized formula or a hashing scheme to assign a specific address to each record. A formula generates the specific address for each record. When that record is requested, the formula can be recalculated to find the address of the requested record. If records are to be accessed randomly, then random access is a more efficient access method than sequential access.

There are situations where the same files may sometimes be accessed either way, sequentially or randomly. In cases where both access methods are necessary, some systems use the **indexed sequential access method** (ISAM). ISAM files are stored sequentially, but can also be accessed randomly because an index allows random access to specific records.

There are also two modes of processing transactions in accounting systems: batch processing and online processing. **Batch processing** requires that all similar transactions are grouped together for a specified time, and then this group of transactions is processed as a batch. Batch processing is best suited to applications which have large volumes of similar transactions that can be processed at regular intervals. Payroll processing is a good example of a system well suited to batch processing. All time cards can be grouped together for a two-week period, and all payroll processing takes place on the entire set, or batch, of time cards.

Online processing is the opposite of batch processing. Transactions are not grouped into batches, but each transaction is entered and processed one at a time. Some online processing systems are also **real-time processing** systems. Real-time processing means that the transaction is processed immediately, and in real time, so that the output is available immediately. Online processing is best suited to applications in which there is a large volume of records, but only a few records are needed to process any individual transaction.

Batch processing is best suited to sequential access files, and online processing is best suited to random access files. If transactions are to be processed online and in real time, then the computer must access a single record immediately. An online, real-time system requires direct access files. As an example, think about placing a telephone call to reserve an airline ticket. The airline employee must be able to access the specific flight that you request. If flight records were stored sequentially, the computer system would need to read all records in sequence until it reached the record. This system would be too inefficient. If the flight records are stored randomly, a hashing index exists to locate any single record quickly.

Online processing usually requires random access files, but batch processing can use either random or sequential access files. In many cases, ISAM files are used, since they offer both random and sequential access. For example, payroll processing requires access to employee records in sequence. This operation would be most efficient as a batch processing system that accesses and processes records sequentially. However, the human resources department would occasionally need to access a single employee's records. For example, when an employee receives a raise, the employee record must be accessed to update the *pay rate* field. Random access would allow the system to quickly locate that single employee record.

DATA WAREHOUSE AND DATA MINING

A **data warehouse** is an integrated collection of enterprise-wide data that includes five to ten fiscal years of nonvolatile data, used to support management in decision making and planning. The data warehouse can be better understood by comparing it with the operational database. The **operational database** contains the data that are continually updated as transactions are processed. Usually, the operational database includes data for the current fiscal year and supports day-to-day operations and record keeping for the transaction processing systems. Each time a new transaction is completed, parts of the operational database must be updated. For example, recording a sale means that sales, inventory, and receivables balances must be updated. This type of update does not occur in a data warehouse.

The data in the data warehouse are said to be enterprise-wide because the data are pulled from each of the operational databases and maintained in the data warehouse for many fiscal periods, ideally, five to ten years. The data in the data warehouse are retrieved from sales order processing, inventory systems, receivables, and many other transaction-processing systems within the organization. The data in a data warehouse are called nonvolatile because they do not change rapidly in the same way that operational data change. Periodically, new data are uploaded to the data warehouse from the operational data; but other than this updating process, the data in the data warehouse do not change.

The data warehouse is used by management to do data mining. **Data mining** is the process of searching data within the data warehouse for identifiable patterns that can be used to predict future behavior. Although there are many reasons a company might want to know future behavior, the most popular use of data mining is to predict the future buying behavior of customers. If businesses are able to more accurately predict customer buying trends, they can plan appropriately to produce, distribute, and sell the right products to customers at the right time. For example, by examining customer buying patterns from the past few periods of sales, a grocery chain might be able to more accurately predict which products sell better during hot-weather periods. The company might find that ice cream sales increase by a large percentage when the temperature exceeds 80 degrees, and therefore it would be able to better plan the amount of ice cream to buy as the weather changes.

NETWORKS AND THE INTERNET

A computer **network** is two or more computers linked together to share information and/or resources. There are several types of computer networks, but the types most important to the topic of accounting information systems are local area network (LAN), the Internet, extranet, and intranet. A **LAN** is a computer network that spans a relatively small area. Most LANs are confined to a single building or group of buildings and are intended to connect computers within an organization. However, one LAN can be connected to other LANs over any distance via other network connections. A system of LANs connected in this way is called a WAN, or wide area network.

The **Internet** is the global computer network, or "information super-highway." The Internet developed from a variety of university- and government-sponsored computer networks that have evolved and are now made up of millions upon millions of computers and subnetworks throughout the world. The Internet is the network that serves as the backbone for the World Wide Web (WWW).

An **intranet** is a company's private network accessible only to the employees of that company. The intranet uses the common standards and protocols of the Internet. However, the computer servers of the intranet are accessible only from internal computers within the company. The purposes of an intranet are to distribute data or information to employees, to make shared data or files available, and to manage projects within the company.

An **extranet** is similar to an intranet except that it offers access to selected outsiders, such as buyers, suppliers, distributors, and wholesalers in the supply chain. Extranets allow business partners to exchange information. These business partners may be given limited access to company servers and access only to the data necessary to conduct supply chain exchanges with the company. For example, suppliers may need access to data pertaining to raw material inventory levels of the company to which they sell, but they would not need access to finished product inventory levels. Conversely, a wholesaler within the supply chain may need access to the manufacturer's finished product inventory, but it would not need access to raw material inventory levels.

These networks are an important part of the infrastructure that allows organizations to effectively use IT systems. The networks allow the IT enablement of business processes. For example, the remote order-taking system described at the beginning of this chapter employs voice-over IP (VoIP) technology. VoIP uses the Internet to transmit voice telephone data. The IT enabling technologies described in the next section utilize some or all of these types of networks.

EXAMPLES OF IT ENABLEMENT (STUDY OBJECTIVE 6)

As described earlier, computers and IT can be used to enable business processes, and applying IT to business processes offers companies the opportunity to do business process reengineering. The manner in which companies complete their processes can be changed to take advantage of the efficiency, effectiveness, or cost savings inherent in IT systems. The examples that follow are systems applied by companies today that use IT-enabled business processes.

E-BUSINESS

E-business is the use of electronic means to enhance business processes. E-business encompasses all forms of online electronic trading—consumer-based e-commerce and business-to-business electronic trading—and business-to-business process integration, as well as the internal use of IT and related technologies for process integration inside organizations. E-business is therefore a very broad concept that includes not only electronic trading with customers, but also servicing customers and vendors, swapping information with customers and vendors, and electronic recording and control of internal processes. IT systems, Internet, and websites, as well as wireless networks, are the common means of enabling e-business to occur. E-commerce is the type of e-business that we are familiar with as consumers. Buying a book at Amazon.com and clothes at LandsEnd.com are examples of engaging in e-commerce. E-business has so many other forms that it is difficult to explain its entire breadth. Chapter 14 describes e-business in more detail.

ELECTRONIC DATA INTERCHANGE

Electronic data interchange (EDI) is the intercompany, computer-to-computer transfer of business documents in a standard business format. Three parts of this definition highlight the important characteristics of EDI: (1) "Intercompany" refers to two or more companies conducting business electronically. For example, a buyer of parts may use EDI to purchase parts from its supplier. (2) The computer-to-computer aspect of the definition indicates that each company's computers are connected via a network. (3) A standard business format is necessary so that various companies, vendors, and sellers can interact and trade electronically by means of EDI software. EDI is used to transmit purchase orders, invoices, and payments electronically between trading partners.

POINT OF SALE SYSTEM

A **point of sale system** (POS) is a system of hardware and software that captures retail sales transactions by standard bar coding. Nearly all large retail and fast food stores use POS systems that are integrated into the cash register. As a customer checks out through the cash register, the bar codes are scanned on the items purchased, prices are determined by access to inventory and price list data, sales revenue is recorded, and inventory values are updated. All of these processes occur in real time, and through POS-captured data the store can provide to its managers or home office daily summaries of sales by cash register or by product. Many companies adopt POS systems because they enhance customer satisfaction by enabling faster and more accurate sales processing.

AUTOMATED MATCHING

Automated matching is a computer hardware and software system in which the software matches an invoice to its related purchase order and receiving report. Traditional systems rely on a person to do this matching, whereas an automated matching system does not. To institute an automated matching system, all of the relevant files must be online and constantly ready for processing; the purchase order and receiving files and records must be in online files or databases. When an invoice is received from a vendor, an employee enters the details into the accounting system by completing the fields in the invoice entry screen, including the purchase order number that usually appears on the invoice. The system can then access the online purchase order and receiving files and verify that the items, quantities, and prices match. The system will not approve an invoice for payment unless the items and quantities match with the packing slip and the prices match the purchase order prices. This ensures that the vendor has billed for the correct items, quantities, and prices. Automated matching reduces the time and cost of processing vendor payments. The real-world example of Ford Motor Company described earlier illustrated an automated matching system.

EVALUATED RECEIPT SETTLEMENT

Evaluated receipt settlement (ERS) is an invoice-less system in which computer hardware and software complete an invoice-less match that is a comparison of the purchase order with the goods received. If the online purchase order matches the goods, payment is made to the vendor. This eliminates the need for the vendor to send an invoice, since payment is approved as soon as goods are received (when they match a purchase order). The name ERS signifies that the receipt of goods is carefully evaluated and, if it matches the purchase order, settlement of the obligation occurs through this system. This IT enabled system reduces the time and cost of processing vendor payments.

E-PAYABLES AND ELECTRONIC INVOICE PRESENTMENT AND PAYMENT

E-payables and **electronic invoice presentment and payment** (EIPP) are both terms that refer to Web-enabled receipt and payment of vendor invoices. EIPP enables a vendor to present an invoice to its trading partner via the Internet, eliminating the paper, printing, and postage costs of traditional paper invoicing.

ENTERPRISE RESOURCE PLANNING SYSTEMS

Enterprise resource planning (ERP) is a multi-module software system designed to manage all aspects of an enterprise. ERP systems are usually broken down into modules such as financials, sales, purchasing, inventory management, manufacturing, and human resources. The modules are designed to work seamlessly with the rest of the system and to provide a consistent user interface between modules. These systems usually have extensive set-up options that allow some flexibility in the customizing of functionality to specific business needs. ERP systems are based on a relational database system.

ERP systems became popular in the 1990s, and many large corporations implemented ERP systems in preparation for the year 2000 to avoid the potential programming and operations problems expected to be caused by older software that was not Y2K compliant. An ERP software system is much more comprehensive and encompassing than traditional accounting software. ERP systems include modules to handle accounting functions, but, as previously mentioned, they also incorporate modules for manufacturing, marketing, logistics, and human resources. Before ERP, these types of modules usually were in separate software systems and were not well integrated with accounting software. This caused the need for some data requests to be answered by the accessing of data or reports from several different systems. If a customer asked whether a particular product was in stock, the accounting system could be accessed to answer that request. If it was not in stock, the customer might ask when it is scheduled to be manufactured. To answer that request, a completely separate software system, the production planning and control system, would need to be accessed. Under this kind of operation, with separate and nonintegrated software systems, a single employee usually did not have access to the separate systems to answer such requests. Customers might have been bounced from department to department to get answers to questions that should be answered by one person. The integration of all modules and business processes into a single ERP system is intended to be a solution to these types of problems. (Chapter 15 provides more details about ERP systems.)

THE INTERNAL CONTROL STRUCTURE OF ORGANIZATIONS (STUDY OBJECTIVE 7)

All organizations face risks in both day-to-day operations and long-term management. Some risks may be beyond the control of management. For example, management would be unable to reduce the risk of an earthquake occurring, which could interrupt operations or destroy buildings and equipment. However, managers can undertake steps to lessen the negative impact of an earthquake. For example, they can ensure that buildings are designed to be resistant to earthquake damage. This ability to lessen risks or risk impacts is true of nearly all risks that organizations face. Management can undertake steps to lessen the risk or reduce the impact of the risk. These processes are called controls.

Accountants have a long history of being the professionals within the organization who help design and implement controls to lessen risks that have an impact on the financial standing of the organization. Accountants are usually experts in controls that can reduce risks in the following broad categories:

1. The risk that assets will be stolen or misused
2. The risk of errors in accounting data or information

3. The risk of fraudulent activity by employees, managers, customers, or vendors
4. The risks inherent in IT systems, such as
   a. Erroneous input of data
   b. Erroneous processing of data
   c. Computer fraud
   d. Computer security breaches
   e. Hardware or software failure
   f. Natural disasters that can interrupt computer system operations

Although management has the ultimate responsibility to establish a control environment to the extent it can reasonably do so, accountants are heavily involved in assisting management in the creation, implementation, and monitoring of the control environment. Management should ensure that the following types of control structures exist:

1. Enterprise risk management (summarized in the next subsection)
2. Code of ethics (Chapter 3)
3. COSO accounting internal control structure (Chapter 3)
4. IT system control structure (Chapter 4)
5. Corporate governance structure (Chapter 5)
6. IT governance structure (Chapter 6)

ENTERPRISE RISK MANAGEMENT

The Committee of Sponsoring Organizations of the Treadway Commission, commonly known as COSO,[3] issued a comprehensive report on enterprise risk management in September of 2004. The purpose of the report was to assist managers in meeting the challenge of managing risk in their organizations. A proper response to risk that all organizations face is to establish formal processes and procedures to manage risk. **Enterprise risk management** (ERM) is defined as

> . . . a process, effected by an entity's board of directors, management and other personnel, applied in strategy setting and across the enterprise, designed to identify potential events that may affect the entity, and manage risk to be within its risk appetite, to provide reasonable assurance regarding the achievement of entity objectives.[4]

[3]COSO was originally formed in 1985 to sponsor the National Commission on Fraudulent Financial Reporting. The National Commission was jointly sponsored by five major professional associations in the United States: the American Accounting Association, the American Institute of Certified Public Accountants, Financial Executives International, The Institute of Internal Auditors, and the National Association of Accountants (now the Institute of Management Accountants). The Commission was wholly independent of each of the sponsoring organizations and contained representatives from industry, public accounting, investment firms, and the New York Stock Exchange. The Treadway Commission was named for James C. Treadway, the National Commission's first chairman and former Commissioner of the Securities and Exchange Commission. (www.coso.org)

[4]"Enterprise Risk Management—Integrated Framework," Committee of Sponsoring Organizations, September 2004. (www.coso.org)

This definition has several critical components. First, notice that ERM is effected (put into place) by top management and the board of directors. This emphasizes that ERM is the responsibility of management. Second, ERM is an ongoing *process*. Therefore, it is not something that occurs once and is forgotten—it is an ongoing assessment of risks, determining acceptable levels of risk, and managing risks to that acceptable level. Finally, ERM must involve not only management, but personnel across the enterprise.

ERM requires that management set policies and procedures related to the following:[5]

- *Internal Environment*—The internal environment encompasses the tone of an organization and sets the basis for how risk is viewed and addressed by an entity's people, including risk management philosophy and risk appetite, integrity and ethical values, and the operational environment.
- *Objective Setting*—Objectives must exist before management can identify potential events affecting their achievement. Enterprise risk management ensures that management has in place a process to set objectives and that the chosen objectives support and align with the entity's mission and are consistent with its risk appetite.
- *Event Identification*—Internal and external events affecting achievement of an entity's objectives must be identified, with distinction made between risks and opportunities. Opportunities are channeled back to management's strategy or objective-setting processes.
- *Risk Assessment*—Risks are analyzed by likelihood and impact, as a basis for determining how they should be managed. Risks are assessed on both an inherent and a residual basis, meaning that the likelihood of errors is considered both before and after the application of controls.
- *Risk Response*—Management selects risk responses—avoiding, accepting, reducing, or sharing risk— by developing a set of actions to align risks with the entity's risk tolerances and risk appetite.
- *Control Activities*—Policies and procedures are established and implemented to help ensure that the risk responses are effectively carried out.
- *Information and Communication*—Relevant information is identified, captured, and communicated in a form and a time frame that enable people to carry out their responsibilities. Effective communication also occurs in a broader sense, flowing down, across, and up the entity.
- *Monitoring*—The entirety of enterprise risk management is monitored and modified as necessary. Monitoring is accomplished through ongoing management activities, separate evaluations, or both.

To achieve the objective of managing risk, management should establish control structures that include at least accounting internal controls, IT controls, corporate governance, and IT governance. These control structures are briefly sketched next and are described in more detail in later chapters.

[5] *Ibid.*

A CODE OF ETHICS

A company's developing and adhering to a code of ethics should reduce opportunities for managers or employees to conduct fraud. This will only be true, however, if top management emphasizes this code of ethics and disciplines or discharges those who violate it. Managers who emphasize and model ethical behavior are more likely to encourage ethical behavior in their employees.

COSO ACCOUNTING INTERNAL CONTROL STRUCTURE

Many years prior to the COSO ERM report, COSO sponsored a committee to study, document, and describe internal controls. The 1992 COSO report, "Internal Controls—Integrated Framework," explains what has become the standard accepted by the accounting and business community as the definition and description of internal control. According to the report, there are five interrelated components of internal control: the control environment, risk assessment, control activities, information and communication, and monitoring. Notice that to achieve ERM, an organization must include these five components of internal control in its enterprise risk management processes. (These five components are described in detail in Chapter 3.)

IT CONTROLS

Threats and risks that interrupt or stop computer operations can be severely damaging to the organization. Not only can they stop or disrupt normal operations; they can lead to incorrect or incomplete accounting information. In addition, computer processing of accounting data leads to the risks of erroneous accounting data due to erroneous or incomplete input or processing of data, computer fraud, and computer security breaches. An organization must institute controls to limit these risks in IT systems.

IT controls can be divided into two categories, general controls and application controls. **General controls** apply overall to the IT accounting system; they are not restricted to any particular accounting application. An example of a general control is the use of passwords to allow only authorized users to log into an IT-based accounting system. Without regard to processing data in any specific application, passwords should be employed in the IT system. **Application controls** are used specifically in accounting applications to control inputs, processing, and output. Application controls are intended to ensure that inputs are accurate and complete; processing is accurate and complete; and outputs are properly distributed, controlled, and disposed of. (General and application controls in IT systems are described in Chapter 4.)

CORPORATE GOVERNANCE

Corporate governance is a relatively new concept that has evolved over recent years. It is generally recognized as involving many diverse aspects of business; thus, many definitions of corporate governance exist to cover each different aspect of interest. For instance, when economists define corporate governance, they recognize factors affecting the supply and demand of corporate leaders and tend to emphasize the importance of motivating leaders through the use of incentive programs. On the other hand, financiers tend to emphasize the role of corporate leaders to provide a good rate of return, while accountants focus on the responsibility of corporate leaders to provide effective internal controls and accurate records.

If forced to provide a single definition, accountants would characterize **corporate governance** as an elaborate system of checks and balances whereby a company's leadership is held accountable for building shareholder value and creating confidence in the financial reporting processes. This system of checks and balances includes several corporate functions that are interrelated within the corporate governance system. These functions include management oversight, internal controls and compliance, financial stewardship, and ethical conduct.

Corporate governance has been tremendously affected by the Sarbanes–Oxley Act of 2002. The purpose of the Act was to improve financial reporting and reinforce the importance of corporate ethics. The legislation was enacted in an effort to curb the corruption and accounting blunders that had been recently discovered in connection with the bankruptcies of such corporate giants as Enron Corp. and WorldCom Inc. The Sarbanes–Oxley Act places a huge responsibility on top management to establish and maintain internal controls. (Corporate governance and the Sarbanes–Oxley Act are described in detail in Chapter 5.)

IT GOVERNANCE

The proper management, control, and use of IT systems are known as IT governance. The IT Governance Institute defines **IT governance** as follows:

> [IT governance] consists of the leadership, organizational structure, and processes that ensure that the enterprise achieve(s) its goals by adding value while balancing risk versus return over IT and its processes. IT governance provides the structure that links IT processes, IT resources and information to enterprise strategies and objectives.[6]

In summary, the board of directors and top-level, executive managers must take responsibility to ensure that the organization uses processes that align IT systems to the strategies and objectives of the organization. IT systems should be chosen and implemented to support the attainment of strategies and objectives. To fulfill the management obligations that are inherent in IT governance, management must focus on the following aspects:

- Aligning IT strategy with the business strategy
- Cascading strategy and goals down into the enterprise
- Providing organizational structures that facilitate the implementation of strategies and goals
- Insisting that an IT control framework be adopted and implemented

(IT governance is further described in Chapter 6.)

[6]Control Objectives for IT (COBIT) 4.1, Executive Summary and Framework p. 5. (www.isaca.org)

THE IMPORTANCE OF ACCOUNTING INFORMATION SYSTEMS TO ACCOUNTANTS (STUDY OBJECTIVE 8)

Anyone pursuing an accounting career must study and understand accounting information systems and the related concepts. No matter which particular career path is chosen within accounting, it will in some manner involve the use of an accounting information system. Accountants have several possible roles related to accounting information systems: They may be users of the AIS, part of the design or implementation team of an AIS, and/or auditors of an AIS.

USERS OF THE AIS

Accountants within any organization must use the accounting information system to accomplish the functions of accounting, generating accounting reports, and using accounting reports. For example, a controller in an organization must oversee a staff of accountants who record all accounting transactions, do the monthly closing of the accounting records, and generate the reports needed by management and external users. The accounting information system is the mechanism that allows the accounting staff to accomplish those functions. Accountants must therefore understand AIS concepts in order to perform these accounting jobs.

DESIGN OR IMPLEMENTATION TEAM

Accountants are usually part of a multiple-discipline team that designs and/or implements accounting information systems. When an organization considers a change to its AIS, accountants must be involved in decisions related to such matters as evaluating which software to purchase, how to design software or systems, and the implementation of software or systems.

AN AUDITOR OF THE AIS

Auditors conduct assurance services such as a financial audit. To conduct an audit, the auditor must collect evidence and make judgments regarding the completeness and accuracy of accounting information. The auditor cannot make informed decisions necessary to complete the audit without an understanding of the accounting information system. The auditor cannot judge the accuracy and reliability of accounting data without understanding how the data are entered, processed, and reported in the accounting information system.

THE RELATION OF ETHICS TO ACCOUNTING INFORMATION SYSTEMS (STUDY OBJECTIVE 9)

Unfortunately, there are many opportunities for unethical or fraudulent behavior related to accounting information systems. Accounting information systems can be misused to assist in committing unethical acts or helping to hide unethical acts. That is, the AIS is often the tool used to commit or cover up unethical behavior.

THE REAL WORLD

In an anonymous company that sold computer software, the following unethical behavior occurred:

> Top management set very ambitious monthly targets in order to meet annual revenue goals. Sales could not be booked as revenue until the product was shipped to customers. As it got closer to the end of a month and it appeared that monthly goals would not be met, salespersons were asked to call customers and ask them to take receipt of their orders earlier than anticipated. If these efforts did not produce enough revenue, there were instances where products were shipped to customers who had not ordered, knowing that customers would immediately ship them back to the company. The revenue, however, would already be recognized for the current month, which resulted in meeting the monthly sales goal.[7]

Notice that those who engaged in the unethical behavior described presumed that there was an accounting information system that would record ("book") sales when orders were shipped to customers. These individuals were taking advantage of the AIS by forcing products to be shipped early and thereby artificially inflating revenue. Those involved in the deception knew that the shipping of goods to customers would trigger processes that would lead to revenue being recorded. The accounting information system would have captured and recorded data as if a sale were proper, because the system is set up to record shipments to customers as sales.

This is only one example of how an accounting information system can be misused to conduct unethical acts. Other examples of some potential unethical behaviors are as follows:

- Fraudulent financial reporting
- Revenue inflation
- Expense account fraud
- Inflating hours worked for payroll purposes
- Computer fraud
- Hacking
- Browsing confidential data

This is just a brief set of examples. In many cases, unethical acts have also been made illegal. For example, fraudulent financial reporting is unethical, and it is also illegal. However, using a 3% bad debt percentage as opposed to a more realistic 4% rate to "fudge the numbers" may not be criminal; yet it is unethical. For many reasons, accountants must become aware of the potential unethical behaviors. Some of those reasons are that accountants

1. assist in developing and implementing internal control structures that should lessen the chance of unethical actions. Those in this role must understand the nature of the various kinds of unethical actions before they can design a system to lessen the risk.
2. are often pressured to assist in, or cover up, unethical actions. Therefore, accountants must understand what actions are ethical and unethical so that they can avoid being coerced into unethical actions.

[7]Joseph F. Castellano, Kenneth Rosenzweig, and Harper A. Roehm, "How Corporate Culture Impacts Unethical Distortion of Financial Numbers," *Management Accounting Quarterly*, Summer 2004, vol. 5, issue 4, p. 39.

3. deal with assets or records that could easily tempt accountants to engage in unethical behavior. For example, someone who handles cash every day may be tempted to steal some of the cash. Accountants have control over or recording responsibilities for many assets. When professional accountants face ongoing temptation, having a better understanding of which actions are unethical may help them to resist temptation to commit unethical acts.

(These unethical behavior examples and many other unethical actions related to AIS will be discussed in the remaining chapters.)

SUMMARY OF STUDY OBJECTIVES

An overview of business processes. There are many different business processes that occur in organizations. A business process is a prescribed sequence of work steps completed in order to produce a desired result for the organization. A business process is initiated by a particular kind of event, has a well-defined beginning and end, and is usually completed in a relatively short period. Many business processes have direct or indirect effects on accounting records, and these can be categorized into revenue processes, expenditure processes, conversion processes, and administrative processes.

An overview of an accounting information system. The accounting information system comprises of the processes, procedures, and systems that capture accounting data from business processes; records the accounting data in the appropriate records; processes the detailed accounting data by classifying, summarizing and consolidating; and reports the summarized accounting data to internal and external users. As business processes occur, accounting data from those processes is entered into the accounting information system, processed, and reported to the appropriate internal and external parties. The internal reports can be used as feedback to monitor and control business processes.

The business process linkage throughout the supply chain. Not only do business processes occur within an organization, but business processes can also be linkages to related organizations. For example, when an organization buys raw materials, it is engaging in a business process linked to the vendor's selling process. Business processes occur throughout the supply chain. The supply chain is the organizations, processes, and information flows that involve the movement of materials, funds, and related information through the full logistics process, from the acquisition of raw materials to delivery of finished products to the end user. Supply chain management is the management and control of all materials, funds, and related information in the logistics process, from the acquisition of raw materials to the delivery of finished products to the end user (customer).

The IT enablement of business processes. Processes throughout the supply chain can benefit from information technology enablement. IT enablement is the leveraging of the capabilities of IT to improve the efficiency of a process, reduce the cost of a process, or both. For example, when an organization sells goods on a website, it is using IT to improve the efficiency and reduce the costs of its sales processes.

Basic computer and IT concepts. To understand an AIS and IT enablement of processes, it is important for us to have an understanding of basic computer and IT concepts. These concepts include the data hierarchy, databases, relational databases, and networks.

Examples of IT enablement. There are many different types of IT enablement used in organizations. Some examples introduced in this chapter are e-business, electronic data interchange, point of sale systems, automated matching of purchasing documents, evaluated receipt settlement, e-payables, and enterprise resource planning systems. IT enablement is described in more detail in later chapters.

The internal control structure of organizations. To maintain a strong control environment, there are at least six control-related structures that management should develop and maintain. These are Enterprise risk management (ERS), a code of ethics, a set of internal controls, a set of IT controls, a corporate governance structure, and an IT governance structure.

The importance of accounting information systems to accountants. Accountants must understand accounting information systems because they are users, participants in the design and implementation, and auditors of the AIS.

The relation of ethics to accounting information systems. The accounting information system can be misused so as to conduct or cover up unethical or fraudulent behavior. Accountants must understand the types of behavior within an organization that are unethical in order to professionally and ethically complete their duties.

KEY TERMS

Accounting information system
Application controls
Automated matching in purchasing
Batch processing
Bit
Business process
Business process reengineering
Byte
Corporate governance
Data mining
Data warehouse
Database
E-business
Electronic data interchange
Electronic invoice presentment and payment
Enterprise resource planning software
Enterprise risk management
E-payables
Evaluated receipt settlement
Field
File
General controls
Indexed sequential access method
Information technology
Internal controls
IT enablement
IT governance
LAN
Master file
Online processing
Operational database
Point of sale systems
Random access
Real-time processing
Record
Sequential access
Supply chain
Supply chain management
Transaction file
Vendor

END OF CHAPTER MATERIAL

CONCEPT CHECK

1. When a customer returns goods that were purchased, the business process to accept the return would most likely be a(n)
   a. administrative process
   b. conversion process
   c. expenditure process
   d. revenue process
2. Which of the following is least likely to be an output of the accounting information system?
   a. a check
   b. a report
   c. an invoice
   d. a bar code
3. Which of the following is not true of the supply chain?
   a. The supply chain includes vendors.
   b. The supply chain excludes customers.
   c. The supply chain includes information flows.
   d. The supply chain includes secondary suppliers.
4. Which of the following is not an objective of IT enablement?
   a. increased accuracy of data
   b. reduced cost
   c. reduced security problems
   d. increased efficiency
5. The correct order of the computer data hierarchy is
   a. byte, bit, record, field, file, database
   b. bit, byte, record, field, file, database
   c. bit, byte, field, record, file, database
   d. bit, byte, field, record, database, file
6. The process of searching for identifiable patterns in data is called
   a. sequential processing
   b. data warehousing
   c. data mining
   d. real-time processing
7. An IT enabled system for purchasing that is an "invoice-less" system is called a(n)
   a. automated matching system
   b. evaluated receipt settlement
   c. e-payables
   d. point of sale system

8. The COSO report written for the purpose of assisting managers in the challenge of managing risk in their organizations is entitled
   a. "Internal Controls—Integrated Framework"
   b. "Enterprise Risk Management—Integrated Framework"
   c. "Corporate Governance"
   d. "IT Governance"
9. Accountants have some form of use of the AIS in all but which role?
   a. user
   b. programmer
   c. auditor
   d. designer
10. Which of the following is not true of unethical behavior?
   a. The only category of unethical behavior for accountants is inflating revenue.
   b. Accountants are often pressured to help commit or cover up unethical behavior.
   c. Hacking is an unethical behavior that accountants should be concerned about.
   d. An accounting information system can be used to cover up unethical behavior.

DISCUSSION QUESTIONS

11. (SO 1) How might the sales and cash collection processes at a Wal-Mart store differ from the sales and cash collection processes at McDonald's?
12. (SO 1) Can you think of any procedures in place at McDonald's that are intended to ensure the accuracy of your order?
13. (SO 1) How might the sales and cash collection process at Boeing Co. (maker of commercial passenger jets) differ from the sales and cash collection processes at McDonald's?
14. (SO 1) Are there business processes that do not in some way affect accounting records or financial statements?
15. (SO 2) Briefly describe the five components of an accounting information system.
16. (SO 2) Describe how sales data are captured and recorded at a restaurant such as Applebee's.
17. (SO 2) What occurs in an accounting information system that classifies accounting transactions?
18. (SO 2) What are the differences between internal reports and external reports generated by the accounting information system?
19. (SO 3) What types of businesses are in the supply chain of an automobile manufacturer?
20. (SO 3) When a company evaluates a supplier of materials, what kinds of characteristics might be evaluated?
21. (SO 3) How do you think a company may be able to influence a supplier to meet its business processing requirements?

22. (SO 4) Describe any IT enablement that you have noticed at a large retail store such as Wal-Mart or Target.
23. (SO 4) How do you think the World Wide Web (WWW) has led to business process reengineering at companies such as Lands End or J. Crew?
24. (SO 4) What two kinds of efficiency improvements result from business process reengineering in conjunction with IT systems?
25. (SO 5) Explain the differences between a field, a record, and a file.
26. (SO 5) Explain why random access files would be preferable to sequential access files when payroll personnel are changing a pay rate for a single employee.
27. (SO 5) Why do real-time systems require direct access files?
28. (SO 5) Why is data contained in the data warehouse called non-volatile?
29. (SO 5) How is an extranet different from the Internet?
30. (SO 6) Prepare a list of the types of businesses that you have been involved in that use point of sale systems.
31. (SO 6) What do you think would be the advantages of an e-payables system over a traditional system that uses paper purchase orders and invoices?
32. (SO 7) Describe why enterprise risk management is important.
33. (SO 7) What is the difference between general controls and application controls?
34. (SO 7) In what way is a code of ethics beneficial to an organization?
35. (SO 8) What roles do accountants have in relation to the accounting information system?

BRIEF EXERCISES

36. (SO 1) For each category of business processes (revenue, expenditure, conversion, administrative), give an example of a business process.
37. (SO 2) Think of a company that you have worked for or with which you have done business. Which departments within the company need reports generated by the accounting information systems?
38. (SO 3) Explain a supply chain linkage and give an example.
39. (SO 4) Explain how business process reengineering occurs. Also, explain how it differs from the typical changes in company policies.
40. (SO 5) For an accounts receivable system, what kind of data would be found in the master files and transaction files, respectively?
41. (SO 5) Describe the differences in the following three types of processing:
    a. batch processing
    b. online processing
    c. real-time processing
42. (SO 5) The networks discussed in this chapter were LANs, Internet, intranet, and extranet. Explain each.
43. (SO 7) Give a brief summary of each of the following:
    a. enterprise risk management
    b. corporate governance
    c. IT governance

44. (SO 9) Describe why accountants should be concerned about ethics.

45. (SO 9) Adrienne Camm is currently pursuing her accounting degree at Ridge University. She has excelled in each of her major courses to date; however, she has always struggled in her computer classes and with assignments requiring use of computer technology. Nevertheless, Adrienne confidently claims that she will become an excellent accountant. Comment on the practical and ethical implications of her position.

PROBLEMS

46. (SO 2) If an accounting information system were entirely a manual system (no computers used), explain how data would be captured, recorded, classified, summarized, and reported. Discuss how the sophistication of the company's computer system impacts the accounting output and, alternatively, how the requirements for accounting outputs impact the design of the accounting information systems.

47. (SO 1,3) Classify each of the following as a revenue process, expenditure process, conversion process, or administrative process:
    a. selling common stock to raise capital
    b. purchasing electronic components to manufacture DVD players
    c. moving electronic components from the stockroom to the production floor to begin making DVD players
    d. paying employees at the end of a payroll period
    e. preparing financial statements
    f. receiving cash payments from customers
    g. buying fixed assets
    h. moving manufactured DVD players from the production floor to the warehouse

48. (SO 1) Business processes are composed of three common stages: an initial event, a beginning, and an end. For each of the processes a through h in Problem 47, identify the applicable initial event, beginning, and end of the process.

49. (SO 1,2,7) Each of the points listed next represents an internal control that may be implemented within a company's accounting information system to reduce various risks. For each point, identify the appropriate business process (revenue, expenditure, conversion, administrative). In addition, refer to the description of business processes under Study Objective 2 in this chapter, and identify the appropriate subprocess. (Some subprocesses may be used more than once, and others may not be used at all.)
    a. Customer credit must be authorized before a business transaction takes place.
    b. An authorized price list of goods for sale is provided.
    c. A shipping report is prepared for all shipments of goods so that customers may be billed in a timely manner.

d. Access to personnel files and paycheck records is available only in accordance with management specifications.

e. New vendors are required to be authorized before a business transaction takes place.

f. Access to cash is restricted to those employees authorized by management.

g. Costs of goods manufactured is properly summarized, classified, recorded, and reported.

h. Amounts due to vendors are reconciled by comparing company records with statements received from the vendors.

i. Employee wage rates and paycheck deductions must be authorized by management.

j. Specific procedures such as the performance of a background check are carried out for all new employee hires.

k. The purchasing manager is notified when stock levels are low so that items may be restocked to prevent backorders.

l. Two signatures are required on checks for payments in excess of $5000.

m. When excess cash is on hand, the funds are invested in short-term securities.

n. Goods received are inspected and damaged, or unmatched items are promptly communicated to the vendor.

o. The monthly bank statement is reconciled to the company's cash records by an outside accountant.

50. (SO 3) Using an Internet search engine (Google, Dogpile, Lycos, etc.) search for the terms "RFID" and "supply chain." Put both of these terms in your search and be sure that "supply chain" is in quotation marks. Read some of the resulting websites you find and answer these questions:

a. What is RFID?

b. How is RFID related to the supply chain?

c. How will RFID improve the accuracy of data from the supply chain?

51. (SO 7) Go to the COSO website and find the executive summary of the article "Enterprise risk management—Integrated Framework." Read the sections titled "Roles and Responsibilities" and "Use of this Report." Describe the roles that various parties should play in enterprise risk management.

52. (SO 9) Using an Internet search engine (Google, Dogpile, Lycos, etc.) search for the term (in quotations) "earnings management." From the items you read, answer the following questions:

a. Is earnings management always criminal?

b. Is earnings management always unethical?

53. (SO 9) Using an Internet search engine (Google, Dogpile, Lycos, etc.) search for "HealthSouth" and "fraud" or "Scrushy" (the name of the company's CEO) and explain the fraud that occurred at HealthSouth Corporation. What was the ultimate result of the prosecution of HealthSouth officials?

CASES

54. The Gas-n-Go Mart is a gas station and convenience market similar to any BP, Shell, or Speedway gas and convenience stores. Gas-n-Go is a regional chain of gas and convenience marts located in the St. Louis area, with 14 locations.

    Required:

    The section of this chapter identified as Learning Objective 2 describes five work steps, or processes, in the accounting information system. Based on your experience in using similar kinds of gas and convenience marts, briefly describe your impression of how these five work steps would be accomplished at Gas-n-Go if you buy gas, a bottled soft drink, and a candy bar.

55. The fast food industry has been dramatically altered through IT enablement. Fast food restaurants include franchise operations such as McDonald's, Wendy's, and Burger King. However, IT enablement has not completely eliminated manual processes in fast food franchise restaurants.

    Required:

    Using your experience in visiting fast food restaurants, answer the two questions that follow:

    a. List and describe four different activities that are manual parts of business processes at a restaurant such as Wendy's.

    b. List and describe four different activities that are IT enabled parts of business processes at a restaurant such as Wendy's.

56. Consider any recent purchase you made at a department store such as Target, Wal-Mart, or Kmart. A business process that occurred was the sale of a product to you. However, to make that sale, the department store had to engage in many other processes that support that sales process, or result from that sales process. These other processes may precede or occur after that sales process.

    Required:

    a. Describe any necessary supporting processes that precede the sale of a product to you.

    b. Describe any necessary supporting processes that occur after a sale to you.

57. Cool's Cues Co. is a regional manufacturing operation that makes and sells pool cues for sporting goods stores and billiard halls in Baltimore, Maryland, and the surrounding local area. John Cool and his wife, Rebecca, are the owners and only employees.

    John Cool purchases all of the materials needed to make pool cues, including wood, paint, hardware, and supplies. All purchases are made from local suppliers, and all payments are made in cash at the time of the purchase. John Cool is responsible for making the pool cues. He also handles all telephone calls and replacements, and he personally delivers all finished products.

    All sales are conducted on account via the Internet. Orders are received electronically through the company's website at www.coolscues.com. Rebecca Cool prints the orders and forwards them to her husband in the workshop. Mrs. Cool is also responsible for website design and maintenance, as well as all accounting and customer collections.

Address the following questions regarding Cool's Cues:

a. What are the business processes that apply to this business?
b. How would the business processes change if Cool's Cues expanded to a regional focus?
c. How would the business processes change if Cool's Cues began selling pool balls and other billiard equipment in addition to cues?

CONTINUING CASE: SPATELLI'S PIZZERIA

INTRODUCTION

On the morning of October 31st, Peter Greyton, Chief Information Officer at Spatelli's Pizzeria, was waiting for both Jim Saxton, database administrator, and Elaine Black, operations manager, to come to his office for a meeting. While waiting, Peter was thinking about the surge of telephone and Internet orders expected to be received through the company's customer order center within the next 12 hours. Halloween had always been the most popular day of the year for people in the greater Pittsburgh area to order pizza from Spatelli's. There were 49 restaurant locations to serve these customers, but only one location to receive all of the orders and forward them to the right restaurant. Peter's thoughts were interrupted as Jim and Elaine entered his office. The following conversation took place:

PETER: Well, guys, it's here again, our biggest day of the year. Not only is Halloween a busy day, but we have the upcoming day after Thanksgiving, the week before Christmas, and Super Bowl Sunday. Can our current computer system's infrastructure and people keep pace with the orders we expect?

JIM: I think our systems are all running at peak performance. We shouldn't have any computer concerns for today or those other busy days.

ELAINE: Everyone in the customer order center is focused on making sure that our customers get their pizzas as ordered. We have plenty of people scheduled to work tonight, so we're good to go.

PETER: Terrific. But every time we face one of these peak sales days, I start wondering about the long-term capacity and effectiveness of our computer systems. Jim, we need to think long term about our computer system. I was just reading an article that I'd like you to take a look at. It's about Anheuser-Busch Companies and their use of data mining.

JIM: I do agree with you, Pete; we should always be thinking about how newer IT systems can help us. Could you e-mail me the link to the article?

PETER: Sure, and I would like you to think about how we might use the same approach in our business. Elaine, your order center people are doing a great job, but again there's something I'd like us to think about in the long run. As you know, we now have to manually enter all customer order center sales and store sales into our general ledger (GL). I think we could improve a lot of things if those sales fed automatically into our GL software. Why don't you think about any advantages you see for an automatic interface, and we'll look at the costs compared to those advantages. How's that sound?

ELAINE: I'll do that. I'll give it some thought and work on a report about an automatic interface between our GL software and the point of sale systems in our restaurants as well as the phone and Internet sales. How soon do you want to meet again to look at these issues?

PETER: Let's say in two weeks at the same time.

As Jim and Elaine left his office, Peter continued to think about the features of the company's accounting information systems and whether or not data extracted from these systems could facilitate the multiple needs of the company. The focus had always been on providing accurate financial accounting information from the various locations; however, the company's aggressive growth strategies meant increased emphasis on the system's ability to analyze detailed customer information that could be translated into increased sales opportunities.

Peter knew the challenges they faced could very well affect the company's ability to maintain its competitive advantage. He realized that his department must continually improve the company's information systems to help it achieve growth strategies. Operating state-of-the-art systems was imperative to position the company to execute those growth plans. However, he was concerned about the possibility that restrictions of the current information systems could actually prevent the company from doing what it wanted to do. Allowing restrictive systems to prevent them from achieving business strategies was a risk that Peter would not tolerate!

BACKGROUND

Spatelli's Pizzeria is a great American success story. Started by Dino Spatelli in the 1960s, the business impetus was a family pizza recipe. Introduced to the public at a church festival in Pittsburgh's Little Italy, Spatelli's pizzas are now a recognized tradition in the Greater Pittsburgh area. A full menu and local expansion have led to its growing popularity over the years and have helped it achieve nearly 50% of the area market share. Annual sales now exceed $100 million. Following is a timeline of milestones in the company's history:

1962 Dino and Gloria Spatelli contributed $500 and the family pizza recipe to a partnership that opened the first Spatelli's Pizzeria.

1965 The Spatellis bought out their business partners.

1967 The first Spatelli's franchise opened.

1971–77 Dozens of new Spatelli's franchises opened throughout the surrounding region.

1983 Home delivery service began.

1992 A central, one-number calling system for all restaurants was launched.

2003 Internet ordering began. The first "prototype pizzeria" opened.

Today A total of 49 locations are in operation.

The company has been known for its ability to get ahead of national trends. For instance, in the early 1980s, Spatelli's began offering delivery service; however, while the competitors were merely delivering pizzas, Spatelli's delivered many additional items from its extensive menu. The company was also on the cutting edge when it launched its one-number telephone ordering system whereby a single telephone number was used to service sales orders for the entire region. Additional conveniences became available about ten years later when Spatelli's introduced online ordering. Recently, it has expanded its menu offerings and opened prototype restaurants specially designed with new features (such as a full-service bar and a retail counter) that appeal to various customer groups. Each of these advancements has propelled Spatelli's growth over the past four decades.

Dino Spatelli's name is also well known for its tradition of supporting neighborhood organizations. Spatelli's promotes schools, amateur athletics, and other community groups. Interestingly, some local student athletes were a tremendous help to Spatelli's in 1971 when the business was in trouble. A fire had destroyed much of the building containing Spatelli's original pizzeria and commissary. The commissary made menu ingredients for all of the Spatelli's pizzerias, so the entire business was in jeopardy when this facility became inoperable. Area students and coaches helped with the clean-up and rebuilding efforts that made it possible for the facility to be reopened in a fraction of the anticipated time. Dino Spatelli thanked them by establishing a hall of fame that has become a fixture of Greater Pittsburgh high school athletics.

Spatelli's reputation for great Italian food and innovations in both customer service and community service have contributed to the company's ability to grow into the most popular pizzeria in the Greater Pittsburgh region. Spatelli's sales include an average of 110,000 pizzas per week. It has managed to stay ahead of the national competitors, which is an unusual feat. In fact, many people in and around Pittsburgh believe that pizza can only be Spatelli's!

MULTIPLE SYSTEMS, MULTIPLE FUNCTIONS, MULTIPLE USES OF INFORMATION

There are three ways to place an order at Spatelli's: in-store, via telephone, or online. The order processing systems are illustrated in Figure 1. Here's how they work:

In-store orders

In-store orders are taken by restaurant staff serving patrons dining in one of Spatelli's restaurants or walking in to place an order. Servers manually complete an order ticket at the tableside and input the information into the company's point of sales system through computer terminals located in the food preparation stations. Walk-in orders are typically entered directly into the system by staff using the computer terminal located at the counter.

Telephone orders

Approximately two-thirds of the company's business is processed via the telephone. Spatelli's phone ordering system is called a one-number system, referring

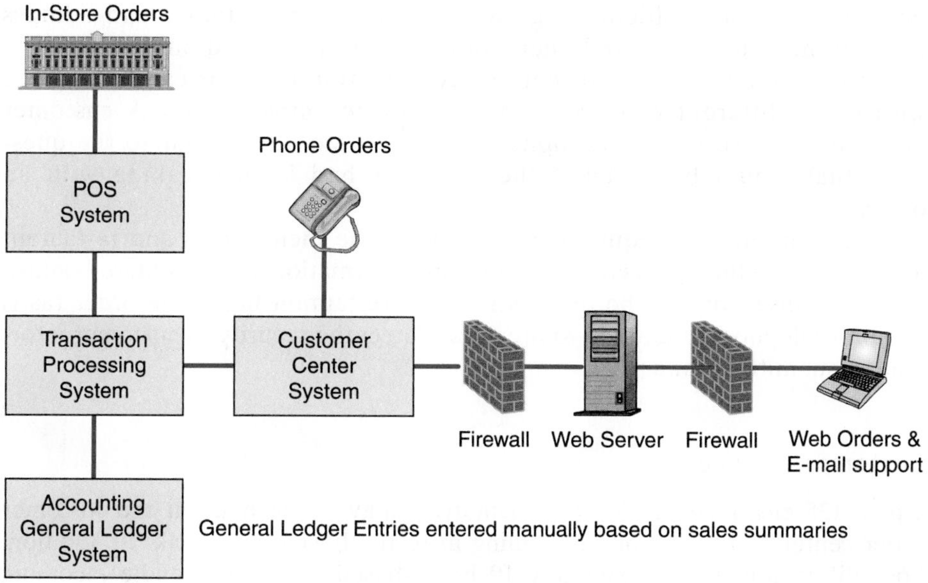

Figure 1
Spatelli's Order Processing Systems

to the convenience of ordering through a single phone number, regardless of the restaurant location nearest the customer.

Most phone orders are received by an operator, who enters the order directly into a computer terminal while speaking with the customer. Customer phone numbers are used to present the customer with his or her choice of the nearest pizzeria for preparation and carry-out or delivery. The software in the system references a street database to verify that the street address exists. Credit card numbers are obtained from customers paying by credit card. The customer service representative verifies the order and credit card number before ending the call.

Upon confirmation of an order, the order is sent directly to the restaurant, where it is processed through the company's transaction processing system and printed at the appropriate food preparation station(s). Credit card numbers are included in the transmission, and all credit card transactions are processed at the restaurants at the time the order is received.

There are several advantages of handling phone orders through a customer order center rather than at individual restaurant locations. Above all, the reduction in background noise improves the accuracy of the order-taking process. In addition, the customer's wait time is greatly reduced. Before Spatelli's implemented its one-number system, customers' wait time at peak could be up to 15 minutes. The order center's average wait time goal is now one minute or less.

Internet orders

To place an online order, a customer must be registered. Registration is a simple process that can occur anytime during business hours. Customers are asked to provide identifying information that will be retained in the system. Repeat customers will not have to go through the registration process again.

Web-based ordering is tied to the company's one-number system. When a customer enters an order online, customer information is pulled from the one-number system. Identifying data such as phone number and address does not have to be entered. Menu offerings are presented on the screen in various drop-down boxes so that any combination of items can be ordered with many different choices of toppings or accompaniments. A customer must answer a series of questions regarding the order, similar to the questions that would be asked if the customer had been speaking with an operator.

Online orders also require confirmation of the menu items and restaurant location before the call is ended. Credit card information may be entered online, and the transaction will be processed at the restaurant filling the order (as is done for telephone orders). Two firewalls protect the security of customer information submitted online.

Customer Service

Up to 135 customer service representatives may be on hand at the customer order center to process orders coming in to the business at peak. In addition, Spatelli's employs approximately 10 home-based agents to handle incoming orders. Home-based agents may perform any of the customer service functions from a computer terminal located within their homes.

All operators are required to undergo a one-week training program before they begin serving customers. After the training program, operators are subject to one week of supervised on-the-job training, followed by ongoing performance evaluations. Supervisors at the customer order center perform order scanning, whereby orders are randomly reviewed for reasonableness. Order scanning is performed more frequently for orders taken by new operators. Supervisors also follow up on errors and customer complaints, and may listen in on calls to review the operator's performance.

If customers are in need of customer service, they may call or e-mail the company. Supervisors handle these types of calls and e-mail messages, and will respond either via telephone or reply e-mail. Restaurant managers can also print customer complaints at their respective locations.

Accounting functions

Spatelli's ordering systems and transaction processing systems are the source of all sales information sent to the accounting department. Restaurant managers prepare daily sales summaries and submit them to the company's administrative offices on the following day. These summaries are transmitted electronically via the intranet and are received in the accounting department. Accounting staff prepare general ledger entries based upon these sales summaries and key the information into the company's accounting software. The transaction processing system provides sales by restaurant for call-in and Internet orders, which are reconciled to the restaurant summaries on a daily basis. Once the accounting system is updated and the daily reconciliations are performed, the data is stored in an on-site server.

Although there is a lot of information to manage, coming from many different locations, the capacity of the system is nearly 25 times its current load.

Information Technology

The information technology staff at Spatelli's is continuously engaged in system maintenance activities. Because the business changes so frequently, systems maintenance is an ongoing process. Every time a new coupon is offered, a price is changed, or a new menu item becomes available, the related information must be integrated into the transaction processing system.

Each menu addition has its own level of complexity, and many of the items include options to customize to individual tastes in a plethora of combinations. This poses a challenge in ordering; however, the menu presentation continues to be improved to eliminate chances of an incomplete or incorrect order. The options are available online and to customer service representatives via drop-down boxes on their computer screens. Most screens require an entry, even if it is "none," in order to ensure that no part of the order is forgotten.

Required:

1. After reading the Spatelli's case information, list and briefly describe (two to three sentences) each business process included in the case description.
2. Think about, list, and briefly describe other business processes that probably occur at Spatelli's.

SOLUTIONS TO CONCEPT CHECK

1. (SO 1) When a customer returns goods that were purchased, the business process to accept the return would most likely be **d. revenue process**. Customer returns are part of the sales return process, which is a revenue process.
2. (SO 2) Of the choices presented, **d. a bar code** would be least likely to be an output of the accounting information system: A bar code is usually an input to the accounting information system. For example, the bar code on a grocery product is scanned to process a sale. The other options are outputs of an accounting information system.
3. (SO 3) The following is not true of the supply chain: **b. The supply chain excludes customers**. The supply chain includes vendors, customers, and all intermediaries.
4. (SO 4) The following is not an objective of IT enablement: **c. reduced security problems**. IT systems usually have increased security problems. The other three answers are objectives of IT enablement.
5. (SO 5) The correct order of the computer data hierarchy is **c. bit, byte, field, record, file, database**.
6. (SO 5) The process of searching for identifiable patterns in data is called **c. data mining**.
7. (SO 6) An IT enabled system for purchasing that is "invoice-less" is called **b. evaluated receipt settlement**.

8. (SO 7) The title of the COSO report that was written for the purpose of assisting managers in the challenge of managing risk in their organizations is **b. "Enterprise Risk Management—Integrated Framework."**
9. (SO 8) Accountants have some role in the AIS as all of the given choices, except **b. programmer.** The programming role involves formulation of the AIS to meet users' needs. It uses input and feedback from a variety of people within the organization and the supply chain to determine its components.
10. (SO 9) The following is not true of unethical behavior: **a. The only category of unethical behavior for accountants is inflating revenue.** This is only one of the many forms of unethical behavior that may take place.

CHAPTER 2

Foundational Concepts of the AIS

Study Objectives

This chapter will help you gain an understanding of the following concepts:

1. The interrelationships of business processes and the AIS
2. Types of accounting information systems
3. Accounting software market segments
4. Input methods used in business processes
5. The processing of accounting data
6. Outputs from the AIS related to business processes
7. Documenting processes and systems
8. Client-server computing
9. Ethical considerations at the foundation of accounting information systems

Appendix: Basic concepts of the Resources, Events, Agents (REA) Model

THE REAL WORLD

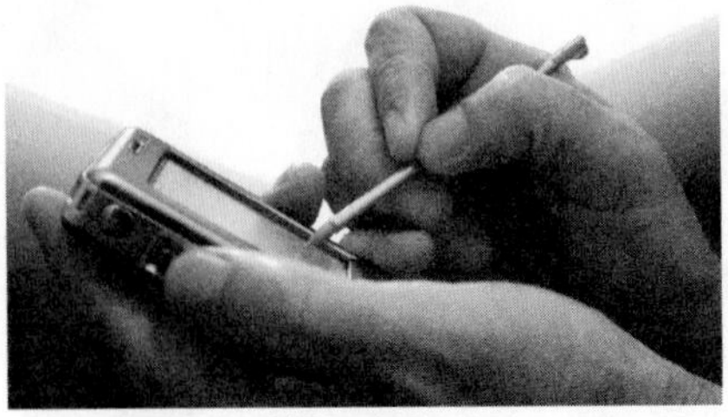

Vasiliki Varvaki/iStockphoto

Medieval Times is a dinner-theater chain that has locations on both the east and west coasts of the United States. Each location seats over 1000 people and offers guests the unique opportunity to watch jousting knights in the arena while enjoying dinner and drinks. Dinner is the same meal for each guest, but guests may order drinks from the bar. Medieval Times gives each cocktail server a handheld wireless computer terminal, which looks and works like a PDA, to relay orders to the bar. This order-taking system "gave us a faster, higher-quality service," said Richard Dunn, the senior vice president of merchandising.[1]

Under a traditional drink-ordering system, prior to the use of handheld devices, servers took orders manually by writing them on a slip, then walked to a terminal to place the order. The new wireless system eliminates that paperwork and legwork because the order is transmitted wirelessly to the bar. When numerous guests desire cocktail service at the same time, the handheld wireless system tremendously speeds up the process of taking and delivering orders. The efficiency increase was so great that Medieval Times was able to increase revenue by adding an extra round of beverage service to each event.

Traditional restaurants are also adopting the handheld wireless systems. Culver's, the franchisor of the Better Burger and frozen custard fame, is experimenting with these systems to sell its frozen custard at the customer's table during peak hours. Many casual eateries, such as Tony Roma's and TGI Friday's, use these systems to take customer orders and then transmit the orders directly from the table to the kitchen. In addition, the kitchen can send messages to servers, and the check can be prepared at the tableside. Not only does this save much time and legwork for servers, but it also increases the efficiency of the kitchen and the accuracy of the order and order pricing.

As illustrated here, technology has allowed the hospitality industry to provide better, faster, and higher quality service to customers. This is an example of using IT to enable business processes. In addition to the changes in terms of enhanced customer service and increased efficiencies, the business processes and the accounting information systems must adapt to these new technologies. Handheld wireless order-taking systems improve the business process of taking and filling customer orders, in addition to changing the way the data for each sales transaction is captured. The older method of writing abbreviations for food orders on a handwritten ticket and then taking that ticket to a terminal to key in the order is not only less efficient, but more prone to errors. IT systems that reduce errors result in more accurate information in the accounting information system.

The point of these examples is to illustrate that business processes, IT systems, and the accounting information system are inextricably linked. Using IT to enable business processes will change these business processes as well as the manner in which accounting data are collected. All industries have been affected by technology and have in most cases revised business processes and accounting information systems for the better. IT systems have dramatically affected the input of data into accounting information systems, the manner in which those data are processed, and the outputs of the accounting information system. This chapter begins by revisiting the fundamental concepts of business processes and accounting information systems, emphasizing the interrelationships between the two. It also describes accounting software and the various data input methods, processing, and output of accounting information systems. In addition, important tools used in accounting information systems—the

[1]Alan J. Liddle, "Handheld POS Usage Clicks with Operators," *Nations Restaurant News,* April 11, 2005.

methods to document accounting information systems and client-server computing—are described.

INTERRELATIONSHIPS OF BUSINESS PROCESSES AND THE AIS (STUDY OBJECTIVE 1)

Chapter 1 introduced an accounting information system as a system that captures, records, processes, and reports accounting information. The information captured is generated by financial transactions within the organization or between the organization and its customers and vendors. When a transaction occurs, there are systematic and defined steps called business processes that take place within the organization to complete the underlying tasks of the transaction. A business process is a prescribed sequence of work steps completed in order to produce a desired result for the organization. A business process is initiated by a particular kind of event, has a well-defined beginning and end, and is usually completed in a relatively short period of time. Business processes occur so that the organization may serve its customers.

Every organization exists to serve customers in some way. Some organizations make and sell products, while others provide services to customers. Nearly everything that an organization does to fulfill its day-to-day activities is part of a business process. When organizations buy, sell, produce, collect cash, hire employees, or pay expenses they are engaged in business processes, all of which support the objective of serving customers. The examples of beverage or food service to customers are business processes.

Each business process has a set of systematic steps undertaken to complete it. Some business processes you see in your everyday life. For example, when you eat at a restaurant, the restaurant must have established a systematic set of steps that employees perform to serve you. A host meets you at the door to seat you, and a server has been preassigned to that table. The server takes your order and relays the order to the kitchen. The kitchen personnel have a predesigned set of activities to prepare your meal. The server then delivers your meal, checks on you periodically throughout the meal while you are eating, and presents a bill; then you pay the bill. All of these activities are business processes for a restaurant.

As these many business processes occur, the corresponding data generated must be collected by the accounting information system. The restaurant must have a system to capture and record the revenue generated by your meal, the details of your credit card payment, the food used in your meal and its cost, the wages paid to the server and host, and any tips. From nearly all of the business processes in an organization, there are accounting effects. As the systematic steps are undertaken in a business process, the accounting information system must capture and record the related financial data.

Exhibit 2-1 shows the relationships among transactions, business processes, and the reporting of information. As transactions occur, business processes are undertaken to complete the transaction and record any relevant data. Within any business, there may be hundreds of business processes. Moreover, these business processes may vary from company to company. For example, the business processes of a local, family restaurant are probably very different from the business processes of a global fast food franchise like McDonald's. In addition, the business processes of McDonald's would be vastly different from, for example, the business processes of Nokia Corp., a cell phone manufacturer.

Exhibit 2-1
Overall View of Transactions, Processes, and Resulting Reports

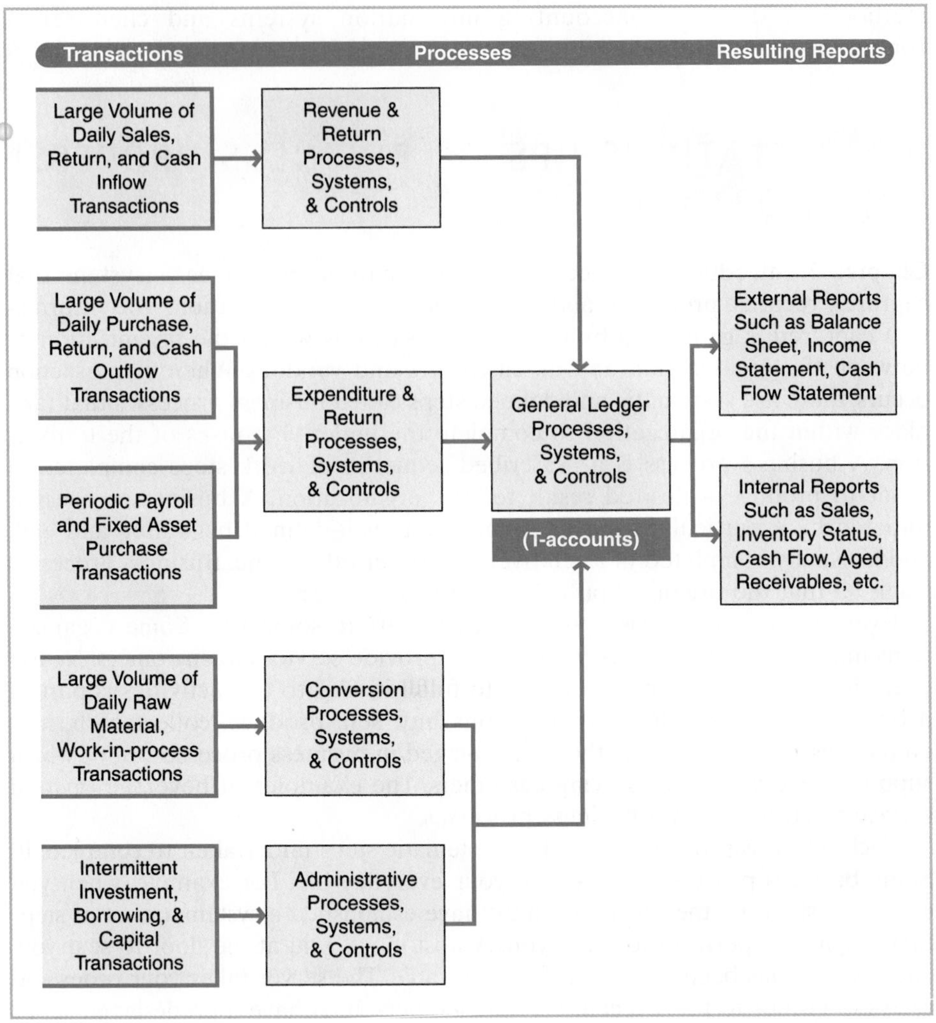

However, regardless of the type of business, as you will recall from Chapter 1, the general categories of business processes and subprocesses that are used to organize the concepts of most business processes include revenues processes, expenditure processes, conversion processes, and administrative processes.

To properly capture and record all relevant financial data, an accounting information system must maintain both detail and summary information. In traditional, manual accounting systems, the detailed transaction data are taken from source documents, special journals, and subsidiary ledgers and are summarized and posted to the general ledger. Exhibit 2-1 depicts the processes that summarize the detailed data into general ledger accounts.

Most accounting systems today are computerized to some extent, but there still remains a need for paper documents in many systems. Regardless of the extent of computerization, all accounting information systems must capture data from transactions within business processes, complete the necessary processing of that data, and provide outputs.

TYPES OF ACCOUNTING INFORMATION SYSTEMS (STUDY OBJECTIVE 2)

There are very many different types of accounting information systems used in business organizations today. The size of the organization, the nature of its processes, the extent of computerization, and the philosophy of management all affect the choice of system. Simply to organize the study of accounting information systems, we have divided the systems in place into three categories, as follows:

1. Manual systems
2. Legacy systems
3. Modern, integrated IT systems

MANUAL SYSTEMS

Certainly, most large or medium-size organizations use computerized accounting systems rather than manual record-keeping systems. However, there are many small organizations that use manual systems, in whole or in part, to maintain accounting records. In addition, even those larger organizations that have computerized aspects of the accounting information system may still have parts of their processes that involve manual records. For example, even if the calculation and printing of a paycheck in an organization are computerized, the employee time card may be completed by hand.

Because small organizations often use manual record-keeping systems—and even computerized systems may rely on some manual record keeping—it is important to examine manual processes in accounting information systems. An entirely manual system would require source documents and paper-based ledgers and journals.

A **source document** is a record that captures the key data of a transaction. The data on a source document usually include the date, purpose, entity, quantities, and dollar amount of a transaction. Some examples of source documents are employee time cards, purchase orders, sales orders, and cash receipts. A source document usually serves three important functions in the accounting system: First, the source document provides the input data necessary for the accounting system to record the transaction. Second, the source document triggers business processes to begin. For example, a purchase order triggers the business processes that will fill the order and ship goods to the customer. Third, the source document serves as part of the permanent audit trail. If necessary, the organization can look up the original source document of a transaction to determine the status of the transaction.

A **turnaround document** is an output of the accounting system that can be used as an input in a different part of the accounting system. An example is your credit card statement, which is a computer output of the system your credit card company uses. The part of that statement you return with your payment is an input that can be used by the company's accounting system to determine account number. The computer system scans the document to read your account number, and it is not necessary for a person to manually type in your number. The turnaround document improves input efficiency and accuracy by eliminating human error.

These source documents become the inputs to record transactions in ledgers and journals. The **general ledger** provides details for the entire set of accounts used in the organization's accounting systems. Transactions or transaction summaries are posted to the general ledger from the general journal and special journals. The **general journal** is the place of original entry for any transactions that are not recorded in special journals. The general journal is used to record nonroutine transactions and adjusting and closing entries. **Special journals** are established to record specific types of transactions. For example, a sales journal records all sales. Other special journals could include a purchases journal, payroll journal, cash receipts journal, and cash disbursements journal. At regular intervals, such as at the end of each week or month, the subtotals of the special journals are posted to the general ledger. **Subsidiary ledgers** maintain detailed information regarding routine transactions, with an account established for each entity. For example, the accounts receivable subsidiary ledger maintains all detailed information regarding customer purchases, payments, and balances due. An account exists for each customer, and the total of those customer accounts equals the balance in the accounts receivable general ledger account.

The source documents, journals, and ledgers comprise the manual records in a manual accounting system. To record in these journals and ledgers, there must be established processes that employees follow in collecting source documents and entering information from source documents into the appropriate journals and ledgers.

As accounting information systems became computerized, the manual processes of record keeping and posting were transferred to automated systems. Automated systems maintain the same structure of subsidiary ledgers and general ledger accounts; however, the difference is that automated ledgers are computer files rather than paper records. Newer IT systems may not use the same structure and are much more likely to use fewer paper documents and records.

When IT is part of the accounting information system, it is important to understand that the hardware and software are not the *entire* accounting information system. In addition to the hardware and software, the human processes that capture, record, and process information are an integral part. The real-world example at the beginning of this chapter described a handheld wireless order-taking system. However, even that advanced technology needs a human to enter the order. The established process of entering the order is part of the accounting information system because it is part of the business process that captures accounting data. Therefore, accounting information systems include human as well as IT processes.

Until the 1990s, most accounting software consisted of modules, or separate programs, for each business process. Accounting software usually has modules for accounts receivable, accounts payable, payroll, and, possibly, other processes. These modules achieve essentially the same purpose as special journals and subsidiary ledgers. For example, the accounts receivable module processes and records all credit sales and maintains detailed information about customer account balances, collections, and balances due. Traditional accounting software systems, often called legacy systems, are described in the next section.

LEGACY SYSTEMS

A **legacy system** is an existing system in operation within an organization. A legacy system uses older technology in which the organization has a considerable investment and that might be entrenched in the organization. Some legacy systems have been in place for many years; perhaps the organization spent much time developing, maintaining, and customizing the system. Often, legacy systems are based on old or inadequate technology. In large companies, many legacy systems run on host-based mainframe computers. "Host based" means that all significant computer processing takes place on the mainframe host computer. Accounting software systems running on such computers are often written in programming languages that are nearing obsolescence. Examples of these software languages are COBOL, RPG, Basic, and PL1.

During the last couple of decades, even as technology advances have made these systems more outdated, many companies have been reluctant to abandon their legacy systems because they were customized to meet the specific needs of the organization and the process to replace them is expensive and time consuming. Legacy systems may have served companies very well over many periods. In 2002, an estimate by systems professionals indicated that at least 80% of organizations had legacy systems that they were attempting to maintain. There are both advantages and disadvantages to maintaining the older systems. The advantages are that legacy systems

1. have often been customized to meet specific needs in the organization;
2. often support unique business processes not inherent in generic accounting software;
3. contain invaluable historical data that may be difficult to integrate into a new system; and
4. are well supported and understood by existing personnel who are already trained to use the system.

There are also many disadvantages to maintaining older systems. The disadvantages are that legacy systems

1. are costly to maintain in both dollars and time;
2. often lack adequate, up-to-date supporting documentation;
3. may not easily run on new hardware, and the old hardware and parts needed to maintain it may become obsolete;
4. are not usually based on user-friendly interfaces such as Microsoft Windows or Apple's Mac OS;
5. tend to use software written in older computer languages, and fewer programmers are available to maintain it;
6. are often difficult to modify to make them web based or user friendly; and
7. become difficult to integrate when companies merge or acquire other companies, in which case consolidating subsidiary company information into one set of financial statements and reports can involve many manual and error-prone steps.

Often, companies are faced with the decision whether to replace or update legacy systems. When the benefits outweigh the costs, organizations typically decide to replace legacy systems. Many large corporations replaced legacy systems just prior to the year 2000 to ensure Y2K compatibility.

THE REAL WORLD

Bowen Workforce Solutions Inc. is a staffing agency that arranges administrative and contract placements. Until recently, the company was relying on an older accounting and payroll system that it implemented in 1999. Bowen had purchased the source code of this legacy accounting system and hired a consulting firm to modify the program code to revamp the entire system. Bowen was spending approximately $200,000 per year to maintain and update custom features in its system. Even with these modifications, Bowen found that it was doing manual and duplicate entries.

To modernize its accounting system, Bowen purchased and implemented Microsoft Business Solutions–Great Plains, HireDesk, and BizTalk Server 2004. Descriptions of these software systems are as follows:

Microsoft Business Solutions–Great Plains manages and integrates finances, e-commerce, supply chain, manufacturing, project accounting, field service, customer relationships, and human resources. It is easy to deploy and configure the functions currently needed, with the option of adding users and additional capabilities in the future.[2]

HireDesk is used by human resources professionals to integrate all the information and tools necessary to effectively manage such tasks as job assignments/position openings, selecting candidates, and building effective relationship.[3]

BizTalk allows HireDesk and Great Plains to exchange data. This eliminates the manual and duplicate entries that were part of Bowen's older legacy system.

Organizations do not always completely replace legacy systems with newer hardware and software systems, but try to use new technology to enhance the existing systems. One approach is to use **screen scrapers,** or frontware, which add modern, user friendly screen interfaces to legacy systems. There are limitations to this approach because mainframe systems are not as efficient at handling data entry by multiple, simultaneous users as newer technology is.

A second approach to upgrading is to use software that bridges legacy systems to new hardware and software systems and interfaces. These interface bridges are called **enterprise application integration,** or EAI. EAI is a set of processes, software and hardware tools, methodologies, and technologies to integrate software systems. When EAIs are implemented, they are intended to consolidate, connect, and organize all of the computer applications, data, and business processes (both legacy and new) into a seamlessly interfaced framework of system components. The EAI allows real-time exchange, management, and reformulation of all of the critical information and business processes. EAIs are developed and sold to companies to put a modern, advanced technology front on older legacy systems, accomplishing the necessary integration of legacy systems with user friendly and modern processing of data.

The third method is the complete replacement of legacy systems. If the organization can afford the time and money required, the purchase and implementation of modern, integrated systems may be the best approach. Management must weigh the cost and benefits of these alternative methods when facing the decision whether to update or replace legacy systems.

[2]http://www.microsoft.com/businesssolutions/greatplains/productoverview.mspx

[3]http://www.hiredesk.com/pdf/HireDesk_Fact_Sheet.pdf

MODERN, INTEGRATED SYSTEMS

In today's AIS environment, numerous accounting software systems are available for purchase that integrate many or all of the business processes within an organization. In the early days of computer automation of accounting, much of the accounting software was developed and written internally by the organization's IT staff. Today, companies more frequently purchase software rather than develop it internally. Often, purchased systems are modified by the IT staff to meet specific needs of the organization.

The new programs sold by software development companies are more user friendly than legacy accounting systems, typically utilize the latest technology in data storage and Internet interfaces, and offer clients powerful, technologically advanced systems that serve as an important part of the accounting information system.

There are many advantages to purchasing accounting software rather than developing software in-house. Purchased software has a lower cost, shorter implementation time, and fewer bugs. The cost is lower because the development cost can be spread across the many companies that purchase the software, rather than being absorbed completely by the company that developed the software. Implementation time is shorter because it is no longer necessary for the companies to design and program their own accounting systems. Finally, these software systems have fewer bugs because they are not sold until they are fully developed, tested, and proven reliable.

THE REAL WORLD

Cole Haan, a wholly owned subsidiary of Nike, Inc., is one of North America's premier designers and marketers of quality footwear, accessories, and outerwear. The company, headquartered in New York City and Yarmouth, Maine, employs about 1100 people.

Prior to implementing its current system in 1999, the legacy system in place at Cole Haan was not integrated with the company's other key business systems, including its sales and distribution legacy system. Fresh data entered the accounting system just once a day, as data were processed in batches. This lack of real-time processing of accounting data made it difficult to base business decisions on timely information. In addition, the company found that it was "spending 99% of its time just keeping nonintegrated systems in synch," said Bob Cheney, Cole Haan's director of information technology.[4]

The time required to synchronize the systems was wasted time for employees using the financial systems. In addition, the legacy systems did not provide real-time data to product managers and sales representatives about how specific products, colors, and styles were performing in the marketplace.

To integrate all business processes and systems, and to have real-time data available for decision making, Cole Haan implemented SAP ERP Financials. SAP is the largest software company in the world, and its enterprise resource planning (ERP) products help companies access the data, applications, and analytical tools needed for efficient business management. The features of SAP ERP Financials address financial control as well as automation and integration of financial and managerial accounting applications. Currently, approximately 200 users throughout Cole Haan access the SAP system on a regular basis.

Accounting software that is sold today is generally categorized into market segments, described in the next section.

[4]http://www.sap.com/solutions/business-suite/erp/financials/pdf/CS_Cole_Haan.pdf

ACCOUNTING SOFTWARE MARKET SEGMENTS (STUDY OBJECTIVE 3)

The accounting software market today is categorized into four market segments: small company systems, midmarket company systems, beginning ERP systems, and tier 1 ERP systems. Each segment is based on the size of the organization in terms of the amount of its revenue.

THE REAL WORLD

Hobie Cat Company, headquartered in Oceanside, California, manufactures and sells fiberglass catamarans that have transformed the sport of sailing. There are currently over 100,000 Hobie Cats in use around the world. To improve the efficiency of its accounting and manufacturing processes, Hobie selected an ERP software system for medium-size companies, MAS 200 by Sage Software Inc.

MAS 200 handles Hobie's financial information, operations, and manufacturing, by automating order-taking, work orders, labor routings, inventory processing, bill of material, receivables, payables, and manufacturing resource planning. Hobie uses three Microsoft Windows servers and 30 Windows PCs to run MAS 200. Hobie is considering purchasing and implementing the e-commerce module of MAS 200.[5]

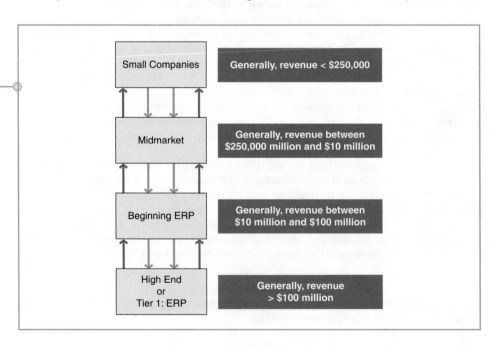

Exhibit 2-2 illustrates the four software market segments. Within this hierarchy of market segments, a company with revenue of $200,000 would probably be classified within the small companies market segment, and would therefore be likely to purchase accounting software that fits in that segment. On the other hand, a large, Fortune 500 corporation might purchase accounting software systems in the tier 1 market segment—that is, an ERP system. Most

Exhibit 2–2
The Accounting Software Market Segments and Movement in the Market

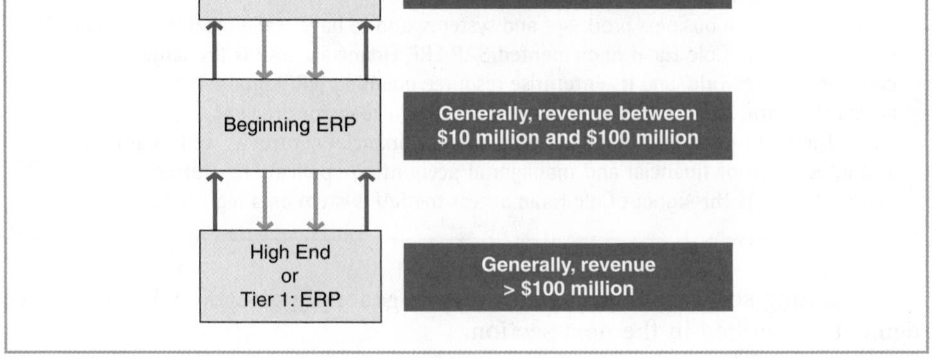

[5] http://www.bestsoftware.com/pdf/mas/ss/mas_hobiecat_ss.pdf

software vendors attempt to increase the appeal of their software to more than one market segment, however, so understanding this market segmentation can be difficult. As an example, while Intuit's Quickbooks has traditionally been sold to small companies, its new software product, Quickbooks Enterprise, is intended to appeal to companies in the midmarket segment.

As accounting software development companies attempt to reach other market segments, the differentiation between products becomes blurred. Therefore, not all accounting software systems fit neatly into a single segment.

Exhibit 2-3 illustrates some of the most popular accounting software systems in each of the four market segments that they most closely fit. Often these software solutions are chosen to more fully integrate business processes across the organization.

The programs listed in Exhibit 2-3 are based on modern technology, and each attempts to integrate many business processes into a single software system. The vendors continue to update these software systems to take advantage of e-commerce, e-business, and integration across business processes. Therefore, even those software systems in small and midmarket segments are becoming more like ERP systems. As described in Chapter 1, ERP systems are multimodule software systems designed to manage all aspects of an enterprise and ERP are usually broken down into modules such as financials, sales, purchasing, inventory management, manufacturing, and human resources. The modules are designed to work seamlessly with the rest of the system and to provide a consistent user interface across modules. Based on a relational database system, ERP systems usually have extensive set-up options that allow some flexibility in customizing their functionality to specific business needs.

Many of the software systems in the small and midmarket categories are not true ERP systems in that their modules are not fully integrated as ERP system would be; the companies that develop and sell these software systems try to assimilate the features of ERP systems. This trend is likely to continue in the future as technological advances allow software development companies to build ever-increasing power and functionality in the software products that they offer.

Because of their size and the many complex processes that make up their businesses, large, multinational corporations have specific needs for accounting software systems. The most widely used tier 1 ERP system for large corporations is SAP. A small sample of the many well-known companies using SAP includes Anheuser-Busch, Daimler–Chrysler, Coca Cola, Exxon, H.J. Heinz, Reebok, and Rubbermaid.

Small	Midmarket	Beginning ERP	Tier 1 ERP
ACCPAC Simply	AccountMate	ACCPAC Corporate	Lawson
ACCPAC Discover	ACCPAC Small	Axapta	Oracle
BusinessWorks	ACCPAC ProSeries	Dynamics GP®	PeopleSoft
Cougar Mountain	Dynamics GP®	Navision Financials	SAP
M.Y.O.B.	Macola Progression	Epicor	
NetLedger	MAS 90 and MAS 200	Macola ES	
One Write Plus	Navision Financials	MAS 500	
Peachtree	TRAVERSE	SAP Business One	
QuickBooks	Platinum for Windows	Solomon	
	Solomon	TRAVERSE Enterprise	

Exhibit 2–3
Popular Accounting Software Programs within the Market Segments

Regardless of the type of accounting software used, computer processing is involved in the input of data, the processing of that data, and the outputs from the system. The next section describes many of the input and processing methods used in IT systems today. In addition, the types of outputs produced are described.

INPUT METHODS USED IN BUSINESS PROCESSES (STUDY OBJECTIVE 4)

As the steps in a business process occur, accounting data are generated that must be captured and recorded in the accounting information system. Accounting data are the input of the accounting information system. For example, a sale generates much accounting data that must be collected and recorded, such as customer identification information, identifying information for items and quantities sold, and information on discounts offered and taken. Most of the business processes in an organization generate accounting data. Because those processes—and the organizations themselves—can differ greatly, there are many different methods to capture and record accounting data, which is the purpose of an input method. Some of the input methods used in organizations today are described in this section, including source documents and keying, bar coding, point of sale systems, EDI, and e-business.

SOURCE DOCUMENTS AND KEYING

Within business processes, the accounting data are often initially captured and recorded on a source document. Source documents are usually preprinted and sequentially prenumbered—preprinted to have an established format to capture data and prenumbered for control purposes to ensure that there are no duplicate or missing source documents and that all source documents are accounted for. One example of capturing data on a source document is the use of an employee time card. As an employee begins and ends a workday, he or she records start and end times on the time card. At the end of the pay period, this source document is forwarded to the payroll department to generate a paycheck. In a computerized system, the start and end work times are keyed into the software, meaning that the payroll employee uses a keyboard to input the data. Exhibit 2-4 shows the input screen in Microsoft Dynamics GP® for entering employee hours worked. To key in hours worked, the person keying the data would need to enter the information from the source document—the employee time card.

This is only a single example of source document and keying. While many organizational business processes use this type of input method, it is time consuming and error prone due to the human efforts required to write on the source documents and to manually key in the data. IT technology has enabled input methods that reduce the time, cost, and errors of data input. The specific type of IT technology used to enable the input of data varies depending on the type of organization and the type of business process. Bar codes, POS systems, EDI, and e-business systems are technology systems that enable the input of data.

BAR CODES

A **bar code** is a printed code consisting of a series of vertical, machine-readable, rectangular bars and spaces that vary in width and are arranged in a specific way to represent letters, numbers, and other human-readable symbols. Bar codes

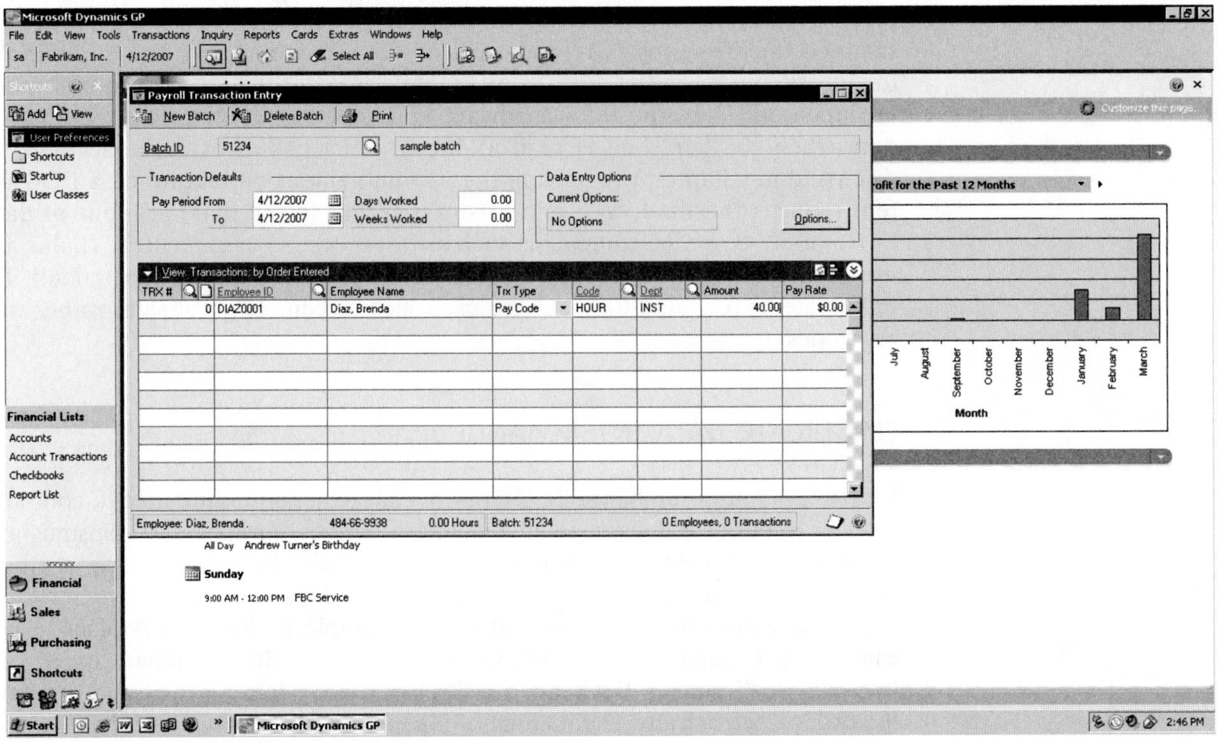

Exhibit 2–4
Keying Hours Worked in Microsoft Dynamics GP® Software

are "read" and decoded by bar code scanners. Bar codes are used to identify retail sales products, identification cards, and other items. They also manage work in progress, track documents, and facilitate many other automated identification applications. To track work in process and inventory movement, a bar code tag (a small white label printed with a bar code) is placed on each inventory part and work in progress.

When inventory parts are counted or moved, a bar code scanner reads the bar code to input the necessary identification of that part. That is, the method of inputting data is not a manual keying of data, but a machine reading data by the bar code scanner. Another example of the use of bar codes to input accounting data is employee ID badges. When an organization uses a bar code system on employee IDs, the bar code reader can record the start and ending work times as the employee enters and leaves the workplace. The bar code scanner becomes the method of capturing and recording hours worked, eliminating the manual steps of writing the data on a source document and then later keying the data into software. Eliminating these manual processes reduces the time, cost, and errors of inputting data.

The most well-known use of bar codes, the point of sale system, is in retail sales.

POINT OF SALE SYSTEMS

A point of sale system (POS) is a method of using hardware and software that captures retail sales transactions by standard bar coding. The bar code label on the products is usually called the universal product code, or UPC.

Nearly all large retail stores use POS systems integrated into the cash register. As a customer checks out through the cash register, the bar codes are scanned on the items purchased, prices are determined by the accessing of inventory and price list data, sales revenue is recorded, and inventory values are updated. Thus, the POS hardware and software automatically inputs the data when the bar code is read as the product passes over the scanner. As discussed in Chapter 1 regarding the IT enablement of data input, a POS system reduces the time, cost, and errors inherent in the manual input of data.

Retail food service companies such as fast food and casual eatery chains also use point of sale systems; however, the food products are not bar coded. The POS systems for retail food service use touch screens to input sales rather than bar codes.

ELECTRONIC DATA INTERCHANGE

Electronic data interchange (EDI) is the intercompany, computer-to-computer transfer of business documents in a standard business format. EDI transmits purchase orders, invoices, and payments electronically between trading partners. Since transmission is electronic, the paper source documents and the manual keying of those documents are eliminated. For example, if Company A plans to purchase from Company B via EDI, Company A transmits a purchase order electronically to Company B. Company B's computer system receives and processes the order electronically. The mailing of a paper purchase order and the keying of that order by Company B has been eliminated. Therefore, we can see that EDI is a method of electronically inputting data into the accounting system. As was true of the other IT enabled input methods, this reduces time, cost, and errors.

E-BUSINESS AND E-COMMERCE

Data are also electronically exchanged between trading partners in e-business and e-commerce. Recall from Chapter 1 that e-business relates to all forms of online electronic business transactions and processing, whereas e-commerce is a type of e-business that is specific to consumer online buying and selling. A major difference between EDI and e-business (including e-commerce) is that EDI uses dedicated networks, while e-business uses the Internet. As is true for EDI, when data are exchanged electronically between trading partners, much of the manual data input process is eliminated, thereby reducing time, cost, and errors.

PROCESSING ACCOUNTING DATA (STUDY OBJECTIVE 5)

After accounting information has been input into the accounting system, it must be processed. Processing accounting data involves calculations, classification, summarization, and consolidation. In manual accounting systems, this processing occurs through the established manual methods and the recording, posting, and closing steps in the journals and ledgers. Automated processing can be accomplished by batch processing or online and real-time processing. These methods are described next.

BATCH PROCESSING

Batch processing requires that all similar transactions are grouped together for a specified time, and then this group of transactions is processed together as a batch. Batch processing is best suited to applications having large volumes of similar transactions that can be processed at regular intervals. Payroll processing is a good example of a system that is well suited to batch processing. All time cards can be grouped together for a two-week period, for example, and all payroll processing then takes place on the entire set, or batch, of time cards.

Many legacy systems use batch processing to handle large volumes of routine transactions. As described in Chapter 1, batch processing is best suited for business processes where the transactions are stored in sequential access files. The business processes that are often batch oriented in legacy systems are payroll, accounts payable, and accounts receivable. These processes and legacy systems have master files and transaction files. An example of a master file for accounts receivable is a file that maintains detailed customer information such as name, address, credit limit, and current balance. The transaction file would contain the set of customer transactions for a certain period such as the week. For high-volume, routine transaction processes, batch processing offers many advantages; but there are also disadvantages to this method.

Advantages to batch processing:

1. It is very efficient for large volumes of like transactions where most items in a master file are used during each processing run.
2. The basic accounting audit trail is maintained, because there are well-defined beginning and ending periods and a set of documents to reconcile to the batch being processed.
3. Such systems generally use less costly hardware and software than other methods.
4. The hardware and software systems are not as complicated as on-line systems and are therefore easier to understand.
5. It is generally easier to control than other types of computerized systems. Batch totals can be used to ensure the batch was processed correctly.
6. When personnel are dedicated to batch processing, they become specialized and efficient in processing those routine transactions.

Disadvantages to batch processing:

1. Processing can take longer than normal if the master files are large and not all records in the master file are used. For example, if only a few customer payments are to be processed from a large master file of customer records, it may take a legacy system with older hardware (that reads all master file records in sequence) as long to deliver the output as it would take if all the customer records were demanded.
2. In legacy systems with older hardware, adding or deleting records takes much computer maintenance time due to the sequential structure of the files.
3. In legacy systems with older hardware, some data duplication is likely because each batch process often uses its own separate master file. Accounts payable and purchasing may be separate batch processes with separate master files, but in both master files vendor information, for example, would be duplicated.

4. Integration across business processes is difficult in legacy systems that are batch oriented. The isolated master files and separate batch processing systems make integration very difficult.
5. By necessity, batch systems have a time lag while all transactions in a batch are collected. This means that available information in files will not always be current, as it would in real-time systems.
6. Legacy systems with older hardware may require that both the transaction files and master files be sorted in the same sequential order. This leads to less flexibility in record storage and retrieval.

Even when the hardware and software systems are new, some business processes may still be best suited to batch processing. Because of the periodic nature of payroll, it is probably best processed in a batch even if the hardware and software allow real-time processing.

ONLINE AND REAL-TIME PROCESSING

Most modern, integrated systems frequently use online and real-time processing. With online processing, transactions are not grouped into batches; rather, each transaction is entered and processed individually. Some online processing systems are also real-time processing systems. Real-time processing means that the transaction is processed immediately, and in real time, so that the output is available immediately. Online processing is best suited to applications in which there is a large volume of records, but only a few records are needed to process any individual transaction. Thus, online processing requires that data from the related business processes be stored in random access files, as described in Chapter 1. Real-time processing usually requires a database and database management software systems.

The advantages to real-time processing are as follows:

1. As data are entered in real time, the system checks for input errors. Therefore, errors can be corrected immediately.
2. Information is provided to users on a timely basis, without the time lag inherent in batch systems.
3. Since all data are in a database system and are updated in real time, all files are constantly up to date.
4. The business processes are integrated into a single database so that a single system is achieved.

The disadvantages of real-time systems are as follows:

1. The hardware and software are more expensive than those used for batch systems.
2. A single database that is shared is more susceptible to unauthorized access of data, unless extensive controls are implemented to prevent unauthorized access.
3. Real-time systems can be difficult to audit because of the complexity of the system.

As computer hardware has become more powerful and less expensive, real-time systems have become more prevalent. The advantages of these real-time systems usually far outweigh their extra cost and complexity.

OUTPUTS FROM THE AIS RELATED TO BUSINESS PROCESSES (STUDY OBJECTIVE 6)

An accounting information system generates many different types of output. There are so many potential outputs that it is not possible to cover all of them in detail here. This section will describe the following general categories of outputs:

1. Trading partner documents such as checks, invoices, and statements
2. Internal documents
3. Internal reports
4. External reports

Some of the outputs of the accounting information system are documents exchanged with trading partners such as customers and vendors. Invoices and statements are examples of documents sent to customers. Checks are outputs sent to vendors. These outputs may be in electronic or paper form. For example, electronic outputs include checks sent to vendors via electronic funds transfer and customer invoices sent via electronic data interchange.

Internal documents are another form of output from an accounting information system. Examples of internal documents include credit memorandums, receiving memorandums, production routing documents, and production scheduling documents. These documents may be printed paper forms, or they may be in the form of screen outputs viewed on the user's computer.

Accounting information systems also generate outputs in the form of reports for either internal or external users of accounting information. External reports are usually financial statements that include a balance sheet, income statement, and statement of cash flows. There are an unlimited number of potential internal reports, as this category comprises any information that management determines is useful to the business. Internal reports provide feedback to managers to assist them in running the business processes under their control. For example, an aged accounts receivable report may be prepared for the manager responsible for accounts receivable; the managers who oversee inventory would be interested in an inventory status report identifying those products that are at low stock levels.

Internal reports vary by process, by manager level, and by the type of organization. They are designed specifically for the function that is the subject of the report. Internal reports may be printed on paper, viewed on a computer screen, or created (either on screen or paper) as customizable queries that allow a manager to "drill down" into the details of the process being managed.

DOCUMENTING PROCESSES AND SYSTEMS (STUDY OBJECTIVE 7)

Systems professionals and accountants must understand the documentation and charts that describe accounting systems. Such documentation allows the accountant to analyze and understand the procedures and processes of a business process and the systems that capture and record accounting data. The old adage that a picture is worth a thousand words is true for users documenting processes and systems. A picture, or chart, of the system is a concise, complete, and easy-to-understand way to analyze a process or system. The various types of popular pictorial representations of processes and systems used in businesses today include the following:

1. Process maps
2. System flowcharts
3. Document flowcharts
4. Data flow diagrams
5. Entity relationship diagrams (ER diagrams)

PROCESS MAPS

Process maps are pictorial representations of business processes in which the actual flow and sequence of events in the process are presented in diagram form—the start of a process, the steps within the process, and a finish of the process. Process maps are becoming a popular way to represent business processes, particularly as organizations undergo business process reengineering. Five symbols are used in process maps, as shown in Exhibit 2-5.

With these five symbols, any business process can be depicted. Exhibit 2-6 is a sample process map that depicts a typical course-registration process for

Exhibit 2–5
Process Map Symbols

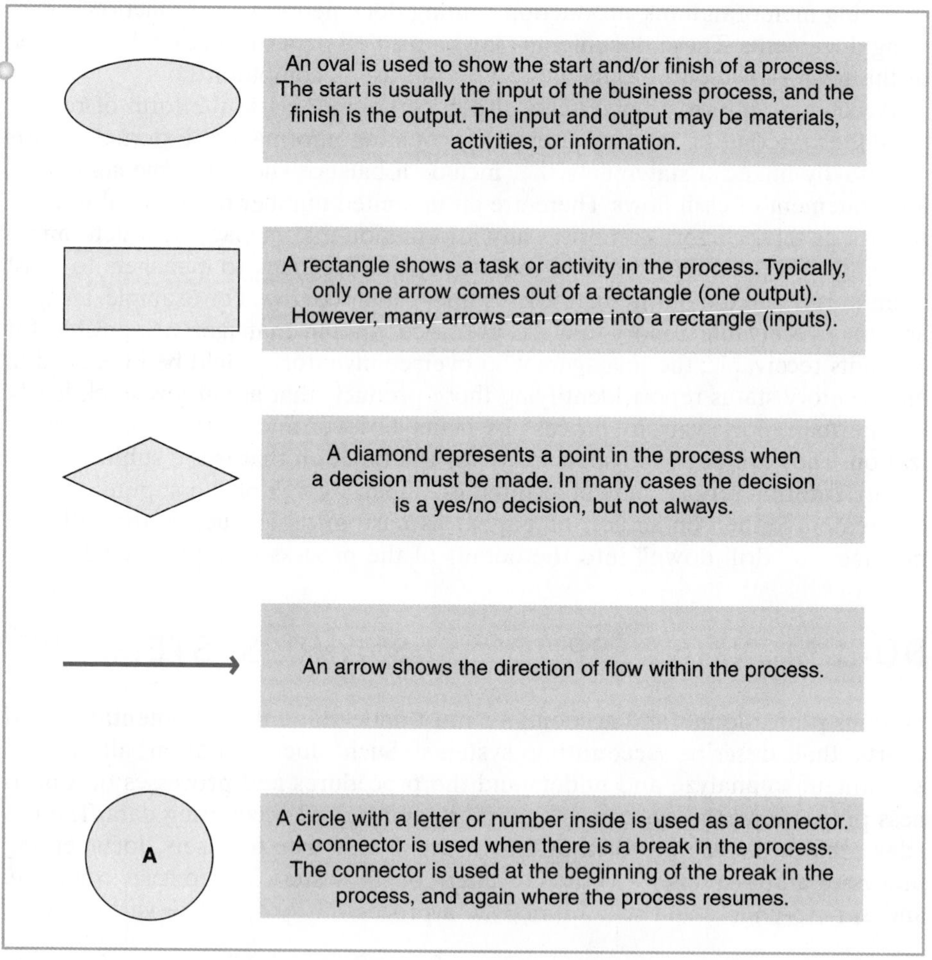
An oval is used to show the start and/or finish of a process. The start is usually the input of the business process, and the finish is the output. The input and output may be materials, activities, or information.
A rectangle shows a task or activity in the process. Typically, only one arrow comes out of a rectangle (one output). However, many arrows can come into a rectangle (inputs).
A diamond represents a point in the process when a decision must be made. In many cases the decision is a yes/no decision, but not always.
An arrow shows the direction of flow within the process.
A
A circle with a letter or number inside is used as a connector. A connector is used when there is a break in the process. The connector is used at the beginning of the break in the process, and again where the process resumes.

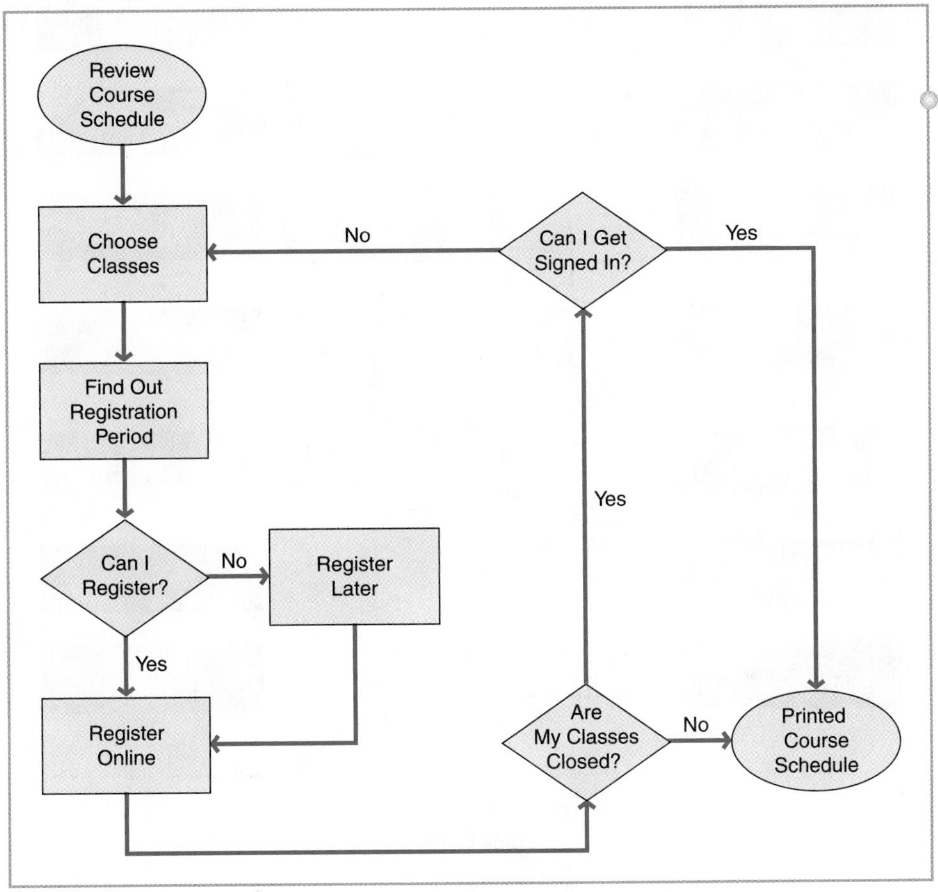

Exhibit 2–6
Process Map of Class Registration

college classes. This process map is easy to comprehend because the underlying process is fairly simplistic. For some processes, however, where numerous activities may be performed in multiple departments or functional areas throughout the organization, process maps may be enhanced to depict varying levels of complexity. Each activity or department within a business process may be presented in either a horizontal or a vertical format.

In later chapters, process maps are presented as pictorial representations of the business and accounting processes. Some of these examples are horizontally formatted process maps, while others are shown in a vertical format.

SYSTEM FLOWCHARTS

A **system flowchart** is intended to depict the entire system, including inputs, manual and computerized processes, and outputs. System flowcharts do not necessarily show details of each process, but display the overall sequence of processes and the media used for processing and storage. Processing and storage are shown as manual or computerized. Inputs can be documents, keying of input, electronic input, or processes that feed data to other processes. Outputs may be documents, statements, reports, data stored in files, or data fed into other processes. The symbols used in system flowcharts appear in Exhibit 2-7. An example of a system flowchart appears in Exhibit 2-8.

Exhibit 2-7
Common System Flowchart Symbols

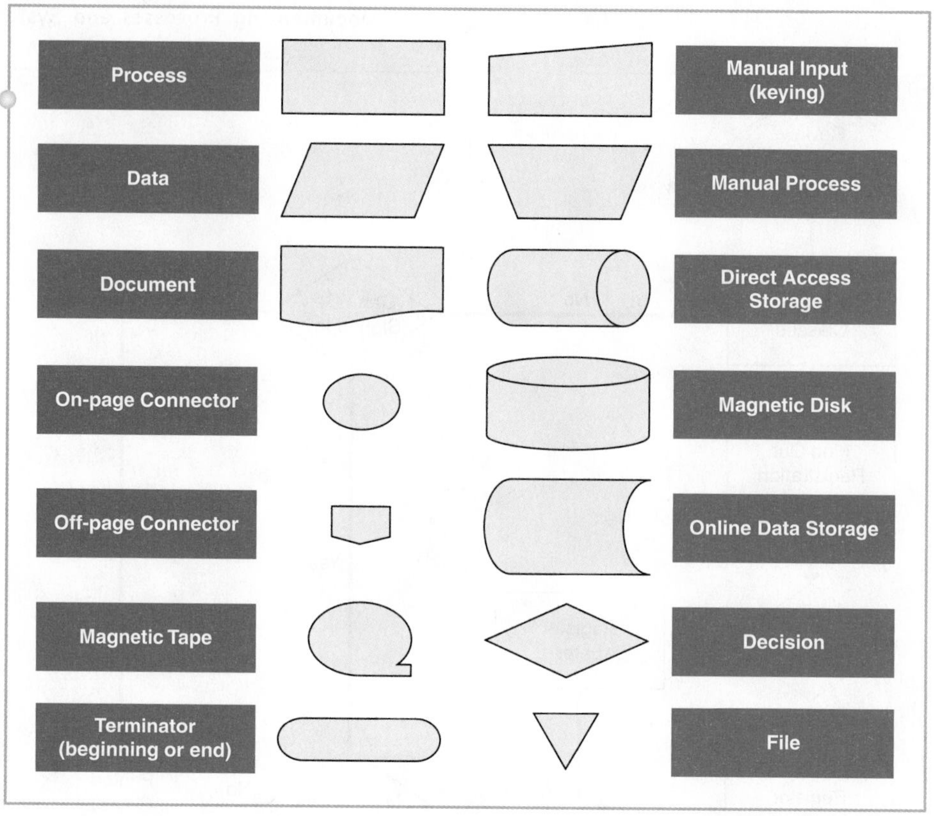

Exhibit 2-8
Payroll System Flowchart

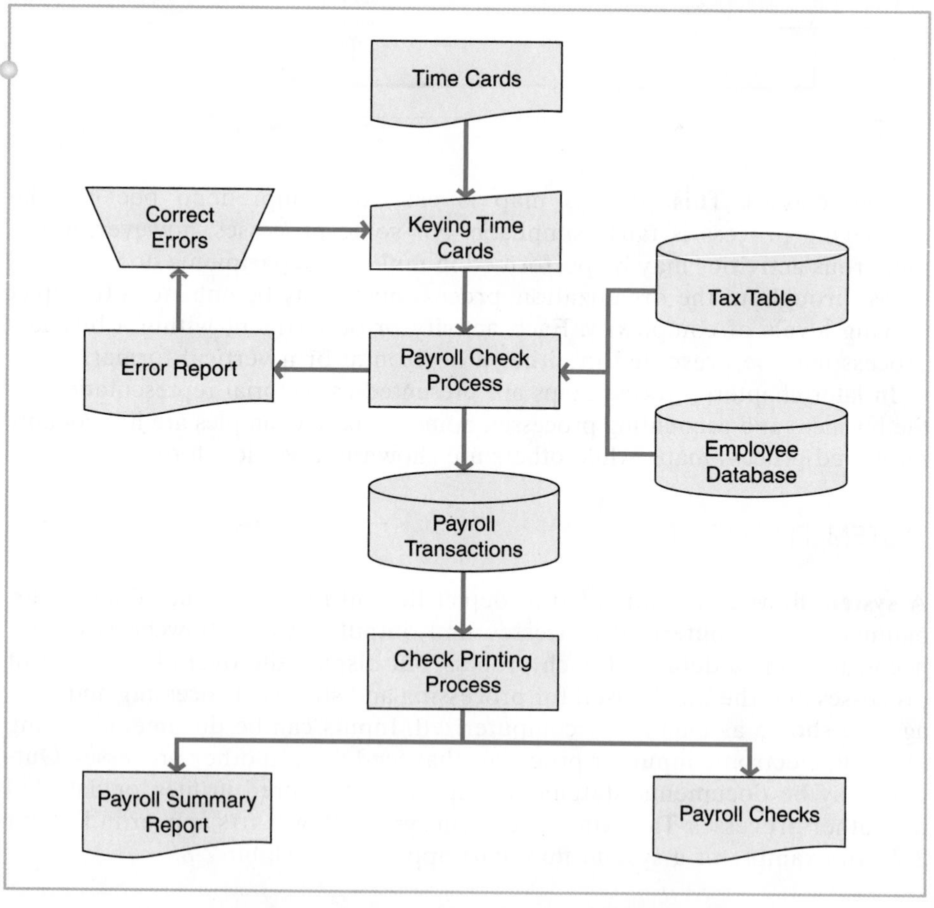

System flowcharts are used by systems professionals in the design and maintenance of IT systems. In general, accountants and auditors do not use system flowcharts extensively. Accountants and auditors are more likely to use process maps, data flow diagrams, and document flowcharts.

DOCUMENT FLOWCHARTS

A **document flowchart** shows the flow of documents and information among departments or units within an organization. Document flowcharts are usually divided into columns, each representing a department or unit of the organization. Document flowcharts trace each document in a process from its origin to its final destination. Thus, the document flowchart shows the origin of a document, the units to which it is distributed, the ultimate disposition of the document, and everything that happens as it flows through the system. For documents prepared in duplicate, the document flowchart shows the flow for each copy of the document.

A document flowchart is a special kind of system flowchart that depicts only document flows. However, document flowcharts do not necessarily show all the related business processes. Document flowcharts are useful for not only understanding the flow of documents, but also in understanding internal controls. The symbols used in documents flowcharts are similar to those used for system flowcharts, as presented in Exhibit 2-7.

Document flowcharts, data flow diagrams, and process maps will be used in selected chapters of this book to illustrate business processes. The next three exhibits are examples of how these methods of documenting systems are used to illustrate processes for a small, local restaurant. Exhibit 2-9 is a process map in which the system for processing records and documents is manual rather than computerized. Exhibit 2-10 shows the corresponding document flowchart, and

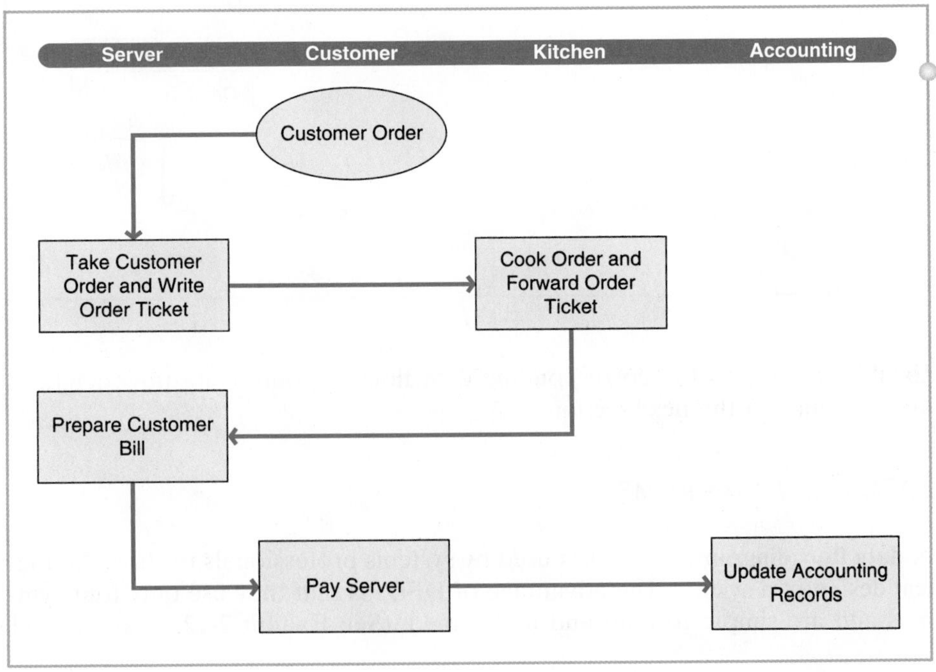

Exhibit 2–9
Restaurant Process Map

Exhibit 2-10
Restaurant Document Flowchart

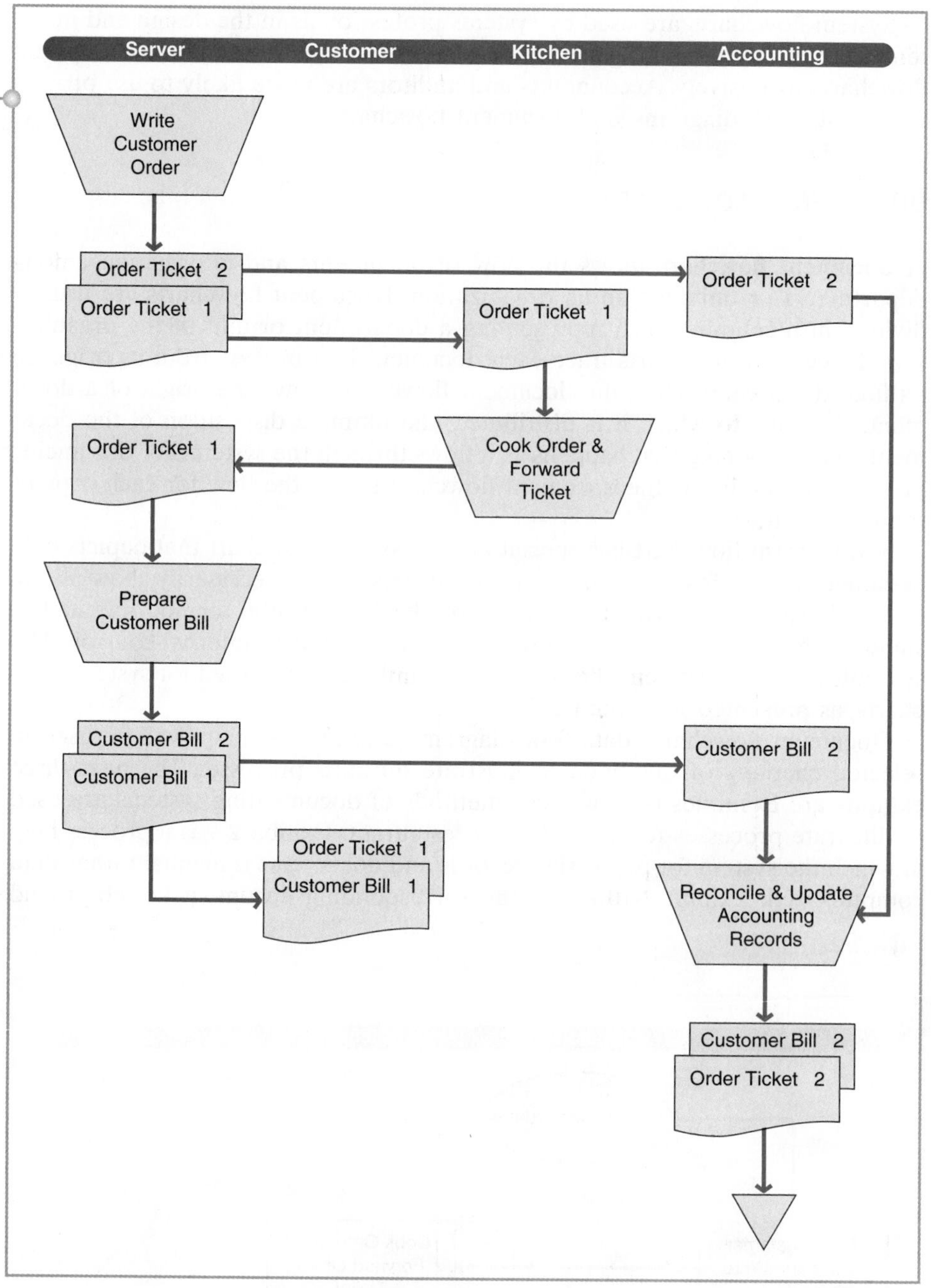

Exhibit 2-11 shows the corresponding data flow diagram. Data flow diagrams are explained in the next section.

DATA FLOW DIAGRAMS

A **data flow diagram**, or DFD, is used by systems professionals to show the logical design of a system. The advantage of DFDs is that they use only four symbols and are simple to read and understand. (See Exhibit 2-12.) Exhibit 2-11

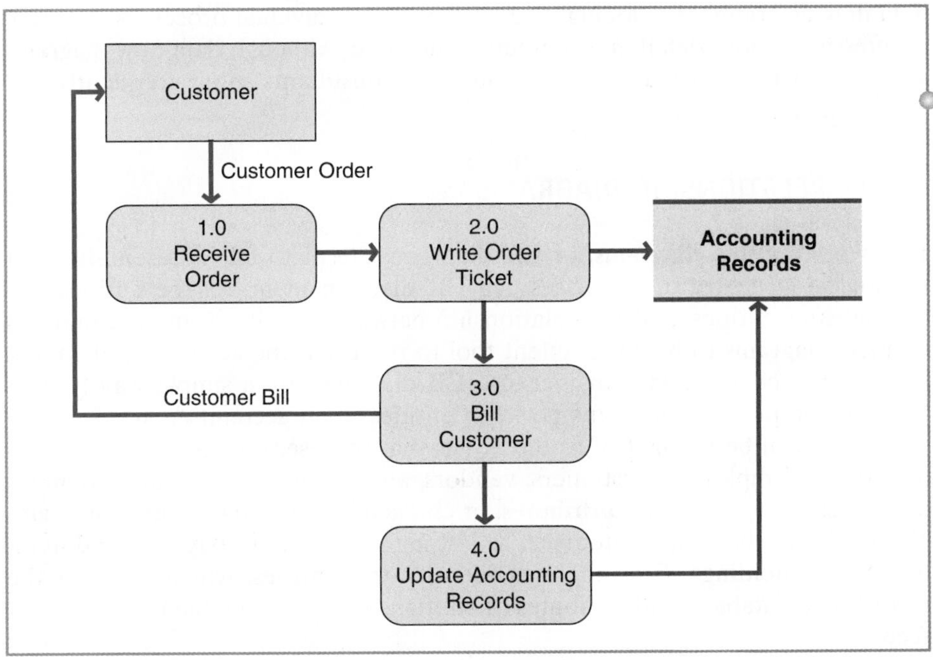

Exhibit 2–11
Restaurant Data Flow Diagram

is a sample data flow diagram of the restaurant process shown in Exhibits 2-9 and 2-10.

Data flow diagrams are used as tools in many of the chapters that follow. Systems professionals use data flow diagrams in structured system design, a process wherein the logical system is diagrammed at a high, conceptual level first. In succeeding steps, the data flow diagrams are exploded into more levels of detail until the logical structures of all detailed tasks been shown in successive

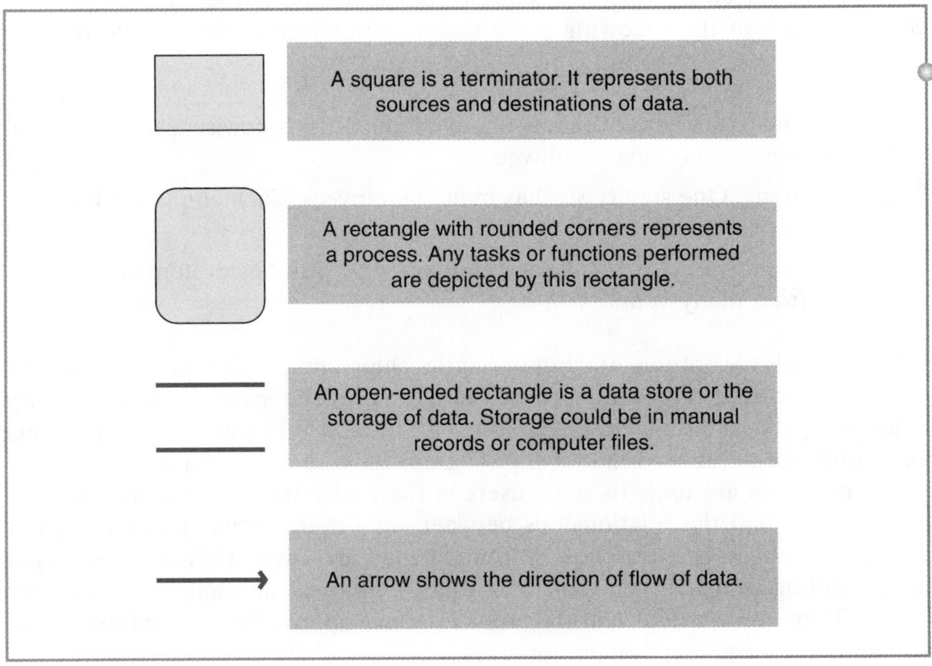

Exhibit 2–12
Data Flow Diagram Symbols

data flow diagrams. "Exploding" means that each individual process is shown in progressively more detail in a subsequent diagram. Although data flow diagrams are easy to read, accountants and business consultants more frequently use process maps.

ENTITY RELATIONSHIP DIAGRAMS

Entity relationship diagrams, or ER diagrams, are pictorial representations of the logical structure of databases. An ER diagram identifies the entities, the attributes of entities, and the relationship between entities. Some accountants find ER diagrams to be an excellent tool to represent the accounting data and entities in accounting systems because ER diagrams are a simple way to analyze the complex relationships between entities in an accounting system.

Entities can be thought of as the nouns that represent items in the accounting system. Employees, customers, vendors, and inventory items are examples of entities. Each entity has **attributes**, or characteristics of the entity. For example, employees have attributes such as last name, first name, pay rate, and number of withholdings. ER diagrams identify the entities, which become the records in a database, and attributes of entities, which become the fields of those records.

Database structures tend to be complex because entities are related to each other, and these relationships can be complex. For example, vendors and inventory items are two sets of entities that are related because the business buys inventory items from vendors. Any individual inventory item could be purchased from many vendors, and any single vendor could sell many different items to the business. Another example is the relationship between customers and orders. Each customer can have many orders, but any one order belongs to only one customer. The relationships between entities in ER diagrams are depicted by a concept called cardinality. **Cardinality** refers to how many instances of an entity relate to each instance of another entity. Cardinality describes each of the following three manners in which entities relate to each other:

1. One to one: Each employee has one personnel file. Likewise, each personnel file belongs to only one employee.
2. One to many: One supervisor has many employees. Each employee has only one supervisor.
3. Many to many: Each vendor can sell many items, and each item can be purchased from many vendors.

Using symbols for entities, attributes, relationships, and cardinality, ER diagrams provide a pictorial representation of the database. The symbols used in entity relationship diagrams appear in Exhibit 2-13. Exhibit 2-14 (on page 64) presents an example of an entity relationship diagram for a sales database.

ER diagrams are tools to assist users in the understanding of complex database systems and the relationships between data items; however, they are not used in the chapters that follow. Although they are currently not widely used in accounting practice, you may find them employed at some point in your future. They are a useful learning tool in some approaches to understanding accounting information system concepts.

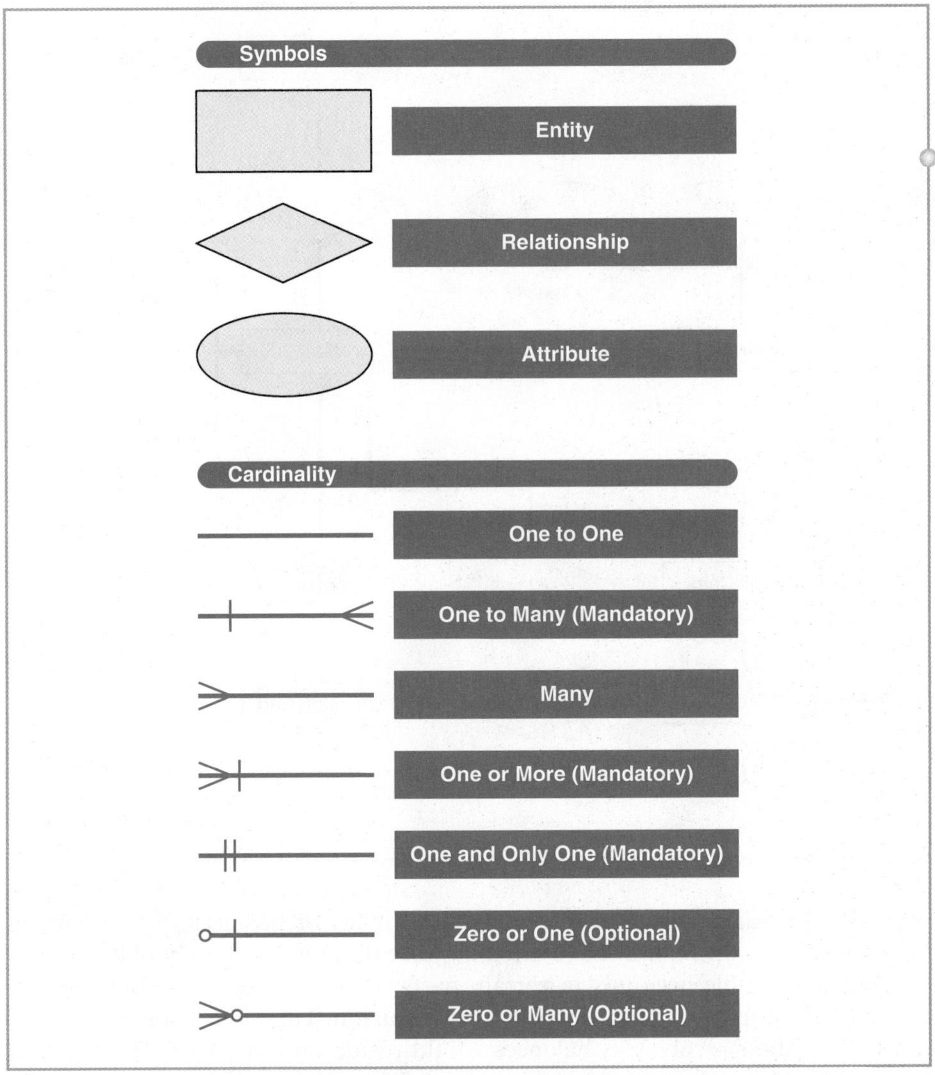

Exhibit 2–13
Entity Relationship Diagram Symbols
Adapted from examples at www.smartdraw.com

CLIENT–SERVER COMPUTING (STUDY OBJECTIVE 8)

In the last couple of decades, the client server model of networks has become common. **Client–Server** computing means that two types of computers are networked together to accomplish the application processing. The server is usually a large computer that contains the database and many of the application programs. Client computers, usually PC-type computers, are networked to the server and work with the server in such a way that the network appears to be one integrated system for users. The advantage of client–server computing is that the PC clients perform as "smart" terminals that can accomplish some share of the processing tasks. In most client–server networks, the server manages and stores the large database, extracts data from the database, and runs the large, complex application programs. The client PC usually works with a subset of data that has been extracted from the server database to accomplish some local processing tasks.

For an example of client–server computing, let us assume that a large national corporation has several regional managers. Each regional manager

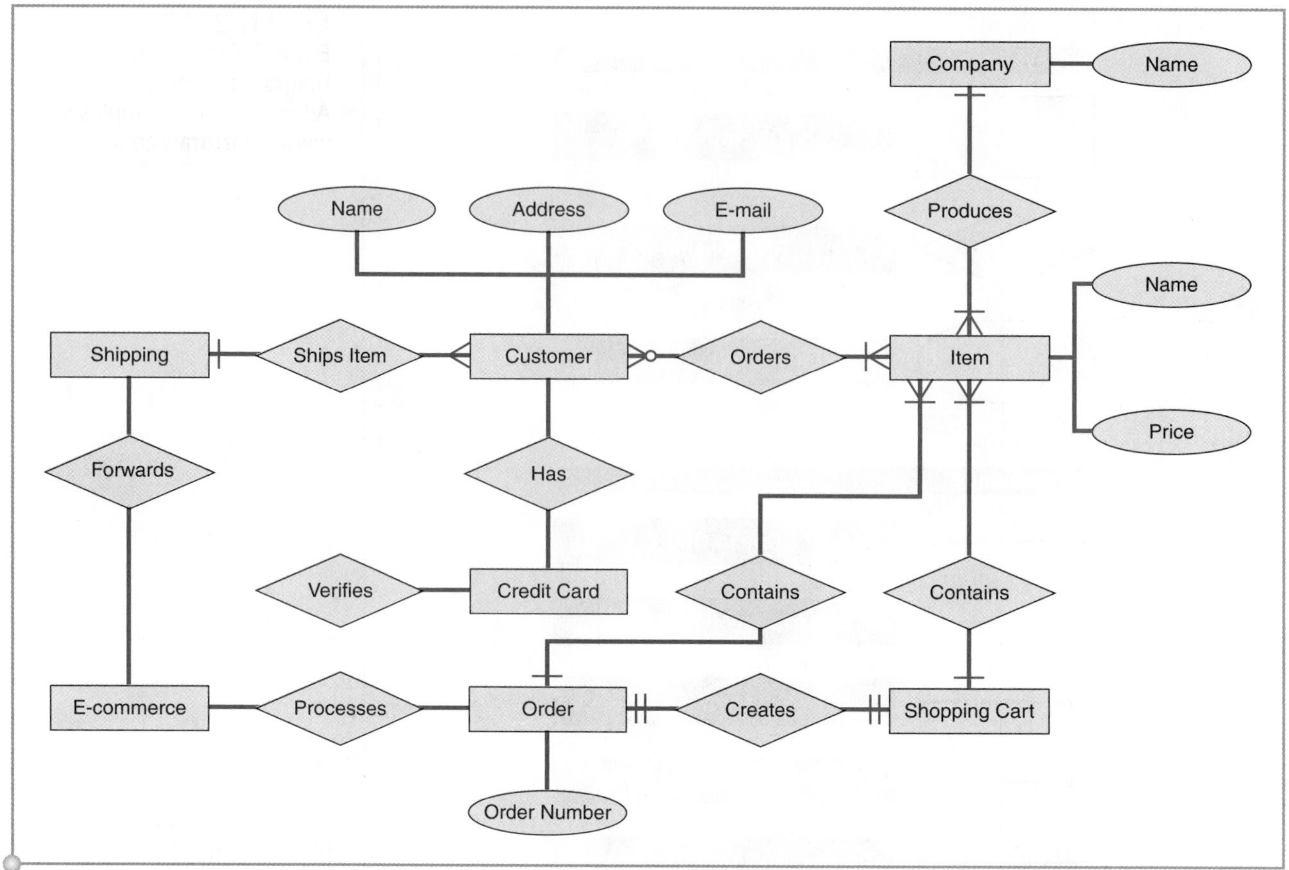

Exhibit 2-14
Entity Relationship Diagram of Internet Sales Adapted from examples at www.smartdraw.com

oversees sales and collection of receivables for his or her area. A manager in Milwaukee, Wisconsin, may have a feeling that there is an extremely high number of uncollectible accounts in certain parts of Milwaukee and would like to examine a report to confirm or allay this suspicion. The large database of customers and their receivables balances would reside on the server. The regional manager in Milwaukee would use her client PC to write a query to extract the overdue customer accounts in Milwaukee from the server. This query travels through the network to the main server, which extracts the customer records requested. This subset of customer records is sent to the client PC, where the regional manager can use software to map locations of overdue accounts. Such a map would help the manager review and manage the uncollectible accounts. This scenario is an example of client–server computing, and it exhibits the main characteristics of client–server systems. Those characteristics are as follows:

1. Client and server computer are networked together.
2. The system appears to users to be one integrated whole.
3. Individual parts of processing are shared between the server and client.
4. The client computer participates in the processing or data manipulation in some meaningful way.

In client–server computing, the tasks are assigned to either the server or the client on the basis of which one can handle each task most efficiently. The server is more efficient in managing large databases, extracting data from databases, and running high-volume transaction processing software applications. The client is more efficient at manipulating subsets of data and presenting data to users in a user-friendly, graphical-interface environment.

Client–server computing can be divided into two levels: distributed presentation and distributed applications.

In **distributed presentation**, the client PC manipulates data for presentation, but does not do any other significant processing. The client PC frequently is used to manipulate a subset of data for presentation in a more user-friendly format such as in a spreadsheet, graphing software, mapping software, or some other type of presentation software. The client PC does not update or change any data that reside on the server, but is used simply as a tool to present or report data. This method of client–server computing is the simpler of the two levels.

In **distributed applications**, the client PC does participate in application processing beyond that described for the distributed presentation method. The client PC updates or changes data that reside on the server. Such data changes may not always be instantaneous, but are more likely to occur as scheduled, periodic updates of the database on the server.

Many client–server applications are now moving toward a web-based model. For example, tier 1 ERP systems such as SAP and PeopleSoft use a web browser interface, where users who enter or view data from a business process do so through the web browser on their desktop computers. Many experts believe that this will continue as a trend and more accounting software systems will be based on web browser interfaces.

ETHICAL CONSIDERATIONS AT THE FOUNDATION OF ACCOUNTING INFORMATION SYSTEMS (STUDY OBJECTIVE 9)

Several important topics have been presented in this chapter regarding the various features and options for an organization's accounting information systems. Most of these topics relate to business processes that are computerized, at least in part. The existence of computerized accounting information systems presents specific challenges for accountants in terms of the potential for unethical behavior.

Recall from Chapter 1 that the accounting information system is often the tool used to commit or cover up unethical behavior. This is true regardless of the extent of computerization. However, it can be especially difficult to detect instances of computer fraud within certain computerized environments, especially if there is only one person or a limited number of IT personnel within the organization with responsibility for maintaining these computer systems. For instance, if an organization's business processes involve the use of sophisticated software programs, the number of personnel with sufficient expertise to recognize wrongdoing within the system may be limited. Likewise, if an organization continues to maintain legacy systems and the number of personnel trained to administer the older computer system becomes limited, the company's ability to detect unethical conduct is compromised. Fraud could be perpetrated and go undetected for a long time if these systems are not carefully monitored.

Accountants should be aware of opportunities for unethical behaviors within the various business processes. If accountants are well informed about these risks, they can be better prepared to control such exposure. As a company chooses features and options for its accounting information systems, the importance of monitoring those systems should not be overlooked as a factor in decision making.

SUMMARY OF STUDY OBJECTIVES

The interrelationships of business processes and the AIS. As transactions occur, the systematic and defined steps that take place within the organization to complete the underlying tasks of the transaction are called business processes. These business processes generate accounting information that must be captured, recorded, and processed. The accounting information system comprises the processes, procedures, and systems that capture accounting data from business processes; record the accounting data in the appropriate records; process the detailed accounting data by classifying, summarizing and consolidating; and report the summarized accounting data to internal and external users. Business processes, IT systems, and the accounting information system are inextricably linked.

The types of accounting information systems. Simply as a way to organize the study of accounting information systems, we classify the systems in place into three categories: manual systems, legacy systems, and modern integrated systems. Manual systems use paper documents and records, including journals and ledgers. Legacy systems employ older technology in which the organization has a considerable investment and that might be entrenched in the organization. Modern, integrated accounting software offers companies powerful, technologically advanced systems to serve as accounting information systems that integrate business processes across the organization.

Accounting software market segments. The market for accounting software can be categorized into four market segments: small companies, midmarket, beginning ERP, and tier 1. There is much movement within these market segments as software development companies attempt to appeal to other segments of the accounting software market.

Input methods used in business processes. In manual systems, input is initially captured on source documents. In IT systems, many different methods are available for inputting data. Some of these methods include manual keying of source documents, bar code scanners, point of sale systems, EDI, and e-business. These input methods for IT systems reduce cost, time, and errors in data input.

The processing of accounting data. Data can be processed by batch processing or online and real-time processing. Batch processing is less complex, but due to its time lag, the accounting data are not always current. Online and real-time systems process data individually as business transactions occur, making outputs available immediately.

Outputs from the AIS related to business processes. The outputs of an accounting information system include trading partner documents, internal documents, internal reports, and external reports. These outputs may be in electronic or paper form.

Documenting processes and systems. A useful way to document processes and systems is to prepare a pictorial representation system. There are many methods of documenting processes and systems, including process maps, data flow diagrams, system flowcharts, document flowcharts, and entity relationship diagrams. Process maps, data flow diagrams, and document flowcharts appear in selected chapters of this book to illustrate business processes.

Client–server computing. Client–server computing means that there are two types of computers networked together to accomplish application processing. The important characteristics of client–server computing are as follows: Both client and server computers are networked together; the system appears to users to be one integrated whole; individual parts of processing are shared between the server and client; and the client computer participates in the data processing or data manipulation in some meaningful way.

Ethical considerations at the foundation of accounting information systems. Detecting fraud may be difficult in a computerized environment, especially when there are a limited number of people responsible for maintaining the computer systems. Accountants must recognize the opportunities for unethical behavior within computerized processes, and must carefully monitor those systems.

KEY TERMS

Accounting information system
Attribute
Bar code
Batch processing
Business process
Cardinality
Client–server computing
Data flow diagram
Distributed application
Distributed presentation
Document flowchart
Electronic data interchange
Enterprise application integration
Entity
Entity relationship diagram
ERP system
General journal
General ledger
Legacy system
Online processing
Point of sale system
Process map
Real-time processing
Screen scraper
Source document
Special journal
Subsidiary ledger
System flowchart
Turnaround document

APPENDIX

RESOURCES EVENTS AGENTS (REA) IN ACCOUNTING INFORMATION SYSTEMS

The chapters of this book explain accounting information systems from the traditional viewpoint of accounting, which is based on a debit and credit model with ledgers and journals. Data from transactions are captured on source documents, recorded in ledgers and journals using debits and credits, and then summarized into reports and financial statements.

An accounting system can be examined through other models. A popular alternative is the REA model. REA is an acronym for resources, events, and agents. The REA model views accounting data collection as a system to collect data about the resources, events, and agents within business processes. Business processes involve *events* in which *resources* are exchanged by *agents.* An example of such an event is a sale. The resources exchanged are inventory and cash. The agents are the company (seller) and the customer (buyer). An REA model suggests that the basic data collected should be the resources, events, and agents in this exchange. Debits, credits, ledgers, and journals are not necessary in such a model. The data are collected and stored in a database that can then be used to provide reports and financial statements. The data include the details about the resources, events, and agents involved in the exchange.

An example of an REA pattern of an exchange is shown in Exhibit 2-15, which demonstrates the basic aspects of REA. First, notice in the middle of Exhibit 2-15 that there is a duality to the exchange. That is, the customer is willing to exchange cash for goods, while the company is willing to exchange an inventory item for cash. In this exchange, there is both outflow and inflow. From the company's perspective, it is an outflow of inventory and an inflow of cash. These are the two events in the duality: a sale and a cash receipt. The resources involved are the inventory of goods and cash. The agents are the salesperson, the customer, and the cashier.

The preceding paragraphs present only a simple explanation of the basics of REA. REA is a rich, complex subject that would require many pages to fully explain. As a model of an accounting system, it is used by some accounting instructors to help students understand the relationship between business processes and the accounting data resulting from the business processes because some faculty members believe it is an excellent model to teach accounting information systems. To properly use it as a model to teach and accounting information system concepts, REA should be integrated into the foundation of the entire course and become a part of all or at least most of the concepts covered.

On a different note, the practical application of REA in accounting systems in real companies or organizations has not become popular. There are at least

Exhibit 2-15
An REA Pattern for Sales

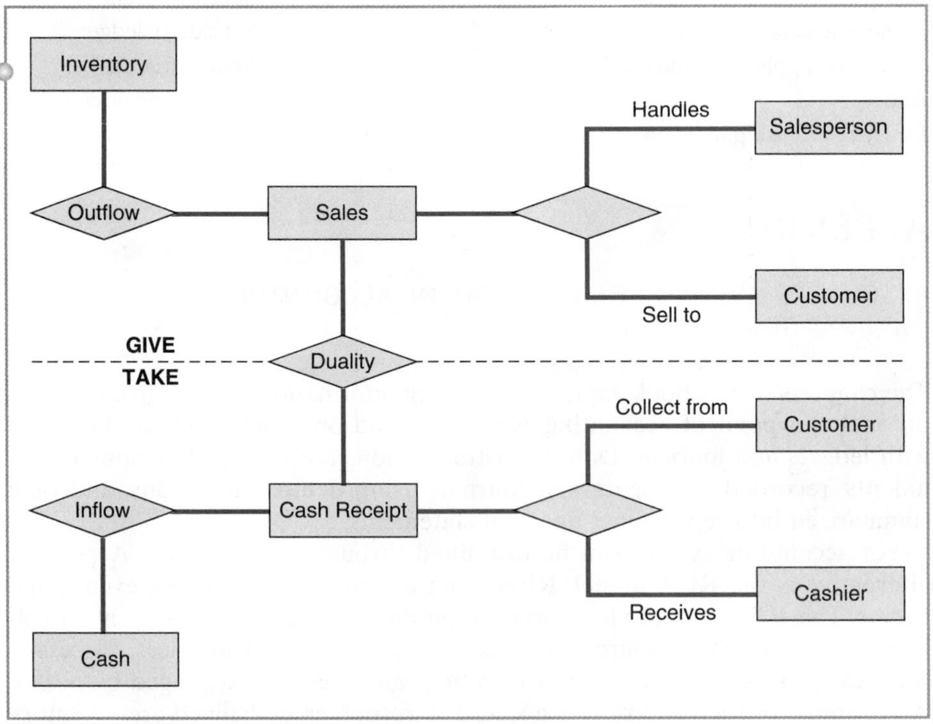

three reasons that REA has not been widely adopted as a model for real-world accounting systems. First, it does not fit well with traditional accounting systems. As described previously, REA offers a perspective completely different from the traditional view of accounting systems. Therefore, it would be very difficult to integrate REA into legacy systems. Second, the restrictions within REA may not fit all aspects of current accounting conventions. For example, resources in REA are akin to assets. However, a strict interpretation of REA resources would not include goodwill, which is considered an asset in traditional accounting concepts. Finally, some have suggested that the accounting profession is too conservative to adopt such a radically different model of accounting systems.

However, REA is continually being further developed and may someday be an important foundation of accounting systems. Currently, REA is an important basis for concepts being developed for e-business exchanges. A working group entitled the eBusiness Transitionary Working Group (eBTWG) is using REA to develop models for detailed information collection and exchange within e-business. REA is a good fit with the low-level detail required for a purchase order in an e-business exchange, but may not fit as well with an overall accounting system based on traditional accounting concepts. As REA continues to be developed and as business and accounting change in the future, REA may at some point become an important foundation of accounting information systems in businesses and organizations.

END OF CHAPTER MATERIAL

CONCEPT CHECK

1. Which of the following statements is not true?
   a. Accounting information systems must maintain both detail and summary information.
   b. Business processes may vary from company to company.
   c. Regardless of the extent of computerization, all accounting information systems must capture data from the transactions within business processes.
   d. Business processes categorized as expenditure processes are not intended to be processes that serve customers.
2. In a manual system, an adjusting entry would most likely be initially recorded in a
   a. special journal.
   b. subsidiary ledger.
   c. general journal.
   d. general ledger.
3. Which of the following is not a disadvantage of maintaining legacy systems?
   a. There are fewer programmers available to support and maintain legacy systems.
   b. They contain invaluable historical data that may be difficult to integrate into newer systems.
   c. Hardware or hardware parts may be unavailable for legacy systems.

d. It can be difficult to integrate various legacy systems into an integrated whole.

4. Which of the following is a disadvantage of purchased accounting software, compared with software developed in-house?
   a. It is custom designed for that company.
   b. It is less costly.
   c. The implementation time is shorter.
   d. There are fewer bugs.
5. Which of the following is not a method of updating legacy systems?
   a. Enterprise application integration
   b. Backoffice ware
   c. Screen scraper
   d. Complete replacement
6. When categorizing the accounting software market, a company with revenue of $8 million would most likely purchase software from which segment?
   a. small company
   b. midmarket
   c. beginning ERP
   d. tier 1 ERP
7. An IT system that uses touch-screen cash registers as an input method is called
   a. electronic data interchange.
   b. e-business.
   c. point of sale system.
   d. source documents and keying.
8. When similar transactions are grouped together for a specified time for processing, it is called
   a. online processing.
   b. real-time processing.
   c. batch processing.
   d. group processing.
9. Which of the following is not correct regarding the differences in the ways that real-time systems differ from batch systems?

	Real-time Systems	**Batch Systems**
a.	Must use direct access files.	Can use simple sequential files.
b.	Processing occurs on demand.	Processing must be scheduled.
c.	Processing choices are menu-driven.	Processing is interactive.
d.	Supporting documents are prepared as items are processed.	Supporting documents are prepared during scheduled runs.

10. In documenting systems, which pictorial method is described as a method that diagrams the actual flow and sequence of events?

a. system flowchart
b. process map
c. data flow diagram
d. entity relationship diagram

11. (CMA Adapted) A company in Florida provides certified flight training programs for aspiring new pilots of small aircraft. Although awarding a pilot's license requires one-on-one flight time, there is also much preparatory training conducted in classroom settings. The company needs to create a conceptual data model for its classroom training program, using an entity-relationship diagram. The company provided the following information:

    Floridian Flight Inc. has 10 instructors who can teach up to 30 pilot trainees per class. The company offers 10 different courses, and each course may generate up to eight classes.

    Identify the entities that should be included in the entity-relationship diagram:

    a. Instructor, Floridian Flight Inc., pilot trainee.
    b. Instructor, Floridian Flight Inc., course, enrollment, class.
    c. Floridian Flight Inc., enrollment, course, class, pilot trainee.
    d. Instructor, course, enrollment, class, pilot trainee.

12. In a client–server system, when the client PC manipulates data for presentation, but does not do any other significant processing, it is called
    a. distributed presentation.
    b. distributed application.
    c. distributed database.
    d. distributed processing.

DISCUSSION QUESTIONS

13. (SO 1) What is the relationship between business processes and the accounting information system?
14. (SO 1) Why is it sometimes necessary to change business processes when IT systems are applied to business processes?
15. (SO 2) Are manual systems and processes completely outdated?
16. (SO 2) What is the purpose of source documents?
17. (SO 2) What are some examples of turnaround documents that you have seen?
18. (SO 2) Why would the training of employees be an impediment to updating legacy systems?
19. (SO 2) Why is it true that the accounting software in and of itself is not the entire accounting information system?
20. (SO 2) How is integration across business processes different between legacy systems and modern, integrated systems?
21. (SO 3) Why do you think there are different market segments for accounting software?
22. (SO 3) How would accounting software requirements for large corporations differ from requirements for small companies?

23. (SO 3) What are some of the differences between ERP systems and accounting software for small companies?
24. (SO 3) Why would accounting software development companies be interested in expanding their software products into other market segments?
25. (SO 4) Given the business and accounting environment today, do you think it is still important to understand the manual input of accounting data?
26. (SO 4) What are the advantages to using some form of IT systems for input, rather than manual input?
27. (SO 4) Why would errors be reduced if a company switched input methods from manual keying of source documents to a bar code system?
28. (SO 5) In general, what types of transactions are well suited to batch processing?
29. (SO 5) Why might the time lag involved in batch processing make it unsuitable for some types of transaction processing?
30. (SO 5) How would real-time processing provide a benefit to managers overseeing business processes?
31. (SO 6) How do internal reports differ from external reports?
32. (SO 6) What are some examples of outputs generated for trading partners?
33. (SO 6) Why might it be important to have internal documents produced as an output of the accounting information system?
34. (SO 7) How does documenting a system through a pictorial representation offer benefits?
35. (SO 8) How does client–server computing divide the processing load between the client and server?
36. (SO 8) Why do you think the client computer may be a better computer platform for presentation of data?

BRIEF EXERCISES

37. (SO 1) Think about your most recent appointment at the dentist's office. Describe the business processes that affected you as the patient/customer. In addition, describe the administrative and accounting processes that are likely to support this business.
38. (SO 2) Describe the purpose of each of the following parts of a manual system:
    a. source document
    b. turnaround document
    c. general ledger
    d. general journal
    e. special journal
    f. subsidiary ledger
39. (SO 2) Consider the accounting information system in place at an organization where you have worked. Do you think that it was a manual system, legacy system, or an integrated IT system? Describe one or two characteristics of that accounting information system that lead you to your conclusion.

40. (SO 2) Suppose that a company wants to upgrade its legacy system, but cannot afford to completely replace it. Describe two approaches that can be used.

41. (SO 3, SO 5) Consider the real-world example of Hobie Cat Company presented in this chapter.
   a. Use Exhibits 2-2 and 2-3 to help you determine the approximate range of Hobie Cat's annual revenues.
   b. What are the advantages Hobie Cat likely realized as a result of having real-time data available?

42. (SO 4) Using IT systems to input accounting data can reduce costs, time, and errors. Give an example showing how you think IT systems can lead to these reductions (cost, time, and errors).

43. (SO 6) Identify whether the following reports would be categorized as trading partner documents, internal documents, internal reports, or external reports:
   a. daily cash receipts listing
   b. accounts receivable aging
   c. wire transfer of funds to a vendor
   d. customer price list
   e. general ledger
   f. statement of cash flows
   g. sales invoice
   h. production schedule
   i. customer address list
   j. payroll journal

44. (SO 6) Which type of accounting information system reports would likely be prepared most frequently by financial accountants? by managerial accountants?

45. (SO 7) Identify which of the cardinal relationships apply, from the following:
   a. component part—product
   b. customer—product
   c. employee ID badge—employee
   d. employee—supervisor
   e. vendor—check

46. (SO 8) Differentiate distributed presentation computing and distributed applications computing. Which of these forms of client server computing is most likely to be used by the sales clerks at a regional sales office for a large retail organization?

PROBLEMS

47. (SO 2) Suppose that a large company is considering replacing a legacy system that is nearing obsolescence. Describe any aspects of this decision that the company should consider.

48. (SO 1, SO 7) Visit the campus bookstore at your university. From what you see happening at the bookstore, try to draw a process map of how the processes at that store serve students, the customers.

49. (SO 3) Look at Exhibit 2-3 and pick one accounting software product from the midmarket segment and one software product from the tier 1 ERP segment. Using those brand names of software, search the Internet for information about those products. Based on your investigation, what are the differences between the two software products you chose? (Hint: To begin your search, you might try examining the following web sites. www.accountingsoftware411.com, www.findaccountingsoftware, and www.2020software.com.)

50. (SO 4) Using an Internet search engine (such as Google, Dogpile, or Lycos), search for the term "RFID." From the results you find, describe how RFID will be used as an input method.

51. (SO 8) Using an Internet search engine (such as Google, Dogpile, or Lycos), search for the terms "client–server" and "scalable." From the results you find, explain why client–server systems are scalable.

CASES

52. In both Chapters 1 and 2, examples of restaurants and fast food chains were used to describe business processes, as they are deemed to be readily familiar to many students. On the basis of your experiences from using the drive-through window at a fast food chain, prepare one each of the three listed pictorial representations of the food-ordering and delivery processes. Your drawings should portray the restaurant's perspective—that is processing a sales transaction via the drive–through window.

    a. process map
    b. document flowchart
    c. data flow diagram

53. Marie Morgan is a college student. Each Monday through Thursday, she commutes to her classes at Tarrey Technical College (TTC). Each semester, Marie pays for on-campus parking privileges. Before Wednesday of the week prior to each new semester, Marie writes a check to TTC Parking Services for $150. She writes her student identification number on the check's memo line and then mails the check to the TTC Parking Services Office.

    Upon receipt of student checks, TTC's Parking Services Office clerk issues a current semester parking decal and a receipt for payment received. These items are mailed to each student at the address noted on the check. A daily listing of checks received is prepared and filed by date. A photocopy of the check is made and placed in a file organized by the student's last name. Accordingly, each student has a parking file maintained in the TTC Parking Services office. The checks are endorsed and deposited in the bank on a daily basis. Once each month, the TTC Parking Services office manager reconciles the bank statement.

    Prepare the following pictorial presentations of TTC's parking services processes:

    a. process map
    b. document flowchart
    c. data flow diagram

CONTINUING CASE: SPATELLI'S PIZZERIA

Reread the Spatelli's case material at the end of Chapter 1 and then consider the following additional information:

This chapter presented a process map (Exhibit 2-9), a document flowchart (Exhibit 2-10), and a data flow diagram (Exhibit 2-11) for a small, local restaurant. In those exhibits manual records and documents as well as manual processes are depicted. On the basis of the case information and the three chapter exhibits mentioned, complete the following requirements:

Required: Describe how each of the following types of orders at Spatelli's differs from the processes and document flow mentioned in Exhibits 2-9 through 2-11.

1. in-store orders
2. telephone orders
3. Internet orders

SOLUTIONS TO CONCEPT CHECK

1. (SO 1) Which of the following statements is not true? **d. Business processes categorized as expenditure processes are not intended to be processes that serve customers** is not a true statement. All business processes either directly or indirectly serve customers. For example, the process to purchase inventory is necessary for stocking inventory to sell to customers.
2. (SO 2) In a manual system, an adjusting entry would most likely be initially recorded in a **c. general journal.** The general journal is the book of original entry for nonroutine transactions, closing entries, and adjusting entries.
3. (SO 2) The choice that is not a disadvantage of maintaining legacy systems is **b. they contain invaluable historical data that may be difficult to integrate into newer systems.** Since legacy systems may have a large amount of historical data that is difficult to integrate into newer systems, it may be an advantage to keep the legacy system and not lose access to the historical data.
4. (SO 2) The choice that is not an advantage of purchased accounting software, compared with software developed in-house, is **a. It is custom designed for that company.** Purchased software is developed to suit the needs of a broad range of customers. Often, companies will purchase and then modify accounting software to meet their specific needs, but the software is not purchased already customized.
5. (SO 3) The choice that is not a method of updating legacy systems is **b. backoffice ware.** Screen scrapers, EAIs, and replacement are all methods to update a legacy system. Backoffice ware is not.
6. (SO 3) When categorizing the accounting software market, a company with revenue of $8 million would most likely purchase software from the **b. midmarket.** Of the four market segments, midmarket is generally considered to comprise companies ranging from $250,000 to $10 million in revenue.

7. (SO 4) An IT system that uses touch-screen cash registers as an input method is called a **c. point of sale system.** Point of sale systems are popularly used at retail stores and fast food restaurants. In retail locations, POS systems use bar code readers; but in fast food and casual eating establishments, POS systems, the server enters customer orders on a touch screen.
8. (SO 5) When similar transactions are grouped together for a specified time for processing, it is called **c. Batch processing.**
9. (CMA Adapted) (SO 5) The choice that is **not** true regarding the differences in the ways that real-time systems differ from batch systems is

	Real-time Systems	Batch Systems
c.	**False: Processing choices are menu-driven.**	**False: Processing is interactive.**

10. (SO 7) In documenting systems, the pictorial method described as a method that diagrams the actual flow and sequence of events is a **b. process map.**
11. (CMA Adapted) (SO 7) A company in Florida provides certified flight training programs for aspiring new pilots or small aircraft. Although awarding a pilot's license requires one-on-one flight time, there is also much preparatory training conducted in classroom settings. The company needs to create a conceptual data model for its classroom training program, using an entity-relationship diagram. The company provided the following information:

    Floridian Flight Inc. has 10 instructors who can teach up to 30 pilot trainees per class. The company offers ten different courses, and each course may generate up to eight classes.

    The entities that should be included in the entity-relationship diagram are **d. instructor, course, enrollment, class, pilot trainee.**
12. (SO 8) In a client–server system, when the client PC manipulates data for presentation, but does not do any other significant processing, it is called **a. distributed presentation.** This is the definition of distributed presentation.

CHAPTER 3

Fraud, Ethics, and Internal Control

Study Objectives

This chapter will help you gain an understanding of the following concepts:

1. An introduction to the need for a code of ethics and internal controls
2. The accounting related fraud that can occur when ethics codes and internal controls are weak or not correctly applied
3. The nature of management fraud
4. The nature of employee fraud
5. The nature of customer fraud
6. The nature of vendor fraud
7. The nature of computer fraud
8. The policies that assist in the avoidance of fraud and errors
9. The maintenance of a code of ethics
10. The maintenance of accounting internal controls
11. The maintenance of information technology controls

Appendix A: The recent history of internal control standards

Appendix B: Control objectives for information technology (CobIT)

INTRODUCTION TO THE NEED FOR A CODE OF ETHICS AND INTERNAL CONTROLS (STUDY OBJECTIVE 1)

During the latter part of 2001 and all of 2002, a wave of information appeared in the news regarding company after company named in fraudulent financial reporting. Among the names were Enron Corp., Global Crossing USA, Inc., Adelphia Communications Corp., WorldCom Inc., and Xerox Corporation. In the case of Enron alone, fraudulent financial reporting led to the loss of billions of dollars for investors, job and retirement-fund losses for employees, the collapse of the Arthur Andersen LLP audit firm, and a further depressing of an already weak stock market. There are many other examples of such problems. An infamous example of fraud and bankruptcy is Phar-Mor, Inc. An examination of the Phar-Mor case illustrates the linkages among ethics, fraud, and internal control.

THE REAL WORLD

Jacob Hamblin/iStockphoto

The drugstore chain Phar-Mor is a classic example of fraud leading to a bankruptcy and many other problems for investors and auditors. At the time Phar-Mor filed bankruptcy, it represented one of the largest cases of fraud in U.S. history. In that bankruptcy, investors lost nearly one billion dollars and Phar-Mor closed many stores and dismissed thousands of workers. The fraud began when top management attempted to make its earnings match the budgeted amounts. Management, desperately trying to overstate revenues or understate expenses to meet expected earnings targets, used illegal accounting tricks such as falsifying inventory. Phar-Mor's top management behaved unethically and fraudulently in an attempt to achieve a desired result.

When management is unethical, fraud is likely to occur. On the other hand, if the top management of a company emphasizes ethical behavior, models ethical behavior, and hires ethical employees, the chance of fraud or ethical lapses can be reduced. In the case of a company such as Phar-Mor, management did not act ethically and did not encourage ethical behavior. Although the company had written and adopted a code of ethics, most of the officers in the company were not aware that it existed.[1] This is an indication that ethics were only "window dressing" and that management did not wish to emphasize and model ethical behavior.

Another way that the Phar-Mor fraud could have been avoided or detected was through the proper operation of the accounting system and internal controls. For example, a good accounting system will process all checks through a bank account that is part of the normal payment approval process. In the case of Phar-Mor, management maintained a separate bank account and used it for fraudulent purposes. Checks drawn on this account did not go through a regular approval process. In summary, maintaining high ethics and following proper procedures can help prevent or detect many kinds of fraud.

In addition to acting ethically, the management of any organization has an obligation to maintain a set of processes and procedures that assure accurate and complete records and protection of assets. This obligation arises because many groups have expectations of management. First, management has a stewardship obligation to those who provide funds to, or invest in, the company.

[1]Stephen D. Williger, "Phar-Mor—A Lesson in Fraud," *The Wall Street Journal*, March 28, 1994.

Stewardship is the careful and responsible oversight and use of the assets entrusted to management. This requires that management maintain systems which allow it to demonstrate that it has appropriately used these funds and assets. Investors, lenders, and funding agencies must be able to examine reports showing the appropriate use of funds or assets provided to management. Management must maintain accurate and complete accounting records and reports with full disclosure. Second, management has an obligation to provide accurate reports to those who are not owners or investors, such as business organizations with whom the company interacts and governmental units like the Internal Revenue Service (IRS) and the Securities and Exchange Commission (SEC).

Finally, to efficiently and effectively manage an organization, management and the board of directors must have access to accurate and timely feedback regarding the results of operations. An organization cannot determine whether it is meeting objectives unless it continuously monitors operations by examining reports that summarize the results of operations. In many cases, these reports are outputs of the computerized system. Therefore, IT systems must provide accurate and timely information in reports. When a vice president at Phar-Mor became concerned about the adequacy of the IT system and the resulting reports, he formed a committee to address the problems; however, the committee was squelched by members of senior management who were involved in the fraud.

The management obligations of stewardship and reporting point to the need to maintain accurate and complete accounting systems and to protect assets. To fulfill these obligations, management must maintain internal controls and enforce a **code of ethics.** If these two items are operating effectively, many types of fraud can be avoided or detected. Internal controls have been defined by several bodies, but perhaps the most encompassing description of accounting internal controls is contained in the Committee of Sponsoring Organizations'[2] (COSO's) report on internal control.[3] The COSO report defines internal control as follows:

> a process, affected by an entity's board of directors, management, and other personnel, designed to provide reasonable assurance regarding the achievement of objectives in the following categories:
>
> - effectiveness and efficiency of operations
> - reliability of financial reporting
> - compliance with applicable laws and regulations.

These internal control processes and procedures will assist in protecting assets and ensuring accurate records. In addition to the accounting internal controls, an organization should also have internal controls covering its IT systems. If not properly controlled, IT systems may become exposed to the risks of unauthorized access, erroneous or incomplete processing, and interruption of service. Guidelines for IT controls are provided by the AICPA, and are discussed later.

[2]The Committee of Sponsoring Organizations includes the following organizations: AICPA, AAA, FEI, IIA, and IMA. The purpose of COSO is to improve the quality of financial reporting through business ethics, effective internal controls, and corporate governance. The COSO web site is www.coso.org.

[3]Committee of Sponsoring Organizations of the Treadway Commission (CSOTC), *Internal Control-Integrated Framework* (COSO Report), 1992.

To help assure accurate and complete accounting systems and reports, an organization should have good accounting internal controls, good IT controls, and an enforced code of ethics. A code of ethics is a set of documented guidelines for moral and ethical behavior within the organization. It is management's responsibility to establish, enforce, and exemplify the principles of ethical conduct valued in the organization. The importance of an ethics code is perhaps easier to see by looking at it from the opposite perspective. As has become obvious with the recent flood of accounting fraud scandals at companies such as Enron, Worldcom, Global Crossing, and others, top management does not always exhibit ethical behavior. If management does not demonstrate ethical behavior, employees at all levels are much more likely to follow suit in their disregard for ethical guidelines. Of course, the opposite should also be true. Management that emphasizes and models ethical behavior is more likely to encourage ethical behavior in employees.

In summary, a company that maintains a good system of accounting and IT internal controls and values ethical behavior will be more likely to avoid fraud, other ethical problems, and errors in accounting records. This chapter describes some types of fraud that can occur and provides details of internal control systems and ethics codes. It is not possible for a single chapter to include all potential types of fraud or the controls to prevent them. The purpose of this chapter is to explain some of these fraud schemes to help you see the nature of the risks involved. With an understanding of the risks, you will find it easier to learn the nature of accounting and IT internal control systems intended to prevent or detect errors and fraud.

ACCOUNTING RELATED FRAUD (STUDY OBJECTIVE 2)

Fraud can be defined as the theft, concealment, and conversion to personal gain of another's money, physical assets, or information. Notice that this definition includes theft and concealment. In most cases, a fraud includes altering accounting records to conceal the fact that a theft occurred. For example, an employee who steals cash from his employer is likely to alter the cash records to cover up the theft. An example of conversion would be selling a piece of inventory that has been stolen. The definition of fraud also includes theft, not only of money and assets, but also of information. Much of the information that a company maintains can be valuable to others. For example, customer credit card numbers can be stolen. An understanding of the nature of fraud is important, since one of the purposes of an accounting information system is to help to prevent fraud.

In fraud, there is a distinction between misappropriation of assets and misstatement of financial records. **Misappropriation of assets** involves theft of any item of value. It is sometimes referred to as a **defalcation,** or **internal theft,** and the most common examples are theft of cash or inventory. Restaurants and retail stores are especially susceptible to misappropriation of assets because their assets are readily accessible by employees. **Misstatement of financial records** involves the falsification of accounting reports. This is often referred to as **earnings management,** or **fraudulent financial reporting.**

In order for a fraud to be perpetrated, three conditions must exist, as shown in Exhibit 3-1. These three conditions, known as the **fraud triangle,** are as follows:

- *Incentive* to commit the fraud. Some kind of incentive or pressure typically leads fraudsters to their deceptive acts. Financial pressures, market pressures, job-related failures, or addictive behaviors may create the incentive to commit fraud.

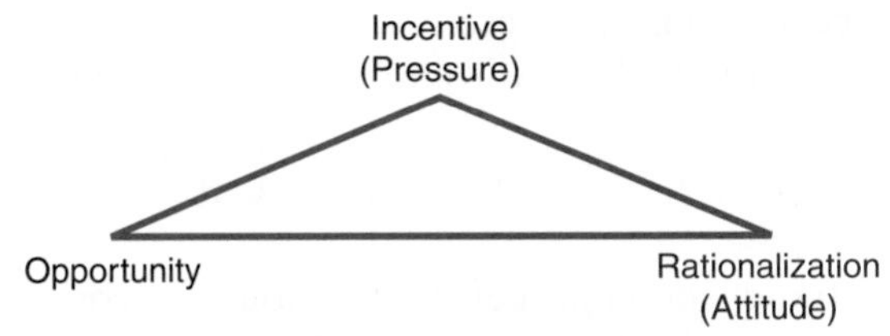

Exhibit 3-1
The Fraud Triangle

- *Opportunity* to commit the fraud. Circumstances may provide access to the assets or records that are the objects of fraudulent activity. Only those persons having access can pull off the fraud. Ineffective oversight is often a contributing factor.
- *Rationalization* of the fraudulent action. Fraudsters typically justify their actions because of their lack of moral character. They may intend to repay or make up for their dishonest actions in the future, or they may believe that the company owes them as a result of unfair expectations or an inadequate pay raise.

Understanding these conditions is helpful to accountants as they create effective systems that prevent fraud and fraudulent financial reporting. Fraud prevention is an increasingly important role for accounting and IT managers in business organizations, because instances of fraud and its devastating effects appear to be on the rise.

THE REAL WORLD

The Association of Certified Fraud Examiners publishes studies of occupational fraud cases. Some statistics from its most recent reports follow:[4]

- Certified fraud examiners estimate that 5–6% of revenues will be lost annually as a result of occupational fraud and abuse. Applied to the U.S. Gross Domestic Product, this translates to losses of approximately $650 billion, or about $4500 per employee.
- Up to half of the frauds in these studies caused losses of at least $100,000, and several caused losses in excess of $1 million.
- Over 80% of occupational frauds involve asset misappropriations. Cash is the targeted asset 90% of the time.
- Corruption schemes perpetrated by company executives and owners cause over $1million in losses, on average. This is up to 13 times as large as the average loss caused by managers and employees.
- The average scheme in this study lasted 18 months before it was detected.
- The most common method for detecting occupational fraud is by a tip from an employee, customer, vendor, or anonymous source. The second most common method is by accident.
- Small businesses are the most vulnerable to occupational fraud and abuse. The average scheme in a small business causes $190,000 in losses, which is even higher than the average loss in the largest companies.

[4]*Report to the Nation on Occupational Fraud and Abuse,* Association of Certified Fraud Examiners, 2006, 2004, and 2002 <acfe.com/fraud/report.asp>.

As indicated by the 2002 fraud report from the Association of Certified Fraud Examiners, fraud occurs in many different ways. The general categories of fraud and examples of these are explained in the sections that follow.

CATEGORIES OF ACCOUNTING-RELATED FRAUD

In an organization, fraud can be perpetrated by four categories of people: management, employees, customers, and vendors. (See Exhibit 3-2.)

Fraud Category	Example	Can Internal Control Be Effective in Preventing or Detecting?	Example of an Internal Control That Can Be Effective
Management fraud	Misstating financial statements	Usually not, because of management override	n/a
Employee fraud	Inflating hours worked on time card	Yes	Require supervisor to verify and sign time card
Customer fraud	Returning stolen merchandise for cash	Yes	Provide refund only if proper sales receipt exists
Vendor fraud	Requesting duplicate payment for one invoice	Yes	Pay only those invoices that have a matching purchase order and receiving report, and mark documents as paid or cancelled

Exhibit 3-2
Categories of Accounting Related Fraud

THE NATURE OF MANAGEMENT FRAUD (STUDY OBJECTIVE 3)

Management fraud, conducted by one or more top-level managers within the company, is usually in the form of fraudulent financial reporting. Oftentimes, the chief executive officer (CEO) or chief financial officer (CFO) conducts fraud by misstating the financial statements through elaborate schemes or complex transactions. Managers misstate financial statements in order to receive such indirect benefits as the following:

1. Increased stock price. Management usually owns stock in the company, and it benefits from increased stock price.
2. Improved financial statements, which enhance the potential for a merger or initial public offering (IPO), or prevent negative consequences due to noncompliance with debt covenants or decreased bond ratings.
3. Enhanced chances of promotion, or avoidance of firing or demotion.
4. Increased incentive-based compensation such as salary, bonus, or stock options.
5. Delayed cash flow problems or bankruptcy.

Management fraud may involve overstating revenues and assets, understating expenses and liabilities, misapplying accounting principles, or any combination of these. While there are numerous examples of management fraud, two examples follow.

THE REAL WORLD

Enron was forced to restate (reduce) earnings by approximately $600 million because of improper financial reporting. Enron's top management had been hiding debt and losses by using a complex set of special purpose entities (SPEs). These SPEs were partnerships controlled by members of Enron's top management, such as the CEO and CFO. The SPEs were treated as unrelated entities and, therefore, were not included in the Enron financial statements.

Shortly after the restatement of financial statements, Enron filed the biggest bankruptcy in history. The company had previously been considered by many to be one of the largest and most successful companies ever. The unraveling of Enron caused the stock price to fall from $90 in 2000 to less than $1 by the end of 2001. Many investors and employees were devastated by their losses. This fraudulent misstatement led not only to the demise of Enron, but also the dissolution of Arthur Andersen, one of the oldest and most prestigious audit firms in the world.

THE REAL WORLD

On April 11, 2002, the SEC filed a civil fraud suit against Xerox Corporation,[5] alleging that top managers at Xerox approved and encouraged accounting practices that violated GAAP and accelerated revenue recognition. These bad accounting practices included the following:

1. Incorrectly counting service and financing lease revenue at the beginning of the contract rather than over the life of the lease.
2. Shifting revenue from financing to equipment sale, which increased gross margin.
3. Improperly recognizing a gain from a one-time event, usually called establishing "cookie jar" reserves.

The effect of this fraud on the financial statements was to artificially increase pre-tax earnings by $1.5 billion over the four-year period of 1997 to 2000. Top management encouraged these practices so that the company could meet expected earnings targets. As a result of the SEC action, Xerox agreed to pay a $10 million fine and restate earnings.

These two examples illustrate that management fraud typically

1. is intended to enhance financial statements;
2. is conducted or encouraged by the top managers;
3. involves complex transactions, manipulations, or business structures; and/or
4. involves top management's circumvention of the systems or internal controls that are in place—known as **management override.**

Management fraud, like the examples at Enron and Xerox, is conducted by top-level managers and usually involves manipulation of the financial statements so that the manager can benefit by such things as increases in compensation or

[5]Securities and Exchange Commission, Litigation Release No. 17465, April 11, 2002.

stock price. Many management frauds include complex transactions or entities, such as Enron's use of SPEs. Moreover, managers operate above the level of internal controls; that is, internal controls can be overridden or circumvented by managers. Therefore, a good set of internal controls may not be as effective in reducing the chance of management fraud as it would be in reducing the chance of fraud committed by an employee, vendor, or customer. The most effective measure to prevent or detect management fraud is to establish a professional internal audit staff that periodically checks up on management activities and reports to the audit committee of the board of directors.

THE NATURE OF EMPLOYEE FRAUD (STUDY OBJECTIVE 4)

Employee fraud is conducted by nonmanagement employees. This usually means that an employee steals cash or assets for personal gain. While there are many different kinds of employee fraud, some of the most common are as follows:

1. *Inventory theft.* Inventory can be stolen or misdirected. This could be merchandise, raw materials, supplies, or finished goods inventory.
2. *Cash receipts theft.* This occurs when an employee steals cash from the company. An example would be the theft of checks collected from customers.
3. *Accounts payable fraud.* Here, the employee may submit a false invoice, create a fictitious vendor, or collect kickbacks from a vendor. A **kickback** is a cash payment that the vendor gives the employee in exchange for the sale; it is like a business bribe.
4. *Payroll fraud.* This occurs when an employee submits a false or inflated time card.
5. *Expense account fraud.* This occurs by an employee submitting false travel or entertainment expenses, or charging an expense ledger account to cover the theft of cash.

Cash receipts theft is the most common type of employee fraud. It is often pulled off through a technique known as **skimming,** where the organization's cash is stolen before it is entered into the accounting records. This type of theft is the most difficult to discover, since there is no internal record of the cash. For example, consider the case of a ticket agent in a movie theater who accepts cash from customers and permits those customers to enter the theater without a ticket. The cash collected could be pocketed by the agent, and there would be no record of the transaction.

Fraudsters also steal the company's cash after it has been recorded in the accounting records. This practice is known as **larceny.** Consider an example of an employee responsible for making the bank deposit who steals the cash after it has been recorded in the accounts receivable records. This type of fraud is uncommon because the fraudster is likely to be caught, since the accounting reports provide evidence of the existence of the cash. Larceny is typically detected when the reconciliation of cash counts (to the accounts receivable or payable records) is performed or when the bank reconciliation is prepared.

In some cases, fraud may involve collusion. **Collusion** occurs when two or more people work together to commit a fraud. Collusion can occur between two or more employees, employees and customers, or employees and vendors. Collusion between employees within a company is the most difficult to prevent or detect because it compromises the effectiveness of internal controls. This is true because collusion can make it much easier to conduct and conceal a fraud or theft even when segregation of duties is in place. For example, if a warehouse employee were to steal inventory and an accounting clerk were to cover it up by altering the inventory records, the fraud would be difficult to detect.

THE REAL WORLD

A recent article described fraud investigation at Dow Chemical Company, much of which is related to detecting employee fraud. The author indicated that the most common frauds at Dow are expense report fraud, kickback schemes, and embezzlement. Dow identifies the following examples of warning signs during its fraud investigations.[6]

Expense Report Fraud

- Excessive amount of expenses without receipts or supporting documentation
- Handwritten rather then computer-generated receipts
- Purchases from retail establishments including toy stores and sporting-goods stores, which may indicate personal expenses
- Excessive cash advances taken against a company credit card
- Numerous expenses under the minimal amount requiring a receipt, which is usually less than $25

Kickback Schemes

- Vendor contracts awarded without bids
- Repeated use of the same vendor
- Excessive complaints about product quality
- Invoiced prices that differ from prices listed in the contract
- Employee living beyond his/her means
- Employee not taking any vacation time
- Photocopied invoices
- Vendor address listed as a P.O. box
- Continual instances of missing inventory

Embezzlement

- Discrepancies between invoice amount and amount paid
- Invoices for unusual items, with no supporting documentation
- Unexplainable cost variances between budgeted amounts and actual amounts
- Duplicate or invalid employee Social Security numbers or addresses (may indicate ghost employees)
- Inflated salaries or travel expenses

[6] Paul Zikmund, "Ferreting Out Fraud," *Strategic Finance*, April 2003, pp. 3–4.

THE NATURE OF CUSTOMER FRAUD (STUDY OBJECTIVE 5)

Customer fraud occurs when a customer improperly obtains cash or property from a company, or avoids a liability through deception. Although customer fraud may affect any company, it is an especially common problem for retail firms and companies that sell goods through Internet-based commerce. Examples of customer fraud include credit card fraud, check fraud, and refund fraud. **Credit card fraud** and **check fraud** involve the customer's use of stolen or fraudulent credit cards and checks. **Refund fraud** occurs when a customer tries to return stolen goods to collect a cash refund.

THE NATURE OF VENDOR FRAUD (STUDY OBJECTIVE 6)

Vendor fraud occurs when vendors obtain payments to which they are not entitled. Unethical vendors may intentionally submit duplicate or incorrect invoices, send shipments in which the quantities are short, or send lower-quality goods than ordered. Vendor fraud may also be perpetrated through collusion. For example, an employee of a company could make an agreement with a vendor to continue the vendor relationship in the future if the employee receives a kickback.

More and more companies are conducting vendor audits as a way to protect themselves against unscrupulous vendors. **Vendor audits** involve the examination of vendor records in support of amounts charged to the company. Since many vendor contracts involve reimbursement for labor hours and other expenses incurred, the company can review supporting documentation for these expenses incurred by its vendor. This could reveal whether or not the vendor is honest in reporting expenses, and may be the basis for continuing or terminating the business relationship.

THE NATURE OF COMPUTER FRAUD (STUDY OBJECTIVE 7)

In addition to the frauds described in previous sections, organizations must also attempt to prevent or detect fraudulent activities involving the computer. Again, there are so many different kinds of computer fraud that it is not feasible to describe all the possibilities in this chapter. In some cases, the computer is used as a tool to more quickly and efficiently conduct a fraud that could be conducted without a computer. For example, an individual could perpetrate **industrial espionage,** the theft of proprietary company information, by digging through the trash of the intended target company. However, it would probably be more efficient for a hacker to gain access to the information through the target company's computer system. In other cases, the fraud conducted is unique to computers. For example, a computer is required to accomplish **software piracy,** the unlawful copying of software programs.

Another characteristic of computer fraud is that it can be conducted by employees within the organization or unauthorized users outside the organization. We categorize these two sources of computer fraud into internal computer fraud and external computer fraud.

INTERNAL SOURCES OF COMPUTER FRAUD

When an employee of an organization attempts to conduct fraud through the misuse of a computer-based system, it is called internal computer fraud. Internal computer fraud concerns each of the following activities:

1. Input manipulation
2. Program manipulation
3. Output manipulation

Input manipulation usually involves altering data that is input into the computer. For example, altering payroll time cards to be entered into a computerized payroll system is a type of input manipulation. Other examples of input manipulation would be creating false or fictitious data inputs, entering data without source documents, or altering payee addresses of vendors or employees.

Program manipulation occurs when a program is altered in some fashion to commit a fraud. Examples of program manipulation include the salami technique, Trojan horse programs, and trap door alterations.

A fraudster uses the **salami technique** to alter a program to slice a small amount from several accounts and then credit those small amounts to the perpetrator's benefit. For example, a program that calculates interest earned can be altered to round down to the lower ten-cent amount; that small excess of interest earned can be deposited to the perpetrator's account. Although it would take many transactions of this type to be of much benefit, the nature of interest calculation is such that it occurs frequently on many accounts; therefore, the amount of the fraud benefit could build quickly.

A **Trojan horse program** is a small, unauthorized program within a larger, legitimate program, used to manipulate the computer system to conduct a fraud. For example, the rogue program might cause a certain customer's account to be written off each time a batch of sales or customer payments are processed.

A **trap door alteration** is a valid programming tool that is misused to commit fraud. As programmers write software applications, they may allow for unusual or unique ways to enter the program to test small portions, or modules, of the system. These entranceways can be thought of as hidden entrances, or trap doors. Before the program is placed into regular service, the trap doors should be removed, but a programmer may leave a trap door in place in order to misuse it to commit fraud.

Computer systems generate many different kinds of output, including checks and reports. If a person alters the system's checks or reports to commit fraud, this is known as output manipulation. This kind of fraud is often successful simply because humans tend to trust the output of a computer and do not question its validity or accuracy as much as they might if the output were manually produced.

EXTERNAL SOURCES OF COMPUTER FRAUD

In most cases, external computer frauds are conducted by someone outside the company who has gained unauthorized access to the computer. These fraudsters are commonly known as hackers. However, it is possible that someone within the organization—essentially, anyone who can gain access to an organization's computer system—could attempt these frauds. Two common types of external computer fraud are hacking and spoofing.

Hacking

Hacking is the term commonly used for computer network break-ins. Hacking may be undertaken for various reasons, including industrial espionage, credit card theft from online databases, destruction or alteration of data, or merely thrill-seeking. Regardless of the purpose of the break-in, tremendous damage can be done to a company in terms of immediate financial loss or loss of customer confidence.

THE REAL WORLD

A computer hacking incident occurred at Data Processors International, a firm that processes credit card transactions for retailers, when a hacker broke into the computer system and gained access to approximately eight million credit card numbers belonging to consumers.

A hacker usually gains access to a network through the various network connections that most businesses and organizations now have. Most companies are connected to networks for many reasons, such as to conduct Internet commerce, to connect various geographic locations of the same company, to allow telecommuting for employees who work at home, and to connect to the computer systems of vendors or customers. The existence of any of these types of network connections opens an opportunity for hackers to violate that connection. This is the paradox faced in today's computer world. To operate efficiently, organizations need to connect to networks, but such connections increase security risks exponentially.

DoS Attacks

A particular kind of hacking that has increased dramatically in recent years is denial of service (DoS) attacks. A **denial of service attack** is intended to overwhelm an intended target computer system with so much bogus network traffic that the system is unable to respond to valid network traffic. A hacker takes advantage of the automated, repetitive nature of computers to accomplish a DoS attack by taking control of one or more computers on a network and using those computers to continually send bogus network traffic to a target computer. If the hacker can take over several computers and force each of them to send bogus traffic to one targeted computer system, the targeted system becomes overwhelmed. Attacks such as these that use several computers to attack one computer are called distributed denial of service attacks, or DdoS attacks.

THE REAL WORLD

In February of 2000, several high-profile companies were the targets of DoS attacks. Companies including Yahoo Inc., Turner Broadcasting System Inc., Ebay Inc., and Amazon.com. experienced DoS attacks that shut down their websites for hours as they worked to wipe out the harmful effects on their computer servers and network.

Spoofing

Spoofing occurs when a person, through a computer system, pretends to be someone else. There are two kinds of spoofing that are currently popular: Internet spoofing and e-mail spoofing. Internet spoofing is the most dangerous to the accounting and control systems, because a spoofer fools a computer into thinking that the network traffic arriving is from a trusted source. Within the Internet, each computer server is identified by a unique Internet protocol (IP) address. Any network traffic between computers is broken into small "packets" of data. Each packet includes the IP addresses of both the sender and receiver of the packet. In spoofing, the originating IP address is intentionally changed to make it appear that the packet is coming from a different IP address. Many computer systems include a security system that accepts packets only from known and trusted sources—essentially, an address book of trusted IP addresses. A spoofer circumvents that system by pretending that the packet originates from a trusted source. These packets can contain malicious data such as viruses, or programs that capture passwords and log-in names.

While e-mail spoofing is not typically as problematic as Internet spoofing is to the direct financial interests of most business organizations, it is nevertheless a source of irritation and inconvenience at the workplace. E-mail spoofing might flood employees e-mail boxes with junk mail, but usually does not result in defrauding their company. E-mail spoofing is usually used in an attempt to scam consumers. For example, a bank customer might get an e-mail that looks as if it comes from the customer service department, asking recipients to provide confidential information such as their log-in and password. With these fake e-mails, the sender is hoping that unsuspecting customers will reply and divulge the confidential information that will allow the spoofer to commit fraud. This type of fraud must be controlled by the consumer and police authorities. Internal control systems within a company can do little or nothing to prevent e-mail spoofing.

POLICIES TO ASSIST IN THE AVOIDANCE OF FRAUD AND ERRORS (STUDY OBJECTIVE 8)

Following are three critical actions that an organization can undertake to assist in the prevention or detection of fraud and errors:

1. Maintain and enforce a code of ethics;
2. Maintain a system of accounting internal controls; and
3. Maintain a system of information technology controls.

These ongoing actions will not entirely prevent or detect all fraud or errors, but they can greatly reduce the chance of fraud and errors. Each of these actions is discussed next.

MAINTENANCE OF A CODE OF ETHICS (STUDY OBJECTIVE 9)

In response to the many fraudulent financial reports generated in 2001, the United States Congress passed the **Sarbanes–Oxley Act** of 2002. The Act was intended to reform accounting, financial reporting, and auditing functions of

Exhibit 3-3
Concepts in a Code of Ethics

Establishing and maintaining a culture where ethical conduct is recognized, valued and exemplified by all employees. This includes:

- Obeying applicable laws and regulations that govern business.
- Conducting business in a manner that is honest, fair, and trustworthy.
- Avoiding all conflicts of interest.
- Creating and maintaining a safe work environment.
- Protecting the environment.

companies that are publicly traded in stock exchanges. Chapter 5 describes the Act's major requirements regarding fraud and internal controls. One requirement is that public companies adopt and disclose a code of ethics for directors, officers, and employees. Documenting and adhering to a code of ethics should reduce opportunities for managers or employees to conduct fraud. This will only be true, however, if top management emphasizes this code of ethics and disciplines or discharges those who violate the code. Exhibit 3-3 presents the type of concepts that are usually found in a business organization's code of ethics.

THE REAL WORLD

In a recent survey of management accountants and financial managers, the effect of ethics codes on management behavior was studied. The survey concluded, in part, "Nearly 62% of the respondents (13 out of 21) from corporations reporting that ethics don't matter also report pressure to alter or 'manage' financial results. In contrast, in corporations where the tone at the top favors ethical conduct, only 19% (35 out of 189) reported pressure to alter results. Similar results were shown with specific financial reporting measures, such as income, balance sheet, and return on investment."[7]

MAINTENANCE OF ACCOUNTING INTERNAL CONTROLS (STUDY OBJECTIVE 10)

Much of the early part of this chapter focused on the nature and sources of fraud. Understanding fraud makes it easier to recognize the need for policies and procedures that protect an organization. Internal control systems provide this framework for fighting fraud. However, attempting to prevent or detect fraud is only one of the reasons that an organization maintains a system of internal controls.

The objectives of an internal control system are as follows:

1. Safeguard assets (from fraud or errors).
2. Maintain the accuracy and integrity of the accounting data.
3. Promote operational efficiency.
4. Ensure compliance with management directives.

To achieve these objectives, management must establish an overall internal control system, the concept of which is depicted in Exhibit 3-4. This control

[7] Barbara Lamberton, Paul H. Mihalek, and Carl Smith, "The Tone at the Top and Ethical Conduct Connection," *Strategic Finance*, March 2005, p. 38.

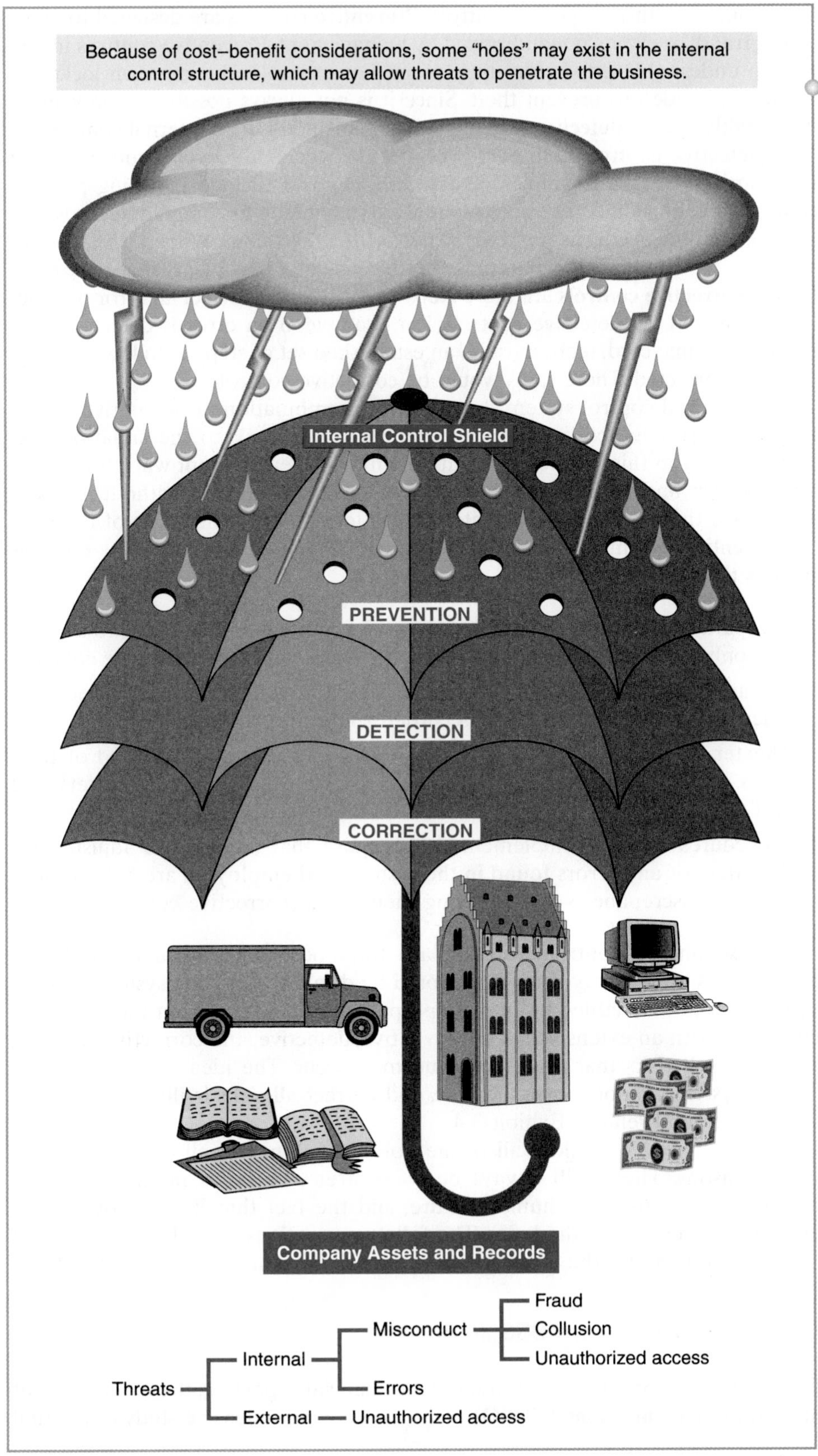

Exhibit 3-4
Internal Controls as Shields to Protect Assets and Records

system includes three types of controls. **Preventive controls** are designed to avoid errors, fraud, or events not authorized by management. Preventive controls intend to stop undesirable acts before they occur. For example, keeping cash locked in a safe is intended to prevent theft. Since it is not always possible to prevent all undesirable events, **detective controls** must be included in an internal control system. Detective controls help employees to uncover or discover errors, fraud, or unauthorized events. Examples of detective controls include matching physical count to inventory records, reconciling bank statements to company records, and matching an invoice to its purchase order prior to payment. When these types of activities are conducted, it becomes possible to detect problems that may exist. Finally, **corrective controls** are those steps undertaken to correct an error or problem uncovered via detective controls. For example, if an error is detected in an employee's time card, there must be an established set of steps to follow to assure that it is corrected. These steps would be corrective controls.

Any internal control system should have a combination of preventive, detective, and corrective controls. As an example, refer back to the situation presented earlier in this chapter involving the movie-theater agent who stole a customer's cash and allowed the customer to enter the theater without a ticket. The movie theater could protect itself from losses due to this type of fraud by implementing a combination of preventative, detective, and corrective controls such as the following:

- A separate ticket taker could be employed who would allow access to the theater only to those customers who present a valid ticket (preventative control).
- An automated system could be used whereby tickets are dispensed only when payment is received and recorded (detective control).
- Theater agents could be required to reconcile activities at the end of their shifts, such as comparing payments received with the number of tickets sold and the number of occupied seats in the theater (detective control).
- Procedures could be implemented to require that records are adjusted for the effect of any errors found in the system, and employees are held responsible for discrepancies found during their shifts (corrective control).

If these kinds of controls were in place, fraud occurrences would be reduced, because it is more likely that fraud would be disallowed by the system, spotted by employees, or rectified before any perpetrator could carry out the act. However, even with an extensive set of preventive, detective, and corrective controls, there are still risks that errors or fraud may occur. The idea that the internal control system cannot prevent, detect, and correct all risks is illustrated by the holes in the umbrella in Exhibit 3-4.

It is not possible to close all of the holes (or eliminate all of the risks) for many reasons. There will always be weak areas, or holes in the umbrellas because of human error, human nature, and the fact that it may not be cost effective to close all of the holes. The following sections describe the details of internal controls and the risk exposures, or holes, in those internal controls.

THE DETAILS OF THE COSO REPORT

Due to ongoing problems with fraudulent financial reporting, the **Committee of Sponsoring Organizations (COSO)** undertook a comprehensive study of internal control and in 1992 issued the COSO report. The **COSO report** has become the standard definition and description of internal control accepted by the accounting industry. According to the COSO report, there are five interrelated components of internal control: the control environment, risk assessment, control activities, information and communication, and monitoring. Each of these components is discussed next.

Control Environment

The **control environment** sets the tone of an organization and influences the control consciousness of its employees. The control environment is the foundation for all other components of internal control, and it provides the discipline and structure of all other components. Control environment factors include the following:

- the integrity, ethical values, and competence of the entity's people
- management's philosophy and operating style
- the way management assigns authority and responsibility
- the way management organizes and develops its people
- the attention and direction provided by the board of directors

In each of these areas, management could establish an operating style that is either risky or more conservative. Exhibit 3-5 shows characteristics of internal

Exhibit 3-5
Factors of the Control Environment

Factor	Example of a Less Risky Control Environment	Example of a More Risky Control Environment
Integrity and ethics	The company has a code of ethics, and it is rigidly enforced.	The company does not have a code of ethics, or if it has one, it is not enforced.
Philosophy and operating style	Management is very conservative in its approach to things such as mergers.	Management is very aggressive and risk taking in its approach to things such as mergers.
Assignment of authority and responsibility	Lines of authority are well established, and managers' jobs and duties are clear to them.	Managers have overlapping duties, and oftentimes managers are not quite sure whether or not they have certain responsibilities and authority.
Organization and development of people	Management carefully trains and cultivates employees to be able to take on more responsibility.	Management does not spend any money or time on the training of employees.
Attention and direction by the board of directors	Members of the board examine reports and hold top management accountable for the accuracy of the reports.	Members of the board do not prepare for the meetings they attend and are merely "big-name" figureheads.

control environments that are considered more risky and less risky. These examples are not intended to indicate that a company with characteristics such as those in the right-hand, "more risky" column will always experience fraud. It implies only that companies represented in the right-hand column are more likely to experience fraud because of risks in the control environment. Conversely, companies with characteristics such as those in the "less risky" column are less likely to experience fraud, because they are more conservative in their approach to the establishment of a control environment; in others words, these companies tend to play it safe by implementing protective measures.

The philosophy and operating style of management is evident in how it approaches the operation and growth of its company. For example, some managers are very aggressive in setting high earnings targets, in developing new products or markets, or in acquiring other companies. Such companies may reward management with incentive compensation plans that award bonuses for increased earnings. Management, therefore, has more motivation to be aggressive in achieving earnings growth. In this environment where aggressive growth is sought, there can be pressure to "fudge the numbers" to achieve those targets.

The operating environments as described previously are established by top management. A company's CEO can either encourage or discourage risky behaviors. Thus, the tone at the top flows through the whole organization and affects behavior at every level. For this reason, the control environment established by management is a very critical component of an internal control system. COSO identifies the tone set by management as the most important factor related to providing accurate and complete financial reports. The control environment is the foundation upon which the entire internal control system rests. No matter how strong the remaining components are, a poor control environment is likely to allow fraud or errors to occur in an organization.

Risk Assessment

Every organization continually faces risks from external and internal sources. These risks include factors such as changing markets, increasing government regulation, and employee turnover. Each of these can cause drastic changes in the day-to-day operations of a company by disrupting routines and processes in the company, including those processes that should help prevent or detect fraud and errors. In order for management to maintain control over these threats to its business, it must constantly be engaged in **risk assessment,** whereby it considers existing threats and the potential for additional risks and stands ready to respond should these events occur. Management must develop a systematic and an ongoing way to do the following:

1. Identify the sources of risks, both internal and external.
2. Determine the impact of such risks in terms of finances and reputation.
3. Estimate the chances of such risks occurring.
4. Develop an action plan to reduce the impact and probability of these risks.
5. Execute the action plan and continue the cycle, beginning again with the first step.

Control Activities

The COSO report identifies **control activities** as the policies and procedures that help ensure that management directives are carried out and that management objectives are achieved. A good internal control system must include control activities that occur at all levels and in all functions within the company. The control activities include a range of activities that can be divided into the following categories:

1. Authorization of transactions
2. Segregation of duties
3. Adequate records and documents
4. Security of assets and documents
5. Independent checks and reconciliation

Authorization of Transactions In any organization, it is important to try to ensure that the organization engage only in transactions which are authorized. **Authorization** refers to an approval, or endorsement, from a responsible person or department in the organization that has been sanctioned by top management. Every transaction that occurs must be properly authorized in some manner. For example, some procedure should be followed to determine when it is allowable to purchase goods, or when it is permissible to extend credit. A common example that you may have encountered occurs at some grocery and department stores. If you have ever stood in a long check-out line while the shopper in front tried to pay with an out-of-state check, you probably groaned silently, knowing that the line would be further delayed while the check-out clerk waited for a manager to approve the payment method. Notice that in this example, for the transaction that carries extra risk (the possibility of a bounced out-of-state check), the company has established a procedure to discourage bad check-writing. This procedure is the requirement for a specific authorization from a manager before the transaction can be completed.

The preceding example also helps illustrate the difference between specific authorization and general authorization. **General authorization** is a set of guidelines that allows transactions to be completed as long as they fall within established parameters. In the example of a grocery or department store, the established guidelines are that the check-out clerk can process anyone through the line as long as the customer pays by cash, credit card, debit card, or an in-state check. If any customer is an exception to these payment methods, as in the case of an out-of-state check, the transaction requires specific authorization. **Specific authorization** means that explicit authorization is needed for that single transaction to be completed.

Another example of the difference between these two types of authorization can be seen in the procedures that a company uses when making purchases. Management usually has established reorder points for inventory items, and when inventory quantities drop to that predetermined level, purchasing agents have general authority to initiate a purchase transaction. However, if the company needs to purchase a new fleet of vehicles, for instance, a specific authorization from upper-level management is likely to be required.

Any organization should establish and maintain clear, concise guidance as to procedures that fall under general authorization as opposed to those requiring specific authorization. Not only does such a practice assure that all transactions are properly authorized; it also makes the organization more efficient. In our example of a grocery store, the check-out line can move quickly and efficiently for low-risk transactions involving payment by cash, credit card, debit card, or in-state check. However, when high-risk transactions are encountered, the extra risk warrants a brief inefficiency (the slowdown in the line) to assure that the risk is controlled by a specific authorization. Another important aspect is that the employee must be well trained and must understand when this specific authorization is needed.

In summary, a part of the control procedures is the guidelines regarding general and specific authorization. Top managers must appropriately delegate the authorization of transactions and establish authorization procedures and practices to assure that the guidelines are followed. They must ascertain that managers and employees have been trained to understand and carry out these policies and practices.

Segregation of Duties When management delegates authority and develops guidelines as to the use of that authority, it must assure that the authorization is separated from other duties. This separation of related duties is called **segregation of duties**. For any transaction, there are usually three component parts: authorization of the transaction, recording the transaction, and custody of the related asset(s). Ideally, management should separate these three components by assigning each component to a different person or department within the organization. The person or department authorizing a transaction should neither be responsible for recording it in the accounting records nor have custody of the related asset. To understand the possible effect of not segregating these duties, consider a payroll example. If a foreman were allowed to hire employees, approve their hours worked, and also distribute the paychecks, then authorization would not have been segregated from custody of the checks. This would give a dishonest foreman the perfect opportunity to make up a fictitious employee and collect the paycheck. However, if paychecks were distributed to employees by someone other than the foreman, the opportunity for this kind of payroll theft would be reduced.

When it is reasonably possible to do so, all three components—authorization, recording, and custody—should be segregated. Exhibit 3-6 illustrates this segregation of duties.

It may not always be possible or reasonable to segregate all three components. This is especially true in small organizations where there may not be enough workers to adequately segregate. However, in smaller companies there is usually much closer supervision by the owner or manager, which helps compensate for the lack of segregation. Thus, supervision is a **compensating control** that lessens the risk of negative effects when other controls are lacking. Supervision as a compensating control is appropriate in larger organizations, too, where there may be situations in which it is difficult to fully segregate duties.

Adequate Records and Documents When management is conscientious and thorough about preparing and retaining documentation in support of its accounting transactions, internal controls are strengthened. Accounting documents and records are important because they provide evidence and establish responsibility.

Exhibit 3-6
Segregation of Duties

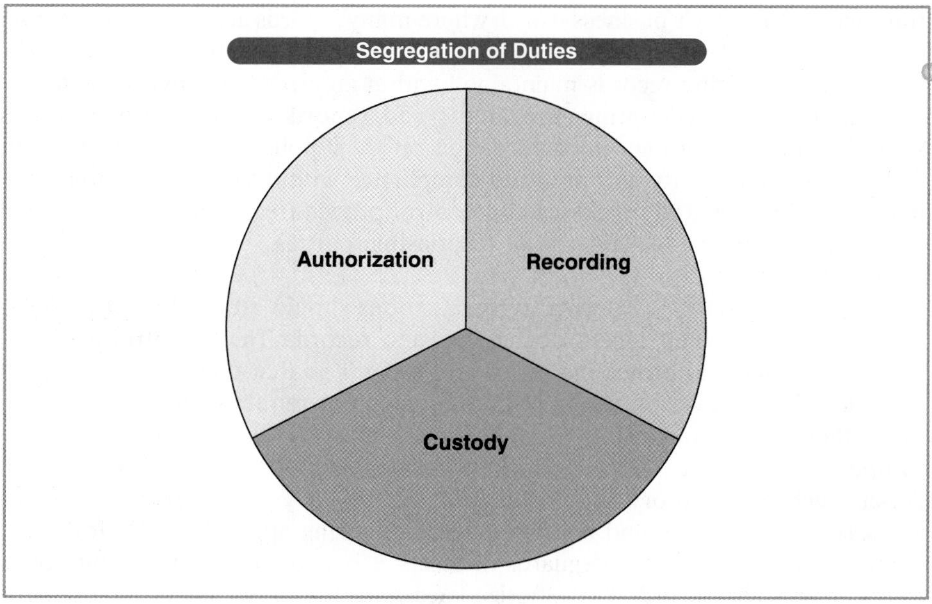

In general, a good system of internal controls includes the following types of documentation:

- Supporting documentation for all significant transactions, including orders, invoices, contracts, account statements, shipping and receiving forms, and checks. Whenever possible, original documentation should be retained as verification of authenticity. Specific types of documentation are discussed in subsequent chapters within the presentations of the various business processes.
- Schedules and analyses of financial information, including details of account balances; reconciliations; references; comparisons; and narrative explanations, comments, and conclusions. These documents should be independently verified from time to time in order for their accuracy to be assessed.
- Accounting cycle reports, including journals, ledgers, subledgers, trial balances, and financial statements.

Documents and records provide evidence that management's policies and procedures, including internal control procedures, are being carried out. They also provide an **audit trail,** which presents verifiable information about the accuracy of accounting records. If accurate, sufficient documentation is maintained, then an audit trail can be established, which can re-create the details of individual transactions at each stage of the business process in order to determine whether proper accounting procedures for the transaction were performed.

All paper documentation should be signed or initialed by the person(s) who authorized, recorded, and/or reviewed the related transactions. This practice establishes responsibility within the accounting function. When records are maintained in electronic format, the organization should take steps to control access to the related files and ensure that adequate backup copies are available in order to reduce the risk of alteration, loss, or destruction. In a computerized system, the audit trail usually includes a detailed transaction log, because the computer system automatically logs each transaction and the source of the transaction. In today's business world, where many records are maintained within computerized systems, managers and auditors must understand, access, and control those accounting records maintained within an electronic environment.

In addition to accounting documents and reports, business organizations should maintain thorough documentation on their policies and procedures. In order to provide clarity and promote compliance within the organization, both manual and automated processes and control procedures should be formalized in writing and made available to all responsible parties.

Security of Assets and Documents Organizations should establish control activities to safeguard their assets, documents, and records. These control activities involve securing and protecting assets and records so that they are not misused or stolen. In the case of assets, physical protection requires limiting access to the extent that is practical. For example, cash must be on hand for a company to operate, but this cash can be locked in safes or cash registers until needed. Assets such as inventory should be protected by physical safeguards such as locks, security cameras, and restricted areas requiring appropriate ID for entry.

In addition to physical safeguards of assets, it is also important to limit access to documents and records. Unauthorized access or use of documents and records allows the easy manipulation of those documents or records, which can result in fraud or cover-up of theft. For example, unauthorized access to blank checks can lead to fraudulent checks being written. All blank documents must be controlled by the limiting of access to only those who require access as part of their job duties.

In both cases—protecting physical assets and protecting information—there is a trade-off between limited access and efficiency. The more access is limited, the harder it becomes to do a job efficiently. This is a good example of why controls must have a benefit greater than their cost. For example, a company could have all employees searched as they leave at the end of their shifts in order to discourage inventory theft. However, the cost of this intrusion in terms of its impact on employee morale and turnover may be greater than the savings from theft avoidance. This concept of the **cost–benefit** comparison of controls is discussed later in the chapter in terms of *reasonable assurance.*

Independent Checks and Reconciliation Independent checks on performance are an important aspect of control activities. **Independent checks** serve as a method to confirm the accuracy and completeness of data in the accounting system. While there are many procedures that accomplish independent checks, examples are as follows:

- Reconciliation
- Comparison of physical assets with records
- Recalculation of amounts
- Analysis of reports
- Review of batch totals

An example of each of these independent checks on performance follows. A **reconciliation** is a procedure that compares records from different sources. For instance, a bank *reconciliation* compares independent bank records with company records to assure the accuracy and completeness of cash records. Similarly, a *comparison of physical assets with records* occurs when a company takes a physical count of inventory and compares the results to the inventory records. Any differences are recorded as adjustments to inventory and result in correct inventory records. *Recalculation of amounts* can help uncover math or program logic errors. For example, recalculating price times quantity may uncover errors in invoices that were caused by either human error or bad program logic. *Analysis of reports* is the examination of a report to assess the accuracy and reliability of the data in that report. A manager who regularly reviews reports is likely to notice errors that crop up in the reports; the manager may not always notice such errors, but many times will. Finally, *review of batch totals* is an independent check to assure the accuracy and completeness of transactions processed in a batch. Batch processing occurs when similar transactions are grouped together and processed as a group. For example, time cards can be collected from all employees within a department and processed simultaneously as a batch. In batch processing, it is possible to calculate a **batch total,** which is merely a summation of key items in the batch (such as hours worked), and compare this batch total along various stages of processing. If at some stage of processing the batch totals no longer match, this means that an error has occurred in processing.

These descriptions of independent checks are examples of control activities, but they only scratch the surface of the number and types of independent checks that may be necessary in an organization. Such independent checks can serve as both detective and preventative controls. They are detective in that they uncover problems in data or processing; they are preventive in the sense that they may help discourage errors and fraud before they occur. For example, employees know that when a company regularly takes a physical inventory and compares the counts with records, shortages are more likely to come to light. Therefore, employees may be less likely to steal inventory, because they presume they will get caught. This preventive effect becomes more obvious if you consider the opposite environment, in which a company never takes a physical inventory. When employees know this, they recognize that it would be easier to carry out a fraudulent act without getting caught.

Information and Communication

To assess, manage, and control the efficiency and effectiveness of operations of an organization, management must have access to feedback information and reports. The feedback consists of operational and financial information, much of it generated by the accounting system. An effective accounting system will provide accurate and complete feedback. Therefore, the better the accounting system, the better management can assess and control operations.

The entire accounting system is therefore a very important component of the internal control system. An ineffective accounting system can generate inaccurate or incomplete reports, and this leads to more difficulty in properly controlling activities. An effective accounting system must accomplish the following objectives:

1. Identify all relevant financial events (transactions) of the organization.
2. Capture the important data of these transactions.
3. Record and process the data through appropriate classification, summarization, and aggregation.
4. Report this summarized and aggregated information to managers.

Whether an accounting system is manual or computerized, it must achieve these objectives to be effective. In addition to maintaining an effective accounting system, the entity must implement procedures to assure that the information and reports are communicated to the appropriate management level. The COSO report describes this communication as "flowing down, across, and up the organization." Such a flow of communication assists management in properly assessing operations and making changes to operations as necessary.

Monitoring Any system of control must be constantly monitored to assure that it continues to be effective. **Monitoring** involves the ongoing review and evaluation of the system. For example, your home may have a heating system with a thermostat. The thermostat constantly measures temperature and turns the heat on or off to maintain the desired temperature. Thus, the thermostat is a control system. However, due to wear and tear or other changes, the thermostat and heater may begin to malfunction. To keep them operating at peak effectiveness, there must be periodic checks on the thermostat and heating system to make sure they are working correctly. The same is true of an internal control system in an organization. To keep the controls operating effectively, management must monitor the system and attempt to improve any deficiencies encountered. This is especially important as organizations undergo changes. Employee and management turnover, new business processes or procedures, and market changes may all affect the functionality of internal controls.

There are many ways an organization can monitor its internal control system. To be most effective, both continuous and periodic monitoring should take place. As managers carry out their regular duties of examining reports, they are performing a type of continuous monitoring. Management should notice major weaknesses or breakdowns in internal controls as they accomplish their duties. In computerized systems, there may be continuous monitoring within the system itself. That is, the computerized accounting system may include modules within the software that review the system on an ongoing basis. In addition, some monitoring, such as internal and external audits, occurs on a regular periodic basis. These audits include examinations of the effectiveness of internal controls. As weaknesses or problems are uncovered through continuous and periodic monitoring, these issues must be reported to management to allow for appropriate changes to be made.

All five internal control components prescribed by the COSO report are necessary for the establishment and maintenance of a capable system of internal controls. The control environment, risk assessment procedures, control activities, information and communication processes, and ongoing monitoring of the system each play a part in strengthening the overall system. There is an old saying that a chain is only as strong as its weakest link. This is also true of the five components of internal control. If any one of the five is weak, the entire system of internal controls will be weak. Much as the links of a chain work together, these components work together to make an effective control system.

REASONABLE ASSURANCE OF INTERNAL CONTROLS

A company that is well managed will maintain a good system of internal controls because to do so makes good business sense. An appropriate internal control system can help an organization achieve its objectives. However, there are limits to what an internal control system can accomplish. Internal controls provide reasonable assurance of meeting the control objectives. **Reasonable assurance** means that the controls achieve a sensible balance of reducing risk when compared with the cost of the control. It is not possible for an internal control system to provide absolute assurance, because there are factors that limit the effectiveness of controls, such as the following:

1. Flawed judgments are applied in decision making.
2. Human error exists in every organization.
3. Controls can be circumvented or ignored.
4. Controls may not be cost beneficial.

No matter how well an internal control system is designed, it is limited by the fact that humans sometimes make erroneous judgments and simple errors or mistakes. Even when a person has good intentions, an error in judgment or a mistake, such as simply forgetting to do a step that provides an internal control, can cause harm. For example, it would be easy for a supervisor to simply forget to sign time cards for a particular pay period.

Another limit to the effectiveness of internal controls is that they can be circumvented. One way to circumvent internal controls is through collusion. Two people working together can thwart internal control procedures. For example, assume that one employee prepares time cards and a second employee distributes paychecks. Working alone, the first employee cannot easily make up a fake employee, submit a fake time card, and get access to the resulting paycheck. But if these two employees agree to work together and split the resulting paycheck, it would be very difficult to prevent. In this example, collusion negates the control effect of segregation of duties.

For every control procedure that an organization wishes to use, the benefits must outweigh the costs. Benefits can be measured by the positive effect the control has. For example, if a control reduces the chance of errors, then an assessment could be made of the savings that would result from lower errors. The cost of the control procedure can be monetary or measured in terms of reduced operating efficiency. For example, a control procedure that requires all purchase transactions of any size to be approved by the CEO would dramatically slow the pace of purchasing. The CEO's desk would become a bottleneck of purchase requests waiting to be approved. This approval procedure would not be cost effective. However, it may be cost effective to have the CEO approve only those purchases involving very large dollar amounts or highly unusual orders. Before adoption, every control procedure should be analyzed to be sure that it results in benefits that exceed the costs of implementing the control.

MAINTENANCE OF INFORMATION TECHNOLOGY CONTROLS (STUDY OBJECTIVE 11)

Over time, the cost of computer hardware and software has dramatically decreased, while computing power has vastly increased. This means that today most small companies can afford to maintain computerized accounting systems, while larger companies place even greater reliance on computer-based systems.

Information technology now plays such an important role in organizations that any failure in these systems can halt such ongoing operations as sales, manufacturing, or purchasing. IT systems have become the lifeblood of operations for most companies.

There is a paradox in this increased use of information technology. Computerized systems increase the efficiency and effectiveness of the organizations that use them; but at the same time, they increase vulnerability. The more that an organization relies on information technology, the greater the risks are, including unauthorized access, hackers, business interruption, and data inaccuracies. These extra risks call attention to the need for internal controls over and above those described in the COSO report.

In response to this need, the Information Systems Audit and Control Association (ISACA) developed an extensive framework of information technology controls, entitled **COBIT,** for Control Objectives for Information Technology.[8] COBIT is extremely important guidance for those who design or audit IT systems. The AICPA and the Canadian Institute of Chartered Accountants have jointly developed IT control guidelines, related to COBIT, commonly referred to as the Trust Service Principles.[9] This guidance addresses risks and opportunities of information technology, and the most recent version became effective in 2006. The **Trust Services Principles** are designed to be the written guidance for CPAs who provide assurance services for organizations. Many types of work performed by CPAs can be called assurance services, but the specific types covered by the Trust Services Principles are Trust Services, SysTrust®, and WebTrust®. For these services, a CPA firm is hired to examine the company's IT and Web-based systems and to issue a subsequent opinion and recommendations about the security, availability, processing integrity, privacy, and confidentiality of the systems. In other words, these principles describe the type of IT controls that an IT auditor would expect to find in an audit of IT systems.

In the subsequent chapters of this text that include business processes and controls, the Trust Services Principles' internal control structure will be used as the context in which IT internal controls are described. For any business process, there should be both accounting internal controls as in COSO, and IT controls as in the Trust Services Principles. The following section describes the Trust Services Principles.

Risk and controls in IT are divided into five categories in the Trust Services Principles, as follows:

1. ***Security.*** The risk related to security is unauthorized access, which may be both physical access and logical access. An example of unauthorized physical access would be a person breaking into the computer room and damaging computer equipment. An example of logical access would be an unauthorized hacker stealing data such as credit card numbers. Internal controls must be designed and implemented to limit both types of unauthorized access.
2. ***Availability.*** The risk related to availability is system or subsystem failure due to hardware or software problems. An example of a risk that can cause interruptions to the system would be a virus that causes the system to slow

[8] COBIT 4.1, IT Governance Institute, Rolling Meadows, IL, 2007.

[9] Trust Services, Principles, Criteria and Illustrations for Security, Availability, Processing Integrity, Confidentiality, and Privacy (Including WebTrust® and Systrust®), American Institute of Certified Public Accountants, Inc. and Canadian Institute of Chartered Accountants, 2006 (www.aicpa.org).

down or fail. Internal controls can be implemented to limit the chances of failure and thereby help improve availability of the system to process information and support ongoing business.

3. ***Processing integrity.*** The risk related to processing integrity could be inaccurate, incomplete, or improperly authorized information. An example of this type of risk would be an error in entering hours worked for a worker's pay. The person keying hours worked into the payroll software might accidentally type an incorrect number of hours. Controls should be implemented to reduce erroneous, incomplete, or unauthorized transactions or data.
4. ***Online privacy.*** The risk in this area is that personal information about customers may be used inappropriately or accessed by those either inside or outside the company. An example is the theft of credit card numbers when orders are placed through the company website. Internal controls should be implemented to limit the chance of personal information being misused.
5. ***Confidentiality.*** The risk related to confidentiality is that confidential information about the company or its business partners may be subject to unauthorized access during its transmission or storage in the IT system. Examples of confidential information are banking information and price lists. Most companies do not wish to allow price lists to be available to competitors. Controls can be implemented to limit unauthorized access to confidential information.

When IT controls are being considered, it is important to understand the nature of the risks so that the controls can be designed and used to limit these risks. As in the case of COSO accounting controls, any IT control implemented should have benefits that exceed the costs of the control. As the risks and controls are described, many controls can be effective in several of the five categories. For example, the use of a password when a user logs in should be of assistance in limiting risks related to security, availability, processing integrity, privacy, and confidentiality. That is, the use of passwords helps limit unauthorized access that could result in security problems (security), theft of private or confidential data (privacy and confidentiality), unauthorized transactions being processed (processing integrity), and hacking that interrupts system processing (availability). The next chapter describes risks and controls in the first four categories: security, availability, processing integrity, and confidentiality. Since privacy is more closely related to e-commerce, they are discussed in the chapter on e-business and e-commerce later in the text.

SUMMARY OF STUDY OBJECTIVES

An introduction to the need for a code of ethics and internal controls. Managers of organizations are entrusted with the assets and funds of their organizations; therefore, they have an ethical duty to appropriately protect and use those assets and funds. As stewards of assets and funds, managers must ensure that policies and procedures are in place to provide protection and to accurately record and report the flow and use of assets and funds. Codes of ethics and strong systems of internal control are important parts of these policies and procedures. Properly enforced codes of ethics and internal controls can establish an operating environment that discourages fraud and errors.

The accounting related fraud that can occur when ethics codes and internal controls are weak or not correctly applied. In organizations where codes of ethics are not enforced or when proper controls are not correctly applied, fraud and errors are much more likely to occur. There are many kinds of fraud that can occur, including management fraud, employee fraud, customer fraud, and vendor fraud.

The nature of management fraud. Management fraud is conducted by upper-level managers and usually involves fraudulent financial statements. Managers are above the level of most internal controls; therefore, internal controls are usually not effective in preventing or detecting management fraud.

The nature of employee fraud. Employee fraud is conducted by non-management employees and usually involves theft or misuse of assets. Internal accounting controls such as the five components of internal control in COSO are intended to assist in the prevention or detection of employee fraud.

The nature of customer fraud. Customer fraud occurs when customers engage in credit card fraud, check fraud, or refund fraud. Internal controls can assist in the prevention or detection of some customer fraud.

The nature of vendor fraud. Vendor fraud is usually conducted by vendors requesting fictitious or duplicate payments. Internal controls can assist in the prevention or detection of some vendor fraud.

The nature of computer fraud. Computers can be used internally or by those outside the organization as a tool to conduct such fraud as manipulating transactions or data, and hacking or other network break-ins. Internal controls and IT controls can assist in the prevention or detection of computer fraud.

The policies that assist in the avoidance of fraud and errors. There are three sets of policies that an organization can institute to help prevent or detect fraud, errors, and ethical violations: implementation and maintenance of a code of ethics, accounting internal controls, and IT controls.

The maintenance of a code of ethics. When management is unethical, fraud is likely to occur. On the other hand, if the top management of a company emphasizes ethical behavior, models ethical behavior, and hires ethical employees, the chance of fraud or ethical lapses can be reduced. Maintaining and enforcing a code of ethics helps reduce unethical behavior in an organization.

The maintenance of accounting internal controls. The components of accounting internal controls are defined by the COSO report as the control environment, risk assessment, control activities, information and communication, and monitoring. Control activities include authorization, segregation of duties, adequate record keeping, security over assets and records, and independent verifications.

The maintenance of information technology controls. IT controls can be categorized as designated within the AICPA's Trust Services Principles. The risk categories are security, availability, processing integrity, online privacy, and confidentiality.

KEY TERMS

Audit trail
Authorization
Availability
Batch totals
Check fraud
COBIT
Code of ethics
Collusion
Compensating control
Computer fraud
Confidentiality
Control activities
Control environment
Corrective controls
COSO
Cost–benefit
Credit card fraud
Customer fraud
Defalcation
Denial of service attack
Detective controls
Earnings management
Employee fraud
Foreign Corrupt Practices Act
Fraud
Fraud triangle
Fraudulent financial reporting
General authorization
Hacking
Independent checks
Industrial espionage
Information and communication
Information criteria
Internal controls
Internal theft
IT resources
Kickbacks
Larceny
Management fraud
Management override
Misappropriation of assets
Misstatement of financial records
Monitoring
Preventive controls
Privacy
Processing integrity
Reasonable assurance
Reconciliation
Refund fraud
Risk assessment
Salami technique
Sarbanes–Oxley Act
Security
Segregation of duties
Skimming
Software piracy
Specific authorization
Spoofing
Stewardship
Trap door alteration
Trojan horse program
Trust Services Principles
Vendor audit
Vendor fraud

APPENDIX A

RECENT HISTORY OF INTERNAL CONTROL STANDARDS

The written documentation regarding internal control has evolved over many years, and many parties have been involved in the effort. An example of earlier descriptions of internal control is provided by the AICPA in its Statements on Auditing Standards (SAS). One of the functions of an auditor is to examine and assess the effectiveness of internal controls. Thus, the AICPA provided guidelines as to proper internal controls and the auditor's responsibility in regard to internal controls. In 1977, the United States Congress passed the **Foreign Corrupt Practices**

Act (FCPA) that was intended to prevent U.S. corporations from bribing foreign officials while soliciting business. That Act required corporations that sell stock in an SEC regulated stock exchange to maintain a system of internal controls. The FCPA incorporated some language from the AICPA internal control guidelines. In 1988, the AICPA issued SAS 55, which further emphasized management's obligation to maintain internal controls. In 1992, the Committee of Sponsoring Organizations (COSO) issued the COSO report, which details the findings of a comprehensive study of internal control and is recognized within the accounting industry as the definition and description of internal control.

Since that time, the AICPA has rewritten SAS guidelines to incorporate COSO concepts. SAS 55 was replaced by SAS 78 in 1994, and in 2002 SAS 78 was amended by SAS 94, the current internal control guide in SAS 94 maintains the COSO internal control concepts. In addition, SAS 99 expands the auditor's duties with regard to internal control and fraud. An auditor must now approach all audits with skepticism about management's honesty and assume that management fraud might have occurred. This means that the auditor must think about the risks and controls in the company and try to determine what kind of frauds could occur. The auditor must also test for management override of controls.

SOX

In the summer of 2002, the United States Congress passed the Sarbanes–Oxley Act in an attempt to curb the fraud and stock market abuses of the previous two years. Section 302 of this bill designates management (specifically, the chief executive officer, chief financial officer, and others performing similar functions) of the company as having responsibility for the establishment and maintenance of an effective system of internal controls. This system must be evaluated on an ongoing basis. Any significant changes or deficiencies in the system, as well as all instances of fraud within the company, must be reported to the SEC. Compliance with these requirements must be confirmed by management in writing.

Section 404 of the Sarbanes–Oxley Act requires every company to include an internal control report within its annual report to stockholders. This report must include the following:

1. A statement that acknowledges management's responsibility to establish and maintain an adequate system of internal controls.
2. An assessment of the effectiveness of the internal control structure.

Thus, legislation underscores the idea that not only is the establishment and operation of an internal control system a good practice, but it also is legally mandatory for publicly traded companies.

This history of internal control emphasizes the increasing importance placed on the role of internal controls in preventing or detecting fraud, including financial statement fraud.

APPENDIX B

CONTROL OBJECTIVES FOR INFORMATION TECHNOLOGY (COBIT)

The COBIT framework is a comprehensive description of the risks and controls in IT environments. The framework establishes what COBIT terms four domains of "High Level Control Objectives":

Domain and Process	Information Criteria: Effectiveness	Efficiency	Confidentiality	Integrity	Availability	Compliance	Reliability	IT Resources: Applications	Information	Infrastructure	People
Domain: Plan and organize, Assess risks	P	P						✓		✓	✓
Domain: Acquire and implement, Acquire & maintain software	P	P		S			S	✓			
Domain: Deliver and support, Ensure continuous service	P	S			P			✓	✓	✓	✓
Domain: Monitor and evaluate, Provide IT governance	P	P	S	S	S	S	S	✓	✓	✓	✓

P = Primary S = Secondary

Exhibit 3-7
Examples of COBIT Domains and Processes

1. Planning and organization
2. Acquisition and implementation
3. Delivery and support
4. Monitoring

In each of these four domains, COBIT provides a description of the processes, the underlying information criteria that apply to those processes, and the related IT resources. COBIT includes 34 processes across the four domains. Rather than discuss all of these processes, four are provided in Exhibit 3-7 as examples.

For each domain, controls over processes can be categorized as to the information criteria that apply to the process and the IT resources managed by the process. COBIT defines **information criteria** as effectiveness, efficiency, confidentiality, integrity, availability, compliance, and reliability. These factors are represented across the top in the first part of the matrix in Exhibit 3-7. As an example, one process that occurs in an IT environment is acquiring and maintaining software. The matrix of information criteria indicates that in this process, effectiveness and efficiency are the primary criteria. This means that as an organization acquires and maintains software, it must establish and follow IT controls that assure the effectiveness and efficiency of that software. An example of a specific control to achieve this objective is to test the software prior to purchasing it. Testing can help ensure that it is effective and efficient. Also, notice the secondary criteria of integrity and reliability. Controls should also be employed to ensure that software is reliable and has integrity (accuracy and completeness). Again, a control such as testing the software assists in assuring the reliability and integrity of the software acquired.

The second part of the matrix shown in Exhibit 3-7 identifies the IT resources. IT resources provide the information needed by business processes. COBIT defines **IT resources** as applications, information, infrastructure, and people. In the previous example, the applications are the only factors that are directly managed in the process of acquiring and maintaining software.

END OF CHAPTER MATERIAL

CONCEPT CHECK

1. The careful and responsible oversight and use of the assets entrusted to Management is called
   a. the control environment.
   b. stewardship.
   c. preventive controls.
   d. security.
2. Which of the following is **not** a condition in the fraud triangle?
   a. rationalization
   b. incentive
   c. conversion
   d. opportunity
3. There are many possible indirect benefits to management when management fraud occurs. Which of the following is **not** an indirect benefit of management fraud?
   a. delayed exercise of stock options
   b. delayed cash flow problems
   c. enhanced promotion opportunities
   d. increased incentive-based compensation
4. Which of the following is **not** an example of employee fraud?
   a. skimming
   b. larceny
   c. kickbacks
   d. earnings management
5. Which of the following is **not** a common form of employee fraud?
   a. inventory theft
   b. expense account fraud
   c. payroll fraud
   d. refund fraud
6. Segregation of duties is a fundamental concept in an effective system of internal controls. Nevertheless, the effectiveness of this control can be compromised through which situation?
   a. a lack of employee training
   b. collusion among employees
   c. irregular employee reviews
   d. the absence of an internal audit function
7. The most difficult type of misstatement to discover is fraud that is concealed by
   a. over-recording the transactions.
   b. nonrecorded transactions.
   c. recording the transactions in subsidiary records.
   d. related parties.

8. The review of amounts charged to the company from a seller that it purchased from is called a
   a. vendor audit.
   b. seller review.
   c. collusion.
   d. customer review.
9. Which of the following is generally an external computer fraud, rather than an internal computer fraud?
   a. spoofing
   b. input manipulation
   c. program manipulation
   d. output manipulation
10. Which control activity is intended to serve as a method to confirm the accuracy or completeness of data in the accounting system?
    a. authorization
    b. segregation of duties
    c. security of assets
    d. independent checks and reconciliations
11. COSO describes five components of internal control. Which of the following terms is best described as "policies and procedures that help ensure management directives are carried out and management objectives are achieved"?
    a. risk assessment
    b. information and communication
    c. control activities
    d. control environment
12. Proper segregation of duties calls for separation of the functions of
    a. authorization, execution, and payment.
    b. authorization, recording, and custody.
    c. custody, execution, and reporting.
    d. authorization, payment, and recording.
13. The AICPA Trust Services Principles identify five categories of risks and controls. Which category is best described by the statement, "Information processes could be inaccurate, incomplete, or not properly authorized"?
    a. security
    b. availability
    c. processing integrity
    d. confidentiality
14. A company's cash custody function should be separated from the related cash recordkeeping function in order to
    a. physically safeguard the cash.
    b. establish accountability for the cash.
    c. prevent the payment of cash disbursements from cash receipts.
    d. minimize opportunities for misappropriations of cash.

DISCUSSION QUESTIONS

15. (SO 1) Management is held accountable to various parties, both internal and external to the business organization. To whom does management have a stewardship obligation and to whom does it have reporting responsibilities?
16. (SO 2, SO 4) If an employee made a mistake that resulted in loss of company funds and misstated financial reports, would the employee be guilty of fraud? Discuss.
17. (SO 2, SO 3) Do you think it is possible that a business manager may perpetrate fraud and still have the company's best interest in mind? Discuss.
18. (SO 7) Distinguish between internal and external sources of computer fraud.
19. (SO 7) Identify and explain the three types of internal source computer fraud.
20. (SO 7) Describe three popular program manipulation techniques.
21. (SO 7) Distinguish between Internet spoofing and e-mail spoofing.
22. (SO 10) What are the *objectives* of a system of internal control?
23. (SO 10) Name and distinguish among the three *types* of internal controls.
24. (SO 10) Identify the COSO report's five interrelated *components* of internal controls.
25. (SO 10) Name the COSO report's five internal control *activities*.
26. (SO 10) Distinguish between general and specific authorization.
27. (SO 10) Due to cost/benefit considerations, many business organizations are unable to achieve complete segregation of duties. What else could they do to minimize risks?
28. (SO 10) Why is a policies and procedures manual considered an element of internal control?
29. (SO 10) Why does a company need to be concerned with controlling access to its records?
30. (SO 10) Many companies have mandatory vacation and periodic job rotation policies. Discuss how these practices can be useful in strengthening internal controls.
31. (SO 10) Name the objectives of an effective accounting system.
32. (SO 10) What does it mean when information flows "down, across, and up the organization"?
33. (SO 10) Provide examples of continuous monitoring and periodic monitoring.
34. (SO 10) What are the factors that limit the effectiveness of internal controls?
35. (SO 11)Identify and describe the five categories of the AICPA Trust Services Principles.
36. (SO 11) Distinguish between the Trust Services Principles of privacy and confidentiality.
37. (Appendix B) Identify the four domains of high-level internal control.

BRIEF EXERCISES

38. (SO 2, SO 3) What possible motivation might a business manager have for perpetrating fraud?

39. (SO 5) Discuss whether any of the following can be examples of customer fraud:
    - An employee billed a customer twice for the same transaction.
    - A customer remitted payment in the wrong amount.
    - A customer received merchandise in error, but failed to return it or notify the sender.

40. (SO 7) Explain the relationship between computer hacking and industrial espionage. Give a few additional examples of how hacking could cause damage in a business.

41. (SO 9) What are some ways in which a business could promote its code of ethics?

42. (SO 10) Describe why the control environment is regarded as the foundation of a business' system of internal control.

43. (SO 10) Think of a job you have held, and consider whether the control environment was risky or conservative. Describe which you chose and why.

44. (SO 10) Identify the steps involved in risk assessment. Do you think it would be effective for an organization to hire external consultants to develop its risk assessment plan? Why or why not?

45. (SO 10, SO 11) Discuss the accuracy of the following statements regarding internal control:
    - The more computerized applications exist within a company's accounting system, the lower the risk will be that fraud or errors will occur.
    - The more involved top management is in the day-to-day operations of the business, the lower the risk will be that fraud or errors will occur.

PROBLEMS

46. (SO 10) Identify whether each of the following accounting positions or duties involves authorization, recording, or custody:
    - cashier
    - payroll processor
    - credit manager
    - mailroom clerk
    - data entry clerk
    - deliver paychecks
    - deliver the bank deposit
    - prepare the bank reconciliation
    - check signer
    - inventory warehouse supervisor
    - staff accountant

47. (SO 10) Identify whether each of the following activities represents preventive controls, detective controls, or corrective controls:
    - job rotation
    - preparation of a bank reconciliation
    - segregation of duties
    - recalculating totals on computer reports
    - use of passwords
    - preparing batch totals for check processing
    - establishing a code of ethics
    - use of a security guard
    - verifying source documents before recording transactions
    - matching supporting documents before paying an invoice
    - independent review of accounting reports
    - performing comparisons of financial statement items
48. (SO 10) Shown are a list of selected sources of internal control guidelines, given in order of issuance, followed by a list of primary purposes. Match each guideline with its primary purpose.

    I. Foreign Corrupt Practices Act

    II. COSO

    III. SAS 99

    IV. Sarbanes–Oxley Act

    V. Trust Services Principles

    a. Required auditors to focus on risks and controls and to conduct audits with skepticism.

    b. Prevented bribery and established internal control guidelines.

    c. Curbed fraud by requiring additional internal control reporting within annual reports.

    d. Established internal control concepts based on comprehensive study.

    e. Established essential criteria for evaluating reliability of business systems.
49. (SO 1, 3, 10) Using a search engine on the Internet, find articles or descriptions of the collapse of Enron. The collapse began in November 2001, and many articles appeared over the next two to three years.

    Required:

    a. Briefly describe the fraud that occurred.

    b. Discuss what you see as weaknesses in the control environment.
50. (SO 3) Using a search engine on the Internet, search for articles on fraud that occurred in 2000 to 2002 in the following companies:

    Adelphia

    Enron

    Global Crossing

    WorldCom

    Xerox

Try to locate articles or information about stock prices, how the fraud was conducted. You might wish to look at the following websites: www.hoovers.com, www.forbes.com

Required:

a. Find information to help you complete the following table:

Company Name	Brief Description of Fraud	Position of Those Conducting Fraud	Stock Price When Fraud Was Uncovered	Stock Price One Year Later	Shares Outstanding	Loss to Investors
Adelphia						
Enron						
Global Crossing						
WorldCom						
Xerox						

b. Discuss the common characteristics that you see in each of these examples.

CASES

51. At the old city hall, mail was sorted in a glorified closet—not the sort of place you'd expect to be frequented by a high-ranking city official with multiple degrees. But the city of Springfield's chief financial officer, Ed Sims, had an unusual interest in the mail. He was often known to greet the postal carrier at the door to receive the day's delivery, take it to the mail closet, then immediately remove selected envelopes and parcels and take them to the privacy of his own office. Other times, he would request hand delivery of incoming payments, circumventing the mail closet altogether.

These activities were part of an elaborate embezzlement scheme that resulted in the loss of million of dollars for the city. Mr. Sims was intercepting checks written to the city and endorsing them to his personal bank account.

The procedural manual for Springfield's accounting department described mailroom policies, including the requirement for a clerk to log checks into a computer file and prepare a receipt. Another employee was responsible for preparing an independent verification of the amount of the receipts, and a third employee made the bank deposit. Despite these written guidelines, Mr. Sims was often known to carry out some of these tasks himself or claim to be doing so.

In response to the news of this fraud, the CFO of a neighboring community commented that many cities are unable to achieve strong internal controls because of the limitations of small staff size and tight operating budgets. Rather, small cities often have no choice but to rely on the integrity of their employees.

Required:

a. Which internal control activity was violated in order for Mr. Sims to perpetrate this fraud?

b. Do you consider this case to be an example of management fraud or employee fraud?

c. Was the city's procedural manual adequate for prescribing internal controls to prevent this type of fraud? Why or why not?

d. Why do you think no one reported the unusual mailroom practices of Mr. Sims? To whom would such a violation be reported?

e. Do you think a business in Springfield could be guilty of customer fraud if it agreed to deliver its payments to Mr. Sims personally rather than send them to the city's mailing address?

f. The comments made by the neighbor CFO express which type of limitation of internal control systems discussed in this chapter?

52. The following description is excerpted from "Coupon Accounting Abuse," *Management Accounting*, January 1993, p. 47.

It's November 15, and Larry, brand manager for a major consumer products firm, is contemplating his year-end bonus. It is becoming increasingly obvious that, unless he takes action, he will not achieve his brand profitability target for the year. Larry's eyes fall to the expense estimate for the new coupon "drop" slated for later in the month. His hand trembles slightly as he erases the 4% anticipated redemption rate on his estimate sheet and replaces the figure with 2%. Larry knows from experience that 2% is an unrealistically low figure, but he also knows that neither the firm's independent nor internal auditors will seriously challenge the estimate. This way, Larry's product profitability report will reflect the increased revenue associated with the coupon "drop" this year, but the entire redemption cost will not be expressed until next year.

"That should put me over," he muses. A wry smile crosses his face. "If the auditors question the rate, I'll give them a story about seasonality and shifting consumer patterns. They won't know enough about marketing to question my story." Eventually, of course, the real cost of the coupon drop will have to be expensed, and that will hurt next year's profit figure. "But, that's next year," Larry reasons, "and I can always figure out a way to make it up. Besides, by the end of next quarter, I'll be handling a bigger brand—if I can show a good profit this year."

A brief description of coupons and proper accounting for coupons might help us to interpret the situation just presented. Coupons are "cents-off" privileges, such as $0.50 off when you buy a certain brand of yogurt. When a company offers coupons to consumers, it must estimate the redemption rate and record an expense and the corresponding liability. This is similar in concept to warranty expenses.

Required:

a. Discuss whether the situation described can happen to a company with a good control environment.

b. Describe any steps a company could take to prevent such abuse.

c. List those parties who might be harmed by this situation.

d. Do you consider this example to be management fraud or employee fraud? Describe how it fits the definition of your choice.

53. The CEO of Mega Motor Company, Leland Brocamp, resigned on November 1, 2002. His resignation had been negotiated with the Board of Directors

of Mega Motor after it was revealed that Mr. Brocamp violated the company's corporate ethics policy by having an affair with a subordinate employee. The policy forbids intimate relationships with anyone who "works through his or her management chain." This resignation essentially forced him into early retirement.

During the next year, the College of Business at Bozeman State University hired Mr. Brocamp as a part-time instructor to teach business strategy courses. The dean of the college suggested that the relationship was a personal matter and that Mr. Brocamp's wealth of experience is beneficial to students. Some who supported the hiring pointed out that other faculty members are not questioned about their personal lives. Others suggested that, since management ethics is so important, someone who violated a company ethics policy should not be teaching students about the proper management of organizations.

Required:

a. Discuss whether Mr. Brocamp's violation of corporate ethics policy affects or reflects the control environment of the company.

b. Since the violation is personal in nature, should Mr. Brocamp have been forced to resign?

c. Should Bozeman State have hired him to teach business strategy courses?

54. Janie Ray frequently makes purchases from mail-order catalogs. Recently, she ordered a dress she intended to wear to her cousin's wedding. Unfortunately, she did not receive the package on time, and on the evening before the wedding, Janie went shopping and purchased another outfit at a local dress shop.

Janie's neighbor, Steve, actually received the mail order package intended for Janie. Because Steve had been out of town last week, he had not had the chance to promptly bring the package to Janie's house. Even though the box correctly showed Janie's name and address, it appears that the carrier merely left the package on the doorstep of the wrong house.

Disgusted with this chain of events, Janie decided to claim that she had never received the package. After all, she was not able to wear the dress for its intended purposes; she should not have to pay for it. Moreover, the carrier was not able to provide proof of delivery.

Required:

a. Discuss which type of fraud is involved in this case, from the perspective of the mail order company.

b. Which of the AICPA Trust Services Principles most closely relates to this situation?

c. Describe a preventive control that could be performed by the carrier to avoid the possible recurrence of this type of fraud.

55. Evan Charter agreed to help his fraternity obtain sponsors for its annual charitable event to be held during Homecoming week. He accepted this responsibility at the recommendation of last year's fund-raiser, who told Evan that the task would require approximately ten hours of time and would likely result in total sponsorships of $1000.

After spending approximately ten hours calling on previous sponsors, Evan felt that he had hit a brick wall. For many reasons, most of last year's sponsors were unwilling to continue their involvement with this annual fund-raiser. Evan needed to look for additional sources of funding. He spent several hours researching potential new contributors and finally located a database containing a list of businesses within the local zip code. Since the list included e-mail addresses, Evan developed a letter of request and e-mailed it to all these businesses.

The response was overwhelming. Evan collected over $3000 from this new pool of business contacts. While compiling the checks received to turn over to the fraternity treasurer, Evan noticed that one business had made its $200 check payable to Evan personally.

Rationalizing that the additional time he had spent on the project and the success he was able to achieve were worthy of compensation, Evan decided to keep this one check. He wrote a letter of acknowledgment to the donor and deposited the $200 in his personal account.

Required:

a. Do you think Evan's actions were justified? What would you have advised him to do in this situation?

b. What internal control activities could the fraternity have implemented in order to prevent Evan's actions?

c. Can you think of a detective control that could uncover the omission of the $200 check?

CONTINUING CASE: SPATELLI'S PIZZERIA

Reread the Spatelli's case material at the end of Chapter 1, and then answer the following questions:

Required:

a. Considering the nature of the relationship between Spatelli's home office and its franchise owners, the company may be quite vulnerable to theft or fraudulent financial reporting committed by these franchise owners. Describe the three components of the fraud triangle and how each would relate to a franchise owner's likelihood to defraud Spatelli's.

b. Identify three types of fraud to which Spatelli's may be susceptible. For each of your three responses, indicate whether the fraud is classified as management fraud, employee fraud, vendor fraud, customer fraud, or computer fraud. In addition, for each of your three responses, suggest an internal control that could be implemented to prevent or detect the potential fraud.

SOLUTIONS TO CONCEPT CHECK

1. (SO 1) The careful and responsible oversight and use of the assets entrusted to management is called **b. stewardship.**

2. (SO 2) **c. Conversion** is **not** a condition in the fraud triangle. Incentive, opportunity, and rationalization make up the fraud triangle.
3. (SO 3) **a. Delayed exercise of stock options** is **not** an indirect benefit of management fraud. When managers conduct fraud, they are expecting indirect benefits such as delayed cash flow problems, enhanced promotion opportunities, and increased compensation. However, delaying stock option exercise is not a benefit.
4. (SO 4) **d. Earnings management** is **not** an example of employee fraud. Earnings management is a type of management fraud. The other answers are examples of employee fraud.
5. (SO 4) **d. Refund fraud** is **not** a common form of employee fraud. Refund fraud is a form of customer fraud, not employee fraud.
6. (CMA Adapted) (SO 4) Segregation of duties is a fundamental concept in an effective system of internal controls. Nevertheless, the effectiveness of this control can be compromised through **b. collusion among employees**. When employees who perform segregated duties work together, they can circumvent controls and perpetrate fraud.
7. (CPA Adapted) (SO 4) The most difficult type of misstatement to discover is fraud that is concealed by **b. nonrecorded transactions**. If there is no record of the fraud, it is especially difficult to detect.
8. (SO 6) The review of amounts charged to the company from a seller that it purchased from is called a **a. vendor audit**. A vendor audit involves the examination of vendor records in support of amounts charged to the company. Since many vendor contracts involve reimbursement for labor hours and other expenses incurred, the company can review supporting documentation for these expenses incurred by its vendor.
9. (SO 7) **a. Spoofing** is generally an external computer fraud, rather than an internal computer fraud. Spoofing occurs when a person, through a computer system, pretends to be someone else. Internet spoofing is the most dangerous to the accounting and control system.
10. (SO 10) The control activity intended to serve as a method to confirm the accuracy or completeness of data in the accounting system is **d. independent checks and reconciliations**. Independent checks and reconciliations on performance are important aspects of control activities. They usually involve the reconciliation, or comparison, of two sets of records, such as a bank reconciliation's comparison of the bank statement with the company's cash records.
11. (SO 10) COSO describes five components of internal control. **c. "Control activities"** is the term that is best described as "policies and procedures that help ensure management directives are carried out and management objectives are achieved." Control activities involve authorization, segregation, security of assets and records, adequate documentation, and independent checks. Policies and procedures of the organization establish the appropriate authorizations, segregations, security of assets and records, adequate documentation, and independent checks.
12. (CPA Adapted) (SO 10) Proper segregation of duties calls for separation of the functions of **b. authorization, recording, and custody**.
13. (SO 11) AICPA Trust Services Principles identify five categories of risks and controls. **c. Processing integrity** is the category best described by the

statement, "Information processes could be inaccurate, incomplete, or not properly authorized."

14. (CIA Adapted) (SO 2, 10) A company's cash custody function should be separated from the related cash recordkeeping function in order to **d. minimize opportunities for misappropriations of cash**. A lack of segregation of duties makes it possible for assets to be stolen, and the related records may be manipulated to conceal the theft.

CHAPTER 4

Internal Controls and Risks in IT Systems

STUDY OBJECTIVES

This chapter will help you gain an understanding of the following concepts:

1. An overview of internal controls for IT systems
2. General controls for IT systems
3. General controls from a Trust Services Principles perspective
4. Hardware and software exposures in IT systems
5. Application software and application controls
6. Ethical issues in IT systems

THE REAL WORLD

Marc Dietrich/iStockphoto

"On October 26, 2004, at 9:00 p.m., cops swooped in to arrest 28 ShadowCrew members in eight states and six countries. They seized dozens of computers and found 1.7 million credit-card numbers and more than 18 million e-mail accounts. . . ."[1]

ShadowCrew is an organized gang engaged in computer crimes such as identity theft, bank account pillage, and the fencing of stolen goods on the Internet. The gang conducts its illegal activity by hacking into computer networks of companies, banks, credit card providers, Internet service providers, and even individual computers at the homes of ordinary citizens.

These kinds of computer security threats continue to grow in number and severity. In 2004, the estimated total damage from computer security breaches was $17.5 billion, an amount that is 30% higher than 2003.[2]

While it will never be possible to prevent all such computer network breaches, companies must implement proper controls to try to reduce the chance of computer security problems. Controls are necessary to protect company and customer data. This chapter describes the inherent risks in IT systems and the IT controls that should be implemented to reduce them.

AN OVERVIEW OF INTERNAL CONTROLS FOR IT SYSTEMS (STUDY OBJECTIVE 1)

For all but the smallest organizations, computer systems are critical to ongoing operations. One of the critical functions within IT systems is the accounting information system. As described in Chapter 1, the accounting information system collects, processes, stores, and reports accounting information. Companies, government agencies, and nonprofit organizations all depend heavily on their computerized accounting systems to process transactions, store data, answer inquiries, and monitor operations. IT systems have become so critical that organizations would hardly be able to operate if their IT systems were suddenly to fail. Since IT systems are such a crucial and valuable resource for accounting systems, you should learn and understand the types of threats to which they are vulnerable so that these threats can be minimized. As an analogy, when you park your car in a public garage, you give some thought to whether it is susceptible to theft or vandalism and take some precautions such as locking the door or turning on a car alarm. Likewise, it is important for you to consider possible threats to the IT system and to know how to implement controls to try to prevent those threats from becoming reality. Unchecked threats and risks can lead to events that interrupt or stop computer operations, which can be severely damaging to the organization. Not only can they stop or disrupt normal operations, but they can also lead to incorrect or incomplete accounting information. This chapter provides an overview of controls in IT systems, the risks that these controls are intended to reduce, and important hardware and software components of IT systems to which controls should be applied.

Knowledge about IT systems and the related risks and controls are important factors in gaining an understanding of business processes and the recording, summarizing, monitoring, and reporting of results. Later chapters will

[1]Brian Grow, "Hacker Hunters," *BusinessWeek,* May 30, 2005, p. 76.

[2]*Ibid.*

describe the usual business processes such as those involving revenues, expenditures, conversion, and administrative processes. The data resulting from these processes are usually recorded, monitored, and stored in IT systems. The material you learn in this chapter regarding risks and controls in IT hardware and software will prepare you to better understand the systems for revenue, expenditures, conversion, and administrative processes described in later chapters.

An important set of concepts in this chapter is the matching of controls to risks. To master risks and controls and how they fit together, three areas must be understood fully. The first area is the description of the general and application controls that should exist in IT systems. The second is the type and nature of risks in IT systems. Third and most important is the recognition of how these controls can be used to reduce the risks in IT systems. The fit of controls to risks is explained through the use of terminology, concepts, and the framework from the AICPA Trust Services Principles. The Trust Services Principles were briefly described in Chapter 3 and will be covered in more depth in this chapter.

From the early days of computer use in accounting, internal controls for computer-based systems have been described as being of two types: general controls and application controls. (See Exhibit 4-1.) **General controls** apply overall to the IT accounting system; they are not restricted to any particular accounting application. An example of a general control is the use of passwords to allow only authorized users to log in to an IT based accounting system. Without regard to processing data in any specific application, passwords should be employed in the IT system.

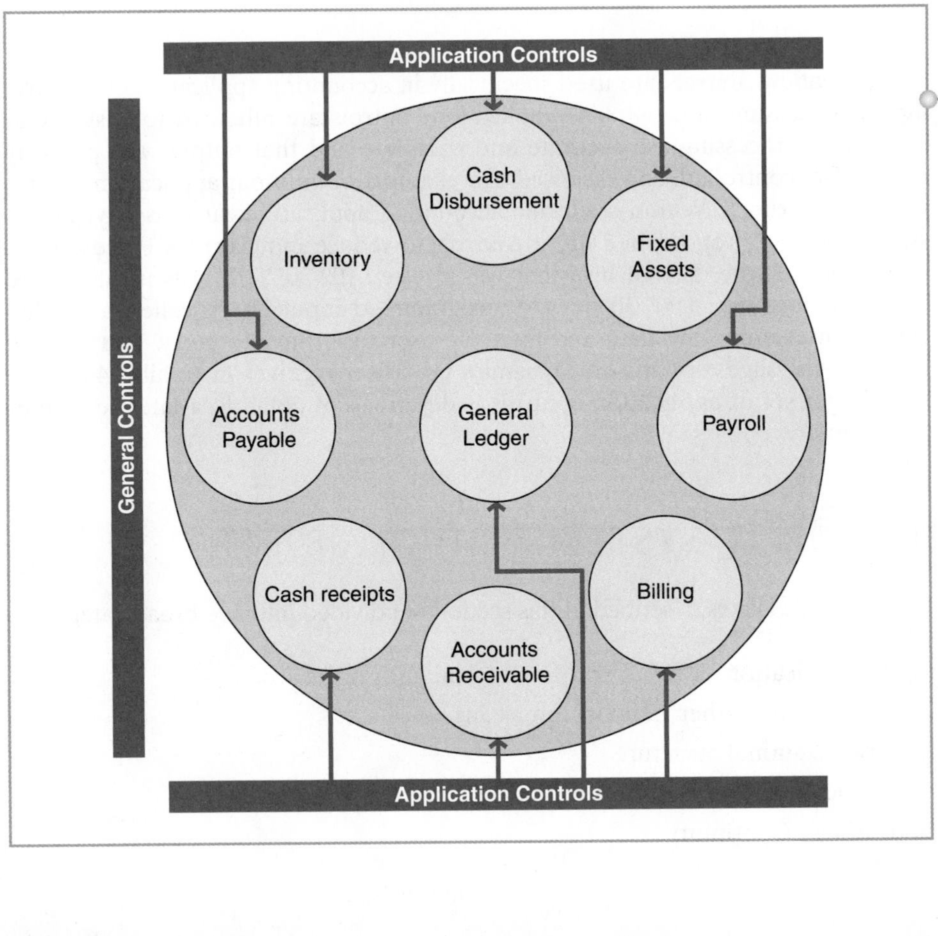

Exhibit 4-1
General and Application Controls in IT Systems

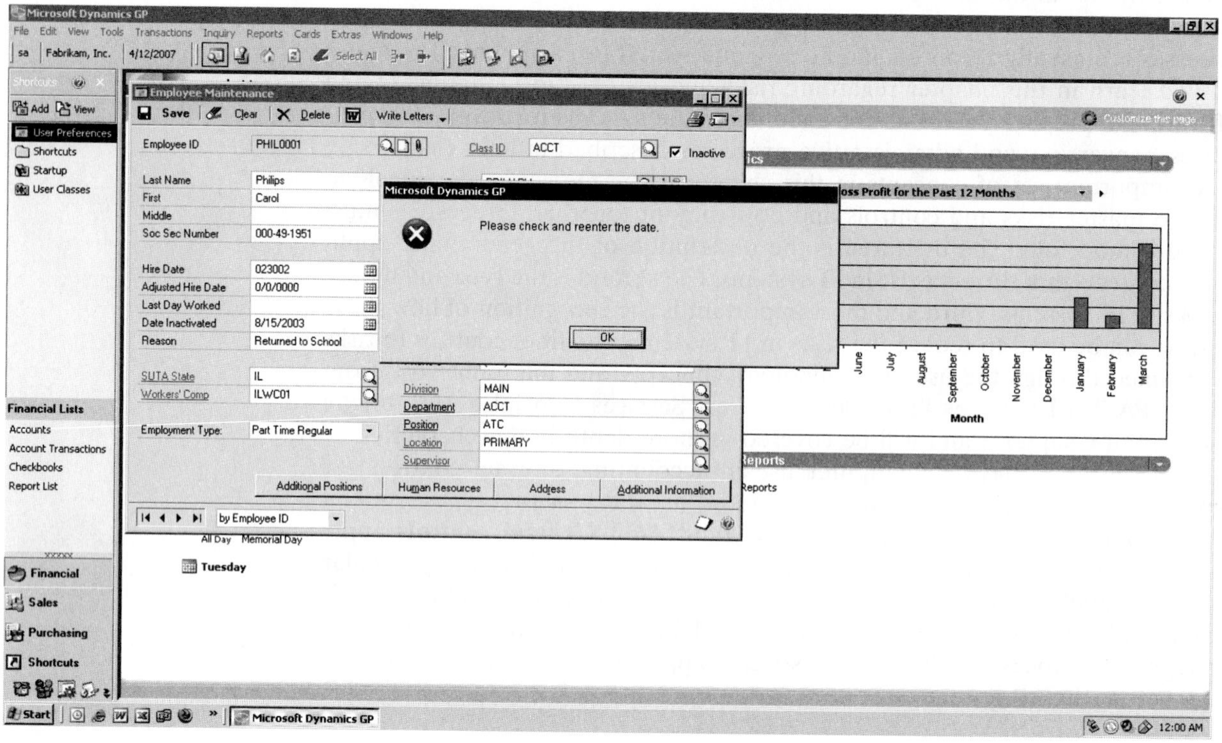

Exhibit 4-2
Validity Check–an Input Application Control

Application controls are used specifically in accounting applications to control inputs, processing, and outputs. Application controls are intended to ensure that inputs and processing are accurate and complete and that outputs are properly distributed, controlled, and disposed. An example of an input application control is a **validity check.** Within a specific accounting application, such as payroll, the system can use programmed input controls to reduce input errors. For example, in Exhibit 4-2, the date of hire that was entered (02/30/2002) was invalid, since February does not have 30 days. A programmed input check called a validity check can examine the date and alert the user to an invalid entry. You can see the error message a Microsoft Dynamics GP® user receives in Exhibit 4-2.

A larger set of application controls is described in detail in a later section of this chapter.

GENERAL CONTROLS FOR IT SYSTEMS (STUDY OBJECTIVE 2)

The general controls described in this section are divided into five broad categories:

1. Authentication of users and limiting unauthorized access
2. Hacking and other network break-ins
3. Organizational structure
4. Physical environment and physical security of the system
5. Business Continuity

AUTHENTICATION OF USERS AND LIMITING UNAUTHORIZED USERS

Authentication of users is a process or procedure in an IT system to ensure that the person accessing the IT system is a valid and authorized user. Unauthorized users trying to access IT systems is a prevalent, difficult, and ongoing problem that organizations must try to control. Unauthorized users may be hackers or people outside the organization, or users within the company trying to gain access to data they are not entitled to. In order to limit unauthorized access, there are many general controls that should be in place.

First, it is important to authenticate users as they attempt to access the IT system. Users may be authenticated in one or more of several ways. An IT system should require that users log-in with a distinct user identification, or user ID, and password**. Log-in** means to make the computer recognize you in order to create a connection at the beginning of a computer session. To increase the effectiveness of log-in restriction, **user IDs** must be unique for each user. A **password** is a secret set of characters that identifies the user as the authentic owner of that associated user ID. Passwords should be at least eight characters in length and contain at least one nonalphanumeric character. Such passwords would be difficult to guess. For example, a password such as xEq7f$23 would be much more difficult to guess than the user's initials. Passwords should also be case sensitive and changed every 90 days. The weak link in passwords is the human aspect. Many people have trouble remembering passwords, particularly if the password meets the strict criteria just mentioned. In addition, many people have several passwords for the different work and private systems they access. Therefore, some users write passwords down and keep them under the keyboard or in a drawer. This, of course, defeats the purpose of having passwords. Due to the weaknesses in passwords, some organizations use passwords in conjunction with other tools such as smart cards, tokens, and biometrics.

The use of passwords can be strengthened by the use of a **smart card** that the user carries. The smart card is plugged into the computer's card reader and helps authenticate that the user is valid. The smart card is a credit-card-size device with an integrated circuit that displays a constantly changing ID code. The user enters her password, and then the smart card displays an ID that she uses to log in. The smart card typically changes the user ID every 5 minutes or so.

A newer technology to authenticate users is a **security token**, which plugs into the USB port and thereby eliminates the need for a card reader. Otherwise, the purpose and use of the security token are the same as those of a smart card. Exhibit 4-3 shows the size and portability of a USB security token.

Exhibit 4-3
A USB Security Token

The use of smart cards or tokens can reduce unauthorized access, since the person who logs in must physically possess and use the smart card or token. The authentication of the user is called **two factor authentication** because it is based on something the user has, the token, and something the user knows, the password. A hacker located several hundred miles away from the organization would not have access to the smart card or token.

Biometric devices can also be used to authenticate users and limit unauthorized access. **Biometric devices** use some unique physical characteristic of the user to identify the user and allow the appropriate level of access to that user. Examples of physical characteristics being used in biometric devices are fingerprint matching, retina scans, voice verification, and face verification. Of these methods, fingerprint recognition is the most widely used technology. For example, it is possible to buy a mouse with a small window for your thumb or finger that scans the fingerprint to authenticate the user. Biometric devices are intended to allow only the authorized user to log in, according to his or her unique fingerprint, iris, voice, or facial features. Biometric devices are becoming more popular as their prices decrease and their reliability increases.

All of the methods described here are intended to limit log-ins exclusively to authorized users. However, none of these methods is foolproof, and it is important to have additional controls. First, all accesses should be logged. The organization should maintain a computer log of all log-ins. This log serves two purposes. The **computer log** is a complete record of all dates, times, and uses for each user. Any abnormalities in log-in or use can be examined in more detail to determine any weaknesses in log-in procedures. Also, the log-in procedures and logs establish nonrepudiation of users. **Nonrepudiation** means that a user cannot deny any particular act that he or she did on the IT system. That is, if a user logged in and changed data fraudulently, the log-in procedures and logs help establish undeniably which user took the action. Nonrepudiation is extremely important in verifying sales to customers. A danger is that a customer could log in via the company website, place an order that is subsequently received, and then deny that he or she initiated the transaction. Log-in of customers and computer logs help establish nonrepudiation of sales transactions.

The log-in procedure should also be established so that the session is terminated after three unsuccessful attempts and that these terminated sessions are also logged. Again, the purpose of the log is to allow proper followup if there are patterns of abnormal log-in or terminated log-ins. To maintain a record of log-in attempts, the system should keep an automated log to detect suspicious or unusual log-in attempts.

After a user logs in with valid authentication, the access granted in the IT system should be limited by the user profile. The **user profile,** which should be established for every authorized user, determines each user's access levels to hardware, software, and data according to the individual's job responsibilities. For example, an employee who enters payroll data does not need access to sales data, so this user's access to sales data should be restricted. In addition, the level of access must be established within the authority tables. An **authority table** contains a list of valid, authorized users and the access level granted to each one. For instance, one user within the payroll area may need to both read and write data, while another may need only read access. These user profiles may be defined in authority tables. Authority tables are an integral part of the

Exhibit 4-4
Authority Table

		Type of Access		
User	Password	Sales Data	Payroll Data	Fixed Asset Data
Chandler	bY5gF$	Read	-	-
Monica	Ybd7#q	-	Read	-
Ross	KfG6!e	-	Read/Write	-
Phoebe	hJ7d*R	-		Read/Write

computer system, and when a user logs in, the system looks up the nature and type of access to which that user is entitled. The authority table defines the type of access that a user has to data within the computer. A sample authority table is illustrated in Exhibit 4-4.

The IT system also has **configuration tables** for hardware, software, and application programs that contain the appropriate set-up and security settings. It is important to limit user access to these configuration tables so that security settings are not changed by unauthorized users. The hardware and operating system configuration table contains security and operating settings for hardware and the operating system. The application software configuration table contains security and operating settings for the application software. In a large-scale IT system, access to configuration tables is limited by the user profile and by control of physical access to the tables. The user ID and password for a particular user should not allow access to the configuration tables unless that user is authorized to change configuration settings.

HACKING AND OTHER NETWORK BREAK-INS

When an IT system is networked to either internal networks or the Internet, those networks are open to opportunities for unauthorized access. The more extensive the series of network connections, the greater chance there is for unauthorized access by hackers, others outside the organization, and unauthorized employees. When an IT system has network connections, the organization should employ one or more firewalls in the network. A **firewall** is hardware, software, or a combination of both that is designed to block unauthorized access. All data traveling between the internal network and the Internet should pass through the firewall first. The firewall examines all data passing through it, and if the firewall detects unauthorized attempts to pass data, it prevents the flow of such data. The firewall can prevent the unauthorized flow of data in both directions, blocking access to data on the network server by preventing unauthorized requests to log in or read data. Ideally, a firewall would be like a brick wall and allow nothing to pass through it. However, this would stop legitimate as well as illegitimate network traffic. Thus, the firewall has to examine data flow and attempt to block only the traffic that appears to be unauthorized. A way to think of the firewall is to compare it to the building security system at a large company. The security system will let employees with the proper badges enter and exit the building, but visitors without ID badges are stopped at the door. Similarly, information passes through a firewall in individual packets, and each packet must have the proper ID. Packets without the proper ID are stopped by the firewall.

Since these authorization and access controls cannot be completely effective, there are still possibilities that unauthorized access will occur. To limit the potential damage of unauthorized access, sensitive data should be encrypted. **Encryption** is the process of converting data into secret codes referred to as cipher text. Encrypted data can only be decoded by those who possess the encryption key or password. Encryption renders the data useless to those who do not possess the correct encryption key.

There are two types of encryption: symmetric encryption and public key encryption. **Symmetric encryption** uses a single encryption key that must be used to encrypt data and also to decode the encrypted data. The sender of the data and the receiver must have the same encryption key. However, it is difficult for the sender to communicate the encryption key to the receiver without compromising the key. **Public key encryption** uses both a public key and a private key. The public key, which can be known by everyone, is used to encrypt the data, and a private key is used to decode the encrypted data. Knowing which public encryption method a receiver uses enables the sender to use that public key to encrypt the data, and the receiver will use her private key to decode the data.

The strength of the encryption refers to how difficult it would be to break the code. Much the same as with passwords, the longer the encryption key is in bits, the stronger the encryption will be and the harder it will be to break the code. Many Internet encryption schemes use 128-bit encryption; that is, the encryption key is 128 bits in length. Under current U.S. standards, the longest encryption keys are 256 bits, but they are not yet widely adopted. Examining the possible combinations of keys proves the difficulty of breaking the encryption key. A 128-bit key size can create 340 undecillion different possible combinations, or 340 followed by 36 zeros. A 256-bit key size can create a combination set of 11 followed by 76 zeros. Someone who wished to randomly guess at the encryption key would potentially have to attempt all of these key possibilities. Even the use of a computer to try the various possibilities is infeasible because of the sheer number of possible combinations.

Encryption is especially important for wireless networks, which send network data as high frequency radio signals through the air. As in the case of radio transmissions, anyone who has the correct receiver can intercept network data waves in a wireless network. Since anyone within range of these radio signals can receive the data, protecting data through encryption is extremely important. A wireless network must have an access point, or a transmitter, that sends the network signals. The computer connected to the wireless network must have a wireless network card to receive the signals. Wireless network equipment, such as access points and wireless network cards, uses an encryption method called **wired equivalency privacy,** or WEP. Depending on the equipment used, WEP employees 64, 128, or 256 encryption methods. The encryption is symmetric in that both the sending and receiving network nodes must use the same encryption key. Because WEP has proven to be susceptible to hacking, the industry has developed a new wireless network security system called **wireless protected access,** or WPA, which has improved encryption and user authentication. With the improved encryption method, WPA can check to see whether encryption keys have been tampered with. WEP is based on a computer-specific address, which is easy for hackers to determine and misuse; a wireless network that uses WPA, on the other hand, requests connection to the network via an access point. The access point then requests the user identity and transmits that identity to an authentication server. Thus, WPA authenticates the computer and the user.

Another important security feature that should be used in wireless networks is a unique **service set identifier,** or SSID. The SSID is a password that is passed between the sending and receiving nodes of a wireless network. Most wireless network equipment sets a default SSID of "any" so that any wireless equipment can connect to it. For example, if you have a laptop computer with wireless network equipment built in, it theoretically can connect to any similarly equipped networks if the same SSID is used in the laptop and other network nodes. However, security is improved if "any" is changed to a unique SSID that only those within the organization use. Using a unique SSID makes it more difficult for an outsider to access the wireless network.

In many organizations, authorized employees may need to access the IT system from locations outside the organization. There are at least two examples of the need for such legitimate outside access. One is employees who telecommute and are permitted to work from home, using a computer connected to the IT system. A second example is sales staff who may be traveling to other cities, but must have access there to the IT system in order to service customers. In these cases, the authorized employees should connect to the IT system by using a virtual private network, or VPN. A **virtual private network** utilizes tunnels, authentication, and encryption within the Internet network to isolate Internet communications so that unauthorized users cannot access or use certain data. A VPN is employed when the employee connects to the IT system through a public network such as the Internet. A VPN uses the Internet,—it is therefore not truly private, but virtually private. The network traffic can be made to be virtually private by technology. Tunnels are end-to-end connections of network cards or other hardware; the VPN traffic can be thought of as traveling through a separate tunnel within the Internet network of public lines.

In addition, network traffic between the organization and all authorized users that is sent via the Internet should limit access by the use of web-based technology called **secure sockets layer,** or SSL. SSL is a communication protocol built into web server and browser software that encrypts data transferred on that website. If you have ever ordered products on a website, you were probably using SSL technology to encrypt personal data such as your credit card number. You can determine whether such sites use SSL technology by examining the URL address. Most website addresses begin with http:// preceding the URL, but SSL addresses begin with https:// preceding the URL.

IT system operations are also threatened by the many network break-in attempts that are undertaken to insert viruses or worms into a system. A **virus** is a self-replicating piece of program code that can attach itself to other programs and data and perform malicious actions such as deleting files or shutting down the computer. A worm is a small piece of program code that attaches to the computer's unused memory space and replicates itself until the system becomes overloaded and shuts down. To avoid destruction of data programs and to maintain operation of the IT system, an organization must employ **antivirus software,** which continually scans the system for viruses and worms and either deletes or quarantines them. Antivirus software renders virus and worm program code harmless.

All of the authentication controls mentioned in this section should assist in limiting unauthorized access. However, people who attempt to access an organization's systems in an unauthorized manner are continually exploiting new ways to gain access. Therefore, an organization must maintain a plan to continually monitor and test the vulnerability of its IT system to unauthorized access.

To monitor exposure long range, the organization should engage in vulnerability assessment, intrusion detection, and penetration testing. **Vulnerability assessment** is the process of proactively examining the IT system for weaknesses that can be exploited by hackers, viruses, or malicious employees. When an organization engages in vulnerability assessment by using manual testing or automated software tools, it can identify weaknesses before they become network break-ins and attempt to fix these weaknesses before they are exploited. **Intrusion detection** systems are specific software tools that monitor data flow within a network and alert the IT staff to hacking attempts or other unauthorized access attempts. An intrusion detection system can be thought of as the burglar alarm for the IT system in that it alerts the appropriate users of break-ins. **Penetration testing** is the process of legitimately attempting to hack into an IT system to find whether weaknesses can be exploited by unauthorized hackers. Penetration testing is sometimes done by the IT staff within an organization, but more often an outside consultant with experience in penetration testing is hired to complete the tests.

ORGANIZATIONAL STRUCTURE

Organizations with extensive IT systems should govern the overall development and operation of IT systems through the use of an **IT governance committee,** usually made up of top executives. Its function is to govern the overall development and operation of IT systems. The committee, which would include officers such as the chief executive officer (CEO), chief financial officer (CFO), chief information officer (CIO), and the heads of business units such as the vice president of marketing, has several important responsibilities, including the following:

1. Align IT investments to business strategy. Investing funds and resources in the most beneficial IT systems should enhance the long-range goal of achieving the business strategy.
2. Budget funds and personnel for the most effective use of the IT systems.
3. Oversee and prioritize changes to IT systems. Within organizations, many user groups will concurrently request improvements or changes to their subsystem within the IT system. The IT governance committee will appoint a stearing committee to prioritize these requests according to the best match to the business strategy and the feasibility of designing, developing, and implementing the necessary changes.
4. Develop, monitor, and review all IT operational policies. The organization should maintain policies and descriptions of procedures for operating and developing its IT systems.
5. Develop, monitor, and review security policies. The organization should maintain policies and descriptions of procedures related to security. For example, the organization should have established procedures to monitor and follow up on security breaches to the IT system.

While there are many types of IT policies that must be in place, the description of policies in this section will focus only on those that are related to general controls over IT systems. It is important to understand that the IT governance committee delegates many of its duties by the policies that it develops. Since the IT governance committee consists of top management, its role is to develop policies and to delegate duties such that those policies are properly implemented. Perhaps the most important factor in controlling IT systems is the competence of the personnel. Thus, it is important that the IT governance committee ensure that the organization maintains hiring and promotion procedures which screen candidates and verify the background and references of applicants. The IT governance committee should also see that the organization maintains written job descriptions and requirements for IT positions.

The manner in which an organization establishes, delegates, and monitors IT system functions is part of the general control over IT systems. The division of duties and the policies of the organization in relation to those duties must be so designed that they strengthen control over IT systems. The functional responsibilities within an IT system must include proper segregation of duties. This segregation is different from the accounting-related segregation described in Chapter 3. In an IT system, the duties to be segregated are those of systems analysts, programmers, operators, and the database administrator. **Systems analysts** analyze and design IT systems, while **programmers** actually write the software, using a programming language. **Operations personnel** are employees who are responsible for processing operating data. The **database administrator** develops and maintains the database and ensures adequate controls over data within the database. In a properly segregated IT system, no single person or department should develop computer programs and also have access to data that is commensurate with operations personnel. Similarly, the database administrator should not develop or write programs.

The IT governance committee should ensure that policies are in place which require the listing of all software used in the organization and that this list include important information such as the level and version of the software and any patches that have been applied. Patches are bug fixes, or security enhancements, to existing software.

In addition, the IT governance committee should develop policies and assign responsibilities to ensure that hardware and software systems are tested annually and that the test results are used to continually improve the security and effectiveness of IT systems. The committee should be established prior to major changes in any IT systems and should meet monthly to review items such as investment decisions, change requests, and security policies. When changes to IT systems are proposed, the IT governance committee should already have in place a system development process that controls the initiation, approval, development, and maintenance of those changes. This process, called the system development life cycle, or SDLC, is described in detail in Chapter 6. The **system development life cycle** can be generally described as the systematic steps undertaken to plan, prioritize, authorize, oversee, test, and implement large-scale changes to the IT system.

PHYSICAL ENVIRONMENT AND SECURITY

The general controls for an IT system should include controls over the physical environment of the system and physical access controls to limit who is in contact with the system. The physical environment includes the location, operating environment, and back-up systems of the IT system. Physical security is intended to limit physical access to computer hardware and software so that malicious acts or vandalism do not disrupt the system and so that data are protected.

Especially for large IT systems, the security of the environment in which they reside and operate is crucial. A large IT system should be physically located in an area and building that are least at risk of natural disasters such as flood, earthquake, hurricane, and fire. Natural disasters can easily destroy or disrupt IT system operations. To the extent possible, IT systems should be installed in locations away from any location likely to be affected by natural disasters.

Computer systems can also be affected by environmental extremes of temperature and humidity. Therefore, a large-scale IT system must be located in a building that properly controls dust, temperature, and humidity. The building should also have a fire protection system that does not use water sprinklers, as water can rain the hardware and data. The fire prevention systems should use a gas such as halon gas that eliminates oxygen in the room, since a fire cannot burn without oxygen.

The computer system should also have both an uninterruptible power supply (UPS) and an emergency power supply (EPS). An **uninterruptible power supply** includes a battery to maintain power in the event of a power outage in order to keep the computer running for several minutes after a power outage. An **emergency power supply** is an alternative power supply that provides electrical power in the event that a main source is lost. An example of an EPS is a gasoline powered generator.

As you may have found with your personal computer, loss of electrical power can result in lost or corrupted data. In the case of an electrical power failure, backup power supplies such as UPS and EPS can keep the IT system operating at least until the individual applications and data can be saved and gradually shut down.

THE REAL WORLD

On August 14, 2003, the largest power blackout in North American history affected eight U.S. States and the Province of Ontario, leaving up to 50 million people with no electricity. Some of the major cities hit included New York City, Cleveland, Toledo, Detroit, Toronto, and Ottawa. Although all electric power from utility systems was out, some telecommunications and wireless networks continued to operate. An Associated Press story explains how they continued to operate:[3]

> Several large telecommunications providers, including the company that supports the vast majority of Internet traffic worldwide, said they immediately switched to backup generators on the East Coast and could continue doing so for several days.
>
> "We lost all utility power out there, but we immediately went to battery power for a few seconds, at which point all of our major generators kicked in," said Margie Backaus, chief business officer of Foster City, Calif.-based Equinix, which operates Internet Business Exchange centers that serve more than 90 percent of the world's Internet routes.

Battery power (UPS) and generators (EPS) served as the uninterruptible power supply and emergency power supply systems that enabled these networks to continue operations during the blackout.

[3]Rachel Konrad, "Wireless Networks Still Work in Blackout," *Associated Press*, August 15, 2003.

The hardware and data in an IT system are also vulnerable to damage, destruction, disruption, or theft if an unauthorized person can physically access them. Large-scale IT systems should be protected by physical access controls. Such controls include the following:

1. Limited access to computer rooms through employee ID badges or card keys
2. Video surveillance equipment
3. Logs of persons entering and exiting the computer rooms
4. Locked storage of backup data and offsite backup data

BUSINESS CONTINUITY

Business continuity planning (BCP) is a proactive program for considering risks to the continuation of business and developing plans and procedures to reduce those risks. Since such a large number of organizations rely on IT systems to operate, the continuation of IT systems is an integral part of business continuity. BCP is a broad type of planning that focuses on key personnel, resources, and activities critical to business continuation.

THE REAL WORLD

In some organizations, loss of a key CEO could spell disaster. For example, Martha Stewart founded and became the CEO of Martha Stewart Living Omnimedia Inc. In June 2003, she was indicted for possible legal violations related to insider trading, and she stepped down as CEO. Some in the financial community wondered if the firm could continue or thrive without Martha Stewart. Part of the business continuity plan for her company should have been a strategy to operate if some event would prevent Martha Stewart from serving as CEO. Martha was convicted, served time in prison, and successfully returned to work.

BCP is a broad concept, but because of the importance of IT systems as a critical business resource, a large part of BCP includes IT continuation. Two parts of business continuity are related to IT systems:

1. A strategy for backup and restoration of IT systems, to include redundant servers, redundant data storage, daily incremental backups, a backup of weekly changes, and offsite storage of daily and weekly backups.
2. A disaster recovery plan.

If IT systems are to continue without interruption, it is important to have backups for both the hardware and software systems, as well as the data. One approach to a backup up processing system is called **redundant servers**—two or more computer network or data servers that can run identical processes or maintain the same data. If one of the servers fails, a redundant server functions in its place. In many IT systems, redundant data storage is accomplished by the use of **redundant arrays of independent disks** (RAIDs), often set up such that two or more disks are exact mirror images. If one disk drive fails, the mirror image on a second drive can serve in its place. In addition to the backup files on a RAID, the organization should maintain daily and weekly incremental backups. This backup protection is improved by **off-site backup,** an additional copy of the backup files stored in an offsite location. In some cases, on-site backups may be destroyed and the offsite backup files would be necessary.

The plan for the continuance of IT systems after a disaster is called a **disaster recovery plan (DRP).** Whereas BCP is proactive planning, DRP is a more reactive plan to restore business operations to normal after a disaster occurs. Disaster recovery plans should include all plans necessary to continue IT operation after a disaster. Although disaster recovery planning has been an important concept in IT systems for many years, there was much more activity regarding disaster recovery planning after the New York City terrorist attacks in September of 2001. Those events reminded companies that catastrophies happen very unexpectedly and can cause IT systems to be damaged or destroyed.

Since disasters can destroy systems and/or data, it is important that organizations maintain backup systems and backup data. Organizations must have regular processes to back up data and to store at least one copy of the backup off site. The off-site backup is necessary in case all data are destroyed at the on-site location.

GENERAL CONTROLS FROM AN AICPA TRUST SERVICES PRINCIPLES PERSPECTIVE (STUDY OBJECTIVE 3)

A reference list for the general controls described in the previous section appears at the end of this chapter as Exhibit 4-11 (page 167). Each of the general controls is intended to prevent, detect, or correct risks and exposures in IT systems. A company may choose not to use all of the controls described previously. Each organization should decide which combination of IT controls is most suitable for its IT systems, making sure that the benefits of each control outweigh its costs. As an example, you probably would not spend money to install an extensive car burglar alarm system in your 1988 Honda Civic. The cost of the burglar alarm would outweigh the benefits.

When considering IT risks, organizations should implement those IT controls which are cost beneficial. As a framework to discuss these IT risks, the AICPA Trust Services Principles categorizes IT controls and risks into five categories:[4]

a. **Security.** The system is protected against unauthorized (physical and logical) access.

b. **Availability.** The system is available for operation and use as committed or agreed.

c. **Processing integrity.** System processing is complete, accurate, timely, and authorized.

d. **Online privacy.** Personal information obtained as a result of e-commerce is collected, used, disclosed, and retained as committed or agreed.

e. **Confidentiality.** Information designated as confidential is protected as committed or agreed.

[4]Trust Services Principles, Criteria and Illustrations for Security, Availability, Processing Integrity, Confidentiality, and Privacy (Including WebTrust® and SysTrust®), American Institute of Certified Public Accountants, Inc. and Canadian Institute of Chartered Accountants, 2006 (www.aicpa.org).

The fourth category, online privacy, applies only to e-business and is discussed in a later chapter on e-business. The other four risk categories are used in this section to describe the concepts of controls and risks in IT systems. For each of these four categories, this section describes some of the risks and the corresponding controls, which are summarized in Exhibit 4-5. This is not a comprehensive list of risks, but a summary of some common risks along the four categories of security, availability, processing integrity, and confidentiality.

Perhaps the best way to understand these risks and the corresponding need for IT controls is to consider the absence of any IT controls. As an analogy, consider the likely negative consequences that could occur if your car doors did not have locks. Car door locks exists to prevent the specific risks of break-in and theft. Car door locks lessen these risks, but do not completely eliminate them. The sections that follow describe some of the potential risks in IT systems and controls that can reduce them. Much like car door locks, controls reduce risks; but it is impossible to completely eliminate risks.

RISKS IN NOT LIMITING UNAUTHORIZED USERS

The top section of Exhibit 4-5 lists eight IT controls related to authentication of users. These were described in the previous section as controls that can lessen the risk of unauthorized users gaining access to the IT system: user ID, password, security token, biometric devices, log-in procedures, access levels, computer logs, and authority tables. Consider the likely results if these controls were completely missing from an IT system: An unauthorized user could easily access data and programs he should not have access to, change data, record transactions, and perhaps even have a company check written directly to himself. Unauthorized users could be from inside or outside the organization. In addition, the lack of a user ID and password would mean that the company would be unable to determine which users accomplish which tasks. There would be no computer log of tasks accomplished by individual users.

There are several *security risks* resulting from unauthorized access. However, it is important first to understand the nature of unauthorized access. While the most popular type of unauthorized access is probably by a person unknown to the organization, employees of the organization also may try to access data to which they do not need access to perform their job duties. For example, a person who works in an accounts receivable department has no need to access payroll data. Data within the organization should be protected from internal unauthorized access as well as from external access. Unauthorized access to the IT system can allow persons to browse through data that is beyond the scope of their job duties, alter data in an unauthorized manner, destroy data, copy the data with the intent to steal and perhaps sell to competitors, or record unauthorized transactions. Establishing log-in procedures that include user IDs, passwords, security tokens, access levels, biometric devices, and authority logs can help prevent or lessen these security risks. These are preventive controls. The computer log of attempted log-ins can be periodically reviewed to determine whether unauthorized access or any attempt to gain unauthorized access has occurred. The organization can then change policies or practices if necessary to prevent further unauthorized access. The computer log serves as a detective control to assist in the discovery of unusual log-in attempts.

Control Category	Security Risks	Availability Risks	Processing Integrity Risks	Confidentiality Risks
Authentication of users	*Unauthorized user can*	*Unauthorized user can*	*Unauthorized user can*	*Unauthorized user can*
User ID Password Security token or smart card Biometric devices Login procedures Access levels Computer logs Authority tables	Browse data Alter data Destroy data Steal data Record nonexistent or unauthorized transactions	Shut down systems Shut down programs Sabotage systems Alter programs	Alter data Alter programs Record nonexistent or unauthorized transactions Repudiate transactions	Browse data Destroy data Steal data
Hacking and other network break-ins	*Person breaking in can*	*Person breaking in can*	*Person breaking in can*	*Person breaking in can*
Firewall Encryption Security policies Security breach resolution Secure socket layers (SSL) Virtual private network (VPN) Wired equivalency privacy (WEP) Service set identifier (SSID) Antivirus software Vulnerability assessment Penetration testing Intrusion detection	Browse data Alter data Destroy data Steal data Record nonexistent or unauthorized transactions	Shut down systems Shut down programs Sabotage systems Alter programs Insert virus or worm that interrupts or slows operations	Alter data Alter programs Record nonexistent or unauthorized transactions Insert virus or worm that alters or destroys data	Browse data Destroy data Steal data
Environmental		*Environmental problems can*	*Environmental problems can*	
Temperature, humidity controls Fire, flood, earthquake controls Uninterruptible power supplies Emergency power supplies		Shut down systems Shut down programs	Cause errors or glitches Cause loss or corruption of data due to power loss	
Physical access	*Unauthorized intruder can*	*Unauthorized intruder can*	*Unauthorized intruder can*	*Unauthorized intruder can*
Card key Operating system configuration tables Hardware configuration tables	Change user access levels	Shut down systems Sabotage or destroy systems Insert virus or worm	Shut down programs Sabotage programs Insert virus or worm	Browse data Destroy data Steal data
Business continuity	*Improper handling of backup data can*	*System interruptions can*	*System interruptions can*	*Improper handling of backup data can*
Disaster recovery plan Backup data Offsite backup	Cause unintended access to data	Shut down systems	Cause errors or glitches Result in incomplete data	Cause unintended access to data

Exhibit 4-5
Control and Risk Matrix in IT Systems

Availability risks must be assessed and controlled by authentication of user controls. Once a person gains unauthorized access, it is conceivable that he may tamper with the IT system in a manner that may shut down systems and/or programs. These interruptions would obviously make the system or program temporarily unavailable for its intended use. An unauthorized user could also sabotage an IT system by inserting malicious program code to be triggered later. For example, suppose Company XYZ fires a disgruntled programmer, but fails to revoke the user ID and password immediately. Before that programmer cleans out his office and leaves, he may insert into the system some malicious instructions that erase the accounts receivable files during its next regularly scheduled run. Many years ago, this happened to a company; it was unable to recover the files and eventually filed for bankruptcy. This type of malicious code can be triggered by a particular date, a scheduled run, or another set of system circumstances. In addition, the unauthorized user may simply change the program itself. Lessening the chance of unauthorized access through authentication controls can help prevent these availability risks. The computer log would assist in tracing the person responsible for shutting down systems and programs, sabotaging systems, or altering programs.

Processing integrity can be compromised without adequate authentication controls. Processing integrity refers to the accuracy, completeness, and timeliness of the processing in IT systems. If unauthorized users access the IT system, they could alter data to change the results of processing. This could occur prior to the transaction being processed, during processing, or after the processing is complete. In all three cases, the accuracy or completeness of processing would be affected. For example, after a sale has been processed, an unauthorized user could delete the amount due to the company in the accounts receivable record. The unauthorized user could also alter programs to affect the results of processing. An unauthorized user might change program instructions to automatically double the hours worked for a particular person every time a payroll check is written for that person. Unauthorized users are sometimes able to circumvent other controls and insert transactions that are fictitious or unauthorized.

Another processing integrity risk is repudiation of real transactions. After a sales transaction has been processed, it may be possible for an unauthorized user to erase traces of the transaction and claim that they do not owe money to the company. Attempting to limit unauthorized users through log-in and authentication controls helps reduce the chances of these risks occurring. Computer logs may facilitate tracing of the alteration of data or unauthorized transactions to the responsible person.

Confidentiality risk, or the risk of confidential data being available to unauthorized users, can occur if authentication controls are weak. An unauthorized user who gains access can browse, steal, or destroy confidential data. Improving authentication and log-in controls helps limit the chances of confidentiality risks. Computer logs can assist in detecting such compromises of data and in tracing them to the responsible person.

Proper use of authentication controls and computer logs can help limit all four categories of these risks. As is always true, these risks cannot be eliminated, but they can be reduced by the use of appropriate controls. Each organization should assess the level of these risks and apply the controls that are cost beneficial for their system.

RISKS FROM HACKING OR OTHER NETWORK BREAK-INS

Hackers or others who break into computer networks are usually thought of as being outside the company. While this is often true, a hacker could be an employee of the organization who hacks in from home or at work. In fact, employees can sometimes be more dangerous because of their knowledge of company operations and potential access to company information or assets. Whether the threat is from an insider or outsider, efforts should be made to reduce the risk of hacking or network break-ins and to limit the harm that can result. The controls that may be applied are firewalls, encryption of data, security policies, security breach resolution, secure socket layers (SSL), virtual private network (VPN), wired equivalency privacy (WEP), wireless protected access (WPA), service set identifier (SSID), antivirus software, vulnerability assessment, penetration testing, and intrusion detection. Intrusion detection is a detective control, while the others are preventive.

The *security risks* related to hacking and network break-ins are the same as those identified in the previous section on unauthorized users. Those who break into a computer network have obviously breached security and could browse, alter, or destroy data. The use of the controls listed in the previous paragraph and in the second group in Exhibit 4-5 can help reduce the security risks of network break-ins, as well as reduce the potential damage if break-ins do occur.

The *availability risks* are that the network break-in can allow systems or programs to be shut down, altered, or sabotaged. The person who breaks in may also plant a virus or worm into the system. The *processing integrity risks* are that the person breaking in can alter the data or programs to compromise the accuracy or completeness of the data. Recording nonexistent or unauthorized transactions will also compromise data accuracy or completeness, as could planting a virus or worm. Again, there is a *confidentiality risk,* since the person breaking in may access, browse, steal, or change confidential data.

RISKS FROM ENVIRONMENTAL FACTORS

IT systems can be negatively affected by the environment in which they operate. Extremes of temperature or humidity can cause operating problems, especially to large mainframe computers, which are sensitive to heat and high humidity and therefore must be placed in rooms in which the climate is tightly controlled. Interruptions to the electrical power can cause systems to go down. It is not possible to prevent power outages caused by thunderstorms, fire, flood, or earthquake, but building location and construction can reduce the effects of these natural disasters. For example, a computer system should not be located in an area that frequently floods. Uninterruptible and emergency power supplies can be used to continue operations during power outages caused by natural events. Because, for example, a thunderstorm can cause a lengthy power outage without actually being disastrous as people commonly think—in terms of death and destruction.

Any environmental changes that affect the IT system can cause *availability risks* and *processing integrity risks*—the risks that systems can be shut down or errors and glitches in processing can occur which cause lost or corrupted data. Backup power supply systems allow IT systems to be gradually shut down without the loss or corruption of data.

PHYSICAL ACCESS RISKS

Physical access to computer systems and computer rooms should be limited to those who must have access in order to carry out their job assignments. Others who gain access (intruders) pose risks to the IT systems. The *security risk* is that an intruder who gains physical access may change user access levels so that she can later access data or systems through any network attached system. The *availability risks* are that unauthorized physical access would allow an intruder to physically shut down, sabotage, or destroy hardware or software. In addition, physical access may make it possible for an intruder to insert viruses or worms from diskette, CD, or other media. An intruder may interrupt processing and thereby affect the accuracy or completeness of processing. Thus, *processing integrity risks* are that systems or programs may be shut down or sabotaged. Viruses and worms can also affect the accuracy and completeness of processing. An intruder poses *confidentiality risks* in that she may be able to gain access to confidential data to browse, alter, or steal.

BUSINESS CONTINUITY RISKS

Many things can interrupt business continuity, including natural disasters. Due to the critical importance of IT systems to business continuity, there must be controls to limit IT risks related to business continuity and natural disasters. However, as part of continuity planning, an organization must still keep backup copies of data on-site and offsite. The existence of backup data poses a risk in that it affords another opportunity for unauthorized access. The *security risk* is that an unauthorized person may gain access to the backup data. Without proper business continuity planning, disaster recovery planning, and backup data, adverse events can interrupt IT system operation. The *availability risk* is that as events interrupt operations, the system becomes unavailable for regular processing. The *processing integrity risk* is that business interruptions can lead to incomplete or inaccurate data. The *confidentiality risk* is that unauthorized persons may gain access to confidential data if they access backup data. A co-ordinated effort regarding business continuity planning, disaster recovery planning, control over backup data, and correct use of these procedures can limit the risks.

HARDWARE AND SOFTWARE EXPOSURES IN IT SYSTEMS (STUDY OBJECTIVE 4)

The previous sections described and linked risk areas to corresponding controls. To properly understand these risks, we must also understand their possible sources. Consider a burglar alarm analogy. One risk in owning a building is the possibility of break-in and theft of assets from the building. A control to help prevent that risk is a burglar alarm. But to know how to install the sensors for a burglar alarm, the installer must know the potential points of entry, which would be any door or window in the building. Doors and windows serve useful purposes and make the building more efficient, but each one is a risk area and the sensors for the burglar alarm must be placed at each of the windows and doors. In a similar manner, components of an IT system can be thought of as areas that open risks for an organization, or "entry points." In an IT system, there are security, availability, processing integrity, and confidentiality risks. General controls (described earlier) can help limit those risks, but the "entry points" over which these controls should be placed must be identified. This section describes the typical IT system components that represent "entry points" where the risks must be controlled.

There are so many different types of hardware and software that can be used in an IT-based accounting system that no two organizations are likely to have identical hardware and software configurations. Each organization selects and implements hardware and software according to its specific needs. Since this chapter cannot possibly cover all possible hardware and software configurations, it describes typical components in generic terms. The exhibits depicting IT systems are not intended to be literal pictures of exact systems, but simplified depictions of those systems. Exhibit 4-6 depicts many, but not all, of the hardware and software components described in this chapter.

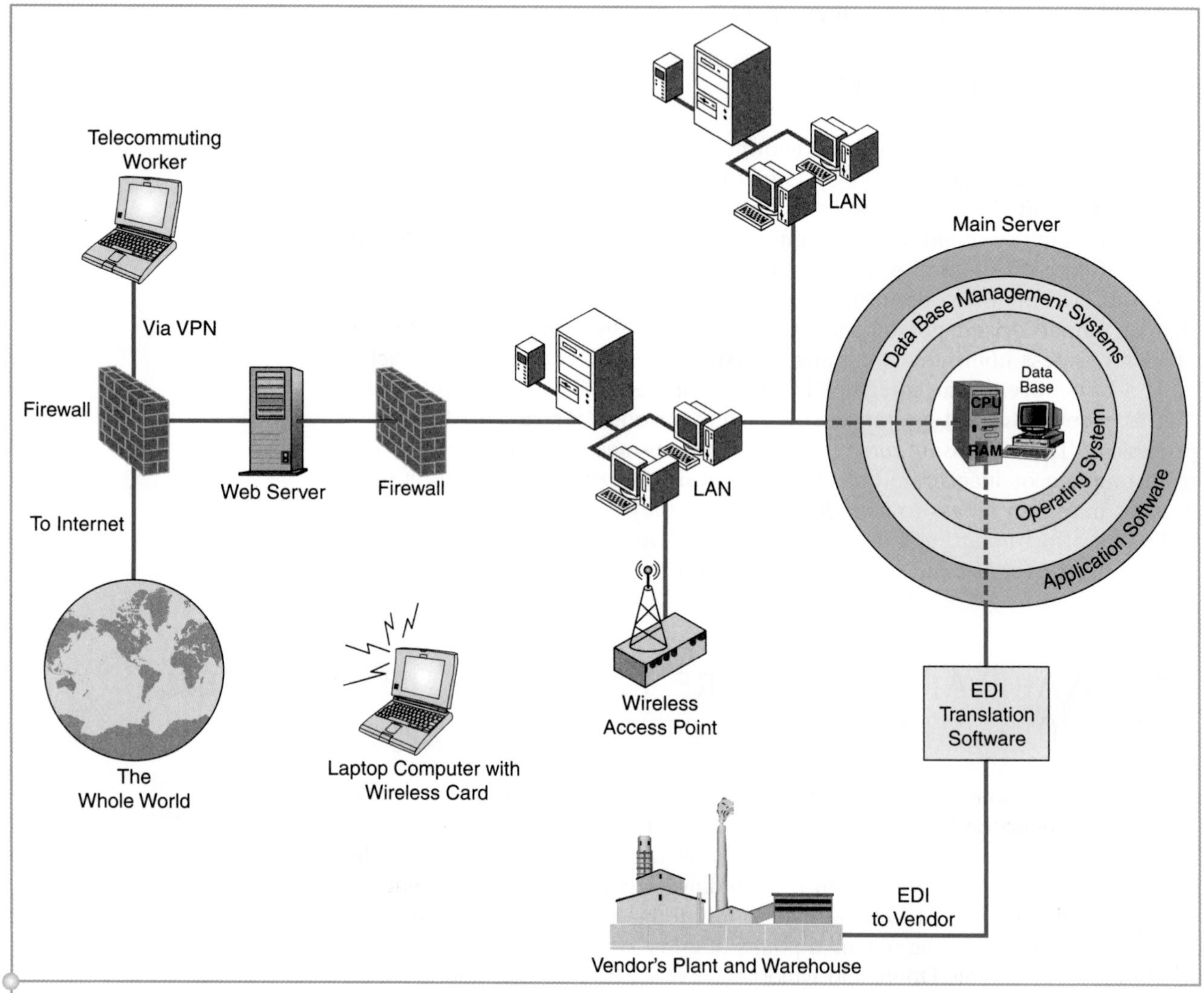

Exhibit 4-6
Exposure Areas in an IT System

The components illustrated in Exhibit 4-6 can increase the efficiency, effectiveness, and economy of conducting business. They can improve sales, performance, and customer service and reduce costs. The existence of each of these components represents an exposure that should be controlled. These IT system exposures are "entry points" that make the organization susceptible to the IT risks described earlier. The exposure areas shown in Exhibit 4-6 are as follows:

1. The operating system
2. The database
3. The database management system (DBMS)
4. Local area networks (LANs)
5. Wireless networks
6. E-business conducted via the Internet
7. Telecommuting workers
8. Electronic data interchange (EDI)
9. Application software

The first eight of these exposure areas can be controlled by the use of appropriate general controls such as those described in previous sections. The next eight sections give a brief description of each of the eight exposure areas. Some of these hardware or software components are described in more detail in other chapters. The ninth exposure area, application software, requires application controls. The description of application controls within application software is presented in the last section of this chapter. The purpose of the descriptions in this chapter is to provide only enough detail to allow an understanding of these exposures.

THE OPERATING SYSTEM

The **operating system** is the software that controls the basic input and output activities of the computer. The operating system provides the instructions that enable the CPU to read and write to disk, read keyboard input, control output to the monitor, manage computer memory, and communicate between the CPU, memory, and disk storage. In large computer systems, the operating system manages memory and CPU functions so that multiple users or multiple applications do not interfere with each other. The operating system handles computer data in binary form, which means that data are in sets of 0 or 1 data bits. That is, data such as dollar balances or passwords are being transmitted or stored in the operating system in binary form—sets of 0 and 1 values. Any knowledgeable person who understands binary data and who gains access to the operating system may be able to scan memory for things such as passwords, employee data, and other sensitive data. Such a person could also manipulate or destroy data. The operating system can be an "entry point" for unauthorized users or hackers.

Operating system access allows a user access to all the important aspects of the IT system. Since all application and database software works through the operating system, access to the operating system also allows access to applications and the database. In addition, all read/write data functions are controlled by the operating system, and any person who has access to the operating system can have full access to data. Essentially, access to the operating system opens access to any data or program in the IT system. Therefore, controlling access to the operating system is critical. If a knowledgeable person is able to access and manipulate the operating system, that person potentially has access to all data passing through the operating system, all processes, and all programs. Thus, the operating system poses *security risks*, *availability risks*, *processing integrity risks*, and *confidentiality risks*.

THE REAL WORLD

As an example of the dangers of threats to operating system software, in 2003 Microsoft Corp announced a critical security flaw in several versions of the Windows operating system for personal computers and servers. An excerpt of an article[5] related to that flaw is as follows:

> "It should be emphasized that this vulnerability poses an enormous threat, and appropriate patches provided by Microsoft should be immediately applied," the group said in an advisory posted to its Web site. The group said that programs designed to exploit the vulnerability will likely be available on the Internet soon.
>
> By sending too much data to other computers that use its operating system, an attacker can cause the system to grant full access to the system.
>
> "This would give the attacker the ability to take any action on the server that they want," Microsoft stated in its advisory. "For example, an attacker could change Web pages, reformat the hard disk, or add new users to the local administrators group."
>
> Jeff Jones, senior director for Microsoft's Trustworthy Computing effort, said that, in addition to applying the patch, users and systems administrators should close down any unused communications channels, or ports.
>
> "Customers should protect their network with a firewall," he said. "Individual users should use the Internet Connection Firewall or some other personal firewall." The Internet Connection Firewall is a feature of Windows XP and Windows 2003 that limits the ways that a potential intruder could attack from the network.

The operating system software is much different from application software. Application software, such as accounting software, usually has programmed controls that limit the types of data a person can see or manipulate. For example, employees in the purchasing department who log in to the accounting system will be able to access vendor information, but not payroll information. Application accounting software is written to limit data access and also accept only a limited type of data to be input. For example, if an employee is entering pay rates, it is not likely that the payroll software would allow her to enter letters in that blank box, or enter a pay rate of $500 per hour. Although software is written to limit data access and input, any knowledgeable person who has access to an operating system can manipulate data without being hindered by these types of input or data limitations.

[5] Robert Lemos, staff writer, "Microsoft warns of critical Windows flaw," CNET News, July 16, 2003 (news.com/2100-1009-1026420.html).

The risks to the operating system related to accounting data include security, availability, processing integrity, and confidentiality risks. Unauthorized access to the operating system would allow the unauthorized user to do the following:

1. Browse disk files or memory for sensitive data or passwords.
2. Alter data through the operating system.
3. Alter access tables to change access levels of users.
4. Alter application programs.
5. Destroy data or programs.

As summarized in Exhibit 4-5, these risks are present in all four categories. Many of the general controls mentioned earlier and shown in Exhibit 4-5 should be in place to help reduce these risks. Since an organization must determine which controls are most cost beneficial, it is not possible to list a complete, inclusive set of general controls recommended for every operating system. At the least, an organization should use user IDs, passwords, log-in procedures, computer logs, and authority tables.

THE DATABASE

In an IT system, all or most accounting records and data are stored in electronic form in the database. There are many different types of databases, but for the purpose of examining the risks to a database, we can assume that the database is a large disk storage for accounting and operating data. The existence of a database offers many operational advantages such as the increased efficiency of IT and easy retrieval of the data. However, the database also is an exposure area. It is a part of the IT system that is susceptible to security, availability, processing integrity, and confidentiality risks. This is true because any unauthorized access to the data can compromise their security and confidentiality and potentially interfere with the availability and normal processing of the IT system. Two examples illustrate these risk areas. An unauthorized user who gains access to the database can browse through the data, compromising the security and confidentiality of the data in the database. The unauthorized user could also destroy or erase data, thereby affecting the accuracy of processing and perhaps making processing unavailable, since some data has been erased.

The exposure of the database may be easier to understand if you compare an IT system with a paper-based system of some 50 years ago. If a person wanted to browse through payroll records back then, he would have to go to the filing cabinet, where the paper payroll records were kept, and use a key to open the file drawer. This means that the only possible unauthorized use of the data could have been by someone with physical access to the file cabinet and the key. However, a sophisticated IT system has data stored in a large database and usually has many computers networked to that database. Hence, it may be possible for someone, including a hacker who might be 3000 miles from the office, to read payroll data from any computer connected to the network. Therefore, the database may be more open to unauthorized access than the physical, paper records, because the database has so many more access points.

General controls such as those outlined in Exhibit 4-5 can help limit the exposure of the database. The use of these controls to authenticate users and limit hacking and network break-ins can reduce the chance of unauthorized access to the data. Again, the organization must determine which specific general controls are best suited to its IT system and may decide not to employ all of the general controls listed in Exhibit 4-5. Controls such as user IDs, passwords, authority tables, firewalls, and encryption are examples of controls that can limit exposures of the database.

THE DATABASE MANAGEMENT SYSTEM

The **database management system (DBMS)** is a software system that manages the interface between many users and the database. Exhibit 4-7 shows a diagram of multiple user groups accessing and sharing the database through the DBMS.

Exhibit 4-7
The Database Management System

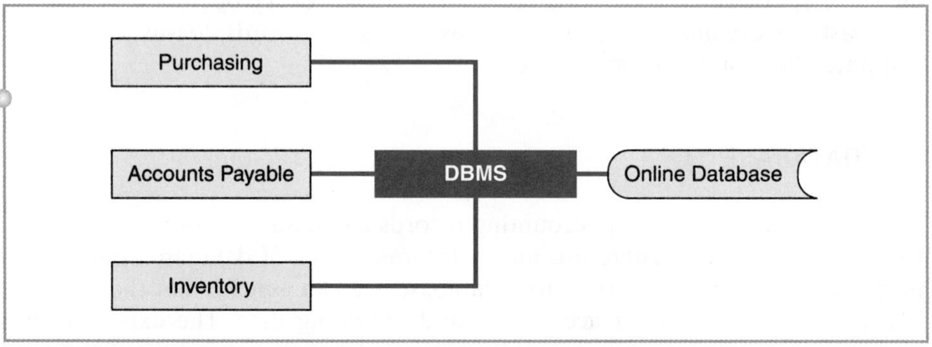

Users in all three application areas—purchasing, inventory, and accounts payable—must be able to access records of inventory items, cost, and other data related to inventory. The inventory data can be stored in the database and shared by all three user groups. Each individual user group may have a different level of access. For example, a purchasing user might need to add a new record when a purchase is placed. However, accounts payable users should not be able to add purchases, but should be able to read the records to determine which items should be paid. In addition, there are other users, such as accounts receivable users, who need access to customer and sales data, but have no need to access purchase records. The database management system manages this interface between users and data. It is the controller of access levels for different users.

As is true of the data, the DBMS poses security, confidentiality, availability, and processing integrity risk exposures. Since the database management system reads from and writes to the database, unauthorized access to the DBMS is another exposure area. An unauthorized user who is able to access the DBMS may browse, alter, or steal data. Authentication controls and controls over hacking and network break-ins can limit the chance of unauthorized access to the DBMS.

Both the data and the database management system are critical components that must be adequately guarded to protect business continuity. Loss of the data or alteration to the DBMS can halt operations. Therefore, the physical access, environmental, and business continuity controls are very important for these two components.

LANS AND WANS

A **local area network**, or **LAN,** is a computer network covering a small geographic area. In most cases, LANs are within a single building or a local group of buildings. Most LANs are sets of personal computers or workstations that are connected in order to share data and devices such as printers. Typically, the LAN is connected to a larger computer, the server, where data and some programs reside and are shared over the LAN. A group of LANs connected to each other to cover a wider geographic area is called a **wide area network,** or **WAN.**

Since LANs and WANs are connected into the larger network of servers and computers within a company, the LANs represent risk exposure areas. Anyone with access to a workstation on the LAN can access data and devices on the entire network within the organization. LANs represent an "entry point" where an unauthorized user may gain access to the network. LANs pose security, confidentiality, availability, and processing integrity risks. An unauthorized user on the LAN may browse, alter, or steal data and thereby compromise the security and confidentiality of data. Any unauthorized manipulation of data or programs through the LAN can affect the availability and processing integrity of the IT system.

In addition to the workstations, the network cabling also poses risks. Any of the network cables or connections represents a spot where an intruder could tap into the network for unauthorized access. The workstations on the LAN and all network connections should be protected by general controls that limit unauthorized users. Firewalls, encryption, and virtual private networks are important controls when the local area network is connected to networks outside the organization, such as the World Wide Web.

WIRELESS NETWORKS

Wireless networks have become very popular in organizations because they allow workers to connect to the network without being tethered to a network cable. A wireless network can save much time, cost, and effort in running network cables. In addition, it allows workers to roam and continue working via the network.

THE REAL WORLD

Boeing Co. uses wireless networks on the floor of the large shop where it manufactures airplanes. This wireless network with notebook computers allows Boeing workers to move around the plane while they are working and view engineering drawings or parts availability during the manufacturing processes. The employees do not have to walk to a desk or workstation, away from the manufacturing flow, to access these things. Wireless networks can make employees more efficient by allowing them to roam.

The wireless network represents another potential "entry point" of unauthorized access and therefore poses the four risk exposures of security, confidentiality, availability, and processing integrity. The wireless network has the same kind of exposures as described in the previous section about local area network. In fact, a wireless network is simply a special case of a LAN. In the wireless network, signals are transmitted through the air rather than over cables. These network signals are similar to radio signals; therefore, anyone who can receive those radio signals may gain access to the network. In fact, there are those who specifically take notebook computers and travel around or near company buildings, hoping to gain access to the company's wireless network. If they can intercept the network signals, they may be able to use the network to gain free Internet access at the least and hack into the company's network in the worst case. In fact, a popular activity is to find a company whose network signal bleeds outside the building to the sidewalk around it. Potential abusers of this network make identifiable chalk marks on the sidewalks so that others can find the network access. This activity has become known as "warchalking." A double curve symbol on the sidewalk indicates that you can access an open wireless network at that point. The legality and ethics of warchalking are debatable, but a company might avoid it by instituting proper controls, such as wired equivalency privacy (WEP) or wireless protected access (WPA), station set identifiers (SSID), and encrypted data.

THE INTERNET AND WORLD WIDE WEB

Many companies use the Internet to buy or sell via a website or to better serve customers and/or employees. A later chapter on e-business will focus on the specifics of web-based commerce. This section provides only basics about business use of the Internet so that risk exposures and controls can be examined. While there are many advantages for companies, using the Internet poses security, confidentiality, availability, and processing integrity risks. In addition, the existence of e-commerce in an organization poses online privacy risks, which are described in a later chapter.

The Internet connection required to conduct web-based business can open the company network to unauthorized users, hackers, and other network break-in artists. The sheer volume of users of the World Wide Web dramatically increases the potential number of hackers or unauthorized users who may attempt to access an organization's network of computers. An unauthorized user can compromise security and confidentiality, and affect availability and processing integrity by altering data or software or by inserting virus or worm programs.

A typical network configuration for Internet connection to a company's network was presented in Exhibit 4-6. Notice in the figure that there is a separate computer serving as the web server. This computer web server is isolated from the company network via a firewall. The exhibit shows a dual firewall system, with a firewall between the Internet and the web server, and a firewall between the web server and the organization's network. The use of dual firewalls can help prevent hackers or unauthorized users from accessing the organization's internal network of computers.

TELECOMMUTING WORKERS

An increasing number of employees in the United States work from home, using some type of network connection to the office. This work arrangement is commonly called **telecommuting** or teleworking. The International Telework Association and Council[6] reports that telecommuting work arrangements are used by approximately 22% of workers over the age of 18. Telecommuting can offer benefits to both employer and employee. The employee gains flexibility and

[6]The website of the association is www.workfromanywhere.org.

other advantages of being at home, while the employer may save office space and overhead expenses for the worker. The potential disadvantages of telecommuting are that the teleworker loses daily face-to-face interaction and may miss meetings with other employees or supervisors.

Telecommuting workers cause two sources of risk exposures for their organizations. First, the necessary network equipment and cabling can be an "entry point" for hackers and unauthorized users. Second, the teleworker's computer is also an "entry point" for potential unauthorized users; it is not under the direct control of the organization, since it is located in the teleworker's home. Therefore, the organization must rely on the teleworker to maintain appropriate security over that computer and to correctly use firewalls and virus software updates to keep security current. These two "entry points" pose security, confidentiality, availability, and processing integrity risks. The organization's security policy should address the security expectations of workers who telecommute, and such workers should connect to the company network via a virtual private network.

ELECTRONIC DATA INTERCHANGE

Electronic data interchange (EDI) is the company-to-company transfer of standard business documents in electronic form. EDI is widely used by businesses to buy and sell goods and materials. Rather than mailing copies of purchase orders and invoices, companies send these kinds of standard business documents back and forth electronically. To conduct EDI with business partners, a company must use a dedicated network, a value added network, or the Internet. The specific details and advantages of EDI are explained in a later chapter on e-business.

Regardless of the type of network used, the EDI network entails security, confidentiality, availability, and processing integrity risks, as it is another "entry point" for unauthorized users or hackers. EDI transactions must be properly guarded and controlled by general controls including authentication, computer logs, and network break-in controls. Exhibit 4-5 lists these controls and the corresponding risks.

APPLICATION SOFTWARE AND APPLICATION CONTROLS (STUDY OBJECTIVE 5)

Applications software accomplishes end user tasks such as word processing, spreadsheets, database maintenance, and accounting functions. All application software runs on top of the operating system software and uses the basic input, output, and data storage functions of the operating system. Any accounting software is considered application software. Application software represents another "entry point" through which unauthorized users or hackers could gain access. As is true of the eight exposure areas described so far, the application software has security, confidentiality, availability, and processing integrity risks. Many of the general controls listed in Exhibit 4-5 can help minimize those risks. For example, authentication of the user through user IDs and passwords can reduce the chance of unauthorized access. Application software processes inputs into accounting information and therefore carries specific processing integrity risks not inherent in the eight previous IT components described. The specific processing risks are inaccurate, incomplete, or unsecure data as it is input, is processed, or becomes output. Another risk of application software is the addition and processing of unauthorized transactions. For these specific risks, application controls should be part of accounting applications.

Many of the general controls in Exhibit 4-5 can help limit access to application software; specific application controls should also be incorporated. **Application controls** are internal controls over the input, processing, and output of accounting applications. Exhibit 4-1 illustrated that application controls apply to specific accounting applications such as payroll, sales processing, or accounts receivable processing. In any of these accounting applications, data are entered through some method of input, those data are processed, and outputs such as reports or checks are produced. Application controls intended to improve the accuracy, completeness, and security of input, processing, and output are described as follows:

1. **Input controls** are intended to ensure the accuracy and completeness of data input procedures and the resulting data.
2. **Processing controls** are intended to ensure the accuracy and completeness of processing that occurs in accounting applications.
3. **Output controls** are intended to help ensure the accuracy, completeness, and security of outputs that result from application processing.

INPUT CONTROLS

In IT systems, data must be converted from human readable form to computer readable form. This process is called data input. Data can be input into a computer application in many different ways. For example, data can be keyed into blank fields on a computer screen from a keyboard; data can be read from bar codes; or data can be received electronically via EDI or the web. No matter the manner of input, controls should be in place to ensure that the data entered are accurate and complete. You probably know the old computer acronym GIGO, which stands for "Garbage in, garbage out"—a short-hand method of saying that if you enter incorrect data, you will obviously get incorrect results. Input controls are intended to prevent or detect the "garbage in" so as to avoid incorrect output, or "garbage out."

To illustrate some input controls, Exhibit 4-8 presents a Microsoft Dynamics GP® screen capture of the input screen to add a new employee to the payroll records.

As the data input person prepares to enter data for a new employee, input controls should be in place to ensure the authorization, accuracy, and completeness of that data input. These input controls are of four types:

1. Source document controls
2. Standard procedures for data preparation and error handling
3. Programmed edit checks
4. Control totals and reconciliation

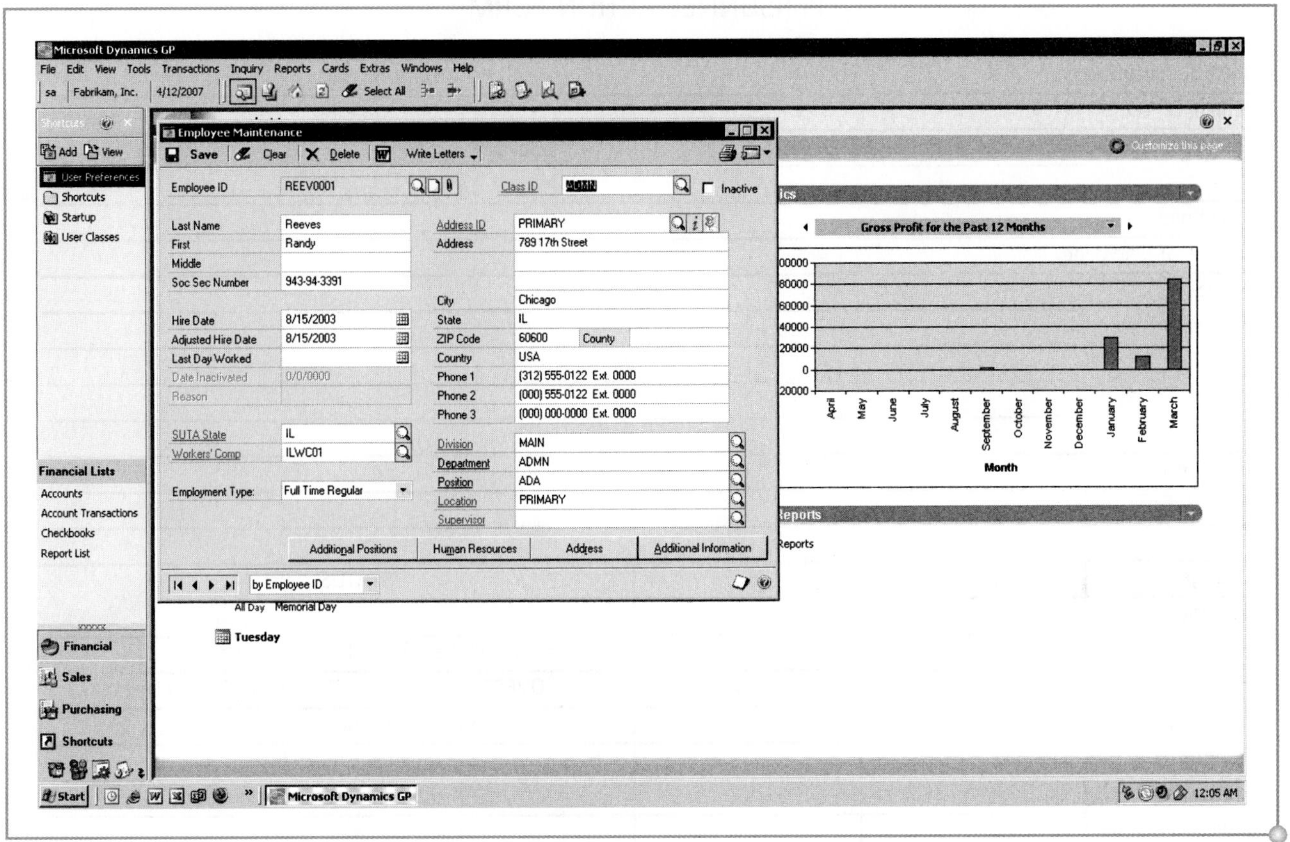

Exhibit 4-8
Employee Maintenance Screen in Microsoft Dynamics GP®

Source Document Controls

In many IT systems and applications, data are keyed in to input screens similar to the Microsoft Dynamics GP® example in Exhibit 4-8. Before those data can be keyed in, the data must be captured and recorded on a source document. A **source document** is the paper form used to capture and record the original data of an accounting transaction. For example, before filling in the blank fields in Exhibit 4-8, the data entry person needs to know the new employee's name, address, hire date, and many other pieces of information. For new employees, the source document would be a personnel action form, a sample of which appears as Exhibit 4-9.

The data entry person often refers to a copy of the source document to enter the data into the blank fields on the screen. It should also be noted that many IT systems do not use source documents. In cases where the input is automatic, such as web-based sales, no source documents are generated. Where no source documents are used, the general controls described earlier, such as computer logging of transactions and making and keeping backup files, become more important. Where source documents are used, to minimize the potential for errors, incomplete data, or unauthorized transactions as data are entered from source documents, several source document controls should be used.

Form design: Both the source document and the input screen should be well designed so that they are easy to understand and use, logically organized into

FORM DATE 6/12/2007

PERSONNEL ACTION FORM

Part A–Employee | **Date of Hire**

Employee Name	Birth Date
Address	Gender
	SS#

Telephone

In Case of Emergency Notify

Name

Address

Home Phone | Work Phone

Relationship | Cell

Part B–Employer

Change	**From**	**To**	**STATUS**	
Job Title				
Pay Rate			Please check the status of the employee:	
Hourly			**OVERTIME STATUS** ❒ Exempt ❒ Non Exempt	
Billing Rate			❒	Administrative
Salary			❒	Direct with benefits
Status (FT/PT)			❒	Indirect with no benefits
Project Assigned				

Reasons for Change

_______ New Hire Effective _______

_______ Merit Increase Effective Date _______

_______ Project Transfer to _______ Effective Date _______

_______ Termination_______ (Date)

_______ Other (please explain below)

Comments:

*NOTE-2 SIGNATURES REQUIRED

Payroll change requested by: _______

Date: _______

Reviewed and authorized by: _______

Date: _______

SAFETY REQUIREMENTS:

VIEWED SAFETY FILMS:

	TEST SCORE
HAZCOM	
CONFINED SPACE	_______
PERSONAL PROTECTIVE EQUIPMENT	_______
BLOODBORNE PATHOGENS	_______
SCAFFOLD	_______

THIS FORM WILL NOT PROCESS WITHOUT SCORES:

Exhibit 4-9
Personnel Action Form

groups of related data. For example, notice that employee name and address blanks, or fields, are located very close to each other, since they are logically related. Source documents should have clear and direct instructions embedded into the form. The personnel action form in Exhibit 4-9 has the following instruction line: "Please check the status of the employee." Finally, the source document design and input screen design should match each other. Ideally, the fields on both forms should be the same and the fields should be in the same order. The closer the source document matches the input screen, the easier it is for the data entry person to complete the input screen without uncertainty and errors.

In many applications, it is not possible to fit all necessary data on a single input screen. This problem is solved by having several related input screens to enter all data. Exhibit 4-10 illustrates a second screen for new employees that allows the input of pay rate data on a pay code screen.

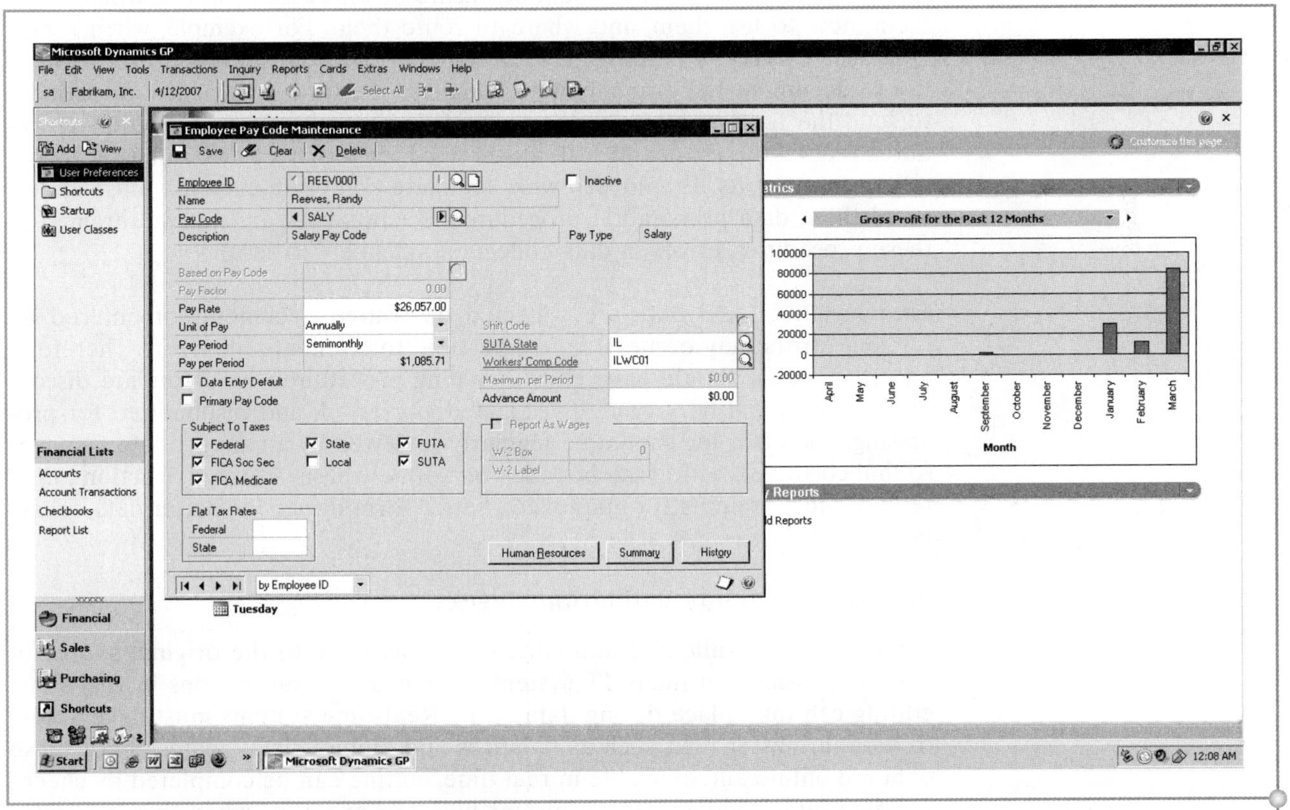

Exhibit 4-10
Related Input Screens for a New Employee

Form authorization and control: The source document should contain an area for authorization by the appropriate manager, such as the bottom left of the form in Exhibit 4-9. The source document forms should be prenumbered and used in sequence. Prenumbering allows for ongoing monitoring and control over blank source documents. If the source document sequence is monitored to ensure that there are no missing numbers in the sequence, most likely no transactions will be lost. Finally, blank source documents should be controlled by being kept in a secure area so as to prevent their being misused to initiate an unauthorized transaction.

Retention of source documents: After data from source documents have been keyed into the computer, the source documents should be retained and filed in a manner that allows for easy retrieval. Filed source documents serve as the historical, original records of transactions and can be used to reconstruct transactions if necessary, or can be used to answer questions that arise about transaction processing. These source documents are part of the audit trail. The audit trail, defined in Chapter 3, is defined here also as a reminder. The audit trail recreates the details of individual transactions at each stage of the business process in order to establish whether proper accounting procedures for the transaction were performed.

Standard Procedures for Data Input

Data preparation: The procedures to collect and prepare source documents are called **data preparation** procedures. Without well-defined source data preparation procedures, employees would be unsure of which forms to use, when to use them, how to use them, and where to route them. For example, when a new employee is hired, the human resources department must know which form to use to document the hiring, how to complete the form, and which department to send the form to after it is completed. The standard data collection procedures reduce the chance of lost, misdirected, or incorrect data collection from source documents. Employees who complete source documents must understand these data preparation procedures. If employees are not well-trained in these procedures, errors in data collection are likely to result.

Error handling: As data are collected on source documents or entered on screens, errors may occur. It is not possible to eliminate all errors. Therefore, an organization should have error handling procedures. As errors are discovered, they should be logged, investigated, corrected, and resubmitted for processing. The error log should be regularly reviewed by an appropriate manager so that corrective action can be taken on a timely basis. Corrective action might require more training for employees, better form design, or better data collection procedures.

Programmed Input Validation Checks

Data should be validated and edited to be as close to the original source of data as possible. In many IT systems that process transactions in real time, editing can take place during data entry. Real-time systems must have access to data in master files, such as balances and employee pay rates. Since these data are online and available in real time, editing can be completed by checking data input against data in master files. For example, when the data entry person enters an employee number in the corresponding field, a real-time system would find the employee record and fill in the appropriate fields with the employee data such as name, address, and pay rate. If an invalid employee number is entered, the real-time system can alert the user that the entry is invalid. In addition to real-time data editing, the application software can include input validation checks to prevent or detect input errors. These checks are pre-programmed into accounting application software and are intended to check a field, or fields, for errors. Exhibit 4-2 illustrated an example of an input validation called a validity check. Input validation checks include the following:

1. Field check
2. Validity check
3. Limit check
4. Range check
5. Reasonableness check
6. Completeness check
7. Sign check
8. Sequence check
9. Self-checking digit

Any particular field may require only numbers, only letters, or a combination of numbers and letters. A pay rate field should accept only numbers, while the last name field should be only letters. A **field check** examines a field to determine whether the appropriate type (alpha or numeric) of data was entered. If the wrong data type is entered, the application should reject that data and alert the user with an error message. There are some fields, such as inventory part numbers, that might be a combination of alpha and numeric data. For those fields, a field check would not be an appropriate input validation. A **validity check** examines a field to ensure that the data entry in the field is valid compared with a preexisting list of acceptable values. For example, there may be only two choices for acceptable values for a field named Pay Type: "hourly" and "salary". The application can be pre-programmed to check input into that field to make sure it is either "h" or "s." Any other values should be rejected as not valid, and the user should see an error message on the screen if the data is not valid. Exhibit 4-2 shows such a message. Limit checks and range checks are very similar. Both check field input against a preestablished limit or limits. A **limit check** has only an upper limit; for example, hours worked cannot exceed a value of as 70 hours per week. Hours worked would never be negative, and it is conceivable that it could be zero in some cases. Therefore, there is no need for a lower limit in that field, and a limit check would be appropriate. A **range check** has both an upper and a lower limit. Some fields, such as quantity requested, may logically suggest that the entry cannot be less than 1. Therefore, a range check could be pre-programmed into the application to accept values between one and some upper limit. A **reasonableness check** compares the value in a field with those fields to which it is related to determine whether the value is reasonable. For example, pay rate could be compared with job category code. A **completeness check** assesses the critical fields in an input screen to make sure that a value is in those fields. For example, when a new employee is processed, a Social Security number must be entered. The completeness check scans only to make sure that a value has been entered; it cannot ensure that the *correct* value was entered. A **sign check** examines a field to determine that it has the appropriate sign, positive or negative. All of these checks examine a field or fields against some preestablished expected values.

Programmed input checks can be used not only for data input that is keyed in but also for some forms of electronic input such as EDI transactions or web-based sales. In the case of web sales, the customer enters data into fields, where programmed input validations can ensure proper input. In EDI transactions, data are imported into the application software through the EDI translation software. These programmed checks can help confirm the accuracy and completeness of imported data.

The programmed input checks just described are appropriate for real-time or batch systems. The final two programmed input validation checks discussed next are more appropriate for transactions that are processed in batches. In batch systems with legacy software and hardware, the master files are not necessarily always online and/or available in real time. Transactions are entered and edited as a batch and run against a master file as a batch. Therefore, the batch of transactions must be in the same order as the master file. For payroll, both transaction and master files are probably sorted by employee number. A **sequence check** ensures that the batch of transactions is sorted in order, but does not help find missing transactions because it checks only sequence, not completeness. In any particular pay period, there may be employees who will not be paid perhaps because they are on a monthly, rather than bi-weekly, pay period, or they may be on unpaid leave. The sequence check just skips over the missing employee number and verifies only that the remaining employees in the batch are sorted in the correct order. A **self-checking digit** is an extra digit added to a coded identification number, determined by a mathematical algorithm. For example, if a vendor number is to be 6453, then an extra digit is added to the end to make it 64532, where the "2" is generated by a mathematical formula. For any data entry tasks, the vendor number 64532 is always used. During an edit run, the computer recomputes the same formula to ensure that the self-checking digit still equals 2. If the data entry person accidentally typed 65432 rather than 64532, the self-checking digit would not match and the input could be flagged as erroneous.

Control Totals and Reconciliation

Control totals are useful in any IT system in which transactions are processed in batches. **Control totals** are subtotals of selected fields for an entire batch of transactions. For a batch of similar transactions, such as payroll transactions for a pay period, control totals can be calculated before data are processed. For example, the total number of hours worked on all time cards can be summed. After the time card data are keyed into the application software, a printed report can provide the computer-generated subtotal of hours worked. This reconciliation of manually-generated subtotals to computer-generated subtotals should result in the same total from both sources. If they do not agree, this indicates that an error has occurred, such as adding extra transactions, skipping transactions, or entering the wrong hours for one or more transactions. Control totals are of three types: record counts, batch totals, and hash totals. **Record counts** are a simple count of the number of records processed. The records can be counted prior to and after input, and the totals should agree. **Batch totals** are totals of financial data, such as total gross pay or total federal tax deducted. **Hash totals** are totals of fields that have no apparent logical reason to be added. For example, the summation of all Social Security numbers in a batch of payroll transactions would provide a control total for comparison, but the total would have no other practical use. Both batch and hash totals are subtotals of certain fields.

PROCESSING CONTROLS

Processing controls are intended to prevent, detect, or correct errors that occur during the processing in an application. First and foremost, it is important to ensure that the application software has no errors. Software that incorrectly processes data can be dangerous, because it can consistently make the same errors and thus cause many errors in the data. To verify the accuracy of application software, the company should be sure the software is tested prior to implementation; and it must be regularly tested thereafter. Application software can be tested by reprocessing actual data with known results or by processing test data. Whether actual or test data are used, the results of processing the data are compared with known results to make sure that there are no errors in processing.

Many input controls also serve as processing controls. Control totals, limit and range tests, and reasonableness and sign tests can prevent or detect processing errors. Control totals such as record counts, batch totals, and hash totals can be reconciled during stages of processing to verify the accuracy and completeness of processing. This reconciliation of control totals at various stages of the processing is called **run-to-run control totals.** During processing, some calculations such as addition or multiplication must occur. Limit, range, and reasonableness checks can be used to ensure that the results of these mathematical manipulations are within expected ranges or limits.

Computer logs of transactions processed, production run logs, and error listings can be regularly examined to prevent, detect, and correct other errors. These logs allow management to find patterns of errors and take action to correct erroneous procedures or application software.

OUTPUT CONTROLS

Many outputs in an IT system are reports from the various applications. An example of an output report is a payroll check register. There are two primary objectives of output controls: to assure the accuracy and completeness of the output, and to properly manage the safekeeping of output reports to ascertain that security and confidentiality of the information is maintained. To ensure accuracy and completeness, the output can be reconciled to control totals. In addition, it is extremely important that users of the reports examine the reports for completeness and reasonableness. Users of the reports are the most familiar with the nature of the output reports and are therefore most likely to notice if there are errors. Any errors detected must be logged and corrected. Management should watch for patterns of errors and follow up with corrective action.

Output reports contain data that should not fall into the wrong hands, as much of the information is confidential or proprietary. Therefore, an organization must maintain procedures to protect output from unauthorized access, in the form of written guidelines and procedures for output distribution. In the case of sensitive data, the procedures might include a requirement that users sign off on the receipt of outputs. Under this procedure, users must sign a log to indicate that they received the output, and the output is not released without the signature. The organization should also establish procedures to guide the retention and disposal of output, such as how output reports are to be stored and the length of time they are to be retained. Outputs scheduled for disposal should be properly removed, depending on the nature of the output. Sensitive output reports should be shredded.

In many cases, the output from IT systems is viewed on a screen rather than examined from a printed copy. In the case of screen outputs, the authentication of user controls described earlier help protect the security and confidentiality of output. Authentication controls help assure that only authorized users have access to such output.

ETHICAL ISSUES IN IT SYSTEMS (STUDY OBJECTIVE 6)

A strong set of internal controls can assist in discouraging unethical behavior such as fraud and abuse. Management has a duty to maintain internal controls over IT systems for several reasons. Mainly, managers have a stewardship responsibility to safeguard assets and funds entrusted to them by the owners of the organization, and meeting this responsibility requires that controls be in place to safeguard assets. IT systems themselves, such as computer hardware and software, are assets that must be protected from theft, abuse, or misuse. Without proper controls on IT systems, the computer systems can be easily misused by outsiders or employees.

THE REAL WORLD

An interesting case of computer abuse occurred at a state agency in Kentucky. A news article included the following details:[7]

> Gov. Paul Patton on Wednesday blamed the Transportation Cabinet for laxity that allowed its computers to be hacked and allegedly used for viewing pornography. Government-wide policies and procedures to prevent those very occurrences were not followed, Patton said in a joint statement with Aldona Valicenti, his chief information officer. The statement came one day after state Auditor Ed Hatchett reported that hackers, apparently from France, used the Transportation Cabinet's computers to store pirated computer files, including movies and games, and to serve as host for a chat room.
>
> An audit also showed that 35 state computers were used to gain access to pornographic Web sites 6,000 times on four randomly chosen days.

While such cases are somewhat amusing, they expose a serious misuse of government funds. The taxpayers of Kentucky paid for computers that were being diverted from their intended use. As indicated in the article, the agency managers have a duty to enforce policies that protect the computers and the IT systems. Similarly, a company has a duty to its owners to enforce policies and controls to prevent misuse.

In addition to computer assets being misused, access to IT systems may give unauthorized users access to other assets. Management must try to prevent theft conducted through the IT system, such as theft accomplished by fraudulent-transaction data entries. Both misuse of computers and theft through the computer systems are unethical behaviors that management must discourage through proper internal controls.

[7] "Patton Blames Agency for PC breach," *Cincinnati Enquirer*, July 31, 2003.

Besides fraud, there are many kinds of unethical behaviors related to computers, such as the following:

- Misuse of confidential customer information stored in an IT system
- Theft of data, such as credit card information, by hackers
- Employee use of IT system hardware and software for personal use or personal gain
- Using company e-mail to send offensive, threatening, or sexually explicit material

The controls described in this chapter can help set an environment in which many of these unethical behaviors are discouraged. Authentication controls, network break-in controls, and computer logging of use can help prevent or detect such behaviors.

SUMMARY OF STUDY OBJECTIVES

An overview of internal controls for IT systems. Threats and risks that interrupt or stop computer operations can be severely damaging to the organization. Not only can they disrupt or shut down normal operations, but they also can lead to incorrect or incomplete accounting information. There are three important areas of knowledge regarding threats and risks to IT systems: The first is the description of the general controls and application controls that should exist in IT systems. The second is the type and nature of risks in IT systems. Third, and most important, is the recognition of how these controls can be used to reduce the risks to IT systems.

General controls for IT systems. These are controls on the overall IT system and can be categorized by the following risk areas they are intended to lessen: unauthorized access; hacking and other network break-ins; exposures in organizational structure; threats in the physical environment and physical security of the system; and disruption to business continuity.

General controls from a Trust Services Principles perspective. The AICPA Trust Services Principles define five objectives for IT controls: security, availability, processing integrity, confidentiality, and online privacy. Security means that the system is protected against unauthorized (physical and logical) access. Availability means the system is available for operation and use as committed or agreed. Processing integrity means that the system processing is complete, accurate, timely, and authorized. Online privacy means that personal information obtained as a result of e-commerce is collected, used, disclosed, and retained as committed or agreed. Confidentiality means that information designated as confidential is protected as committed or agreed.

Hardware and software exposures in IT systems. The various hardware and software parts of IT systems are sources of risk or exposure. Examples of these risks are altered, deleted, or stolen data; systems that are shut down or rendered unusable; and virus or worm infections. The parts of the IT system that have these potential exposures are the operating system, the database, the database management system (DBMS), a local area network (LAN), a wireless network, e-business systems, telecommuting workers, electronic data interchange (EDI) systems, and application software.

Application software and application controls. These are input controls, processing controls, and output controls. Input controls are intended to prevent, detect, or correct errors during data input; thus, they should help ensure the accuracy and completeness of any data that are input. Processing controls are intended to ensure accurate and complete processing. Output controls are intended to ensure that output is properly distributed and disposed of, and that it is accurate and complete.

Ethical issues in IT systems. IT systems and computers within IT systems can be used unethically. Examples of unethical behavior with IT systems are misuse of confidential customer information, theft of customer or company data, employee use of IT systems for personal use, and misuse of company e-mail systems to send offensive, threatening, or sexually explicit material.

KEY TERMS

Antivirus software
Application controls
Authentication of users
Authority table
Availability
Backup data
Batch total
Biometric device
Business continuity planning
Completeness check
Computer log
Confidentiality risks
Control totals
Data preparation procedures
Database administrator
Database management system (DBMS)
Disaster recovery plan
Electronic data interchange (EDI)
Emergency power supplies (EPS)
Encryption
Field check
Firewall
General controls
Hash totals
Input controls
Intrusion detection
IT governance committee
Limit check
Local area network (LAN)
Log in
Nonrepudiation
Off-site backup
Online privacy
Operating system
Operations personnel
Output controls
Password
Penetration testing
Processing controls
Processing integrity
Programmers
Public key encryption
Range check
Reasonableness check
Record counts
Redundant array of independent disks (RAID)
Redundant servers
Run-to-run control totals
Secure sockets layer (SSL)
Security
Security token
Self-checking digit

Sequence check
Service set identifier (SSID)
Sign check
Smart card
Source document
SSL
Symmetric encryption
System development life cycle (SDLC)
Systems analyst
Telecommuting
Two factor authentication
Uninterruptible power supplies (UPS)
User ID
User profile
Validity check
Virtual private network (VPN)
Virus
Vulnerability assessment
Wide area network (WAN)
Wired equivalency privacy (WEP)
Wireless protected access (WPA)

END OF CHAPTER MATERIAL

CONCEPT CHECK

1. Internal controls that apply overall to the IT system are called
   a. overall controls.
   b. technology controls.
   c. application controls.
   d. general controls.
2. In entering client contact information in the computerized database of a telemarketing business, a clerk erroneously entered nonexistent area codes for a block of new clients. This error rendered the block of contacts useless to the company. Which of the following would most likely have led to discovery of this error at the time of entry into the company's computerized system?
   a. limit check
   b. validity check
   c. sequence check
   d. record count
3. Which of the following is not a control intended to authenticate users?
   a. user log-in
   b. security token
   c. encryption
   d. biometric devices
4. Management of an Internet retail company is concerned about the possibility of computer data eavesdropping and wiretapping, and wants to maintain the confidentiality of its information as it is transmitted. The company should make use of
   a. data encryption.
   b. redundant servers.
   c. input controls.
   d. password codes.

5. An IT governance committee has several responsibilities. Which of the following is least likely to be a responsibility of the IT governance committee?
   a. Develop and maintain the database and ensure adequate controls over the database.
   b. Develop, monitor, and review security policies.
   c. Oversee and prioritize changes to IT systems.
   d. Align IT investments to business strategy.
6. AICPA Trust Services Principles describe five categories of IT risks and controls. Which of these five categories would best be described by the statement, "The system is protected against unauthorized access"?
   a. security
   b. confidentiality
   c. processing integrity
   d. availability
7. The risk that an unauthorized user would shut down systems within the IT system is a(n)
   a. security risk.
   b. availability risk.
   c. processing integrity risk.
   d. confidentiality risk.
8. The risk of an unauthorized user gaining access is likely to be a risk for which of the following areas?
   a. telecommuting workers
   b. Internet
   c. wireless networks
   d. all of the above
9. Which programmed input validation check compares the value in a field with related fields to determine whether the value is appropriate?
   a. completeness check
   b. validity check
   c. reasonableness check
   d. completeness check
10. Which programmed input validation check determines whether the appropriate type of data, either alphabetic or numeric, was entered?
    a. completeness check
    b. validity check
    c. reasonableness check
    d. field check
11. Which programmed input validation makes sure that a value was entered in all of the critical fields?
    a. completeness check
    b. validity check
    c. reasonableness check
    d. field check

12. Which control total is the total of field values that are added for control purposes, but not added for any other purpose?
    a. record count
    b. hash total
    c. batch total
    d. field total
13. A company has the following invoices in a batch:

Invoice no.	Product I.D.	Quantity	Unit price
401	H42	150	$30.00
402	K56	200	$25.00
403	H42	250	$10.00
404	L27	300	$5.00

    Which of the following numbers represents a valid record count?
    a. 1
    b. 4
    c. 70
    d. 900

DISCUSSION QUESTIONS

14. (SO 1) What is the difference between general controls and application controls?
15. (SO 1) Is it necessary to have both general controls and application controls to have a strong system of internal controls?
16. (SO 2) What kinds of risks or problems can occur if an organization does not authenticate users of its IT systems?
17. (SO 2) Explain the general controls that can be used to authenticate users.
18. (SO 2) What is two-factor authentication with regard to smart cards or security tokens?
19. (SO 2) Why should an organization be concerned about repudiation of sales transactions by the customer?
20. (SO 2) A firewall should inspect incoming and outgoing data to limit the passage of unauthorized data flow. Is it possible for a firewall to restrict too much data flow?
21. (SO 2) How does encryption assist in limiting unauthorized access to data?
22. (SO 2) What kinds of risks exist in wireless networks that can be limited by WEP, WPA, and proper use of SSID?
23. (SO 2) Describe some recent news stories you have seen or heard regarding computer viruses.
24. (SO 2) What is the difference between business continuity planning and disaster recovery planning? How are these two concepts related?
25. (SO 2) How can a redundant array of independent disks (RAID) help protect the data of an organization?

26. (SO 2) What kinds of duties should be segregated in IT systems?
27. (SO 2) Why do you think the uppermost managers should serve on the IT governance committee?
28. (SO 4) Why should accountants be concerned about risks inherent in a complex software system such as the operating system?
29. (SO 4) Why is it true that increasing the number of LANs or wireless networks within an organization increases risks?
30. (SO 4) What kinds of risks are inherent when an organization stores its data in a database and database management system?
31. (SO 4) How do telecommunicating workers pose IT system risks?
32. (SO 4) What kinds of risks are inherent when an organization begins conducting business over the Internet?
33. (SO 4) Why is it true that the use of EDI means that trading partners may need to grant access to each other's files?
34. (SO 5) Why is it critical that source documents be easy to use and complete?
35. (SO 5) Explain some examples of input validation checks that you have noticed when filling out forms on websites you have visited.
36. (SO 5) How can control totals serve as input, processing, and output controls?
37. (SO 5) What dangers exist related to computer output such as reports?

BRIEF EXERCISES

38. (SO 2, SO 5) Categorize each of the following as either a general control or an application control:
    a. validity check
    b. encryption
    c. security token
    d. batch total
    e. output distribution
    f. vulnerability assessment
    g. firewall
    h. antivirus software
39. (SO 5) Each of the given situations is independent of the other. For each, list the programmed input validation check that would prevent or detect the error.
    a. The zip code field was left blank on an input screen requesting a mailing address.
    b. A state abbreviation of "NX" was entered in the state field.
    c. A number was accidentally entered in the last name field.
    d. For a weekly payroll, the hours entry in the "hours worked" field was 400.
    e. A pay rate of $50.00 per hour was entered for a new employee. The job code indicates an entry-level receptionist.
40. (SO 3) For each AICPA Trust Services Principles category shown, list a potential risk and a corresponding control that would lessen the risk. An example is provided.

EXAMPLE

Security:

Risk: A hacker could alter data.

Control: Use a firewall to limit unauthorized access.

In a similar manner, list a risk and control in each of the following categories:

a. security
b. availability
c. processing integrity
d. confidentiality

41. (SO 4) For each of the following parts of an IT system of a company, write a one-sentence description of how unauthorized users could use this as an "entry point":
    a. a local area network (LAN)
    b. a wireless network
    c. a telecommuting worker
    d. a company website to sell products
42. (SO 5) Application controls include input, processing, and output controls. One type of input control is source document controls. Briefly explain the importance of each of the following source document controls:
    a. form design
    b. form authorization and control
    c. retention of source documents
43. (SO 5) Explain how control totals such as record counts, batch totals, and hash totals serve as input controls, processing controls, and output controls.
44. (SO 6) Briefly explain a situation at your home, university, or job in which you think somebody used computers unethically. Be sure to include an explanation of why you think it was unethical.

PROBLEMS

45. (SO 1, SO 2) Explain why an organization should establish and enforce policies for its IT systems in the following areas regarding the use of passwords for log-in:
    a. length of password
    b. the use of numbers or symbols in passwords
    c. using common words or names as passwords
    d. rotation of passwords
    e. writing passwords on paper or sticky notes
46. (SO 2) The use of smart cards or tokens is called two-factor authentication. Answer the following questions, assuming that the company you work for uses smart cards or tokens for two-factor authentication.

    Required:

    a. What do you think the advantages and disadvantages would be for you as a user?

b. What do you think the advantages and disadvantages would be for the company?

47. (SO 4) Many IT professionals feel that wireless networks pose the highest risks in a company's network system.

    Required:

    a. Why do you think this is true?
    b. Which general controls can help reduce these risks?

48. (SO 5) Control totals include batch totals, hash totals, and record counts. Which of these totals would be useful in preventing or detecting IT system input and processing errors or fraud described as follows?
    a. A payroll clerk accidentally entered the same time card twice.
    b. The accounts payable department overlooked an invoice and did not enter it into the system because it was stuck to another invoice.
    c. A systems analyst was conducting payroll fraud by electronically adding to his "hours worked" field during the payroll computer run.
    d. To create a fictitious employee, a payroll clerk removed a time card for a recently terminated employee and inserted a new time card with the same hours worked.

49. (SO 5) Explain how each of the following input validation checks can prevent or detect errors:
    a. field check
    b. validity check
    c. limit check
    d. range check
    e. reasonableness check
    f. completeness check
    g. sign check
    h. sequence check
    i. self-checking digit

50. (SO 2) The IT governance committee should comprise top level managers. Describe why you think that is important. What problems are likely to arise with regard to IT systems if the top level managers are not involved in IT governance committees?

51. (SO 2) Using a search engine, look up the term "penetration testing." Describe the software tools you find that are intended to achieve penetration testing. Describe the types of systems that penetration testing is conducted upon.

52. (SO 3) Visit the AICPA website at www.aicpa.org. Search for the terms "WebTrust" and "SysTrust." Describe these services and the role of Trust Services Principles in these services.

53. (SO 2) Using a search site, look up the terms "disaster recovery," along with "9/11." The easiest way to search for both terms together is to type into the search box the following: "disaster recovery" "9/11." Find at least two examples of companies that have changed their disaster recovery planning

since the terrorist attacks on the World Trade Center on September 11, 2001. Describe how these companies changed their disaster recovery plans after the terrorist attacks.

54. (SO 5) Go to any website that sells goods. Examples would be BestBuy, Staples, and J. Crew. Pretend that you wish to place an order on the site you choose and complete the order screens for your pretend order. **Do not** finalize the order; otherwise, you will have to pay for the goods. As you complete the order screens, attempt to enter incorrect data for fields or blanks that you complete. Describe the programmed input validation checks that you find that prevent or detect incorrect data input.

CASES

55. The EnviroCons Company, a small business with 100 employees, sells environmental consulting services to large companies around the United States. It employs 40 consultants who travel the United States, assisting clients with environmental compliance. To conduct business, the company must maintain a website so that potential customers can learn of its services and contact its consultants. The company maintains an internal network with an extensive database of environmental regulations and environmental data. Each of its consultants carries a laptop computer; the company has installed a wireless network so that when the consultants are in the office they can easily connect to the company's network. Consultants visit off-site clients much of the time, but while on-site consulting with clients, they must use their laptops to access the company database to look up environmental regulations and data.

    Required:

    a. From the list of general controls shown in Exhibit 4-5, list each authentication and hacking control that you think the EnviroCons Company should have in place.

    b. Explain how each control that you list can prevent IT related risks for EnviroCons.

    c. Are there any general controls that you think would not be cost-beneficial?

56. Plaskor Inc. is a manufacturer of plastic knobs for lawn and garden tractors and lawn mowers. The company has always used traditional paper-based systems to conduct transactions with its customers. For example, when a customer ordered knobs, Plaskor personnel filled out a sales order acknowledgement and mailed it to the customer. Plaskor would like to expand its business opportunities by becoming a supplier, as management believes the company can manufacture interior parts for automotive manufacturers. Automotive manufacturing companies use EDI extensively as they transact business with suppliers and expect any suppliers that they buy from to have the appropriate systems to conduct transactions via EDI. Therefore, Plaskor must buy or develop systems that would allow it to use Internet EDI.

    Required:

    a. Describe the extra IT system risks that Plaskor should consider as it evaluates whether to buy or develop an Internet EDI system.

    b. Describe the IT internal controls that should be incorporated into an Internet EDI system.

57. In the early days of computers, Jerry Schneider was a very enterprising young man who, while attending UCLA, was also conducting a major fraud against Pacific Telephone and Telegraph Company (PT&T). At the height of his fraud in 1971, he was collecting approximately $30,000 a day from PT&T. In total, it was estimated that he stole as much as $900,000 from PT&T. Jerry's fraud was fairly simple in concept, but he did work very hard at it. In 1969, he began a legitimate company refurbishing phone equipment for PT&T. As a supplier to PT&T, he became familiar with some of their operations. He also spent much time digging through dumpsters at PT&T and was able to salvage many reports that helped him understand the inventory and ordering systems. He purchased a telephone truck at an auction, and since he was a valid supplier to PT&T, he had keys to the loading dock. He began tapping into PT&T's touch-tone ordering system, ordering equipment to be dropped off at certain locations. Using his truck, he would pick up the equipment and sell it, either to PT&T or to other companies, as refurbished equipment. His knowledge of computers and PT&T systems allowed him to alter their programs to erase any traces of his illicit activity. His operation became so large that he needed employees to assist him. One of his employees became disgruntled and tipped off police to Jerry's illegal activities in 1972. Jerry was convicted of grand theft, burglary, and receiving stolen property and served 40 days in jail, with a three-year probation. He eventually became a computer security consultant.

Required:

List and describe internal controls from this chapter that may have helped prevent or detect Jerry Schneider's fraud. Keep in mind that this case occurred before there was an Internet and large company computer networks.

CONTINUING CASE: SPATELLI'S PIZZERIA

Reread the Spatelli's Pizzeria Continuing Case in Chapter 1. Notice that only a couple of years prior to the case time frame, the management of Spatelli's had begun an Internet order system. As management of Spatelli's considered the advantages of the Internet order system, it should also have considered the inherent risks of conducting business via the Internet.

Required:

1. Describe the new risks of Internet orders that Spatelli's management should have considered. The risks you describe should be specific to the Internet order system.
2. Describe internal controls that Spatelli's should have implemented to lessen the risks you identify in part 1.

SOLUTIONS TO CONCEPT CHECK

1. (SO 1) Internal controls that apply overall to the IT system are called **d. general controls.** There are two categories of IT internal controls. General controls apply overall to the IT system, such as passwords, encryption of data, and physical security controls. Application controls are input, processing, and output controls applied to each specific IT application system.

2. (CMA Adapted) (SO 1) In entering client contact information in the computerized database of a telemarketing business, a clerk erroneously entered nonexistent area codes for a block of new clients. This error rendered the block of contacts useless to the company. The control that would most likely have led to the discovery of this error at the time of entry into the company's computerized system is a **b. validity check**. A validity check can examine the data entered and alert the user to an invalid entry.
3. (SO 2) **c. Encryption** is not a control intended to authenticate users. Encryption can render data unreadable and useless to those without the encryption key, but it does not prevent unauthorized users from accessing the IT system. User logins, security tokens, and biometric devices do authenticate users and are intended to prevent unauthorized access.
4. (CMA Adapted, CIA Adapted) (SO 2) Management of an Internet retail company is concerned about the possibility of computer data eavesdropping and wiretapping, and wants to maintain the confidentiality of information as it is transmitted. The company should make use of **a. data encryption**. Since encryption renders data unreadable, it prevents eavesdropping and makes wiretapping useless.
5. (SO 2) An IT governance committee has several responsibilities. The option least likely to be a responsibility of the IT governance committee is to **a. develop and maintain the database and ensure adequate controls over the database**. This is a description of the responsibilities of the database administrator, not the IT governance committee.
6. (SO 3) AICPA Trust Services Principles describe five categories of IT risks and controls. Of the five given categories, the one best described by the statement "The system is protected against unauthorized access" is **a. security**. Availability means that the system is available for operation and use as committed or agreed. Processing integrity means that system processing is complete, accurate, timely, and authorized. Confidentiality means that information designated as confidential is protected as committed or agreed.
7. (SO 3) The risk that an unauthorized user would shut down systems within the IT system is an **b. availability risk**. The shutdown of all or part of the IT system would make the IT system unavailable for use as intended, and it is therefore an availability risk.
8. (SO 4) The risk of an unauthorized user gaining access is likely to be a risk for **d. all of the above**. Each of these areas of an IT system is a potential "entry point" for unauthorized users.
9. (SO 5) **c. A reasonableness check** is the programmed input validation check that compares the value in a field with related fields to determine whether the value is appropriate. An example would be that pay rate could be compared with job category code to make sure that the pay rate is reasonable.
10. (SO 5) The programmed input validation check that determines whether the appropriate type of data, either alphabetic or numeric, was entered is a **d. field check**. A field check is intended to ensure that only numeric data are entered in numeric fields and only alphabetic data are entered in alphabetic fields.
11. (SO 5) The programmed input validation which verifies that a value was entered in all of the critical fields is a **a. completeness check**. When a user is completing an input screen, a completeness check would not allow the user to finish the input and move to the next screen or step until all critical fields contain a value.

12. (SO 5) The control total which is the total of field values added for control purposes, but not added for any other purpose, is a **b. hash total**. As an example, a hash total might be the total of all Social Security numbers, a field that would not be summed for any purpose other than control.
13. (CPA Adapted) (SO 5) A company has the following invoices in a batch:

Invoice no.	Product i.d.	Quantity	Unit price
401	H42	150	$30.00
402	K56	200	$25.00
403	H42	250	$10.00
404	L27	300	$ 5.00

Of the numbers presented, the one that represents a valid record count is **b. 4**. This represents the number of records (invoices) included for processing in the batch.

		Term	Reference Location
General Controls		Access	S 1.2; S 3.1; A 1.2; A 3.4; P 1.2
		Access levels	S 1.2; S 3.1; A 1.2; P 3.5
		Antivirus	S 3.4; A 3.7; P 3.8; O 3.10; C 3.7
		Authentication of users	S 1.2; S 3.1
		Backup data	S 3.1; A 3.2; A 3.3; P 3.18; P 3.19; C 3.4
		Business continuity	A 1.2; A 3.2; P 3.18
		Card key	S 3.2; A 3.5; P 3.6; O 3.8; C 3.5
		Disaster recovery	A 3.2; A 3.3; A 3.11; P 3.18
		Encryption	S 3.5; A 3.8; P 3.1; P 3.8
		Environmental factors	A 3.1; P 3.17; P 4.3
		Firewall	S 3.2; S 3.3; A 3.6; P 3.7; O 3.8; O 3.9; C 3.6
		Intrusion detection	S 3.3; S 3.6; A 3.6; A 3.9; P 3.7; P 3.10; C 3.6; C 3.9
		IT steering committee	S 3.10; A 2.5; P 2.5; O 3.16; C 2.3
		Log-in attempts	S 3.3; A 3.4; A 3.6; P 3.5; C 3.4; C 3.6
		Logs	S 3.2; S 3.6; A 3.4; A 3.5; A 3.6; A 3.9; P 3.10; P 4.2; C 3.5
		New users	S 1.2; S 3.1; A 1.2; A 3.4; P 1.2; P 3.5
		Offsite backup	S 3.2; A 3.3; P 3.6
		Operating system	S 3.8; A 3.4; P 3.5; O 3.7; C 3.4
		Output distribution	S 3.1; P 3.3; P 3.5; O 3.7; C 3.4
		Passwords	S 3.1; A 3.4; P 3.5; O 3.7; C 3.4
		Physical access	S 3.2; A 3.1; A 3.5; P 3.6
		Router	S 3.2
		SDLC	S 3.8; S 3.10; A 3.11; P 3.2; P 3.12; O 3.14; C 3.11
		Security breach resolution	S 1.2; S 3.6; A 2.4; A 3.5; O 3.8; C 3.10
		Security policy	S 1.1; S 1.2; S 1.3; S 3.7; A 4.1
		Segregation of duties	S 3.11; A 3.4; P 3.5; O 3.17
		Server	S 3.2
		SSL	S 3.5; A 3.8; P 3.1; P 3.9; O 3.11; C 3.8
		Terminated employees	S 3.1; A 3.4
		Testing systems	S 1.2; S 3.10; S 3.11; A 1.2; A 3.11; A 3.13; P 1.2
		User profiles	S 3.1; A 3.4; P 3.5; C 3.4
		Utility programs	A 3.4; P 3.5
		Virus	S 3.4; A 3.7; P 3.8
		VPN	S 3.3; A 3.6; P 3.1; P 3.7; O 3.9; C 3.6
		Vulnerability assessment	S 3.3; A 3.6
Application Controls	Input	Control totals	P 3.1; P 3.3
		Data entry	P 3.1
		Data preparation procedures	P 3.1
		Error handling procedures	P 3.1
		Field edits	P 3.1
		Hash totals	P 3.1
		Input form design	P 3.1
		Range checks	P 3.1
		Record counts	P 3.2
		Source documents authorized	P 3.1
		Source documents maintained (imaged)	P 3.1
		Validity checks	P 3.1
	Processing	Error handling procedures	P 3.2
		Processing	P 3.2
		Production run logs	P 3.10
		Record counts	P 3.2
		Standard review procedures	P 3.11
	Output	Exceptions logged, investigated, resolved	P 3.3
		Output distribution	P 3.3
		Outputs stored based on classification	P 3.5
		Reconcile control totals to outputs	P 3.3

Reference (S = Security; A = Availability; P = Processing Integrity; C = Confidentiality, O = Online Privacy)

Exhibit 4–11
AICPA Trust Services Principles Reference List for IT Control Terms

CHAPTER 5

Corporate Governance and the Sarbanes-Oxley Act

STUDY OBJECTIVES

This chapter will help you gain an understanding of the following concepts:

1. An overview of corporate governance
2. Participants in the corporate governance process
3. The functions within the corporate governance process
4. The history of corporate governance
5. The Sarbanes–Oxley Act of 2002
6. The impact of the Sarbanes–Oxley Act on corporate governance
7. The importance of corporate governance in the study of accounting information systems
8. Ethics and corporate governance

THE REAL WORLD

Photodisc/Getty Images

The Procter & Gamble Company (P&G) is well known for its best selling brands such as Jif® peanut butter, Crest® toothpaste, and Pampers® diapers. In addition to its successful consumer products, P&G has also gained recognition for its success in the area of corporate governance.

In 2001, P&G was named the "Best Corporate Citizen" by *Business Ethics* magazine. In 2004 and 2005, P&G received the highest possible rating for corporate governance by Governance Metrics International (GMI), an independent research and ratings agency. Thousands of companies have been rated by GMI, with only 1% earning this top rating.

P&G's reputation is so impressive because it focuses on doing what is right; all levels of personnel stress integrity in all aspects of their work. Its commitment to corporate governance is based upon the following components:[1]

- A hard-working and experienced board of directors provides effective oversight and interaction with management and investors.
- Strong internal controls protect the company's assets and information, and ensure compliance with applicable regulations and accounting standards.
- A financial stewardship program provides discipline in decision-making, responsibility to investors, and accountability for actions.
- A code of conduct sets forth ethical standards for all business matters.

Companies like P&G can benefit from being recognized as leaders in corporate governance. Rewards may be realized in terms of increased loyalty from investors, customers, and employees. Research indicates that when companies stress corporate governance, they tend to reap financial benefits such as higher returns and lower cost of capital.

The pages that follow demonstrate that there are many ways of defining corporate governance. However, regardless of the variations in the definition, the essence of corporate governance is embodied in P&G's framework of commitment to corporate governance, as previously described. The four points used in P&G's framework will provide the basis for defining corporate governance in this text.

The remainder of this chapter addresses the importance of corporate governance in a modern business environment, as well as some related historical, legal, and ethical perspectives.

AN OVERVIEW OF CORPORATE GOVERNANCE (STUDY OBJECTIVE 1)

Corporate governance is a concept that has recently received increased attention and is evolving. The purpose of corporate governance is to encourage the efficient use of resources and to require accountability for those resources. The aim is to balance the interests of individuals, corporations, and the community. Individuals such as shareholders desire high return on their investment, while the community desires responsible corporate behavior that benefits the community. At the same time, the corporation and those within it desire long-term

[1]www.pg.com//company/our_commitment/corp_gov/

preservation of the corporation. Often, the needs of these various groups conflict with each other. Good corporate governance properly balances the needs and desires of these groups.

Corporate governance is generally recognized as involving many diverse aspects of business. Thus, a different definition of corporate governance exists to cover each different aspect of interest. For instance, when economists define corporate governance, they recognize factors affecting the supply and demand of corporate leaders and tend to emphasize the importance of motivating leaders through the use of incentive programs. On the other hand, financiers tend to emphasize the role of corporate leaders to provide a good rate of return, while accountants focus on the responsibility of corporate leaders to provide effective internal controls and accurate records. If forced to provide a single definition, accountants would characterize **corporate governance** as an elaborate system of checks and balances whereby a company's leadership is held accountable for building shareholder value and creating confidence in the financial reporting processes.

Although there are diverse definitions for corporate governance and multiple connected functions within the company, overall corporate governance is a system with many components working together for a common cause. In summary, corporate governance involves the manner in which companies manage and conduct themselves to achieve financial discipline. In order to be effective, governance should be engaged, ongoing, and diligent.

Building value and creating confidence are key ingredients in the preceding definitions; a related concept that is an integral part of corporate governance is "tone at the top." **Tone at the top** refers to the set of values and behaviors in place for the corporate leaders. It must be reinforced through each function of corporate governance, not only through written policies, but through the actions and attitudes of the company's leadership. Tone at the top must be established over time by the building of trust through integrity, consistency, and clarity, and by the diligent involvement of corporate leaders with various groups of people and organizations connected to the company.

In order to explain corporate governance in more detail, it is first necessary to introduce the participants in the governance process and the related functions that are performed. The next two sections focus on these topics.

PARTICIPANTS IN THE CORPORATE GOVERNANCE PROCESS (STUDY OBJECTIVE 2)

Recall from the previous section that corporate governance can be defined as an elaborate system of checks and balances. Corporate governance is considered elaborate not only because it is multifunctional, but also because of the variety of people involved in the system. The participants in the corporate governance process are often referred to as stakeholders. **Stakeholders** are all of the different people who have some form of involvement or interest in the business. They participate in or with the business in a manner that puts them in a position of financial interest or risk, or is otherwise significant to the overall strategies and operations of the business.

Stakeholders can be internal or external. Exhibit 5-1 presents an example of the various internal and external stakeholders of a typical corporation. Each of

Exhibit 5-1
Stakeholders as Participants in the Corporate Governance Process

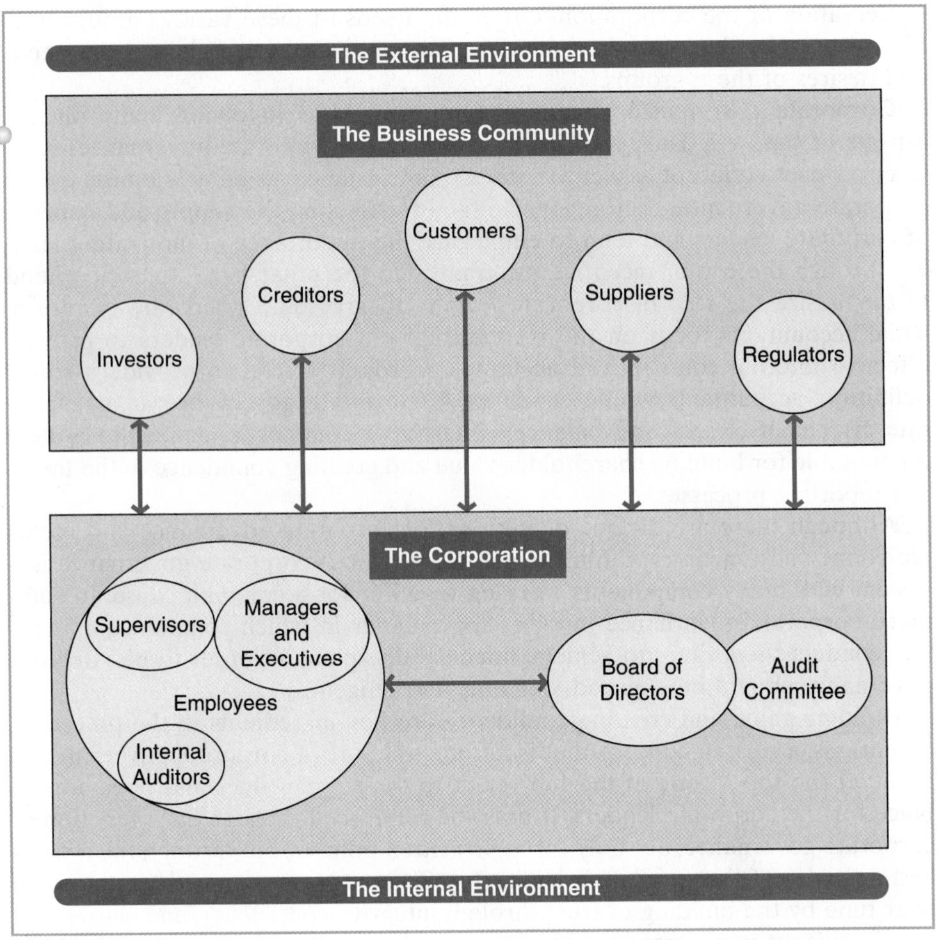

these stakeholder groups affect, or is affected by, corporate governance. For example, management has a huge direct impact on corporate governance, while the community is likely to be more indirectly affected by corporate governance. To understand corporate governance, it is important to grasp not only who the stakeholders are, but what their functions are, relative to the organization. The stakeholder groups from Exhibit 5-1 are described next, and the section that follows these descriptions explains their functions.

Internal stakeholders must work together in a proactive manner to foster continuous improvements in the company's reporting systems. The following parties are considered internal stakeholders:

The *management* team of a typical corporation is often divided into layers: top management, middle management, and supervisors. Top management is made up of the company's president and chief executive officer (CEO), as well as the remaining executive officers. This generally includes a vice president for each functional area of the company. Although the main responsibility of top managers has historically been corporate strategy and supervision, this is changing in the modern business world. Top managers are becoming more accountable for the details of the business. Middle managers coordinate a number of different departments or groups within the company by leading the supervisors in their respective areas of responsibility. Supervisors guide the work of a number of employees doing similar tasks within a given department or group.

Employees carry out the day-to-day operations and administrative functions of the company. The jobs performed by individual employees are each important, yet they make up a small component of the company's overall business. Employees rely on supervisors to oversee and coordinate their activities in order for them to work effectively to accomplish the company's overall objectives.

Internal auditors are employees of the corporation who help management establish and monitor internal controls by continuously looking for "red flags." They rotate throughout the company, reviewing the policies, procedures, and reports in each area to determine whether or not they are working as planned. The internal audit function is usually a separate department within the business, comprising a number of managers, supervisors, and employees (depending upon the size of the company).

The *board of directors* is elected by the shareholders to direct the corporation. Its role is to align the interests of shareholders and management. Although not typically involved in day-to-day decision-making, the board of directors should have the highest level of authority with respect to the company's objectives and strategies. The board of directors is generally made up of a chairman and secretary, as well as several members who are independent from the company. A board of directors will often have subcommittees made up of a subset of the board's membership to handle specific tasks. Members should be professionally experienced so that they can effectively serve as advisors to the company.

THE REAL WORLD

EMC Corporation is a provider of information storage products and services. It has also established policies for its board of directors that make it an icon of good corporate governance. EMC has in place corporate governance guidelines that clarify the roles and responsibilities of its board of directors. Included in these guidelines are such topics as eligibility for membership, frequency of meetings, continuous education, and performance assessment. In order to be sure that the board of directors has the necessary level of expertise to perform its duties, EMC implemented a directors training program. The training covers the company's operations, strategies, finances, etc., and requires that the directors spend time with company officials and outside business advisors. In addition, board members undergo annual reviews on their performance at the individual, committee, and full board levels. These policies make it possible for the board to practice continuing improvement and to be more effective in its work for the company.[2]

The *audit committee* is a subcommittee of the board of directors. The audit committee is responsible for financial matters, including reporting, controls, and the audit function. The role of the audit committee is discussed in more detail later in this chapter.

Shareholders own a portion, or share, of the corporation. As owners, they have the ability to influence the company by voting on significant matters. Otherwise, shareholders are often not involved in daily operations, except in small companies. Because many corporations have millions of ownership shares, a typical individual shareholder owns a very small fraction of the company and therefore has little influence. Because of the lack of involvement and limited influence of individual shareholders, these parties are sometimes regarded as external stakeholders.

[2] www.emc.com/about/governance

External stakeholders are people and organizations outside the corporation who have a financial interest in the corporation. In most situations, external stakeholders work with the company and are therefore interested in its inputs, outputs, and/or financial success. The following parties are generally considered external stakeholders:

The *communities* in which corporations are located have a stake in those corporations because of their impact on social, environmental, charitable, and employment practices in their areas. Companies may have a big influence in the communities in which they operate; therefore, the people and organizations that make up those communities tend to have a connection to the business, even if they are not otherwise involved as employees, customers, etc.

Investors are those who have an ownership interest in the company or who consider obtaining an ownership share. Although all shareholders are investors of the company, not all investors are shareholders. Investors are included as external stakeholders because this group includes potential shareholders, those people or organizations considering becoming shareholders. Investors, as well as each of the remaining external stakeholders to be described later, depend on the financial information presented by the company to serve as a basis for making decisions about their involvement (or potential involvement) with the company.

Creditors are those who help finance the company by lending money. They are genuinely interested in the company's financial health because it determines the company's ability to repay its obligations.

Customers and *suppliers* are involved with the company on a day-to-day basis by buying and selling, respectively. Customers purchase the company's products and services, whereas suppliers provide the resources needed for the company to do business.

One special type of supplier who provides important services for the company is the external auditor. *External auditors* lend credibility to the financial statements and are responsible for evaluating whether or not the company's financial information is prepared according to established accounting rules. External auditors must be independent from the company so that they can perform their work without bias. Accordingly, they should approach every audit with a skeptical attitude and think about ways that fraud might be carried out within client companies. This attitude allows auditors to be more thorough and objective.

Regulators are important stakeholders in the corporate governance process because they are responsible for the regulations and guidelines that govern the company. Some of the most influential governing bodies in the area of corporate governance include the following:

- The **Securities and Exchange Commission** (**SEC**) is the federal regulatory agency responsible for protecting the interests of investors by making sure that public companies provide complete and transparent financial information.
- The **Treadway Commission** formed the Committee of Sponsoring Organizations (COSO) that created the framework for internal controls evaluations. The Treadway Commission was established by five organizations that are influential in the practice of accounting, including the American Institute of CPAs, The Institute of Internal Auditors, Financial Executives International, the Institute of Management Accountants, and the American Accounting Association. Chapter 4 introduced COSO and its importance in laying a foundation for establishing and monitoring internal controls.

- The **Financial Accounting Standards Board** (**FASB**) and **International Accounting Standards Board** (**IASB**) in the United States and globally, respectively, are responsible for establishing applicable financial accounting and reporting standards. FASB and IASB are private organizations that have been influential in establishing accounting principles which provide information useful in business decision making.

An important feature of corporate governance is the need for the corporation to be conscientious about maintaining good working relationships with each group of stakeholders, both internal and external. One way to enhance good relationships is to ensure that certain stakeholders remain independent with respect to the company's financial reporting. For instance, the audit committee and external auditors should not allow any financial connections to influence the decisions they make about the company's financial statements or disclosures. Even the internal auditors should maintain an independent attitude. Although internal auditors are employees of the company and cannot therefore remain completely independent, the corporation should be structured in such a way that internal auditors do not have any reporting relationships or conflicting roles that impact their objectivity on the job.

The systems of checks and balances that constitute corporate governance involve the internal stakeholders working to perform several interrelated functions. Moreover, the company's success in maintaining good working relationships with each group of stakeholders will enhance the corporate governance functions. The next section describes these functions.

FUNCTIONS WITHIN THE CORPORATE GOVERNANCE PROCESS (STUDY OBJECTIVE 3)

The system of checks and balances in corporate governance includes several interrelated functions, including management oversight, internal controls and compliance, financial stewardship, and ethical conduct.

MANAGEMENT OVERSIGHT

Who leads a company's leaders? This question relates to the concept of the management oversight function of corporate governance. There must be a level of supervision that oversees the company's leaders, including its board of directors, chief executives, and management team. **Management oversight** encompasses the policies and procedures in place to lead the directorship of the company.

The directorship of a company is generally considered to be its supervisors, managers, officers, and directors. A corporate organizational chart is typically structured in such a way that supervisors must report to managers, managers must report to an officer, and officers are responsible to the board of directors. The key to the effectiveness of this structure is the level of commitment from those in the positions of authority. Good management oversight involves leaders who are good communicators, attentive and responsive to those both above and below in the chain of command. These features make it possible for leaders to be effective at recruiting, motivating, evaluating, problem solving, and decision making. Overall, good leaders guide by example.

Management at every level within a company should communicate, both through words and by example, the importance of the policies and procedures that are in place and the ethical conduct that is required to achieve the company's goals. In order for this communication to be effective, a top-down approach must be in full force. This means that management's commitment must be demonstrated at the executive level, with the CEO at the forefront, and that every subordinate level within the company must recognize this commitment. In other words, the tone at the top is key to effective management oversight.

Even though the CEO is the top-ranking employee, he or she is not the "end-all" in terms of management insight. The CEO must report to the company's board of directors and must feel a sense of responsibility to the board. The board of directors is therefore an important and active component of management and control. As such, it must take responsibility for overseeing the company's executive management team. In order to do this effectively, the board of directors must be engaged in the business. Although the board is not typically involved in all day-to-day activities, its involvement must be sufficient for its members to truly serve as directors rather than merely pose as figureheads. The board must have a thorough understanding of the company's business so that it can take part in strategic decision making and spearhead the systems of communication and accountability that management oversight is made of.

THE REAL WORLD

Undoubtedly, the two most noteworthy bankruptcy cases in U.S. history have been those of Enron and WorldCom. The problems that led to the demise of these two corporations can be traced to poor management oversight. Although policies and procedures were well documented in both of these companies, the reality was that top management and/or the board of directors did not live by the methods that were documented.

In the case of Enron, the board of directors was criticized for its lack of engagement. Its meetings were few and brief, it did not challenge the company's aggressive accounting policies, and it allowed senior executives to be exempted from the company's policies regarding conflicts of interest.

In the case of WorldCom, the message communicated by the CEO was for employees to do whatever was necessary to make sure that the company's stock price did not go down.[3]

As these real-world examples demonstrate, management oversight cannot be taken for granted. Consistent reporting and oversight relationships should be in full force at every level of management to make sure that corruption does not bleed into the corporation. This is a tall order that requires a lot of support. One way that it can be realized is for the company to implement a thorough system of internal controls.

INTERNAL CONTROLS AND COMPLIANCE

As described in Chapters 3 and 4, internal controls are the systems by which companies control risks. Although the details of internal controls are addressed in previous chapters, some of the related concepts are worth reinforcing

[3]Colleen Cunningham, "Section 404 Compliance and 'Tone at the Top,'" *Financial Executive,* vol. 21, issue 5, June 1, 2005, p. 6.

because they are a fundamental part of corporate governance. Of particular importance are the control mechanisms that

- dictate the manner in which rights and responsibilities are assigned to different people within the organization, and
- ensure that the company is fulfilling its obligations with respect to adherence to accounting conventions and regulatory requirements.

The goal of corporate governance, with respect to internal controls and compliance, is to ensure that financial information is accurate and transparent. **Accuracy** relates to the correctness of the information presented; it is concerned with whether the financial information is verifiable and proper. **Transparency** relates to how clearly the financial information can be understood; it requires a straightforward, consistent, and timely approach. Companies that emphasize accuracy and transparency will have controls in place to make sure that their financial reports do not contradict one another. There will be fewer opportunities for errors or fraud. This does not necessarily mean that the company cannot be aggressive in its operating approach; but a strong system of checks and balances would be more likely to prevent opportunities for potential wrongdoers to cross the line into areas of fraud. If handled properly, this level of diligence in the preparation and presentation of financial information can help the company be more focused on the timely collection and use of data in a forward-thinking manner, which is likely to put the company in a better position to deal successfully with potential investors and creditors.

Establishing an internal control system to ensure accurate and transparent financial reporting requires a process approach. The following approach is suggested:

Six-step process for internal controls:[4]

1. Define the key activities and resources involved in each business activity. This should answer the question, "What is the related activity and who is involved?"
2. Define the objectives of each activity. This step should answer the question, "Why is the activity being performed?"
3. Obtain input from experienced users and advisors on the effective design of controls.
4. Formally document the details of controls. Make sure that the documentation is thorough enough to identify
   - Where, when, and how are activities being performed?
   - What records are being prepared?
   - Where, when, and how are records (both paper and electronic) being retained?
5. Test the effectiveness of controls to make sure they are operating as designed. Testing should be done by a combination of users, internal auditors, and external auditors.
6. Engage in continuous improvement to fix problems and upgrade controls.

[4]J. Stephen McNally, "Assessing Company-Level Controls: Another Hurdle on the Road to Compliance," *Journal of Accountancy,* June 2005, pp. 65–68.

These steps should be carried out for the most routine components of operations and should continue until they pervade the entire organization. When such processes are well planned and completed carefully and thoroughly, the outcome for the company should be a reliable system of internal controls that supports its compliance requirements.

Maintaining effective internal controls and ensuring compliance is an ongoing process. Many companies conduct surveys and organize task groups to monitor the effectiveness of internal controls and to determine whether the priorities communicated by their superiors are consistent with the company's official, documented goals. Companies that take part in this kind of ongoing monitoring often recognize the direct link between transparency and the relationships with external stakeholders. The next section addresses the importance of these relationships within the realm of corporate governance.

FINANCIAL STEWARDSHIP

Corporate governance is focused on the roles of managers and directors, who hold unique positions of responsibility. Managers and directors have a fiduciary duty to the shareholders of the company. A **fiduciary duty** is a special obligation of trust, especially with respect to the finances of another. In the corporate environment, "fiduciary" is a term which means that management has been entrusted with the power to manage the assets of the corporation, owned by the shareholders. The financial affairs of a corporation are expected to be managed in such a way as to maximize shareholders' wealth. Corporate leaders are required to be loyal to the shareholders; the personal interests and welfare of managers cannot overshadow this commitment to the shareholders. Since the business is owned and financed by the shareholders, the corporate leaders must serve as agents or stewards for the shareholders, leading the business in the best interest of the shareholders. Financial **stewardship** refers to the manner in which an agent handles the affairs and/or finances of another. Discipline, respect, and accountability encourage good financial stewardship.

Good communication and open dialogue are undoubtedly the most important factors for a leader to successfully fulfill the duty of financial stewardship. Corporate executives and managers must have frequent contact with the board of directors and shareholders in order to keep them informed of all that is going on in the business. The information provided must be thorough, accurate, and transparent.

To cultivate an environment where corporate leaders can be good financial stewards, there must be in place well-defined rules and procedures for making decisions on corporate affairs. Objectives must be considered at the starting point. Furthermore, any decision must be based on objectives that serve the interest of the shareholders. Finally, a means of monitoring performance, obtaining feedback, and continuous improvement should be part of the process. Accordingly, the six-step process described previously may serve as a guide to facilitating good financial stewardship.

In addition to their knowledge of good corporate governance techniques, corporate leaders should be aware of some warning signs that may indicate the occurrence of faulty practices. For instance, if management is resorting to earnings management techniques as a means of maintaining a positive environment of financial stewardship, it could actually be putting the company at risk. **Earnings management** is the act of manipulating financial information in such a way as to shed more favorable light on the company or its management than is actually warranted. Some typical earnings management techniques include the following:

- early recognition of revenues
- early shipment of products
- falsification of customers
- falsification of invoices or other records
- allowing customers to take products without taking title to the products

Earnings management is unethical because it involves stretching the rules beyond their intended bounds. In addition, earnings management tends to have a snowball effect, meaning that once it is started, it must be continued in order to prevent a negative result in terms of financial stewardship.

These components of financial stewardship and the related processes are very closely tied to the other functions of corporate governance. In order to enhance financial stewardship, effective management oversight and internal control procedures must be in working order. Furthermore, an ethical foundation must be in place. The next section addresses the ethical considerations for corporate governance.

ETHICAL CONDUCT

From the preceding presentations on the functions of corporate governance, it should be clear that creating a culture of honesty is a fundamental part of the model of effective corporate governance. Integrity, fairness, and accountability are the underlying concepts in each of the other roles of corporate governance, including the descriptions for sound systems of management oversight, internal controls, and financial stewardship. Because of its widespread relevance, ethical conduct is often valued as the most important part of corporate governance.

Good corporate governance must rely on the professional integrity of the company's leaders. A system of corporate governance can be only as good as the people in charge (regardless of the policies and procedures in place to enhance the various functions within the structure). Although many suggestions have been published for enhancing corporate conduct through strong management oversight, internal controls, and financial stewardship, there is no replacement for integrity and ethical behavior.

The next section introduces some of the most significant laws that have influenced the changing face of corporate governance over the years.

THE HISTORY OF CORPORATE GOVERNANCE (STUDY OBJECTIVE 4)

Corporate governance has changed over the years as the focus of the business world has changed. In addition, since compliance is such an important function within the corporate governance process, changes in legislation have had a big impact on corporate governance. The pace of change has been fast in recent years, especially since the turn of the century in the year 2000. This section presents a chronology of significant developments that have influenced corporate governance.

The origin of the corporate governance concept in the United States coincides with the establishment of the SEC and enactment of the securities laws, in response to pressure from investors following the stock market crash of 1929 and the Great Depression of the 1930s. Investors wanted greater protection against misleading accounting and reporting practices. The **Securities Act of 1933** requires full disclosure of financial information through the filing of registration statements before securities can be sold in the financial markets. The **Securities Exchange Act of 1934** requires ongoing disclosures for registered companies, as well as regulation of stock exchanges, brokers, and dealers.

In the subsequent decades, as companies were rebuilding and recovering from the Great Depression, more emphasis was placed on the accounting function. Up until the 1970s, sharp focus was on materiality as companies and their auditors concentrated on the transactions and accounts that were most significant to the overall business. By the 1980s, however, it became clear that market pressures were a bigger influence on accountants and corporate leaders. There was intense pressure for companies to meet or beat their earnings targets. As a result, earnings management and other creative accounting practices became more common. Even after the release of COSO's internal control framework in 1992, the number of accounting irregularities was still on the rise. In fact, the irregularities became so severe that, in the early 2000s, a series of high-profile corporate scandals erupted, including the most noteworthy cases at Enron and WorldCom. These scandals robbed thousands of people of their jobs and retirement savings and caused major corporations to file bankruptcy. In response, many investors demanded that new legislation be introduced to avoid repeat instances of these types of accounting-based scandals.

The Sarbanes–Oxley Act of 2002 is the legislation enacted to combat deceptive accounting practices. This Act is so extensive that its details and impacts are presented in the next two sections of this chapter.

In addition to the Sarbanes–Oxley Act, many other new guidelines were implemented in the early 2000s. For instance, the U.S. Patriot Act (2001) and the Basel II regulations (2004) were put into practice to provide for improved financial systems for banks and financial institutions. Other industries have followed suit, with the goal of improving corporate governance in their companies.

THE SARBANES–OXLEY ACT OF 2002 (STUDY OBJECTIVE 5)

The Sarbanes–Oxley Act was signed into law on July 30, 2002, for the purpose of improving financial reporting and reinforcing the importance of corporate ethics. The legislation was enacted in an effort to curb the corruption and accounting blunders that had been recently discovered in connection with the bankruptcies of such corporate giants as Enron and WorldCom. In these cases, many Americans suffered tremendously as the values of stock prices and employee retirement plans plunged. It became apparent that change was needed to improve investor faith in America's financial reporting systems.

The Sarbanes–Oxley Act ("the Act") applies to public companies and the auditors of public companies. In order to carry out the provisions of the Act,

Exhibit 5-2
Summary of the Key Provisions of the Sarbanes–Oxley Act of 2002

Title I	**Public Company Accounting Oversight Board**—establishment and responsibilities of the PCAOB	
Title II	**Auditor Independence**—requirements to enhance auditor objectivity	
	Sec. 201	Services outside the scope of practice of auditors
	Sec. 203	Audit partner rotation
	Sec. 206	Conflicts of interest
Title III	**Corporate Responsibility**—requirements for a company's securities to be listed on a national securities exchange	
	Sec. 301	Public company audit committees
	Sec. 302	Corporate responsibility for financial reports
Title IV	**Enhanced Financial Disclosures**—requirements for improved accuracy of financial statements and supporting financial disclosures	
	Sec. 401	Disclosures in periodic reports
	Sec. 404	Management assessment of internal controls
	Sec. 406	Code of ethics for senior financial officers
	Sec. 409	Real-time issuer disclosures
Title V	**Analysts' Conflicts of Interest**—requirements to enhance the objectivity of securities analysts	
Title VI	**Commission Resources and Authority**—funding authority for hiring professionals to oversee public audit services	
Title VII	**Studies and Reports**—research authority for the General Accounting Office and Securities Exchange Commission to perform studies on financial reporting	
Title VIII	**Corporate and Criminal Fraud Accountability**—penalties for destruction or falsification of records and protection for whistleblowers	
	Sec. 802	Criminal penalties for altering documents
	Sec. 806	Protection for employees who provide evidence of fraud
Title IX	**White-Collar Crime Penalty Enhancements**—requirements and violations for CEO/CFO regarding financial certification	
	Sec. 906	Corporate responsibility for certification of financial reports
Title X	**Corporate Tax Returns**—requirements for CEO regarding tax returns	
Title XI	**Corporate Fraud and Accountability**—further penalties for fraud	
	Sec. 1102	Tampering with records or impeding an official proceeding

the Public Company Accounting Oversight Board (PCAOB) was established. The PCAOB comprises five members who are appointed by the SEC. The PCAOB governs the work of auditors of public companies by providing standards related to quality controls. The PCAOB has investigative and disciplinary authority over the performance of public accounting firms.

The Act includes 11 "titles," or categories of provisions. Each title includes several sections. Exhibit 5-2 summarizes the titles and certain key sections within each title. The sections identified in the exhibit are discussed in detail in this chapter because of their relevance to corporate governance and other topics within this text.

Certain sections of the Act pertain to audit services. Audit services, including IT auditing, are addressed in Chapter 7. Titles II and III address the following auditing topics, among others:

Section 201—Services outside the scope of practice of auditors. Auditors of public companies are now prohibited from providing nonaudit services to their audit clients. Nonaudit services include the following:

- Bookkeeping or preparation of accounting records and financial statements
- Designing or implementation of accounting information systems
- Appraisal or other valuation services
- Actuarial services
- Internal audit outsourcing services
- Management advisory services or human resource management
- Investment advisory, investment banking, or brokerage services
- Legal advisory services

In the past, it was customary for auditors to perform many of these nonaudit services. In fact, a company could realize efficiencies by having its auditors involved in these areas, since the auditors were already familiar with these areas of the business. However, each of these services is now prohibited because of its potential to impair the auditor's objectivity. These types of services are deemed to put the auditor in the role of management or an employee or advisor of the client company. The Act recognizes that auditors who perform these types of services for their audit clients are likely to be placed in a situation of auditing their own work. An auditor who performs nonaudit services would therefore be faced with a conflict of interest; the auditor cannot be completely impartial while auditing financial information that he or she prepared. Likewise, if the auditor advises a client on financial matters, the auditor could not be neutral with respect to those matters with which he or she is already familiar.

It is particularly noteworthy that an auditor's involvement with the design and implementation of a client's accounting information systems can cause problems. Since auditors must be thoroughly familiar with a client's financial systems, they are often in a perfect position to advise clients regarding system improvements. However, if the auditor's involvement expands into areas of systems development, then the auditor is considered to have impaired independence. It is presumed that it would be difficult for that auditor to remain objective when auditing information that was processed by the system that he or she developed.

For other nonaudit services not included in this list, an auditor must obtain advance approval from the client's audit committee. For instance, auditors may perform income tax services for their audit clients as long as such services are preapproved by the board of directors.

Other sections of the Act address additional requirements for auditors to improve their impartiality with respect to their audit clients. One of the most significant changes affecting auditors includes a provision within Section 203 for the lead partner on a public company audit to rotate off the engagement after five years. This allows for a new partner to take over periodically and provide a fresh perspective on the overall audit. Section 206 introduces another requirement applicable to auditors who are hired away from the audit firm in order to take a job with the client. Such an auditor must take a "cooling off" period of one year if the new job is in a key accounting role. This is to allow for the separation of roles of accountant and auditor.

Section 301—Public company audit committees. Public companies must have an audit committee as a subcommittee of the board of directors. Although many companies had audit committees even before the Act was enacted, the audit committee now has more responsibility. The audit committee is responsible for hiring, firing, and overseeing the external auditors and serving as the liaison between both internal and external auditors and management on any points of disagreement. Hence, the auditors report directly to the audit committee on all matters related to the audit.

The members of the audit committee must be independent, meaning that they cannot be affiliated with the company, its employees, or its subsidiaries (other than through their service on the audit committee). In order to remain independent, members of the audit committee may not receive compensation from the company for their service to the company.

Certain sections of the Act that relate to enhanced financial disclosures are particularly important in the study of accounting information systems. Since accountants are responsible for the collection and presentation of financial information included in the reports, it is imperative that the underlying systems receive adequate attention. Financial statements can be only as good as the underlying systems that are used in their preparation. The following sections are not necessarily presented in the order that they appear in Exhibit 5-2; however, they appear along with other relevant sections of the Act.

Section 302—Corporate responsibility for financial reports. The CEO, CFO, and other responsible officers of the company must submit a certified statement accompanying each annual and quarterly report. The purpose of the certification is for the officers to acknowledge responsibility for the contents of the financial reports and for the underlying system of internal controls. This section requires that the top managers actually sign this statement. Their signatures indicate their acceptance of the responsibilities outlined in the following six points of acknowledgement that must be included in the certification:

1. The signing officers have reviewed the report in detail.
2. Based on the officer's knowledge, the report does not misstate any facts.
3. Based on the officer's knowledge, the financial statements and related disclosures are fairly presented.
4. The signing officers are responsible for the establishment, maintenance, and effectiveness of internal controls.
5. The signing officers have disclosed to the auditors and audit committee any instances of fraud or internal control deficiencies.
6. The signing officers indicate whether or not any significant changes in internal controls have occurred since the date of their most recent evaluation.

Notice that the fourth item on this list makes top management responsible for the internal control system. The types of internal controls discussed in Chapters 3 and 4 must be established and maintained. The Act requires that the certifications be prepared to accompany financial statements every time they are filed with the SEC. Accordingly, the certifications must be updated on a quarterly basis. It is expected that the certifications may be modified from period to period to reflect changes in internal controls as new systems are implemented and prior weaknesses and deficiencies are corrected.

Section 906—Failure of corporate officers to certify financial reports. If an officer of a public company does not comply with the requirements of Section 302 or if the officer certifies financial statements that are known to be misleading, stiff penalties may apply. Fines and/or prison terms may be imposed up to $5,000,000 and 20 years, respectively.

Section 401—Disclosures in periodic reports. The Act introduces new requirements for additional information to be disclosed along with the financial statements. Specifically, a company must disclose any off-balance-sheet transactions, including obligations or arrangements that may impact the financial position of the company. This requirement is intended to prevent repeated incidents like the problems encountered at Enron, where special-purpose entities were used to conceal off-balance-sheet transactions.

Section 404—Management assessment of internal controls. An internal control report is required to accompany each financial statement filing. The internal control report must establish management's responsibility for the company's internal controls and related financial reporting systems. It must also include an assessment of the effectiveness of the company's internal controls and related financial reporting systems. If there are any weaknesses in internal controls, they must be disclosed in this report.

The SEC defines internal controls over financial reporting as a process that is the responsibility of the company CEO and CFO, to provide reasonable assurance that the financial reporting systems are reliable. A reliable system of internal controls must include policies and procedures to provide reasonable assurance that

- detailed records accurately reflect the underlying transactions,
- transactions are recorded in accordance with generally accepted accounting principles,
- transactions are being carried out only in accordance with management's authorization, and
- unauthorized transactions are being prevented or detected.

Management's internal control evaluation must be based on a recognized framework. The framework that is used by most U.S. companies is COSO's Internal Control–Integrated Framework. Again, notice that these provisions of the Sarbanes–Oxley Act require establishment of the internal controls described in Chapters 3 and 4.

In addition to management's increased responsibility regarding internal controls, there are also new legal requirements for the auditors of public companies regarding the internal control structure of their clients. As part of their audit procedures, auditors must now attest to the internal control effectiveness. This means that an auditor's report on the overall fairness of financial statements must now include a statement regarding the effectiveness of the company's controls over financial reporting.

Section 406—Code of ethics for senior financial officers. The Act requires all public companies to have in place a code of ethics covering its CFO and other key accounting officers. The code must include principles that advocate honesty and moral conduct, fairness in financial reporting, and compliance with applicable governmental rules and regulations.

Section 409—Real-time disclosures. The Act requires that certain issues must be reported immediately if they involve information necessary to protect investors. This requirement allows for better and more timely information to be provided to the public regarding important corporate events such as bankruptcy, new contracts, acquisitions and disposals, and changes in control. Such events must be reported within four business days following their occurrence.

Titles VIII and XI of the Act address the issues of corporate fraud and accountability, discussed next.

Section 802—Criminal penalties for altering documents. It is a felony to knowingly alter, destroy, falsify, or conceal any records or documents with the intent to influence an investigation. The provisions of this section apply to both the company and its auditors, so it affects company records as well as the auditor's working papers.

Since the provisions of Section 802 prohibit document destruction, it follows that documents must be maintained for a relevant length of time. Specifically, auditors are required to retain working papers for five years. Similarly, many companies are making sure that they maintain supporting financial records for a given period. Document retention and storage are also discussed in Chapters 2 and 13.

Section 1102—Tampering with a record or otherwise impeding an official proceeding. If a person or firm is found to be in violation of Section 802, stiff penalties may apply. Violations are punishable by both monetary fines and lengthy (10- to 20-year) prison sentences.

Section 806—Protection for employees of publicly traded companies who provide evidence of fraud. This section is often referred to as the "whistleblower protection" provision of the Act. A **whistleblower** is someone who reports instances of wrongdoing or assists in a fraud investigation. To protect a whistleblower from retaliation by the fraudulent company or its employees, the Act prohibits any form of ridicule or harassment, demotion, discrimination, or termination of employment against a person who has provided such information in a lawful manner.

As can be inferred from the descriptions of the various sections, the Sarbanes–Oxley Act has had a tremendous impact on the regulatory environment of public companies. It has reformed corporate governance and financial reporting. Many corporate customs that were previously thought of as "best practices" or supplemental controls are now required by law. The next section provides additional information about the corporate changes that have come about as a result of the Act.

THE IMPACT OF THE SARBANES–OXLEY ACT ON CORPORATE GOVERNANCE (STUDY OBJECTIVE 6)

As you consider the many instances of change in the corporate governance process that have resulted from the Sarbanes–Oxley Act, bear in mind the functional context that was introduced earlier in this chapter. As a reminder, the four functional areas of corporate governance include management oversight, internal controls and compliance, financial stewardship, and ethical conduct. Each of these is revisited next.

Management oversight. The Act changes management's focus from one of strategic decision making and risk management to overall accountability. With the requirement for signed certifications of financial information, members of upper management must now be knowledgeable about many details of the organization. In the past, managers were rarely well versed on operating statistics and financial details of the company, as these types of responsibilities were often delegated to subordinates.

With the introduction of the PCAOB into the realm of management oversight, the board of directors and audit committee are also more accountable. The changes brought about by the PCAOB are significant in comparison with the public accounting profession's history of self-regulation. The Act has put an end to the times when members of the board of directors could be mere figureheads, as they are now held accountable to a variety of stakeholders. In particular, the audit committee's new role places it in a unique position within the domain of management oversight. As the point of contact on financial matters, the audit committee serves as the supervisor of the board of directors. Similarly, the board of directors serves as the supervisor of corporate management. Exhibit 5-3 illustrates the management oversight relationships established as a result of the enactment of Sarbanes–Oxley.

Overall, business leaders at all levels have increased responsibilities as a result of Sarbanes–Oxley. They must be more knowledgeable about accounting principles and the company's financial systems. In addition, the new requirements for management certification of financial information and the rigid penalties for noncompliance have had a tremendous impact on the attitudes of corporate managers. Their jobs now carry significantly more risk. The days of being able to plead ignorance are gone, as the new financial reporting era demands more responsibility and accountability.

Internal controls and compliance. The Act is forcing companies to comply with a wide range of new management and financial reporting requirements. This is creating a lot of extra work for accountants, IT departments, and executives. More paperwork is now prepared, retained, and filed with the SEC. More timely information is required. In order to comply with this provision, it is essential that every public company have in place financial reporting systems which can provide current information, in real time, concerning its operations and financial condition.

Section 404 requires companies to monitor their systems to find weaknesses in internal controls. The company's response must be to establish tighter controls, especially where temptation for fraud is greatest. Many companies are making changes in their IT systems and in their workforce in order to improve their controls. Testing is now required to make sure that company objectives

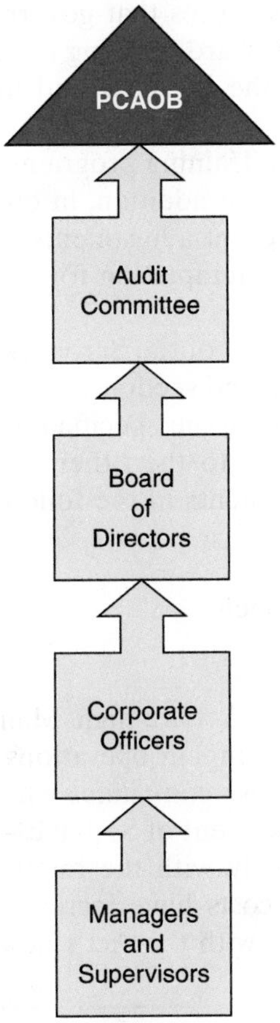

Exhibit 5-3
The Chain of Management Oversight for Corporate Financial Matters

are being met and that a transparent way of preparing and disclosing financial information is in place. Strict internal control procedures and consistency in reporting have never been more important.

Strong internal controls allow top managers to be in a better position to handle their new responsibilities regarding executive certification. Tight controls enable them to answer questions about operating details with which they may not have previously been familiar, including questions such as "Can you monitor supplier performance?" "Do you know precisely where the company's money is being spent?" and "Who is notified when a contract is violated?"

A substantial side effect of compliance with these sections of the Act is the huge increase in the amount of accounting information now required of public companies in order to support the new reporting requirements. Some companies are compiling enough paperwork to fill bookcases with binders containing the documentation that describes and tests the company's financial systems. In addition, there are now stricter requirements for retaining these documents. Accordingly, the corporate associates who are responsible for the development and maintenance of the underlying accounting information systems have become increasingly important.

Financial stewardship. The Act has caused many companies to take a deeper look at their policies and procedures that govern corporate conduct, including the attitudes of management toward fulfilling their fiduciary duties to the shareholders. The introduction of the PCAOB and increased responsibility of the audit committee have put greater pressure on managers to demonstrate their accountability to shareholders. Training programs are on the rise in an effort to reinforce these responsibilities. In addition, in order to enhance accountability, some companies have made recent adjustments to management incentive compensation packages so that the temptation for managing earnings is reduced.

Ethical conduct. The overall goal of the Sarbanes–Oxley Act is to improve ethical conduct. Nearly every title and section within the Act ties to the company's foundation of ethical behavior. Some specific changes that have not been previously mentioned with respect to the other corporate governance functions include increases and improvements in the following areas:

- codes of conduct
- performance evaluation models
- communications

The costs of complying with the Act are high. Many companies have been faced with the challenging task of changing operations in order to comply with the provisions of the Act. Even those companies who had some of the "best practices" in place prior to the enactment of Sarbanes–Oxley are finding it time consuming and expensive to comply with the reporting requirements of the new provisions. In addition, audit costs have increased as audit firms have had to hire more auditors to keep up with the Act's new demands.

THE REAL WORLD

Guidant Corporation is a manufacturer of pacemakers, defibrillators, and therapeutic devices used in the cardiovascular health care industry. With nearly $4 billion in annual revenues, dozens of worldwide locations, and over 12,000 employees, Guidant has expended a significant amount of resources in order to meet the new requirements of the Sarbanes–Oxley Act. Most of the effort and expense was related to preparation for the internal control certifications required by Section 404.

Guidant used a process-owner strategy to address the demands of Section 404. This means that employees and managers who are responsible for the various business processes were also held accountable for the documentation and testing of those processes. This approach involves many people throughout the company. In addition, consultants were hired to coordinate the project and assist with training and technical inquiries.

Even though Guidant used its own employees to prepare the internal control documentation and perform the testing, and even though no new computers were purchased, the costs of the project were still significant. Guidant estimates that its first-year costs of complying with the Act included $200,000 in consulting fees, an 80% increase in audit fees, and over 28,000 employee hours (including the hiring of two full-time professionals).[5]

Whether the increases in cost are worthwhile and whether the Act will be effective at deterring fraud is yet to be seen. Many accountants and corporate leaders have criticized the extreme requirements and minimal benefits of

[5]Ramona Dzinkowski, "Keeping Pace with SOX 404: Internal Control Certification at Guidant Corporation," *Strategic Finance,* September 2004, pp. 46–50.

the Sarbanes–Oxley Act. Opponents claim that it was enacted hastily in response to a few bad cases of corruption that are not necessarily representative of America's corporate control environment as a whole. They warn of the negative consequences that may result when management shifts attention from the company's big, strategic issues in an effort to fulfill the Act's new, detailed requirements.

On the other hand, many supporters of the Act argue that it provides a necessary opportunity to enhance performance by improving controls and visibility and reducing risk. Although costly, it can provide value in terms of increased efficiency, decision making, public confidence, and ultimately, overall business performance. Proponents tend to believe that the benefits are likely to be realized gradually as the company increases its awareness of internal controls and streamlines its business processes accordingly.

THE IMPORTANCE OF CORPORATE GOVERNANCE IN THE STUDY OF ACCOUNTING INFORMATION SYSTEMS (STUDY OBJECTIVE 7)

Consistent reporting and management of information has never been more important, considering the recent increases in government oversight and audit requirements. In addition to the Sarbanes–Oxley Act and other new corporate governance guidelines, even the income tax code has become increasingly complex. Overall, there is more focus on accounting information and improvements within financial systems.

CEOs and corporate managers must now be more in tune with the ever-changing financial picture of the company. IT departments are expected to help management achieve compliance by leveraging technology. Companies must be equipped with well-managed financial processes and related technological enhancements to make sure that corporate leaders have information readily available. Managers cannot be expected to sort through volumes of supporting documents when they need to get answers. Electronic record keeping is essential, but it depends upon an IT infrastructure that supports the company's strategies and goals. Even in nonpublic companies, in which compliance with the Sarbanes–Oxley Act is not required, IT managers are becoming increasingly popular as they provide corporate governance solutions to management.

THE REAL WORLD

The Dow Chemical Company and BASF have more in common than chemical products; these companies are each using the Internet to deliver training on their ethics codes. Advanced technology and information systems make it possible for a code of ethical conduct and the underlying principles to be disseminated to employees in such a way that they can be tied to day-to-day operations. These companies are extending their reach to reinforce their values so that employees understand what an important role ethical conduct plays in their jobs. Their strategy also provides a monitoring device for issues such as conflicts of interest and other items that are increasingly important in today's era of corporate compliance. This is quite a feat, considering that the use of dozens of different languages is involved to reach hundreds of thousands of employees located all around the globe.[6]

[6] "Making a Code of Conduct Central to the Enterprise" at www.lrn.com

Data mining software (discussed in Chapter 13) is becoming more important to the participants in the corporate governance process because it can help signal fraud. For example, the software provides analytical data that can help uncover suspicious patterns which might indicate fraud. Although this type of analysis is not required by Sarbanes–Oxley, many top managers are now demanding that this type of information be available. Managers typically do not have time to spend collecting data; they need to have information readily accessible so that they can devote ample time to traditional management roles such as strategic decision making.

Those with insight into the study of accounting information systems realize that information has business value. As such, accounting information is key to the corporate governance process, as well as to the overall economic health of the company. In addition, corporate governance is closely related to the other accounting information systems topics in this text; it serves as a link between the coverage of the control environment in Chapters 3 and 4 and IT governance in Chapter 6.

ETHICS AND CORPORATE GOVERNANCE (STUDY OBJECTIVE 8)

Creating a corporate governance system is a matter of doing what is right. However, maintaining positive corporate governance during tough times is an extremely challenging task. Corporate leaders may be faced with situations where their corporate governance principles and their ethical values are tested "when the going gets tough."

Arguably, the most challenging ethical issue within corporate governance is the potential conflict of interest for managers in their role as financial stewards of the corporation. It may become difficult for managers to always act in the best interest of the shareholders, especially in times when shareholder interests and management interests are not aligned. Managers are often placed in a very difficult position because their jobs include lofty goals that are tied to the company's earnings. Thus, managers may be inclined to act in ways that protect their jobs or the jobs of their employees. Actions taken in the personal interest of management often come at the expense of the shareholders.

In recent years, a troubling number of accounting executives have abandoned or ignored their fiduciary responsibility to the corporate shareholders. In most cases, these executives did not set out to do wrong, but they let their personal interests take priority over their corporate duties. Unfortunately, this is often how fraud unfolds: A high-ranking corporate official, with help from those working for him, may become somewhat desperate in his attempts to make his goal. His intentions are not dishonest at first, but eventually he shifts his focus and his actions become fraudulent. He thinks there will be a way out of the deception in the near future, but that break never comes. Instead, the fraud grows. Some subordinates may become reluctant to continue with the crime, but none has the courage to blow the whistle. Eventually, they will be discovered, the company's stock price will drop, and the shareholders will lose a lot of money. Ultimately, the perpetrators will be looking for new jobs, and some may go to jail because of their involvement.[7]

[7] Carol J. Loomis, "Lies, Damned Lies, and Managed Earnings," *Fortune*, August 2, 1999 vol. 140, issue 3, pp. 74–83.

Participating in earnings management is a very risky activity for managers. Although the motivation is for the company to realize sustained or improved earnings, the reality is that greater harm than good will result if the means of achieving the positive outcome is not honest.

The corporate governance structure plays a significant role in maintaining an environment of honesty. Corporate governance includes the function of internal controls and compliance, which is responsible for minimizing opportunities for collusion and management circumvention of controls. In reality, however, the success of the system depends on the integrity of the company's leaders. What matters most is the personal moral character and technical competence of the people who make up the financial systems. If top managers are intent upon doing wrong, it would be nearly impossible to develop a set of checks and balances that could completely prevent them from doing so.

Another example where corporate governance may be challenged in times of hardship pertains to management's role regarding oversight of the company's workforce. In times of trouble, changes may be needed in the workforce, and management may be placed in the painstaking position of firing and reorganizing personnel. An ethical approach to this difficult task is important to develop.

THE REAL WORLD

> Motorola Corporation, a worldwide electronics conglomerate, has a longstanding reputation of being a great place to work. In addition to its economic success, it is well known for its model social and environmental performance. The company's corporate citizenship programs support philanthropy, diversity, wellness, and community outreach. The company prides itself on being a great corporate citizen.
>
> Motorola's favorable reputation of strong ethics was threatened, however, when the company was forced to downsize in order to maintain its competitive edge (like many high-tech companies) in the early 2000s. In carrying out this difficult task of reducing its workforce, management made sure that affected people were treated with respect, protecting employee benefits for as long as possible during the transition period. It offered placement counseling and provided extended medical coverage and severance packages. Ed Zander, Motorola's CEO, claims that times of hardship prove how important corporate governance is to a corporation.[8]

The Motorola case exemplifies a company upholding its commitment to corporate governance during difficult financial times. Motorola's approach focused on preserving the morale and welfare of its human resources. It is sometimes challenging to balance personnel issues with stewardship obligations. Some managers may be inclined to make swift, drastic cuts in order to protect shareholder resources. However, a compassionate approach is likely to be more effective than a quick fix, in terms of protecting the company's reputation.

Another concept that is extremely significant to corporate governance and ethical conduct is independence. With the changes imposed by the Sarbanes–Oxley Act, it is more important than ever for a corporation's audit committee to maintain independence when it performs its duties. The audit committee is responsible for financial oversight, which requires it to challenge financial decisions and presentations of related information. Even though the board of directors demands ethical conduct from the company, the audit committee cannot be too trusting of the company's management. Members of the audit committee cannot let their

[8]www.motorola.com

connection to the company overshadow their objectivity with regard to financial matters. They must thoroughly understand the company's underlying transactions, especially any nonroutine transactions that may have by-passed the normal system of internal controls.

Although there are now many legal changes to corporate governance that mandate a more ethical business environment, there is no substitute for the integrity and ethics of a company's leaders.

SUMMARY OF STUDY OBJECTIVES

An overview of corporate governance. Corporate governance is the body of policies and procedures in place to make sure that all of the corporation's employees and leaders are held accountable for their actions on the job. Its purpose is to ensure the efficient use of the company's resources so as to protect the economic wealth of the shareholder and the overall health of the corporation. An effective system of corporate governance depends on the tone at the top.

Participants in the corporate governance process. Many stakeholders are important to the corporate governance process. Internal stakeholders consist of shareholders, the board of directors and its audit committee, and all of the company's layers of personnel, including managers, supervisors, staff members, and internal auditors. External stakeholders consist of external auditors, regulators, investors, creditors, customers, suppliers, and the overall business community in which the company operates.

The functions within the corporate governance process. There are four primary functions of the corporate governance process: management oversight, internal controls and compliance, financial stewardship, and ethical conduct. Management oversight involves the various positions of internal and external stakeholders monitoring the responsibilities of others under their direction. Internal control and compliance involve safeguarding corporate assets and establishing accurate financial reports in an effort to maintain compliance with accounting principles and other regulations. Financial stewardship is the overall responsibility for protecting the financial interest of the company's shareholders. Ethical conduct is the foundation of the corporate governance system, as each of the other functions depends on the honest and conscientious efforts of the people involved.

The history of corporate governance. Corporate governance first came to light in the 1930s with the creation of the Securities and Exchange Commission and in reaction to the accounting problems connected with the market crash of 1929 and the Great Depression. Over the years, the concept has evolved as the business world has shifted focus from materiality to earnings pressures and, most recently, to the requirements of the Sarbanes–Oxley Act.

The Sarbanes-Oxley Act of 2002. This federal law was enacted in an effort to improve financial reporting and to reinforce the importance of corporate ethics. The most significant provisions of the Act include the establishment of the Public Company Accounting Oversight Board (PCAOB) to monitor and discipline public accountants and audit committees, increased information requirements for financial reporting purposes with stiff penalties for noncompliance, requirements for management to certify the financial statements and internal controls of the company, and increased responsibilities for auditors to report on the effectiveness of their client's internal controls and restrict the types of nonaudit services they perform for audit clients.

The impact of the Sarbanes–Oxley Act on corporate governance. The Act has resulted in widespread change in the corporate environment, as it involves all of the participants and functions within the corporate governance process. Never before has there been so much attention placed on the roles of corporate leaders and their diligent involvement in the company's financial information. Many of the responsibilities of management and the board of directors now have greater importance, especially with respect to management oversight, maintenance of effective internal controls to support compliance, and increased focus on financial stewardship and ethical conduct. Gone are the days when corporate managers and boards could perform solely the task of strategic decision making; the Act requires these corporate leaders to be well versed in many details of the company's financial systems.

The importance of corporate governance in the study of accounting information systems. The Sarbanes–Oxley Act heightens the business value of financial information. Since the Act requires more financial information and faster financial reporting, there is more attention than ever on the importance of the accountants and IT personnel who provide financial information for the company. In addition, it is increasingly important that this data be readily accessible to the auditors and members of corporate management who are responsible for certifying the information.

Ethics and corporate governance. Internal stakeholders may sometimes have difficult ethical choices to make when their personal interests conflict with the interests of shareholders. Corporate governance must provide the structure to make sure that a system of financial stewardship is maintained, even when times get tough.

KEY TERMS

Accuracy
Corporate governance
Earnings management
Fiduciary duty
Financial Accounting Standards Board (FASB)
International Accounting Standards Board (IASB)
Sarbanes–Oxley Act of 2002
Securities Act of 1933
Securities and Exchange Commission (SEC)
Securities Exchange Act of 1934
Stakeholder
Stewardship
Tone at the top
Transparency
Treadway Commission
Whistleblower

END OF CHAPTER MATERIAL

CONCEPT CHECK

1. Which of the following is **not** considered a component of corporate governance?
   a. board of directors oversight
   b. IRS audits
   c. internal audits
   d. external audits
2. Good corporate governance is achieved when the interests of which of the following groups are balanced?
   a. internal auditors and external auditors
   b. shareholders and regulators
   c. shareholders, the corporation, and the community
   d. regulators and the community
3. Over time, corporate leaders establish trust by being active leaders, stressing integrity, clarity, and consistency. This is referred to as
   a. internal control.
   b. corporate governance.
   c. fiduciary duty.
   d. tone at the top.
4. Corporate governance is primarily concerned with
   a. enhancing the trend toward more women serving on boards of directors.
   b. promoting an increase in hostile takeovers.
   c. promoting the legitimacy of corporate charters.
   d. emphasizing the relative roles, rights, and accountability of a company's stakeholders.
5. The governing body responsible for establishing the COSO framework for internal controls evaluations is the
   a. Treadway Commission.
   b. SEC.
   c. PCAOB.
   d. FASB.
6. When financial information is presented properly and its correctness is verifiable, it is
   a. transparent.
   b. compliant.
   c. accurate.
   d. accountable.
7. Which of the following nonaudit services may be performed by auditors for a public-company audit client?
   a. IT consulting regarding the general ledger system for a newly acquired division

b. programming assistance on the new division's general ledger system

c. human resource consulting regarding personnel for the new division

d. income tax return preparation for the new division

8. Which of the following is **not** true regarding the requirements for reporting on internal controls under Section 404 of the Sarbanes–Oxley Act of 2002?

   a. Management must accept responsibility for the establishment and maintenance of internal controls and provide its assessment of their effectiveness.

   b. The independent auditor must issue a report on the effectiveness of internal controls.

   c. Management must identify the framework used for evaluating its internal controls.

   d. Management must achieve a control environment that has no significant deficiencies.

9. In the corporate governance chain of command, the audit committee is accountable to

   a. the company's vendors and other creditors.

   b. management and employees.

   c. governing bodies such as the SEC and PCAOB.

   d. the external auditors.

10. Section 806 of the Sarbanes–Oxley Act is often referred to as the whistleblower protection provision of the Act because

    a. it offers stock ownership to those who report instances of wrongdoing.

    b. it specifies that whistleblowers must be terminated so as to avoid retaliation.

    c. it protects whistleblowers' jobs and prohibits retaliation.

    d. it provides criminal penalties for the alteration or destruction of documents.

11. Which of the following is true regarding the post-Sarbanes–Oxley role of the corporate leader?

    a. More emphasis is placed on strategic planning and less emphasis on financial information.

    b. The corporate leader must be more in tune with IT to provide corporate governance solutions.

    c. The corporate leader must be more focused on merger and acquisition targets.

    d. The corporate leader tends to be less involved with the board of directors.

12. Many corporate frauds involve

    a. managers soliciting assistance from their subordinates.

    b. a small deceptive act that intensifies into criminal behavior.

    c. an earnings management motive.

    d. all of the above.

DISCUSSION QUESTIONS

13. (SO 1) Why is tone at the top so important to corporate governance?
14. (SO 1) Why do you think companies that practice good corporate governance tend to be successful in business?
15. (SO 2) Which stakeholder group, internal or external, is more likely to be affected by corporate governance, and which has a direct affect on corporate governance?
16. (SO 2) Explain how it is possible that a shareholder could be considered both an internal and an external stakeholder.
17. (SO 2) Why is the board of directors considered an internal stakeholder group, when it is required to have members who are independent of the company?
18. (SO 2) How can internal auditors maintain independence, since they are employees of the company?
19. (SO 3) Identify the four functions of the corporate governance process.
20. (SO 3) Describe the key connection between tone at the top and management oversight.
21. (SO 3) Explain the connection between fiduciary duty and financial stewardship.
22. (SO 4) Why do many accountants claim that corporate governance was born in the 1930s?
23. (SO 4) What is the primary difference between the Securities Act of 1933 and the Securities Exchange Act of 1934?
24. (SO 5, SO 6) Why did the SEC establish the PCAOB?
25. (SO 5) Why can auditors no longer be involved in helping their audit clients establish accounting information systems?
26. (SO 5) Under what conditions are auditors permitted to perform nonaudit services for their audit clients?
27. (SO 5, SO 6) How has the Sarbanes–Oxley Act increased the importance of audit committees in the corporate governance process?
28. (SO 5) Identify the six financial matters that must be certified by a company's top officers under the requirements of Section 302 of the Sarbanes–Oxley Act.
29. (SO 5) Explain the relationship between Section 401 of the Sarbanes–Oxley Act and the concept of transparency.
30. (SO 5) Explain the difference between management's responsibility and the company's external auditors' responsibility regarding the company's internal controls under Section 404 of the Sarbanes–Oxley Act.
31. (SO 5) Explain why Section 409 of the Sarbanes–Oxley Act has placed more pressure on members of IT departments within public companies.
32. (SO 5) How is the Sarbanes–Oxley Act forcing corporations to become more ethical?
33. (SO 6) Why do corporate leaders see their jobs as more risky since the Sarbanes–Oxley Act became effective?
34. (SO 6) Which governing body holds the top position of management oversight?

35. (SO 6) Identify two ways that companies are making efforts to improve the financial stewardship of their managers.
36. (SO 7) How can IT departments assist corporate managers in fulfilling their corporate governance roles?
37. (SO 8) How is it that management's role as financial stewards may be considered a conflict of interest with their position as employees of the company?

BRIEF EXERCISES

38. (SO 2) Why are shareholders sometimes considered internal stakeholders and sometimes considered external stakeholders?
39. (SO 3) Is it possible for financial information to be accurate, but not transparent? Similarly, is it possible for financial information to be transparent, but not accurate? Explain.
40. (SO 3) Earnings management involves lying about the company's financial results in order to provide a more favorable impression to investors. Earnings management is discussed in the section on financial stewardship. Explain how the other three functions of corporate governance can work together to help prevent earnings management within a corporation.
41. (SO 4) Describe how the characteristics of the financial markets in the 1980s eventually led to the creation of the Sarbanes–Oxley Act of 2002.
42. (SO 5) Although the Sarbanes–Oxley Act of 2002 applies to public companies, many private business organizations have been impacted by this legislation, especially if they are suppliers to a public company. Explain how this external stakeholder relationship can lead to the widespread application of Section 404 of the Act.
43. (SO 6, SO 7) Describe at least three ways that the Sarbanes–Oxley Act and the increased attention to corporate governance have put more emphasis on the role of those responsible for the company's accounting information systems.
44. (SO 8) Why do you think it is particularly challenging for companies to maintain ethical behavior during difficult financial times?

PROBLEMS

45. (SO 3) List the six steps for establishing internal controls and describe how this process leads to stronger overall corporate governance.
46. (SO 5, SO 6) List the items that must be certified by corporate management in accordance with the provisions of the Sarbanes–Oxley Act. Discuss how these responsibilities have likely changed the period-to-period activities of the certifying managers.
47. (SO 6) Identify the costs and benefits of complying with the Sarbanes–Oxley Act of 2002. Do you think the costs are justified?
48. (SO 2, SO 5) Using an Internet search engine, determine who the whistleblower was at Enron. Summarize the circumstances. What was the relationship of this person with the company? Was this an internal or external stakeholder?

49. (SO 3, SO 8) Using an Internet search engine, search for the terms "guilty as charged" + "California Micro Devices" in order to find an article about the company, California Micro Devices. Identify the related corporate governance issues.

50. (SO 3, SO 8) There are five types of earnings management techniques presented in this chapter. Provide two or three specific examples of how corporate leaders could pull off these types of fraud, as well as the internal control activities that could be used to prevent them.

CASES

51. Do you think the tone at the top of organizations like Enron and WorldCom led to their demise? In support of your answer, identify specific actions of top managers at each of these companies. In order to answer this question, you may wish to perform research on the conditions that brought these companies down.

52. Through online research, locate the code of conduct for the top management of a real-world company. Discuss the importance of each component of this code in terms of ethics and its relation to the concept of corporate governance.

CONTINUING CASE: SPATELLI'S PIZZERIA

Refer to the Spatelli's Pizzeria case at the end of Chapter 1. Answer the following questions:

a. From the facts of the case, identify Spatelli's internal and external stakeholders.

b. Other than by its product offerings (pizza, etc.), identify any ways that Spatelli's Pizzeria influences its business community.

SOLUTIONS TO CONCEPT CHECK

1. (SO 1, SO 2) **b. IRS audits** are not considered a component of corporate governance. Although income tax returns are a form of financial reporting, they are not considered part of the corporate governance structure because management does not have the same level of responsibility for tax returns.

2. (SO 1) Good corporate governance is achieved when the interests of **c. shareholders, the corporation, and the community** are balanced. For each of the other responses, the stakeholder groups are not expected to have aligned interests; rather, they each have diverse interests in the corporation.

3. (SO 1) Over time, corporate leaders establish trust by being active leaders, stressing integrity, clarity, and consistency. This is referred to as **d. tone at the top.**

4. (CIA Adapted) (SO 1) Corporate governance is primarily concerned with **d. emphasizing the relative roles, rights, and accountability of the company's stakeholders.** This response is consistent with the definition of corporate governance which states that the company's leadership is held accountable for building shareholder value and creating confidence.
5. (SO 2) The governing body responsible for establishing the COSO framework for internal controls evaluations is the **a. Treadway Commission.**
6. (SO 3) When financial information is presented properly and its correctness is verifiable, it is **c. accurate.**
7. (SO 5) **d. Income tax return preparation for a new division** is a nonaudit service that may be performed by auditors for a public-company audit client. Each of the other services is expressly prohibited by Section 201 of the Sarbanes-Oxley Act.
8. (CPA Adapted) (SO 5) The statement **d. Management must achieve a control environment that has no significant deficiencies** is not true regarding the requirements for reporting on internal controls under Section 404 of the Sarbanes–Oxley Act of 2002. Although management would certainly strive for a control environment free of deficiencies, there is no requirement for such. Each of the other responses represents a requirement of Section 404 of the Act.
9. (SO 6) In the corporate governance chain of command, the audit committee is accountable to **c. governing bodies such as the SEC and PCAOB.** Refer to Exhibit 5-3.
10. (SO 5) Section 806 of the Sarbanes–Oxley Act is often referred to as the whistleblower protection provision of the Act because **c. it protects whistleblowers' jobs and prohibits retaliation.**
11. (SO 6) The post-Sarbanes–Oxley role of the corporate leader is **b. more in tune with IT to provide corporate governance solutions.** Each of the other answers is more characteristic of the CEO's role prior to the Act.
12. (SO 8) Many corporate frauds involve **d. all of the above,** including managers soliciting assistance from their subordinates, small deceptive acts that intensify into criminal behavior, and an earnings management motive.

CHAPTER 6

IT Governance

STUDY OBJECTIVES

This chapter will help you gain an understanding of the following concepts:

1. An introduction to IT governance and its role in strategic management
2. An overview of the system development life cycle (SDLC)
3. The elements of the systems planning phase of the SDLC
4. The elements of the systems analysis phase of the SDLC
5. The elements of the systems design phase of the SDLC
6. The elements of the systems implementation phase of the SDLC
7. The elements of the operation and maintenance phase of the SDLC
8. The critical importance of IT governance in an organization
9. Ethical considerations related to IT governance

THE REAL WORLD

Sean Locke/iStockphoto

Keeping technology initiatives aligned with business direction is a challenge facing every company, but the larger the company, the bigger the challenge will be. As a global corporation with multiple subsidiaries, United Parcel Service Inc. (UPS) has faced the challenge and fashioned an award-winning IT organization consistently aligned with the company's core business strategy.

UPS formed an information and technology strategy committee (ITSC) composed of 15 senior managers from all functional areas within the company. ITSC was chartered with the tasks of studying the impacts and application of new technologies and understanding near-term technology direction.

A cross-functional committee has approval and oversight on all projects and programs, while a senior executive heads them and an IT owner helps prioritize needs and resource requirements across functions. Projects are prioritized on the basis of the strength of their business cases (e.g., service to UPS customers) and financial metrics (e.g., return on investment, net present value), but nonfinancial metrics are also considered so that noncore projects can be given adequate resources.

UPS also formed an IT governance committee to oversee day-to-day IT operations. In addition to formalizing the project prioritization and budgeting processes, the IT governance committee established standards and designed the architecture, policing itself to ensure that all work was in tune with business requirements and direction. Composed of the chief information officer and senior IT managers, the IT governance committee more closely aligns IT to the business, establishing stringent management processes and enforcing technology standards and processes. The committee has oversight into all key IT decisions and provides a forum to raise critical issues.[1]

INTRODUCTION TO IT GOVERNANCE (STUDY OBJECTIVE 1)

In the business environment of today, IT systems are critical to the success of the organizations that use them. IT systems can improve efficiency and effectiveness, and reduce costs. Companies that fail to take proper advantage of the potential benefits of IT systems can lose market share to competitors or in some cases, become bankrupt. To ensure that a company is using IT to its competitive advantage, it must continually investigate and assess the viability of using newer information technologies. The company must ensure that its long-term strategies, and its ongoing operations, properly utilize appropriate IT systems. But how does a company decide which IT systems are appropriate to its operations? Moreover, how does a company decide, for example,

- which accounting software package to buy?
- when the company has outgrown its accounting software or when to upgrade that accounting software?
- whether to use IT systems to sell products on the web?
- whether to establish a data warehouse for analyzing data such as sales trends?
- whether to use ERP systems or customer relationship management (CRM) software?

[1] Excerpts from a United Parcel Service press release, http://www.pressroom.ups.com/mediakits/factsheet/0,2305,1043,00.html

Each of these decisions is likely to have a long-run strategic impact on the company. Decisions the company makes about the IT systems it will use will affect the efficiency and effectiveness of the organization in achieving strategic goals. IT systems must be chosen that support management's strategic goals and the daily operational management. IT systems must be strategically managed. **Strategic management** is the process of determining the strategic vision for the organization, developing the long-term objectives, creating the strategies that will achieve the vision and objectives, and implementing those strategies. Strategic management requires continuous evaluation of, and refinements to, the vision, objectives, strategy, and implementation. To achieve the purposes of strategic management, an organization must also properly manage, control, and use IT systems that enable the organization to achieve its strategies and objectives. The proper management, control, and use of IT systems is IT governance. The IT Governance Institute defines **IT governance** as follows:

> [A] structure of relationships and processes to direct and control the enterprise in order to achieve the enterprise's goals by adding value while balancing risk versus return over IT and its processes. IT governance provides the structure that links IT processes, IT resources and information to enterprise strategies and objectives.[2]

A summary of this definition is that the board of directors and top-level executive managers must take responsibility to ensure that the organization has processes that align IT systems to the strategies and objectives of the organization. IT systems should be chosen and implemented that support attainment of strategies and objectives. To fulfill the management obligations that are inherent in IT governance, management must focus on the following activities:

- aligning IT strategy with the business strategy
- cascading strategy and goals down into the enterprise
- providing organizational structures that facilitate the implementation of strategy and goals
- insisting that an IT control framework be adopted and implemented
- measuring IT's performance

There is no single method of achieving each of these management obligations. Different companies may choose different approaches. There are, however, three popular models of an IT control framework:

1. Information Systems Audit and Control Association (ISACA) control objectives for IT (COBIT)
2. The International Organization for Standardization (ISO) 17799, Code of Practice for Information Security Management
3. The Information Technology Infrastructure Library (ITIL)

These three are very comprehensive models of an IT control framework, and their details are beyond the scope of this book. The Appendix to Chapter 3 briefly described the components of COBIT. The major focus of this chapter is

[2]Control Objectives for information and Related Technology (COBIT) 4.1, Executive Summary Framework, IT Governance Institute, Rolling Meadows, IL, 2007 (www.itgi.org), p. 5.

to highlight the first three of the preceding objectives: aligning IT strategy with business strategy; cascading strategy down into the enterprise; and providing organizational structures to facilitate implementation. Therefore, this chapter will focus only on three selected aspects of IT governance: the definition of IT governance, the role of the IT governance committee, and the system development life cycle.

IT governance must be an important issue for all management levels, from the board of directors to lower level managers. To meet its obligation of corporate governance, the board must oversee IT. IT systems are critical to the long-term success of the organization, and board involvement in IT oversight is therefore necessary. The board should do the following:

- Articulate and communicate the business direction to which IT should be aligned. The board should set and communicate long-term company strategy and objectives.
- Make sure it is aware of the latest developments in IT, from a business perspective.
- Insist that IT be a regular item on the agenda of the board and that it be addressed in a structured manner.
- Be informed about how and how much the enterprise invests in IT compared with its competitors' investments.
- Ensure that the reporting level of the most senior information technology manager is commensurate with the importance of IT. For example, the chief information officer (CIO) may need to report directly to the CEO.
- Ensure that it has a clear view of the major IT investments, from a risk-and-return perspective. Each IT investment will have risks—for example, increased security risks. However, each IT investment will also generate return in the form of cost savings, such as increased efficiency. The board members should be informed about the risks and returns.
- Receive regular progress reports on major IT projects.
- Receive IT performance reports illustrating the value of IT.
- Ensure that suitable IT resources, infrastructures, and skills are available to meet the required enterprise strategic objectives.[3]

To ensure that IT systems support long-term strategic objectives as well as daily operations, management must constantly assess its current situation, where it plans to go, and which IT systems will help it get there. To be effective, this assessment should be part of an ongoing process to evaluate organizational direction and the fit of IT to that direction. The board and top management must ensure that the organization has processes to accomplish the following tasks:

1. Continually evaluate the match of strategic goals to the IT systems in use.
2. Identify changes or improvements to the IT system that will enhance the ability to meet strategic organizational objectives.
3. Prioritize the necessary changes to IT systems.

[3]Adapted from "Board Briefing on IT Governance," 2nd Ed., IT Governance Institute. Rolling Meadows, IL, 2003 (www.itgi.org).

4. Develop the plan to design and implement those IT changes that are of high priority.
5. Implement and maintain the IT systems.
6. Continually loop back to step 1.

The managerial obligation to evaluate strategic match and to implement IT systems begins with the board of directors and must cascade down into the organization. This means that the board, top executive management, and lower level managers all must work toward the same goal of ensuring IT systems and strategy align with the organization's strategic goals. To match company strategy to IT systems, the company should have an IT governance committee and a formal process to select, design, and implement IT systems. The **IT governance committee** is a group of senior managers selected to oversee the strategic management of IT. The formal process that many organizations use to select, design, and implement IT systems is the **system development life cycle,** or **SDLC.** Both of these management tools, the IT governance committee and the SDLC, are necessary in the strategic management of IT systems.

By analyzing similar management situations, we may find it easier to see the importance of the IT governance committee and the SDLC. Professional sports teams can be used as an analogy to IT management. For a professional football team to be a consistent winner over many seasons, two kinds of important management process must occur. First, the general manager, scouts, and coaches must draft and trade for players who fit into the organization. When drafting and trading players, these team managers must be considering their long-term strategy. They must assess the strengths and weaknesses of the team, the style of offense and defense they will play in the future, and the types of players that will best fit those playing styles and the coaching structure. In addition to this long-term management of team strategy and player choices, the coaches must make shorter-term decisions to develop and use the players of the team. Coaches must decide which players are starters and which serve as back-up players. They must decide which players play which positions and which types of offensive and defensive plays most effectively use the skills of their players. In other words, to consistently be successful in winning games, team managers must not only have a proper long-term strategy, but, within any sports season, must manage the players in a way that takes best advantage of team strengths and weaknesses. They must fit all the pieces of the team together in a way that maximizes team success. That is, they must implement the best mix of players and plays to maximize the effectiveness of the team in achieving the objective: winning games. The managers and coaches have systematic, regular steps that they consistently apply to manage the long-term and short-term success of the team. Without these systematic, regular steps, the team would not be successful when playing against other well-managed teams. The team play would be too chaotic and unorganized to play successfully. For example, a playground, pick-up basketball team could never hope to succeed against a professional NBA basketball team.

These two processes of long-term development and short-term management are similar to the functions of the IT governance committee and the SDLC. The IT governance committee should constantly assess the long-term strategy of the company and determine the type of IT systems to purchase, develop, and use that will help the organization achieve its objectives. Once the IT governance committee has determined the priority it places on various IT systems, the SDLC is the process that manages the development, implementation, and use of those IT systems. Much like players on a team, the various parts of the IT system must fit together in a way that maximizes the overall effectiveness and efficiency of the company operations. In addition, much like the salary caps in professional sports, there is a limit to the funds that a company can spend to purchase, develop, and implement IT systems. With limited funds available, the proper long-term and short-term management of IT systems becomes very critical. The organization must strategically manage IT systems to achieve maximum effectiveness of the systems at a cost that matches the IT budget. Similar to the sports team example, the lack of systematic, regular steps to strategically manage the IT systems leads to chaotic and unorganized IT systems. In such an unorganized environment, the company is less likely to be successful in competing against other companies and may not survive.

AN OVERVIEW OF THE SDLC (STUDY OBJECTIVE 2)

The systems development life cycle (SDLC) is a systematic process to manage the acquisition, design, implementation, and use of IT systems. The oversight and management of the SDLC is normally the responsibility of the IT governance committee. The IT governance committee is usually made up of the top managers of the organization, including the chief executive officer (CEO), the chief financial officer (CFO), the chief information officer (CIO), top managers from user departments, and top management from internal audit. In addition to developing a long-term vision and objectives for IT systems, the IT governance committee oversees the SDLC.

In the early days of computers, most organizations had to develop, program, and implement accounting software in-house. It was not feasible to buy accounting software, nor was it available at a reasonable price. During that time, the SDLC was a systematic set of regular steps to accomplish the IT systems selection, design, programming, and implementation. The phases of the SDLC are depicted in Exhibit 6-1 and are briefly defined as follows:

Exhibit 6-1
An Overview of the Systems Development Life Cycle

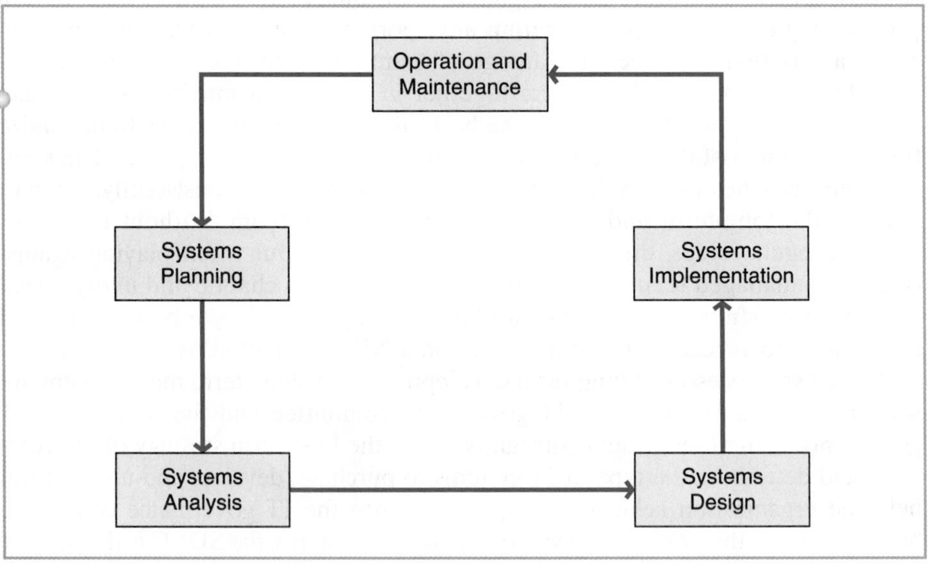

1. **Systems planning** is the evaluation of long-term, strategic objectives and the prioritization of the IT systems in order to assist the organization in achieving its objectives. Systems planning also involves the planning and continuing oversight of the design, implementation, and use of those IT systems.
2. **Systems analysis** is a study of the current system to determine the strengths and weaknesses and the user needs of that system. Analysis requires the collection of data about the system and the careful scrutiny of those data to determine areas of the system that can be improved.
3. **Systems design** is the creation of the system that meets user needs and incorporates the improvements identified by the systems analysis phase.
4. **Systems implementation** is the set of steps undertaken to program, test, and activate the IT system as designed in the system design phase.
5. **Operation and maintenance** is the regular, ongoing functioning of the IT system and the processes to fix smaller problems, or "bugs," in the IT system. During operation, management should request and receive ongoing reports about the performance of the IT system.

Notice that the SDLC is a cycle that eventually loops back to systems planning. This is true because the IT governance committee must continually evaluate how well the current IT systems match the company's strategic objectives. At some point, the IT governance committee will most likely find it necessary to go back through the phases of the SDLC to design new and improved IT systems.

As computers and IT systems have become more complex, more comprehensive, and more common, some steps in the phases in the SDLC have evolved to be slightly different. The major difference now, compared with earlier days of computers, is that the majority of companies purchase the accounting software they use rather than designing and programming the software in-house. However, even when accounting software is purchased, it may require extensive modification to make it fit the organization's needs. Therefore, even when purchasing accounting software, it is important to use a systematic, regular set of steps to evaluate, purchase, modify, and implement the software. The SDLC phases may be slightly different, but still comprise necessary steps for the proper strategic management of IT systems.

The remaining sections of this chapter describe the phases and steps of the SDLC in the modern IT environment. A process map overview of a typical SDLC appears in Exhibit 6-2. Not every organization follows each of these steps in the exact sequence shown; the SDLC phases can vary from organization to organization. The more important factor is that an organization follows a set of logical, systematic steps when modifying or adopting new systems. The exact steps and their sequence are not as critical as the need to formalize and conduct those steps completely and consistently. As a corollary, think about how companies conduct their budgeting procedures. Different companies may go about building their budgets in different ways. Some may use a bottom-up approach where lower level managers build budgets for their area and those budgets are submitted up the chain of management where they are consolidated into one overall budget. Other companies may budget from the top down. In either case, the method chosen should fit the company. The important factor is that the company has a working budgeting process, not whether it uses a particular method. Likewise, it is important that the SDLC

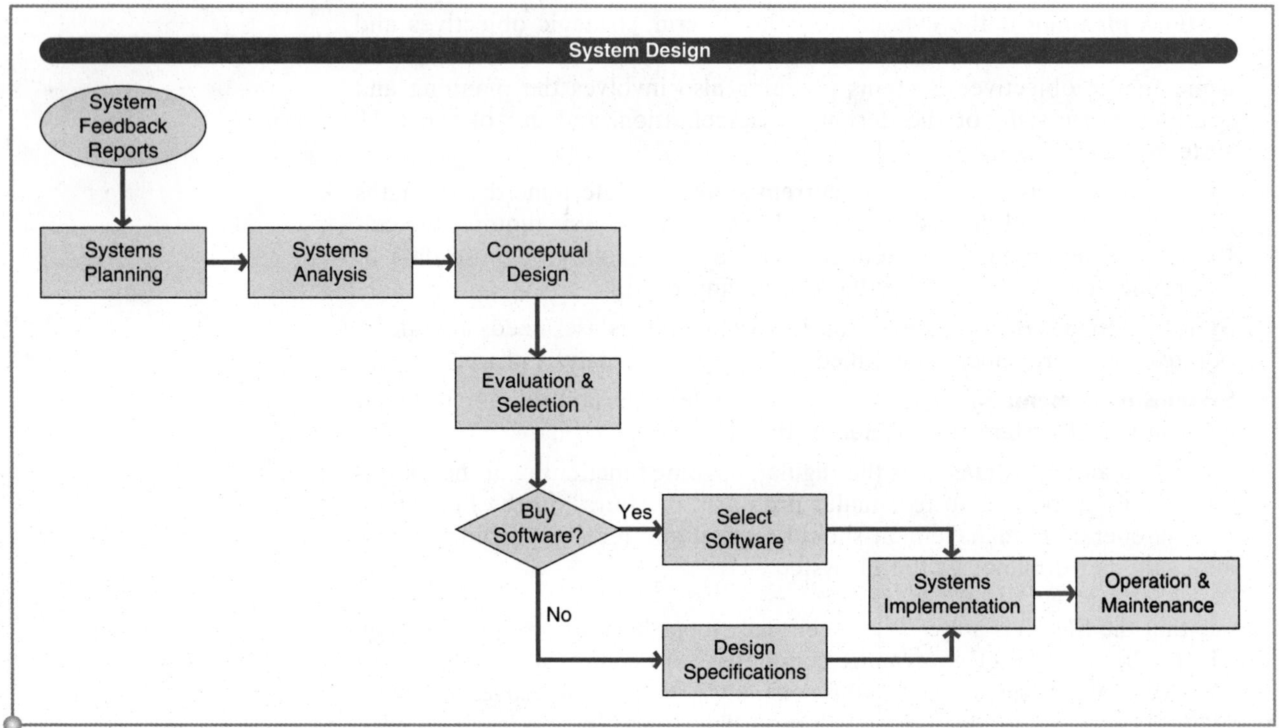

Exhibit 6-2
Process Map of the System Development Life Cycle (SDLC)

has a logical sequence of phases, but those phases may vary slightly from company to company.

The process map shows the same phases as the SDLC overview in Exhibit 6-1, but with an expanded set of processes within the system design phase. These expanded processes are necessary because there is usually more than one software or system type that meets the needs of the organizations. For example, if a company wishes to modify the payroll processes and systems in use, there are several ways to approach the modification. The company could do timekeeping in-house, but outsource the actual payroll processing to a payroll processing firm. Second, the company could buy or write a stand-alone payroll processing program. As a third alternative, the company could buy or write an integrated payroll system as part of a more comprehensive human-resource-management software system. To guide this process of designing a new payroll system, the company should have defined steps that identify the alternative system approaches, evaluate the fit of each alternative to the company's needs, select the best fit, and design or buy that system.

The process map in Exhibit 6-2 shows these alternative phases of system design. **Conceptual design** is the process of matching alternative system models to the needs identified in the system analysis phase. **Evaluation and selection** is the process of assessing the feasibility and fit of each of these alternative conceptual approaches and selecting the one that best meets the organization's needs. The best system may be either software that can be purchased, or a system designed and developed in-house. If software is to be purchased, the company must undergo a set of steps called **software selection** to select the best software for its needs. When systems are to be developed in-house, the company must undertake steps to design the details of that system. **Detailed design** is the process of designing the outputs, inputs, user interfaces, databases, manual procedures, security and controls, and documentation of the new system.

THE PHASES OF THE SDLC

The sections that follow build upon the overview of the SDLC phases, examining each phase in detail. As mentioned previously, it is important to remember that the description presented here is of a typical set of phases and steps within the SDLC and is not intended to imply that every organization must follow these exact steps.

ELEMENTS OF THE SYSTEMS PLANNING PHASE OF THE SDLC (STUDY OBJECTIVE 3)

Systems planning is a managerial function of the IT governance committee. The IT governance committee must constantly monitor the IT system through feedback about network utilization, security breaches, and reports on the operation of the system. This constant monitoring allows the IT governance committee to determine whether the current system meets organizational needs. When the committee determines that a part or parts of the IT system are not meeting organizational needs, it should begin the process to study and evaluate the feasibility of modifying or updating those parts of the system. The IT governance committee will also receive specific requests from those who use the IT system to modify or upgrade parts of the system. This means that at any one time the IT governance committee may be considering not only modifications or upgrades that they have noted need attention, but also upgrades or modifications requested by users. Usually, it is not possible to simultaneously modify or upgrade all of these areas. The IT governance committee must have procedures to follow that will assist it in prioritizing the most important needs of the IT system for immediate modification or upgrade.

THE REAL WORLD

Before Allstate Insurance Co. formed a capital spending committee with IT governance responsibilities, the process of prioritizing IT projects typically was decided by "whoever spoke the loudest or whoever had the biggest checkbook," said Chief Technology Officer Cathy Brune.[4]

Now Brune and some top Allstate executives, including the chairman and CEO and the chief financial officer, collectively decide how to prioritize IT initiatives based on business needs. "They help me decide where to spend our money," Brune said, noting that the new approach to IT governance gives the business executives a better understanding of the IT spending process.[5]

[4]Thomas Hoffman, "IT Governance Is on the Hot Seat," *ComputerWorld*, July 12, 2004, pp. 6–8.
[5]*Ibid.*

The old approach at Allstate did not lead to selecting the IT systems that best empowered the company to achieve its strategic objectives. A better approach is to follow a system for prioritizing IT changes. To prioritize these projects, the IT governance committee should consider two broad aspects: (1) the assessment of IT systems and their match to strategic organizational objectives, and (2) the feasibility of each of the requested modifications or upgrades. In addition, the IT governance committee must plan and manage the design, implementation, and use of those IT systems. Exhibit 6-3 details the systems planning process.

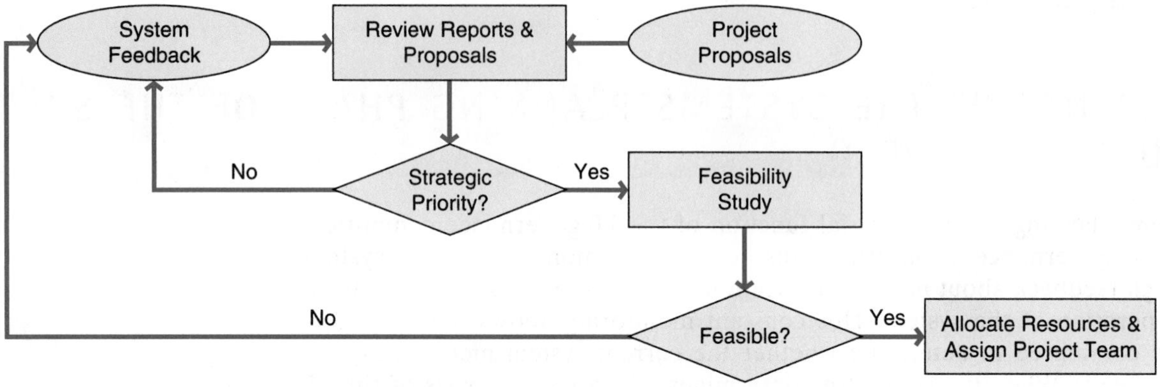

Exhibit 6-3
Systems Planning Process Map

THE MATCH OF IT SYSTEMS TO STRATEGIC OBJECTIVES

The IT governance committee must evaluate proposed changes to IT systems in terms of their usefulness in assisting the organization to achieve its objectives. Evaluating the match of proposed IT changes to strategic objectives will allow the IT governance committee to begin prioritizing the desired changes. For example, suppose that a company has decided that a main strategic objective is to improve customer satisfaction. If the IT governance committee has received requests to begin modifications of the customer-order entry system and the payroll system, they are likely to place a higher priority on the customer-order entry system, since it will affect the service and satisfaction of customers. The payroll system modifications may be of a lower priority because such a change does not match as well with the strategic objective of improved customer satisfaction.

This need to match IT systems to organizational objectives also highlights the need for the IT governance committee to include as its members top management such as the CEO, CFO, CIO, and other high-level managers. Since these managers establish strategic objectives, they are in the best position to assess the fit of IT systems to those objectives. In addition, top management has the authority to allocate resources and time to these projects that will modify or upgrade IT systems. Lower level managers would not have the authority or gravitas within the organization to push through IT changes.

THE REAL WORLD

Recently, the top management at Anheuser Busch Companies, Inc. became very determined to use IT to improve beer sales. This was a major change for the company and would require significant investments of time, effort, and money to achieve the goal.

"As recently as six years ago, the beer industry was a technological laggard. Distributors and sales reps returned from their daily routes with stacks of invoices and sales orders, which they would type into a PC and dial in to breweries. They, in turn, would compile them into monthly reports to see which brands were the hottest. But Anheuser changed the rules in 1997, when chairman August Busch III vowed to make his company a leader in mining its customers' buying patterns."[6]

This data-mining example is discussed in more detail in Chapter 10, but included here to emphasize that the use of sophisticated IT systems to do data mining was a strategic objective of the company championed by the chairman, August Busch III. Such initiatives cannot be successful without the support of high-level managers, who control the resources necessary to successfully implement IT systems. Top-level managers must become strong supporters of improved IT systems if problem-solving systems are to be successfully integrated into the organization.

FEASIBILITY STUDY

In addition to examining the match of IT systems to strategic objectives, the IT governance committee should evaluate the feasibility of each competing proposal. Feasibility refers to the realistic possibility of affording, implementing, and using the IT systems being considered. There are four feasibility aspects that should be considered—remember them by the acronym TOES:

1. **Technical feasibility**—assessment of the realism of the possibility that technology exists to meet the need identified in the proposed change to the IT system.
2. **Operational feasibility**—assessment of the realism of the possibility that the current employees will be able to operate the proposed IT system. If the operation will require new training of employees, this assessment should include an evaluation of the feasibility of providing enough training to existing employees.
3. **Economic feasibility**—assessment of the costs and benefits associated with the proposed IT system. Is it realistic to conclude that the benefits of the proposed IT system outweigh the costs?
4. **Schedule feasibility**—assessment of the realistic possibility that the proposed IT system can be implemented within a reasonable time.

As the IT governance committee studies and assesses each of these aspects of feasibility, it can come to a better understanding of which proposed changes should have higher priorities. As an analogy to this process, think about how you chose your major in college. There are several majors that might have been possible for you. Perhaps you were considering an accounting major, a marketing major, and future law school as potential choices. To narrow your alternatives,

[6]Kevin Kelleher; "66, 207, 879(6) Bottles of Beer on the Wall," *Business 2.0*, January 1, 2004 (http://money.cnn.com/magazines/business2/business2_archive/2004/01/01/359602/index.htm).

you had to think about which major best fit your skills, talents, knowledge, and abilities. You had to assess the realistic possibilities of each major. It was probably true that you could rule out some majors as not at all feasible. But there may have been three or four that were realistically possible for you. You had to assess each of those potential majors from several aspects and decide which single major was best for you. Likewise, the IT governance committee may rule out some proposed changes to the IT system as not feasible at all. Among those that remain, some IT changes are more feasible than others. The studies of technical, operational, economic, and schedule feasibility allow the IT governance committee to decide which proposed IT changes should have the highest priority.

Using both the strategic objective match and the feasibility study, the IT governance committee can prioritize the various proposed changes to the IT system.

PLANNING AND OVERSIGHT OF THE PROPOSED CHANGES

After the IT governance committee has prioritized the proposed changes, it must decide which of the changes can be undertaken at the current time. Basing its decisions on the budget, resources, and time available, the IT governance committee may find that there are only one or two proposed changes that can be undertaken. Those proposed changes that must be delayed may be reviewed again in the future when the IT governance committee reassesses the strategic match of IT and feasibility. These processes are ongoing.

For the sake of further analysis, let us assume that the IT governance committee has decided that only one proposed IT system change can be undertaken at this time. The committee should do several things to initiate the next phases of the SDLC:

1. Formally announce the project they have chosen to undertake.
2. Assign the project team that will begin the next phase, the systems analysis.
3. Budget the funds necessary to complete the SDLC.
4. Continue oversight and management of the project team and proposed IT changes as the remaining SDLC phases occur.

ELEMENTS OF THE SYSTEMS ANALYSIS PHASE OF THE SDLC (STUDY OBJECTIVE 4)

Exhibit 6-4 illustrates typical steps within the systems analysis phase of the SDLC: a preliminary investigation, a survey of the current system, a determination of user information needs, analysis, and business process reengineering. At the end of this phase, the project team will prepare and deliver a systems analysis report.

PRELIMINARY INVESTIGATION

The preliminary investigation occurs within a short period ranging from a few hours to a few days and should not exceed two to three days. The purpose of

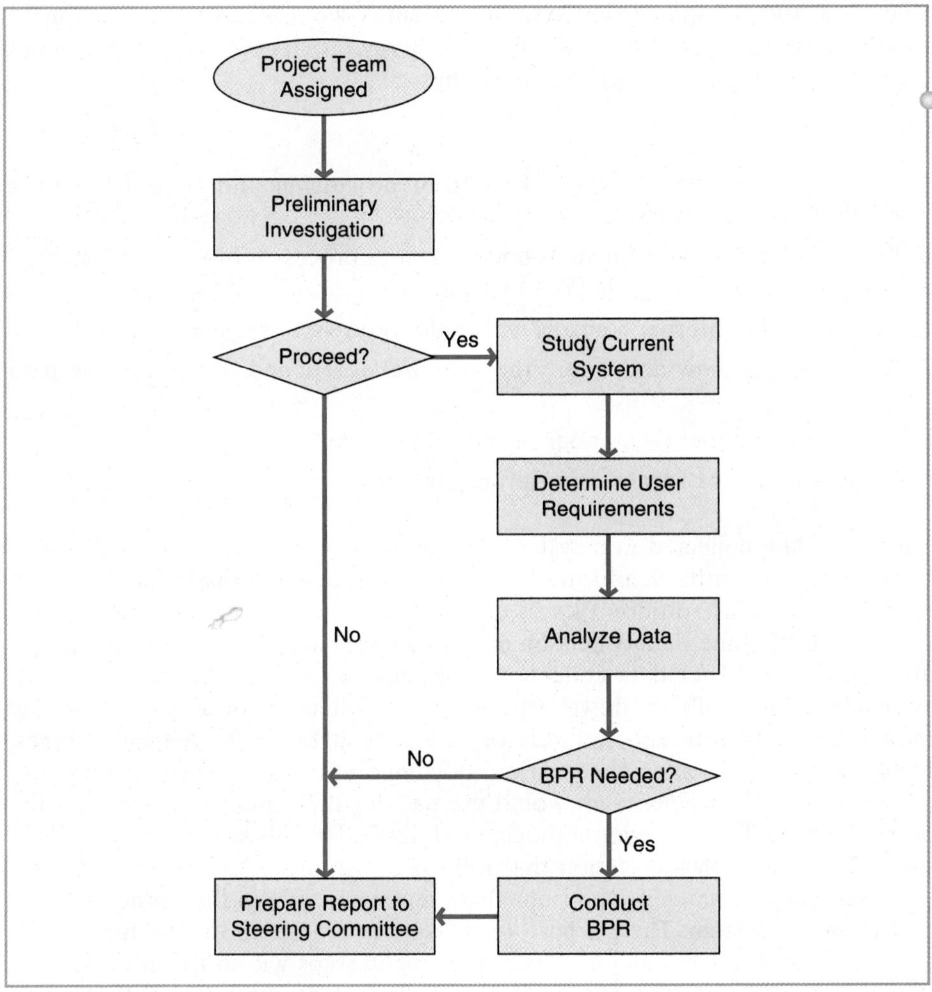

Exhibit 6-4
Systems Analysis Process Map

the preliminary investigation is to determine whether the problem or deficiency in the current system really exists. The project team may reexamine some of the feasibility aspects of the project. At this point, the purpose is to make a "go" or "no-go" decision. The end result is a decision to proceed further or to abandon the project.

SYSTEM SURVEY: THE STUDY OF THE CURRENT SYSTEM

In most cases, it is easier to improve something only when you have a good understanding of it. For example, it would be difficult for you to improve on the fuel efficiency of a car if you did not know details about how gas is used in the car, what quantities of gas the car uses, and which characteristics of the car affect fuel efficiency. Likewise, we cannot improve the efficiency and effectiveness of the IT system in use without first knowing such details about the system as transaction volumes, processes within the system, and controls within the system. All of these factors and others affect the throughput of an accounting system. **Throughput** is a measure of transactions per period. The **systems survey** is a detailed study of the current system to identify weaknesses to improve upon and strengths to be maintained. A systems survey requires collecting data about the current system, including the following:

- Inputs—sources of data
- Outputs—the uses of information from processing and outputs such as checks, reports, or forms
- Processes—the individual steps undertaken to process transactions, including both manual and computerized processes
- Controls—the internal controls within the processing system
- Data storage—how and where the data are stored, and the size of the data storage
- Transaction volumes—number of transactions per day or per hour
- Errors—number of transaction processing errors

The exact data collected in a systems survey may vary from project to project or company to company, and the foregoing list shows the usual data collected. As noted in this list, different kinds of data must be collected from several different sources. Some data collection may involve asking employees or managers questions, while other data collection may require examining documents such as operating manuals or flowcharts. The data collection in a systems survey requires several different methods of collecting data from different sources. Data collection involves observation, documentation review, interviews, and questionnaires. A project team would use each of these methods to collect the necessary data. The first two methods are described in this section, and the final two are described in the section that follows.

Observation is watching the steps that employees take as they process transactions in the system. The purpose of the observation is to enable the project team to gain an understanding of the processing steps within the system. **Documentation review** is the detailed examination of documentation that exists about the system to gain an understanding of the system under study. The project team would examine any relevant documentation about the system such as flowcharts, run manuals, operating manuals, input forms, reports, and outputs.

DETERMINATION OF USER REQUIREMENTS

While observation and documentation review are important methods of data collection, neither method actually seeks the views or thoughts of users of the system. By these methods, the project team members capture only those strengths and weaknesses within the system that they notice. To gain a complete understanding of the system under study, the project team should not only observe and review documentation, but also seek the opinions and thoughts of those who use the system.

Interviews and questionnaires are data collection methods that solicit feedback from users of the system. These are critical parts of the data collection, because it is of utmost importance that users have input into the development of a new or revised system. Since users are the people who input data or use output reports on a daily basis, the system must satisfy the needs of these users.

The user perspective and perception about the current system are an important part of the information that the project team needs to collect in order to benefit from a system survey. Interviews are a data collection method that help the project team in determining user needs.

Interviews are the face-to-face, verbal questioning of users to determine facts or beliefs about the system. The questions asked can be structured, unstructured, or some mixture of the two. A structured question is designed such that the format and range of the answer is known ahead of time. An unstructured question is completely open ended, and the respondent is free to answer in any way that he feels addresses the question. The difference between structured and unstructured questions is similar to the difference between multiple choice and essay questions. The multiple choice question has predetermined answers in a certain format, whereas the format and content of an essay answer are much more flexible for the person answering the question. Both types of questions can be used in interviews to solicit feedback from users about how they use the system and about strengths and weaknesses in the current system. The face-to-face nature of interviews provides advantages. The interviewer can clarify any misunderstandings about the question and can follow up with more questions, depending on the response of the interviewee. Both the interviewer and interviewee are more certain that they understand each other when communication is verbal and face to face.

Questionnaires are also used to solicit feedback from users. However, **questionnaires** are a written, rather than an oral, form of questioning of users to determine facts or beliefs about the system. Questionnaires can also include both structured and unstructured questions. There are advantages to the use of questionnaires. Questionnaires can be answered anonymously, which allows the respondent to be more truthful without fear of negative consequences. Similar to the anonymous instructor-evaluation forms used in college classes—wherein the student can be completely frank in his or her evaluation of a professor, since responses are anonymous—a respondent to a systems questionnaire can answer the questionnaire fully and truthfully. The other advantage to questionnaires is efficiency; that is, it is much easier and less time consuming to process 100 questionnaires than it is to personally interview 100 users.

ANALYSIS OF THE SYSTEM SURVEY

The analysis phase is the critical-thinking stage of the systems analysis. The purpose is to question the current approaches used in the system and to think about better ways to carry out the steps and processes in the system. The project team studies the information collected in the system survey phase and attempts to create improvements to the system.

In many cases, the analysis phase and the attempt to create improvements may lead to **business process reengineering (BPR)**. BPR has been defined as *"fundamental rethinking and radical redesign of business processes to bring about dramatic improvements" in performance.*[7] Business processes are the many sets of activities within the organization performed to accomplish the functions necessary to continue the daily operations. For example, every organization has

[7]Michael Hammer and James Champy, *Reengineering the Corporation, Revised Edition*, New York: HarperCollins Publishers, Inc., 1993 p. 32.

a process to collect and record the revenue earned. In a smaller company, the revenue collection process may simply be a single person who mails out bills, receives customer checks in the mail, totals the checks, records them in the accounting records, and deposits the funds. Through rethinking and redesigning this process, the company may be able to improve the process and thereby speed up the collection of revenue earned. This rethinking and redesign is especially aided by the use of IT. When technology or computers are introduced, the processes can be radically redesigned to take advantage of the speed and efficiency of computers to improve processing efficiency. IT and BPR have a mutually enhancing relationship. IT capabilities should support the business processes, and any business process should be designed to match the capabilities that the IT system can provide. BPR should leverage the capabilities of IT to improve the efficiency of processes. As discussed earlier, Anheuser Busch uses extensive IT systems to improve the forecasting of customer buying patterns. This IT system and the new processes that match it enable Anheuser Busch to keep customer store shelves stocked with the right amount of its various beer brands.

BPR will probably begin at this stage of the SDLC, but it may continue through several phases of the SDLC. As the project proceeds through the phases of the SDLC and the team begins to design and implement improvements to the system, more BPR may be necessary to match the processes to the system.

SYSTEMS ANALYSIS REPORT

The last step in the systems analysis phase is to prepare a systems analysis report for delivery to the IT governance committee, which will inform the IT governance committee of the results of the systems survey, user needs determination, and BPR. The report will make recommendations to the IT governance committee regarding the continuation of the project.

ELEMENTS OF THE SYSTEMS DESIGN PHASE OF THE SDLC (STUDY OBJECTIVE 5)

The nature of the steps within the design phase of the SDLC is different, depending on whether the organization intends to purchase software or design the software in-house. Much of the software used by organizations today is purchased. However, even when software is purchased, it is likely to be modified or customized to suit the specific needs of the organization. Therefore, there are similarities in the steps of the system design phase when software is purchased and when it is designed and written in-house. Exhibit 6-5 shows the typical steps undertaken when software is purchased.

THE PURCHASE OF SOFTWARE

When the project team has reached the design phase, user needs and system requirements have previously been determined in the systems analysis phase. Therefore, the project team is ready to solicit proposals from different software vendors for accounting systems that satisfy the identified user needs and meet the system requirements.

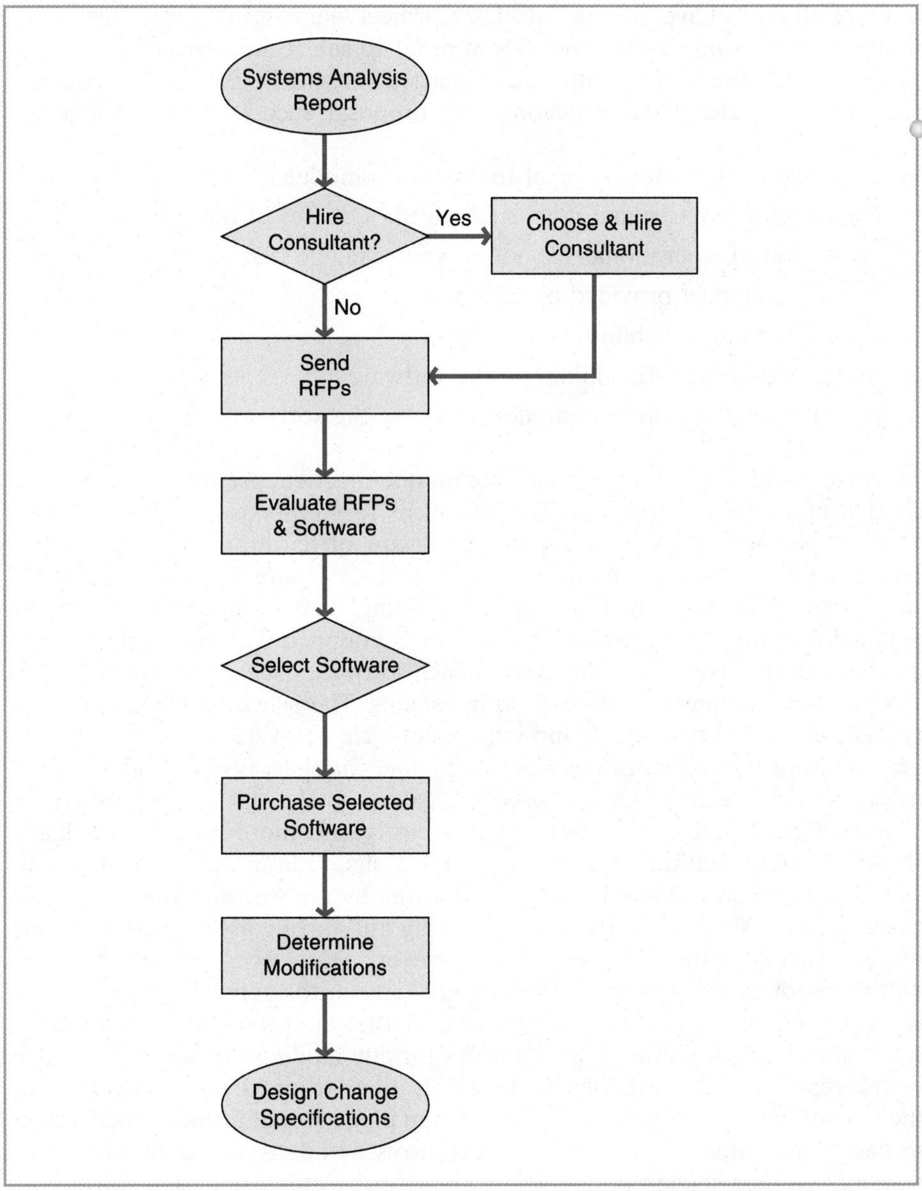

Exhibit 6-5
System Design Process Map for Purchased Software

Often, an organization hires a consultant to assist in the selection, design, and implementation of purchased software. If the organization intends to hire a consulting firm, such hiring may take place at this point. However, it is important to understand that a consultant could be hired for any part or parts of the SDLC. The hiring of the consultant is mentioned at this point (see Exhibit 6-5) to show how consulting firms may be used throughout the SDLC.

The process to solicit proposals is called a **request for proposal,** or **RFP.** An RFP may be sent to each software vendor offering a software package that meets the system and user needs. When the vendor returns the RFP, it will include details such as a description of the software that it intends to sell, the technical support that it intends to provide, and the related prices.

Once all RFPs have been received, the project team and IT governance committee should evaluate the proposals in order to select the best software package. There are many things that the project team and IT governance committee should consider when evaluating each proposal, such as the following:

1. The price of the software or of the software modules
2. The match of system and user needs to the features of the software
3. The technical, operational, economic, and schedule feasibility
4. Technical support provided by the vendor
5. Reputation and reliability of the vendor
6. Usability and user friendliness of the software
7. Testimonials from other customers who use the software.

The project team or IT governance committee must choose one of the several competing software products. The technical feasibility is an assessment of whether or not the existing computer hardware, or hardware to be purchased, represents adequate computing power to run the software. The operational feasibility refers to the capability of the existing staff of employees and any planned new hires to use the software as it is intended. The economic feasibility refers to the cost–benefit analysis of each software package. The cost–benefit analysis is a comparison of costs with benefits. The schedule feasibility is an analysis of the time to install and implement each software package. From the evaluation of these factors, the software system that best fits the organization's needs will be selected and purchased.

In general, purchased software is less costly and more reliable and has a shorter implementation time than software designed in-house. Purchased software has these advantages because it is written by the software vendor, its cost is spread over several clients, and the coding and testing are already complete when a customer buys the software. However, nearly every organization has unique needs or circumstances that may not match the software exactly. There is often a need to customize the software or the reports within it. The project team should develop design specifications for any modifications to the software or the reports. In the case of major modifications to purchased software or in the case of in-house design, the system design phase would include specific steps to design the outputs, inputs, processes, controls, and data storage of the revised system. The next section describes the steps of the in-house design phase.

IN-HOUSE DESIGN

As discussed in the previous section, the systems analysis report identifies user needs and system requirements. Exhibit 6-6 shows a process map for the in-house design of accounting system software, with the systems analysis report containing the input information to begin this phase.

Hiring a Consultant

As discussed, while it is not necessary to hire a consulting firm, many organizations find that the special expertise of consulting firms is most beneficial in the design and implementation of accounting system software. Such firms have

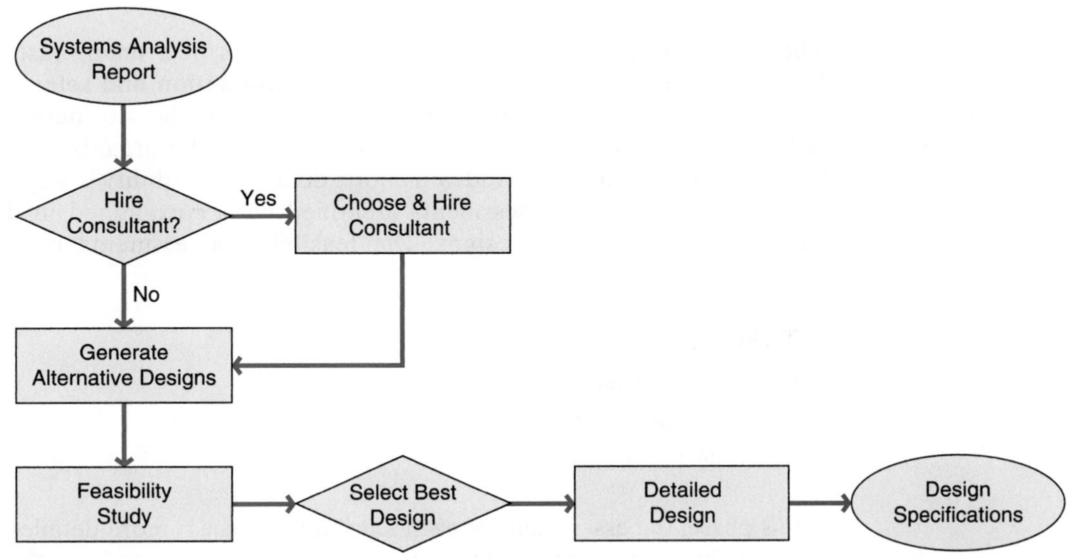

Exhibit 6-6
System Design Process Map for In-House Design

a broad range of expertise, assisting many different types of organizations with many different types of software systems. The choice of whether to use a consultant and the point at which to hire one are fully dependent on the extent of in-house expertise available within the organization.

CONCEPTUAL DESIGN

Whether or not a consulting firm is hired, the next step would be the **conceptual design** phase, which involves identifying the alternative conceptual design approaches to systems that will meet the needs identified in the system analysis phase. This step could be viewed as a sort of "brainstorming" to generate the different conceptual approaches in a system design that will meet the identified needs. In the case of purchased software, this step is taken by sending RFPs to several software vendors. In the case of in-house design, the project team must identify different conceptual design approaches. For example, there are different types of payment processing available to organizations to receive and pay invoices. The different approaches range from a traditional system that matches the purchase order, receiving, and invoice documents and involves relatively little complex technology to a web-based electronic invoice presentment and payment (EIPP) system. The EIPP system is a "matchless" system in which invoices are paid as soon as they are electronically delivered; there is no matching of documents prior to the approval and payment of the invoice. While both of these systems accomplish the payment of invoices, they each rely on differing amounts of technology and complexity. The EIPP system requires more complex and advanced technology and fewer manual steps. The traditional document matching requires simpler technology and involves more manual tasks. These are examples of different conceptual design approaches. The project team should identify the different conceptual designs that meet the identified needs.

EVALUATION AND SELECTION

When the conceptual designs are identified, the project team must evaluate the alternatives and choose the best design. **Evaluation and selection** is the process of assessing the feasibility and fit of each of the alternative conceptual approaches and selecting the one that best fits the organization's needs. The evaluation process includes a more detailed feasibility study, with the same set of feasibility assessments identified earlier examined in detail for each of the conceptual designs. The feasibility assessments in the study include the following:

1. Technical feasibility
2. Operational feasibility
3. Economic feasibility
4. Schedule feasibility

In this phase, the assessment of each feasibility aspect is more detailed and the scope of the study is much different from the feasibility study in the systems planning phase.

As you may recall, the purpose of the feasibility study in the systems planning phase was to assist the IT governance committee in determining which of the several different systems within the organization has the highest priority. For example, the IT governance committee might have been trying to determine whether revising the order entry system is more important than revising the invoice payment system. Assume that the IT governance committee decided that the invoice payment system is the higher priority. The end result of the system planning phase would be to announce this decision and to assign resources and a project team to begin the revision of the invoice payment system. Now we move forward through the other phases. In the conceptual design phase, the project team identified a traditional invoice-matching system and a web-based invoice payment system as the alternative conceptual designs. At the point of evaluation within the design phase, the project team must now evaluate whether the matching or web-based system better meets organizational needs and select the optimal system.

Since the project team has a more narrow and defined scope, the estimates of the technology needed, the operational requirements, the economic aspect, and the schedule for implementation can be more precise than in the systems planning phase. The project team may now be able to attach quantifiable measurements such as dollars, weeks, or number of employees needed to these feasibility assessments.

The project team should study each aspect of the feasibility assessment for each of the alternative conceptual designs. Examples of the type of assessments and analysis the project team would make are described in the following list:

1. *Technical feasibility*. The project team will assess the technical feasibility of each alternative conceptual design. In general, designs that require more complex technology have a lower feasibility than designs with less complex technology. The project team may place a numeric score on the technical feasibility. For example, on a scale of 1 to 10, the invoice-matching system may be scored as a 10 because the lower technology requirements make it much

easier and less risky to acquire and/or implement. The web-based system may be scored as a 5, since the technology is more complex and thus more risky to acquire and implement.

2. *Operational feasibility.* The project team will assess the realism of the possibility of operating each of the alternative designs. During this process, the team must consider the number of employees, their capabilities and expertise, and any supporting systems necessary to operate each alternative design. The team attempts to determine whether existing staff and support systems are adequate to operate the systems. For example, with a given staff size, a highly computerized system such as a web-based system may be more operationally feasible because it would require fewer staff members to operate. However, the staff using the system probably needs more computer expertise. Also, to implement a web-based system, there must be an adequate number of highly reliable vendors and a high degree of trust between the company and its vendors. This is true because any invoice presented is paid, without matching supporting documents. In summary, all of the support staff and underlying supporting systems must be examined, with the intention of assessing how easily the company could operate each alternative system design. Again, the project team may assign numerical assessment on a scale to indicate the relative operational feasibility.
3. *Economic feasibility.* The project team must estimate the costs and benefits of each alternative design. The costs and benefits can be compared by a formal cost–benefit method such as net present value, internal rate of return, or payback period. The purpose of this analysis is to determine which of the alternative designs is most cost effective. The costs of the system designs might include hardware and software costs, training expenses, and increases in operating and supplies costs. These examples of systems-related costs do not represent a complete list. Benefits might include cost savings from reductions in staff, increased operating efficiency, and elimination of non-value-added steps. Cost savings should be compared with the cost of a system by a formal analysis that allows the organization to determine whether tangible benefits outweigh costs. When a company is revising systems, there are also intangible benefits that are difficult to estimate in dollars. For instance, an improved accounting system might result in better feedback to management and, therefore, improved decision making. However, it is very difficult to place a dollar value on improved decision making. Since it may not be possible to estimate the dollar amount of intangible benefits, they cannot be included in an analysis such as net present value. The project should not ignore the intangible benefits, however. The report of the project team should include a written description of the intangible benefits.
4. *Schedule feasibility*. For each alternative design, the project team must estimate the total amount of time that will be required to implement the revised system. The designs that take longer to implement are less feasible.

The project team must summarize and analyze the results of these four feasibility tests for the purpose of selecting the single best design from the alternatives available. The task of summarizing and analyzing can become difficult because there may be conflicting signals across the four feasibilities. For example, a system may have high benefits when costs are compared (economic feasibility), but it may also require a longer time to implement (schedule feasibility). The team must then assess the trade-offs involved in higher cost–benefit, but longer implementation time. In most cases, the cost–benefit analysis is the most important of the four tests. However, any one of the four feasibilities can cause the team to drop an alternative design. For example, a design that meets all other feasibilities, but cannot be operated by the company's staff (operational feasibility) would not be selected.

DETAILED DESIGN

The end result of the evaluation and selection phase of the SDLC is that the best alternative design is selected. Once the design has been selected, the details of that alternative must be designed. The purpose of the **detailed design** phase is to create the entire set of specifications necessary to build and implement the system. The various parts of the system that must be designed are the outputs, inputs, processes, data storage, and internal controls. Each of these parts must be designed in enough detail so that programmers and analysts can develop the program code necessary to build the software system. However, the actual writing of program code is not part of the design phase. The coding of software occurs in the implementation phase.

Outputs of the system are reports and documents, such as income statements, aged accounts receivable listings, inventory status reports, and sales by product. Other outputs are documents or turn-around documents. For example, checks printed by the accounts payable system and invoices printed by the billing system are outputs. Each output of the system being revised must be designed in detail. The form and format must be designed. The form may be a printed report or a report viewed on the screen. The format is the actual layout of the report or document. The details of the rows and columns of data and how they appear on the report must be crafted. Since users need these reports on an ongoing basis as part of their jobs, it is critical to have user feedback in designing the details of output reports. If output reports do not meet the needs of the intended users, they are not very useful.

The organization needs customized output reports even when software is purchased rather than designed in-house. Therefore, when software is purchased, it is often necessary for the customer company to design detailed formats of output reports.

Inputs are the forms, documents, screens, or electronic means used to put data into the accounting system. There are many ways that data can be input, ranging from the manual keying in of data on a keyboard to computerized input such as bar code scanning. The project team must design the input method to fit the system being revised. For example, if the evaluation and selection phase results in the selection of an EIPP system, then invoices will be received electronically and there is no matching of the related documents. Therefore, there is no reason to design a paper copy of a receiving report. Instead, the project team must design the systems that will receive, read, and convert the electronic invoice. There are so many different forms of input that it is not possible to describe here the details of all possible forms. The overriding concern, regardless of the form of input, is ensuring the efficiency and accuracy of input. That is, the inputs must be designed to work efficiently and with as few errors as possible. Samples of the different methods of data input are as follows:

1. Keying in data with a keyboard from data on a paper form. The person operating the keyboard must enter data from a paper form into an input screen on the computer.
2. Magnetic ink character recognition (MICR) is used on checks and turnaround documents such as the portion of your credit card bill that you return. The computer system reads the magnetic ink to determine information such as account number.
3. Electronic data interchange (EDI), in which standard business documents are transmitted electronically.
4. Internet commerce, in which the customer enters customer and order data.
5. Bar code scanning, such as in the point-of-sale systems used by grocery and department stores.

In general, the manual input from item (1) is more error prone and much slower than the other electronic methods of input. Regardless of the method, internal controls should be incorporated to reduce input errors. Input controls were described in the application control section of Chapter 4 and include electronic data validation controls such as validity checks, limit checks, and completeness checks.

In the case of purchased software, input screens are often modified to better suit the specific needs of the organization. Before the screens are modified, the project team should follow the process of detailed design of the input screens and solicit user involvement. Lack of user input can result in screens that are difficult to use, resulting in input errors.

All details of the processes of the system must also be designed. As you may recall from your study of processes, there are many different processes in an accounting system. Each one usually requires many detailed steps. For example, processing payroll checks requires many steps, including timekeeping, calculation of gross pay and deductions, approvals for the payroll, and printing and distribution of checks. In the detailed design phase, all of the individual steps within a process must be designed. The project team again should have user input in designing these processes. Without user input, the processes may be designed in a way that makes it difficult or undesirable for users to use the system. Any such difficulties or reluctance by users to use the system can lead to efficiency problems or errors in the process.

The internal controls within the system must be designed during the detailed design phase. Internal controls are much more effective when they are designed into the processes from the beginning. Adding internal controls after the system has been implemented is much more difficult. To understand why this is true, let's think about the global positioning systems (GPSs) that are now built into some cars. When those cars were designed, the electronics, dashboard space, and dashboard controls had to be designed simultaneously. If you buy a car without the GPS and decide to add it later, your add-on system is likely to be less effective than a built-in GPS. Likewise, internal controls that are initially designed into the system are more effective. Chapter 4 described the types of controls that should be a part of IT systems.

An IT system must also have the proper amount and type of data storage to accomplish the functions it was designed to do. The data storage method and size must match the design of the inputs, processes, and outputs. The project team must design the method, size, and format of the data storage. For example, if data are to be stored in a relational database, the team must design all the elements, including the tables, the rows and columns within the tables, and the relationships between the tables. Chapter 13 on databases includes details about the storage and use of data in a relational database.

When the project team has completed the detailed design of outputs, inputs, processes, internal controls, and data storage, the implementation phase can begin.

ELEMENTS OF THE SYSTEMS IMPLEMENTATION PHASE OF THE SDLC (STUDY OBJECTIVE 6)

There are many individual tasks that must be undertaken to implement a new or revised accounting system. This is true regardless of whether the software is purchased or designed in-house. Implementation time would be much shorter for purchased software, since the software has already been written and tested by the vendor. However, even purchased software is often modified, and those modifications should be coded and tested in the implementation phase. Exhibit 6-7 is a process map of the systems implementation and operation phase.

There are so many different tasks within the implementation and operation phase that it would be impossible to describe all of them in this chapter. Instead, a few of the critical steps are described.

As depicted in Exhibit 6-7, some tasks can occur simultaneously. The employee training, program testing, and documentation can all be undertaken at the same time. For example, the documentation does not need to begin after employee training.

SOFTWARE PROGRAMMING

Using the design specifications developed in the detailed design phase, the programming staff would write the program code for the new or revised system. In the case of purchased software, the programming staff would modify the program code as necessary to meet the design specifications. While accountants may not be directly involved in programming, they would have frequent interaction with the programming staff to ensure that the programming meets the identified accounting requirements.

TRAINING EMPLOYEES

As the programming is completed or near completion, employees should be trained to use the new system. Depending on the changes from the old system, employees may need training in the use of new input screens, output reports, and processes.

SOFTWARE TESTING

As programmers complete the programming of the new system, the programs and the modules that make up the programs must be tested. Software should never be implemented before it is tested; otherwise, it can cause errors or problems in

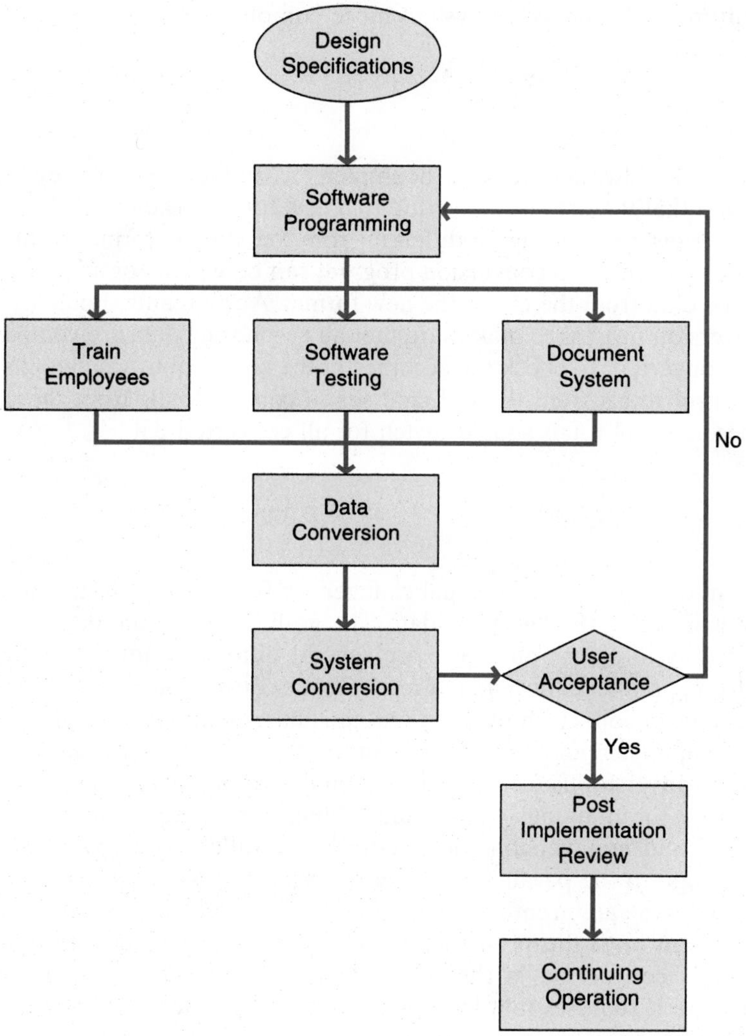

Exhibit 6-7
Implementation and Operation Process Map

the accounting system and thereby result in erroneous accounting data. The most common way to test software is to use test data, which are specially created and entered into the software to ensure that the software works correctly. The test data approach is described in Chapter 7.

DOCUMENTING THE SYSTEM

Since inputs, outputs, and processes are very likely to change as systems are revised, it is important to write the documentation that matches the new inputs, outputs, and processes. There are many kinds of documentation necessary to operate and maintain an accounting system, including flowcharts, data flow diagrams, entity relationship diagrams, process maps, operator manuals, and data dictionaries. Unfortunately, many companies do not always rewrite documentation at this stage, even though they should. The lack of up-to-date documentation makes it much more difficult for new employees to understand the system and makes future revisions to the system more complicated.

DATA CONVERSION

Though it is not always necessary, the implementation of a new or revised system may require that the data be converted to a new format. The file or database storage for the new system may be different from the storage format of the old system. In most instances, a conversion program can be written or acquired that will convert the data from the old to the new format. Accountants should oversee the data conversion process to make sure that all accounting data are completely and correctly converted. To check the accuracy of the conversion, accountants can reconcile control totals from the old data set to control totals from the converted data. These control totals should match for all converted data.

SYSTEM CONVERSION

The system conversion is the actual changeover from the old to the new system. Often, this is called the "go-live" date. The go-live date is the day that the new system is fully in operation. There are several different conversion methods to choose from: parallel conversion, direct cutover conversion, phase-in conversion, and pilot conversion. Each of these methods has advantages and disadvantages, and the company should choose the method that best fits its situation.

Parallel conversion is a conversion method in which the old and new systems are operated simultaneously for a short time. For example, the company may run the old and new versions of a system in parallel for a one-month period. The advantage to the parallel conversion is that it is the least risky. If errors or problems become apparent in the new system, the company can continue to use the old system until the problems are resolved. However, the disadvantage is that parallel conversion is the most costly and time-consuming conversion method, since it requires that the operating staff operate two systems and input all data twice—once in each system.

Direct cutover conversion means that on a chosen date the old system operation is terminated and all processing begins on the new system. This method is in many ways the opposite of parallel conversion. Direct cutover is the most risky method, but the least costly and time consuming. Since systems are not run in parallel, there is no backup in the form of the old system if problems occur.

The **phase-in conversion** is a method in which the system is broken into modules, or parts, which are phased in incrementally and over a longer period. As an example, assume that a company is implementing an entirely new accounting system, using a phase-in approach. The company might first implement only the order-entry part of the system. If that is successful, it may then choose to phase in the accounts receivable module. When that is working well, it may then phase in the cash receipts module. The phase-in approach is a low-risk approach, as it does not disrupt large parts of the organization at the same time. However, it will take longer to phase in all the parts of the accounting system.

In a **pilot conversion,** the system is operated in only one or a few sub-units of the organization. For example, suppose that a bank intends to implement new loan processing software at its branch offices. The bank may choose a few of its locations as pilot test sites for the software. The bank would implement the new software at the selected pilot sites and work out any problems in the system at those sites. Once the bank is satisfied with the operation at the pilot sites, the system can be implemented at the remaining sites.

USER ACCEPTANCE

To ensure that user needs have been met, many organizations require a user acceptance at the end of the implementation of a new system. **User acceptance** means that when the manager of the primary users of the system is satisfied with the system, he will sign an acceptance agreement. The enforcement of user acceptance makes it much more likely that project teams will seek user input and that the project team will work hard to meet user needs.

POST-IMPLEMENTATION REVIEW

A few months after implementation, the project team should review the SDLC steps for the project that was implemented. This **post-implementation review** is a review of the feasibility assessments and other estimates made during the process. The purpose of the review is to help the organization learn from any mistakes that were made. The review does not correct any errors made, but it helps the company avoid those same errors in the future.

ELEMENTS OF THE OPERATION AND MAINTENANCE PHASE OF THE SDLC (STUDY OBJECTIVE 7)

After implementation, the company will operate and maintain the system for some length of time. This part of the SDLC is the longest and most costly part, since it may last for several years. At some point, the company will need to make major revisions or updates to the system, which will trigger the SDLC to begin again to revise the system.

During the ongoing operation, management should receive regular reports regarding the performance of the IT system. The reports are necessary to monitor the performance of IT and to enable management to determine whether IT is aligned with business strategy and meets the objectives of the IT system. Some examples of these IT reports are the following:

- IT performance
  - IT load usage and excess capacity
  - Downtime of IT systems
  - Maintenance hours on IT systems
- IT security and number of security breaches or problems
- IT customer satisfaction, from both internal and external customers. Internal customers are the various users of IT systems within the organization.

These reports are an important part of IT governance, as they drive the continual monitoring of the IT system.

THE CRITICAL IMPORTANCE OF IT GOVERNANCE IN AN ORGANIZATION (STUDY OBJECTIVE 8)

The establishment and use of an IT governance committee and an SDLC are critically important for an organization to accomplish IT governance. Three major purposes are served by the continual and proper use of the IT governance committee and the SDLC:

1. The strategic management process of the organization
2. The internal control structure of the organization
3. The fulfillment of ethical obligations

The manner in which the SDLC accomplishes these three purposes is described in the sections that follow.

SDLC AS PART OF STRATEGIC MANAGEMENT

As discussed in the introduction of this chapter, IT systems are an extremely important resource in most organizations. IT systems improve efficiency, effectiveness, and long-term success of operations. Each organization may approach IT governance in a slightly different manner, but each organization should establish procedures for IT governance. The models presented in this chapter of an IT governance committee and a systems development life cycle are typical of IT governance. An SDLC process serves as the mechanism to continually assess the fit of IT systems to long-term strategy and short-run goals of the organization. Once the IT governance committee has identified which types of IT systems are appropriate for the organization, the SDLC becomes the mechanism to properly manage the development, acquisition, and implementation of IT systems.

SDLC AS AN INTERNAL CONTROL

Chapter 4 provided an overview of the AICPA Trust Services Principles and their role in the internal control structure of IT systems. These Trust Services Principles include many details about an IT governance committee and the SDLC and the role of these two strategic management processes in the internal control structure. The Trust Services Principles illustrate that the SDLC and an IT governance committee are an important part of the IT system of an organization. Without the use of an IT governance committee and the SDLC, the process of revising or updating systems can be chaotic and uncontrolled. The organization is likely to find that an uncontrolled approach results in poorly designed and documented systems. In addition, systems that result from such a chaotic process would probably not meet user needs and would not be likely to support the strategic objectives of the company.

A few excerpts from the Trust Services Principles are presented in Exhibit 6-8 as examples of the role of an IT governance committee and the SDLC in internal

Exhibit 6-8
Selected Sections[8] of the AICPA Trust Principles[9]

Security 4.3 Environmental and technological changes are monitored and their effect on system security is assessed on a timely basis. *Senior management*, as part of its annual IT planning process, considers developments in technology and the impact of applicable laws or regulations on the entity's security policies. The entity's IT security group monitors the security impact of emerging technologies. Users are proactively invited to contribute to initiatives to improve system security through the use of new technologies.

Availability 2.5 Changes that may affect system availability and system security are communicated to management and users who will be affected. Planned changes to system components and the scheduling of those changes are reviewed as part of the monthly *IT steering committee* meetings.

Availability 3.9 Procedures exist to identify, report and act upon system availability issues and related security breaches and other incidents. Network performance, system availability, and security incident statistics and comparisons to approved targets are accumulated and reported to the *IT steering committee* monthly.

Security 3.8 Design, acquisition, implementation, configuration, modification, and management of infrastructure and software related to system security are consistent with defined system security policies to enable authorized access and to prevent unauthorized access. The entity has adopted a formal *systems development life cycle (SDLC)* methodology that governs the development, acquisition, implementation, and maintenance of computerized information systems and related technology. The SDLC methodology includes a framework for classifying data and creating standard user profiles that are established based on an assessment of the business impact of the loss of security. Users are assigned standard profiles based on needs and functional responsibilities.

Process Integrity 3.2 The procedures related to completeness, accuracy, timeliness, and authorization of system processing, including error correction and database management, are consistent with documented system processing integrity policies. The entity's documented *systems development life cycle (SDLC)* methodology is used in the development of new applications and the maintenance of existing applications. The methodology contains required procedures for user involvement, testing, conversion, and management approvals of system processing integrity features.

controls. The term "steering committee" is becoming less popular in the IT industry than the more recent term "IT governance committee."

These excerpts illustrate that an IT governance committee and the SDLC are used as internal control mechanisms to monitor and control security, availability, acquisition, implementation, and maintenance of IT systems. These internal control mechanisms allow management to ensure that IT systems meet organizational needs and that the development and implementation of new IT systems is properly controlled.

[8]Emphasis added.

[9]Trust Services Principles, Criteria and Illustrations for Security, Availability, Processing Integrity, Confidentiality, and Privacy (Including WebTrust® and SysTrust®), American Institute of Certified Public Accountants, Inc. and Canadian Institute of Chartered Accountants, 2006 (www.aicpa.org), pp. 12–31.

ETHICAL CONSIDERATIONS RELATED TO IT GOVERNANCE (STUDY OBJECTIVE 9)

ETHICAL CONSIDERATIONS FOR MANAGEMENT

The management of any organization has an ethical obligation to maintain a set of processes and procedures that assure accurate and complete records and protection of assets. This obligation arises because management has a stewardship obligation to those who provide funds or invest in the company. **Stewardship** is the careful and responsible oversight and use by management of the assets entrusted to management. This requires that management maintain systems that allow it to demonstrate that it has appropriately used these funds and assets. Investors, lenders, and funding agencies must be able to examine reports that show the appropriate use of funds or assets provided to management. This is accomplished by the maintenance of accurate and complete accounting records and accounting reports and full disclosure within those reports. Therefore, management should have a mechanism that assists the organization in the development of accurate and complete accounting processes and systems.

In many cases, poorly designed IT systems can allow a fraudster to perpetrate fraud. In the case of the Phar-Mor drugstore chain fraud, a vice president became concerned about the adequacy of the IT system and the resulting reports. This vice president formed a committee to address the problems, but the committee was squelched by members of senior management who were involved in the fraud. Poorly developed IT systems can be used by managers or employees to commit and hide fraud. A management team that is focused on ethics throughout the organization should consistently monitor and improve IT systems. The SDLC is the mechanism to accomplish that. Thus, by diligently adhering to SDLC processes, management is, in part, fulfilling its ethical obligations of stewardship and fraud prevention.

As systems and processes are revised, management must also consider the ethical implications regarding employees. Revising processes and systems can lead to job-related changes for employees. These changes may include changes in job functions or duties, changes in the processes that employees perform, or in some cases, job loss. If managers expect employees to be ethical, then management must be ethical in the treatment of employees. Managers must carefully consider the impact of system changes on employees and be ethical in the manner that it handles employees throughout the processes of change. Although job losses are sometimes unavoidable, management must be especially conscious of the manner that it informs, terminates, and assists employees who experience job loss due to system changes. In addition, managers should maintain confidentiality about the proprietary features and functions of the IT system.

ETHICAL CONSIDERATIONS FOR EMPLOYEES

As managers apply the processes within the SDLC to revise IT systems, employees should not subvert the process. A disgruntled employee may sabotage the SDLC process by not cooperating, providing false information in interviews or questionnaires, or reverting to the old ways of doing things. If management of the organization has made an honest effort to include user feedback and participation in the SDLC processes, employees should likewise make an honest effort to participate, learn new system processes, and properly use the new processes and systems.

For employees who serve on project teams in the revision of IT systems, confidentiality can be an ethical consideration. As they participate in project teams, employees may learn things about people or processes in the organization that they would not otherwise know. These employees should not disclose things that management wishes to keep confidential. However, this can sometimes be a difficult ethical choice. For example, suppose that while serving on a project team, you learn that a friend's job will be eliminated and that management intends to announce the job cuts next week. In the days before the formal announcement, should you tell your friend of the impending job loss? In most circumstances, the project team member should keep this information confidential and allow management to handle the job cuts in a responsible and ethical manner.

ETHICAL CONSIDERATIONS FOR CONSULTANTS

When consultants are employed to assist the organization with phases of the SDLC, they have at least four ethical obligations:

1. Bid the engagement fairly, and completely disclose the terms of potential cost increases.
2. Bill time accurately to the client and do not inflate time billed.
3. Do not oversell unnecessary services or systems to the client just to inflate earnings on the consulting engagement.
4. Do not disclose confidential or proprietary information from the company to other clients.

In the past, many CPA firms offered consulting services to assist organizations in the selection and implementation of accounting system software. The freedom of CPA firms to do such consulting was significantly decreased when Congress enacted the Sarbanes–Oxley Act of 2002, which prohibits CPA firms from offering systems consulting to any organization for which the CPA firm serves as the auditor. An excerpt from the AICPA summary of Section 201 of the Act follows (emphasis added): SOX

> It shall be "unlawful" for a registered public accounting firm to provide any nonaudit service to an issuer contemporaneously with the audit, including: (1) bookkeeping or other services related to the accounting records or financial statements of the audit client; (2) **financial information systems design and implementation;** (3) appraisal or valuation services, fairness opinions, or contribution-in-kind reports; (4) actuarial services; (5) internal audit outsourcing services; (6) management functions or human resources; (7) broker or dealer, investment adviser, or investment banking services; (8) legal services and expert services unrelated to the audit; (9) any other service that the Board determines, by regulation, is impermissible.

As an example, if Pricewaterhouse Coopers (PwC) audits Anheuser Busch, then PwC would be prohibited from providing systems consulting services to Anheuser Busch. However, PwC could provide systems consulting services to The Boston Beer Company, Inc. (brewers of the Samuel Adams® product line) if it does not audit this company. Only CPA firms face this restriction under Sarbanes–Oxley, because CPA firms are the only entities that are permitted to conduct external audits of public company financial statements. Other companies, such as International Business Machines Corp. (IBM), are not restricted in providing system consulting services to organizations.

The restrictions under the Sarbanes–Oxley Act are intended to enhance CPAs' ethical obligation to remain independent with respect to their clients. On the other hand, if CPAs were to implement new IT systems for their audit clients, the perception of objectivity and independence may be compromised.

Because of this restrictive environment for CPA firms in providing consulting services, most large CPA firms have spun off or sold their consulting divisions. There are still CPA firms that provide system consulting services, but they must be careful not to ever provide both consulting and audit services to the same organization.

SUMMARY OF STUDY OBJECTIVES

An introduction to IT governance and its role in strategic management. The board of directors and top-level executive managers must take responsibility to ensure that the organization has processes that align IT systems to the strategies and objectives of the organization. IT systems should be chosen and implemented that support attainment of strategies and objectives. To ensure that IT systems support long-term strategic objectives and also support daily operations, management must constantly assess its current situation, where it plans to go, and which IT systems will help it get there. To be effective, this assessment should be part of an ongoing process to evaluate organizational direction and the fit of IT to that direction. The board and management should establish ongoing processes and procedures to accomplish this IT fit. These processes would include an IT governance committee and a systematic approach to IT system change, such as a systems development life cycle approach.

An overview of the system development life cycle (SDLC). The SDLC is a systematic approach to the change or upgrade of an IT system. While there are many approaches to the SDLC, a popular approach has five phases: systems planning, systems analysis, systems design, systems implementation, and operation and maintenance. These five phases are a structured and systematic way to undertake changing or upgrading IT systems.

The elements of the systems planning phase of the SDLC. Systems planning is the evaluation of long-term, strategic objectives and the prioritization of the IT systems that assist the organization in achieving its objectives. Systems planning also involves the planning and continuing oversight of the design, implementation, and use of those IT systems. The planning phase involves matching organization strategy to IT strategy and selecting IT changes that successfully meet the requirements of the feasibility study. In a feasibility study, the realism of the possibility of each proposed IT change is assessed on four dimensions: technical feasibility, operational feasibility, economic feasibility, and schedule feasibility.

The elements of the systems analysis phase of the SDLC. Systems analysis is a study of the current system to determine the strengths and weaknesses and the user needs of that system. Analysis requires the collection of data about the system and the careful analysis of that data to identify areas of the system that can be improved. Data are collected through observation, documentation review, interviews, and questionnaires.

The elements of the systems design phase of the SDLC. Systems design is the creation of the system that meets user needs and incorporates the improvements identified by the systems analysis phase. The design phase includes generating alternative conceptual designs, evaluating those designs, selecting the best conceptual design, and designing the details of the selected conceptual design.

The elements of the systems implementation phase of the SDLC. Implementation consists of the steps undertaken to program, test, and activate the IT system selected in the system design phase.

The elements of the operation and maintenance phase of the SDLC. Operation and maintenance is the regular, ongoing functioning of the IT system and the processes to fix small problems, or "bugs," in the IT system. During ongoing operation, management should request and receive ongoing reports about the performance of the IT system.

The critical importance of IT governance in an organization. The SDLC serves as the mechanism to continually assess the fit of IT systems to long-term strategy and short-run goals of the organization. As such, it is an important part of the strategic management of the organization. The SDLC process also serves as a mechanism to monitor and control security, availability, acquisition, implementation, and maintenance of IT systems. In addition, the SDLC assists management in ensuring that it maintains accurate and complete accounting records and accounting reports and that it maintains full disclosure within those reports. The SDLC is a mechanism that assists the organization in developing accurate and complete accounting processes and systems.

Ethical considerations related to IT governance. Managers, employees, and consultants all have obligations to act ethically while engaged in changes to IT systems. Managers must ensure that proper IT systems are functioning to meet the stewardship obligation they have for the assets entrusted to them. In addition, they must consider confidentiality and the effects of employee displacement as changes occur. Employees have obligations to provide honest feedback about IT systems and to not disclose confidential information. Consultants have ethical obligations to bid and bill time fairly, to not oversell IT system modules, and to maintain confidentiality.

KEY TERMS

Business process reengineering (BPR)
Conceptual design
Detailed design
Direct cutover conversion
Documentation review
Economic feasibility
Evaluation and selection
Interviews
IT governance
IT governance committee
IT steering committee
Observation

Operation and maintenance
Operational feasibility
Parallel conversion
Phase-in conversion
Pilot conversion
Post-implementation review
Questionnaires
Request for Proposal (RFP)
Schedule feasibility
Software selection
Stewardship
Strategic management
Strategic management of IT
System Development Life Cycle (SDLC)
Systems analysis
Systems design
Systems implementation
Systems planning
Systems survey
Technical feasibility
User acceptance

END OF CHAPTER MATERIAL

CONCEPT CHECK

1. IT governance includes all but which of the following responsibilities?
   a. Aligning IT strategy with the business strategy
   b. Writing programming code for IT systems
   c. Insisting that an IT control framework be adopted and implemented
   d. Measuring IT's performance
2. Which phase of the system development life cycle includes determining user needs of the IT system?
   a. systems planning
   b. systems analysis
   c. systems design
   d. systems implementation
3. Which of the following is **not** part of the system design phase of the SDLC?
   a. Conceptual design
   b. Evaluation and selection
   c. Parallel operation
   d. Detailed design
4. Which of the following feasibility aspects is an evaluation of whether the technology exists to meet the needs identified in the proposed change to the IT system?
   a. Technical feasibility
   b. Operational feasibility
   c. Economic feasibility
   d. Schedule feasibility
5. The purpose of the feasibility study is to assist in
   a. selecting software.
   b. designing internal controls.
   c. designing reports for the IT system.
   d. prioritizing IT requested changes.

6. Within the systems analysis phase of the SDLC, which of the following data collection methods does not involve any feedback from users of the IT system?
   a. Documentation review
   b. Interviews using structured questions
   c. Interviews using unstructured questions
   d. Questionnaires
7. A request for proposal (RFP) is used during the
   a. phase-in period.
   b. purchase of software.
   c. feasibility study.
   d. in-house design.
8. Which of the following steps within the systems implementation phase could not occur concurrently with other steps, but would occur at the end?
   a. Employee training
   b. Data conversion
   c. Software programming
   d. Post-implementation review
9. Each of the following are methods for implementing a new application system except
   a. direct cutover conversion.
   b. parallel conversion.
   c. pilot conversion.
   d. test method conversion.
10. A retail store chain is developing a new integrated computer system for sales and inventories in its store locations. Which of the following implementation methods would involve the most risk?
    a. Direct cutover
    b. Phased-in implementation
    c. Parallel running
    d. Pilot testing
11. The use of the SDLC for IT system changes is important for several reasons. Which of the following is not a part of the purposes of the SDLC processes?
    a. As a part of strategic management of the organization
    b. As part of the internal control structure of the organization
    c. As part of the audit of an IT system
    d. As partial fulfillment of management's ethical obligations
12. Confidentiality of information is an ethical consideration for which of the following party or parties?
    a. Management
    b. Employees
    c. Consultants
    d. All of the above

DISCUSSION QUESTIONS

13. (SO 3) Near the beginning of Chapter 6, the real-world example of Allstate's IT expenditure is mentioned. Prior to the implementation of its IT governance committee, "whoever spoke the loudest or whoever had the biggest checkbook" got to select IT projects. What do you think the problems were with this kind of approach?
14. (SO 1) Why is it important that IT systems be aligned with the business strategy?
15. (SO 1) Why would IT governance include measuring the performance of IT systems?
16. (SO 3) What is the difference between technical feasibility and operational feasibility?
17. (SO 3) How does the analysis of feasibilities in the systems planning phase help to prioritize system changes?
18. (SO 4) What is the advantage of studying the current system during the systems analysis phase?
19. (SO 4) During the systems analysis phase, which two data collection methods help determine user requirements?
20. (SO 5) What are the advantages of purchased software when compared with software developed in-house?
21. (SO 5) Why might it be important to follow some or all of the SDLC phases for purchased software?
22. (SO 5) How is conceptual design different from detailed design?
23. (SO 5)Within the system design phase, what are the purposes of evaluation and selection?
24. (SO 5) Which part of the system design phase would include designing rows and columns of output reports? Why is it important to design reports?
25. (SO 6) What is the purpose of software testing?
26. (SO 6) How are accountants involved in data conversion?
27. (SO 6) Why is a direct cutover conversion risky?
28. (SO 6) Why is parallel conversion costly?
29. (SO 6) Why is user acceptance important?
30. (SO 6) Why is post-implementation review undertaken?
31. (SO 8) How does the SDLC serve as an internal control?
32. (SO 9) What ethical obligations do employees have as IT systems are revised?

BRIEF EXERCISES

33. (SO 1) Describe the role that the board of directors should play in IT governance.
34. (SO 3, SO 5) Two feasibility studies occur during the SDLC: one during systems planning and one during systems design. Describe the differences between these two feasibility studies.

35. (SO 4) There are four methods of data collection used in the study of the current system: observation, documentation review, interviews, and questionnaires. Compare and contrast these four methods.
36. (SO 4) Describe the purpose of business process reengineering during the system analysis phase.
37. (SO 6) There are four methods of system conversion: parallel, direct cutover, pilot, and phase-in. Describe these four methods and how they differ.
38. (SO 7) Operation and maintenance is the longest and costliest part of the SDLC. Explain why this is true.
39. (SO 7) Describe how IT performance reports are important in IT governance.
40. (SO 9) What is the underlying purpose of the restrictions on CPA firms in Section 201 of the Sarbanes–Oxley Act?

PROBLEMS

41. (SO 1) Mega Corporation just became a public corporation when shares of its stock were sold to the public three months ago. A new board of directors has been appointed to govern the corporation. Assume that you will be giving a presentation to the board members on their responsibilities for IT systems. Write a report that could be delivered to the board.
42. (SO 2) Brumarch MultiMedia Stop is a regional retailer of consumer electronics, with warehouses and stores located in several large cities in California. The board and top management of Brumarch are considering updating their accounting, inventory, and retail sales software and hardware. The current systems are approximately 15 years old. Assume that you have been hired as a consultant to guide them through the process of upgrading their systems. Write a document that could be presented to the board of directors and that summarizes the SDLC.
43. (SO 4) Assume that you are the manager of the project team that is engaged in a systems analysis. The company is a large, national retailer with several stores and warehouses located throughout the United States. The corporate headquarters are in Atlanta, Georgia, and all major accounting takes place at the corporate headquarters. Describe how you would use the various data collection techniques of observation, documentation review, interviews, and questionnaires.
44. (SO 5) CEEMCO Corp. is a small, privately owned manufacturing company in Cincinnati, Ohio. CEEMCO manufactures custom products as well as store display products to sell to other companies such as retailers. Using an Internet search engine, do a search on the terms "CEEMCO" and "Cincinnati." Examine the kind of manufacturing the company does. Once you have completed that, study an accounting software site such as www.2020software.com or www.accountingsoftware411.com. Complete the following:
    a. Describe the process CEEMCO should undertake to determine which accounting software might be the best fit for the company.
    b. Although you do not know much about the company, develop a list of requirements you believe that any accounting software should have in order for CEEMCO to consider the software as a viable alternative.

c. Choose an accounting software from your web search, and describe why you believe it is a good match for CEEMCO.

45. (SO 2) There are several approaches to applying an SDLC methodology to IT system change. Using an Internet search engine, search for these terms: SDLC, waterfall, JAD (joint application development), RAD (rapid application development), build and fix, and spiral model. For example, you might try entering these search terms: SDLC waterfall. From your search results, write a brief definition of these various approaches to the system development life cycle.

46. (SO 9) Tannell Johnson is an accounting software consultant at Fipps and Associates Consulting. Fipps is a value-added reseller of accounting software for midsize companies, which normally have revenue between 50 million and 500 million dollars. One of Johnson's responsibilities is to solicit new client companies and to meet with their management to recommend the best accounting software system for them. Midmarket accounting software typically offers several modules that the client may choose from. For example, not all clients would need an e-business module for their accounting software. Since part of Johnson's compensation is a percentage of software sales and consulting revenue that he generates, what are the ethical conflicts he faces when soliciting new clients and recommending software and software modules?

CASES

47. The Electronics Shak is a retailer of electronics such as cell phones, satellite radios, mp3 players, and high-end LCD and plasma TVs. The Electronics Shak is a large chain with stores in strip shopping centers throughout the United States. However, each store is small, with generally five to six employees and a manager. Each store sells much less volume than a large electronic retailer such as Best Buy or Circuit City.

Top management has recently become concerned with what appears to be an excessive amount of inventory loss (shrinkage) at many of its stores. At this point, the management team is uncertain whether the excessive loss is due to weaknesses in its IT system that tracks inventory or to customer and employee theft at the stores. Top managers are concerned that the IT system may be a contributing factor to the loss and would like to study whether a new system should be implemented. Through their industry contacts, they know that large retailers such as Best Buy and Circuit City use much more sophisticated inventory management systems than The Electronic Shak does.

A systems analysis would require a cost–benefit analysis and a feasibility study. Describe steps that The Electronic Shak should take to complete a cost–benefit analysis and a feasibility study for a new IT system to track inventory.

48. Schibey International is in the process of purchasing a new accounting software system. Schibey is in a very specialized industry, with an international market. The company manufactures specialized parts to sell to companies in the oil exploration and drilling industry. The corporate headquarters are in Fort Worth, Texas, and a significant number—approximately one-half—of their operations are U.S. based. They also maintain production plants and a sales and support staff in most oil producing countries. Explain the factors

that Schibey should consider when determining which software system will best suit its needs.

49. Refer to case 48. Describe which parts of the design phase Schibey should undertake to ensure that the purchased software matches with the business processes that it will use.

CONTINUING CASE: SPATELLI'S PIZZERIA

Reread the Spatelli's Pizzeria Continuing Case in Chapter 1 and then read the additional paragraphs that follow.

Back at his desk, Peter Greyton is thinking of the day's developments. He reflects upon his meeting with Jim Saxton and Elaine Black. He considers where the company has been and where it is heading, and ponders the current issues regarding Spatelli's accounting information systems.

Overall, Peter feels that he needs help aligning Spatelli's business strategy with its IT systems. In addition, he is concerned about the limitations of the current accounting information system. Are internal controls strong enough? Would a new, integrated IT system yield improvements? As he contemplates the integration of the POS systems at the restaurant locations with the GL software at the home office, he wonders about the requirements for developing and implementing such a system, and how to best utilize the system to support Spatelli's business strategy. Peter realizes that his ability to address these issues will be critical not only to the success of the company, but also to his career. He asks himself, "What should I do now?"

Required:

Assume that you are Jim Saxton preparing a report for Peter Greyson, the CIO. Address the following:

a. Do you think Spatelli's business strategy is driving the development of its information systems, or vice versa? Use points from the case to support your answer.

b. Describe the steps Spatelli's should take (according to the systems development life cycle stages) to ensure that its IT systems are aligned with its business strategy.

SOLUTIONS TO CONCEPT CHECK

1. (SO 1) IT governance includes all the given choices, except **b. writing programming code for IT systems.** IT governance does include aligning IT strategy with business strategy, insisting that an IT control framework be adopted, and measuring IT performance.
2. (SO 2, SO 4) The phase of the system development life cycle that includes determining user needs of the IT system is **b. systems analysis.** The systems analysis phase includes a study of the current system to determine strengths and weaknesses of the system, and a determination of user needs.
3. (SO 2, SO 5) **c. Parallel operation** is not part of the system design phase of the SDLC. The system design phase can be divided into conceptual design,

evaluation and selection, and detailed design. Parallel operation occurs within the systems implementation phase.

4. (SO 3) The feasibility aspect that is an evaluation of whether the technology exists to meet the need identified in the proposed change to the IT system is **a. technical feasibility.** The purpose of the evaluation of technical feasibility is to assess the realism of the possibility that the technology exists to meet the need identified in the proposed change to the IT system.
5. (SO 3) The purpose of the feasibility study is to assist in **d. prioritizing IT requested changes**. The feasibility study helps determine which proposed IT systems or changes have a realistic possibility of being achievable from the standpoint of technical, operational, economic, and schedule feasibility. Those suggested changes that are less feasible will be ranked lower and, therefore, have a lower priority.
6. (SO 4) Within the systems analysis phase of the SDLC, the data collection method that does not involve any feedback from users of the IT system is **a. documentation review**. Interviews and questions require that users answer either structured or unstructured questions. Therefore, these methods of data collection allow users to provide feedback. Documentation review is a review of documentation for the IT system and does not involve obtaining feedback from users.
7. (SO 5) A request for proposal (RFP) is used during the **b. purchase of software**. An RFP is a request to bid. Organizations use RFPs to request bids on software.
8. (SO 6) The following steps within the systems implementation phase that could not occur concurrently with other steps, but would occur at the end, make up the **d. post-implementation review**. A post-implementation review is a review of the SDLC process to determine whether any estimates or processes were incorrect and must occur after the other implementation processes are completed.
9. (CIA Adapted) (SO 6) Each are methods for implementing a new application system except **d. test**. Although all systems should be tested before implementation, there is no one specific test method for all systems implementation.
10. (CIA Adapted) (SO 6) A retail store chain is developing a new integrated computer system for sales and inventories in its store locations. The implementation method that would involve the most risk is **a. direct cutover**. This approach would be considered risky because it would involve all store locations carrying out a simultaneous implementation. Accordingly, there would be no opportunity to compare results between the old and new systems, and any problems or "bugs" would adversely affect every location.
11. (SO 7) The use of the SDLC for IT system changes is important for several reasons, but, **c. as part of the audit of an IT system**, is not among the SDLC's purposes. The SDLC processes are critical as part of strategic management of the organization, as part of the internal control structure of the organization, and as partial fulfillment of management's ethical obligations. The SDLC helps ensure that IT strategy is aligned with business strategy, that system changes are properly controlled, and that management has attempted to fulfill its ethical obligation to maintain adequate IT systems. The SDLC is not an integral part of an IT audit.
12. (SO 9) Confidentiality of information is an ethical consideration for **d. all of the above**. Management, employees, and consultants all have an ethical obligation to keep proprietary or sensitive information confidential.

CHAPTER 7

Auditing Information Technology-Based Processes

STUDY OBJECTIVES

This chapter will help you gain an understanding of the following concepts:

1. An introduction to auditing IT processes
2. The various types of audits and auditors
3. Information risk and IT-enhanced internal control
4. Authoritative literature used in auditing
5. Management assertions used in the auditing process and the related audit objectives
6. The phases of an IT audit
7. The use of computers in audits
8. Tests of controls
9. Tests of transactions and tests of balances
10. Audit Completion/Reporting
11. Other audit considerations
12. Ethical issues related to auditing

THE REAL WORLD

Andeas Gabler/iStockphoto

A leading distributor of gold jewelry, Aurafin Corporation, faced a challenging situation. It had been experiencing problems with transaction fulfillment and delivery, and its customers, including retail giants like JCPenney and Wal-Mart, were beginning to take notice. In fact, JCPenney had implemented a supplier scorecard system, a type of vendor audit whereby companies like Aurafin, which do business with JCPenney, were evaluated on the basis of the quality of service provided. This system brought to light some significant violations in Aurafin's business processes, including weaknesses in controls and inadequate computer systems.

In order to save its customer relationships, Aurafin took quick action. It underwent a thorough IT audit, which identified the specific causes of its process failures. Aurafin acted swiftly upon the recommendations made by its auditors and implemented a more reliable technology platform that empowered it to apply a variety of new audit and control techniques and to get its systems in sync with its business goals. Aurafin credits the audit processes to its newfound success, including its recent recognition as JCPenney's "Vendor of the Year." This chapter focuses on the various aspects of the IT audit, as well as the accountant's techniques for evaluating information-technology processes, and their importance in business processes.

INTRODUCTION TO AUDITING IT PROCESSES (STUDY OBJECTIVE 1)

Nearly all business organizations rely on computerized systems to assist in the accounting function. Technological advances have transformed the business world by providing new ways for companies to do business and maintain records. This boom in technological developments has increased the amount of information that is readily available. Business managers, investors, creditors, and government agencies often have a tremendous amount of data to use when making important business decisions. However, it is often a challenge to verify the accuracy and completeness of the information.

Accountants have an important role in the business world because they are called upon to improve the quality of information provided to decision makers. Accounting services that improve the quality of information are called **assurance services.** Many types of services performed by accountants are considered assurance services because they lend credibility to the underlying financial information. An audit is the most common type of assurance service.

TYPES OF AUDITS AND AUDITORS (STUDY OBJECTIVE 2)

An audit is a type of assurance service that involves accumulating and analyzing support for information provided by management. The main purpose of the audit is to assure users of financial information about the accuracy and completeness of the information. To carry out an audit, accountants collect and evaluate proof of procedures, transactions, and/or account balances and compare the information with established criteria. The three primary types of audits include compliance audits, operational audits, and financial statement audits. Although all audits involve an investigation of supporting information, each type of audit has a different purpose. **Compliance audits** determine whether the client has complied with regulations and policies established by contractual agreements, governmental agencies, company management, or other high authority. **Operational audits** assess operating policies and procedures for efficiency and effectiveness. **Financial statement audits** determine whether the company has prepared and presented its financial statements fairly, and in accordance with generally accepted accounting principles (GAAP) or some other financial accounting criteria.

Audits are typically conducted by accountants who have knowledge of the established criteria. For example, financial statement audits are performed by **certified public accountants (CPAs)** who have extensive knowledge of GAAP. There are different types of audit specialization that exist in business practice today, including internal auditors, IT auditors, government auditors, and CPA firms. An **internal auditor** is an employee of the company that he or she audits. Most large companies have a staff of internal auditors who perform compliance and operational audit functions at the request of management. Some internal auditors achieve special certification as certified internal auditors (CIAs). **IT auditors** specialize in information systems assurance, control, and security. Some IT auditors achieve special certification as certified information systems auditors (CISAs). **Government auditors** conduct audits of government agencies or income tax returns. CPA firms represent the interests of the public by performing independent audits of many types of business organizations. Each type of auditor may perform any of the three types of audits described earlier. However, only CPA firms can conduct financial statement audits of companies whose stock is sold in public markets such as the New York Stock Exchange. An important requirement for CPA firms is that they must be neutral with regard to the company being audited. This requirement of neutrality allows the CPA firm to provide a completely unbiased opinion on the information it audits, and it is the foundation of an external audit performed by CPAs. An **external audit** is performed by independent auditors who are objective and neutral with respect to the company and information being audited. To keep their neutrality, CPA firms and their individual CPAs are generally prohibited from having financial connections with client companies and from having personal ties to those working for client companies. A CPA's objectivity could be impaired by having financial and personal relationships with a client company or with anyone having the ability to influence the client's decisions and financial reporting activities.

Any audit may be affected by the amount and type of computerization used by the client. All types of auditors should have knowledge concerning technology-based systems so that they can properly audit IT systems. The remainder of this chapter will concentrate on financial statement audits conducted by CPA firms, as this is the most common type of audit service used in the modern business world. However, many of the topics applicable to financial statement audits conducted by CPA firms are also applicable to other types of audits performed by other types of auditors.

Performing financial statement audits is a main service of CPA firms, and they devote a large portion of time to these audits. Because many companies that are audited now use sophisticated IT accounting systems to prepare financial statements, it is increasingly important for auditors to enhance the quality of their services in auditing those systems. IT auditing is a part of the financial statement audit that evaluates a client's computerized accounting information systems. Since the IT processes are typically a major factor in the financial statement audit, an auditor must gain a sufficient understanding of the characteristics of a client company's IT system. Although auditors do not need to be experts on the intricacies of computer systems, they do need to understand the impact of IT on their clients' accounting systems and internal controls.

As mentioned previously, a financial statement audit is conducted in order to express an opinion on the fair presentation of financial statements in accordance with GAAP. This is the primary goal of a financial statement audit, and this goal is not affected by the presence or absence of IT accounting systems. However, the use of computers may significantly change the way a company processes and communicates information, and it may affect the underlying internal controls. Therefore, the IT environment plays a key role in how auditors conduct their work in the following areas:

- Consideration of risk
- Audit procedures used to obtain knowledge of the accounting and internal control systems
- Design and performance of audit tests

INFORMATION RISK AND IT-ENHANCED INTERNAL CONTROL (STUDY OBJECTIVE 3)

As business environments become more complex, the possibility of receiving unreliable information increases. **Information risk** is the chance that information used by decision makers may be inaccurate. Following are some causes of information risk:

- *The remoteness of information.* Decision makers are typically forced to rely on others for information. When the source of the information is removed from the decision maker, the information stands a greater chance of being misstated. A decision maker may become detached from the source of important information due to geographic distances, organizational layers, or other factors that are often associated with a company's growth.
- *The volume and complexity of the underlying data.* As a business grows, the volume and complexity of its transactions increase. This tends to increase the chance that misstated information may exist undetected.
- *The motive of the preparer.* Those who prepare information may have goals different from those of the decision maker. As a result, the information may be slanted in favor of a particular viewpoint or incentive, which impacts its presentation and decision-making usefulness.

The most common way for decision makers to reduce information risk is to rely upon information that has been audited by an independent party. Because information users generally do not have the time or ability to verify information for themselves, they depend on auditors for accurate and unbiased judgments. Even if decision makers wanted to verify the information, it may be difficult to do so when the financial information is contained in computerized accounting systems. These are the main reasons that a discussion of information-based processing and the related audit function are included in the study of accounting information systems.

Various risks are created by the existence of IT-based business processes. For example, because the details of transactions are often entered directly into the computer system, there may be no paper documentation maintained to support the transactions. This is often referred to as the **loss of audit trail visibility** because there is a lack of physical evidence to visibly view. There is also a greater likelihood that data may be lost or altered due to system failure, database destruction, unauthorized access, or environmental damage. In addition, IT systems do many tasks that previously were manually performed by humans. Since IT systems, rather than humans, do these tasks, there are increased internal control risks, such as a lack of segregated duties and fewer opportunities to authorize and review transactions.

Despite the risks, there are important advantages to using IT-based systems. Internal controls can actually be enhanced if care is exercised in implementing these systems. Computer controls can compensate for the lack of manual controls. In addition, if programs are tested properly before being activated, the risk of human error (such as a mathematical and/or classification mistake) is virtually eliminated because computers process all information consistently.

In addition to internal control enhancements, IT-based processes provide higher quality information to management. Information is higher quality when it is supplied in a timely manner and administered effectively. When high-quality information is used to make decisions, the result is more effective management.

AUTHORITATIVE LITERATURE USED IN AUDITING (STUDY OBJECTIVE 4)

The work of an auditor must be conducted in accordance with several sources of authoritative literature, as described next.

Generally accepted auditing standards (**GAAS**) are broad guidelines for an auditor's professional responsibilities. These ten standards are divided into three categories that include general qualifications and conduct of an auditor (general standards), guidelines for performing the audit (standards of fieldwork), and requirements for the written report communicating the results of the audit (standards of reporting). Exhibit 7-1 summarizes these standards by category.

GAAS provides a general framework for conducting quality audits, but this framework is not specific enough to provide useful guidance in the actual performance of an audit engagement. For such detailed guidance, auditors rely upon standards issued by the Public Company Accounting Oversight Board, the Auditing Standards Board, the International Audit Practices Committee, and the Information Systems Audit and Control Association.

The **Public Company Accounting Oversight Board** (**PCAOB**) was organized in 2003 for the purpose of establishing auditing standards for public companies. These standards are to serve as interpretations of GAAS and guidelines for quality control within CPA firms. The PCAOB was established by the Sarbanes–Oxley Act, which was created in response to several major corporate accounting scandals, including those affecting Enron, Worldcom, and others. Prior to the PCAOB, standard-setting was the responsibility of the **Auditing Standards Board** (**ASB**) of the American Institute of CPAs (AICPA). The ASB has issued Statements on Auditing Standards (SASs) that have historically been widely used in practice and will continue to be the standards applicable to nonpublic companies. The **International Audit Practices Committee** (**IAPC**) was established by the International Federation of Accountants (IFA) to set International Standards on Auditing (ISAs) that contribute to the uniform application of auditing practices on a worldwide basis. ISAs are similar to SASs; however, ISAs tend to extend SASs because of their usefulness in audits of multinational companies. Although

General Standards	Standards of Fieldwork	Standards of Reporting
1. The audit is to be performed by a person or persons having adequate technical training and proficiency as an auditor. 2. Independence in mental attitude is to be maintained in all matters related to the audit engagement. 3. Due professional care is to be exercised in all phases of the audit process.	1. The audit is to be adequately planned and supervised. 2. An understanding of internal control is to be obtained as part of the planning process for the purpose of determining the nature, timing, and extent of tests to be performed. 3. Evidence is to be obtained through inspection, inquiries, observation, and confirmations in order to provide a reasonable basis for forming an overall opinion on the audit.	1. The written report must state whether the financial statements are presented in accordance with generally-accepted accounting principles (GAAP). 2. The written report identifies any circumstances in which GAAP have not been consistently applied in the current period in relation to the prior period. 3. The financial statements are assumed to contain adequate informative disclosures unless otherwise indicated in the written report. 4. The written report expresses an opinion on the fairness of the financial statements as a whole, or an assertion to the effect that an opinion cannot be expressed (and the reasons therefor). The report also describes the character of the auditor's work and the degree of responsibility assumed by the auditor.

Exhibit 7-1
Generally Accepted Auditing Standards

auditors have a primary responsibility to comply with standards issued within their own countries, ISAs are useful in expanding those requirements in order to meet different needs in other countries where the audited information may also be used. The **Information Systems Audit and Control Association (ISACA)** issues Information Systems Auditing Standards (ISASs) that provide guidelines for conducting the IT audit. These standards address audit issues unique to a company's information systems environment, including control and security issues.

Although SASs, ISAs, and ISASs contribute more detailed guidance than is provided by GAAS, they still do not furnish the auditor with specific direction regarding the types of audit tests to use and the manner in which conclusions should be drawn. Auditors must resort to industry guidelines, professional journals, textbooks, and other resources for those purposes. Many CPA firms develop their own specific policies and procedures for designing and conducting effective audit engagements. Still, individual audits must be customized to apply to the specific financial reporting environment of each company. Accordingly, auditors must exercise a considerable amount of professional judgment in performing audits.

MANAGEMENT ASSERTIONS AND AUDIT OBJECTIVES (STUDY OBJECTIVE 5)

Responsibility for the preparation of financial statements lies with management of the company. The financial statements represent a set of management assertions. **Management assertions** are claims regarding the financial condition of the business organization and results of its operations. The role of the auditors is to analyze the financial statements to decide whether they are fairly presented in accordance with GAAP. A CPA firm designs audit tests to analyze information

Exhibit 7-2
Management Assertions and Related Audit Objectives

Management Assertions	Audit Objectives
Existence/occurrence	Determine that recorded transactions, events, and related account balances are real and have been properly authorized.
Valuation and Allocation	Determine that recorded transactions and related account balances are:
Accuracy classification cutoff	• accurate in terms of dollar amounts and quantities, and any related allocation adjustments are properly recorded • classified properly • recorded in the proper period • supported by detailed evidence • correctly summarized and posted to the general ledger • recorded at estimated realizable values
Completeness	Determine that all existing transactions and related accounted balances are recorded—i.e., that none have been omitted.
Rights and Obligations	Determine that transactions and related asset account balances are actually owned. Similarly, determine that liability account balances represent actual obligations.
Presentation and Disclosure	Determine that all required disclosures are properly presented and clearly expressed so the financial statements are understandable.

information supporting the financial statements in order to determine whether management's assertions are valid. To accomplish this, CPAs create audit tests that address general audit objectives. Each audit objective relates to one of management's assertions. Exhibit 7-2 summarizes the relationship between management assertions and general audit objectives.

The general audit objectives described in Exhibit 7-2 may be applied to any category of transaction and the related account balances. Auditors design specific tests to address these objectives in each audit area. For example, an auditor will develop tests to determine whether a company has properly accounted for its borrowing transactions during the period. These tests are specific to the accounts and information systems in place at the company being audited. Audit tests developed for an audit client are documented in an **audit program.** Exhibit 7-3 presents an excerpt from a typical audit program covering notes payable and the related accounts and information systems. The related management assertions are shown in parentheses.

As shown in Exhibit 7-3, a unique set of audit tests determines whether each general objective is met for each major account or type of transaction. For example, a test for completeness of notes payable involves the review of minutes to determine whether additional borrowing arrangements exist that are not recorded. If, instead, the auditor were testing for the completeness objective related to accounts receivable and sales, an appropriate test would be to examine shipping reports and investigate whether each of the related sales transactions was properly included in the accounting records. Thus, audit testing for any single general objective may involve diverse testing techniques with different kinds of information collected to support each different account and transaction.

Procedure:	Performed by:	Reviewed by:
1. Obtain written confirmation from financial institutions regarding the amount of borrowings at year end. (Existence, Obligations, Valuation)		
2. Obtain copies of each loan agreement and:		
• Note the interest rate and interest payment dates. Determine that interest expense and interest payable are recorded in the proper amounts and in the proper period. (Valuation)		
• Note the principal payment dates. Determine that the current and noncurrent classifications are computed correctly. (Valuation, Presentation)		
• Note the existence of any restrictions placed on the company by this agreement. Determine whether the company is in compliance with all such restrictions. (Presentation and Disclosure)		
3. Examine canceled checks for any principal payments made during the period. (Valuation)		
4. Review the minutes of the board of directors meetings to determine whether additional borrowing arrangements exist. (Completeness)		
5. Inquire of management as to the existence of additional borrowing arrangements. (Completeness)		

Exhibit 7-3
Specific Audit Procedures Address General Audit Objectives and Assertions

Auditors must think about how the features of their client's IT systems influence management's assertions and the general audit objectives. These matters have a big impact on the choice of audit methodologies used. The next section relates these IT considerations to the different phases of an audit.

PHASES OF AN IT AUDIT (STUDY OBJECTIVE 6)

An IT audit generally follows the same pattern as a typical financial statement audit. There are four primary phases of the audit: planning, tests of controls, substantive tests, and audit completion/reporting. Exhibit 7-4 provides an overview of these phases.

Through each phase of an audit, evidence is accumulated as a basis for supporting the conclusions reached by the auditors. **Audit evidence** is proof of the fairness of financial information. The techniques used for gathering evidence include the following:

- physically examining or inspecting assets or supporting documentation
- obtaining written confirmation from an independent source
- rechecking or recalculating information
- observing the underlying activities
- making inquiries of client personnel
- analyzing financial relationships and making comparisons to determine reasonableness

The various phases of the audits typically include a combination of these techniques.

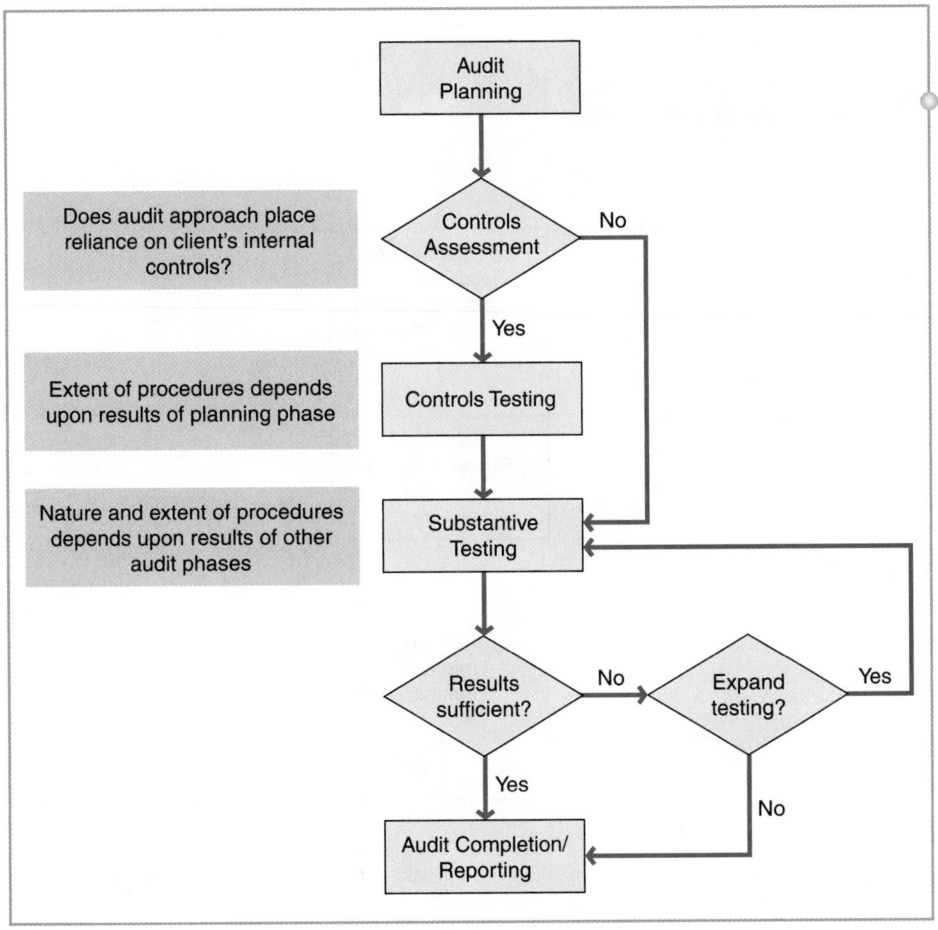

Exhibit 7-4
Process Map of the Phases of an Audit

AUDIT PLANNING

During the **planning phase** of an audit, the auditor must gain a thorough understanding of the client's business and financial reporting systems. In doing so, auditors review and assess the risks and controls related to the business, establish materiality guidelines, and develop relevant tests addressing the objectives (presented earlier). A process map of the planning phase of the audit is presented in Exhibit 7-5.

The tasks of assessing materiality and audit risk are very subjective and are therefore typically performed by experienced auditors. In determining **materiality,** auditors estimate the monetary amounts that are large enough to make a difference in decision making. Materiality estimates are then assigned to account balances so that auditors can decide how much evidence is needed. Transactions and account balances that are equal to or greater than the materiality limits will be carefully tested. Those below the materiality limits are often considered insignificant (if it is unlikely that they will impact decision making) and therefore receive little or no attention on the audit. Some of these accounts with immaterial balances may still be audited, though, especially if they are considered areas of high risk. **Risk** refers to the likelihood that errors or fraud may occur. Risk can be inherent in the client's business (due to such things as the

Exhibit 7-5
Audit Planning Phase Process Map

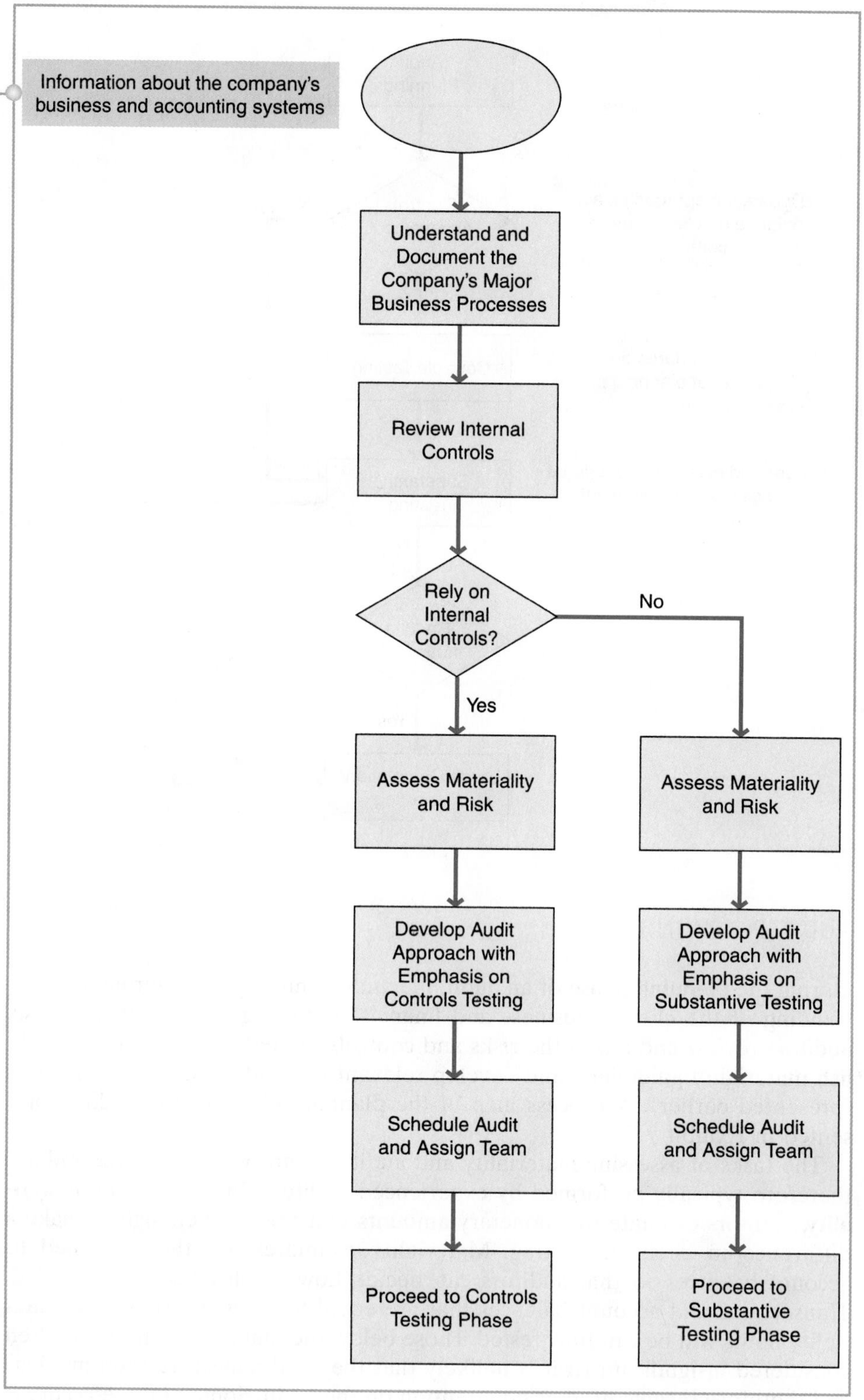

nature of operations, the economy, or management's strategies), or it may be caused by weak internal controls. Auditors need to perform risk assessment to carefully consider the risks and the resulting problems to which its clients may be susceptible. In addition, there will always be some risk that material errors or fraud may not be discovered in an audit. Each of these risk factors and the materiality estimates are important to consider in determining the nature and extent of audit tests to be applied.

A big part of the audit planning process is the gathering of evidence about the company's internal controls. Auditors typically gain an understanding of internal controls by interviewing key members of the accounting and IT staff. They also observe policies and procedures and review IT user manuals and system flowcharts. They often prepare narratives or memos to summarize the results of their findings. In addition, company personnel generally complete a questionnaire about the company's accounting systems, including its IT implementation and operations, the types of hardware and software used, and control of computer resources. The understanding of internal controls provides the basis for designing appropriate audit tests to be used in the remaining phases of the audit. Therefore, it is very important that the auditor understand how complex its clients' IT systems are and what types of evidence may be available for use in the audit.

The process of evaluating internal controls and designing meaningful audit tests is more complex for automated systems than for manual systems. An auditor cannot easily spot the controls that are part of an automated (computer) system. In recognition of the fact that accounting records and files often exist in electronic form, the ASB issued **SAS 94,** "The Effect of Information Technology on the Auditor's Consideration of Internal Control in a Financial Statement Audit." This statement was issued in 2001 to expand the historical concept of audit evidence to include electronic evidence. SAS 94 describes the importance of understanding both the automated and manual procedures that make up an organization's internal controls. SAS 94 also considers how misstatements may occur, including the following:

- how transactions are entered into the computer
- how standard journal entries are initiated, recorded, and processed
- how nonstandard journal entries and adjusting entries are initiated, recorded, and processed

SAS 94 provides useful guidance for auditors in deciding whether IT audit specialists may be needed for the audit. IT auditors may be called upon to consider the effects of computer processing on the audit or to assist in testing those automated procedures.

USE OF COMPUTERS IN AUDITS (STUDY OBJECTIVE 7)

Many companies design their IT systems so that important information such as purchase and sales orders, shipping and receiving reports, and invoices can be retrieved from the system in readable form. This kind of supporting documentation, as well as journals and ledgers, can be printed from the computer system to serve as evidence for auditors. Under these conditions, auditors can compare documents used to input data into the system with reports generated from the system, without gaining extensive knowledge of the computer system logic. In such cases, the use of IT systems does not have a great impact on the conduct of the audit, since the auditor can perform audit testing in the same manner as would be done for a manual system. This practice is known as **auditing around the computer** because it does not require evaluation of computer controls. Sometimes it is also referred to as "the black box approach," because it does not involve detailed knowledge of the computer programs. Auditing around the computer merely uses and tests *output* of the computer system in the same manner as the audit would be conducted if the information had been generated manually. Because this approach does not consider the effectiveness of computer controls, auditing around the computer has limited usefulness.

Auditing through the computer involves directly testing the internal controls within the IT system, whereas auditing around the computer does not. Auditing through the computer is sometimes referred to as "the white box approach," because it requires auditors to understand the computer system logic. This approach requires auditors to evaluate IT controls and processing so that they can determine whether the information generated from the system is reliable. Auditing through the computer is necessary under the following conditions:

- The auditor wants to test computer controls as a basis for evaluating risk and reducing the amount of audit testing required.
- Supporting documents are available only in electronic form.

Auditors can use their own computer systems and audit software to help conduct the audit. This approach is known as **auditing with the computer.** A variety of **computer-assisted audit techniques (CAATs)** are available for auditing with the computer. CAATs are useful audit tools because they make it possible for auditors to use computers to test more evidence in less time.

Next, we will focus on techniques used to audit through the computer and to audit with the computer in the testing phases of the audit.

TESTS OF CONTROLS (STUDY OBJECTIVE 8)

Exhibit 7-6 presents the components of the tests of controls phase of the audit.

The **tests of controls** involve audit procedures designed to evaluate both general controls and application controls. Recall from Chapter 4 that general controls relate to all aspects of the IT environment, whereas application controls relate to specific software applications that cover a particular type of transaction. During audit planning, auditors must learn about the types of controls that exist within their client's IT environment. Then they may test those controls to determine whether they are reliable as a means of reducing risk. Tests of controls are sometimes referred to as "compliance tests," because they are designed to determine whether the controls are functioning in compliance with management's intentions. The following section discusses how these controls are evaluated:

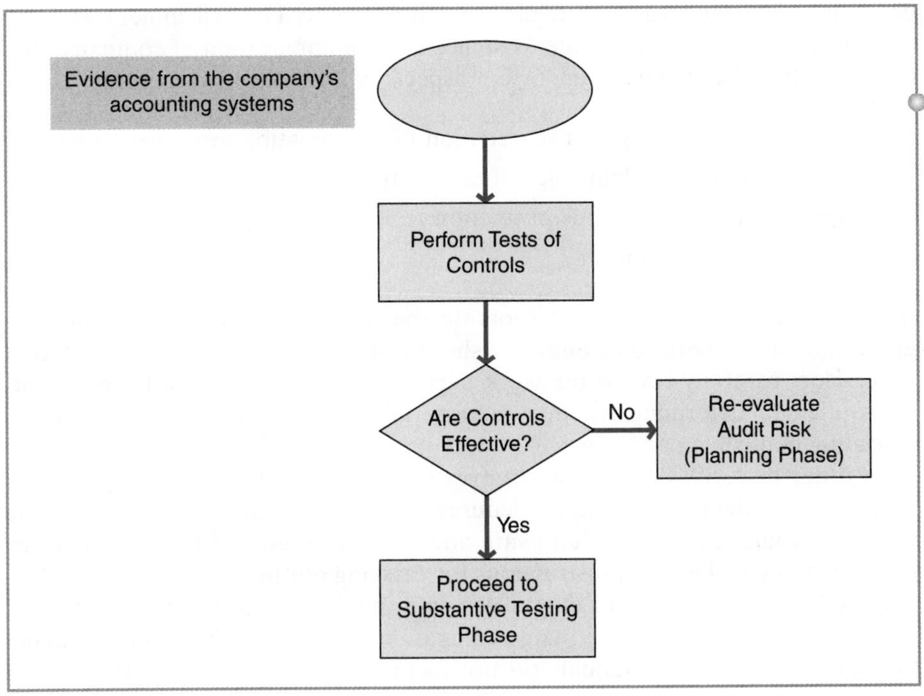

Exhibit 7-6
Controls Testing Phase Process Map

GENERAL CONTROLS

General controls must be tested before application controls are. Since **general controls** are the automated controls that affect all computer applications, the reliability of application controls is considered only after general controls are deemed reliable. In other words, even when application controls are believed to be strong, misstatements may still exist as a result of weak general controls. For example, if there were a lack of physical controls, a company's hardware and software could be accessed by an unauthorized user who could alter the data or the programs. So even if the application controls were working as designed, the general control deficiency could result in errors in the underlying information. Accordingly, the effectiveness of general controls is the foundation for the IT control environment. If general controls are not functioning as designed, auditors will not devote attention to the testing of application controls; rather, they will reevaluate the audit approach (according to Exhibit 7-4) with reduced reliance on controls.

There are two broad categories of general controls that relate to IT systems:

- IT administration and the related operating systems development and maintenance processes
- Security controls and related access issues

Each of these categories and the related audit techniques are described in detail next.

IT Administration

IT departments should be organized so that an effective and efficient workplace is created and supported. Auditors should verify that the company's management promotes high standards with regard to controlling its IT environment. Related audit tests include review for the existence and communication of company policies regarding the following important aspects of administrative control:

- personal accountability and segregation of incompatible responsibilities
- job descriptions and clear lines of authority
- computer security and virus protection
- IT systems documentation

If the client company does not separate the functions of system design, programming, and operations, auditors should observe activities to ensure that supervisors carefully review the work performed by employees with incompatible duties, to determine whether managerial oversight is in place as a compensating control.

In order to verify proper control over operations of the IT system, auditors should review the policies and procedures manuals covering operator tasks. The manuals should identify the hardware and software used and the timetable for performing tasks. Detailed instructions for carrying out the tasks should be documented, along with a list of employees who should have access to the outputs. Also, in order to test for adequate segregation of duties, auditors should make sure that the operator manuals do not include information about the system design or program code.

Details about the internal logic of computer systems should be documented in IT manuals. Auditors should verify that such documentation exists and is kept up-to-date. IT documentation often includes system flowcharts and other systems development data. System operators and users should not have access to this information, in order for the company to maintain good segregation of duties.

In order to evaluate a client company's administrative effectiveness in terms of IT maintenance, auditors should review system documentation to find out whether system maintenance projects are properly authorized. In addition, auditors should determine whether their clients maintain control over systems documentation and programs by using a system librarian. A librarian is responsible for maintaining and controlling access to up-to-date systems documentation and programs. Additional tests to be performed when the company makes changes in its IT environment are described later in this chapter, and other access control issues are discussed in the next section.

Security Controls

Auditors are concerned about whether a client company's computer system has controls in place to prevent unauthorized access to or destruction of information within the accounting information systems. Unauthorized access may occur internally when employees retrieve information that they should not have, or externally when unauthorized users (or hackers) outside the company retrieve information that they should not have. Destruction may occur as a result of natural disasters, accidents, and other environmental conditions. Controls that protect the company from these risks include various access controls, physical controls, environmental controls, and business continuity policies. You may find it helpful to refer back to Exhibit 4-5, which presents the various types of controls that a company may use to prevent risk of loss due to unauthorized use, network break-ins, and environmental problems. As auditors gain an understanding of a company's information systems, they can find out if the types of controls listed in Exhibit 4-5 are being used to prevent or detect the related risk. When controls are in place, they can be tested for effective operation. Following are some ways that an auditor can test these controls.

In order to test internal access controls, auditors should determine that the company has properly segregated IT duties or compensated for a lack of segregation by improving supervisory reviews. The client's authority table should be tested to find out whether access to programs and to data files is limited to authorized employees. Auditors should perform **authenticity tests** for valid use of the client's computer system, according to the authority tables. Policy and procedure manuals should describe control over the use of passwords, security tokens, biometric devices, etc. Employees should be required to have passwords, and their level of access should be consistent with their job responsibilities. Auditors can design controls tests to determine whether access is being controlled in accordance with company policies. Computer logs can also be reviewed for login failures, to gauge access times for reasonableness in light of the types of tasks performed, or to detect any unusual activity that may have occurred. In such cases, audit tests may need to be expanded for appropriate follow up. Many computer systems permit an auditor to view an electronic audit trail to determine whether access to operating systems has taken place according to the company's policies. Auditors should also perform tests to be sure that computer access privileges are blocked for employees who have been terminated. They should also test for whether access has been revised for employees who have changed job responsibilities.

In order to test external access controls, auditors may perform the following procedures:

- Authenticity tests, as previously described.
- **Penetration tests,** which involve various methods of entering the company's system to determine whether controls are working as intended. For example, auditors may search for weaknesses in a client's firewall by attempting unauthorized access to the system.
- **Vulnerability assessments,** which analyze a company's control environment for possible weaknesses. For example, auditors may send test messages through a client's system to find out whether encryption of private information is occurring properly. Special software programs are available to help auditors identify weak points in their clients' security measures.
- Review access logs to identify unauthorized users or failed access attempts. Discuss with IT managers the factors involved in rejecting unauthorized access, and verify the consistency of the managers' explanations with documented policies.

In order to maintain good controls, a client company's managers should not rely on their auditors to test for computer access violations, but should also monitor the systems on their own on an ongoing basis. The auditors can examine security reports issued by the IT department or review its security detection systems as a way to test the effectiveness of the company's access controls. The frequency of reporting and the manner of following up are important elements of the control environment.

One of the most effective ways a company can protect its computer system is to place physical and environmental controls in the computer center. Physical controls include locks, security guards, alarms, cameras, and card keys. Physical controls not only limit access to the company's computers, but also are important for preventing damage to computer resources. In addition to assessing physical controls, auditors should evaluate the IT environment to determine that proper temperature control is maintained, fireproofing systems are installed, and an emergency power supply is in place.

To test another important feature of effective security control, auditors should determine whether the company would be able to continue its accounting processes in the event of a loss due to a catastrophe caused by human error, crime, acts of nature, or other unforeseen events. All possible causes should be considered in deciding whether the company is protected. To make such a determination, audits typically review the company's disaster recovery plan, backup procedures, virus protection procedures, and insurance coverage, and discuss with management the reasonableness of these policies and the supporting documentation.

As mentioned earlier, application controls are tested only after the general controls are proven to be strong. When general controls have been tested and found to be operating effectively, auditors then test applications controls to see if they are also working as intended.

APPLICATION CONTROLS

Application controls are computerized controls over application programs. Since any company may use many different computer programs in its day-to-day business, there may be many different types of application controls to consider in an audit. Auditors test the client's systems documentation to be sure that adequate details exist for all application programs. The details should include a list of all applications critical to financial reporting, along with supporting source code that is kept up-to-date in the IT library. Backup copies should be stored off-site. In addition to testing systems documentation, auditors should test the three main functions of the computer applications, including input, processing, and output.

Input Controls

Auditors perform tests to verify the accuracy and completeness of information input to software programs. Auditors are concerned about whether errors are being prevented and detected during the input stage of data processing. Some of the most widely used computer tests of input controls are summarized in Exhibit 7-7.

Each of the controls presented in Exhibit 7-7 may be used by the company as an internal control measure. In most cases, the same type of function can be performed by auditors as a test of the related control. Auditors test these controls to determine whether control risks are being prevented or detected. Auditors observe controls that the company has in place and perform the comparisons on a limited basis to determine their effectiveness. These tests can be performed manually or by electronic methods.

Processing Controls

IT audit procedures typically include a combination of data accuracy tests, whereby the data processed by computer applications are reviewed for correct

Exhibit 7-7
Input Controls

Control	Description
Financial totals: Financial control totals Batch totals	Mathematical sums of dollar amounts or item counts. Useful because they typically identify the amount of a journal entry made in the financial accounting system. Tested by comparing system-generated totals with totals computed by auditors.
Hash totals	Mathematical sums of data that are meaningless to the financial statements (such as vendor numbers or check numbers), but useful for controlling the data and especially for detecting possible missing items. Tested by comparing system-generated totals with totals computed by auditors.
Completeness tests or redundancy tests: Record counts Sequence verification	Counting the number of entries (record counts) or the order of documents in a series (sequence verification). Useful for determining whether application records are complete or if any items are incorrectly included more than once. Also ensures that processing takes place only when all fields within the data file are filled in. Tested by comparing system-generated counts with counts/listings prepared by auditors.
Limit tests	Scanning entries for reasonable limits, such as predetermined limits on check amounts or a customer's credit. Useful in preventing errors and unauthorized processing. Tested by comparing programmed limits with company policies.
Validation checks	Scanning entries to verify whether there is missing or bogus information. Entries are reviewed for valid dates and labeling, records are reviewed for reasonable values and sequences, and fields are reviewed for valid limits or missing data. Tested by comparing programmed information with predetermined values documented in the program code.
Field checks	Scanning entries to determine that data exist in the proper alpha or numeric format. Useful in preventing processing errors due to unrecognized data. Tested by comparing the data format with program code.

dollar amounts or other numerical values. For example, limit tests, described previously as an input control, can also be an effective processing control. **Run-to-run totals** involve the recalculation of amounts from one process to the next to determine whether data have been lost or altered during the process. **Balancing tests** involve a comparison of different items that are expected to have the same values, such as comparing two batches or comparing actual data against a predetermined control total. **Mathematical accuracy tests** verify whether system calculations are correct. Completeness tests and redundancy tests, introduced earlier, check for inclusion of the correct data. Many other procedures, previously described as input control tests, can be performed again during applications processing to check for the possibility of lost or unprocessed data.

Technique	Summary Description	Advantages	Disadvantages
Test data method	Auditors develop test data and process separately, using client's computer system.	Little technical expertise required.	Risk of client data destruction. Time consuming. Tests only anticipated problems. Provides only a static test of controls.
Program tracing	Auditors follow transactions through all processing steps in sequence.	Efficient because it uses actual client data.	May require special technical expertise to consider all paths of program logic.
Integrated test facility	Auditors develop test data and process simultaneously with client's actual data.	Very effective for simple applications. Used during client's normal processing. Provides ongoing tests of controls.	Risk of client data destruction. Time consuming. Less effective for complex applications.
Parallel simulation	Auditors develop program like client's application, then use it to process a copy of client's actual data.	Independent test that allows for large sample sizes. Moderate technical expertise required.	Practicality depends on the complexity of client's application.
Embedded audit modules	Auditors insert tests within client's application. May be used periodically or continuously.	Identifies processing problems as they occur.	Lacks objectivity because it cannot identify unanticipated activity.

Exhibit 7-8
Comparison of Computer-Assisted Audit Techniques, or CAATs, for Testing Applications Controls

Exhibit 7-8 presents a comparison of several **computer assisted audit techniques (CAATs)**. The **test data method** is an audit and control technique often used to test the processing accuracy of software applications. Test data are fictitious information developed by auditors and entered in the client's application system. Test data are processed under the client's normal operating conditions. The results of the test are compared with predicted results to determine whether the application is functioning properly. Auditors must carefully design the test data to include items that appear authentic, as well as some that are illogical. Therefore, it is expected that the system will accurately process the realistic data and isolate the rejected (nonsense) data in an error report. After this testing is complete, auditors should make sure that test items are removed from the client's system to avoid contaminating its actual data. The test data method is well suited to tests of controls in batch systems. The batch of test data can be processed as a single batch so that it will not interrupt or interfere with regular batch processing. The batch nature of the test data approach makes it a static approach to testing controls. This means that the test data method provides a picture of the operation of the internal controls at only one point in time and not over the entire year. This static nature of the test data method makes it less likely to detect fraudulent transactions. The person conducting fraud through changing an application within the IT system could temporarily change it back to the normal operation at the time the test data are processed. Then, after the data have been tested, the application could be reverted to its fraudulent operation.

A slight variation of the test data method involves the auditor testing fictitious data, using a copy of the client's application. The test data may be processed through the application on a different (nonclient) computer. Under these conditions, an auditor can also use another test data method, **program tracing,** whereby bits of actual data are followed through the application in order to verify the accuracy of its processing.

An **integrated test facility** (**ITF**) may be used to test application controls without disrupting the client's operations. Under this approach, test data are input directly into the client's system along with actual data, but the system is programmed to exclude the test data from its master files. The test data and test master files are often called dummy transactions and dummy entities. The dummy transactions are accumulated in the dummy entity files, which are separate files used only by the auditors. Accordingly, auditors can evaluate the applications in light of predetermined expectations (similar to the test data method) during a client's normal operating conditions, without affecting real accounting results. The ITF method is well suited to testing controls in online—as well as online, real-time—systems. The dummy transactions can be processed at intervals throughout the year. Thus, ITF provides an ongoing analysis, rather than a static picture, of the internal controls.

Parallel simulation is an audit technique that processes client data through a controlled program designed to resemble the client's application. Parallel simulations are run to find out whether the same results are achieved under different systems. Simulated results are compared with the client's actual results. Auditors should be careful in forming conclusions on the basis of differences noted in parallel simulations. Although such differences may be the result of control weaknesses in the client's application, they could also be caused by mistakes in developing the simulation.

The **embedded audit module** approach involves placing special audit testing programs within the client's operating system. The test modules search the data and analyze transactions or account balances that meet specified conditions of interest to the auditor. For instance, transactions with a key customer or those that exceed a given dollar amount may be captured in the audit module. The auditors analyze the evidence in the audit module to determine whether it is being recorded accurately. The embedded audit module approach is similar to parallel simulation, except that the embedded audit module approach can be programmed to work either periodically (at each quarter end, for instance) or continuously throughout the period. Parallel simulations, on the other hand, are conducted at a particular point in time.

THE REAL WORLD

Ernst & Young LLP employs thousands of auditors in its Technology and Security Risk Services group. This specialized group assists with financial statement audits and provides other services concerning its clients' information systems. Information systems assurance services focus on audits of business information systems, assessment of the underlying control environment, and the use of CAATs to verify accounting and financial data.

As one of the Big Four CPA firms, Ernst & Young is responsible for auditing the financial statements of many public companies. It serves clients in over 700 locations in more than 140 countries. These client companies are quite diverse in terms of the type of business they perform, their size, and their complexity, but tend to be alike in their need for timely information. The use of CAATs helps Ernst & Young provide timely service to its clients, while accumulating audit evidence necessary for doing its job as auditor.

Output Controls

Audit tests that evaluate general controls over access and backup procedures may also be used in the testing of specific computer application outputs. It is important that auditors test for proper control of financial information resulting from applications processing. Regardless of whether the results are printed or retained electronically, auditors may perform the following procedures to test application outputs:

- **Reasonableness tests** compare the reports and other results with test data or other criteria.
- **Audit trail tests** trace transactions through the application to ensure that the reporting is a correct reflection of the processing and inputs.
- **Rounding errors tests** determine whether significant errors exist due to the way amounts are rounded and summarized.

At the conclusion of the controls testing phase of the audit, an auditor must determine the overall reliability of the client's internal controls. Auditors strive to rely on internal controls as a way to reduce the amount of evidence needed in the remaining phases of the audit. They can be reasonably sure that financial information is accurate when it comes from a system that is proven to have strong controls. Therefore, once the general and application controls are tested and found to be effective, the amount of additional evidence needed in the next phase of the audit is minimal. It is also worthwhile to note that controls testing can be done nearly anytime during the period, so auditors can schedule their work at a convenient time. This convenience factor, plus the reduction in additional audit evidence required, makes testing controls more efficient than testing transactions and account balances.

TESTS OF TRANSACTIONS AND TESTS OF BALANCES (STUDY OBJECTIVE 9)

The auditor's tests of the accuracy of monetary amounts of transactions and account balances are known as **substantive testing.** Substantive testing is very different from testing controls. Substantive tests verify whether financial information *is accurate,* whereas control tests determine whether the financial information is managed under a system that *promotes accuracy.* Some level of substantive testing is required regardless of the results of control testing. If weak internal controls exist or if important controls are not in place, extensive substantive testing will be required. On the other hand, if controls are found to be effective, the amount of substantive testing required is significantly lower, because there is less chance of error in the accounting records. Exhibit 7-9 presents a process map of the substantive testing phase of the audit.

In an IT environment, the evidence needed to determine the accuracy of transactions and account balances is contained in electronic data files within the computer system, from where it may be pulled by specialized audit techniques. Some techniques used to test controls can also be used to test transactions and financial statement balances. For example, parallel simulations, the test data

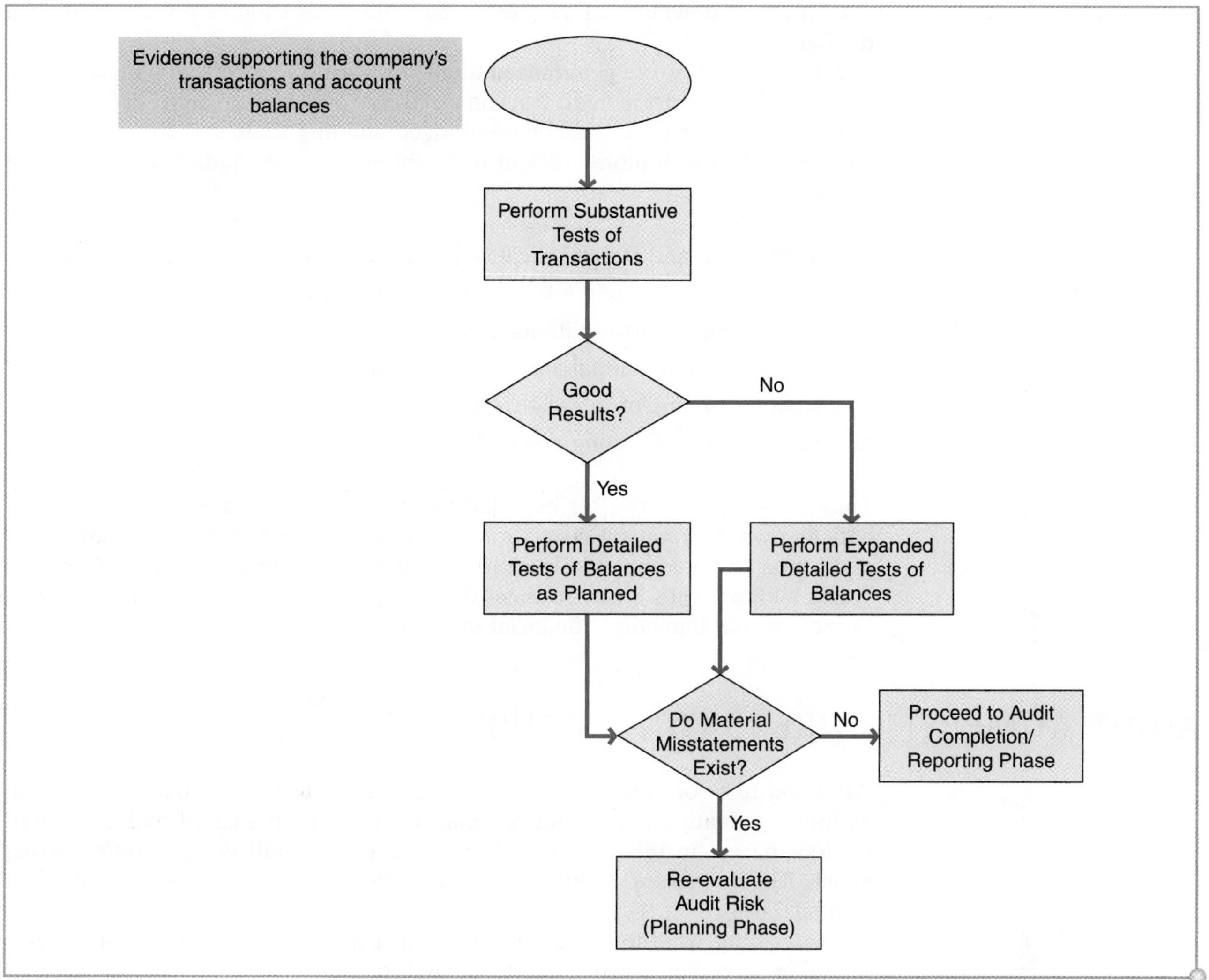

Exhibit 7-9
Substantive Testing Phase Process Map

method, the embedded audit module, and the integrated test facility can be used for both control testing and substantive testing.

Continuous auditing techniques, such those available with the embedded audit module approach, are becoming a very popular form of substantive testing. When companies use e-commerce to conduct business online, auditors know that financial accounting information is produced in real time. Real-time financial reporting has created the need for **continuous auditing,** whereby auditors constantly analyze audit evidence and provide assurance on the related financial information as soon as it occurs or shortly thereafter. The SEC and AICPA also approve of the use of continuous auditing. In response to recent corporate failures, such as those at Enron and WorldCom, continuous auditing helps auditors stay involved with their client's business and perform audit testing in a more thorough manner.

Continuous auditing generally requires that the auditors' access their client's systems online so that audit data can be obtained on an ongoing basis. Audit data are then downloaded and tested by auditors as soon as possible after the data are received.

Most CPA firms use **generalized audit software** (**GAS**) or **data analysis software** (**DAS**) to perform audit tests on electronic data files taken from commonly used database systems. These computerized auditing tools make it possible for auditors to be much more efficient in performing routine audit tests such as the following:

- mathematical and statistical calculations
- data queries
- identification of missing items in a sequence
- stratification and comparison of data items
- selection of items of interest from the data files
- summarization of testing results into a useful format for decision making

The use of GAS or DAS is especially useful when there are large volumes of data and when there is a need for accurate information. These programs allow audit tests to be completed quickly, accurately, and thoroughly, therefore providing auditors with a way to meet the growing needs of decision makers who expect precise, immediate financial information.

AUDIT COMPLETION/REPORTING (STUDY OBJECTIVE 10)

After the tests of controls and substantive audit tests have been completed, auditors evaluate all the evidence that has been accumulated and draw conclusions based on this evidence. This phase is the **audit completion/reporting phase.** The processes within this final phase of the audit are presented in Exhibit 7-10.

In deciding whether a client's financial statements have been fairly presented in accordance with GAAP, the auditors must consider whether the evidence supports the financial information presented. All of the evidence from all phases of the audit and covering all types of accounts and transactions must be combined so that the auditors can make a decision on the fairness of the financial statements as a whole. The auditors must also consider whether the extent of testing has been adequate in light of the risks and controls identified during the planning phase versus the results of procedures performed in the testing phases.

The completion phase includes many tasks that are needed to wrap up the audit. The most important task is obtaining a **letter of representations** from client management. The letter of representations is often considered the most significant single piece of audit evidence because it is a signed acknowledgment of management's responsibility for the fair presentation of the financial statements. In this letter, management must declare that it has provided complete and accurate information to its auditors during all phases of the audit.

When the auditors are satisfied with the extent of testing and a representations letter has been obtained from the client, an audit report must be issued. The audit report expresses the auditors' overall opinion of the financial

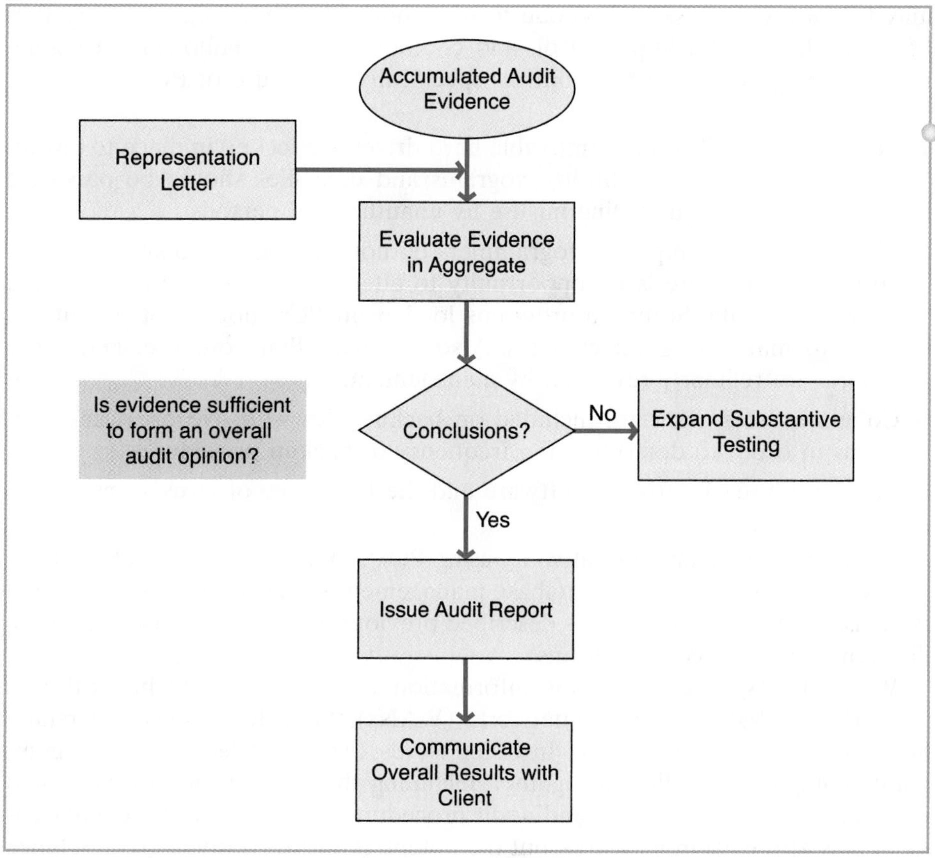

Exhibit 7-10
Audit Completion/Reporting Phase Process Map

statements. There are four basic types of reports that could be issued, including the following:

1. **Unqualified opinion,** which states that the auditors believe the financial statements are fairly and consistently presented in accordance with GAAP
2. **qualified opinion,** which identifies certain exceptions to an unqualified opinion
3. **adverse opinion,** which notes that there are material misstatements presented
4. **disclaimer,** which states that the auditors are unable to reach a conclusion.

Communication is key to the proper conclusion of an audit. In addition to management communicating information in the representations letter and auditors issuing the audit report, auditors must discuss the overall results of the audit with the company's directors.

OTHER AUDIT CONSIDERATIONS (STUDY OBJECTIVE 11)

DIFFERENT IT ENVIRONMENTS

Most companies use microcomputers or personal computers (PCs) in their accounting processes. General controls covering PCs are often less advanced than those covering the mainframe and client–server systems. As a result, PCs may face a greater risk of loss due to unauthorized access, lack of segregation of duties, lack of backup control, and computer viruses. Following are some audit techniques used to test controls specifically in the use of PCs:

- Make sure that PCs and removable hard drives are locked in place to ensure physical security. In addition, programs and data files should be password protected to prevent online misuse by unauthorized persons.
- Make sure that computer programmers do not have access to systems operations, so that there is no opportunity to alter source code and the related operational data. Software programs loaded on PCs should not permit the users to make program changes. Also ascertain that computer-generated reports are regularly reviewed by management.
- Compare dates and data included on backup files with live operating programs in order to determine the frequency of backup procedures.
- Verify the use of antivirus software and the frequency of virus scans.

In addition to, or as an alternative to, using PCs, companies may use IT environments that involve networks, database management systems, and/or e-commerce systems. Most of the procedures described previously may also be used for these different computer configurations.

When clients have accounting information systems organized in local area networks (LANs) or wide area networks (WANs), the auditors must understand how the network is structured. In other words, they must learn how the company's computers are linked together, including the location of all servers and workstations. All of the risks and audit procedures that apply to a PC environment may also exist in networks, but the potential for loss is much greater. Since network operations typically involve a large number of computers, many users, and a high volume of data transfers, any lack of network controls could cause widespread damage. Auditors must apply tests over the entire network. It is especially important for auditors to test the software that manages the network and controls access to the servers.

When companies use database systems, the database management system (including the data, applications, and related controls) replicates or partitions data for many different users. The data will be organized in a consistent way. This tends to make it easier for auditors to select items for testing. However, there are some special considerations for auditors testing database management systems. For example, since many users may have access to the data, the auditors must be sure to evaluate access controls surrounding the database. In addition, it is more important than ever to maintain proper backups in a database environment, because so many people depend on the consistent operation of the database and availability of data. Auditors are responsible for understanding how the data are managed so that they are reliable as a source of financial information. In addition to testing access and backup controls, as discussed earlier in this chapter, the auditors should perform tests to verify that a database administrator is monitoring access to the client's financial data and backing up the database on a regular basis. Since many different applications may access and change the data in the database, database control is especially important.

Security risks always exist in companies that use e-commerce, because their computer systems are linked online with the systems of their business partners. As a result, the reliability of a company's IT system depends upon the reliability of its customers' and suppliers' systems. The audit procedures used to assess controls in e-commerce environments were addressed earlier in this chapter in the discussion on external access controls. In addition, auditors often

- inspect message logs to identify the points of remote access, verify proper sequencing of transactions, and review for timely followup on unsuccessful transmissions between business partners;
- verify that the company has evaluated the computer systems of its business partners prior to doing business over the Internet;
- reprocess transactions to see whether they are controlled properly.

Because of the difficulty of testing all possible points of access in an online system, auditors sometimes find it more cost effective to perform substantive tests rather than extensive tests of controls.

Some client companies may rely on external, independent computer service centers to handle all or part of their IT needs. This is known as **IT outsourcing.** IT outsourcing creates a challenge for auditors, who must gain an adequate understanding of internal controls that are located at an independent service center. However, the service center may have its own independent auditors who report on internal controls. This third-party report can be used as audit evidence about the effectiveness of internal controls. As an alternative, auditors may choose to perform audit tests around the client's computer instead of testing controls at the service center.

CHANGES IN A CLIENT'S IT ENVIRONMENT

When a company changes the type of hardware or software used or otherwise modifies its IT environment, its auditors must consider whether additional audit testing is needed. During its period of change, financial statement information may include data taken from different systems at different times. As a result, auditors should consider applying tests of controls at multiple times throughout the period in order to determine the effectiveness of controls under each of the systems. Specific audit tests include verification of the following items:

- An assessment of user needs
- Proper authorization for new projects and program changes
- An adequate feasibility study and cost–benefit analysis
- Proper design documentation, including revisions for changes made via updated versions, replacements, or maintenance
- Proper user instructions, including revisions for changes made via updated versions, replacements, or maintenance
- Adequate testing before the system is put into use

Overall, auditors need to evaluate a client's procedures for developing, implementing, and maintaining new systems or changes in existing systems. Chapter 6 addressed the systems development life cycle, which involves the various stages of change within the IT function.

When a client company plans to implement new computerized systems, auditors may find it advantageous to review the new features before they are placed in use. This way, the auditors can have a chance to identify controls and make suggestions to management on how to strengthen controls. This may also give the auditors time to develop effective audit tests to be used when the system is activated.

SAMPLING

Auditors cannot possibly evaluate every transaction that makes up an account balance. Auditors rely on **sampling,** whereby they choose and test a limited number of items or transactions and then draw conclusions about the balance as a whole on the basis of the results. Since audit tests do not cover all items in the population, there is some risk that a sample, or subset, of the population may not represent the balance as a whole. Auditors try to use sampling so that a fair representation of the population is evaluated. Computerized software is often employed to help auditors select samples. Random numbers can be generated by special software programs. A sample is random if each item in the population has an equal chance of being chosen. The use of computer programs ensures that there is no bias in selecting the test items. Auditors may also use electronic spreadsheets to generate random numbers or to choose sample items by other methods, such as a selection based on item size. The choice of an appropriate sampling technique is very subjective, and different CPA firms tend to have different policies for using and selecting samples.

ETHICAL ISSUES RELATED TO AUDITING (STUDY OBJECTIVE 12)

Every CPA who is a member of the AICPA is bound by the Code of Professional Conduct, commonly called its code of ethics. This code of ethics is made up of two sections, the principles and the rules. The principles are the foundation for the honorable behavior expected of CPAs while performing professional duties, whereas the rules provide more detailed guidance. Following are the six principles of the code:[1]

1. *Responsibilities.* In carrying out their professional duties, CPAs should exercise sensitive professional and moral judgments in all their activities.
2. *The Public Interest.* CPAs should act in a way that will serve the public interest, honor the public trust, and demonstrate commitment to professionalism.
3. *Integrity.* To maintain and broaden public confidence, CPAs should perform their professional duties with the highest sense of integrity.
4. *Objectivity and Independence.* CPAs should maintain objectivity and be free of conflicts of interest in the performance of their professional duties. CPAs in public practice should be independent in fact and appearance when providing auditing and other attestation services.

[1]Adapted from the *Code of Professional Conduct,* New York: American Institute of Certified Public Accountants, Inc., 2000.

5. *Due Care.* CPAs should observe the profession's technical and ethical standards, strive continually to improve competence and the quality of services, and discharge professional responsibility to the best of their ability.
6. *Scope and Nature of Services.* CPAs in public practice should observe the principles of the Code of Professional Conduct in determining the scope and nature of services to be provided.

The Code of Professional Conduct is voluntarily adopted by the AICPA in recognition of that body's ethical responsibilities to the public, clients, and colleagues. Certified Information Systems Auditors (CISAs) and Certified Internal Auditors (CIAs) also have codes of professional ethics, which can be found at their respective web sites. Compliance with a code of conduct depends primarily upon the understanding and voluntary actions of its members. In the United States, many states have special committees of CPAs that are responsible for enforcing the code of ethics. These committees consider cases of wrongdoing by CPAs practicing within the state. Committee actions may include informal discussions, investigating complaints, issuing warning letters, hearings, trials, and suspension or expulsion of the CPA designation. If a CPA is found guilty of a felony, the committee typically suspends or revokes the CPA's license to practice.

Of all the principles and related rules within the Code of Professional Conduct, the one that generally receives the most attention is independence. The early pages of this chapter described the importance of CPAs being unbiased, which is the essence of independence. The requirement for independence makes the CPA profession unique compared with other business professionals. CPA firms are restricted from performing audit engagements when they have financial or personal relationships with clients or when they have the ability to influence their clients.

THE REAL WORLD

In the case of the Phar-Mor pharmaceutical company fraud, the auditors became too close to the management of Phar-Mor and shared audit information that they should not have. For example, the auditors told management which stores they would select for inventory testing. Phar-Mor managers were then able to move inventory between stores to make sure the inventory counts were correct in the stores that were to be audited by the CPA firm.

The Phar-Mor example illustrates the point that a CPA firm's independence may sometimes be jeopardized simply because the auditors become too friendly with their clients. Auditors have an ethical obligation to never let anything, including friendliness or cozy relationships with their clients, compromise their independence and objectivity.

SOX

Recently, the Sarbanes–Oxley Act placed greater restrictions on CPAs by prohibiting certain types of services historically performed by CPAs for their audit clients. For example, CPAs can no longer perform IT design and implementation services for companies which are also audit clients. The Act regards IT services as involving management decisions that would affect the financial information provided by the company. This would ultimately place the firm in a position of auditing its own work and would therefore violate its objectivity.

The Sarbanes–Oxley Act also increases management's responsibilities regarding the fair presentation of the financial statements. It requires public companies to have an audit committee as a subcommittee of the board of directors. The audit committee is charged with the responsibility for promoting the independence of its auditors, and therefore typically must approve all nonaudit services provided by its auditors. In addition, the Sarbanes–Oxley Act requires top management to verify in writing that the financial statements are fairly stated and that the company has adequate internal controls over financial reporting.

Auditors are responsible for auditing financial statements and for reporting on the effectiveness of their clients' internal controls. Accordingly, auditors should *not* be in a position of making managerial decisions, designing or implementing policies and procedures, or preparing financial information for their clients, as such tasks would jeopardize their independence. If auditors were to be engaged in such tasks, they could not possibly audit the client's underlying financial statements and internal controls in a truly unbiased manner.

In fulfilling their ethical responsibilities, auditors must practice professional skepticism during the audit. **Professional skepticism** means that the auditors should not automatically assume that their clients are honest, but must have a questioning mind and a persistent approach to evaluating evidence for possible misstatements. Misstatements may result from error or fraud, and auditors have equal responsibility for searching for both causes of material misstatements.

Concerning fraud in the business organization, recall from Chapter 3 the distinction between employee fraud and management fraud: Employee fraud involves stealing assets, whereas management fraud is the intentional misstatement of financial information. Fraud may be difficult for auditors to find because the perpetrator often tries to hide the fraud. Auditors must recognize that management may be in a position to override established controls and employees may work in collusion to carry out a fraudulent act. This makes it even more difficult for auditors to detect fraud.

THE REAL WORLD

One of the most widely publicized cases of management fraud involved Crazy Eddie's electronics retail stores in the New York area. This case is particularly outrageous because the management of the company, including Eddie Antar and his family, used nearly every trick in the book to commit financial statement fraud and con its auditors in the process. Some of the tactics used by Antar included the reporting of false sales and overstated inventories, hiding liabilities and expenses, and altering financial statement disclosures. Antar and his family used their employees and suppliers to help carry out their illegal schemes. They also tampered with audit evidence.

Because the auditors were too trusting and did not carefully protect the audit working papers when they went home at the end of the day, the client (Crazy Eddie's) had the opportunity to alter the audit files. Even though this fraud occurred nearly two decades ago, it provides a clear example of how management fraud can be pulled off and how auditors can be deceived.

This example of fraud perpetrated by Crazy Eddie's describes the importance to auditors of knowing their clients well and exercising professional skepticism.

In the exercise of professional skepticism, auditors should make sure that the audit procedures include the following:

- Examination of financial reporting for unauthorized or unusual entries.
- Review of estimated information and changes in financial reporting for possible biases.
- Evaluation of a reasonable business purpose for all significant transactions.

It is important for auditors to consider the conditions under which fraud could be committed, including the possible pressures, opportunities, and rationalization for committing dishonest acts. In the context of a client's IT systems, auditors should also think about the possibility that computer programs could be altered to report financial information in a manner that is favorable for the company.

Modern auditing tends to concentrate on evaluating clients' computer systems and testing the related controls, with reduced emphasis on substantive procedures. Although it is important to understand the company's accounting systems and to determine whether related controls are effective, this type of testing is not enough to satisfy the responsibilities of the audit profession. Auditors should be careful about balancing the mix of audit procedures between tests of controls and substantive tests. Emphasis on computer processes and internal controls may lead to an over-reliance on the accounting system, which could be circumvented by management. Therefore, it is important to also perform substantive procedures that focus on the actual transactions and account balances that make up the financial statements.

THE REAL WORLD

Recent examples of management fraud have been discovered at Enron, Xerox, WorldCom, and other large, well-known companies. In fact, most of the big corporate fraud cases that have been in the news in recent years involved the company's chief executive or top accounting managers. The financial statement misstatements resulting from these frauds have been staggering. At WorldCom, for example, nearly $4 billion in operating expenses were hidden when management decided to capitalize the expenditures rather than report them on the income statement. This illustrates the importance to auditors of varying the mix of audit procedures to include a reasonable combination of tests of controls and substantive tests. Even in large companies with sophisticated systems of internal control, the audit needs to include tests of the accounting balances in order to increase the chances of discovering whether management may have circumvented controls in order to perpetrate fraud.

Accountants are sometimes called upon to perform a specialized type of assurance service called forensic auditing. **Forensic auditing** involves audit testing designed specifically for finding and preventing fraud and is used for companies where fraud is known or believed to exist. Some accountants who work on forensic audits become **certified fraud examiners (CFEs)** and are considered experts in the detection of fraud. Some CFEs specialize in computer forensics, which involves the detection of abuses within computer systems.

SUMMARY OF STUDY OBJECTIVES

An introduction to auditing IT processes. Nearly all companies use computerized systems to conduct business and account for business activities, and many businesses are overwhelmed with the volume of computerized data available for reporting and decision-making purposes. In light of this heightened volume of information and level of information processing, the audit function is as important as ever in improving the quality of information available to decision makers.

The various types of audits and auditors. The three primary types of audits include compliance audits, operational audits, and financial statement audits. Audits may be conducted by CPAs, internal auditors, IT auditors, or government auditors.

Information risk and IT-enhanced internal control. Information risk is the chance that information available to decision makers may be inaccurate. Information risk may be reduced through the use of information that has been audited. Auditors rely on both manual and computer controls to reduce information risk. Computer controls often compensate for weaknesses in manual controls.

Authoritative literature used in auditing. Audit guidance is found in generally accepted auditing standards, as well as standards issued by the Public Company Accounting Oversight Board, the Auditing Standards Board, the International Audit Practices Committee, and the Information Systems Audit and Control Association.

Management assertions used in the auditing process and the related audit objectives. Management makes claims regarding the financial status and results of operations of the business organization, and audit objectives relate to each of these assertions. The assertions include existence, valuation, completeness, rights and obligations, and presentation and disclosure.

The phases of an IT audit. An audit engagement is typically characterized by four phases, including planning, tests of controls, substantive testing, and completion/reporting.

The use of computers in audits. Depending on the nature of a client company's computerized systems, an auditor may perform auditing around the computer, auditing through the computer, or auditing with the computer, using computer assisted audit techniques.

Tests of controls. General controls and application controls can be tested during an audit to determine whether they are working as they were designed to work. This will be done only if the auditor intends to rely on the effectiveness of the client's internal controls as a means of justifying a reduced extent of substantive tests in the remaining phases of the audit.

Tests of transactions and tests of balances. Substantive tests involve the accumulation of evidence in support of transactions that have occurred and the resulting account balances. The extent of substantive testing necessary in an audit depends upon the strength of the client's underlying controls.

Audit completion/reporting. The final phase of an audit involves an evaluation of the evidence accumulated from all audit tests in order to reach an overall conclusion on the fair presentation of the organization's financial statements. Thorough communication is key in this phase; the company's management must issue a letter of representations, the auditors must issue an audit report, and discussions must be held with company directors.

Other audit considerations. Audit procedures need to be tailored to the specific characteristics of each client's business. In particular, extensive testing is generally used when auditing personal computer environments, for companies using extensive database or networking systems, and for companies where significant computer changes have been implemented. To assist in efficient completion of audit tests, sampling techniques are available whereby a subset of the population is tested.

Ethical issues related to auditing. CPAs are bound by a code of conduct that consists of six ethical principles, including professional responsibilities, service to the public interest, integrity, objectivity and independence, the exercise of due care, and the observance of professional conduct.

KEY TERMS

Adverse opinion
Application controls
Assurance services
Audit completion/reporting phase
Audit evidence
Audit program
Audit trail tests
Auditing around the computer
Auditing Standards Board (ASB)
Auditing through the computer
Auditing with the computer
Authenticity tests
Balancing tests
Certified Fraud Examiner (CFE)
Certified Public Accountant (CPA)
Compliance audits
Computer-assisted audit techniques (CAATs)
Continuous auditing
Data analysis software (DAS)
Disclaimer
Embedded audit module
External audit
Field checks
Financial statement audits
Financial totals
Forensic auditing
General controls
Generalized audit software (GAS)
Generally accepted auditing standards (GAAS)
Governmental auditors
Hash totals
Information risk
Information Systems Audit and Control Association (ISACA)
Integrated test facility
Internal auditors
International Audit Practices Committee (IAPC)
IT auditors
IT outsourcing
Letter of representations
Limit tests
Loss of audit trail visibility
Management assertions
Materiality
Mathematical accuracy tests
Operational audits
Parallel simulation
Penetration tests
Planning phase
Professional skepticism
Program tracing
Public Company Accounting Oversight Board (PCAOB)
Qualified opinion
Reasonableness tests

Redundancy tests
Risk
Rounding errors tests
Run-to-run totals
Sampling
SAS No. 94
Substantive testing
Test data method
Tests of controls
Unqualified opinion
Validation checks
Vulnerability assessments

END OF CHAPTER MATERIAL

CONCEPT CHECK

1. Which of the following types of audits is most likely to be conducted for the purpose of identifying areas for cost savings?
   a. Financial statement audits
   b. Operational audits
   c. Regulatory audits
   d. Compliance audits
2. Financial statement audits are required to be performed by
   a. government auditors.
   b. CPAs.
   c. internal auditors.
   d. IT auditors.
3. Which of the following is **not** considered a cause of information risk?
   a. Management's geographic location is far from the source of the information needed to make effective decisions.
   b. The information is collected and prepared by persons who use the information for very different purposes.
   c. The information relates to business activities that are not well understood by those who collect and summarize the information for decision makers.
   d. The information has been tested by internal auditors and a CPA firm.
4. Which of the following is **not** a part of generally accepted auditing standards?
   a. general standards
   b. standards of fieldwork
   c. standards of information systems
   d. standards of reporting
5. Which of the following best describes what is meant by the term "generally accepted auditing standards"?
   a. Procedures used to gather evidence to support the accuracy of a client's financial statements
   b. Measures of the quality of an auditor's conduct
   c. Professional pronouncements issued by the Auditing Standards Board
   d. Rules acknowledged by the accounting profession because of their widespread application

6. In an audit of financial statements in accordance with generally accepted auditing standards, an auditor is required to
   a. document the auditor's understanding of the client company's internal controls.
   b. search for weaknesses in the operation of the client company's internal controls.
   c. perform tests of controls to evaluate the effectiveness of the client company's internal controls.
   d. determine whether controls are appropriately designed to prevent or detect material misstatements.
7. Auditors should design a written audit program so that
   a. all material transactions will be included in substantive testing.
   b. substantive testing performed prior to year end will be minimized.
   c. the procedures will achieve specific audit objectives related to specific management assertions.
   d. each account balance will be tested under either a substantive test or a test of controls.
8. Which of the following audit objectives relates to the management assertion of existence?
   a. A transaction is recorded in the proper period.
   b. A transaction actually occurred (i.e., it is real).
   c. A transaction is properly presented in the financial statements.
   d. A transaction is supported by detailed evidence.
9. Which of the following statements regarding an audit program is true?
   a. A standard audit program should be developed for use on any client engagement.
   b. The audit program should be completed by the client company before the audit planning stage begins.
   c. An audit program should be developed by the internal auditor before audit testing begins.
   d. An audit program establishes responsibility for each audit test by requiring the signature or initials of the auditor who performed the test.
10. Risk assessment is a process designed to
   a. identify possible events that may effect the business.
   b. establish policies and procedures to carry out internal controls.
   c. identify and capture information in a timely manner.
   d. test the internal controls throughout the year.
11. Which of the following audit procedures is most likely to be performed during the planning phase of the audit?
   a. Obtain an understanding of the client's risk assessment process.
   b. Identify specific internal control activities that are designed to prevent fraud.
   c. Evaluate the reasonableness of the client's accounting estimates.
   d. Test the timely cutoff of cash payments and collections.

12. Which of the following is the most significant disadvantage of auditing around the computer rather than through the computer?
    a. The time involved in testing processing controls is significant.
    b. The cost involved in testing processing controls is significant.
    c. A portion of the audit trail is not tested.
    d. The technical expertise required to test processing controls is extensive.
13. The primary objective of compliance testing in a financial statement audit is to determine whether
    a. procedures have been updated regularly.
    b. financial statement amounts are accurately stated.
    c. internal controls are functioning as designed.
    d. collusion is taking place.
14. Which of the following computer assisted auditing techniques processes actual client input data (or a copy of the real data) on a controlled program under the auditor's control to periodically test controls in the client's computer system?
    a. Test data method
    b. Embedded audit module
    c. Integrated test facility
    d. Parallel simulation
15. Which of the following computer assisted auditing techniques allows fictitious and real transactions to be processed together without client personnel being aware of the testing process?
    a. Test data method
    b. Embedded audit module
    c. Integrated test facility
    d. Parallel simulation
16. Which of the following is a general control to test for external access to a client's computerized systems?
    a. Penetration tests
    b. Hash totals
    c. Field checks
    d. Program tracing
17. Suppose that during the planning phase of an audit, the auditor determines that weaknesses exist in the client's computerized systems. These weaknesses make the client company susceptible to the risk of an unauthorized break-in. Which type of audit procedures should be emphasized in the remaining phases of this audit?
    a. Tests of controls
    b. Penetration tests
    c. Substantive tests
    d. Rounding errors tests
18. Generalized audit software can be used to
    a. examine the consistency of data maintained on computer files.
    b. perform audit tests of multiple computer files concurrently.

c. verify the processing logic of operating system software.

d. process test data against master files that contain both real and fictitious data.

19. Independent auditors are generally actively involved in each of the following tasks except:

a. Preparation of a client's financial statements and accompanying notes

b. Advising client management as to the applicability of a new accounting standard

c. Proposing adjustments to a client's financial statements

d. Advising client management about the presentation of the financial statements

20. Which of the following is most likely to be an attribute unique to the audit work of CPAs, compared with work performed by attorneys or practitioners of other business professions?

a. Due professional care

b. Competence

c. Independence

d. A complex underlying body of professional knowledge

21. Which of the following terms is **not** associated with the auditor's requirement to maintain independence?

a. Objectivity

b. Neutrality

c. Professional skepticism

d. Competence

DISCUSSION QUESTIONS

22. (SO 1) What are assurance services? What value do assurance services provide?
23. (SO 2) Differentiate between a compliance audit and an operational audit.
24. (SO 2) Which type of audit is most likely to be performed by government auditors? Which type of audit is most likely to be performed by internal auditors?
25. (SO 2) Identify the three areas of an auditor's work that are significantly impacted by the presence IT accounting systems.
26. (SO 3) Describe the three causes of information risk.
27. (SO 3) Explain how an audit trail might get "lost" within a computerized system.
28. (SO 3) Explain how the presence of IT processes can improve the quality of information that management uses for decision making.
29. (SO 4) Distinguish among the focuses of the GAAS standards of fieldwork and standards of reporting.
30. (SP 4) Which professional standard-setting organization provides guidance on the conduct of an IT audit?

31. (SO 5) If management is responsible for its own financial statements, why are auditors important?
32. (SO 6) List the techniques used for gathering evidence.
33. (SO 6) During which phase of an audit would an auditor consider risk assessment and materiality?
34. (SO 6) What is the significance of Statement on Auditing Standards No. 94?
35. (SO 7) Distinguish between auditing through the computer and auditing with the computer. When are auditors required to audit through the computer as opposed to auditing around the computer?
36. (SO 8) Explain why it is customary to complete the testing of general controls before testing applications controls.
37. (SO 8) Identify four important aspects of administrative control in an IT environment.
38. (SO 8) Think about a place you have worked where computers were present. What are some physical and environmental controls that you have observed in the workplace? Provide at least two examples of each from your personal experience.
39. (SO 8) Batch totals and hash totals are common input controls. Considering the fact that hash totals can be used with batch processing, differentiate between these two types of controls.
40. (SO 8) The test data method and an integrated test facility are similar in that they are both tests of applications controls and they both rely on the use of test data. Explain the difference between these two audit techniques.
41. (SO 9) Explain the necessity for performing substantive testing even for audit clients with strong internal controls and sophisticated IT systems.
42. (SO 9) What kinds of audit tools are used to perform routine tests on electronic data files taken from databases? List the types of tests that can be performed with these tools.
43. (SO 9) Which of the four types of audit reports is the most favorable for an audit client? Which is the least favorable?
44. (SO 9) Why is it so important to obtain a letter of representation from an audit client?
45. (SO 10) How can auditors evaluate internal controls when their clients use IT outsourcing?
46. (SO 11) An auditor's characteristic of professional skepticism is most closely associated with which ethical principle of the AICPA Code of Professional Conduct?

BRIEF EXERCISES

47. (SO 2) Why is it necessary for a CPA to be prohibited from having financial or personal connections with a client? Provide an example of how a financial connection to a company would impair an auditor's objectivity. Provide an example of how a personal relationship might impair an auditor's objectivity.
48. (SO 3) From an internal control perspective, discuss the advantages and disadvantages of using IT-based accounting systems.

49. (SO 4) Explain why standards of fieldwork for GAAS are not particularly helpful to an auditor who is trying to determine the types of testing to be used on an audit engagement.
50. (SO 5) Tyrone and Tyson are assigned to perform the audit of Tylen Company. During the audit, it was discovered that the amount of sales reported on Tylen's income statement was understated because one week's sales transactions were not recorded due to a computer glitch. Tyrone claims that this problem represents a violation of the management assertion regarding existence, because the reported account balance was not real. Tyson argues that the completeness assertion was violated, because relevant data was omitted from the records. Which auditor is correct? Explain your answer.
51. (SO 6) One of the most important tasks of the planning phase is for the auditor to gain an understanding of internal controls. How does this differ from the tasks performed during the tests of controls phase?
52. (SO 8) How is it possible that a review of computer logs can be used to test for both internal access controls and external access controls? Other than reviewing the computer logs, identify and describe two types of audit procedures performed to test internal access controls, and two types of audit procedures performed to test external access controls.
53. (SO 9) Explain why continuous auditing is growing in popularity. Identify and describe a computer-assisted audit technique useful for continuous auditing.
54. (SO 11) Each of the principles of the AICPA Code of Professional Conduct relates to the trustworthiness of the CPA. Distinguish between the fourth principle (integrity) and the fifth principle (objectivity and independence).

PROBLEMS

55. (SO 4) Given is a list of audit standard-setting bodies (shown on the left) and a description of their purpose (shown on the right). Match each standard-setting body with its purpose.

I. PCAOB	a. Established by the AICPA to issue SASs.
II. ASB	b. Issues ISASs to provide guidelines for IT audits.
III. IAPC	c. Established by the Sarbanes–Oxley Act of 2002 to establish audit guidelines for public companies and their auditors.
IV. ISACA	d. Issues ISAs to promote uniformity of worldwide auditing practices.

56. (SO 8) Identify whether each of the following audit tests is used evaluate internal access controls (I), external access controls (E), or both (B):
- Authenticity tests
- Penetration tests
- Vulnerability assessments

- Review of access logs
- Review of policies concerning the issuance of passwords and security tokens

57. (SO 9) Refer to the notes payable audit program excerpt presented in Exhibit 7-3. If an auditor had a copy of this client's data file for its notes receivable, how could a general audit software or data analysis software package be used to assist with these audit tests?

58. (SO 11) In order to preserve auditor independence, the Sarbanes–Oxley Act of 2002 restricts the types of nonaudit services that auditors can perform for their public-company audit clients. The list includes nine types of services that are prohibited because they are deemed to impair an auditor's independence. Included in the list are the following:
    - financial information systems design and implementation
    - internal audit outsourcing

Describe how an auditor's independence could be impaired if she performed IT design and implementation functions for her audit client. Likewise, how could an auditor's involvement with internal audit outsourcing impair her independence with respect to auditing the same company?

59. (SO 2) Visit the AICPA website at www.aicpa.org and click on Becoming a CPA/Academic Resources. Use the Careers in Accounting tab to locate information on audit careers.

60. (SO 4 and 9) Visit the ISACA website at www.isaca.org and click the Students and Educators tab and then the IT Audit Basics tab to find articles covering topics concerning the audit process. Locate an article on each of the following topics and answer the related question:
    a. Identify and briefly describe the four categories of CAATs.
    b. List the factors that contribute to the formation of due care in an auditor.

61. (SO 12) Refer to the example presented in this chapter describing frauds perpetrated by top managers in large companies like Enron, Xerox, and WorldCom. Perform an Internet search to determine the nature of Xerox's management fraud scheme and to find out what happened to the company after the problems were discovered.

CASES

62. Lidia Lune was auditing the financial statements of Lea Wholesale Industries when she was presented with a curious situation. A member of Lea's top management team approached her with an anonymous note that had been retrieved from the company's suggestion box. The note accused unnamed employees in Lea's IT department of altering the accounts payable database by entering bogus transactions involving fictitious vendors. Payments made to this fictitious vendor were being intercepted and cashed by the fraudster.

    Required:

    a. What tests of controls would be effective in helping Lune determine whether Lea's vendor database was susceptible to fraud?

b. What computer-assisted audit technique would be effective in helping Lune determine whether Lea's vendor database had actually been falsified?

63. Leland Tuwe is an auditor for a large CPA firm. Leland was recently assigned to perform a financial statement audit of Guten Meister Industries, a brewery and distributor of German specialty foods. Leland's firm is auditing Guten Meister for the first time. The audit is nearly complete, but it has required more time than expected. The auditors who performed the planning and testing phases have now been assigned to another client engagement, so Leland was called in to carry out the completion/reporting phase.

In discussing the details of the audit engagement with the original audit team, Leland learned that the original team expected that an unqualified audit opinion would be issued. This expectation was based on the extent of audit evidence accumulated, which led to the belief that the financial statements were fairly presented in accordance with GAAP.

Hans Erich Schirmer, Guten Meister's CFO, is unhappy about the change in audit personnel. He is threatening to refuse to furnish a letter of representation.

Required:

a. Would it be appropriate for Leland to reopen the audit testing phases in order to expand procedures, in light of the lack of representative evidence from management? Why or why not?

b. Will Leland's firm still be able to issue an unqualified audit report if it does not receive the representation letter? Research the standard wording to be included in an unqualified audit report, as well as the typical wording included in a client representation letter. Base your answer on your findings.

CONTINUING CASE: SPATELLI'S PIZZERIA

Consider the case of Spatelli's Pizzeria as presented at the end of Chapter 1. Imagine that you have been hired to perform the financial statement audit for Spatelli's Pizzeria. This is the first time the company has had an external audit.

Required:

a. What steps would your firm go through in the planning phase for this initial audit engagement?

b. What computer-assisted audit techniques could you use in conducting this audit? Use details from the case to explain why you believe these techniques would be appropriate for Spatelli's.

SOLUTIONS TO CONCEPT CHECK

1. (CIA Adapted) (SO 2) Of the given types of audits, **b. the operational audit** is most likely to be conducted for the purpose of identifying areas for cost savings. The primary purpose is to enhance efficiency and effectiveness, which is likely to result in cost savings.

2. (SO 2) Financial statement audits are required to be performed by **b. CPAs.** CPAs have extensive knowledge of GAAP, which is the required criteria in

a financial statement audit. On the other hand, government auditors are specialists in governmental regulations, internal auditors work with gauging compliance with management's directives and operating effectiveness, and IT auditors focus on the effectiveness of computerized processes.

3. (SO 3) That **d. the information has been tested by internal auditors and a CPA firm** is not considered a cause of information risk. This is a way to reduce information risk, not a cause of information risk. Answer a. relates to the remoteness of information, b. relates to the motive of the preparer, and c. relates to the complexity of the transactions, which are each associated with increased information risk.
4. (SO 4) **c. Standards of information systems** are not a part of generally accepted auditing standards. The three categories of GAAS are general standards, standards of fieldwork, and standards of reporting.
5. (CPA Adapted) (SO 4) **b. "Measures of the quality of an auditor's conduct"** best describes what is meant by the term "generally accepted auditing standards."
6. (CPA Adapted) (SO 4) In an audit of financial statements in accordance with generally accepted auditing standards, an auditor is required to **a. document the auditor's understanding of the client company's internal control**. Each of the other responses pertain to testing of controls, which are required only if the auditor plans to rely upon the effectiveness of internal controls.
7. (CPA Adapted) (SO 5) Auditors should design a written audit program so that **c. the procedures will achieve specific audit objectives related to specific management assertions.**
8. (SO 5) The audit objective which relates to the management assertion of existence is that **b. a transaction actually occurred (i.e., it is real).** Answers a. and d. relate to valuation; answer c. relates to presentation and disclosure.
9. (SO 5) The statement regarding an audit program which is true is that **d. an audit program establishes responsibility for each audit test by requiring the signature or initials of the auditor who performed the test.** Answer a. is incorrect because audit programs need to be developed to address the unique nature of each client company. Answers b. and c. are incorrect because the client, including its internal auditors, should not be involved in the development or completion of the audit program; rather, the audit is the independent auditor's responsibility.
10. (CMA Adapted) (SO 6) Risk assessment is a process designed to **a. identify possible events that may effect the business.**
11. (CPA Adapted) (SO 6) The audit procedure most likely to be performed during the planning phase of the audit is to **a. obtain an understanding of the client's risk assessment process.** Response b. is performed during tests of controls. Responses c. and d. are performed as part of substantive testing.
12. (CIA Adapted) (SO 7) The most significant disadvantage of auditing around the computer rather than through the computer is that **c. a portion of the audit trail is not tested.** The other three responses would each be considered disadvantages of auditing through the computer.
13. (CMA Adapted) (SO 8) The primary objective of compliance testing in a financial statement audit is to determine whether **c. internal controls are functioning as designed.** Compliance testing is another term for tests of

controls, the purpose of which is to determine whether internal controls are functioning in compliance with management's intentions.

14. (CPA Adapted, CIA Adapted) (SO 8) The computer assisted auditing technique that processes actual client input data (or a copy of the real data) on a controlled program under the auditor's control to periodically test controls in the client's computer system is **d. parallel simulation.** Each of the other responses involves use of the client company's computer system.
15. (CPA Adapted) (SO 8) The computer assisted auditing technique that allows fictitious and real transactions to be processed together without client personnel being aware of the testing process is the **c. integrated test facility.**
16. (SO 8) The general control to test for external access to a client's computerized systems is **a. penetration tests.** Answers b., c., and d. are application controls.
17. (SO 8 and 9) During the planning phase of an audit, the auditor determines that weaknesses exist in the client's computerized systems. These weaknesses make the client company susceptible to the risk of an unauthorized break-in. The type of audit procedures that should be emphasized in the remaining phases of this audit is **c. substantive tests.** Answers a., b., and d. each relate to tests of controls, which are to be performed only when good controls have been found to be in place. It is not worthwhile to test weak or ineffective controls, since the purpose of tests of controls is to prove the usefulness of controls as a basis for reducing substantive testing.
18. (CIA Adapted) (SO 9) Generalized audit software can be used to **a. examine the consistency of data maintained on computer files.** This response applies to the use of generalized audit software to perform comparisons. None of the other responses relates to the uses described under Study Objective 9.
19. (CMA Adapted) (SO 11) Independent auditors are generally actively involved in each of the given tasks except **a. preparation of a client's financial statements and accompanying notes.** Auditors would be placed in a position of auditing their own work if they prepared financial statements for an audit client.
20. (CPA Adapted) (SO 11) The attribute most likely to be unique to the audit work of CPAs, compared with work performed by attorneys or practitioners of other business professions, is **c. Independence.** Most other professionals are advocates for their clients, whereas auditors must be independent with respect to their audit clients.
21. (SO 4 and 11) The term not associated with the auditor's requirement to maintain independence is **d. Competence.** Competence relates to the first general standard within GAAS; each of the other answers relate to independence (the second general standard).

CHAPTER 8

Revenue and Cash Collection Processes and Controls

Study Objectives

This chapter will help you gain an understanding of the following concepts:

1. An introduction to revenue processes
2. Sales processes and the related risks and controls
3. Sales return processes and the related risks and controls
4. Cash collection processes and the related risks and controls
5. An overview of IT systems of revenue and cash collection that enhance the efficiency of revenue processes
6. E-business systems and the related risks and controls
7. Electronic data interchange (EDI) systems and the related risks and controls
8. Point of sale (POS) systems and the related risks and controls
9. Ethical issues related to revenue processes
10. Corporate governance in revenue processes

THE REAL WORLD

Eric Delmar/iStockphoto

Staples®, the large office supply company, sells not only in retail stores, but also to other large corporations. Top management at Staples realizes that these corporate sales are dependent upon customers' satisfaction with their buying experience. Staples must have sales processes that maximize customer satisfaction, because the sales processes are what make up the buying experience. The "customer's total experience starts at the time the order is placed, continues through the time it is delivered to the final destination, addresses the need for easy returns, and ends with the payment of the invoice."[1] Staples must have, monitor, and improve all of the internal processes that generate the sale, deliver to the customer, and collect the payment. These processes must be able to handle walk-in sales, telephone orders, and web orders. To improve performance in filling customer orders and collecting the cash, Staples monitors the following performance measures:

- Order entry accuracy
- Order fill rate versus unit fill rate
- Percent of items mispicked
- Percent of orders delivered next day
- Products delivered undamaged

To perform efficiently in these areas, Staples must have processes within the company to enter customer orders, pick the correct items from the warehouse shelves, package and ship the items correctly, bill the customer correctly, and collect the payment as quickly as possible. If these processes are inefficient or poorly managed, the result may be unhappy customers and reduced sales. This chapter describes these types of revenue processes and the internal controls within those processes.

INTRODUCTION TO REVENUE PROCESSES (STUDY OBJECTIVE 1)

There are many kinds of companies selling many kinds of products and services. Because there is such a variety of types of companies and items for sale, and because there are so many methods of conducting revenue transactions, it is impossible to present an example of revenue and collection business processes that represents all possibilities. For instance, retailers may sell their products to consumers through company-owned department stores, using cash registers with bar coding systems called point of sale (POS) systems. These systems record the sale, collect cash, and update the inventory status all at the time of the sale. On the other hand, a manufacturer may sell products to other companies on 30-day credit terms, deliver the goods and bill the customer at a later date, and collect payment after the 30-day period.

The business processes for a company selling to other companies are likely to be different from a company selling products to consumers. An example of a company that sells to end consumers is Wal-Mart, while an example of a company that sells to other companies is Procter & Gamble (P&G). P&G sells consumer products, such as Crest® toothpaste, to companies (like Wal-Mart) who then resell to consumers. Wal-Mart serves as the middle man who buys toothpaste from P&G and resells to consumers. The business processes that Wal-Mart engages in to generate and collect revenue are much different from those of

[1]Jay Baitler, "The Power of Effective Procurement and Strategic Suppliers," *Strategic Finance*, April 2003, p. 39.

P&G. This chapter begins by describing a common set of revenue and cash collection processes for companies that sell goods to other companies. Business process maps, document flowcharts, and data flow diagrams are included as visual representations of the business activities. However, the processes illustrated and described in this chapter can focus only on common characteristics of such companies. Not all companies conduct business exactly as presented in this chapter.

Exhibit 8-1 shows the revenue processes section of the overall accounting system that is the subject of this chapter. In a large company, there may be thousands or hundreds of thousands of sales transactions occurring each day. The company must have systems and processes in place to capture, record, summarize, and report the results of these transactions. The processes are the polices and procedures that employees follow in completing the sale, capturing customer data and sales quantities, and routing the resulting sales documents to the right departments within the company. The accounting system uses this flow of sales documents to various departments to record, summarize, and report the results of the sales transactions.

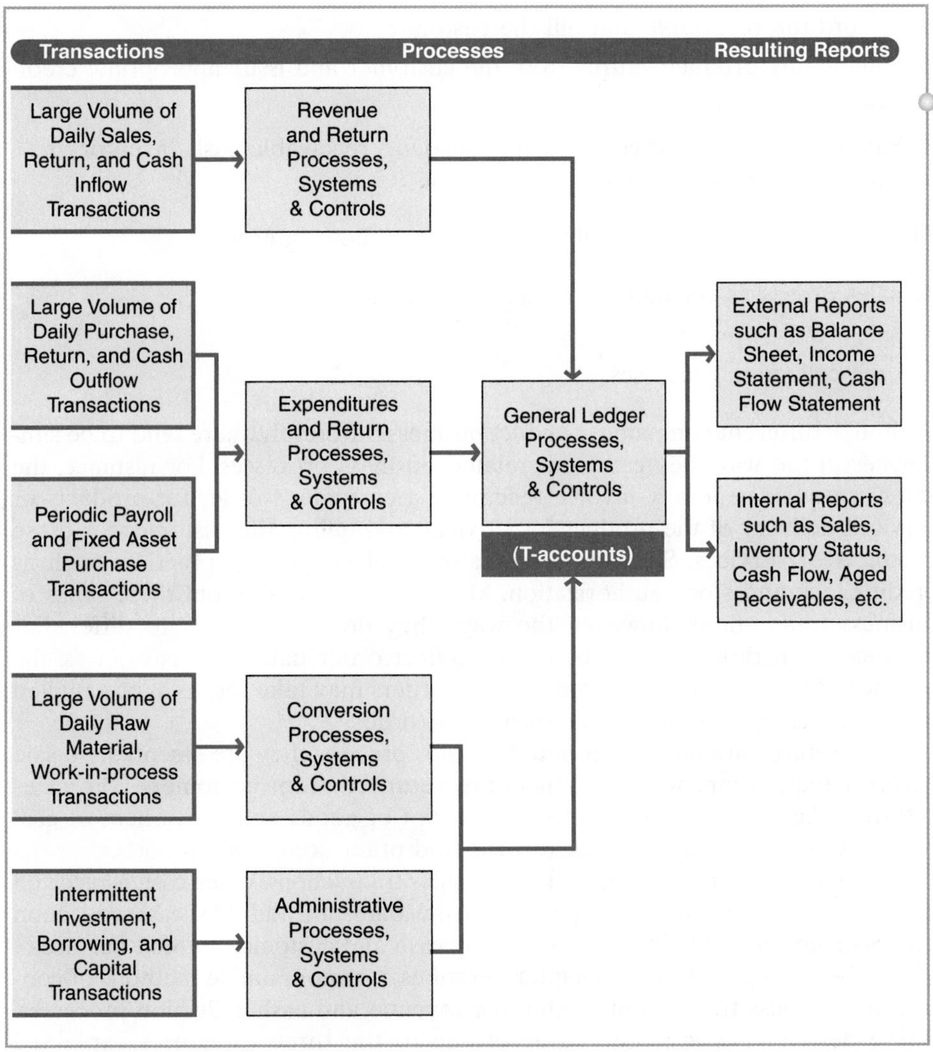

Exhibit 8-1
Revenue Processes within the Overall System

For example, when a sale occurs, the information resulting from that sale must flow into the sales recording systems, the accounts receivable and cash collection systems, and the inventory tracking systems. In IT accounting systems, these recording and processing systems are called **transaction processing systems (TPS).** Thus, there is a set of processes within the company to conduct sales and route sales information, and there is a TPS within the IT system to record, summarize, and report sales transactions.

Sales transactions that occur daily also generate other related transactions. Those transactions are the movement of inventory to customers, the recording of accounts receivable and the subsequent cash inflow, and sales returns from customers. Processes for each of these types of transactions must be in place for the company to carry out transactions on a daily basis. The business processes that are common in company-to-company sales transactions are as follows:

- Collect order data from the customer (another company, not the end-user consumer)
- Deliver goods, often via common carrier such as trucking company or rail carrier
- Record the receivable and bill the customer
- Handle any product returns from the customer and issue appropriate credit
- Collect the cash
- Update the records affected, such as accounts receivable, cash, inventory, revenue, and cost of goods sold

These types of processes are divided into the following groups:

1. sales processes, including ordering, delivery, and billing
2. sales returns processes
3. cash collection processes

Although different companies conduct business differently, there tend to be similarities in the way they carry out related business processes. For instance, the sales processes generally involve receipt of a customer's order for products or services, delivery of the products or services, and billing the customer for those products or services. Sales processes also need supporting practices such as credit check and stock authorization. Most companies carry out these types of business transactions; however, the ways they do so are likely to differ. For instance, even though most companies collect order data from customers, the manner of receiving order data may vary. Orders may take the form of a mailed purchase order, a website order, or an EDI order.

Sales returns are an exception to the sales process; they are essentially a sale reversal that occurs when products are returned from customers. The sales return processes generally involve the receipt of goods and adjustment of customer accounts, inventory stock records, and other accounting reports.

Cash collections result from completed sales transactions. When cash is received from customers, it must be deposited in the bank. In addition, cash collection processes involve updating and reconciling cash and customer account balances.

The beginning part of this chapter describes common, simple methods of conducting business transactions within the revenue and cash collection processes. These descriptions are ordered according to the three categories explained earlier: sales, sales returns, and cash collections.

This chapter also considers the following risks that may affect the revenue and cash collection processes:

- Recorded transactions may not be valid or complete; that is, they may involve a fictitious customer, incorrect quantities or terms, or erroneous duplication.
- Transactions may be recorded in the wrong amount.
- Valid transactions may have been omitted from the records.
- Transactions may have been recorded in the wrong customer account.
- Transactions may not have been recorded in a timely manner.
- Transactions may not have been accumulated or transferred to the accounting records correctly.

The internal control procedures and IT controls that help lessen these risks are presented in exhibits following the discussion of each process category.

After describing the business processes for company-to-company transactions, the latter part of this chapter describes alternative business process models to generate and collect revenue. Examples include e-commerce or web-based sales, EDI systems, and point of sale systems.

SALES PROCESSES (STUDY OBJECTIVE 2)

The business process map in Exhibit 8-2 depicts the activities related to sales processes. Exhibit 8-3 shows a document flowchart for the sales process, and Exhibit 8-4 shows the sales process in a data flow diagram (DFD). The process begins when a buyer, or customer, places an order with the company. The form designating this order is referred to differently by the customer and seller. From the customer's perspective, this order is called a **purchase order** (because it is making a purchase), while the seller refers to this same order as a **sales order** (because it is making a sale). A customer's purchase order is the source document that conveys the details about the order. When a customer's purchase order is received, it must be entered into the seller's system as a sales order. Depending on the extent of computerization of the seller's system, this could be either manually entered or read automatically by the system.

Sales orders are calculated on the basis of current selling prices of the items sold. The source of these prices is the price list. A **price list** is the entire set of preestablished and approved prices for each product. In most accounting software systems, selling prices are attached to each product in the company's inventory. Exhibit 8-5 (on page 291) shows a price list for a product in Microsoft Dynamics GP®. Notice that the same item includes different prices for sales by the case and sales by the individual unit.

Once a sales order is in the system, the customer's credit status must be checked. For existing customers, a new sale on account should be approved only if it is determined that the customer has not exceeded the established credit limit. The **credit limit** is the maximum dollar amount that a customer is allowed to carry as an accounts receivable balance. Each customer should have a preestablished credit limit, which designates the maximum amount of credit the company is willing to extend to that customer. Credit limits may be adjusted on the basis of payment history and the current amount of uncollected sales outstanding.

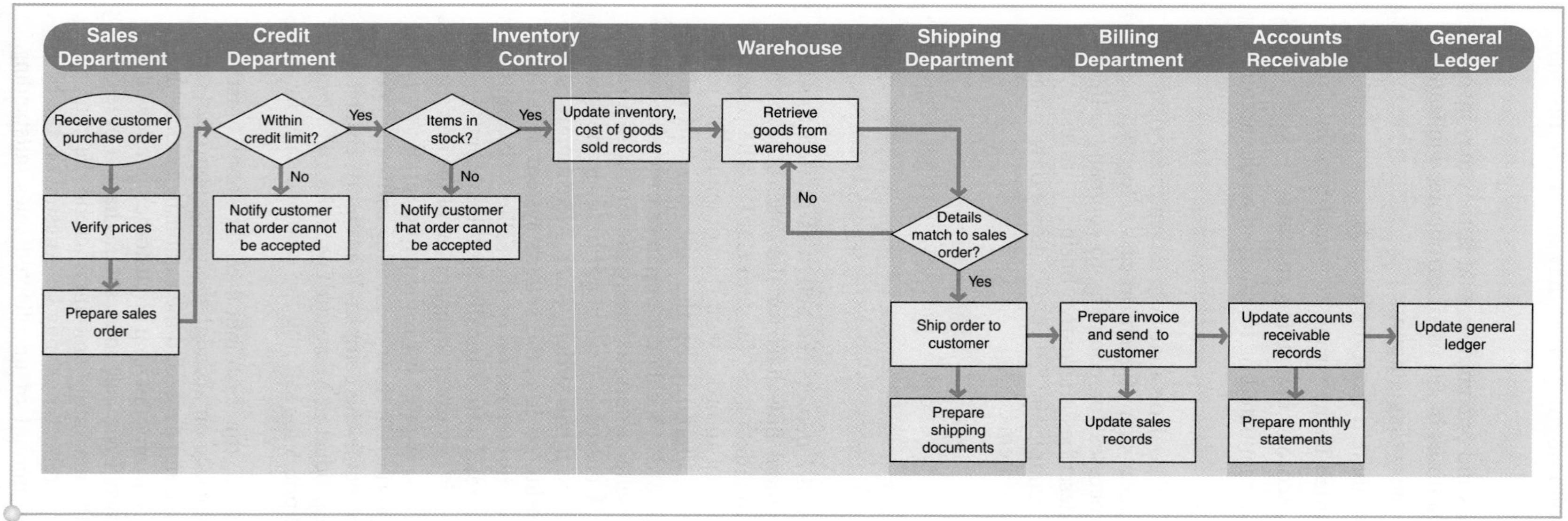

Exhibit 8-2
Sales Process Map

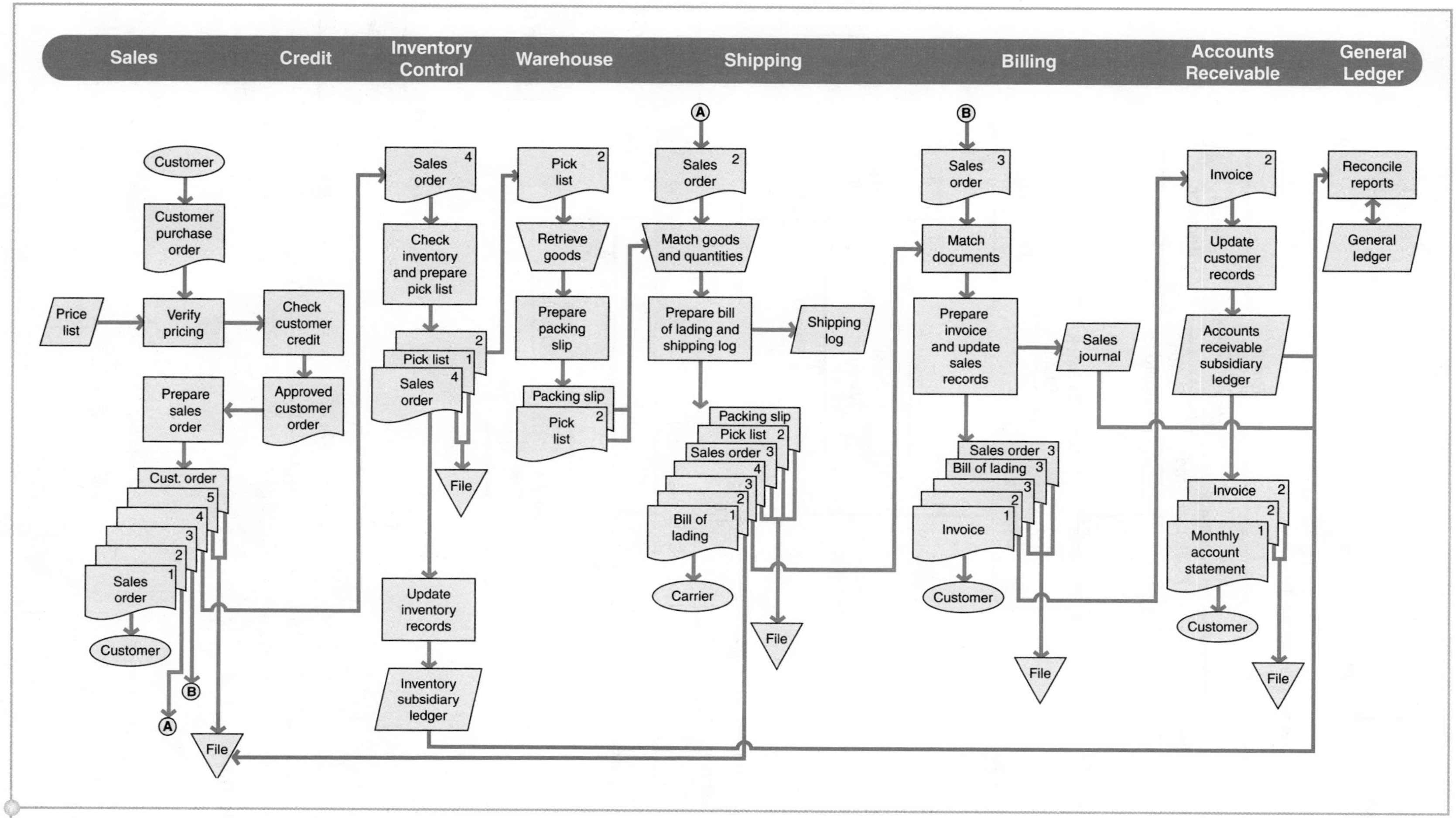

Exhibit 8-3
Document Flowchart of a Sales Process

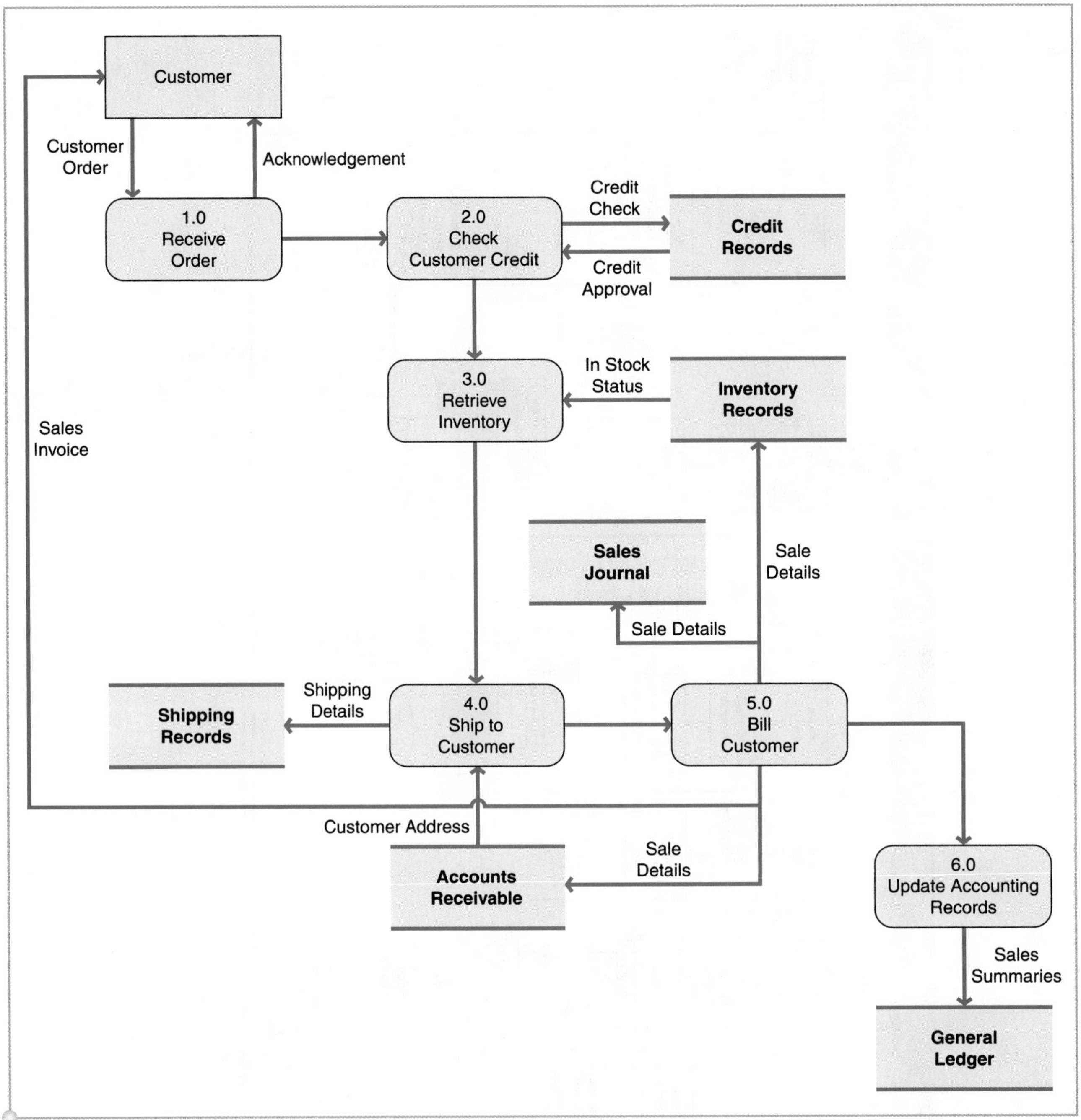

Exhibit 8-4
Sales Processes Data Flow Diagram

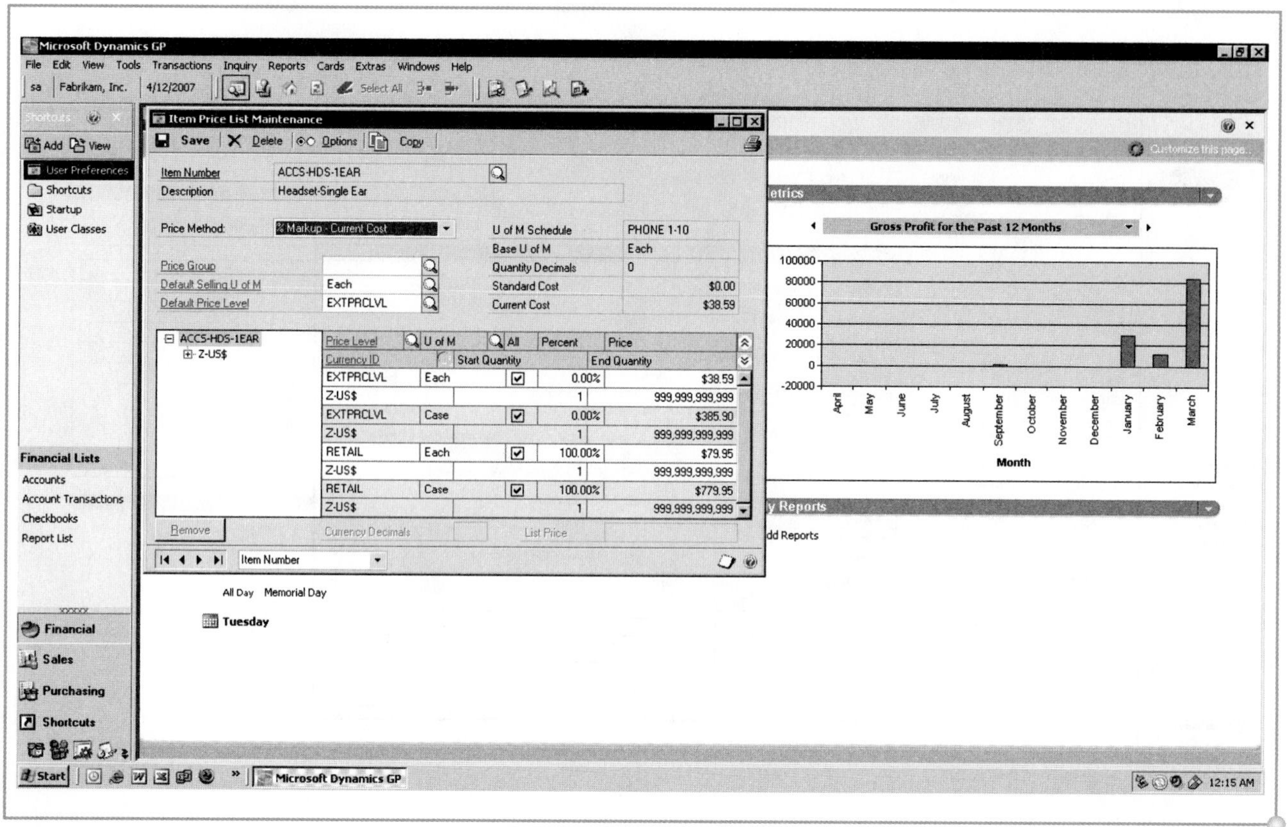

Exhibit 8-5
List Price of a Product in Microsoft Dynamics GP®

If a sales order is for a new customer, the creditworthiness of that customer must be evaluated before the sale is approved. As new customers are entered into the system, a credit limit must be set for them. Exhibit 8-6 shows a credit limit of $20,000 for a customer, Associated Insurance Company, as it would be established in Microsoft Dynamics GP® accounting software. Whether it is a new or an existing customer, customer records must be examined to determine whether to accept the sale.

If the customer has not exceeded the credit limit, the order is accepted and the customer is notified. Again, it is important to determine whether this sale will push the customer over the established credit limit. In reference to Exhibit 8-6, if this customer's account balance showed that it owed $15,000 from a prior sale, the company would not be willing to authorize another sale to this customer for an amount over $5000, as its total resulting account balance would then exceed the established credit limit.

It is also important to check the inventory to determine whether the items ordered are in stock. If the items are in stock, a pick list is prepared. A **pick list** documents the quantities and descriptions of items ordered. Items on the pick list should be pulled from the warehouse shelves and packaged for the customer. A **packing slip** (or packing list) prepared by warehouse personnel lists all items included in a shipment. For a company-to-company sale, the goods are typically shipped by a common carrier such as a trucking company or rail carrier. The terms of the agreement between the company and the carrier are documented in a **bill of lading.** Finally, inventory records are updated to reflect the decrease in inventory, and a shipping log is prepared. A **shipping log** is a

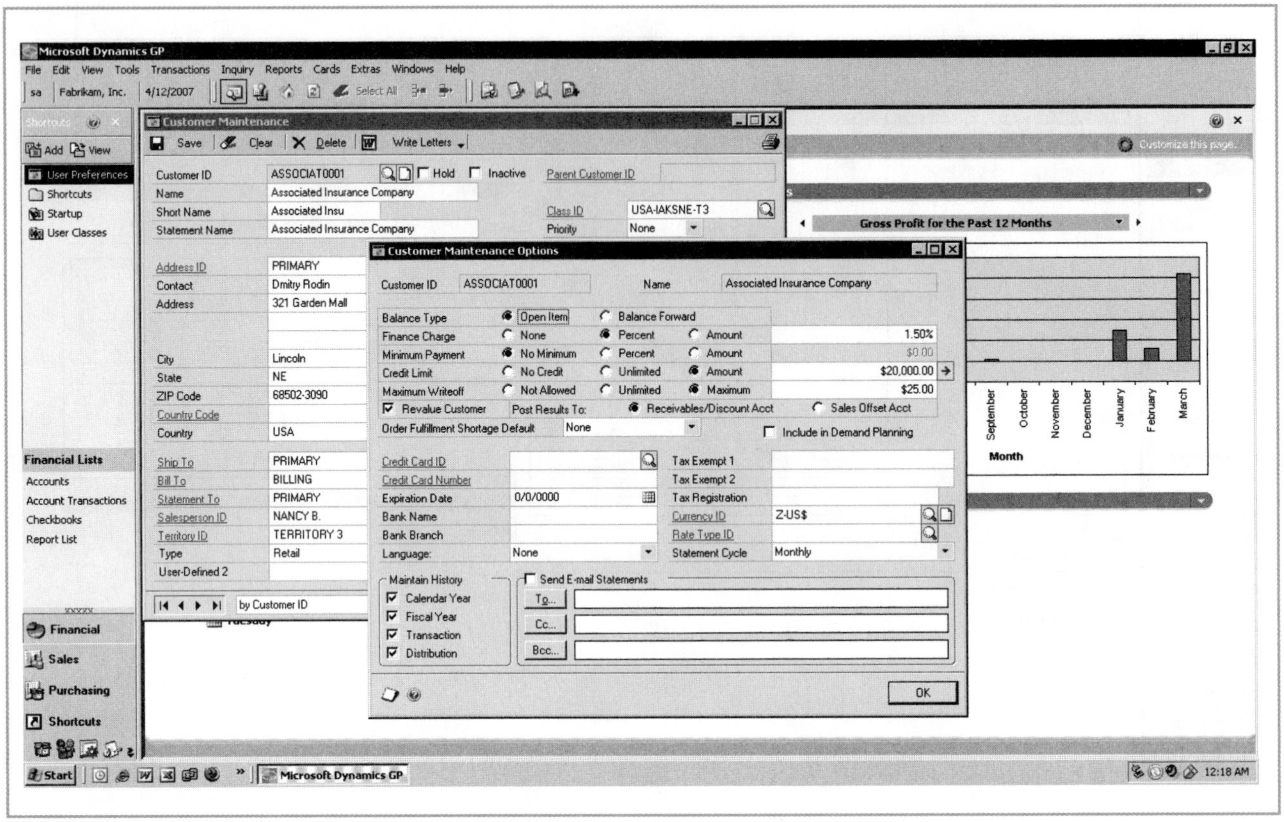

Exhibit 8-6
Establishing a Credit Limit in Microsoft Dynamics GP®

chronological listing of shipments that allows management to track the status of sales and to answer customer inquiries regarding order status.

Once shipment has occurred, customers should be billed for the sale. A sales invoice is prepared and sent to the customer. The **sales invoice** (typically referred to as a **bill**) provides details of the sale and requests payment. The timing of the billing process is important. Since customers will be unhappy if they are billed before they receive the items purchased, billing should not take place prior to shipment. However, it is important to avoid waiting very long after shipping to bill the customer, since that will delay the collection of cash. When customers are billed, accounts receivable records should be updated to reflect the increased amount owed by the customer. Also, the sale should be recorded in a sales journal so that the amount will be included in revenue during the current fiscal period. A **sales journal** is a special journal that records sales transactions. Periodically, the sales amounts in a sales journal are posted to the general ledger. Many companies also prepare customer account statements on a regular basis to accumulate and summarize all the transactions that have taken place between the customer and the company within the period.

RISKS AND CONTROLS IN SALES PROCESSES (STUDY OBJECTIVE 2, continued)

Management should strive to achieve a system of internal controls, using both manual and programmed procedures to minimize the chance of error or fraud. Unfortunately, the existence of good internal controls is not necessarily related to financial success in terms of a company's ability to make money; internal controls do not ensure high sales and profits. However, effective and efficient internal controls may relieve managers of valuable time that might otherwise be spent on accounting or operational problems, thus making it possible for them to devote more attention to revenue growth and cost reduction.

In terms of the five internal control activities described in Chapter 3, following are common procedures associated with the sales process:

AUTHORIZATION OF TRANSACTIONS

Specific individuals within the company should have authoritative responsibility for establishing sales prices, payment terms, credit limits, and guidelines for accepting new customers. Only designated employees should perform these authorization functions. These specific people should have a recognized method of communicating when sales transactions have been authorized. For example, approval is often documented by a signature or initials on a sales order or shipping document. Such a signature indicates that a designated employee has verified that the sale is to an accepted customer, the customer's credit has been approved (i.e., it has not exceeded its credit limit), and the price is correct. Once a sales order has been filled, established procedures should be in place for verifying that the shipment represents items ordered. Thus, proper sales authorization control includes obtaining approval prior to processing an order and again before the order is shipped.

SEGREGATION OF DUTIES

Within the sales process, the accounting duties related to order entry, credit approval, shipping, billing, information systems, and general accounting need to be separated in order to meet the objectives of internal controls. Recall that individuals with authoritative responsibilities should not also have access to the related records or custody of the related assets. In addition to the authorization responsibilities just described, certain information systems duties are included in the sales process, such as data entry, programming, IT operations, and security. The recording function includes the preparation of sales orders, shipping logs, and sales invoices, as well as that of general accounting reports such as the sales journal, accounts receivable subsidiary records and customer statements, the general ledger, and financial statements. Finally, the custody function includes product handling and preparing goods for shipment.

Ideally, good internal controls within the sales process require that accounting for inventory is completely separate from product handling. Also, any person who maintains detailed accounts receivable records should not also be responsible for maintaining the general ledger for or handling cash.

ADEQUATE RECORDS AND DOCUMENTS

Those responsible for recording sales should ensure that supporting documentation is retained and organized. As records are prepared, they should be compared with supporting information to make sure they are accurate and to prevent duplication. Sales orders, shipping logs, invoices, customer account statements, and other related documents should be saved and filed. Record files are often organized by customer name or by the numerical sequence of the documents. When companies account for the numerical sequence of their documents, it is possible to review the list to determine whether omissions have occurred. In addition, if accounting personnel compare the different documents that make up each transaction, they can find out whether the transaction has been carried out properly. For example, when the customer order, packing list, shipping records, and invoice for a single transaction are properly retained, personnel can verify that the records reflect the correct quantities, prices, customer, timing, etc. Maintaining good records also facilitates the performance of independent checks and reconciliations, which will be discussed later.

SECURITY OF ASSETS AND DOCUMENTS

A company's inventory of products should be protected by physical controls in the warehouse. Some examples of physical controls are surveillance cameras, security guards, and alarm systems. Likewise, data files, production programs, and accounting records should each be protected from unauthorized access. Passwords, backup copies, and physical controls (such as locked file cabinets) can protect a company's records.

INDEPENDENT CHECKS AND RECONCILIATION

In order to promote accountability for the sales process, companies should implement procedures whereby independent checks and record reconciliations are performed on a regular basis. These procedures are most effective when they are conducted by someone independent of the related authority, recording, and custody functions. Within the sales process, the most common types of independent checks include the verification of information in the sales journal and on sales invoices, the reconciliation of accounts receivable detail with invoices and with the general ledger, and the reconciliation of inventory records with actual (counted) quantities of products on hand.

COST–BENEFIT CONSIDERATIONS

Companies tend to implement internal controls only if they view the benefits of the control as being greater than the costs of carrying out the task. The extent to which a company implements controls depends upon many factors, including the type of products sold, business or industry factors, and the overall control consciousness of management. Following are some examples of characteristics indicating that a company may be more risky with respect to its sales processes:

- Frequent changes are made to sales prices or customers.
- The pricing structure is complex or based on estimates.
- A large volume of transactions is carried out.
- The company depends on a single or very few key customers.
- Shipments are made by consignees or are under other arrangements not controlled directly by the company.
- The product mix is difficult to differentiate.
- Shipping and/or recordkeeping are performed at multiple locations.

When any of these types of conditions exist, management should be especially mindful of the internal controls that are in place to make sure its system is well controlled.

Control	Minimizes the Related Risk of:
Authorization:	
Approval of sales order prior to shipment, including establishing sales prices, payment terms, and credit limits	Invalid customers, over-extended customers, unapproved pricing, or incorrect amounts
Approval of shipment for proper customer	Fictitious customers or wrong customers
Segregation of Duties:	
Separation of responsibility for authorization of new customers from custody of inventory	Fictitious customers
Separation of custody of inventory from accounts receivable recordkeeping	Invalid sales or omitted transactions
Separation of duties related to order entry, credit approval, shipping, billing, information systems, and general accounting	Invalid transactions, incorrect amounts or accounts, or omitted transactions
Records and Documents:	
Preparation of packing lists and shipping records on prenumbered forms	Omitted transactions
Preparation of shipping log and packing list only when products have actually been shipped	Invalid transactions, omitted transactions, or timing issues
Initiation of the billing function and updating of the sales journal, inventory records, and customer accounts receivable records only when products have actually been shipped	Invalid transactions, omitted transactions, or timing issues
Preparation of customer account statements	Wrong customers or incorrect amounts
Matching of key information on related documents (customers, dates, inventory quantities and descriptions, prices, and account codes) prior to shipment	Invalid transactions, incorrect amounts or accounts, timing issues, or duplicate transactions
Security:	
Physical controls in inventory and shipping areas	Invalid sales or omitted transactions
IT controls over computer records and physical controls in records storage areas	Invalid sales, omitted transactions, incorrect amounts or accounts, timing issues, accumulation issues, or duplicate transactions
Independent Checks and Reconciliations:	
Comparison of shipping records with sales journal and invoices	Omitted transactions, incorrect amounts, wrong customers, or timing issues
Verification of recorded descriptions, dates, quantities, authorized prices, and mathematical accuracy	Incorrect amounts or timing issues
Mathematical verification of sales journal and comparison to accounts receivable subsidiary ledger and general ledger posting	Problems with the accumulation of transactions and transfer to the general ledger and financial statements
Review of accounts receivable records and comparison with sales invoices	Invalid customers, wrong customers, omitted transactions, incorrect amounts, timing issues, or problems with the accumulation of transactions

Exhibit 8-7
Sales Process Controls and Risks

As mentioned earlier, the effectiveness of internal controls is measured by their ability to prevent or detect errors and fraud. In determining the likelihood of errors or fraud, accountants must consider the risks that exist within the company's business processes. Exhibit 8-7 presents a summary of the relationship between controls and risks for the revenue processes. This exhibit does not include all the possible controls and risks surrounding the revenues process, but presents controls used to correct some common problems that may be encountered.

SALES RETURN PROCESSES (STUDY OBJECTIVE 3)

It is nearly always the case that a small portion of sales made to customers will ultimately be returned to the seller. A company must have procedures in place for receiving returned goods, crediting the customer's account, and placing the items back in inventory. Exhibit 8-8 is a process map of a sample sales return process. Exhibit 8-9 shows a document flowchart for the sales return processes, and Exhibit 8-10 shows sales return processes in a data flow diagram (DFD).

When customers return goods, the goods are handled by the receiving department. Returned goods are typically accompanied by documentation from the customer, such as a bill of lading and packing slip. The goods should be inspected for possible damage, and a copy of the original sales invoice should confirm the historical sale of the goods. A **receiving log** is prepared that lists the chronological sequence of all returned items, and a receiving report records the quantity received. A **receiving report** is a source document completed by personnel in the receiving dock that documents the quantity and condition of items received. If the returned goods are accepted, they are placed back in the proper location in the warehouse and the inventory records are updated to reflect the increase in inventory.

A **credit memorandum** is prepared to document the return and to adjust the amount of the customer's credit status. A journal of credit memos should be maintained in order to provide a complete listing of all credits issued. Reference to the original sales invoice and approved price list will assure that the credit is issued for the correct amount. Sometimes, a refund check may be issued to the customer. In other cases, the customer's accounts receivable balance will be adjusted for the returned items.

RISKS AND CONTROLS IN THE SALES RETURN PROCESSES (STUDY OBJECTIVE 3, continued)

In terms of the five internal control activities, the following specific controls should be implemented over the sales returns process:

AUTHORIZATION OF TRANSACTIONS

Certain designated individuals within the company should be assigned the authority to develop sales return policies, authorize sales returns, and approve credit memos. Others within the organization should recognize these specific individuals and should not process returns if they have not been approved by a designated person.

SEGREGATION OF DUTIES

For sales returns, an effective system of internal controls segregates individuals with authoritative duties (such as those already discussed) from those responsible

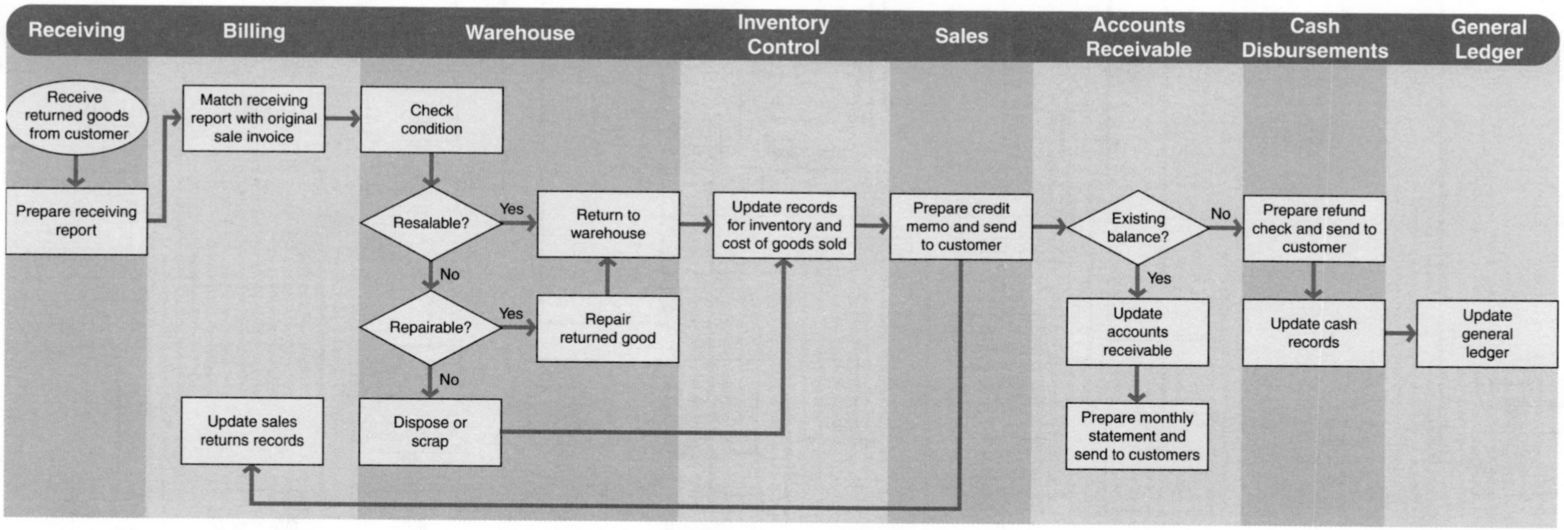

Exhibit 8-8
Sales Return Process Map

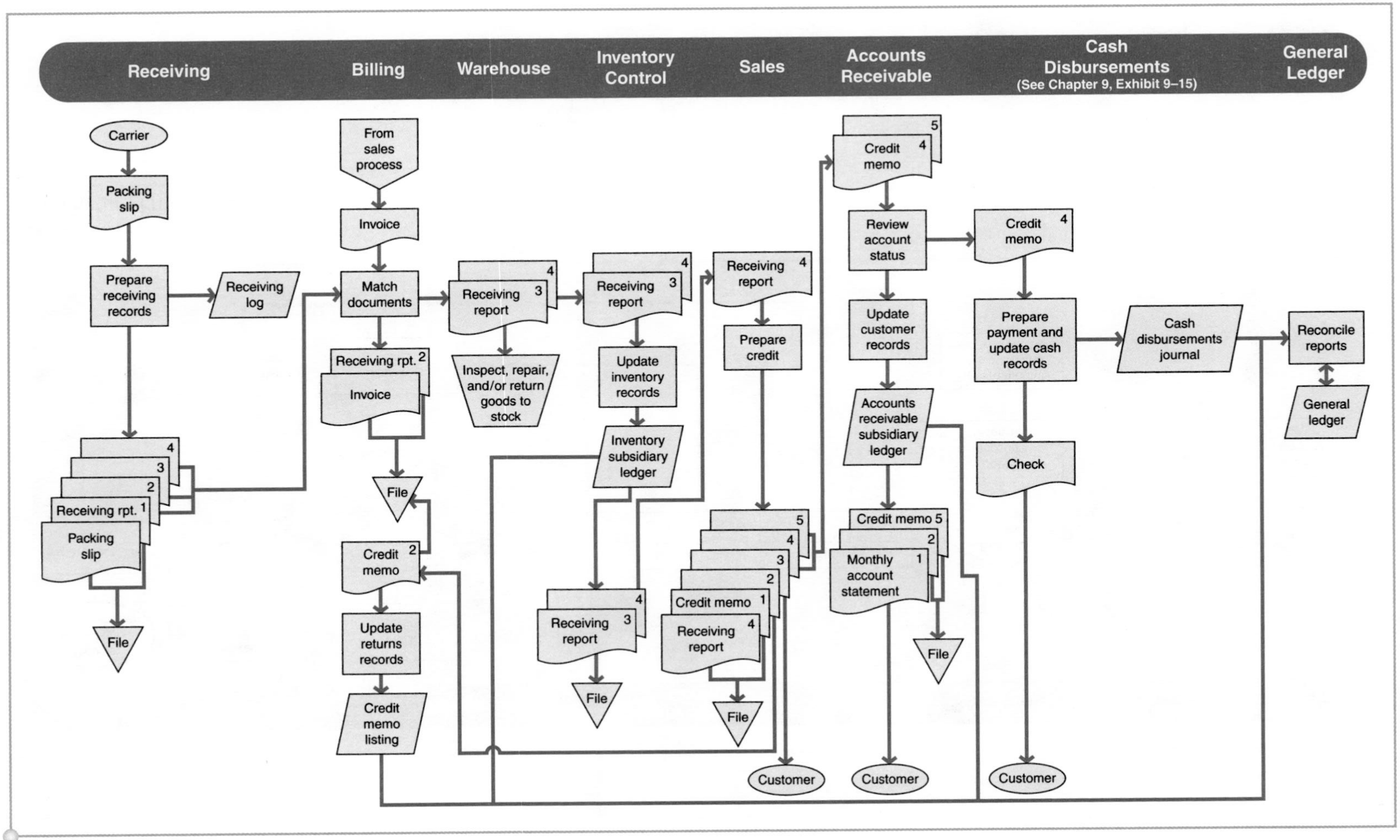

Exhibit 8-9
Document Flowchart of a Sales Return Process

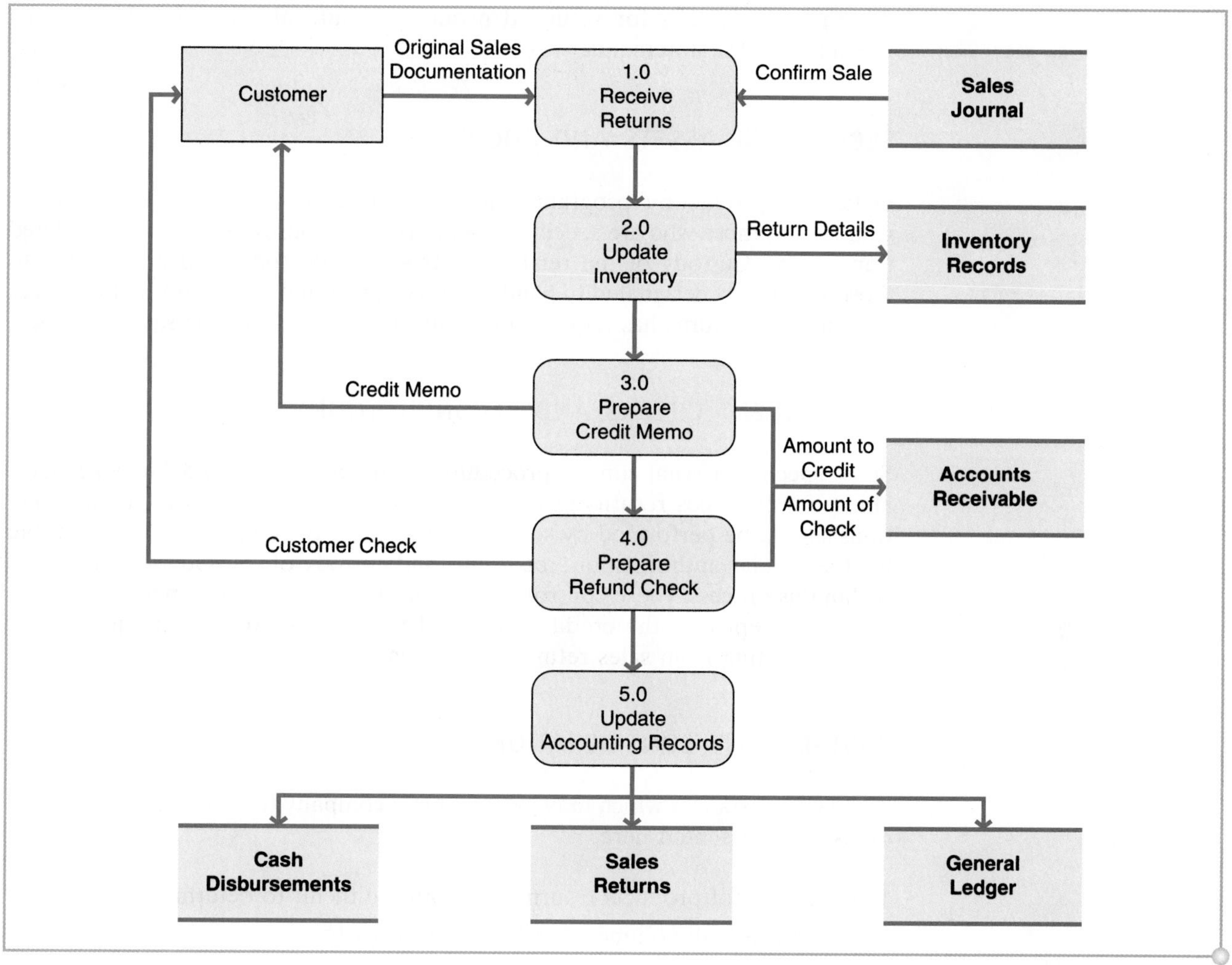

Exhibit 8-10
Sales Return Processes Data Flow Diagram

for recording (initiation of the credit memo and preparation of the credit memo journal) and custody (receiving the returned products and transferring them to the proper area in the warehouse). Ideally, anyone who performs a credit memo activity should not also be responsible for data entry, credit approval, shipping, billing, information systems, or general accounting.

ADEQUATE RECORDS AND DOCUMENTS

Internal controls over sales return records are similar to those for the sales process, whereby the reports documenting movement of the goods and the related notification to the customer should be issued sequentially, organized, and retained. In addition, it is important to match receiving reports for returns with the respective credit memos in order to ensure that the company issues credit for all returns and for the proper amounts. Returns are also matched with the original sales invoices in order to verify quantities, prices, and item descriptions. Credits for returned products should also be included in customers' account statements.

SECURITY OF ASSETS AND DOCUMENTS

Data files, production programs, and accounts receivable records should be restricted to those who are specifically authorized to approve or record the related transactions. Custody of the related assets should be controlled and limited to those specifically designated to handle the receipts or move the returned products. Security over returns has requirements similar to security for the sales process.

INDEPENDENT CHECKS AND RECONCILIATION

Some specific internal control procedures to be performed to achieve accountability for the sales returns process are presented in Exhibit 8-11. These functions should be performed by someone other than the employee(s) responsible for the regular authorization, recording, and custody of transactions and assets within this process. These controls are similar to the ones performed in the sales process, except that the credit memo and receiving report are the new documents resulting from sales return transactions.

COST–BENEFIT CONSIDERATIONS

Some circumstances which may exist within a company that indicate a high level of risk are presented here:

1. Quantities of products returned are often difficult to determine.
2. There is a high volume of credit memo activity.
3. Product prices change frequently, or the pricing structure is otherwise complex.
4. Returns are received at various locations, or the issuance of credit memos may occur at different locations.
5. The company depends on a single customer or very few key customers.
6. Returns are received by consignees or under other arrangements not directly controlled by the company.

A company should always consider the risks of its system to determine whether the costs of implementing a control procedure are worthwhile in terms of the benefits realized from that control. The higher the risks, the more controls are generally required, and the more costly its accounting system may become. Exhibit 8-11 summarizes some common control procedures for the sales returns process and the related risks that are addressed through their implementation.

In addition to sales returns, companies may sometimes issue sales allowances as an accommodation to customers who receive defective merchandise or late shipments. A **sales allowance** is a credit to the customer account made to compensate the customer for a defective product or a late shipment. Sales

Control	Minimizes the Related Risk of:
Authorization:	
Approval of sales return prior to issuing credit memo	Invalid customers, invalid returns, unapproved pricing, or incorrect amounts
Segregation of Duties:	
Separation of responsibility for authorization of customers returns from custody of inventory	Fictitious customers
Separation of custody of inventory from accounts receivable record keeping	Invalid returns or omitted transactions
Separation of duties related to credit memo preparation, credit approval, receiving, information systems, and general accounting	Invalid transactions, incorrect amounts or accounts, or omitted transactions
Records and Documents:	
Preparation of receiving reports and credit memos on prenumbered forms	Omitted transactions
Preparation of receiving report and receiving log only when products have actually been received	Invalid transactions, omitted transactions, or timing issues
Preparation of credit memos and credit memo journal only when products have actually been received	Invalid transactions, omitted transactions, or timing issues
Preparation of customer account statements	Wrong customers or incorrect amounts
Matching of key information on related documents (customers, dates, inventory quantities and descriptions, prices, and account codes) prior to issuing credit	Invalid transactions, incorrect amounts or accounts, timing issues, or duplicate transactions
Security:	
Physical controls in inventory and receiving areas	Invalid returns or omitted transactions
IT controls over computer records and physical controls in records storage areas	Invalid returns, omitted transactions, incorrect amounts or accounts, timing issues, accumulation issues, or duplicate transactions
Independent Checks and Reconciliations:	
Comparison of receiving log with credit memo listing and credit memos	Omitted transactions, incorrect amounts, wrong customers, or timing issues
Verification of recorded descriptions, quantities, dates, prices, and mathematical accuracy	Incorrect amounts or timing issues
Mathematical verification of credit memo listing and comparison to accounts receivable subsidiary ledger and general ledger posting	Problems with the accumulation of transactions and transfer to the general ledger and financial statements

Exhibit 8-11
Sales Return Controls and Risks

allowances and returns are similar; however, the receipt of goods typically does not occur in a sales allowance transaction. Therefore, documentation in a receiving log and the issuance of a receiving report are not necessary. Due to this reduced level of supporting records, many companies require thorough documentation for sales allowances, especially with respect to authorizing the transactions, segregating related duties, and matching original sale documents to ensure proper recording.

CASH COLLECTION PROCESSES (STUDY OBJECTIVE 4)

Company-to-company sales are typically made on account, and a time span is given for the customer to pay. An example of the credit terms of sale would be net 30. This means the customer has 30 days after the invoice date to pay. Therefore, the timing of a cash collection is such that there will be some number of days between invoice date and collection of the cash. The actual number of days depends on the credit terms of the sale and the diligence of the customer in paying on time. When the customer sends a check, the company must have processes in place to properly handle the receipt. The appropriate employees should match the check with the related sales invoice, deposit the funds in a timely manner, and update customer and cash records. Exhibit 8-12 is a process map of a cash collection process. Exhibit 8-13 shows a document flowchart of cash collection processes, and Exhibit 8-14 (on page 305) shows the cash collection processes in a data flow diagram (DFD).

Collections from customers typically include a **remittance advice,** which is the documentation accompanying payment that identifies the customer account number and invoice to which the payment applies. An example of a remittance advice in your personal life is on your credit card statement. Part of your statement is meant to be detached and mailed with your payment. This remittance that you return enables the company to properly apply your payment to your account. In the case of company-to-company sales, a remittance advice identifies the invoice and customer account number to which the payment should be applied. Exhibit 8-15 (on page 306) shows the application of a payment to the appropriate invoice. In Exhibit 8-15, a check mark is placed in the IVC08 invoice box to apply the payment to that invoice.

For each check received, the payment must be matched with the appropriate invoice or invoices. A list of all cash collections is prepared, and the checks received are recorded in the cash receipts journal. A **cash receipts journal** is a special journal that records all cash collections. The listing of collections is to be forwarded, along with the payments received, to a cashier who prepares the bank deposit. The payments are deposited in the company account, and customer records and cash records must be updated.

At the end of the month, an updated statement of account will be prepared and sent to the customer. This statement reflects the invoices that have been paid and the decrease in the customer's balance owed as a result of these collections. Also, the bank will send a monthly statement to the company so that the cash records of the company can be reconciled to the bank records.

RISKS AND CONTROLS IN THE CASH COLLECTION PROCESSES (STUDY OBJECTIVE 4, continued)

We now turn our attention to specific internal controls and related risks associated with cash collections from sales revenues. Some internal controls present within a cash receipts process are as follows:

AUTHORIZATION OF TRANSACTIONS

Appropriate individuals should be assigned responsibility for opening and closing all bank accounts and approving bank deposits or electronic

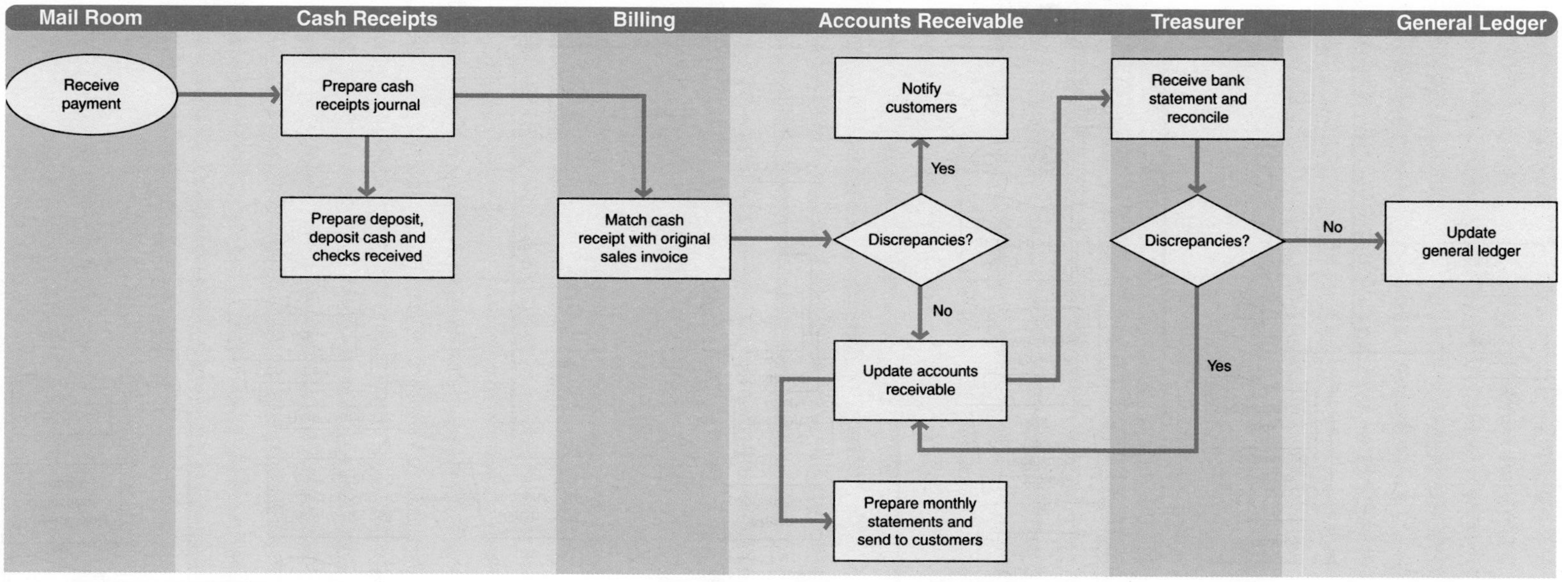

Exhibit 8-12
Cash Receipts Process Map

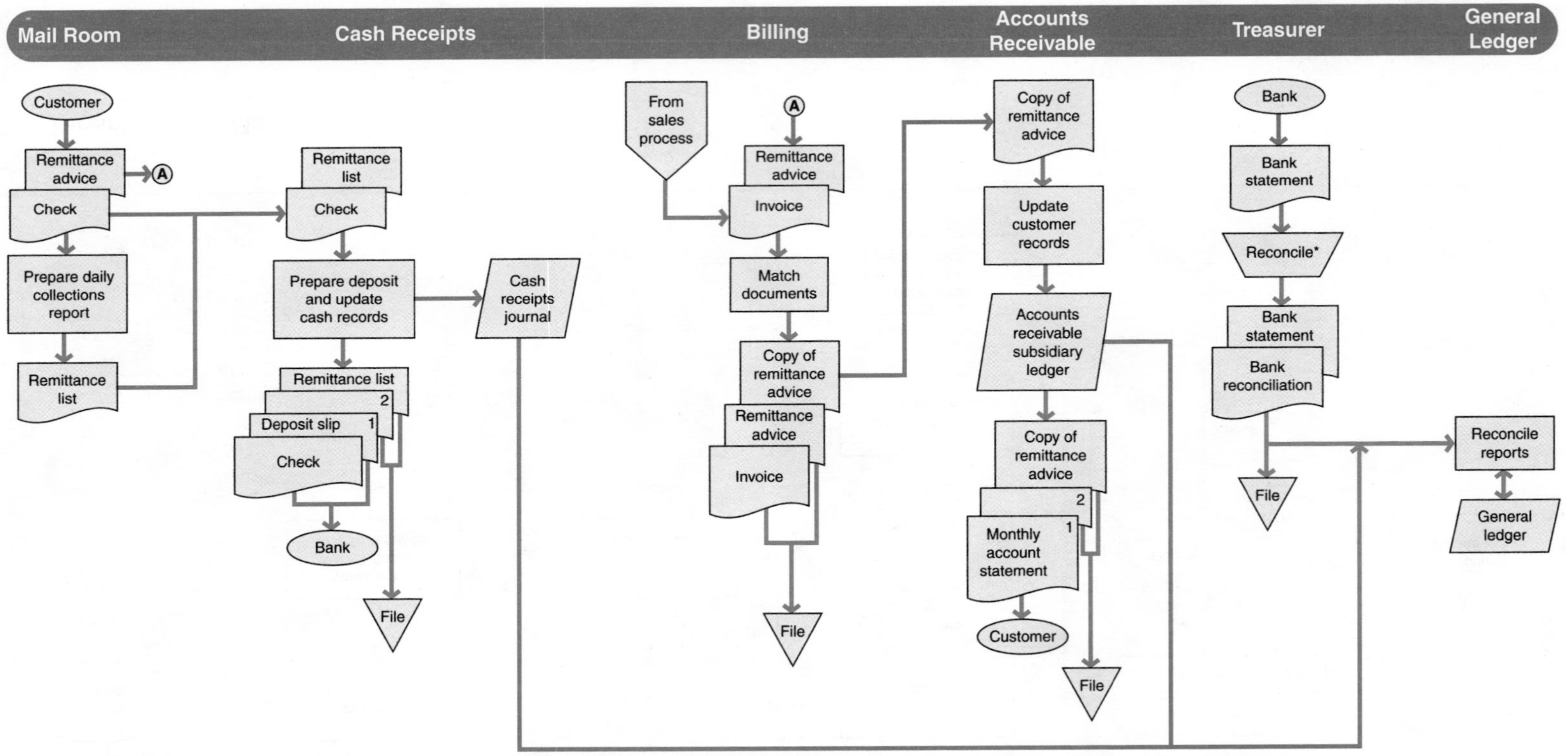

* Involves comparisons of remittance listings, deposit slips, and cash receipts journal with information reported on bank statement.

Exhibit 8-13
Document Flowchart of a Cash Receipts Process

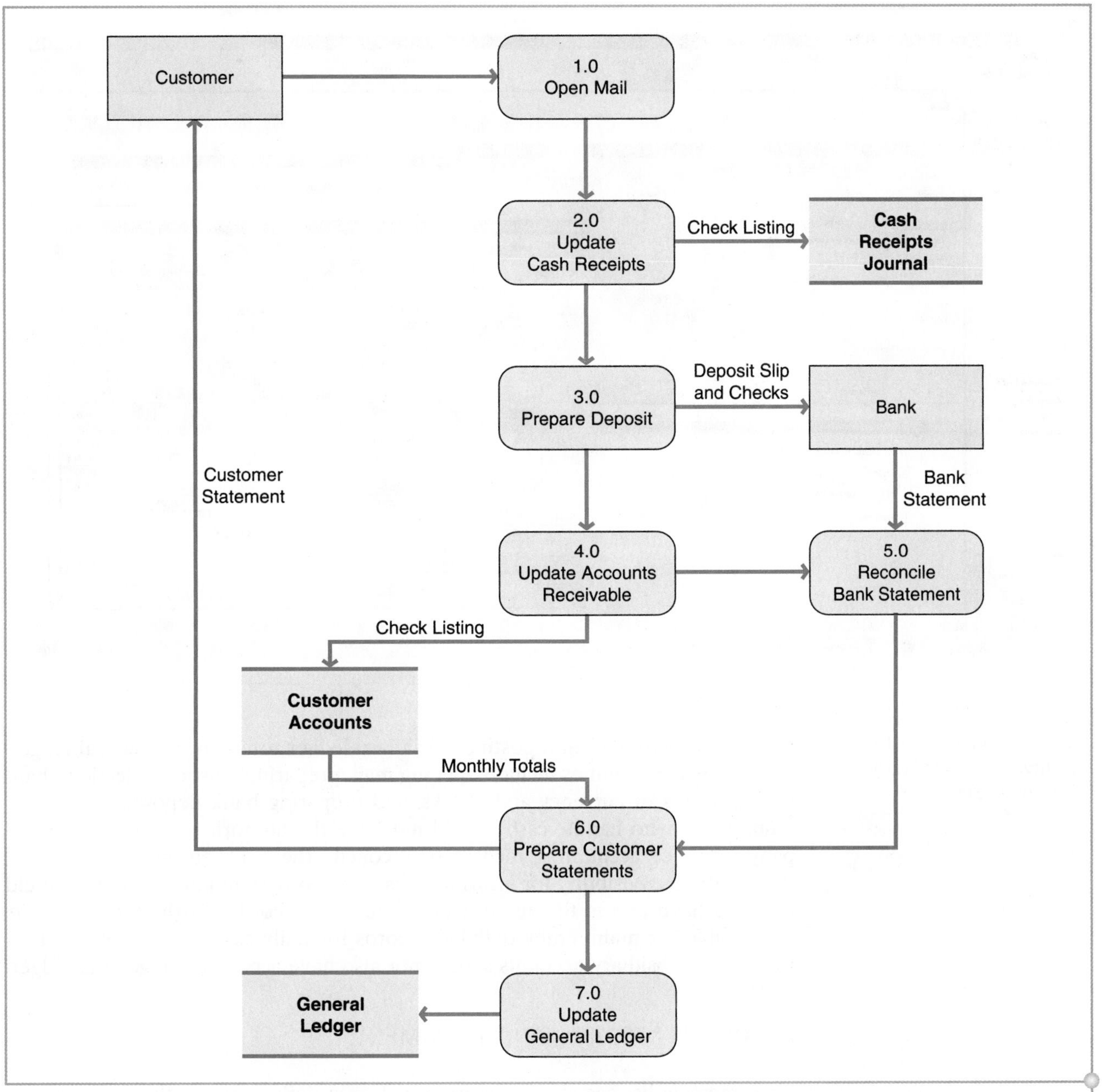

Exhibit 8-14
Cash Receipts Processes
Data Flow Diagram

transfers of funds. This ensures that records are updated only for authorized transactions.

SEGREGATION OF DUTIES

As you know, authorization duties (described previously) need to be kept separate from recording and custody duties. Recording responsibilities include maintaining a cash receipts journal, updating accounts receivable records for

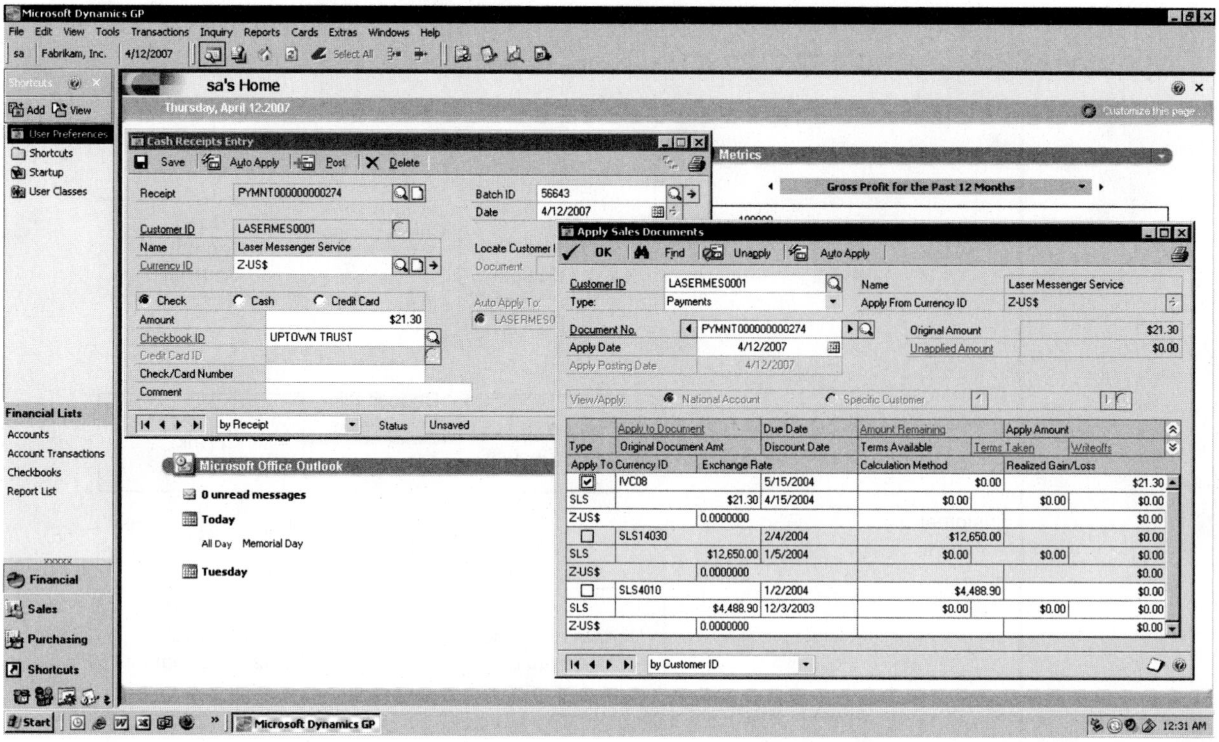

Exhibit 8-15
Applying a Payment to an Invoice in Microsoft Dynamics GP®

individual customers, and posting subsidiary ledger totals to the general ledger. Custody responsibilities include opening mail, preparing a list of collections, handling receipts of currency and checks, and preparing bank deposits. At a minimum, those who handle cash should not have the authority to access the company's cash or accounting records or reconcile the bank account. In addition, those with responsibility for information systems programming or control should not also have access to the cash or accounting records. Furthermore, anyone responsible for maintaining detailed records for daily cash receipts or accounts receivable subsidiary accounts should not also have access to the general ledger.

ADEQUATE RECORDS AND DOCUMENTS

Cash receipts listings should be prepared on a daily basis, so the daily activity of collections should be reconciled to supporting documentation from the bank deposit. Bank deposit receipts should be retained and filed chronologically, and regular, timely bank reconciliations should be prepared and retained. Detailed customer accounts should also be maintained and reconciled with customer statements regularly.

SECURITY OF ASSETS AND DOCUMENTS

Access to cash collections needs to be limited to those who are expressly authorized to handle cash. Controls over cash collections are likely the most important control procedure, because cash is the asset most susceptible to theft or misappropriation. Because of the universal appeal of cash and the difficulty of proving ownership, a company must take extra precautions to protect this asset. Cash collections should be deposited in the bank in a timely manner to prevent the risk of theft. Also, related computerized data files and programs must be protected from unauthorized use.

INDEPENDENT CHECKS AND RECONCILIATION

A physical count of cash needs to be conducted from time to time in order to compare actual cash on hand with the amounts in the accounting records. To maximize effectiveness, cash counts should occur on a surprise basis and be conducted by someone not otherwise responsible for any cash receipts functions. Daily bank deposits should also be compared with the detail on the related remittance advice and in the cash receipts journal.

In addition, it is important that companies regularly reconcile their cash accounts with the respective bank statements. Like cash counting procedures, a bank reconciliation should be performed by someone who has no other responsibility for handling cash or accounting for cash transactions. The bank statements should be received directly by the person who prepares the reconciliation, to make sure it is not altered by other company personnel. Among the bank reconciliation tasks are procedures to ensure that deposits are examined for proper dates and that all reconciling items are reviewed and explained.

COST–BENEFIT CONSIDERATIONS

In addition to the need for tight controls over cash due to its susceptibility to theft, the following circumstances may indicate risks related to cash collections:

1. High volume of cash collections
2. Decentralized cash collections
3. Lack of consistency in the volume or source of collections
4. Presence of cash collections denominated in foreign currencies

Companies often find that maximum internal controls are beneficial with respect to cash collections, due to the great temptation that exists for those in a position to steal cash and the high (and unrecoverable) cost of errors. Even a small company will tend to find ways to segregate duties and implement a variety of internal controls in order to protect its valuable cash. Exhibit 8-16 presents typical procedures used to control cash receipts and the risks that they help to reduce.

In wrapping up the discussion of revenue-related accounting processes, it is important to mention an additional issue that may impact the accounting records related to cash collections for sales transactions. Namely, most companies have occasional problems with customers who fail to pay, leading to the write-off of accounts receivable and the recording of an allowance for uncollectible accounts. Companies should ensure that proper controls are in place to reduce risks related to transactions involving uncollectible accounts. Specifically, responsibilities should be segregated such that no one has the opportunity to

Control	Minimizes the Related Risk of:
Authorization:	
Designated person opens/closes bank accounts	Invalid bank account or omitted transactions
Approval of cash receipt prior to bank deposit	Invalid bank account or incorrect amounts
Segregation of Duties:	
Separation of custody of cash from the responsibility for reconciling the bank accounts	Invalid cash receipts, incorrect amounts, omitted transactions
Separation of custody of cash from accounts receivable record keeping	Invalid cash receipts or omitted transactions
Separation of duties related to cash receipts journal preparation, credit approval, inventory handling, information systems, and general accounting	Invalid transactions, incorrect amounts or accounts, or omitted transactions
Records and Documents:	
Preparation of deposit slips on prenumbered forms	Omitted transactions
Preparation of cash receipts journal and accounts receivable records only when cash has actually been received	Invalid transactions, omitted transactions, or timing issues
Preparation of customer account statements	Wrong customers or incorrect amounts
Matching of key information on related documents (customers, dates, prices, and account codes) prior to reducing customer accounts	Invalid transactions, wrong customer, incorrect amounts or accounts, timing issues, or duplicate transactions
Security:	
Physical controls in areas where cash is received	Lost or stolen cash receipts, invalid receipts, or omitted transactions
IT controls over computer records and physical controls in records storage areas	Invalid receipts, omitted transactions, incorrect amounts or accounts, timing issues, accumulation issues, or duplicate transactions
Cash receipts deposited in bank on a daily basis	Lost or stolen cash receipts
Independent Checks and Reconciliations:	
Cash counts and comparison of daily deposit with cash receipts journal	Invalid receipts, lost or stolen cash, omitted transactions, incorrect amounts or accounts, or timing issues
Preparation of bank reconciliation	Invalid receipts, omitted transactions, incorrect amounts or accounts, timing issues, or lost or stolen cash
Matching of remittance advice with cash receipts journal	Invalid receipts, omitted transactions, incorrect amounts, timing issues, or lost or stolen cash
Mathematical verification of cash receipts journal and comparison with accounts receivable subsidiary ledger and general ledger posting	Problems with the accumulation of transactions and transfer to the general ledger and financial statements

Exhibit 8-16
Cash Receipts Controls and Risks

write off customer accounts as a cover-up for stolen cash or inventory. In addition, since determining the amount of an allowance for uncollectible accounts is very subjective, it is important that thorough guidelines be established for this process. In order to properly monitor customer payments and determine the amount of an allowance for uncollectible accounts, an accounts receivable aging report should be generated to analyze all customer balances and the respective lengths of time that have elapsed since payments were due.

IT ENABLED SYSTEMS OF REVENUE AND CASH COLLECTION PROCESSES (STUDY OBJECTIVE 5)

The previous section described the processes related to revenue transactions. In addition to the activities that take place within those processes, there must also be accounting systems to record, summarize, and report the results of the related transactions. In the majority of organizations, the accounting information system consists of hardware and software within IT systems. However, there is such great variety in accounting software systems in terms of their size, complexity, and extent of automation that it is impossible to describe all of the various kinds of systems. In general, as complexity and automation increase, there are fewer manual processes and more computerized processes. This is usually true regarding size also: Larger IT systems generally have fewer manual processes and more computerized processes. More computerized processes means there would be a greater need for the type of IT controls described in Chapter 4, and it generally means that there are fewer paper documents within the process. As a simple illustration, consider two kinds of restaurants you might visit. A small, family-owned restaurant might not use computers at all, and the server may simply write your order on a pad. On the other hand, a large restaurant chain might have a system completely based on computers, where servers enter orders on the touch screen of a handheld device that transmits the order to the kitchen. The family-owned restaurant would have no need for computer controls, while the restaurant chain would need many computer-based controls.

The following section provides a description of a typical revenue processing system and some specialized IT systems:

Exhibit 8-17 is a system flowchart of a generic version of revenue system with some paper documents. The system flowchart documents a system for company-to-company sales. When the customer's order is received, an employee enters it into the IT system by keying the order into an input screen. With online data files, the input data can be edited, the customer's credit status can be reviewed, and inventory levels can be checked. If the order does not exceed the customer's credit limit and the inventory items are available, the order can be processed.

Order processing updates the sales records and the customer's account records. The appropriate documents needed to fill and ship the order are printed. These documents usually include a pick list, a packing slip, an invoice, and a bill of lading. The pick list is used by warehouse personnel to select items from the warehouse shelves. The packing slip is used by shipping personnel to ensure the correct items are packed. The bill of lading is the agreement between the common carrier and the company. A common carrier is a trucking or rail company. The invoice is sent to the customer.

Usually at the end of the month, customers are billed and regular monthly reports are printed. Customers are billed according to the customer statement. Regular monthly reports would include sales reports, inventory status reports, and accounts receivable reports.

The general and application controls described in Chapter 4 should be used to ensure the security, availability, processing integrity, and confidentiality of this IT system. General controls would include authentication of users, computer logs, physical access controls, and business continuity planning. General controls to prevent network break-ins would be necessary if the system uses any network connections to other systems. The application controls help ensure the

Exhibit 8-17
Revenue Processes System Flowchart

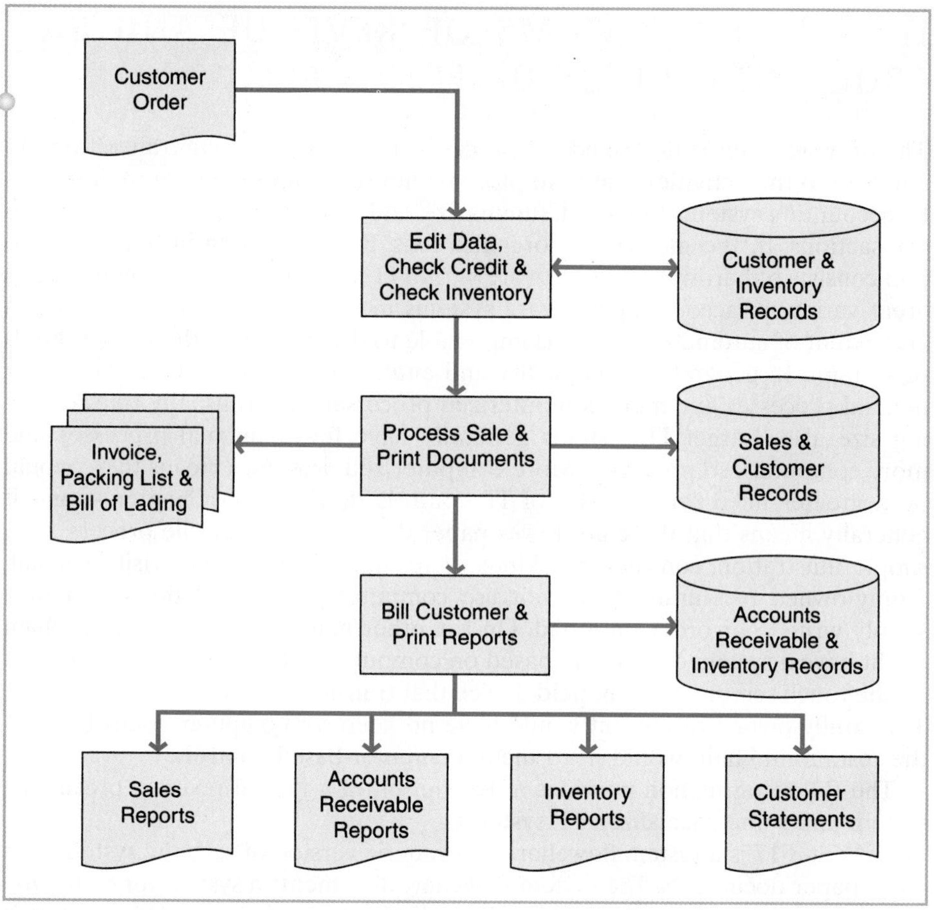

accuracy and completeness of processing. Input controls used in this system would be likely to include data preparation and error handling procedures, programmed input validation checks, and control totals. Well-defined procedures for data preparation and error handling can reduce the chance for mistakes in data entry into the system. The programmed input checks such as field checks, validity checks, limit checks, and reasonableness checks will help prevent or detect keying errors. If customer orders are entered in batches, control totals can help ensure the accuracy and completeness of input and processing. Output controls help to protect data through proper distribution, storage, and disposal of reports.

The system depicted in Exhibit 8-17 uses some manual processes, such as keying of data, and some paper forms. More complex IT systems can reduce or eliminate these manual processes and paper forms. For example, orders placed over the Internet would eliminate manual keying by someone within the company. The customer keys in the order while placing an order on the website. The sections that follow describe some types of systems with fewer manual processes and paper forms.

In many companies today, sophisticated, highly integrated IT systems capture, record, and process revenue and cash collection events. These IT systems are more specialized than the generic system described earlier. Such systems include e-commerce systems, electronic data interchange (EDI) systems, and point of sale (POS) systems. **E-commerce systems** incorporate electronic processing of sales-related activities, and generally, e-commerce sales processes are transacted over the Internet. **Electronic data interchange (EDI)** systems communicate sales documents electronically with a standard business format. **Point of sale (POS)** systems process sales at a cash register in retail stores.

When implementing these types of IT systems, many companies find that they must change the methods used to perform sales and collections. As companies redesign these processes to align with their software systems, they conduct what is known as business process reengineering. **Business process reengineering (BPR)** is the purposeful and organized changing of business processes to make the processes more efficient. BPR not only aligns business processes with the IT systems used to record processes, it also improves efficiency and effectiveness of these processes. Thus, the use of sophisticated IT systems usually leads to two kinds of efficiency improvements. First, the underlying processes are reengineered so as to be conducted more efficiently. Second, the IT systems improve the efficiency of the underlying processes. As an example, Northern Telecom (Nortel Networks Corp.) found that EDI reduced the cost of purchasing from approximately $80 per transaction when paper based to $35 per transaction with EDI.[2]

Explanations of three types of IT systems are included in the sections that follow, including e-commerce, EDI, and POS systems. Each of these systems greatly reduces or eliminates the paper-based documentation used in older manual or automated systems. That is, these systems may eliminate the need for paper-based sales orders or paper-based checks. In these IT systems, information is transmitted electronically and payments are collected electronically, not in paper documents. The elimination of paper completely changes the audit trail and the internal controls. Therefore, the sections that follow will describe the risks and controls for these IT systems.

E-BUSINESS SYSTEMS AND THE RELATED RISKS AND CONTROLS (STUDY OBJECTIVE 6)

Today, there are two popular types of Internet sales, commonly referred to as business to consumer (**B2C**), and business to business (**B2B**). B2C sales are those that most people are familiar with, whereby a retail or service firm sells directly to consumers using a website. This is also called e-commerce. B2B sales, on the other hand, involve companies using websites to sell products and services to each other. These types of sales transactions are known as e-business. A more detailed description of e-commerce and e-business is presented in Chapter 14.

There are numerous B2C examples, including Amazon.com, CDUniverse.com, Lands' End, J. Crew, and Delta Air Lines. In a B2C sale, the company's website and underlying network and software systems capture sales data, authorize credit card payments, and acknowledge the order via e-mail. The details such as customer, shipping address, items ordered, and credit card number are captured on the website and uploaded into the company's accounting and logistic software

[2]F. Borthick and H.P. Roth, "EDI for Reengineering Business Processes," *Management Accounting*, October 1993, pp. 32–37.

systems. The website must interface with the company's data on inventory, customer accounts, prices, and shipping charges.

B2B is not as well known by those in the general public. Like B2C, it involves the use of websites and the Internet to conduct business. The difference is that the transactions are between companies, rather than between a company and consumer. This difference is significant in several ways. First, a B2B sale is between known and trusted parties. The buyer and seller have a preestablished business relationship and may have even negotiated prices and delivery expectations. In a B2C sale, the seller may not have any established relationship with the customer.

THE REAL WORLD

Many large corporations sell to other companies. Staples® is an example of a company selling to other companies via websites. Regarding sales of office supplies to other large corporations, management at Staples realizes that it must support orders in the manner the customer prefers. In a recent article, Jay Baitler, the senior vice president of the Staples Contract Division, said, "Offering Internet-based transactions is now critical."[3] Internet-based sales accounted for 70% of the revenue in the contract division.

In both B2B and B2C sales, the advantages of e-commerce include the following:

1. Reduced cost through lower marketing, employee, and paperwork costs
2. Shorter sales cycles due to reduced time to place an order, deliver the order, and collect payment
3. Increased accuracy and reliability of sales data
4. Increased potential market for products and services

However, the Internet-connected nature of e-commerce sales includes several risks that a company must manage. As described in Chapter 4, the network and Internet connections required to conduct e-commerce are risk exposure areas, or "entry points." The risks involve security, availability, processing integrity, and confidentiality, among others. The risks related to Internet sales are as follows:

Security and Confidentiality

1. Unauthorized access
2. Hackers or other network break-ins
3. Repudiation of sales transactions

Processing Integrity

4. Invalid data entered by customers
5. Incomplete audit trail
6. Errors when integrating data into back end systems such as accounting, payment processing, and order fulfillment software systems

[3] Jay Baitler, "The Power of Effective Procurement and Strategic Suppliers," *Strategic Finance*, April 2003, p. 40.

Availability

7. Hardware and software system failures that block customers from access to the website
8. Virus and worm attacks
9. Denial-of-service attacks by hackers

In addition, there are many online privacy risks to customers. Customer data must be safeguarded by internal controls. The specifics of online privacy risks and controls appear in a later chapter on e-commerce.

Controls should be in place to reduce the security, availability, processing integrity, and confidentiality risks. The controls that can lessen these risks are described in the next several sections.

SECURITY AND CONFIDENTIALITY RISKS

To protect the security of the IT system and the confidentiality of the data, it is important to ensure that those accessing the website and conducting sales transactions are valid and authorized users. User authentication is an important control for Internet sales when it is possible to use it. In the case of retail sales to end-user consumers, user authentication may not be appropriate. B2C companies that engage in retail sales do not always ask users to create user IDs and passwords before buying on the website. Customers can perceive this requirement as burdensome or an invasion of privacy. The need to sell to a wide range of unknown customers may prevent online retailers from using authentication controls. The cost of user authentication in terms of lost sales would outweigh any benefit of the controls. In other cases, such as B2B Internet sales, authentication through user IDs and passwords is a more important control.

To lessen the chance of fraudulent sales, sales without payment, and repudiation of sales, a company must institute controls to assure the authenticity of the customer and the sale. A real danger in Internet sales is that a customer will use false or fictitious payment information in placing an order. A second danger is that a customer will repudiate a sale. "Repudiate" means that the customer claims to not have conducted the transaction. In both situations, it is important that a company have controls in place to ensure that the transaction is with a valid customer with valid payment authorization and that an audit trail is maintained to avoid repudiation. Customer authentication through user ID and password should also be used. Credit card authorization procedures must be correctly processed. Digital signatures or digital certificates can be used much like a paper signature is used to authenticate and validate the customer. Finally, transactions should be logged and data trails maintained to avoid repudiation.

PROCESSING INTEGRITY RISKS

As customers enter data on a website to place an order, they may make data entry errors. Controls should be used to minimize these errors. The programming within the website should include steps to check the completeness, accuracy, and validity of the data. You have probably noticed the effect of these controls when ordering items on a website. As two examples, consider what happens if you enter an incorrect state abbreviation or do not complete all necessary fields. Usually, the website provides feedback to you that the state abbreviation is not valid or all necessary fields have not been completed. These are programmed data input checks that should be built into any web-based sale systems. The programmed checks should include many of those described in Chapter 4, such as field checks, validity checks, limit checks, range checks, reasonableness checks, and sign checks.

In a web-based sale system, there probably is no trail of paper documents to serve as an audit trail. Therefore, the company must capture all relevant data and maintain those data in a form that constitutes an audit trail. Logging transactions can help establish an audit trail in an electronic environment.

Dynamically programmed websites that capture sales data can be considered the front end of the sales process. A company must develop a method to integrate the data captured into the back end processes and applications. An example of a back end process is one that actually pulls items from warehouses and ships to customers. The data from the website must either be manually entered, or integrated into these back end processes. Controls must exist to ensure the accuracy of data as it is integrated across back end processes. Such controls include reconciliations and verifications. Data can be totaled as they come from the website and retotaled after they are integrated into the back end system. These two totals can be reconciled to make sure they agree.

AVAILABILITY RISKS

Any interruptions to the system can cause critical problems for companies that sell via e-commerce. Any time the website is unavailable to customers probably means lost sales. Therefore, the company should put controls in place to minimize service disruptions. These controls can include redundant systems, disaster recovery plans; testing of software changes; and capacity planning and testing. Redundancy is needed for servers, data, and networks.

A redundant server system requires maintaining one or more computers as extra, back-up web servers that can operate if the main server goes down. Data redundancy is usually accomplished by having data stored in RAID (redundant array of inexpensive disks). A RAID storage maintains one or more disk drives that mirror each other. In this manner, one or more exact duplicates of the data are maintained. A backup network structure should be in place if communication is lost through the regular network.

Disaster recovery plans must be in place to ensure uninterrupted customer access even through natural disasters such as fire, flood, or earthquake. The company must have plans to continue service when disasters occur.

As changes are made to the website or the underlying software to process sales, it is important that the changes be tested before they are implemented. If such changes are not tested, they may fail and disrupt operations.

Finally, managers must properly plan for sufficient capacity in the e-commerce system and servers to ensure that the system is not overwhelmed by the number of users accessing it. A slow or stalled website can result in lost sales. Managers should consistently monitor, test, and adjust the capacity of the system to meet its needs.

ELECTRONIC DATA INTERCHANGE (EDI) SYSTEMS AND THE RISKS AND CONTROLS (STUDY OBJECTIVE 7)

Electronic data interchange is the inter-company, computer-to-computer transfer of business documents in a standard business format. Three parts of this definition highlight the important characteristics of EDI. Inter-company refers to two or more companies conducting business electronically. The computer-to-computer aspect of the definition indicates that each company's computers are connected via a network. A standard business format is necessary so that companies can interact and trade with a variety of vendors and sellers using EDI. The standard business format allows all vendors and sellers to "speak the same language." The American National Standards Institute (ANSI) has developed standard formats for the usual documents needed in a sales process, including purchase orders, sales invoices, price quotations, and shipping schedules. The standard in the United States is ANSI X.12.

ANSI X.12 standards divide EDI data transmissions into three parts: header and trailer data, labeling interchanges, and data segments. **Header data** contain information about the file or transmission being sent. The header identifies the beginning and end of a particular transaction data set. **Trailer data** also contain data about the file or transmission and identify the end of a particular transaction data set. **Labeling interchanges** identify the type of transactions in the set, such as a set of sales invoices. **Data segments** include the actual data within the invoices, such as quantities and prices.

Although two companies may have a network connection that allows them to be directly linked to each other, it is expensive to develop and maintain such a system. The majority of companies using EDI communicate with trading partners by a third-party network like the one illustrated in Exhibit 8-18.

The two companies in Exhibit 8-18 are not directly connected to each other, but they communicate EDI data through a third-party network via mailboxes in the third party's computer system. These third-party networks are termed **value added networks (VANs)** because they provide other valuable services such as translation and encryption of the EDI data and authentication of a valid and authorized trading partner.

There are many advantages to an EDI system within the revenue and cash collection processes:

1. Reduction or elimination of data keying
2. Elimination of keying errors
3. Elimination of costs related to keying and keying errors

Exhibit 8-18
EDI Using a Third-Party Network

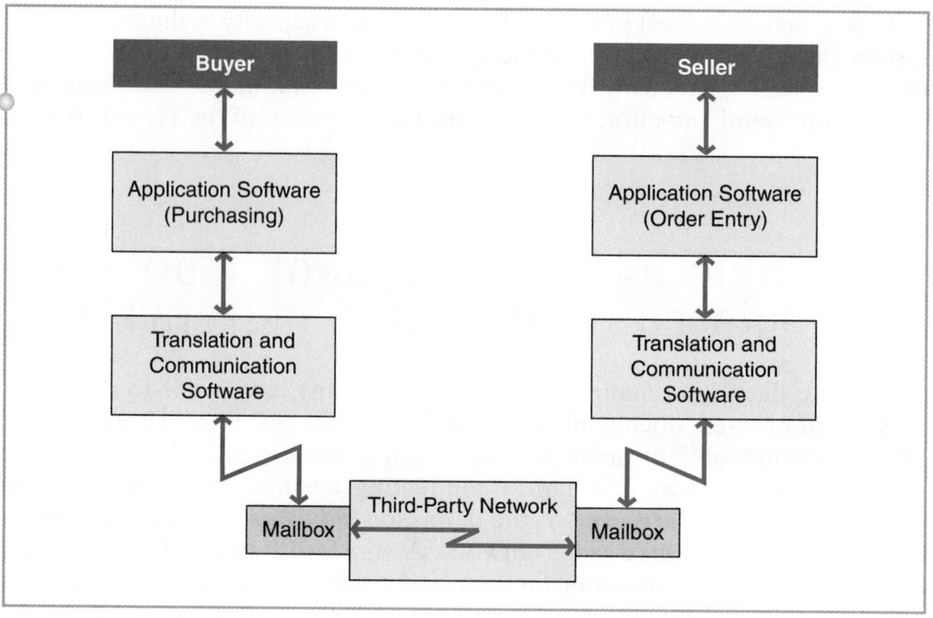

4. Elimination of the time needed to key in orders
5. Elimination of mail delays
6. Elimination of postage costs
7. Reduction in inventory levels as a result of shorter order cycle
8. Competitive advantage through better customer service
9. Preservation of business with existing customers who have adopted EDI

The first four advantages listed relate to time and costs savings from reducing or eliminating data keying. Since EDI transmits data between computers without paper documents, no data entry clerks are needed to key details of a sale from paper documents into the computer system. This saves time and dollars, as well as the errors that are inherent in keying data. Advantages numbered five and six arise because data are sent electronically rather than by mail. Mail delays and the costs of mailing are completely avoided. Advantage number seven occurs because there is a significant amount of time saved by avoiding keying, keying errors, and mail delays. This time savings can cut days from the time cycle to enter an order, ship it, and receive payment. Thus, the seller can maintain lower inventory levels and replenish those inventory levels more quickly. Finally, the last two advantages relate to getting or keeping competitive advantages. Sometimes, a company needs EDI in order to survive—for example, to satisfy the vendors or sellers it already deals with. In other cases, EDI offers a competitive advantage by allowing a seller to more quickly and accurately service customers.

Newer EDI systems use the Internet, rather than third-party networks, to transmit EDI documents. Companies using Internet EDI realize large cost savings because they avoid the fees paid to a third-party network.

THE REAL WORLD

Northern Telecom (Nortel) switched to an Internet EDI system in the late 1990s. Nortel has customers all over the globe, and the use of the Internet by Nortel customers to transmit purchase orders is a low-cost transmission option for those customers. This was especially beneficial to Nortel in expanding its customer base in Europe and Asia. As Nortel works to gain new customers, a low-cost way to order is an enticement to those customers.

There are also other benefits to Nortel. The use of Internet EDI eliminated the need for customers to fax purchase orders or supplier information to Nortel. Michael Keef, the senior manager of electronic business solutions at Nortel, said, "Errors occur when people fax things. We won't have to rekey shipment notices."[4] Details of Internet EDI are described in a later chapter on e-commerce.

EDI systems cause risks that may be different from those found in traditional manual or IT systems. EDI eliminates much of what would be the traditional paper audit trail of documents, such as sales orders, shipping documents, and invoices. Risks in an EDI system are as follows:

Security and Confidentiality

1. Unauthorized access
2. Trading partners gaining access to unauthorized data
3. Hackers or other network break-ins
4. Repudiation of sales transactions

Processing Integrity

5. Invalid data entered by trading partners
6. Incomplete audit trail
7. Errors when integrating data into back end systems such as accounting, payment processing, and order fulfillment software systems

Availability

8. System failures such as hardware and software failures that block customers from access to the EDI system

IT controls can lessen these risks. Exhibit 8-19 summarizes these risks and controls for e-commerce and EDI. The controls are authentication, encryption, transactions logging, control totals, and acknowledgements. **Authentication** is the process of user identification to ensure that only authorized users are accessing the IT system. Authentication occurs through the use of user ID, password, and other unique identifiers. Only valid, authorized trading partners should be allowed to initiate or receive EDI communication. For example, a company would not want an employee to log in from a home computer and submit false orders to be delivered to her home address. Limiting communication to authorized trading partners is accomplished by authentication that uses software-

[4]Ellen Messmer, "Nortel embraces Net EDI," *Network World*, March 17, 1997, p. 69.

based authentication techniques such as user account IDs and passwords. Authentication can occur at the VAN log-in, within the translation software, and within the application software.

Since data travel over network data lines and third-party networks, they are susceptible to network break-ins. **Encryption,** the coding of data that makes data unreadable to those without the encryption key, is a control that limits risk. Encryption of the data will not prevent these breaches, but will render the data useless. **Transaction logging** occurs when the IT system automatically produces a log of users and the actions they undertake within the IT system. As a computer conducts EDI transactions, it should automatically log each transaction, and this log should be regularly examined and reconciled to ensure that no transactions are lost or unaccounted for.

Control totals are subtotals of selected fields for an entire batch of transactions. For example, quantity ordered could be added for a batch of orders. The **acknowledgment** is a reply that echoes the data control totals. The use of acknowledgments and matching control totals can reduce the risk of erroneous or invalid EDI data in transactions. When an EDI transaction is transmitted, the receiving computer should transmit an acknowledgment. These totals can be compared with original data to make sure it was not garbled or lost during transmission.

Risk	Controls
Security and Confidentiality	
Unauthorized access Hackers or other network break-ins Repudiation of sales transactions	Authentication: user ID, password, log-in procedures, access levels, authority tables Firewall, encryption, vulnerability assessment, intrusion detection, penetration testing Computer logs
Processing Integrity	
Invalid data entered by customers Incomplete audit trail Errors integrating into back end systems	Input controls: field check, validity check, limit check, reasonableness check Computer logs Software testing
Availability	
System failures Virus and worm attacks Denial of service attacks by hackers	Business continuity planning, backup data and systems Firewall, encryption, vulnerability assessment, intrusion detection, penetration testing

Exhibit 8-19
Risks and Controls for E-commerce and EDI Revenue Processes

POINT OF SALE (POS) SYSTEMS AND THE RELATED RISKS AND CONTROLS (STUDY OBJECTIVE 8)

For retail operations there is a type of accounting software categorized as point of sale (POS) systems. These systems capture all relevant sales data at the point of sale: the cash register. You have seen POS systems on your shopping visits to grocery or department stores. As you checked out, the bar codes are scanned on the items you purchased, prices were determined by the accessing of inventory and price list data, sales revenue was recorded, and inventory values were updated. All of these processes occur in real time, and the store can provide to its managers or home office daily summaries of sales by cash register or by product. Many companies adopt POS systems because they enhance customer satisfaction by enabling faster and more accurate checkouts. In addition, POS systems have many features that assist accountants and managers in the company, including the following:

1. Touch screen menus for easy training and use by employees lead to fewer errors and more accurate sales and inventory data.
2. Bar code scanning of products eliminates the need to manually enter product codes, quantities, or prices.
3. Real-time access to inventory and price data allows for more accurate pricing at check-out, as well as quick and efficient price updates. List prices can be changed online by a manager and reflected instantly at the checkout register.
4. Credit card authorizations during the sale save time and help prevent credit card fraud.
5. Real-time update of cash, sales, and inventory records allows for immediate analysis of sales trends, inventory needs, and cash on hand.
6. Immediate summaries and analyses can be provided to on-site management or the home office.
7. Integration with the company's general ledger system to post sales, cost of goods sold, inventory, and receivables accounts saves many manual steps.

POS systems are not usually connected to trading partners outside the company. The system is an internal system that may have network connections from individual stores or locations to corporate headquarters. Since it usually does not involve outside network connections, it does not pose as many security or confidentiality risks as e-commerce or EDI systems. The POS software system can actually reduce some processing integrity risks within revenue and cash collection processes. The risks lessened are as follows:

1. Pricing errors for products sold
2. Cash overage or shortage errors
3. Errors in inventory changes—less chance of an incorrect product number
4. Erroneous or invalid sales voids or deletions

Since a POS system does use extensive computer hardware and software, there are availability risks. Hardware or software failures can make the system unavailable for use and interrupt or halt business operations. Therefore, it is important for a company to institute controls to lessen the availability risks. Backup systems and backup data procedures should be in place. The organization should also have business continuity and disaster recovery plans in place.

There are many examples of POS systems in the companies you probably buy from regularly. Retail stores such as department stores, grocery stores, and bookstores, as well as restaurants, may all use POS systems.

THE REAL WORLD

Several years ago, Pizza Hut, Inc. switched all company restaurants to a POS system.[5] The system tremendously increased control over sales, cash, and inventory. Item prices for all of the possible menu combinations are determined at the home office and downloaded into the POS system at each restaurant. These downloaded prices reduce errors such as charging incorrect prices to customers. As the order is entered in the system, a copy of the order is printed in the kitchen so that the kitchen can prepare the pizza correctly with the requested combination of toppings.

Procedures at the end of the day improve control over cash. A report of cash received can be compared with the bank deposit amount of that day, and any differences can be reconciled or investigated. Also, at the end of the day, Pizza Hut's POS system prepares a report that can be reviewed by the managers and staff of that restaurant before the start of the next day. That report shows managers a comparison of carryout, delivery, and in-store sales. It also categorizes sales by type of product such as pizza, sandwich, or salad.

More recently, some Pizza Hut franchises have adopted the newest versions of POS software. In February 2005, Restaurant Management Company (RMC) of Wichita, Kansas, selected SpeedLine Solutions, Inc. as its exclusive POS provider. RMC operates over 160 Pizza Hut, KFC, Long John Silver's and other restaurants across the U.S. Speedline is the top provider of POS software for pizza restaurants.

POS software also interfaces with the company's general ledger software and makes appropriate entries to record sales, cash, and inventory changes. These processes within the POS system allowed Pizza Hut to improve several aspects of its performance by giving management better feedback. As a result, management is able to use the system to forecast labor needs, control inventory levels, and determine popular sales items to promote via marketing.

ETHICAL ISSUES RELATED TO REVENUE PROCESSES (STUDY OBJECTIVE 9)

A sad fact of the business and accounting environment is that many deceptions and fraudulent acts relate to revenue measurement and recognition. Many managers or owners succumb to the temptation to inflate (overstate) revenues so

[5]R.M. Young, "Accounting for Remote Locations," *Management Accounting*, November 1991, pp. 58–60.

that they can make the company's financial performance appear better than it is. Intentional revenue inflation is unethical, and many types of revenue inflation are illegal.

THE REAL WORLD

In the early days of personal computers, one of the manufacturers of hard drives was MiniScribe Corporation. The chief executive officer of MiniScribe, Q.T. Wiles, was convicted of fraud in 1994 and subsequently served 30 months in prison for falsifying revenue. To inflate revenues, Q.T. Wiles came up with a novel idea. He made the employees ship bricks, rather than hard drives, in boxes that were sent to distributors. The company also shipped scrapped parts in boxes that were labeled as hard drives. The company inflated revenue by recording completely fictitious, fraudulent sales of these bricks and scrap materials. In addition to the CEO being sentenced to jail time, the chief financial officer, a CPA, was disciplined by the Securities and Exchange Commission. The company ultimately failed.[6]

There are many examples of companies inflating revenue. The MiniScribe example points out an unfortunate truth: If top management is intent on falsifying financial statements by inflating revenue, it does not matter how good the underlying processes and accounting systems are; it can still often find ways to misstate revenue despite the effectiveness of the accounting system. Accurate financial reports can only be an output of an accounting system if management desires accurate financial reports. Unethical managers can easily cause fictitious or inflated sales revenues to be recorded, although doing so requires the assistance of those who work for the top managers. Since top managers have so much control over those whom they employ, it is possible for them to convince employees to assist in the deception. If MiniScribe's employees had been more ethical, it would have been more difficult for its leaders to conduct the fraud.

In addition to the novel approach of MiniScribe, there are more mundane ways to inflate revenue. Two popular approaches are "channel stuffing" and "leaving sales open" beyond the end of the fiscal period. **Channel stuffing** is intentionally persuading a customer to buy more than needed, thereby "stuffing" more product into the sales channel. "**Leaving sales open**" is a term that refers to moving a period cut-off date forward to include sales that rightly would occur in a future period. This means that the company records sales revenue that should actually be recorded in the following fiscal year. From an accounting system perspective, it is important that the system properly account for revenue in the proper period. This can become complex when the order, shipment, and payment dates occur near or after the fiscal year end. The system that records revenue transactions must be so designed that it includes in current period revenues only those items that were actually shipped before year-end. Any shipments occurring after year-end must be counted in the subsequent fiscal

[6]Andy Zipser, "Cooking the Books: How Pressure to Raise Sales Led MiniScribe to Falsify Numbers" *The Wall Street Journal*, 9/11/1989.

year. The system should be tested to make sure that it handles this sales revenue cutoff correctly.

THE REAL WORLD

Sunbeam Corp. is another recent example of a company involved in intentional revenue misstatements. Sunbeam's former chief executive, Albert "Chainsaw Al" Dunlap, and former CFO, Russell Kersh, devised a series of schemes to inflate revenues via channel stuffing.[7] Sunbeam reported tens of millions of dollars in fraudulent sales that were a result of improper bill and hold transactions, whereby sales invoices were sent to customers for items that they intended to purchase at a later date and Sunbeam claimed to be holding the items for them. Other techniques used by Sunbeam included offering customers extraordinary discounts in order to accelerate sales, and the premature recognition of contingent sales arrangements.

Management has a responsibility to maintain an accounting system that properly recognizes revenue. If management chooses to do so, inflating revenues by shifting revenue cutoffs is easy. This emphasizes the fact that the ethics of management and the control environment are the most important factors in accurate and complete financial statements. Without ethical management at the top of a company, financial reports must be suspect.

In many cases where revenue is intentionally overstated, accountants or CFOs have participated in the deception. In the cases of MiniScribe and Sunbeam, the chief financial officers were involved in the fraud. Accountants throughout an organization should try to ensure that the department, area, or division they work in does not overstate revenues. Overstated revenues mislead the general public as they make investment decisions regarding stocks to buy. If any department or subunit within the company overstates revenue, it can mislead investors. Therefore, accountants must make sure that the accounting systems used to record revenue are accurate. Secondly, accountants must not allow managers to coerce them into assisting in the overstatement of revenue through the use of accounting tricks or deceptions. Unfortunately, an accountant or CFO can be swayed by arguments advanced by top managers. For example, a CEO might say that the revenue overstatement is only temporary until earnings targets are met. The CEO might even say that the company will have to cut back its workforce if revenues deception is not carried out. These arguments can be very persuasive, and many accountants have agreed to participate in such deceptions involving revenue. Obviously, it is best to be vigilant about resisting involvement in revenue overstatement. Once it begins, it usually seems to snowball into more and more overstatements as pressure mounts to report continued revenue growth. Accountants must continually guard against persuasion to participate in such frauds.

[7]John A Byrne, "How Al Dunlap Self-Destructed: The Inside Story of What Drove Sunbeam's Board to Act," BusinessWeek, June 25, 1998, www.businessweek.com/1998/27/63585090.htm

THE REAL WORLD

A recent example of accountants being involved in revenue misstatement in an accounting fraud scheme occurred at HealthSouth Corp. Richard Scrushy, the CEO, and five different financial officers were accused of inflating profits by $1.4 billion. An excerpt of a news report described the accountants' involvement.[8]

> Acting on Scrushy's orders to "fix" earnings, senior accountants gathered in what they called "family meetings" to falsify results when HealthSouth's performance failed to meet Wall Street forecasts.

In June of 2005, to the surprise of federal prosecutors, Scrushy was found not guilty of all counts against him even though the five other HealthSouth officials had plead guilty and testified that Scrushy ordered the actions. Although a jury found him not guilty, Scrushy's job prospects as a CEO are severely damaged. At a minimum, he tolerated and failed to prevent unethical behavior, even though it was not proven beyond a reasonable doubt that he participated in the events.

CORPORATE GOVERNANCE IN REVENUE PROCESSES (STUDY OBJECTIVE 10)

Chapter 5 identified four primary functions of the corporate governance process: management oversight, internal controls and compliance, financial stewardship, and ethical conduct.

The systems, processes, and internal controls described in this chapter are part of the corporate governance structure. When management designs and implements processes for sales, sales returns, and cash collections, they assign responsibility for executing those functions to various managers and employees. As management assigns and oversees these revenue processes, it is carrying out the corporate governance function of proper management oversight.

As described in this chapter, management should also establish appropriate internal controls for revenue processes to accomplish the objectives of safeguarding assets within those processes and ensuring the accuracy and completeness of the data produced by the processes. These internal controls are also part of the corporate governance structure.

When management has designed and implemented processes and internal controls and then continually manages them, it is helping to ensure proper stewardship of the company's assets. Corporate governance requires proper financial stewardship. The processes, internal controls, and feedback data from these systems help management report to owners and other stakeholders about proper stewardship of assets within the revenue processes. These assets would include inventory, cash, receivables, and operating assets.

Finally, good corporate governance requires ethical conduct. This chapter described some of the ethical issues that management must consider and address within the revenue processes. When top management acts ethically and encourages ethical behavior throughout the organization, stronger corporate governance is the result. There are usually fewer cases of frauds, errors, or ethical problems in an organization when top management behaves ethically and encourages ethical behavior.

[8] Jay Reeves, Associated Press, "HealthSouth, chairman accused of massive fraud," March 20, 2003.

Perhaps it would be easier to understand the way this chapter's topics fit into corporate governance if you think of it from a negative perspective. For example, if management of a particular organization did not establish sound processes, good internal controls, and ethical policies, it would lack good corporate governance. In that organization, revenue processes would be poorly executed and weakly controlled. Management would not be exercising proper financial stewardship. Therefore, stakeholders such as investors, creditors, and owners would have little or no trust in the resulting financial statements. The organization would not represent the type of organization in which we would wish to invest our own money. On the other hand, when an organization has good corporate governance, the stakeholders can correctly have more confidence that proper stewardship is occurring. Establishing proper processes, internal controls, and ethical guidelines leads to better corporate governance and, therefore, good financial stewardship.

SUMMARY OF STUDY OBJECTIVES

An introduction to revenue processes. The three typical types of processes related to revenues are sales processes, sales return processes, and cash collection processes.

Sales processes and the related risks and controls. Sales processes include checking customer credit and authorizing the sale if credit is not exceeded, checking inventory to determine whether goods are in stock, picking the correct goods from the warehouse, shipping goods to the customer, billing the customer, and updating accounting records. Sales process controls can be categorized into authorization, segregation, adequate records, security of assets and records, and independent checks.

Sales return processes and the related risks and controls. Sales return processes include receiving returned goods, matching goods to the original invoice, preparing credit memorandum, returning goods to the warehouse, reducing accounts receivable and increasing inventory records, issuing credit or a check to the customer, and updating accounting records. Sales process controls can be categorized into authorization, segregation, adequate records, security of assets and records, and independent checks.

Cash collection processes and the related risks and controls. Cash collection processes include receiving checks in the mailroom, comparing checks with the remittance advice, preparing a check prelist and a deposit slip, depositing the funds, updating cash, accounts receivable, and general ledger records, and reconciling the bank records to the organization's records. Cash collection process controls can be categorized into authorization, segregation, adequate records, security of assets and records, and independent checks.

An overview of IT systems of revenue and cash collection that enhance the efficiency of revenue processes. As complexity and automation in IT systems increases, there are fewer manual processes and more computerized processes. This is usually true regarding size also; larger IT systems generally have fewer manual processes and more computerized processes. More computerized processes means there would be a greater need for the IT controls to reduce IT risks. IT risks can be categorized into security, availability, processing integrity, and confidentiality risks. General and application IT controls can reduce these risks.

E-business systems and the related risks and controls. E-business can include both business-to-business (B2B) and business-to-consumer (B2C) sales. In either case, the advantages include reduced cost through lower marketing, employee, and paperwork costs, shorter sales cycles due to reduced time to place an order, deliver the order, and collect payment, increased accuracy and reliability of sales data, and increased potential market for products and services. The Internet connected nature of e-commerce sales includes several risks that a company must manage. These risks include security, availability, processing integrity, and confidentiality risks.

Electronic data interchange (EDI) systems and the related risks and controls. Electronic data interchange is the inter-company, computer-to-computer transfer of business documents in a standard business format. The network connected nature of EDI sales includes several risks that a company must manage, including security, availability, processing integrity, and confidentiality risks.

Point of Sale (POS) systems and the related risks and controls. For retail operations, there is a type of accounting software categorized as point of sale (POS) systems. These systems capture all relevant sales data at the point of sale: the cash register. As items are checked out through a register, the bar codes are scanned on the items purchased, prices are determined by the accessing of inventory and price list data, sales revenue is recorded, and inventory values are updated. All of these processes occur in real time, and the store can provide its managers or home office with daily summaries of sales by cash register or by product. Some risks, including pricing errors, cash shortages, inventory discrepancies, and erroneous sales invoices or voids, can be lessened by POS systems.

Ethical issues related to revenue processes. Revenue processes are very susceptible to unethical revenue inflation schemes. Such schemes include fraudulent or fictitious sales, improper sales cutoff periods, and channel stuffing.

Corporate governance in revenue processes. The revenue processes described in this chapter—sales process, sales return process, and cash collection process—are part of the management oversight of corporate governance. The internal controls and ethical tone and procedures within the revenue processes are also part of the corporate governance structure. Establishing and maintaining reliable revenue processes, internal controls, and ethical practices help insure proper financial stewardship.

KEY TERMS

Acknowledgment
Authentication
Bill of lading
Business process reengineering (BPR)
B2B Sales
B2C Sales
Cash receipts journal
Channel stuffing
Control totals
Credit limit

Credit memorandum
Data segments
Disaster recovery plan
E-commerce systems
Electronic data interchange (EDI)
Encryption
Header data
Labeling interchanges
Packing list or packing slip
Pick list
Point of Sale (POS)
Price list
Programmed data input checks
Purchase order
Receiving log
Receiving report
Remittance advice
Sales allowance
Sales invoice
Sales journal
Sales order
Shipping log
Trailer data
Transaction logging
Transaction processing systems (TPS)
Value added network (VAN)
Virtual private network (VPN)

END OF CHAPTER MATERIAL

CONCEPT CHECK

1. Within the revenue processes, a signed approval of a sales order indicates all of the following except:
   a. The date of delivery.
   b. The sale is to an accepted customer.
   c. The customer's credit has been approved.
   d. The sales price is correct.
2. An example of an independent verification in the sales process is
   a. preparation of packing lists on prenumbered forms.
   b. initialing the sales order.
   c. proof of recorded dates, quantities, and prices on an invoice.
   d. physical controls in record storage areas.
3. The purpose of tracing shipping documents to prenumbered sales invoices would be to provide evidence that
   a. shipments to customers were properly invoiced.
   b. no duplicate shipments or billings occurred.
   c. goods billed to customers were shipped.
   d. all prenumbered sales invoices were accounted for.
4. The purpose of tracing sales invoices to shipping documents would be to provide evidence that
   a. shipments to customers were properly invoiced.
   b. no duplicate shipments or billings occurred.
   c. goods billed to customers were shipped.
   d. all prenumbered sales invoices were accounted for.
5. To ensure that all credit sales transactions of an entity are recorded, which of the following controls would be most effective?

a. On a monthly basis, the accounting department supervisor reconciles the accounts receivable subsidiary ledger to the accounts receivable control account.

b. The supervisor of the accounting department investigates any account balance differences reported by customers.

c. The supervisor of the billing department sends copies of approved sales orders to the credit department for comparison of authorized credit limits and current customer balances.

d. The supervisor of the billing department matches prenumbered shipping documents with entries recorded in the sales journal.

6. Under a system of sound internal controls, if a company sold defective goods, the return of those goods from the customer should be accepted by the

a. receiving clerk.

b. sales clerk.

c. purchasing clerk.

d. inventory control clerk.

7. The source document that initiates the recording of the return and the adjustment to the customer's credit status is the

a. pick list.

b. sales journal.

c. credit memorandum.

d. sales invoice.

8. Which of the following is **not** a document that is part of the cash collection process?

a. Remittance advice

b. Cash receipts journal

c. Bank deposit slip

d. Packing slip

9. Which of the following would represent proper segregation of duties?

a. The employee who has custody of cash also does accounts receivable record keeping.

b. The employee who has custody of cash completes the bank reconciliation.

c. The employee who opens mail containing checks prepares a list of checks received.

d. The employee who opens mail containing checks records transactions in the general ledger.

10. Immediately upon receiving checks from customers in the mail, a responsible employee working in an environment of adequate internal control should prepare a listing of receipts and forward it to the company's cashier. A copy of this cash receipts listing should also be sent to the company's

a. treasurer for comparison with the monthly bank statement.

b. internal auditor for investigation of any unusual transactions.

c. accounts receivable clerk for updating of the accounts receivable subsidiary ledger.

d. bank for comparison with deposit slips.

11. If a company does not prepare an aging of accounts receivable, which of the following accounts is most likely to be misstated?

a. Sales revenues

b. Accounts receivable

c. Sales returns and allowances

d. Allowance for uncollectible accounts

12. When a company sells items over the Internet, it is usually called e-commerce. There are many IT risks related to Internet sales. The risk of invalid data entered by a customer would be a(n)

a. availability risk.

b. processing integrity risk.

c. security risk.

d. confidentiality risk.

13. When a company sells items over the Internet, there are many IT risks. The risk of hardware and software failures that prevent website sales would be a(n)

a. availability risk.

b. processing integrity risk.

c. security risk.

d. confidentiality risk.

14. The use of electronic data interchange (EDI) to conduct sales electronically has both risks and benefits. Which of the following is a benefit of EDI, rather than a risk?

a. Incomplete audit trail

b. Repudiation of sales transactions

c. Unauthorized access

d. Shorter inventory cycle time

15. An IT system that uses touch screens, bar coded products, and credit card authorization during the sale is called a(n)

a. electronic data interchange system.

b. e-commerce system.

c. point of sale system.

d. e-payables system.

16. Which of the following is **not** a method of unethically inflating sales revenue?

a. Channel stuffing

b. Holding sales open

c. Premature recognition of contingent sales

d. Promotional price discounts

DISCUSSION QUESTIONS

17. (SO 2) Why is it important to establish and monitor credit limits for customers?
18. (SO 2) Distinguish between a pick list and a packing slip.
19. (SO 2) How can an effective system of internal controls lead to increased sales revenue?
20. (SO 2) Why should the person responsible for shipping goods to customers not also have responsibility for maintaining records of customer accounts?
21. (SO 3) What is the purpose of a credit memorandum?
22. (SO 3) How are sales invoices used (in a manual system) in the preparation of credit memos?
23. (SO 2) How can a security guard in a warehouse be considered an important component of a company's accounting system?
24. (SO 3) How could fraud be perpetrated through the sales returns process?
25. (SO 6, 7, 8) Identify and distinguish between the three types of IT systems used in the sales process.
26. (SO 6) Distinguish between B2B sales and B2C sales. Other than those presented in this chapter, name a company from your personal experience that uses B2C sales.
27. (SO 6) List the advantages of e-commerce systems.
28. (SO 6) Identify two of the biggest risks to companies who use e-commerce, along with controls to prevent these risks.
29. (SO 6,7) What controls should a company implement to ensure consistency of sales information between the front end and back end of its systems?
30. (SO 6) Why is a redundant server system needed in an e-commerce environment?
31. (SO 6) Why should a company continuously monitor the capacity of its e-commerce system?
32. (SO 7) What are the three important characteristics of the EDI definition?
33. (SO 7) What are the three standard parts of an EDI data transmission?
34. (SO 7) How could it be possible for two companies to conduct EDI if they are not directly connected with each other?
35. (SO 7) List the advantages of an EDI system.
36. (SO 6, 7, 8) What is the purpose of maintaining transaction logs? Why are they especially important in IT systems?
37. (SO 8) List some advantages of a POS system.
38. (SO 8) Why are backup systems one of the most important controls for POS systems?
39. (SO 9) Describe a popular fraud scheme where company employees misuse the sales revenues cutoff.

BRIEF EXERCISES

40. (SO 2, SO 4) Describe what is likely to occur if company personnel erroneously recorded a sales transaction for the wrong customer. What if a cash receipt were applied to the wrong customer? Identify internal controls that would detect or prevent this from occurring.

41. (SO 4) Debate the logic used in the following statement: The person responsible for handling cash receipts should also prepare the bank reconciliation because he is most familiar with the deposits that have been made to the bank account.
42. (SO 7) Revenue systems are crucial in the health care industry, where hundreds of billions of dollars are spent annually reconciling revenues and billing data from the perspectives of providers (doctors and clinics, etc.) and payers (insurance companies). Briefly describe how EDI would be beneficial in this industry. Describe the purpose of the header data and trailer data.
43. (SO 2, SO 3, SO 4) Use the process maps in this chapter to answer the following questions:
    a. What would a credit manager do if a sales order received caused a customer to exceed its credit limit?
    b. What happens after the shipping department verifies that the quantities and descriptions of goods prepared for shipment are consistent with the sales order?
    c. What would an accounts receivable clerk do if a $100 credit memo is issued to a customer whose accounts receivable balance is $1000?
    d. When is it necessary for an accounts receivable clerk to notify a customer?
44. (SO 2) Describe how the matching of key information on supporting documents can help a company determine that its revenue transactions have not been duplicated.
45. (SO 2, 3) Describe how the use of prenumbered forms for receiving reports and credit memos can help a company determine that sales return transactions have not been omitted from the accounting records.
46. (SO 8) Describe how a POS system could be useful to a company's marketing managers. How could it be useful to purchasing agents?
47. (SO 8) Briefly describe an example from your personal experience where you purchased something from a company that uses a POS system. How might your experience have been different if the POS system did not exist in the experience you described?

PROBLEMS

48. (SO 6) In 1956, Junior DeLucca opened a pizza restaurant that he named DeLucca's in St. Louis, Missouri. Over the years, he opened both company and franchise locations and grew the business to include over 40 restaurants that serve the three states around the St. Louis area. In 1993, DeLucca introduced a centralized phone ordering system with one phone number for customers to use. This meant that the customer did not need to look up the phone number of a local restaurant and call that restaurant to order. Rather, customers call one number, and the employees taking the order can determine the closest DeLucca's location and process the order. This system also centralized the pricing, ordering, and inventory systems for DeLucca's. In 2004, DeLucca's began offering online pizza orders through its website. DeLucca's advertises this web ordering as more convenient for the customer. For example, its ads suggest that a customer can examine the entire menu on the website prior to ordering, something that is not possible with phone orders.

While there are many customer advantages of web ordering, there are also many advantages to the company. From an accounting and internal control perspective, describe the advantages of Delucca's system and any risks that it reduces.

49. (SO 8) You are the recent heir of $20,000 cash, with which you are considering opening a sushi bar in the university community. You would accept cash and credit card payments, which would be handled primarily by your servers. You also plan to offer introductory specials to attract customers during the initial months of business. Identify some advantages and disadvantages of investing in a POS system as part of this new business venture. What internal controls should be implemented to reduce the risk of theft or error related to the handling of cash, credit card payments, and coupons?

50. (SO 2, 4, 6) Aaron Preswick is the owner of AP's Instant Replay, a consignment shop for used sporting goods. Aaron accepts consigned goods and offers them for sale to the general public. Aaron rents business space, including a retail store where the consigned goods are displayed and sold, with adjoining office space where an Internet site is maintained and other administrative functions are performed. The Internet site includes photos and descriptions of items available for sale worldwide. If the goods sell, Aaron's consignment fee is 40% of the sale price, and 60% is remitted to the consignor. Shipping costs on electronic orders are paid by the customers.

Required:

Identify internal control considerations for the following:

a. the e-commerce portion of the business

b. the retail portion of the business, assuming that the accounting systems are mostly manual and handled by Aaron and his wife

51. (SO 2, 3, 4) Identify an internal control procedure that would reduce each of the risks that follow in a manual system. Also, describe how (or if) an IT system could reduce these risks:

a. Revenues may be recorded before the related shipment occurs.

b. Employees responsible for shipping and accounts receivable may collude to steal goods and cover up the theft by recording fictitious sales.

c. Credit memos may be issued at full price, when the goods were originally sold at a discount.

d. Sales invoices may contain mathematical errors.

e. Amounts collected on accounts receivable may be applied to the wrong customer.

f. Duplicate credit memos may be issued for a single sales return.

g. Sales invoices may not be prepared for all shipments.

h. Shipments may contain the wrong goods.

i. All sales transactions may not be included in the general ledger.

52. (SO 3, 4, 5) The following list presents various internal control strengths or risks that may be found in a company's revenues and cash collection processes:

_____ Credit is authorized by the credit manager.

_____ Checks paid in excess of $5000 require the signatures of two authorized members of management.

_____ A cash receipts journal is prepared by the treasurer's department.

_____ Collections received by check are received by the company receptionist, who has no additional record-keeping responsibilities.

_____ Collections received by check are immediately forwarded unopened to the accounting department.

_____ A bank reconciliation is prepared on a monthly basis by the treasurer's department.

_____ Security cameras are placed in the shipping dock.

_____ Receiving reports are prepared on preprinted, numbered forms.

_____ The billing department verifies the amount of customer sales invoices by referring to the authorized price list.

_____ Entries in the shipping log are reconciled with the sales journal on a monthly basis.

_____ Payments to vendors are made promptly upon receipt of goods or services.

_____ Cash collections are deposited in the bank account on a weekly basis.

_____ Customer returns must be approved by a designated manager before a credit memo is prepared.

_____ Account statements are sent to customers on a monthly basis.

_____ Purchase returns are presented to the sales department for preparation of a receiving report.

Required: In the space provided, indicate whether each of these items represents a strength (S) or risk (R) related to internal controls in the revenues and cash collection processes. Alternatively, indicate whether the item is not applicable (N/A), meaning that it either has no impact on the strength of internal controls or does not pertain to the revenues and cash collection processes.

53. (SO 2) Following is the April 30th Accounts Receivable Subsidiary Ledger of Gerrett, Inc., a retailer of tents and camping equipment.

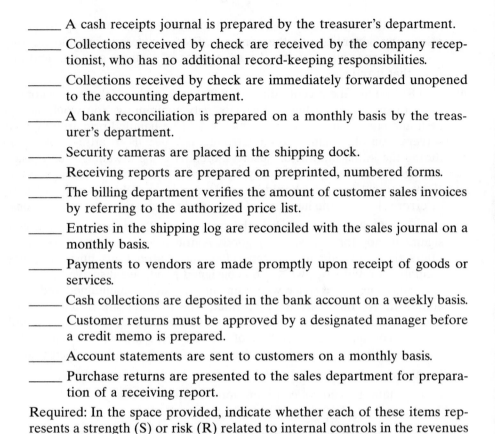

Accounts Receivable Subsidiary Ledger
Gerrett, Inc.
April 30, 20xx Open Receivables

Customer: **Acme Sporting Goods Central**
4726 Interstate Highway 2L
Devron, Kansas 76588
507-945-8800

Account 43985
Credit Terms: 30 days
Credit Limit: $15,000

Invoice Number	Invoice Date	Due Date	Amount	Customer Total
77341	April 27	May 27	$1,366.48	
75118	April 1	May 1	4,975.00	
70698	March 15	April 14	4,017.15	
65287	January 14	February 13	659.59	$11,018.22

(continued)

Customer: **Brufton Outdoors**
623 Main Street NW
Devron, Kansas 76588
507-945-1844

Account 41772
Credit Terms: 30 days
Credit Limit: $15,000

Invoice Number	Invoice Date	Due Date	Amount	Customer Total
67915	February 20	March 22	$1,946.40	
61190	January 2	February 1	6,763.10	$8,709.50

Customer: **Jafferty Sporting Goods**
8466 State Route 33
Elkton, Kansas 76541
507-312-9469

Account 30966
Credit Terms: 15 days
Credit Limit: $5,000

Invoice Number	Invoice Date	Due Date	Amount	Customer Total
74555	March 22	April 6	$4,067.99	$4,067.99

Customer: **Kansas Department of Recreation and Safety**
8466 State Route 33
Gray Mountain, Kansas 76529
507-226-6881

Account 29667
Credit Terms: 30 days
Credit Limit: $25,000

Invoice Number	Invoice Date	Due Date	Amount	Customer Total
78021	April 30	May 30	$10,646.20	
77216	April 16	May 16	6,653.15	
77089	April 15	May 15	975.63	
75663	April 1	May 1	299.00	
74277	March 15	April 14	1,104.13	
73586	March 7	April 6	655.31	
67644	February 20	March 22	1,843.83	$22,177.25

Customer: **Pup Scouts of Devron**
9064 State Route 16
Devron, Kansas 76588
507-312-3126

Account 33117
Credit Terms: 15 days
Credit Limit: $10,000

Invoice Number	Invoice Date	Due Date	Amount	Customer Total
77911	April 20	May 5	$9,737.91	
75559	March 29	April 13	220.04	$9,957.95

Customer: **Regents Athletic Club**
22 West Adams Way
Devron, Kansas 76588
507-945-2149

Account 30846
Credit Terms: 30 days
Credit Limit: $5,000

Invoice Number	Invoice Date	Due Date	Amount	Customer Total
66268	January 25	March 24	$2,678.59	
61119	January 2	February 1	862.35	$3,540.94

Customer: **Buddy's Sports Buff**
212 Oak Street
Silver Horn, Kansas 76557
507-399-7761

Account 16200
Credit Terms: 30 days
Credit Limit: $10,000

Invoice Number	Invoice Date	Due Date	Amount	Customer Total
77115	April 15	May 15	$8,046.40	
70564	March 15	April 14	1,774.92	$9,821.32

Required:

Use Microsoft Excel to prepare an electronic spreadsheet of an accounts receivable aging report for Gerrett for April 30. Organize the spreadsheet with the following column headings:

Customer Name	Total Account Balance	Current Balance		Past Due Balances					
				1–30 days		31–60 days		Over 60 days	
		Invoice #	Amount	Invoice #	Amount	Invoice #	Amount	Invoice #	Amount

Be sure to include each individual invoice for each customer, and show column totals for each customer. Also show report totals for each column and be certain that the report totals cross-foot and agree with the ending Total Account Balance for all customers.

54. (SO 2) Following is a sales order form for Weston's World of Wines, Inc. This form is prepared manually by a sales clerk and based on a telephone order from a customer. This form represents the source document that triggers the revenues process at Weston's World of Wines.

Sales Order

Weston's World of Wines, Inc.
802 Ashmore Ave.
Weston, CA 95718

No. 35610

Bill to:
La Cheaux Partners
412 Bridge Blvd.
Bridgetown, AK 37616

Cust. # 42004

Ship to:
La Cheaux Magnique
8212 Hampton Place
Bridgetown, AK 37615

Date: 5/27/2006

Preferred Shipping Method:
2-day USP
Payment Terms: 30 days

Item Number	Description	Quantity	Unit Price	Extended Price
1046R	Merlot	12	6.99	$83.88
1047R	Zinfandel	12	7.99	95.88
1049R	Cabernet Sauvignon	24	7.49	179.76
2025W	Pinot Grigio	24	7.49	179.76
2027W	Riesling	12	6.49	77.88
				$617.16

Authorized by: H.B Clayton

Date: 5/27/06

Required:

Use Microsoft Excel to perform the following:

a. Design an appropriate format for a data entry screen that could be used in the accounting department to enter information from the sales order in the company's revenues software program.

b. Prepare a sales journal with appropriate column headings. Enter the relevant information from the preceding sales order into your spreadsheet.

55. (SO 2, 4) Following are ten internal control failures related to the revenues and cash collection processes:

_____ A customer ordered 12 boxes of your product (total of 144 items) for express shipment. Your data entry clerk inadvertently entered 12 individual items.

_____ You enter sales and accounts receivable data in batches at the end of each week. Several problems have resulted recently as a result of invoices being recorded to the wrong customer account.

_____ In an effort to boost sales, you obtain some of the stock of unissued shipping reports and create a dozen fictitious shipments. You submit these documents to the billing department for invoicing.

_____ Checks are received by the mail room and then forwarded to the accounts receivable department for recording. The accounts receivable clerk holds the checks until the proper customer account has been identified and reconciled.

_____ Several shipping reports have been misplaced en route to the billing department from the shipping department.

_____ Several sales transactions were not invoiced within the same month as the related shipment.

_____ A sales clerk entered a nonexistent date in the computer system. The system rejected the data and the sales were not recorded.

_____ Upon entering sales orders in your new computer system, a sales clerk mistakenly omitted customer numbers from the entries.

_____ A computer programmer altered the electronic credit authorization function for a customer company owned by the programmer's cousin.

_____ Customer orders were lost in the mail en route from the sales office to the accounting department (located at the company's headquarters).

Required:

From the list that follows, select one internal control would be most effective in the prevention of each listed failure. Indicate the letter of the control next to each failure. Letters should not be used more than once, and some letters may not be used at all.

a. Preformatted data entry screens

b. Prenumbered documents

c. Programmed edit checks

d. 100% check for matching of customer orders and sales orders

e. 100% check for matching of sales orders, pick list, and packing slips

f. 100% check for matching of sales orders and invoices

g. 100% check for matching of deposit slip and customer check

h. Prompt data entry immediately upon receipt of customer order

i. Customer verification

j. Independent authorization for shipments

k. Independent authorization for billing

l. Reasonableness check

m. Hash totals

n. Data back-up procedures

o. Program change controls

p. Sequence verification

q. Periodic confirmation of customer account balances

56. (SO 2, 3, 4) Brathert Company is a small company with four people working in the revenue processes. One of the four employees supervises the other three. Some tasks that must be accomplished within the revenue processes are the following:

a. Accounts receivable record keeping

b. Approving credit of customers

c. Authorizing customer returns

d. Authorizing new customers

e. Billing customers

f. Cash receipts journal posting

g. Entering orders received

h. Inventory record keeping

i. Maintaining custody of cash

j. Maintaining custody of inventory

k. Reconciling records to the bank statement

Required:

From the preceding list, assign all the duties to each of four employees: supervisor, employee 1, employee 2, and employee 3. No employee should have more than three tasks, no two employees should have any of the same tasks, and there should be a proper separation of duties to achieve appropriate internal control. List the four people, the duties you assign to each employee, and a description of why those assignments achieve proper separation of duties.

57. (SO 6) Refer to the Ethical Dilemma: Mail Order Case presented in Chapter 3. What term introduced in this chapter applies to the type of mail order deceit? What could the mail order company do to avoid a loss resulting from an event, assuming that it uses an e-commerce system?

58. (SO 9) Visit the financial education website created by Equade Internet Ltd. at www.e-commerceguide.com. Note the definition for channel stuffing. According to this site, what is the primary motivation for channel stuffing?

59. (SO 6) Visit the e-commerce website for Jupitermedia Corporation at www.ecommerce.guide.com and perform the following:
    a. Use the News and Trends tab to find a news article posted during the current month concerning developments in e-commerce.
    b. Use the Research tab to find statistics or trends in e-commerce. Report on your findings.
60. (SO 9) Refer to the example presented in this chapter regarding fraudulent revenue reporting perpetrated at Sunbeam Corp. Conduct an Internet search to determine what happened to the company and its CEO and CFO subsequent to the 1998 discovery of this financial fiasco.

CASES

61. ReSound Company is a regional retail chain that sells used CDs. The company has eight stores throughout the Philadelphia region. At each store, customers can bring in used CDs to sell to ReSound or to trade for used CDs already in stock. Also, customers can buy used CDs from the large selection on racks in the stores. ReSound also carries older LP records for collectors.

    When a used CD or LP record arrives at a ReSound store, it is checked for damage, labeled with a bar code, and entered into the extensive inventory. A customer buying a used CD or record takes it to the cash register, where it is scanned through a bar code reader and the customer's cash, check, or credit card payment is processed.

    ReSound has decided to establish a website and to begin selling used CDs and records on its website. The company believes there is a niche market for collectors of CDs or records that it can reach via the web.

    Required:
    a. Describe any differences in the sales processes of the online sales in comparison with in-store sales processes.
    b. Describe any data collected about customers in the in-store sales.
    c. Describe any data collected about customers in the online sales process.
    d. Describe any data you believe ReSound should collect from online sales to help improve customer service or profitability.
    e. Describe any data you believe ReSound should collect from online sales to help improve customer service or profitability.
62. At Jamison Manufacturing, the revenue processes are conducted by five employees. The five employees are the sales clerk, warehouse clerk, accountant 1, accountant 2, and the collection clerk. A description of their duties is as follows:
    a. The sales clerk receives customer orders by phone. She prepares a four-copy sales order form. She files one copy, one copy goes to the warehouse clerk, one copy goes to accountant 1, and one copy is mailed to the customer.
    b. After0 receiving a sales order, the warehouse clerk prepares a packing slip, takes the proper items from the warehouse, and ships them with the packing slip enclosed. The sales order is stamped with the ship date, and the shipping log is updated. The sales order is filed by customer number.

c. After receiving the sales order from the sales clerk, accountant 1 reviews the customer records and either approves or disapproves customer credit. If he approves the customer's credit, he stamps the sales order "approved" and forwards it to accountant 2. Accountant 1 prepares a three-copy invoice. One copy is mailed to the customer, one copy is forwarded to accountant 2, and one copy goes to the collection clerk.

d. Accountant 2 matches the approved sales order to the invoice and files these by customer number.

e. After receiving a copy of the invoice, the collection clerk posts the sale to the sales journal and the accounts receivable subsidiary ledger. Daily totals from the sales journal are sent to accountant 1, and she posts these sales summaries to the general ledger.

f. A mail clerk forwards customer checks to the collection clerk. The collection clerk stamps the check "For Deposit Only" and records it in the accounts receivable subsidiary ledger. The check is also recorded in the cash receipts journal by the collection clerk. The collection clerk deposits checks in the bank account weekly. A weekly summary of cash receipts is forwarded to accountant 2, and she records these summaries in the general ledger.

Required:

a. Draw two process maps to reflect the sales processes and collection processes at Jamison. The student website has a document flowchart in an Excel file for your reference.

b. Describe any weaknesses in these processes or internal controls. As you identify weaknesses, also describe your suggested improvement.

c. Draw two new process maps that include your suggested improvements. One process map should depict the sales processes, and the second process map should depict the cash collection processes.

63. Cluxton, Inc. has five departments that handle all sales, billing, and collection processes. The five departments are sales, billing, accounts receivable, warehouse, and general ledger. These processes occur as follows:

a. A customer mails a purchase order to Cluxton, and it is forwarded to the sales department.

b. A sales clerk in the sales department prepares a four-copy sales order. Two copies are forwarded to billing, one copy to the warehouse, and one copy to general ledger. The sales clerk posts the sale to the sales journal.

c. Upon receiving the sales order, the warehouse picks goods from the warehouse, updates the inventory subsidiary ledger, and ships the goods to customers. The copy of the sales order is given to the common carrier to accompany the shipment.

d. Upon receiving the sales order, the billing department looks up prices in the price list and adds these prices to the sales order. One copy is sent to the customer as the invoice. The second copy is forwarded to accounts receivable.

e. Upon receiving the sales order from billing, the accounts receivable temporarily stores the sales order until the customer mails a check and remittance advice to accounts receivable. The accounts receivable department matches the check to an open sales order, posts to the accounts receivable subsidiary ledger and the cash receipts journal, and deposits checks in the bank daily.

f. Upon receiving the sales order from the sales department, the general journal and general ledger are updated.

Required:

a. Draw two process maps to reflect the business processes at Cluxton. One process map should depict the sales processes, and the second process map should depict the cash collection processes.

b. Describe any weaknesses in these processes or internal controls. As you identify weaknesses, also describe your suggested improvement.

c. Draw two new process maps that include your suggested improvements. One process map should depict the sales processes, and the second process map should depict the cash collection processes.

64. Art's Artist World is a retailer of arts and craft supplies in the suburban Chicago area. It operates a single retail store and also has extensive catalog sales on account to area schools, churches, and other community organizations. Retail customers pay for supplies with cash, check, or credit card at the time of the sale. Occasionally, a credit customer may come into the store and purchase supplies on account. In such cases, the sales clerk is required to have the sale approved by the manager. The manager will authorize the sale if he or she recognizes the customer. The sales clerk must complete a charge slip for each sale on account.

At the end of each shift, the sales clerk prepares a summary of cash collections. This report is forwarded to the accounting department. The charge slips are forwarded to the accounts receivable department at this time.

The supervisor in the accounts receivable department verifies the information on the charge slip. Prices are matched with an approved price list. If errors are found, they are manually noted on the charge slip. A sales invoice is then prepared by the accounts receivable supervisor. The accounts receivable clerk mails the invoice to the customer.

The accounts receivable supervisor enters invoices in the computer system each afternoon. At this point, the accounts receivable subsidiary ledger is created and details of the sale are forwarded to the accounting department. At month's end, the accounts receivable supervisor prints a monthly report of the accounts receivable subsidiary ledger and list of past-due accounts. These reports are filed and referred to in cases of customer complaints or payment problems.

A cashier supervises the sales clerks and performs the basic cash collection functions. The cashier opens the mail each day and stamps the check "For Deposit Only," with the company's endorsement and bank account number. Checks are compared with any supporting remittance advice received with the check, and a daily listing of mail collections is prepared. Two daily deposits are prepared: one for the mail collections and another for cash register collections. A duplicate copy of all deposit slips is maintained by the cashier for use in the preparation of the monthly bank reconciliation.

In the accounting department, a staff accountant receives documentation of cash collections from sales clerks and the cashier. The staff accountant uses the information to prepare the journal entry for posting to the general ledger. When all of the collections have been entered, the remittance information is transmitted electronically to the accounts receivable supervisor for purposes of updating the accounts receivable subsidiary ledger for the day's collections.

Monthly account statements are prepared by the staff accountant and mailed to all customers. If a customer's account remains unpaid for six months, the staff accountant will notify the accounts receivable supervisor to write off the account as uncollectible. At this time, the credit manager is also notified of the account status so that additional credit will not be granted to this customer.

Required:

From the facts of this scenario, describe the internal control risks associated with Art's internal controls over the revenues and cash collection processes. Prepare a business memo, addressed to Art Dusing, the company's owner/operator, describing your recommendations for correcting each of these problems.

65. Jeyco, Ltd. is in the process of updating its revenues and receivables systems with the implementation of new accounting software. Bill Rumya and Associates is an independent information technology consultant who is assisting Jeyco with the project. Bill has developed the following checklist containing internal control points that the company should consider in this new implementation:

- Is the sales department separate from the credit office and the IT department?
- Are all collections from customers received in the form of checks?
- Is it appropriate to program the system for general authorization of certain sales, within given limits?
- Are product quantities monitored regularly?
- Will all data entry clerks and accounting personnel have their own PCs with log-in IDs and password protection?
- Will different system access levels for different users be incorporated?
- Will customer orders be received via the Internet?
- Has the company identified an off-site alternative computer processing location?
- Does the project budget include line items for an upgraded, uninterrupted power source and firewall?
- Will the system be thoroughly tested prior to implementation?
- Will appropriate file backup procedures be established?
- Will business continuity plans be prepared?
- Will an off-site data storage exist?
- Will intrusion detection systems be incorporated?

Required:

Describe the control purpose of each of the points presented.

66. Springtown Pediatric Association is a partnership of six pediatrician owners, two nurse practitioners, ten nurses, three accounting clerks, two receptionists, and an office manager. The office manager and all of the accounting clerks have their own PCs, and the receptionists share a PC.

These PCs are connected through a local area network. They are password protected, and the managing partner keeps a record of all passwords. The practice uses a standard medical-services software package that cannot be modified. Following is a description of the revenues and cash collections processes used in this medical practice:

Most patients receive medical attention after insurance coverage has been verified by the office manager. Upon entering the medical office, the patient presents proof of insurance to a receptionist. The insurance documentation is photocopied and immediately forwarded to the office manager for verification (while the patient is in the waiting room). In some situations, the office manager may extend credit on the basis of special circumstances. Approximately 20% of the patients pay for services with cash or check at the time of the appointment.

The attending physician must prepare a prenumbered service report at the time services are rendered to patients. Completed service reports are immediately forwarded to the first accounting clerk, who updates the report with pricing information. One copy of this report is given to the patient, and the other copy is retained by the second accounting clerk. Depending upon the patient's form of payment, the second accounting clerk will perform one of the following for each service report:

- File an insurance claim and record the related insurance company receivable for any reports that are signed by the office manager as a verification of the patient's insurance coverage.
- Record a patient receivable for any reports that are designated by the office manager as approved credit.
- Receive the cash or check from the patient and record the related cash collection in a cash receipts listing.

The second accounting clerk prepares a daily summary of patient revenues.

The first accounting clerk opens the mail each day and handles insurance company correspondences. When collections are received in the mail from insurance companies and patients, they are forwarded to the second accounting clerk for deposit. The second clerk stamps each check "For Deposit Only" and prepares a daily cash receipts listing (which also includes collections from patients who received services that day). One copy of this list is retained, and a copy is sent to the third accounting clerk. The third clerk prepares the daily bank deposit slip and retains a copy in a chronological file. This clerk also handles patient correspondences and scheduling and maintains a list of patients whose insurance coverage has been approved by the office manager.

When patient accounts are not collected within 60 days, the second clerk notifies the office manager, who analyzes the reasons for all instance of nonpayment. When the insurance company rejects the claim, the office manager reclassifies the receivable from an insurance account to a patient account. The second clerk adjusts the insurance company and patient account files for reclassifications and write-offs. This clerk maintains a listing of patients with uncollectible balances and provides an updated copy each week to the third clerk, who will not allow patients with this status to schedule new appointments.

Springtown Pediatrics Association uses a local CPA firm to perform various accounting functions. On a monthly basis, the firm posts the daily revenues summaries to the general ledger and prepares a trial balance and monthly financial statements. In addition, this firm accounts for the numerical sequence of service reports, files tax returns and payroll forms, and performs the monthly bank reconciliations. The CPA firm reports directly to the managing partner of the practice.

Required:

Evaluate the information in each of the following situations as being either an internal control (1) strength, (2) weakness, or (3) not a strength or weakness.

1. Springtown Pediatrics Association's office manager approves the extension of credit to patients and also authorizes write-offs of uncollectible accounts.
2. Springtown Pediatrics Association's office manager may extend credit based on special circumstances rather than using a formal credit search and established credit limits.
3. Springtown Pediatrics Association extends credit rather than requiring cash or insurance in all cases.
4. The computer software package cannot be modified by the employees of the practice.
5. None of the employees who generate revenues or record revenues are able to write checks.
6. Computer passwords are known only by the individual employees and the managing partner, who has no record-keeping responsibilities.
7. Individual pediatricians document the services they perform on prenumbered reports that are used for both recording revenues and patient receipts.
8. Insurance coverage is verified by the office manager before medical services are rendered.
9. The bank reconciliation is prepared by an independent CPA firm.
10. The sequence of prenumbered service reports is accounted for on a monthly basis by an independent CPA firm.
11. The second accounting clerk receives cash and checks and prepares the daily deposit.
12. The second accounting clerk maintains the accounts receivable records and can add or delete receivables information on the PC.
13. The second clerk receives the cash and checks and also records cash receipts.
14. Springtown Pediatrics Association is involved only in medical services and does not have diversified business operations.

(Excerpt from Adapted CPA Simulation Problem)

67. Slodobon, Inc., processes its sales and cash receipts documents in the following manner:

CASH RECEIPTS

Each morning a mail clerk in the sales department opens the mail containing checks and remittance advices, which are then forwarded to the sales department supervisor, who reviews each check and forwards the checks and remittance advices to the accounting department supervisor. The accounting department supervisor, who also functions as the credit manager, reviews all checks for payments of past-due accounts and then forwards the checks and remittance advices to the accounts receivable clerk, who arranges the advices in alphabetical order. The remittance advices are posted directly to the accounts receivable ledger. The checks are totaled, and the total is posted to the cash receipts journal. The remittance advices are filed chronologically.

After receiving the cash from the preceding day's cash sales, the accounts receivable clerk prepares a three-copy daily deposit slip. The third copy of the deposit slip is filed by date, and the second copy and the original accompany the bank deposit.

SALES

Sales clerks prepare a three-copy sales invoice for each sale. The original and the second copy are presented to the cashier, while the third copy is retained by the sales clerk in the sales book. When the sale is paid for with cash, the customer pays the sales clerk, who presents the money to the cashier with the invoice copies.

A credit sale is authorized by the cashier using an approved credit list after the sales clerk prepares the three-copy invoice. After receiving the cash or approving the invoice, the cashier validates the original copy of the sales invoice and gives it to the customer. At the end of each day the cashier recaps the sales and cash received and forwards the cash and the second copy of all sales invoices to the accounts receivable clerk. The accounts receivable clerk balances the cash received with cash sales invoices and prepares a daily sales summary. The credit sales invoices are posted to the accounts receivable ledger, and then all invoices are sent to the inventory control clerk in the sales department for posting to the inventory control catalog. After posting, the inventory control clerk files all invoices numerically. The accounts receivable clerk posts the daily sales summary to the cash receipts journal and sales journal and files the sales summaries by date.

BANK DEPOSITS

The bank validates the deposit slip and returns the second copy to the accounting department, where the accounts receivable clerk files it by date. Monthly bank statements are reconciled promptly by the accounting department supervisor and filed by date.

Required:

a. Prepare a process map of these processes.

b. Identify internal control weaknesses in these processes.

(Adapted CPA problem)

CONTINUING CASE: SPATELLI'S PIZZERIA

Reread the Spatelli's Pizzeria case in Chapter 1. Consider the following issues related to the revenues processes at Spatelli's:

As Peter Greyton reflects on his meeting with Jim Saxton and Elaine Black, he considers where the company has been and where it is heading, and ponders the current issues regarding Spatelli's accounting information systems and its ability to take and record sales. He is concerned about the limitations of the current accounting information system. Are internal controls strong enough? Would a new, integrated IT system yield improvements? As he contemplates the integration of the POS systems at the restaurant locations with the GL software at the home office, he wonders about the requirements for developing and implementing such a system, and how to best utilize the system to support Spatelli's plans for growth. Peter realizes that his ability to address these issues will be critical not only to the success of the company, but also to his career.

Required:

a. Briefly describe the differences in Spatelli's three order-entry systems (in-store, telephone, and Internet). For each method, specifically identify the employees needed and describe the tasks performed by these employees.

b. Draw three process maps of the ordering and sales processes at Spatelli's. One process map should depict in-store sales, one map should depict phone orders, and one should depict online orders.

c. From the descriptions of Spatelli's various revenue and collection processes, answer the following questions regarding internal controls:

   a. Separately identify at least one internal control strength and/or weakness for each of the three ordering systems (in-store, telephone, and Internet).

   b. What is the control purpose of the drop-down boxes in the Internet ordering system?

SOLUTIONS TO CONCEPT CHECK

1. (SO 2) Within the sales processes, a signed approval of a sales order indicates all except **a. the date of delivery.** When a designated employee approves a sales order, it is an indication that the sale is authorized in accordance with company policies. This means that the customer is approved, the customer's credit status has been verified to indicate that the credit limit is not exceeded, and the sales price is in accordance with established pricing. The date of delivery is typically beyond the control of the authorizing person, as it is dependent upon the amount of inventory in stock.

2. (SO 2) An example of independent verification in the sales process is **c. proof of recorded dates, quantities, and prices on an invoice.** This is the only choice that reflects an independent verification procedure. In option a., preparation of packing lists on prenumbered forms is an example of a control over documents and records; in option b., initialing the sales order is an indication of authorization; and in option d., physical controls in record storage areas is a security measure.

3. (CPA Adapted) (SO 2) The purpose of tracing shipping documents to prenumbered sales invoices would be to provide evidence that **a. shipments to customers were properly invoiced.** The forward direction of this testing verifies that the billing process was completed for this shipping transaction. Response b. is incorrect because an entire sequence of such documents would need to be verified in order to determine that there were no omissions. Response c. is incorrect because its direction of the testing is opposite;

i.e., the proper starting point would be the invoice for this determination (as in question 4.). Response d. is not relevant because it is concerned with the completeness of the accounting records.

4. (CIA Adapted) (SO 2) The purpose of tracing sales invoices to shipping documents would be to provide evidence that **c. goods billed to customers were shipped.** The backward direction of this testing serves the purpose of verifying the existence of the transaction. Response a. is incorrect because its direction of the testing is opposite; i.e., the proper starting point would be the shipping document for this determination (as in question 3.). Response b. is incorrect because a review of all matched invoices and shipping documents would be needed to determine whether any duplicates had occurred. Response d. is not relevant, because it is concerned with the completeness of the accounting records.

5. (CPA Adapted) (SO 2) To ensure that all credit sales transactions of an entity are recorded, the most effective control would be that **d. the supervisor of the billing department matches prenumbered shipping documents with entries recorded in the sales journal.** This test addresses the completeness of accounting records. Response a. is incorrect because agreement of the records does not necessarily ensure that there are no omissions. Responses b. and c. are incorrect because they address the accuracy and authorization of the account balances, respectively, rather than completeness.

6. (CPA Adapted) (SO 3) Under a system of sound internal controls, if a company sold defective goods, the return of those goods from the customer should be accepted by the **a. receiving clerk.** Since the receiving clerk is independent of all related record-keeping functions, this is the correct response. Each of the other responses involves record-keeping functions that would violate internal controls regarding adequate segregation of duties.

7. (SO 3) The source document that initiates the recording of the return and the adjustment to the customer's credit status is the **c. credit memorandum.** Option a., a pick list, provides detail of the items to be pulled from inventory to fulfill a customer's order; option b., a sales journal, is the record of sales transactions; and in option d., a sales invoice, provides details of a sale and requests payment from the customer.

8. (SO 4) The choice which is not a document that is part of the cash collection process is a **d. Packing slip.** This is part of the sales process. Each of the other options relates to a document that is part of the cash collection process.

9. (SO 4) **c. The employee who opens mail containing checks prepares a list of checks received** is the statement that would represent proper segregation of duties. This involves preparation of the daily cash receipts listing, which is typically performed by the person who opens the mail. Each of the other options describes a scenario lacking in proper controls regarding segregation of duties.

10. (CPA Adapted) (SO 4) Immediately upon receiving checks from customers in the mail, a responsible employee working in an environment of adequate internal control should prepare a listing of receipts and forward it to the company's cashier. A copy of this cash receipts listing should also be sent

to the company's **a. treasurer for comparison with the monthly bank statement.** Response b. is incorrect because internal auditors are not part of a company's routine processing. Response c. is incorrect because the accounts receivable subsidiary ledger should not be updated before a cash receipts journal is prepared and the receipt has been matched with an outstanding invoice. Response d. is incorrect because the bank would not be involved in reconciliation of the company's cash transactions.

11. (CIA Adapted) (SO 4) If a company does not prepare an aging of accounts receivable, the account most likely to be misstated is the **d. allowance for uncollectible accounts.** An accounts receivable aging report is used to analyze customer balances according to the respective lengths of time that have elapsed since payment was due. This helps determine the collectibility of customer accounts, which is the foundation of the allowance for uncollectible accounts.
12. (SO 6) When a company sells items over the Internet, it is usually called e-commerce. There are many IT risks related to Internet sales. The risk of invalid data entered by a customer would be a **b. processing integrity risk.** Option a., availability risk, relates to service denial due to system failures or attacks; options c. and d., security risk and confidentiality risk, relate to unauthorized access, network break-ins, and repudiation of sales.
13. (SO 6) The risk of hardware and software failures that prevent website sales would be an **a. availability risk.** Option b., processing integrity risk, relates to invalid, incomplete, or erroneous data; options c. and d., security risk and confidentiality risk, relate to unauthorized access, network break-ins, and repudiation of sales.
14. (SO 7) The use of EDI to conduct sales electronically has risks and benefits. **d. Shorter inventory cycle time** is a benefit of EDI, rather than a risk. This makes it possible for the company to reduce its inventory levels and replenish those inventory levels more quickly, as a result of the time savings realized from avoiding keying, keying errors, and mail delays. Option a., incomplete audit trail, is an example of a processing integrity risk associated with EDI; options b. and c., repudiation and unauthorized access, relate to security and confidentiality risks associated with EDI.
15. (SO 8) An IT system that uses touch screens, bar coded products, and credit card authorization during the sale is called a **c. point of sale system.** Option a., EDI, involves inter-company exchanges of standard business documents; option b., e-commerce, uses electronic processing for Internet-based sales transactions; and d., e-payables, uses electronic processing of payments.
16. (SO 9) **d. Promotional price discounts** are not a method of unethically inflating sales revenue unless the discounts are not part of the company's customary promotions or are used with excessive coercion. Each of the other options is unethical because it involves the artificial inflation of revenue.

CHAPTER 9

Expenditures Processes and Controls–Purchases

STUDY OBJECTIVES

This chapter will help you gain an understanding of the following concepts:

1. An introduction to expenditures processes
2. Purchasing processes and the related risks and controls
3. Purchase return processes and the related risks and controls
4. Cash disbursement processes and the related risks and controls
5. An overview of IT systems of expenditure and cash disbursement processes that enhance the efficiency of expenditures processes
6. Computer-based matching of purchasing documents and the related risks and controls
7. Evaluated receipt settlement systems and the related risks and controls
8. E-business and electronic data interchange (EDI) systems and the related risks and controls
9. E-payables systems
10. Procurement cards
11. Ethical issues related to expenditures processes
12. Corporate governance in expenditures processes

THE REAL WORLD

Christine Balderas/iStockphoto

Organizations not only pay the purchase price of inventory and supplies that they acquire, but they also pay a cost to conduct purchases and to write checks to pay for purchases. This cost is the wages and salaries that organizations pay to employees involved in purchasing and payment activities. Many organizations continuously look for ways to reduce this cost by improving the efficiency of the purchasing and payment processes. General Electric Co. (GE) implemented a web-based electronic invoice presentment (EIP) system in which its small and midsize vendors would send invoices electronically via the web. This process allowed GE to avoid the time and cost of receiving and entering paper invoices into its IT system. GE agreed to pay within 15 days in return for a 1.5% discount for invoices submitted under the EIP system. On the other hand, any paper invoices would be paid in 60 days. Within six months of implementing the new system, "more than 15,000 of GE's vendors, who represented 45% of the company's vendors, signed up for electronic presentment."[1] This change resulted in a 12% reduction in the cost of payables processing.

This chapter describes the processes of purchasing, receiving, and paying for inventories and supplies.

INTRODUCTION TO EXPENDITURES PROCESSES (STUDY OBJECTIVE 1)

In a large company, there may be thousands of purchasing transactions occurring each day. The company must have systems and processes in place to capture, record, summarize, and report these transactions. The processes are the policies and procedures that employees follow in completing the purchase of goods or materials, capturing vendor data and purchase quantities, and routing the resulting purchasing documents to the proper departments within the company. Exhibit 9-1 highlights the expenditures processes section of the overall accounting system.

When a purchase occurs, the information resulting from that purchase must flow into the purchase recording systems, the accounts payable and cash disbursement systems, and the inventory tracking systems. In IT accounting systems, these recording and processing systems are called **transaction processing systems (TPS)**. Thus, there is a set of processes within the company to conduct purchases and route purchasing information, and there is a TPS within the IT system to record, summarize, and report these purchasing transactions.

Every company acquires materials or goods and must therefore have expenditures. It is a fundamental process of all businesses as they buy the resources needed to conduct operations, record the resulting liability, and eventually pay cash to the vendor. This process is somewhat similar to the revenue processes discussed in Chapter 8, except that goods and cash flow in opposite directions. As shown in Exhibit 9-2, goods flow away from the

[1]Suzanne Hurt, "Why Automate Payables and Receivables?" *Strategic Finance*, April 2003, p. 2.

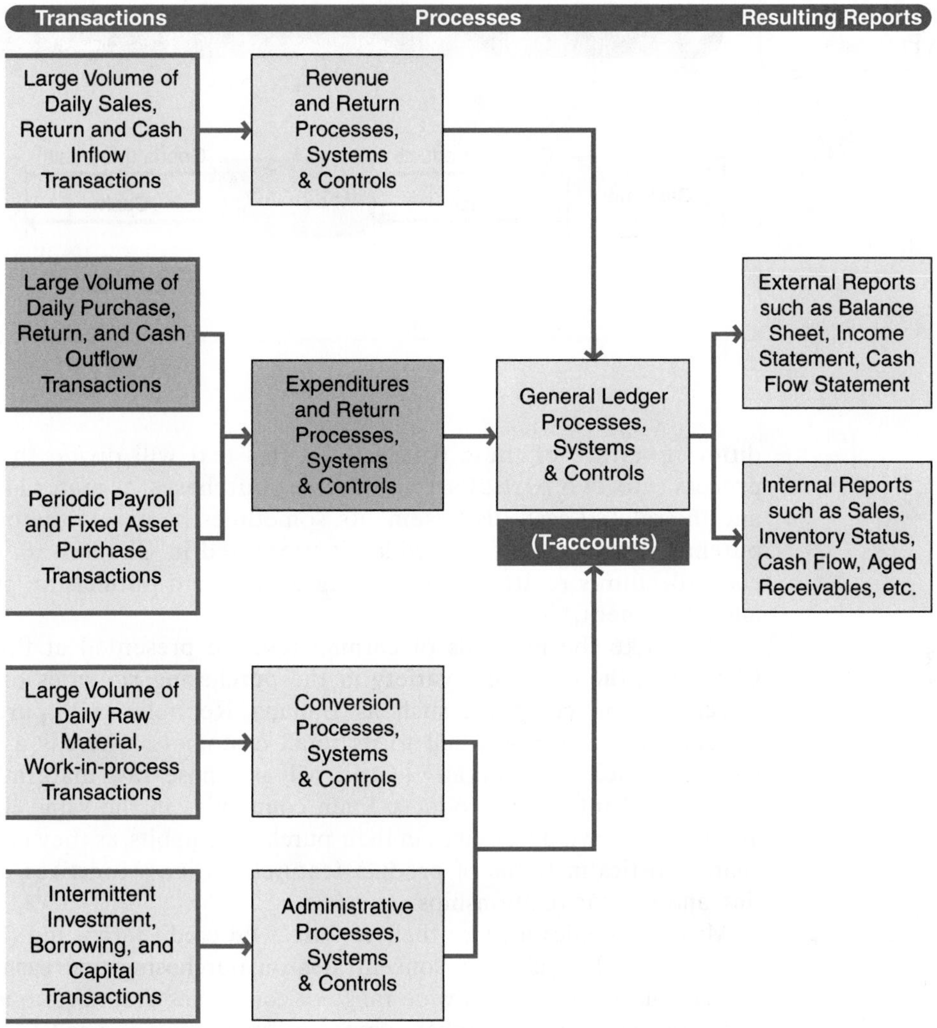

Exhibit 9-1
Expenditures Processes within the Overall System

company in the revenue process, whereas they flow into the company in the expenditures process. Likewise, cash is collected by the company in the revenue process, whereas it is paid out in the expenditures process. Accordingly, the company is a **vendor** from the customer's perspective, and the company is a customer from the vendor's perspective. Accountants must always be mindful of the processing flow of the transaction in order to properly recognize it.

There are many different kinds of resources that may be needed to run a business, such as materials, supplies, equipment, facilities, and a skilled workforce, to name a few readily observable examples. Because of the large volume of expenditures transactions that most companies process and the

Exhibit 9-2
Comparison of the Revenue and Expenditures Processes

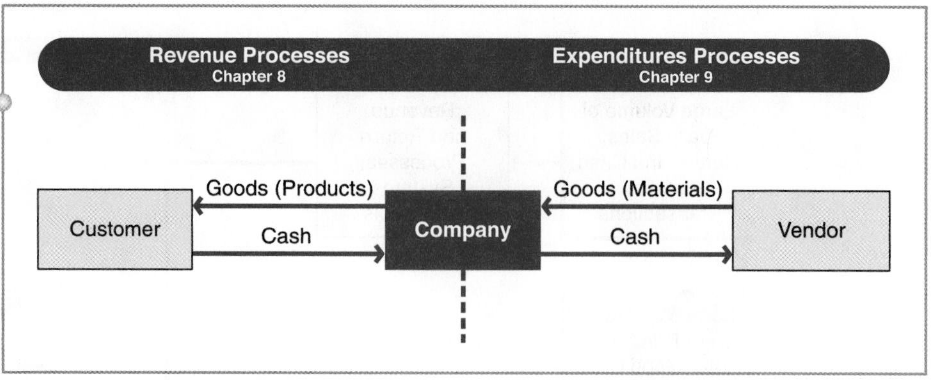

differing nature of these transactions, this text will divide the expenditures process into two parts. Part 1 addresses purchases of materials and supplies and the related cash disbursements, sometimes known as the procurement or purchasing process. Part 2, which is presented in Chapter 10, examines special procedures related to processing payroll and purchasing property, plant, and equipment.

Much like the methods of earning revenue presented at the beginning of Chapter 8, there is great variety in the purchasing activities of businesses. A merchandising company, such as Banana Republic, will purchase finished merchandise that it will sell to its retail customers, whereas a manufacturing company, such as General Electric, will purchase raw materials that will be transformed into new products. Even companies in the same line of business are likely to have differences in their purchasing habits, as they may have unique characteristics in terms of product features, business practices, storage capacities, and vendor relationships.

Most companies acquire their resources on credit terms and pay for them at a later date. This chapter concentrates on purchasing and cash disbursement transactions common to a wide range of companies that acquire an inventory of goods or materials from other companies on account and sell goods or products to other companies. Not every company will carry out its expenditures processes exactly as depicted here, but this chapter provides a practical presentation of a typical approach.

The most common expenditures processes include the following:

- Prepare a purchase requisition and/or purchase order for goods or services needed.
- Notify the vendor (supplier) of goods or services needed.
- Receive goods or services, often via common carrier. A **common carrier** is a trucking, rail, or air freight company.
- Record the payable.
- Pay the resulting invoice.
- Update the records affected, such as accounts payable, cash, inventory, and expenses.

The first part of this chapter describes a typical purchasing system, which includes three primary categories of processes: purchasing processes, purchase return processes, and cash disbursement processes (or payments). In addition, controls and risks related to these processes are presented. For each category, the goal of the system's internal controls is to reduce the following types of business risks:

1. Invalid (fictitious or duplicate) transactions may have been recorded.
2. Transactions may have been recorded in the wrong amounts.
3. Actual transactions may have been omitted from the accounting records.
4. Transactions may have been recorded to the wrong vendor or wrong account number.
5. Transactions may not have been recorded in a timely manner.
6. Transactions may have been accumulated or transferred to the accounting records incorrectly.

This chapter also examines computer-based purchasing and cash disbursement systems. Finally, some prevalent business ethics and corporate governance topics related to the expenditures processes are presented in the latter part of the chapter.

PURCHASING PROCESSES (STUDY OBJECTIVE 2)

The business process map in Exhibit 9-3 illustrates the flow of activities in a typical purchasing system. Exhibit 9-4 is a document flowchart depicting the related records used in a purchasing system. Exhibit 9-5 is a data flow diagram of the purchasing processes. This process begins when an employee of the company recognizes the need to make a purchase, typically as a result of observing low inventory levels or unfilled sales orders. Purchasing needs may change daily with the occurrence of shipping and receiving transactions, production transfers, and new sales orders. It may be that a warehouse attendant notices a particularly low stock level, an accountant detects potential shortages in documented inventory quantities, an operations manager becomes aware of additional quantities that will be needed to produce upcoming sales orders, or an IT system determines an order is necessary. Regardless of the manner in which the purchase is initiated, the appropriate **purchase requisition** form should be prepared to document the need and request that the specific items and quantities be purchased. A purchase requisition must then be authorized by a designated member of management. The purchase requisition triggers the next steps in the purchase process.

Once a purchase requisition has been approved, it will be forwarded to the purchasing department within the company, where a purchase order form is prepared. A **purchase order (PO)** is a document issued to a seller by a buyer that indicates the details—products, quantities, and agreed-upon prices—for products or services that the seller will provide to the buyer.

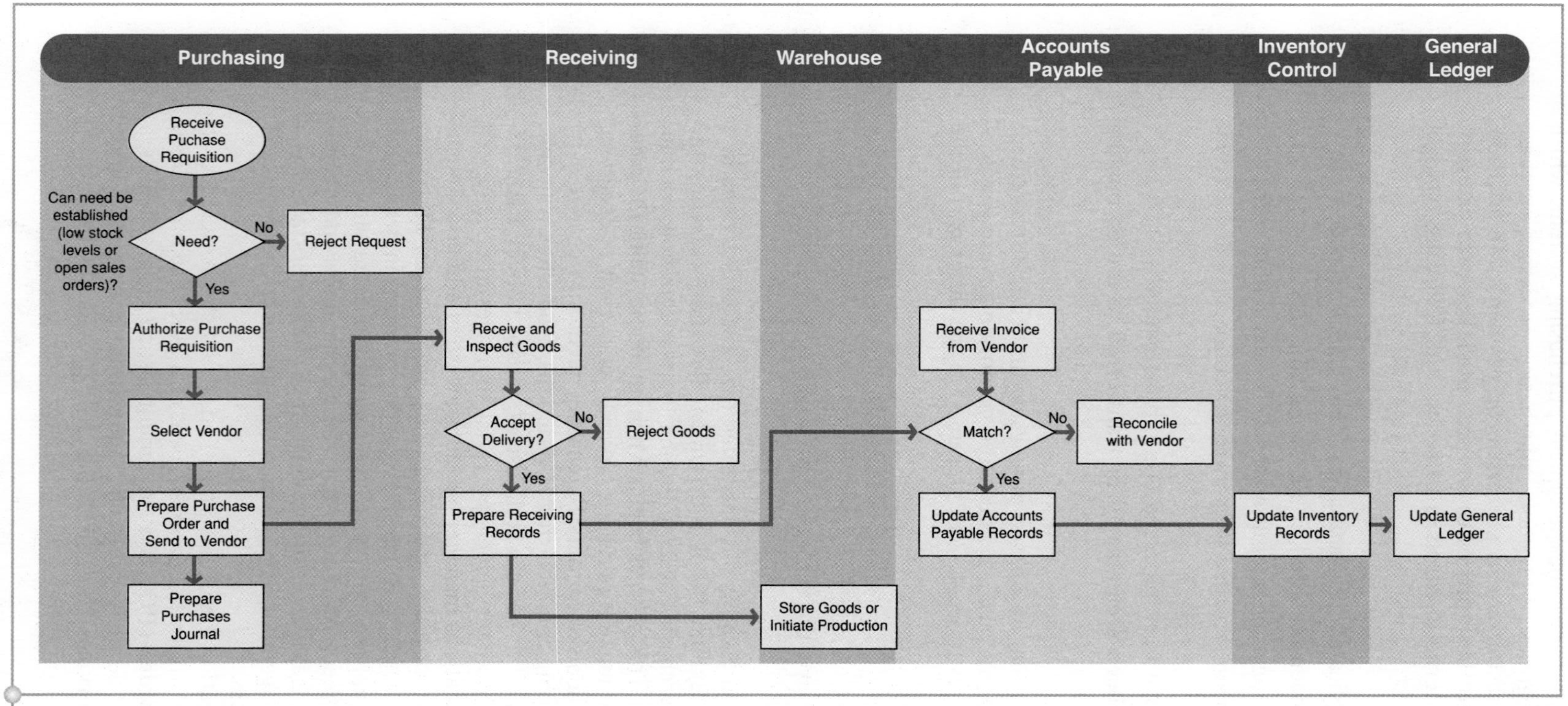

Exhibit 9-3
Purchasing Process Map

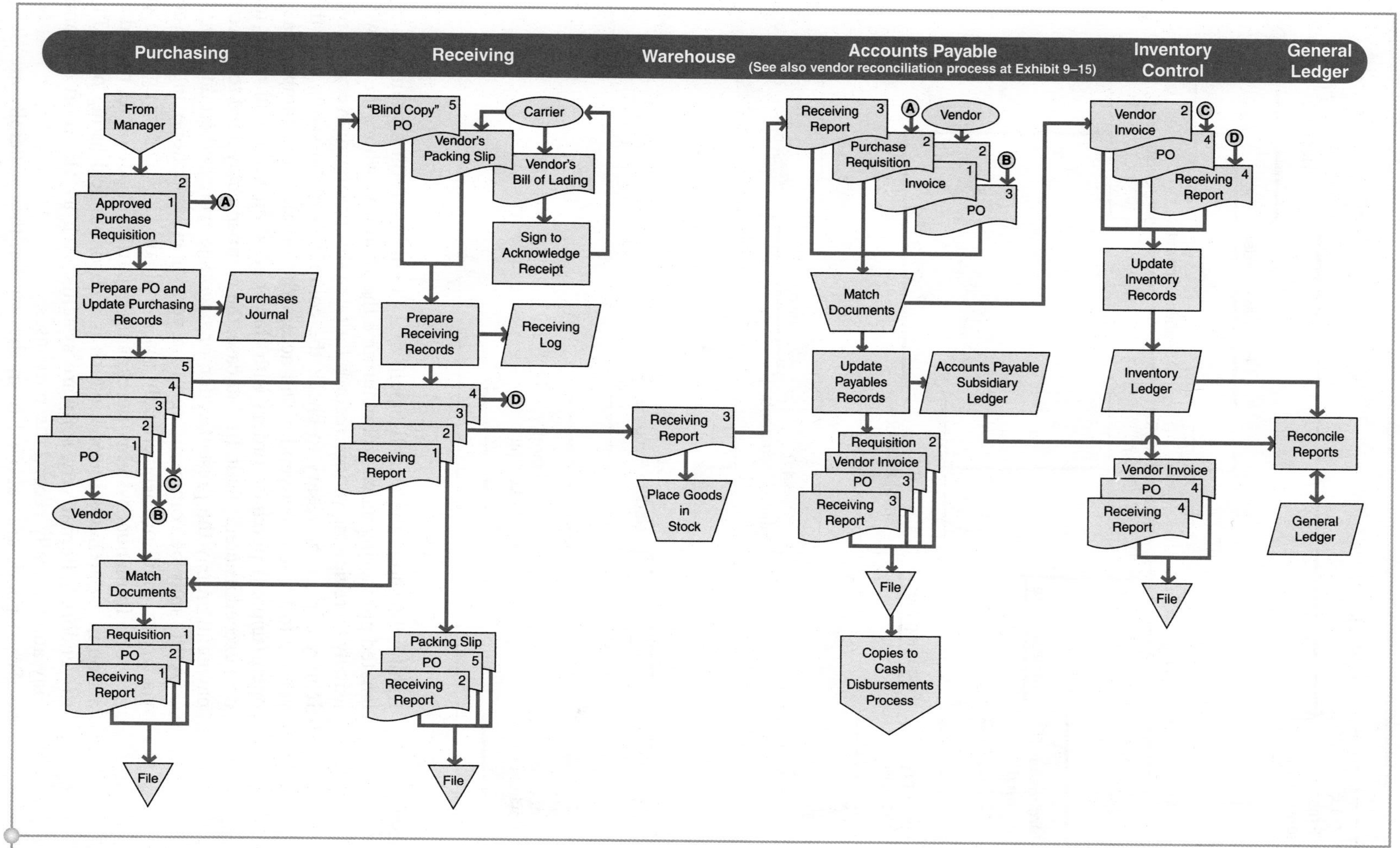

Exhibit 9-4
Document Flowchart of the Purchasing Processes

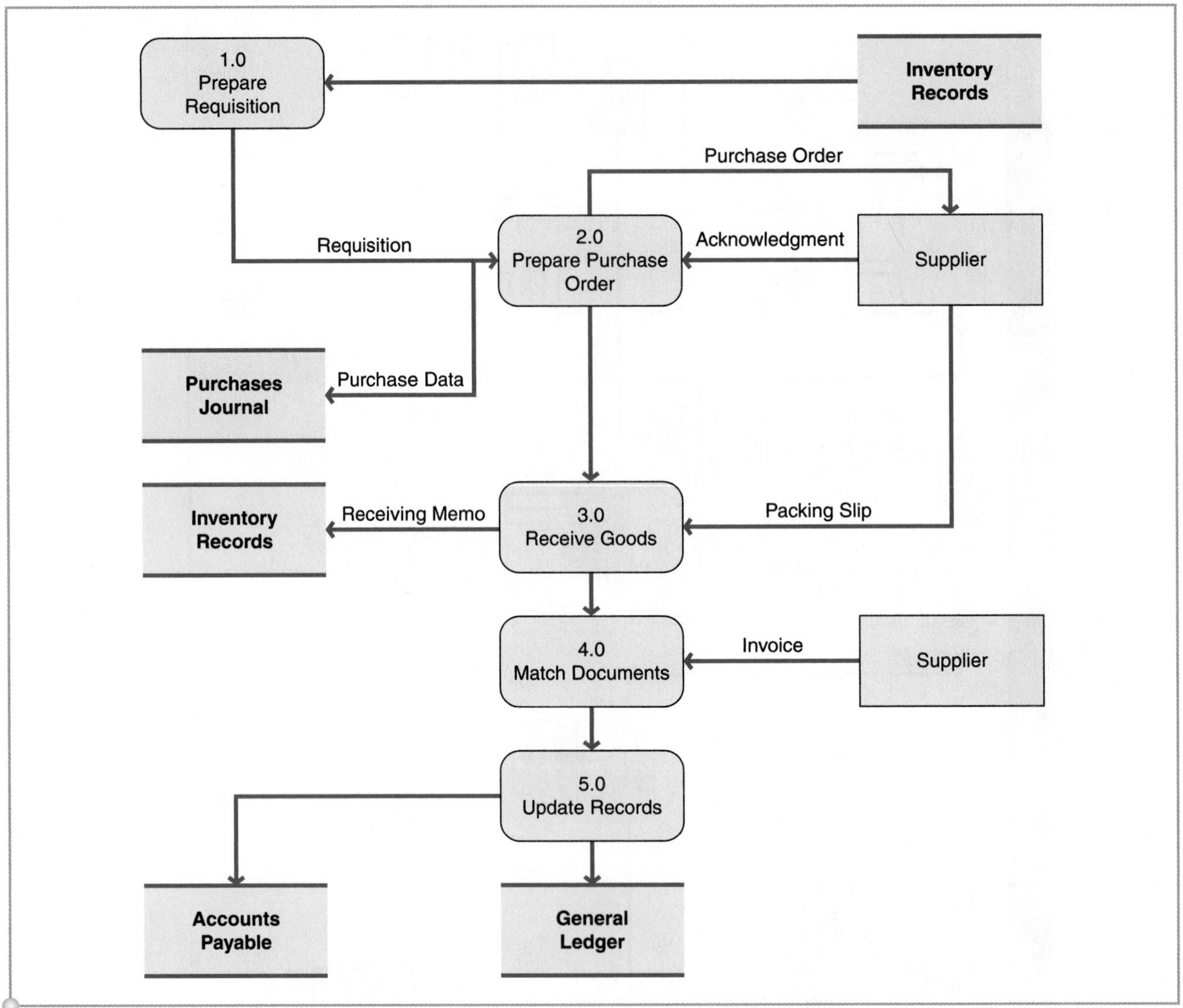

Exhibit 9-5
Purchasing Processes Data Flow Diagram

Exhibit 9-6 shows the establishment of a PO in Microsoft Dynamics GP®. A designated purchasing agent will determine the vendor to whom the PO will be sent, usually by reviewing vendor records for favorable pricing, delivery, or credit terms. It may also be necessary to check the company's credit status with the chosen vendor to be sure the vendor will accept the order. If the company already has open (unpaid) purchase orders with this vendor, an additional order may cause it to exceed its credit limit. In that case, the company may need to make a prompt payment, prepay the present order, or negotiate increased credit terms.

A PO may be communicated to a vendor via telephone, in hard-copy form via fax or mail, or electronically via e-mail or directly through the computer network. In manual systems, purchasing department personnel record the transaction in a **purchases journal,** which is a chronological listing of all POs issued to vendors. Alternatively, software systems, such as Microsoft Dynamics GP®, may automatically record the purchases.

When goods are received from the vendor, they generally are delivered via common carrier, such as a trucking or rail company. All goods received should be

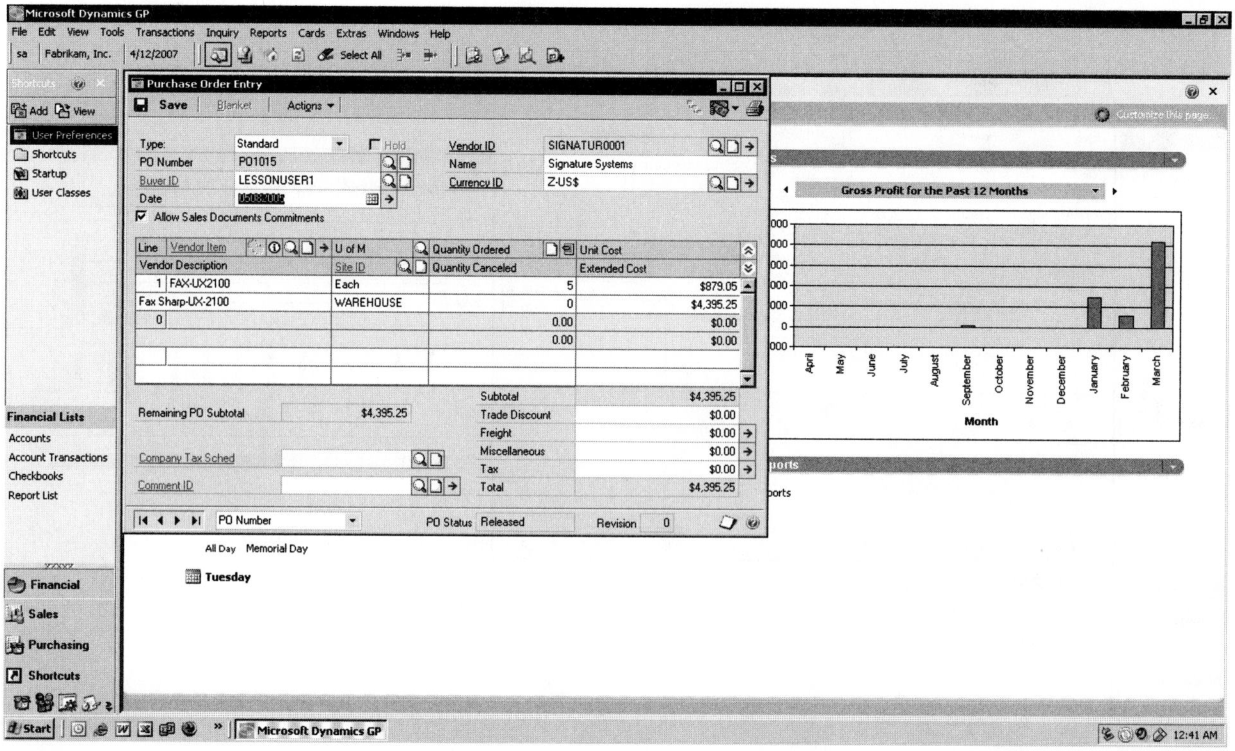

Exhibit 9-6
Establishing a Purchase Order in Microsoft Dynamics GP®

inspected by company personnel in the receiving area. The quantity should be counted, and the useable condition of the goods should be assessed to determine any damage or substitutions. The receiving clerk is responsible for counting and inspecting all items received and documenting the details of the receipt before the carrier leaves. The receiving clerk can help reduce the risk of error or fraud related to purchases by performing special procedures designed to determine the propriety of goods received. The purchasing department can prepare a "blind" copy of each PO. A **blind purchase order** includes information from the PO, but it omits data about the price and quantity of the item(s) ordered. It may also contain critical information such as quantity limits and quality specifications. With a blind PO, the receiving clerk can make sure that the receipt represents a valid PO, yet it still forces the performance of an independent check of the quantity and quality of the delivery. Even when blind copies of POs are not provided, a receiving clerk should not have access to the original POs. When receiving clerks are denied access to PO prices and quantities, it becomes nearly impossible for them to hurriedly accept a delivery without taking time to verify its accuracy.

A copy of the vendor's bill of lading typically accompanies goods received from the common carrier. A **bill of lading** provides details of the items included in the delivery, and the receiving clerk must sign that form as verification of receipt. The vendor's packing slip may also accompany the shipment. The **packing slip** is intended to show quantities and descriptions of items included in the shipment, but it does not generally include prices. A **receiving report** is then prepared by the receiving clerk, detailing the contents and condition of the receipt. A **receiving log** should also be maintained as a sequential listing of all receipts. When accounting software is used to record purchasing and receiving

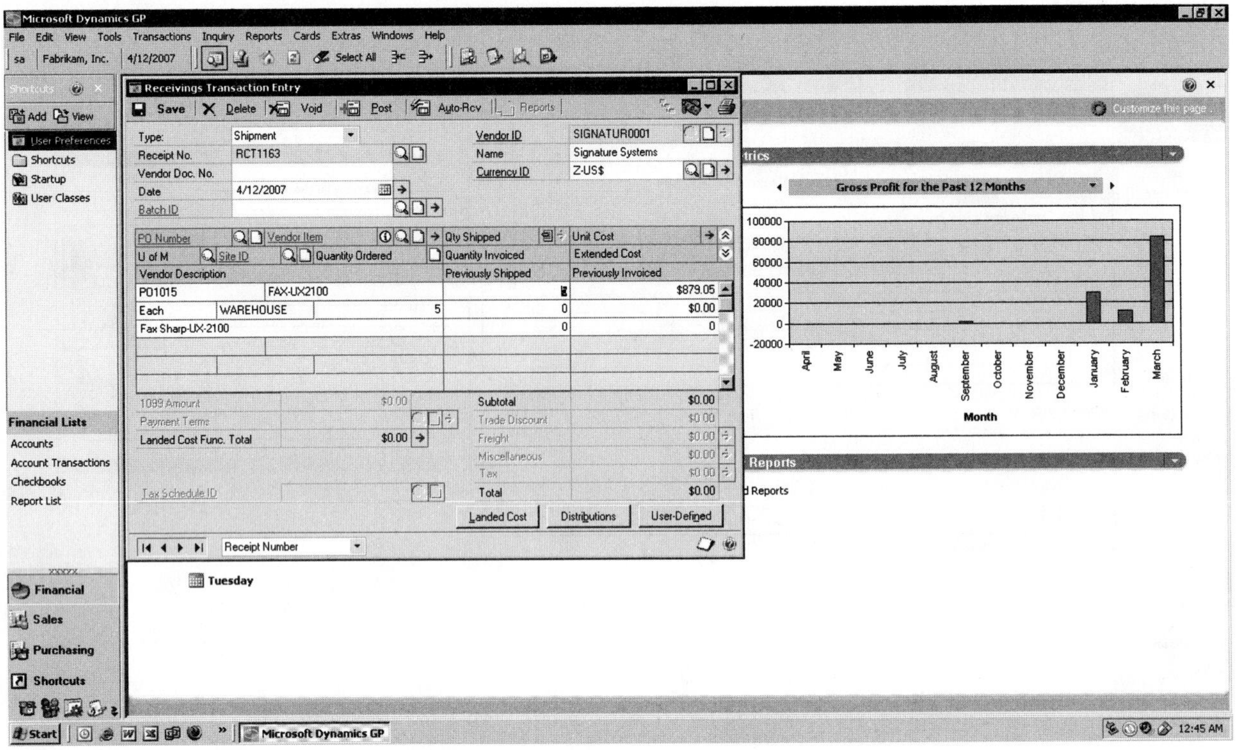

Exhibit 9-7
Entering Purchase Receipts in Microsoft Dynamics GP®

transactions, the software maintains a receiving log and updates inventory balances. Exhibit 9-7 shows the receiving screen in Microsoft Dynamics GP®.

Theoretically, as soon as a company receives goods, it is obligated to pay for those goods. In practice, however, many companies wait to record the liability until the related invoice is received from the vendor. This is typically not a problem when the vendor is prompt in sending its invoice. However, there may be a lag in timing. When a receipt of goods occurs before the end of the period, but the related invoice is delayed until after the end of the period, a problem arises related to recording the liability in the correct period. This is called a cutoff issue. A **cutoff** is the date for the end of the accounting period. The accounts payable department should establish specific procedures to avoid cutoff issues. The liability and the inventory receipt must be recorded in the same period as the physical receipt of goods. If goods have arrived, but the related invoice is still outstanding at the end of the period, the accounts payable department should determine (or estimate) the amount owed to the vendor, in order to accrue the liability and recognize the receipt of these items in the proper period.

The accounts payable department is responsible for recording the liabilities for goods received in the accounting records. Caution must be exercised to be certain that vendor invoices represent goods that were actually ordered and received. The accounts payable department maintains copies of purchase orders and receiving reports so that the documents can be compared before the accounting records are updated. This comparison helps ensure that invoices represent goods actually ordered and received. Also, the accounts payable department will ensure that the correct vendor account is immediately adjusted for each purchase transaction so that the company will know the correct amount owed to the vendor. An **accounts pa yable subsidiary ledger** includes the detail of amounts owed to each vendor. Finally, the accounts payable department maintains a file of outstanding invoices awaiting payment. This file is usually organized in alphabetical order by vendor name. A copy of the invoice is also given to the cash disbursements department, where it is filed by due date or by the discount date, such as ten days after invoicing for 2/10, n/30 terms.

Many of the goods received are likely to be inventory items. Therefore, the inventory control department is part of the purchasing process. The inventory control department maintains inventory records, which must be increased for the proper item, quantity, and dollar amount each time a purchase occurs.

To complete the purchasing process, the general ledger function is designed for posting and reconciling transactions from the respective accounts payable and inventory subsidiary ledgers.

RISKS AND CONTROLS IN THE PURCHASING PROCESS (STUDY OBJECTIVE 2, continued)

As described in previous chapters, management is responsible for implementing internal controls over each business process. Accordingly, the purchasing process needs special attention to reduce the risk of fraud or errors specific to these types of transactions. The next section identifies common procedures, organized according to the five internal control activities discussed in Chapter 3.

AUTHORIZATION OF TRANSACTIONS

Specific individuals within the company should be given authoritative responsibility for the preparation of purchase requisitions and purchase orders, including approval of the specific items to purchase, order quantities, and vendor selection. Only those designated individuals should have the opportunity to carry out these tasks. The company should establish specific procedures to ensure that POs have been properly authorized before the order is officially placed with a vendor. The authorized individual typically includes his or her signature or initials on a purchase requisition to indicate proper authorization. In an automated system, specific authorization for purchase transactions can be controlled by limiting access to the authorization function. This is a critical control in that no purchasing events should begin until the initial authorization occurs. In most organizations, the approval of a purchase requisition is the initial approval that triggers the remaining purchasing processes.

A company should have established guidelines for managing vendor relationships, including securing competitive bids for purchase requisitions, negotiating payment terms, and maintaining current price lists. These functions should be limited to designated individuals within the company.

SEGREGATION OF DUTIES

Within the purchasing process, the accounting duties related to requisitioning, ordering, purchase approval, receiving, inventory control, accounts payable, information systems, and general accounting should be segregated in order to meet the objectives of internal controls. In general, responsibilities for authorization, custody, and record-keeping functions should each be separated in order to prevent the possibility of error or fraud. The authority function includes approval of purchasing transactions and certain information systems tasks such as data entry, programming, IT operations, and security. The custody function includes inventory handling and receiving, as well as the related cash disbursement duties. The record-keeping function includes preparation of POs, as well as the general accounting reports such as the purchases journals, the accounts payable subsidiary ledger, the inventory ledger, the general ledger, and financial statements.

Ideal internal controls involve complete separation of inventory custody from inventory accounting. With respect to the purchasing process, this control is especially important in reducing instances of fraud. If, on the other hand, individuals have an opportunity to both handle inventory and access the related records, theft could occur and be concealed by altering the records. If custody and record keeping are segregated, the person having access to the goods may have an opportunity to conduct the theft, but will not have the capability to alter records.

ADEQUATE RECORDS AND DOCUMENTS

Accounting personnel should ensure that adequate supporting documentation is maintained for purchasing transactions. Files should be maintained for purchase requisitions, POs, receiving reports, invoices, etc. These files should be organized either in chronological order by due date, in numerical sequence by form number or inventory item number, or in alphabetical order by vendor name. When documentation is well organized, a company can establish the validity of its transactions and determine whether omissions have occurred. For instance, if the purchase requisition, PO, receiving report, and invoice are each retained and matched, accounting personnel can determine that each purchasing transaction is carried out properly with respect to quantity, quality, price, vendor, timing, etc. Proper documentation also establishes an audit trail and facilitates the performance of independent checks and reconciliations.

SECURITY OF ASSETS AND DOCUMENTS

Purchasing records and programs must be protected from unauthorized access through the use of electronic controls, such as passwords, and physical controls, such as locked storage cabinets. Physical controls should also be used in the company's storage warehouse and receiving area, in order to protect purchased items from theft.

INDEPENDENT CHECKS AND RECONCILIATION

Some specific internal control procedures to be performed to achieve accountability for this process are presented next. The performance of these functions by someone independent of the related authority, custody, and record-keeping functions for the purchasing process will enhance their effectiveness. For example, periodic physical inventory counts should be reconciled with the inventory ledger and general ledger control account to make sure inventory is being properly accounted for. Significant differences may indicate that purchases have been omitted or theft may have occurred. Independent reconciliation of the accounts payable subsidiary ledger to the general ledger control account also helps ensure that transactions have been properly posted.

COST–BENEFIT CONSIDERATIONS

We know from previous chapters that companies will implement internal controls only if the corresponding benefit exceeds the cost of implementation. Accordingly, the company should evaluate risks prevalent in its system before determining the mix of controls to execute. Some high-risk characteristics that might warrant the need for extensive internal controls are as follows:

1. Goods received are especially difficult to differentiate, count, or inspect.
2. High volumes of goods are often received, or the goods are of high value.
3. Inventory pricing arrangements are complex or based on estimates.
4. Frequent changes occur in purchase prices or vendors.
5. The company depends on one or very few key vendors.
6. Receiving and/or record keeping are performed at multiple locations.

When any of these circumstances exist, management should be especially mindful of related controls that could effectively prevent or detect errors or fraud that could occur.

Exhibit 9-8 summarizes examples of internal controls and the related risks that are minimized in the purchasing process. This exhibit does not include all the possible risks and controls surrounding purchasing transactions, but provides some common problems that may be encountered.

Exhibit 9-8
Purchasing Controls and Risks

Control:	Minimizes the Related Risk of:
Authorization:	
Approval of purchase transaction prior to placing an order	Invalid vendors, over-extended credit limits, unapproved pricing or quantities
Segregation:	
Separation of authorization of purchases and new vendors from custody of inventory in the receiving area	Fictitious purchases
Separation of inventory custody from the accounts payable record keeping	Fictitious purchases
Segregation of the ordering, receiving, inventory control, amounts, accounts payable, information systems, and general accounting functions	Fictitious purchases, omitted purchases, wrong wrong vendor, timing issues
Records & Documents:	
Timely updating of the purchases journal for all purchasing transactions	Fictitious purchases, omitted purchases
Preparation of receiving reports on prenumbered forms so that the sequence of receipts can be reviewed for proper recording	Omitted purchases
Immediate preparation of receiving reports for all actual receipts of goods	Timing issues, omitted transactions, invalid purchases
Prior to recording, matching of vendor invoices with related PO and receiving report for verification of vendors, authorized prices, mathematical accuracy, account coding, quantities, and descriptions of goods	Fictitious purchases, duplicate purchases, incorrect amounts or accounts, wrong vendor, timing issues
Monthly review and reconciliation of vendor statements with accounts payable records	Omitted purchases, fictitious purchases, incorrect amounts, wrong vendor, timing issues
Requirement for accounts payable records to be updated only when receiving report verifies actual receipt of goods	Fictitious purchases, duplicate purchases, incorrect amounts, wrong vendor, timing issues

(continued)

Control:	Minimizes the Related Risk of:
Performance of end of period review to determine whether purchases are recorded in the proper period	Timing issues, duplicate purchases, omitted purchases
Security:	
Physical controls in the warehouse, receiving, and areas with access to inventory items	Stolen goods
Physical and electronic controls covering the purchases and accounts payable records	Fictitious purchases, duplicate purchases, incorrect amounts, omitted transactions, wrong vendor, timing issues, accumulation problems
Independent Checks:	
Comparison of receiving reports with the purchases journal	Omitted purchases, duplicate purchases, incorrect amounts, wrong account numbers, timing issues
Matching of purchase records and verification for item descriptions, quantities, dates, authorized prices, and mathematical accuracy	Incorrect amounts, invalid purchases, timing issues
Review of purchases journal for mathematical accuracy, reconciliation to the accounts payable records, and correct posting to the general ledger	Incorrect amounts, incorrect accumulation or posting, omitted purchases, wrong account numbers, duplicate purchases
Requirement for receipts to be inspected, counted, and compared with "blind copy" POs	Fictitious purchases, duplicate purchases, incorrect quantities
Performance of physical inventory counts and reconciliation with the inventory records	Stolen goods, omitted purchases, fictitious purchases, wrong amounts, duplicate purchases, timing issues
Verification of accounts payable subsidiary ledger for mathematical accuracy and proper posting to the general ledger	Incorrect amounts, incorrect accumulation or posting, omitted purchases, wrong account numbers, duplicate purchases

PURCHASE RETURN PROCESS (STUDY OBJECTIVE 3)

Occasionally, the company may reject goods received and initiate the purchase return process. This may occur for a variety of reasons, including the following:

1. Goods received are unacceptable due to these situations:
    - Quantity or quality discrepancies
    - Damage or defects
    - Errors in the type of goods delivered or ordered
    - Discrepancies in the terms of the purchase
    - Timing issues
2. Changes in the company's needs regarding future sales or production.

The unacceptable-goods circumstances noted in the first item listed are typically detected immediately, since goods are inspected upon receipt. Sometimes, however, unacceptable goods may be discovered at a later date, especially in the case of defective goods, quality discrepancies, and purchase terms discrepancies. Changes in company needs, the second item, may occur at any time, as the company may have unforeseen changes in its business activities. Regardless of the reason for rejecting a purchase or the timing of the return, a company must have specific procedures in place for handling its returns to a vendor. Exhibit 9-9 presents a business process map of the activities related to purchase return transactions. Exhibit 9-10 is a document

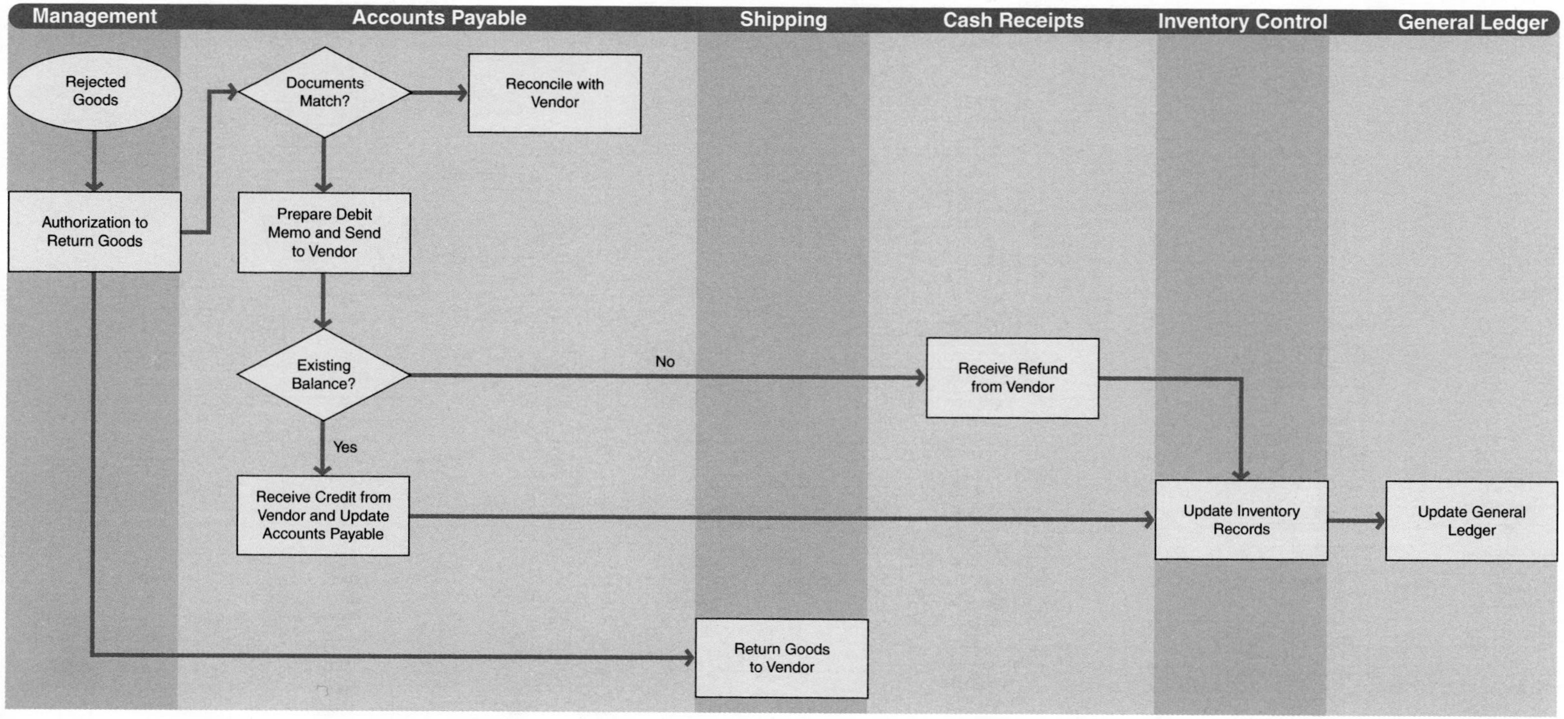

Exhibit 9-9
Purchase Return Process Map

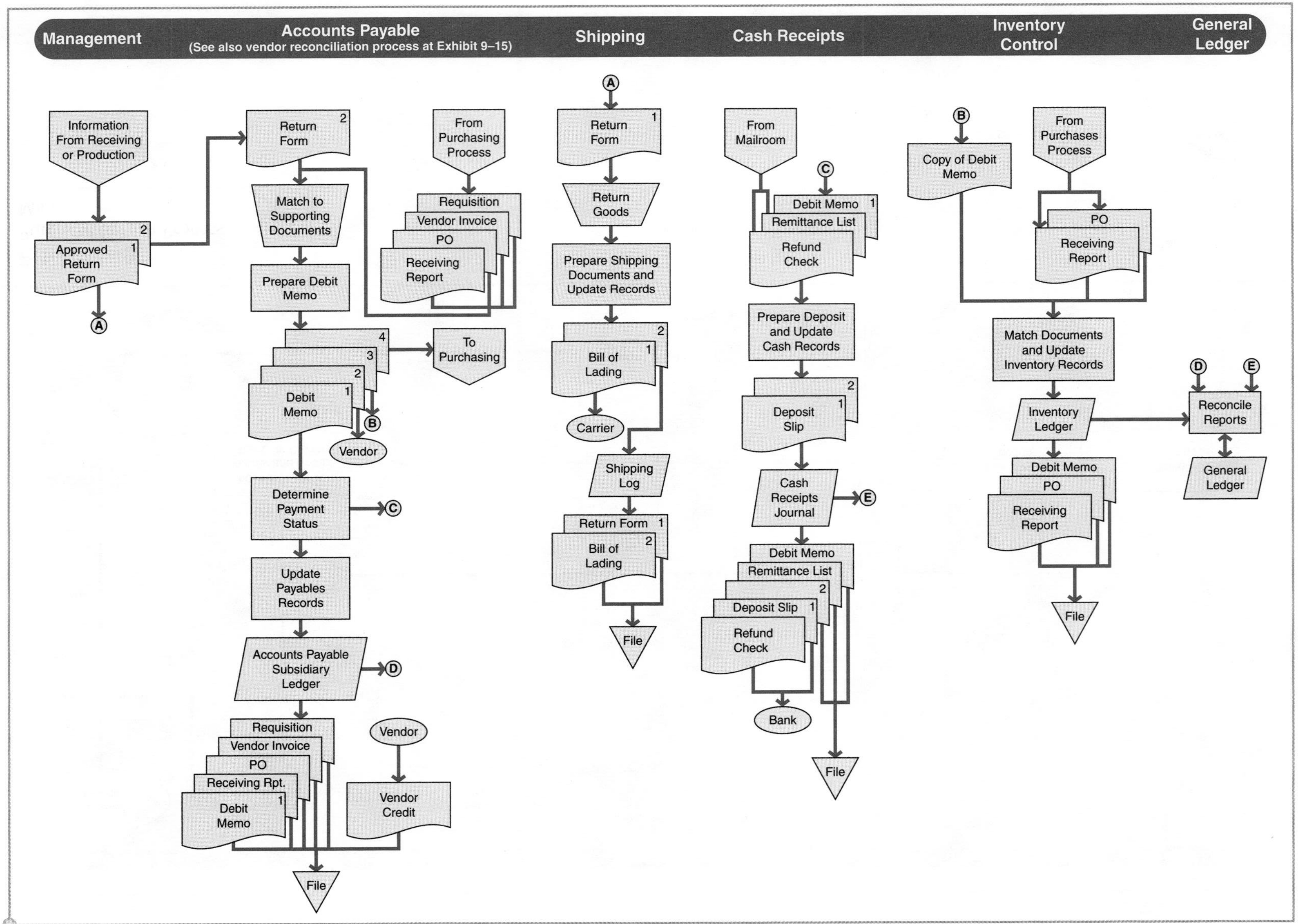

Exhibit 9-10
Document Flowchart of the Purchase Return Processes

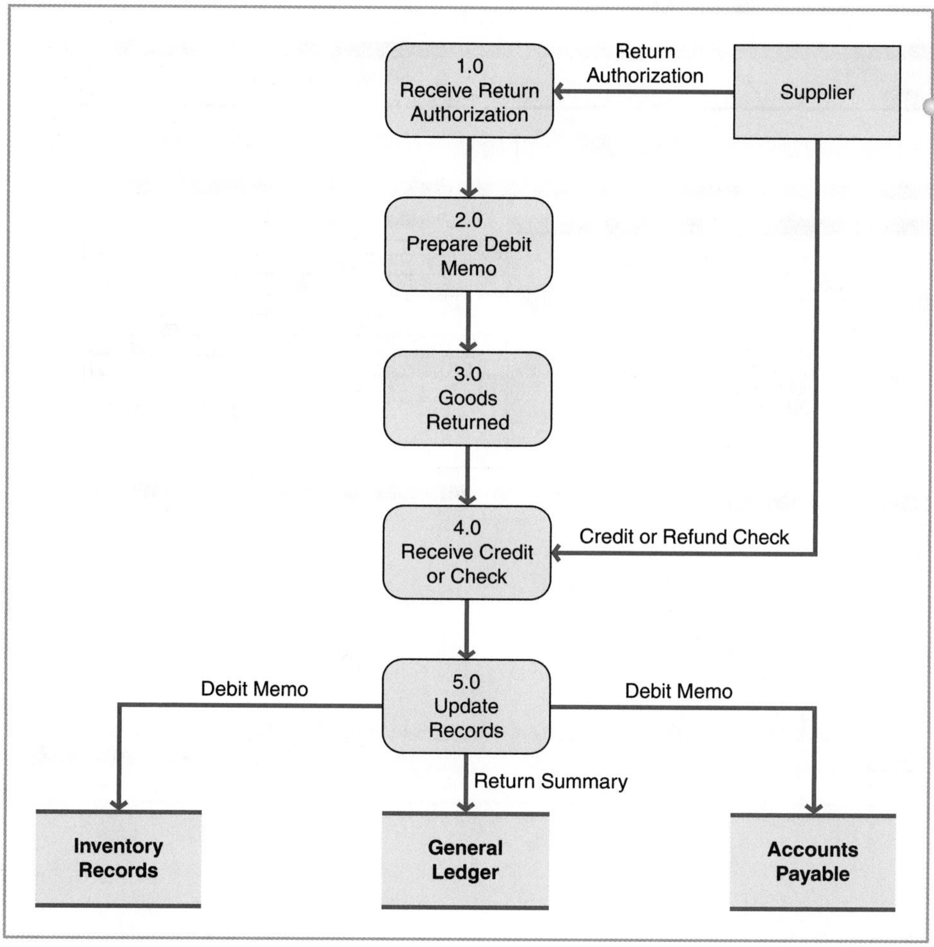

Exhibit 9-11
Purchase Return Processes
Data Flow Diagram

flowchart showing the records used in the purchase return process, and Exhibit 9-11 shows a data flow diagram of purchase returns. These exhibits depict a return process whereby the items being returned had been received and accepted at an earlier time, rather than being rejected immediately upon receipt.

Once rejected goods are identified, management approval must be obtained in order to formally make the decision to return the purchase. A debit memo should then be prepared. A **debit memo** is the document that identifies the items being returned, along with relevant information regarding vendor, quantity, and price. This form should be prepared by the accounts payable department on the basis of information from the related purchasing records, such as the PO, receiving report, and/or invoice. Exhibit 9-12 shows the processing of a purchase return in Microsoft Dynamics GP®.

After the debit memo is prepared, the goods can be physically returned to the vendor. At that point, the company should prepare a record of the return shipment, similar to the procedures described in Chapter 8 for shipments related to the sales process. It is a good practice to keep a record of all shipping

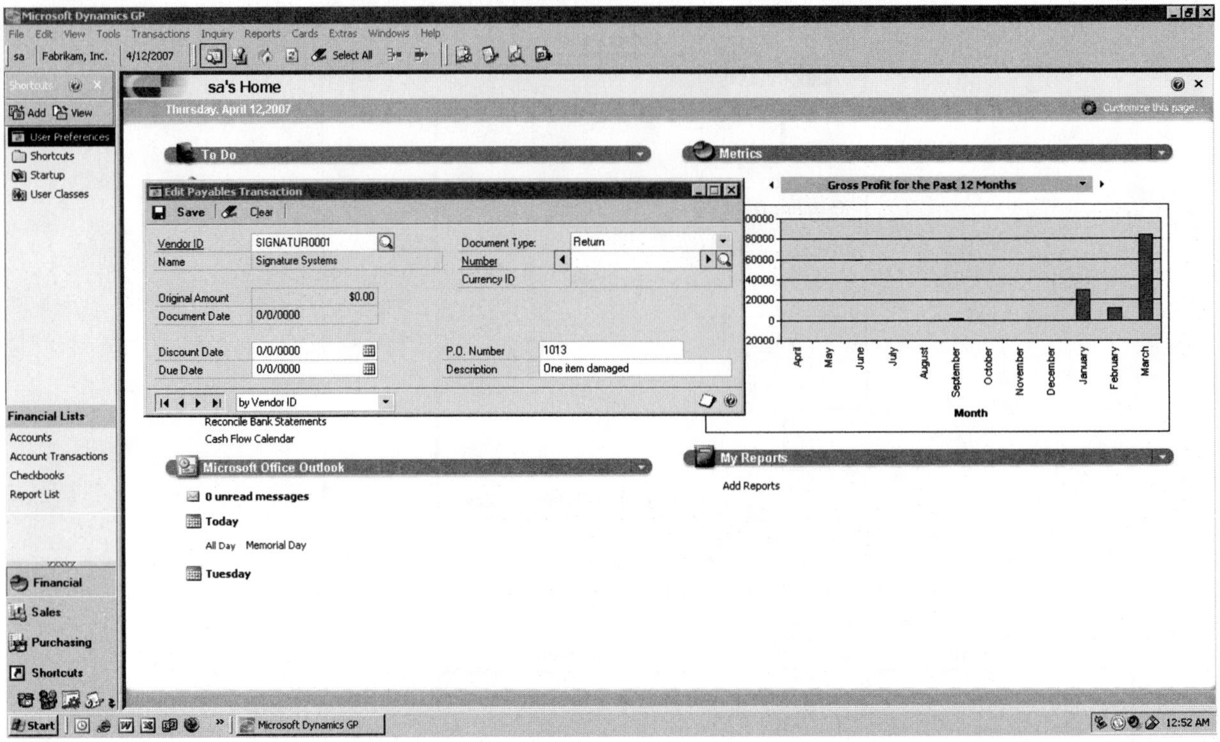

Exhibit 9-12
Entering Purchase Returns in Microsoft Dynamics GP®

activity, whether it is related to sales or purchase return transactions. It is also necessary to update inventory records so that the returned goods are no longer recorded as company assets. (Note that the accounts affected will depend on the type of inventory system used by the company, either perpetual or periodic.)

Occasionally, communications with the vendor regarding purchase returns indicate that there is no need to physically return the goods. In the case of defective goods, for example, a vendor may wish to avoid the costs of shipping the items and may therefore instruct the company to dispose of the goods rather than return them. When this happens, the company may need to implement additional controls to be sure that the disposal is not overlooked in the accounting records. Because there will be no shipping report for this item, company personnel may need to make an extra effort to be sure the debit memo is properly prepared and recorded.

Finally, the company will receive a refund or credit from the vendor for the returned (or disposed) goods. If a cash refund is received, the cash receipts procedures described in Chapter 8 should be implemented. If a credit is received, accounts payable records must be adjusted to reflect a reduction in the amount owed to the vendor.

RISKS AND CONTROLS IN THE PURCHASE RETURN PROCESSES (STUDY OBJECTIVE 3, continued)

AUTHORIZATION OF TRANSACTIONS

Whenever problems are noted with purchases, special authorization should be required to officially reject and return the items and initiate the preparation of a debit memo. All debit memos must be approved by a member of management or other designated individual within the company before the goods are physically returned to the vendor.

SEGREGATION OF DUTIES

The accounts payable employee who prepares the debit memos should not also be responsible for performing duties in the custody or authorization functions of the purchasing process. Accordingly, these individuals should not handle inventory or cash, or approve purchasing or purchase return transactions.

ADEQUATE RECORDS AND DOCUMENTS

The debit memo is the most significant document in the purchase return process. It is important that debit memos include thorough descriptions regarding the items being returned, including quantities and prices, as well as reference to the original purchase invoice. Debit memos should be issued in numerical sequence to enable the verification of complete accounting for purchase return transactions. When debit memos are issued on prenumbered forms, company personnel can account for the sequence and evaluate whether or not the entire sequence has been accounted for.

Debit memos should be filed along with supporting documentation such as the original purchase records. They should also be matched with the refund or credit documentation received from the vendor.

SECURITY OF ASSETS AND DOCUMENTS

Accounts payable records and data files should be restricted to those who are specifically authorized to approve or record the related purchase return. Custody of the returned goods should be controlled and limited to those in the shipping function or others specifically designated to handle the goods.

INDEPENDENT CHECKS AND RECONCILIATION

Companies should have in place specific internal control activities to achieve accountability for purchase returns. Especially important are controls that check for the possibility of unrecorded purchase returns. Physical inventory counts can help detect unrecorded returns. In addition, someone independent of the accounting function should review supporting documents to verify that debit memos represent actual returns.

COST–BENEFIT CONSIDERATIONS

Internal controls should always be a part of a company's accounting system. However, certain exposures may exist within a company that may warrant the need to implement more extensive internal control procedures. A company should evaluate whether the benefits achieved from its internal controls are worthwhile, given the related risks and costs of implementation. In addition to the risks noted under the cost–benefits discussion related to the purchasing process, a company might also consider the need for extensive internal controls related to the purchase return process when it processes a large volume of debit memos.

Exhibit 9-13 presents some common control procedures related to the purchase return process, along with the related risks that they address.

Exhibit 9-13
Purchase Return Controls and Risks

Control:	Minimizes the Related Risk of:
Authorization:	
Approval of purchase return transaction prior to preparation of a debit memo	Invalid returns, incorrect amounts
Segregation:	
Separation of authorization of purchase returns from accounts payable record keeping and custody of inventory	Fictitious returns
Segregate the ordering, shipping, inventory control, accounts payable, information systems, and general accounting functions	Fictitious returns, omitted returns, wrong amounts, wrong vendor, timing issues
Records & Documents:	
Preparation of a debit memo for all purchase return transactions	Fictitious returns, omitted returns
Preparation of debit memos on prenumbered forms	Omitted purchase returns
Preparation of shipping reports on prenumbered forms so that the sequence of returns can be reviewed for proper recording	Omitted purchases
Immediate preparation of shipping reports for all returns of goods	Timing issues, omitted transactions, invalid purchase returns
Prior to preparation of a debit memo, matching of supporting documents (vendor invoices, PO, and receiving report) for verification of vendors, authorized prices, mathematical accuracy, account coding, quantities, and descriptions of goods	Fictitious returns, duplicate returns, incorrect amounts or accounts, wrong vendor, timing issues
Monthly review and reconciliation of vendor statements with accounts payable records	Omitted returns, fictitious returns, incorrect amounts, wrong vendors, timing issues

(continued)

Updating of accounts payable records for returns only when shipping report and debit memo verify actual return of goods	Fictitious returns, duplicate returns, incorrect amounts, wrong vendor, timing issues
Performance of end-of-period review to determine whether returns are recorded in the proper period	Timing issues, duplicate returns, omitted returns
Security:	
Physical controls in the warehouse and shipping areas with access to inventory items	Stolen goods
Physical and electronic controls covering access to the purchase returns and accounts payable records	Fictitious returns, duplicate returns, incorrect amounts, omitted transactions, wrong vendor, timing issues, accumulation problems
Independent Checks:	
Comparison of shipping logs with debit memo activity	Omitted returns, duplicate returns, invalid returns, timing issues
Verification of debit memo listing for mathematical accuracy and posting to the accounts payable records and general ledger	Invalid returns, omitted returns, incorrect amounts, wrong vendor, timing issues, incorrect accumulation or posting
Matching of purchase return records with original purchase documentation and verification for item descriptions, quantities, dates, authorized prices, and mathematical accuracy	Incorrect amounts, invalid purchase returns, timing issues
Performance of physical inventory counts and reconciliation with the inventory records	Stolen goods, omitted returns, fictitious returns, wrong amounts, duplicate returns, timing issues
Verification of accounts payable subsidiary ledger for mathematical accuracy and proper posting to the general ledger	Incorrect amounts, incorrect accumulation or posting, omitted returns, wrong account numbers, duplicate purchase returns

CASH DISBURSEMENT PROCESSES (STUDY OBJECTIVE 4)

The processing flow related to procurement activities requires that payments be made for purchase obligations that have been incurred. The cash disbursements process must be designed to ensure that the company appropriately processes payments to satisfy its accounts payable when they are due.

Cash disbursements may include payments made by check or with currency. Most companies conduct business transactions with checks so that a written record is established of the cash disbursement. Because the practice of writing checks enhances internal control, here we will describe cash disbursements made by check. Exhibit 9-14 presents a business process map of a typical cash disbursement system, while Exhibit 9-15 shows the document flowchart for that process. Exhibit 9-16 is a data flow diagram of cash disbursements.

The accounts payable department is generally responsible for notification of the need to make cash disbursements and the maintenance of vendor accounts. Before payment is made to a vendor, specific steps should be taken to enhance the effectiveness and efficiency of the process. These steps include vendor account reconciliation, cash management techniques, and payment authorization. **Cash management** is the careful oversight of cash balances, forecasted cash

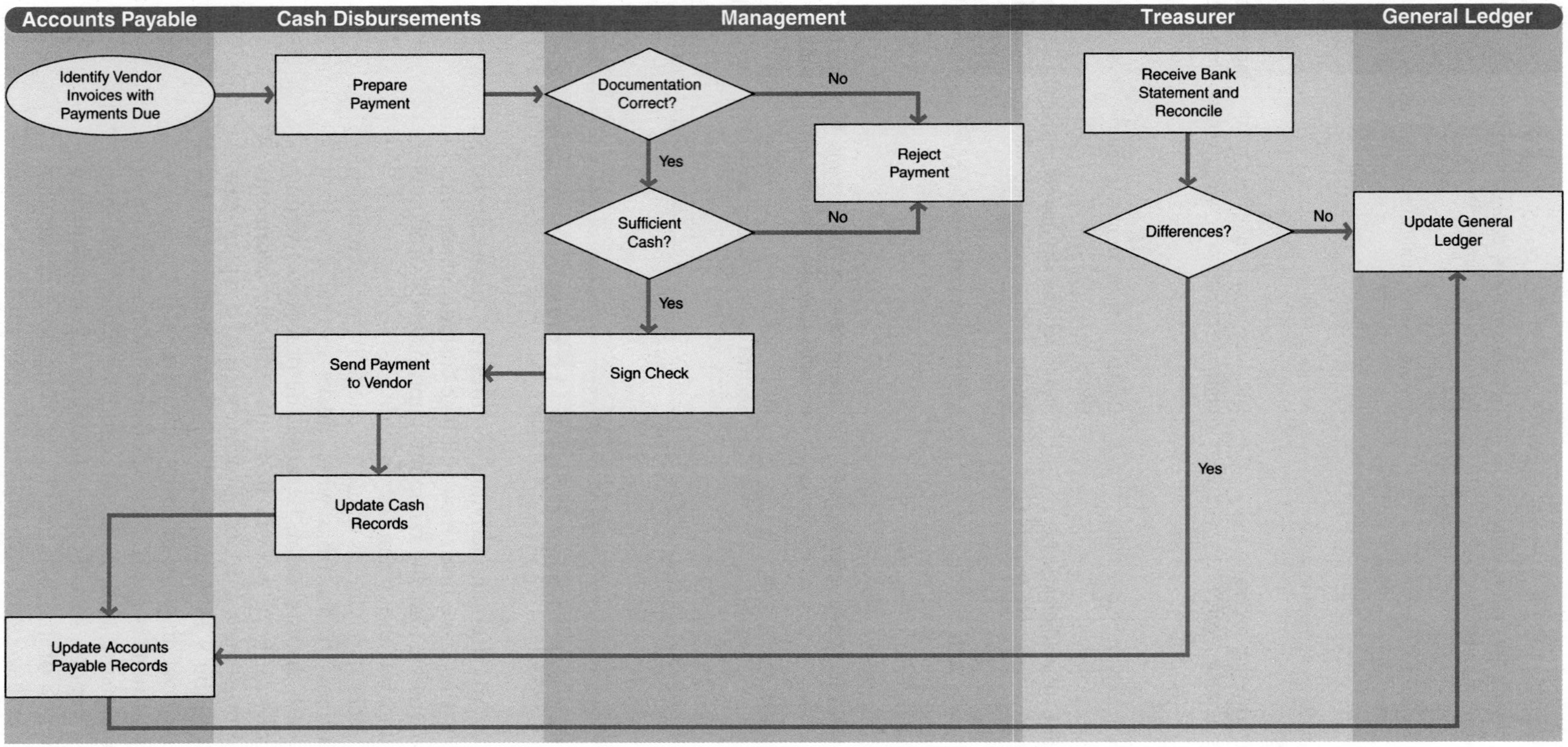

Exhibit 9-14
Cash Disbursement Process Map

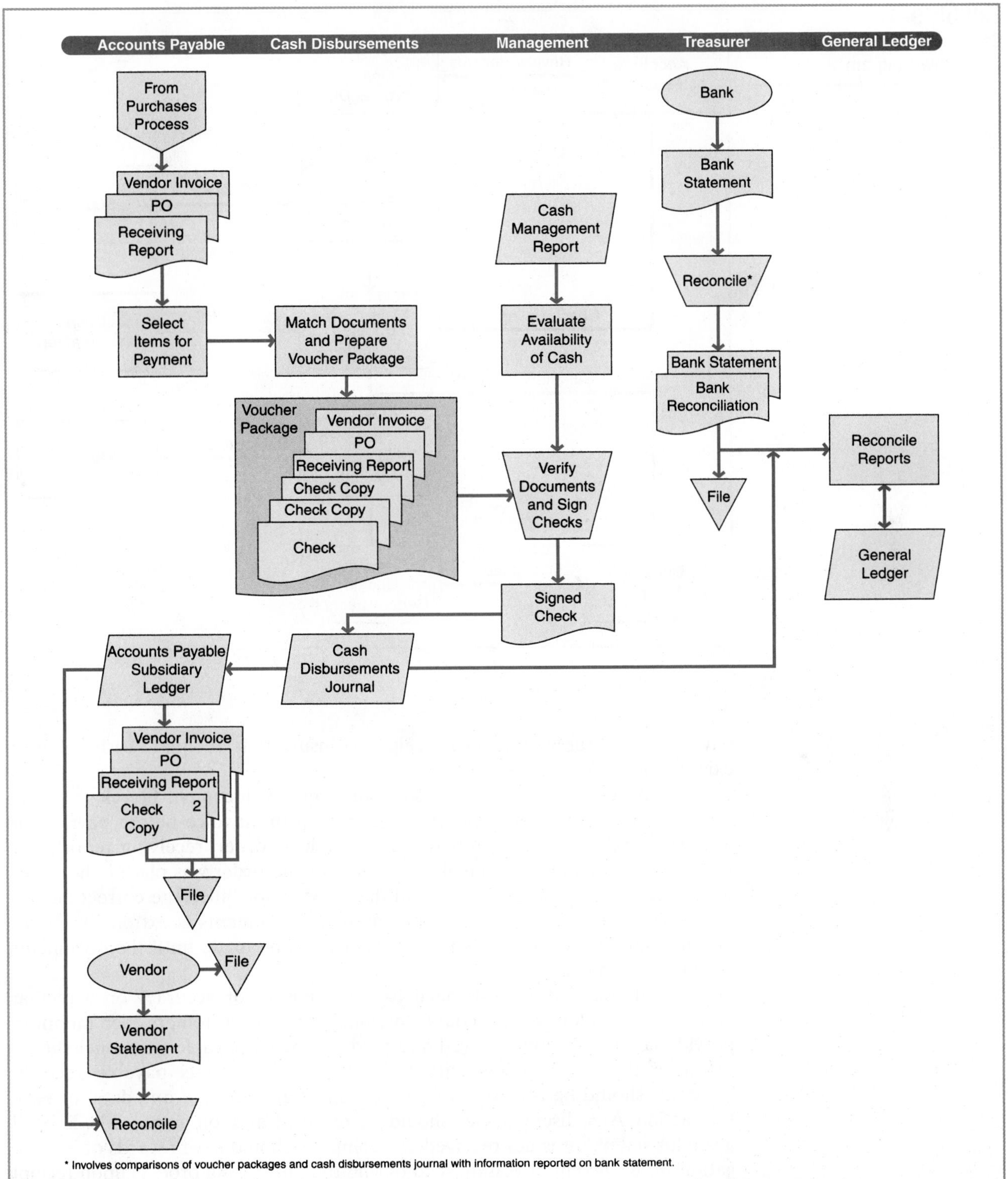

Exhibit 9-15
Document Flowchart of the Cash Disbursement Processes

Exhibit 9-16
Cash Disbursement Processes Data Flow Diagram

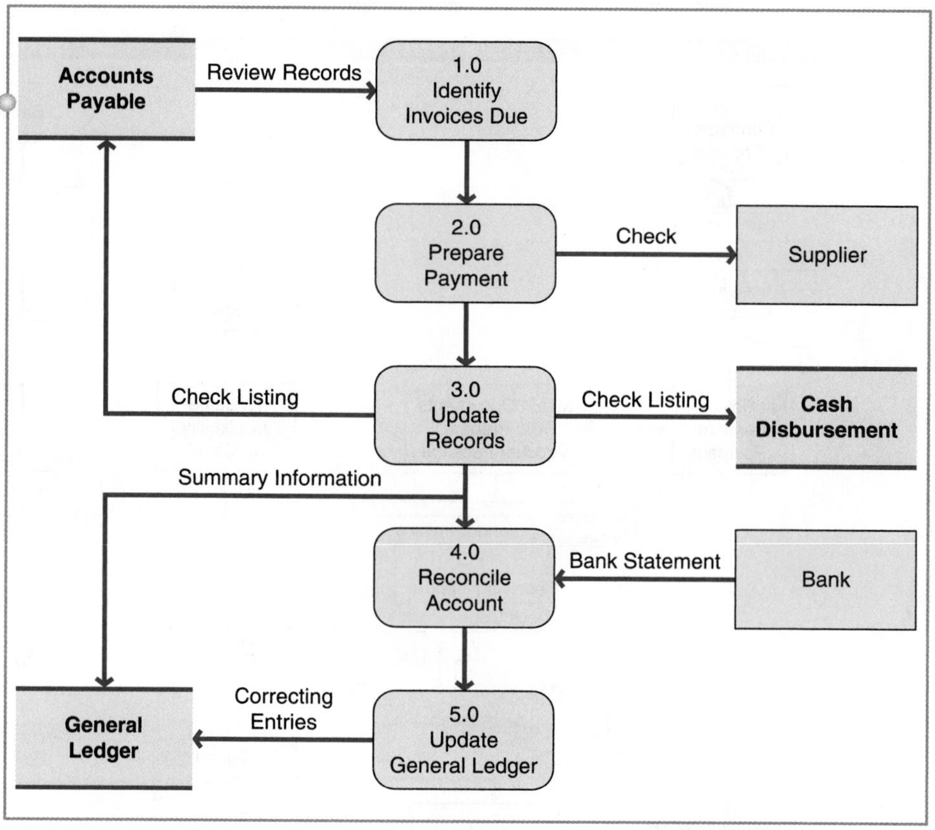

payments, and forecasted cash receipts to insure that adequate cash balances exist to meet obligations.

An important aspect of this cash disbursements document flowchart is that the documentation must support or agree with the invoice before payment is approved and a check is prepared. The purchase order, receiving report, and invoice must be matched to make sure that a valid order was placed, the goods were received in good condition, and that the vendor billed the correct quantities and prices. The process of matching these documents is extremely important in cash disbursements. No payments should be made until the documents are properly matched.

Accounts payable records need to be reviewed for accuracy on a regular basis. Many vendors send account statements to their customers each month to provide detail of amounts owed and paid. Accounts payable personnel should reconcile these statements with the company's accounts payable records. Accounts should be reviewed for agreement of amount and due date for each transaction. Any discrepancies should be resolved as soon as possible. Even if a vendor statement is not received, the company should have records of its obligations to each vendor (established during the purchasing process upon receipt of goods and the related purchase invoice). Some companies streamline the process by using a voucher system, whereby multiple transactions involving the same vendor may be combined into a single cash disbursement.

Copies of invoices should be filed in the accounts payable department in chronological order by due date. Accounts payable personnel should review this file regularly so that disbursements can be initiated in a timely manner. This provides for efficient cash management. A company typically desires to keep its cash for as long as possible. However, it must also be mindful of paying by the due date in order to avoid late payment fees, to establish trust, and to stay on good terms with its vendors.

It is often the case that vendors offer price reductions for prompt payment. When this type of trade discount is offered, it is the responsibility of the accounts payable department to make sure that the company has the opportunity to take advantage of these discounts. If the files are arranged chronologically, the system should consider any accelerated due dates warranted by discounts. The cash disbursements department must be notified to make the payment by the discount date. This is an added responsibility in the cash management process. The company should always weigh the advantages of a discount against the advantages of holding on to its cash in order to meet other operating needs, earn interest, or avoid borrowing. Controlling the timing of payments is therefore a very important managerial task, and accounts payable procedures are fundamental to the company's ability to manage its cash flow.

When an invoice is due for payment, accounts payable personnel will retrieve the invoice from the file and forward it to the cash disbursements department for preparation of the check detail. Supporting documentation should be attached, including a copy of the PO and receiving report. Business checks often include a check stub, or remittance advice, where the invoice number and other relevant information can be documented. A **remittance advice** is usually a tear-off part of a check that has a simple explanation of the reasons for the payment, including invoice numbers and transaction line-item descriptions. Exhibit 9-17 shows the payment screen in Microsoft Dynamics GP®.

Although a cash disbursements clerk prepares checks, the responsibility for signing the check is reserved for members of management. The authorized signer can verify the propriety of the disbursement by reviewing the check in comparison with the supporting documentation. Finally, once the check is signed, it will be sent to the vendor. A copy of the check and supporting documentation will be returned to the cash disbursements and accounts payable departments.

Once a payment is made, the related invoice should be canceled to indicate that it has been paid. To cancel an invoice, a cash disbursements clerk will clearly mark the invoice with information pertaining to the date and check number used to satisfy this obligation. Alternatively, a copy of the check or remittance advice can be attached to the invoice to accomplish this task. Either method provides a written trail of the disbursement and prevents the likelihood of duplicate payments. These documents are filed in the accounts payable department in check-number sequence. The accounts payable department will then update its vendor accounts to reflect the current payment activity.

Cash disbursements should be recorded in the accounting system as soon as the payment is made. A cash disbursements clerk will prepare a **cash disbursements journal,** which is a chronological listing of all payments. This listing is sometimes called a check register and is similar to the record kept for a personal checking account. The cash disbursements journal is used to prepare a

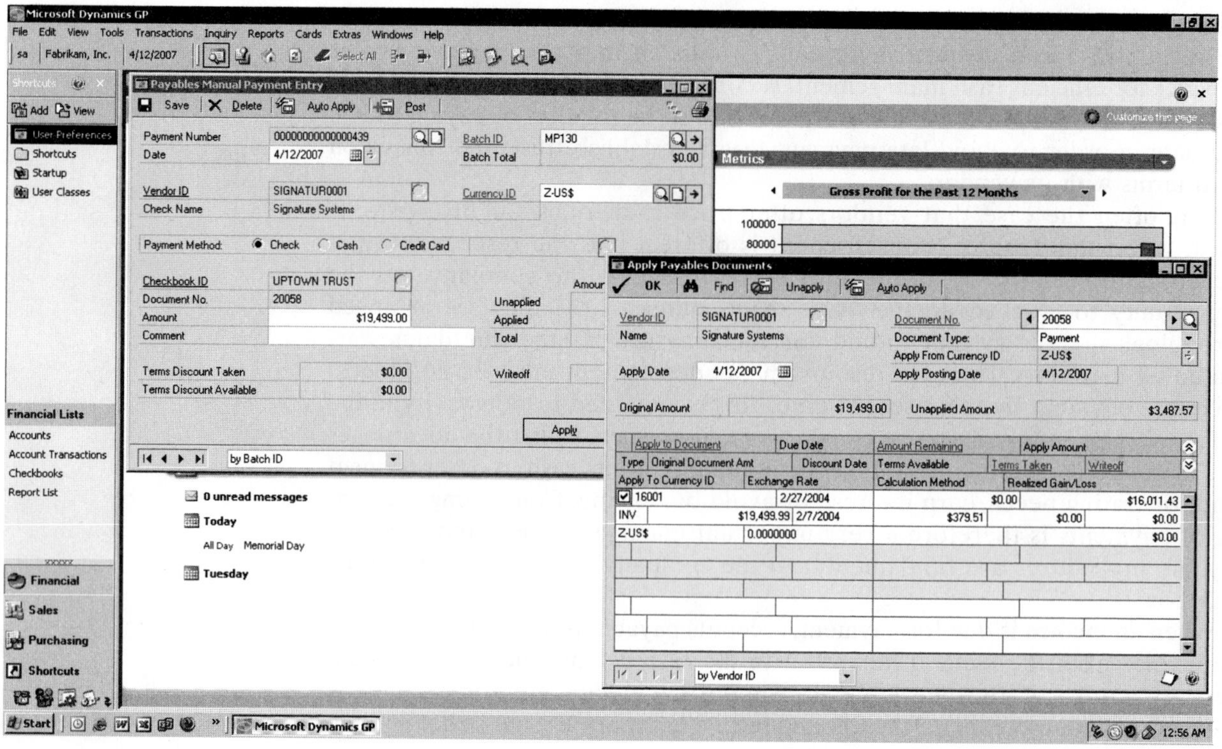

Exhibit 9-17
Establishing a Payment in Microsoft Dynamics GP®

daily journal entry, whereby the cash and accounts payable accounts are updated to reflect the day's payments. Accounting software, such as Microsoft Dynamics GP®, automatically maintains records of checks written and updates cash and accounts payable balances as checks are written. It is important that the accounting records reflect the actual date of the cash disbursement, as shown on the check. Later in the period, the records can be reconciled. Cash and accounts payable records are periodically verified by comparison with bank statements and vendor statements, respectively.

RISKS AND CONTROLS IN THE CASH DISBURSEMENT PROCESSES (STUDY OBJECTIVE 4, continued)

AUTHORIZATION OF TRANSACTIONS

Only the accounts payable department should authorize the processing of a cash disbursement transaction, according to the need to satisfy a vendor obligation. The authorization occurs when the accounts payable department matches the purchase order, receiving report, and invoice, and then forwards these matched documents to the cash disbursements department. In addition, designated members of management should be given responsibility for authorizing the actual payments by their signatures on the face of the check. This means that only one or a few people should have check-signing authority. The bank will keep records of the signatures of those authorized check signers and should not pay a check unless it bears the signature of an authorized party. Finally, all bank accounts that are established in the company's name should be authorized by the board of directors.

Many companies establish special cash disbursement authorization policies and procedures applicable to large checks whereby a dual signature requirement is in place for checks over a specified dollar amount. **Dual signature** means that two people sign the check. This additional control requires the approval and signature of two authorized persons, thus reducing the risk of a significant fraud or error. The company's bank plays a crucial role in enforcing this policy, as it must not pay checks over the threshold amount unless two authorized signatures are included.

SEGREGATION OF DUTIES

Effective segregation of duties reduces the likelihood of undetected errors or fraud by providing accounting control over the cash disbursement processes. If the purchasing, receiving, accounts payable, and cash disbursement functions are segregated, then the opportunity for theft or error within the processes should be minimized. No person should have the ability to initiate a false purchase transaction and simultaneously pay for it and account for it. Ideally, individuals within the cash disbursements department should not have check-signing authority and should not have access to the cash account or to the company's accounts payable records. In addition, information systems operations and programming related to the cash disbursements and accounts payable departments should be separate from those having responsibility for custody, authorization, or record keeping within those functions.

ADEQUATE RECORDS AND DOCUMENTS

An accounts payable subsidiary ledger and a cash disbursements journal are fundamental records in the cash disbursement process. Also, the practice of issuing checks on prenumbered forms creates a record of the sequence of transactions. And the orderly maintenance of accounts payable records facilitates effective cash management techniques.

SECURITY OF ASSETS AND DOCUMENTS

Access to cash should be limited to the authorized check signers. Physical controls should be in place in the areas where cash is retained and disbursed. Similarly, the company's stock of unused checks should be protected and controlled. Access to the records should be limited to designated persons within the accounts payable and cash disbursements functions.

INDEPENDENT CHECKS AND RECONCILIATION

The cash disbursements journal and accounts payable subsidiary ledger should be reconciled to the general ledger control accounts on a regular basis. Also, someone separate from the cash disbursements and accounts payable functions should be responsible for reconciliation of the bank statement on a monthly basis. Procedures for adequate reconciliation of the bank account include the direct receipt of the bank statement by the designated employee so that no others may have an opportunity to alter the document. If copies of checks are returned with the bank statement, these checks should be completely reviewed for dates, payees, and signatures.

COST–BENEFIT CONSIDERATIONS

When a company processes a large volume of cash disbursements, it should consider the implementation of internal control procedures to ensure the accuracy of those transactions. Some other situations that may warrant increased controls include the existence of complex vendor arrangements or discount terms, decentralized or widely dispersed cash disbursements, cash disbursements via currency (rather than by check), high volumes of purchase returns, and cash disbursements denominated in foreign currencies.

Exhibit 9-18 is a summary of certain controls and risks related to the cash disbursement process.

Exhibit 9-18
Cash Disbursement Controls and Risks

Control:	Minimizes the Related Risk of:
Authorization:	
Board of Directors' authorization for all company bank accounts	Invalid payments, stolen cash
Approval of cash disbursement transaction prior to preparation of a check	Invalid payments, incorrect amounts
Dual signature requirement for disbursement of large sums of cash	Invalid payments, incorrect amounts
Segregation:	
Separation of check-signing authority from accounts payable and cash disbursements record keeping and custody of cash	Invalid payments, incorrect amounts, stolen cash
Separation of the ordering, shipping and receiving, inventory control, accounts payable, cash disbursements, information systems, and general accounting functions	Fictitious payments, omitted payments, wrong amounts, wrong vendor, timing issues
Records & Documents:	
Preparation of checks on prenumbered forms	Omitted payments
Prior to preparation of a check, matching of supporting documents (vendor invoices, PO, and receiving report) for verification of vendors, authorized prices, mathematical accuracy, account coding, quantities, and descriptions of goods	Fictitious payments, duplicate payments, incorrect amounts or accounts, wrong vendor, timing issues
Updating of the cash disbursements journal and accounts payable records as soon as checks have actually been disbursed	Invalid payments, duplicate payments, incorrect amounts, timing issues

(continued)

Cancellation of supporting documentation once payment has been made	Duplicate payments
Monthly review and reconciliation of vendor statements with accounts payable records	Omitted payments, fictitious payments, incorrect amounts, wrong vendors, timing issues
Security:	
Physical controls covering cash and the company's supply of checks	Stolen cash
Physical and electronic controls over access to the cash disbursement and accounts payable records	Fictitious payments, duplicate payments, incorrect amounts, omitted transactions, wrong vendor, timing issues, accumulation problems
Independent Checks:	
Monthly performance of bank reconciliation	Invalid payments, incorrect amounts, omitted payments, issues timing
Matching of checks with original purchase documentation and verification for item descriptions, quantities, dates, authorized prices, and mathematical accuracy	Incorrect amounts, invalid payments, timing issues
Verification of cash disbursements journal for mathematical accuracy and proper posting to the general ledger	Incorrect amounts, incorrect accumulation or posting, omitted payments, wrong account numbers, duplicate payments
Verification of accounts payable subsidiary ledger for mathematical accuracy and proper posting to the general ledger	Incorrect amounts, incorrect accumulation or posting, omitted payments, wrong account numbers, duplicate payments

IT SYSTEMS OF EXPENDITURES AND CASH DISBURSEMENT PROCESSES (STUDY OBJECTIVE 5)

Even in computerized accounting systems, there can be many manual tasks. This is usually true for small or midsize companies with small-scale IT systems. The examples shown in the early parts of this chapter of screen captures from Microsoft Dynamics GP® accounting software depict such a system. In purchasing systems, the document matching is often called a three-way match. A **three-way match** is the matching of a purchase order to the related receiving report and invoice. The person operating the computer software must still physically match the purchase order to a receiving report and invoice, deciding which invoices match which purchase orders and receiving reports. The computer automates much of the record keeping and check writing, but a human must still make decisions regarding this matching process, depicted in Exhibit 9-19.

Within small or midsize organizations with accounting software such as Microsoft Dynamics GP®, the following tasks must be completed by employees:

1. The purchasing department orders items from a vendor, and an employee must enter a purchase order into the accounting software by keying data into the fields of a purchase order form on the screen.

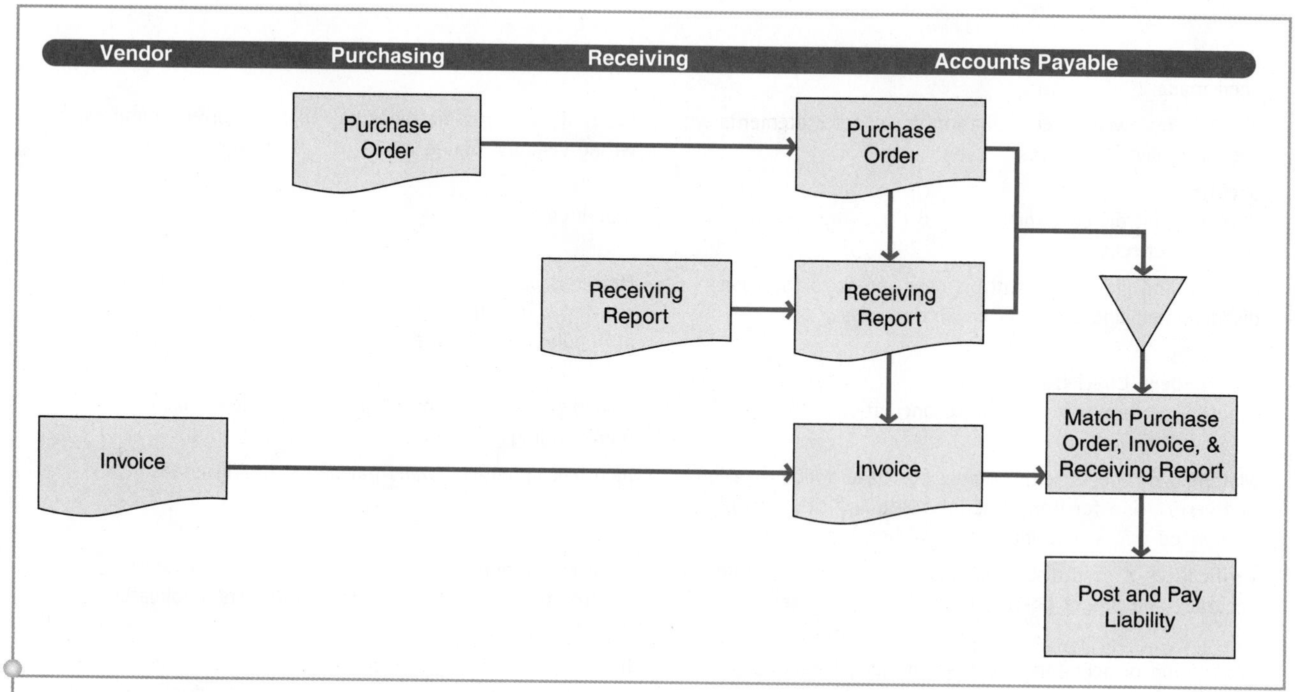

Exhibit 9-19
Flowchart of Document Matching to Approve and Pay for Purchases

2. The receiving department receives the goods and compares the packing slip with the purchase order to confirm part numbers and quantities.
3. A receiving report is prepared by an employee filling in the appropriate fields in a receiving screen in the software. The person completing this screen must choose the purchase order that matches this receiving report. When the vendor name or ID number is entered, the system will list open purchase orders with that vendor.
4. After the vendor has provided an invoice, the invoice must also be entered into an invoice entry screen in the accounting software. Again, the proper purchase order must be chosen from a list of open purchase orders.
5. If the purchase order, receiving report, and invoice match as to part numbers, quantities, and prices, the liability is approved for payment.
6. At the discount date or due date of the invoice, a designated person must select certain invoices to pay and have the system generate a batch of checks.

This manual entry and matching system is extremely time consuming and expensive. It is time consuming due to the complexities of purchases. Purchasing and payments can become complex because a vendor may occasionally substitute items, ship a different quantity (undership or overship), notify the buyer of back orders, or fill a partial order. Thus, matching takes a large amount of human time to reconcile and approve for payment. This is true even if the accounting system is maintaining records and generating checks electronically. The problems with this system are as follows:

1. The total salaries or wages paid to employees who match these three documents can be very expensive.
2. Mismatches as to part numbers, quantities, or prices can take much time to investigate and reconcile, which causes the cost of this manual processing to be even higher.
3. Employees must manually key into the software the details of purchasing, receiving, and invoicing. This also is expensive and time consuming. In addition, keying errors can be made.

Many organizations are using advances in IT systems to reduce the time and expense of purchase and payment processing. With technology, processes can be changed to lessen or eliminate the aforementioned problems. The process undertaken to change processes to enhance efficiency is called business process reengineering. Recall from Chapter 1 that **business process reengineering (BPR)** is an organized change in business processes for the purpose of improving efficiency and effectiveness. BPR aligns business processes with the IT systems in order to accomplish these improvements. In the case of purchasing and paying for purchases, BPR facilitates reductions in paperwork, manual processing, and processing costs. In many cases, IT systems are used to enhance the efficiency of purchasing and payment processes. Implementing these IT systems usually entails BPR to make the processes fit the IT system.

Examples of IT systems that usually involve BPR in purchasing and payments include the following:

- Computer-based matching and checking of purchasing documents
- Evaluated receipt settlement (ERS), an invoice-less processing technique
- Electronic forms of purchase and payment such as e-business, e-payables, and EDI

For example, EDI reduces or eliminates the manual keying of invoices because the invoice is communicated electronically between the buyer and the vendor. The next section describes these IT systems that allow organizations to reduce the time and cost of processing purchases and payments.

COMPUTER-BASED MATCHING (STUDY OBJECTIVE 6)

The IT system used for purchasing and payments can be used to automate the document matching process. **Automated matching** is a computer software technique in which the computer software matches an invoice to its related purchase order and receiving report. Traditional systems rely on a person to do this matching, whereas an automated matching system does not. To institute an automated matching system, all of the relevant files must be available and constantly ready for processing. This means that purchase order and receiving files and records must be online or in databases. When an invoice is received from a vendor, an employee enters the details into the accounting system by completing fields in the invoice entry screen. The purchase order number usually appears on the invoice, and this number is entered as the invoice is entered. The system can then access the online purchase order and receiving files and check the match of items, quantities, and prices. The system will not approve an invoice for payment unless the items and quantities match with the packing slip, and the prices match the purchase order prices. This ensures that the vendor has billed for the correct items, quantities, and prices.

During the matching process, the system will also check for mathematical errors and ensure that there are no previous payments that would make this payment a duplicate one. Without such checking, duplicate invoices can be received and paid. Vendors can accidentally or intentionally invoice the same order twice. The system checks for duplicate invoices by examining the invoice number, the vendor number, and the dollar amount. The system can print any instances it finds as potential duplicate payments, and this list can be reviewed by a manager prior to payment. In addition, the automated system can evaluate the discount terms and select the most advantageous timing of the actual payment. For example, if payment terms are 2/10, net/30, the system can be programmed to determine whether the two-percent discount is advantageous when compared with the company's cost of funds.

An automated matching system can reduce time, costs, errors, and duplicate payments in invoice processing. These improvements over manual matching can decrease the amount of time required to enter invoices and therefore give management more timely information to forecast future cash outflows for payment of invoices. In addition, the system can summarize detailed transactions into summary amounts that are posted to general ledger accounts. Thus, management receives more complete feedback in a much more timely manner,

THE REAL WORLD

Frymaster Corporation is a company in Shreveport, Louisiana that manufactures food-service equipment such as fryers and frying systems, food dispensing equipment, pasta cookers, and toasters. Frymaster uses an automated document-matching system for invoice payment. It is a medium-size company with four people in its accounts payable department. Compared with companies like it, Frymaster has a cost per vendor payment processed that is extremely low: Frymaster's average cost is $3.25, while the overall average for a medium-size company is $13.50. The Institute of Management and Administration (IOMA)[2] gave the following explanation for the low processing costs at Frymaster:

> The company has been using an automated three-way match since 1993. It results in a first-time hit rate of 75% to 80% of the time. This means a high percentage of the invoices with purchase orders fly through the system with little intervention from the accounts payable staff.

Therefore, fewer staff members are needed to process a larger volume of payments, so the staff can focus on exceptions. Documents that are properly matched are processed automatically, and only those with differences require manual steps to reconcile.

[2] "Automation & Air-Tight A/P Procedures Lead to Gold Star Performance," *IOMA's Report on Managing Accounts Payable,* July 2002, Vol. 2, Issue 7, pp. 11–12.

enabling management to better plan and control cash disbursements. While there are many advantages to automated matching, there are also risks, including system errors in the matching process, unauthorized access, fraud, and inadequate backup of files.

RISKS AND CONTROLS IN COMPUTER-BASED MATCHING (STUDY OBJECTIVE 6, continued)

SECURITY AND CONFIDENTIALITY RISKS

Applying automated matching processes means that people do not perform the matching and authorizing functions, because these take place within the system. Therefore, unauthorized access to the system increases the danger of fraudulent or fictitious payments. Someone who gains unauthorized access to the system's ordering and matching functions can insert fictitious vendors and invoices, and thus receive fraudulent payment. This risk can be lessened by authenticating users and limiting the access of authorized users. Passwords and user IDs should be used for any employee accessing the system. If the dollar amounts involved are extremely large or the data are sensitive, the use of biometrics, security tokens, or smart cards might be necessary to improve the strength of user authentication. In addition, authority tables should be established to limit access of authorized users to those subsystems necessary to their jobs. For example, a user who logs in to enter invoices should not have the system access that would allow her to order goods. Computer logs should be maintained in order to have a complete record of users and their histories of use. The computer log will allow monitoring and identification of unauthorized accesses or uses.

PROCESSING INTEGRITY RISKS

Since the system authorizes payment of invoices, it is critical to ensure that it is programmed to correctly accomplish this matching. Errors in system logic can cause systematic and repetitive errors in matching. In simpler terms, if the system mistakenly matches documents, it will mistakenly match documents repetitively. Thus, erroneous system logic can quickly cause cash flow problems. This is also true of the logic used to find duplicate payments. To find duplicate payments, the system must be preprogrammed with the criteria that identify duplicate payments. If the criteria are too tightly defined, it may not identify all duplicate payments. Alternatively, if the criteria are too loose, it may identify duplicate payments that are not really duplicates. For example, if a company were to regularly and frequently order the same items at the same cost, it would become harder to determine which are duplicate invoices and which are not, because the quantities and prices would be the same. These risks of systematic errors in matching or duplicate payments can be lessened by routine tests of the system and through regular management review of reports of invoice payments.

AVAILABILITY RISKS

As is always true of IT systems, the more reliance is placed on the system, the more critical it becomes to make sure that the system is available. Any system breakdowns or interruptions can stop or slow the processing of invoices and payments. Extreme delays in paying invoices could lead to lost discounts, late fees, interest charges, or loss of a vendor. Therefore, it is important to maintain backup systems and backup files. Since the matching is done within the system rather than manually, there may not be a paper trail of transactions processed. Therefore, backup files must be maintained to ensure a complete audit trail. In addition, uninterruptible power supplies and disaster recovery plans should be in place to allow continued operations even in the event of power outages or natural disasters.

EVALUATED RECEIPT SETTLEMENT (STUDY OBJECTIVE 7)

In the middle of the decade prior to 2000, some companies, including those in the automotive industry, began implementing invoice-less matching systems for purchasing and paying vendors. For instance, General Electric Co. began using an invoiceless system for direct material purchases and wished to move other purchases to an invoiceless system.[3] Changing document matching to an invoiceless system is more a process change than it is an application of new technology. However, the capability to achieve an invoiceless matching system is dependent on having extensive IT systems with online, purchase-related files. The simple explanation of an invoiceless match is that a comparison takes place by matching the purchase order with the goods received. If the PO matches the goods, payment is made to the vendor. This eliminates the need for the vendor to send an invoice, since payment is approved as soon goods are received (when they match a purchase order). Thus, it is an invoiceless system and is called **evaluated receipt settlement (ERS)**. The ERS name signifies that the receipt of goods is carefully evaluated and, if it matches the purchase order, settlement of the obligation occurs through this system.

When the purchasing department initiates a purchasing process, a purchase order is entered in the online database of open orders. When goods arrive at the receiving dock, employees in the receiving department will check the online database for the purchase order that matches the vendor, part numbers, and quantities. This means that employees must be able to access online purchase orders immediately, while the delivery person is still at the receiving dock. Thus, extensive IT systems with online purchasing files are necessary. If there is no matching purchase order, the goods are refused and returned to the vendor. If there is a matching purchase order, receiving employees enter a receiving record into the online database and payment is processed according to the payment terms previously negotiated with the vendor.

[3]"The GE Approach to Electronic Invoice & Payment Processing", *IOMA's Report on Managing Accounts Payable*, July 2002, Vol. 2, Issue 7, pp. 11–14.

THE REAL WORLD

The information that follows was excerpted from a large company's website for its vendors to see the company's new policies about ERS. For this illustration, the name of the company has been changed to "Example Company," but the other details are real. The list may give you a better understanding of how ERS works.

> Example Company is implementing ERS—Evaluated Receipt Settlement. With ERS we will pay suppliers based upon the quantity we receive and our purchase order price. Invoices are no longer necessary.
>
> **Requirements:**
>
> 1. Example Company's purchase order, part number, prices, terms and shipping methods must be 100% accurate.
> 2. Packing slips must be 100% accurate with correct items, part number, purchase order number, and correct quantities in the purchase order's unit of measure.
> 3. Goods must be received accurately. Accordingly, packing slips must be clear and easy to read, with bar coded packing slips preferred.
> 4. No invoices are to be received. Suppliers are to put the invoices on hold in their system.
> 5. Charges for supplementary items such as set up, plating, drum charges, etc. must be included in the unit price of the item or must be added as an individual line item on the purchase order.
> 6. Example Company requires the use of its preferred freight carrier. Example Company provides its carrier account numbers to its suppliers.
> 7. The supplier's invoice number, packing slip number, or receipt date will be included on remittance advices. Example Company's standard transaction codes will be used on remittance advices.
> 8. Suppliers must accept electronic fund transfers as payment.
> 9. Specific questions concerning, orders, receivers, rejects, and payments should be directed to the Example Company buyer who placed the order.

RISKS AND CONTROLS IN EVALUATED RECEIPT SETTLEMENT (STUDY OBJECTIVE 7, continued)

Unfortunately, eliminating parts of a manual matching process also eliminates some of the internal controls inherent in a three-document match of purchase order, receiving report, and invoice. Since some internal controls are eliminated, it becomes necessary to compensate for this loss of controls by strengthening other controls or implementing additional controls. First, the receiving procedures must be established to ensure that goods are accepted only when part numbers and quantities match exactly. There is no reconciliation process later for substitutions, overshipments, or partial shipments. Thus, an organization that wishes to institute an invoice-less matching process must also establish close working relationships with vendors and negotiate firm prices prior to ordering. Since goods are accepted only when quantities match, the vendors must understand that receiving personnel will not accept a shipment unless it matches exactly. Payment is based on those prior negotiated prices, not on an invoice. This speeds the entire receiving and paying process and eliminates much time and cost in processing payments. The organization and the vendor must work together to minimize exceptions such as substitutions of product, damaged products, and partial shipments. The organization should also have established procedures to handle the few exceptions quickly.

There are also IT risks inherent in an invoiceless system. These risks are in the categories of security, confidentiality, processing integrity, and availability.

SECURITY AND CONFIDENTIALITY

It is necessary to authenticate user controls in order to prevent unauthorized access to purchase-related files and to prevent fraudulent or fictitious vendor payments. User IDs and passwords should be required of all users of the purchasing and payment systems. Authority tables establish the access levels of authorized users. This prevents unauthorized users from initiating purchase transactions. Computer logs can assist management in monitoring user access and in detecting unauthorized access or misuse of purchase and payment systems.

PROCESSING INTEGRITY

As described in the previous discussion on automated matching system risks, errors in system logic can lead to repetitive errors in authorizing payments. Therefore, the system must be monitored and tested to ensure the accuracy and completeness of the matching and payment approvals. This monitoring and testing should also include tests to ensure that duplicate payments are appropriately avoided.

AVAILABILITY

Since the system relies heavily on an IT system that can quickly access online purchase-order files, a system interruption or slowdown can halt all receiving activity. Receiving processes could not operate without the ability to view online purchase-order files. Therefore, backup systems and backup data are crucial to ensuring availability of the system at all times. The general controls should also include uninterruptible power supplies and extensive disaster recovery plans to allow continued operations without interruptions.

E-BUSINESS AND ELECTRONIC DATA INTERCHANGE (EDI) (STUDY OBJECTIVE 8)

Chapter 8 described e-business and EDI advantages, risks, and controls from the perspective of the seller. In addition, it was explained earlier in this chapter that the buyer and seller exchange goods and cash with each other; the buyer receives goods and pays cash in the exchange, while the seller receives cash and ships goods. When these exchanges are viewed from the buyer's perspective, a mirror image of the seller's perspective can be seen. The electronic exchange of transaction information is much the same for the buyer as for the seller. You should find it useful at this point to reexamine Chapter 8, Exhibit 8-18, regarding

EDI exchanges. The similarity in processes between buyer and seller means that most of the previous description of advantages, risks, and controls from the seller's perspective applies to the same features from the buyer's perspective, as addressed in this chapter. To avoid repeating those entire sections, the description here will focus only on the risks and controls and will cover both e-business and EDI in this single section.

RISKS AND CONTROLS IN E-BUSINESS AND EDI (STUDY OBJECTIVE 8, continued)

Exhibit 8-19 in Chapter 8 summarized the risks and controls from the seller's perspective. That exhibit is presented here as Exhibit 9-20 to summarize risks and controls of electronic purchase transactions from the buyer's perspective, including security and confidentiality risks, processing integrity risks, and availability risks.

SECURITY AND CONFIDENTIALITY

When conducting purchase and payment transactions electronically, there must be an electronic link between buyer and seller IT systems. This electronic link might be in the form of private leased lines, third-party networks, or the Internet. No matter which type of electronic link is employed, the use of electronic links between buyer and seller exposes risks of unauthorized access and hacking or other network break-ins. Therefore, it is important that all users, including trading partners such as vendors, be authenticated

Exhibit 9-20
E-Business and EDI Risks and Controls

Risk	Controls
Security and Confidentiality	
Unauthorized access Hackers or other network break-ins Repudiation of purchase transactions	Authentication: user ID, password, log-in procedures, access levels, authority tables Firewall, encryption, vulnerability assessment, intrusion detection, penetration testing Computer logs
Processing Integrity	
Invalid data entered by vendors Incomplete audit trail Errors integrating into back-end systems	Input controls such as field check, validity check, limit check, reasonableness check Computer logs Software testing
Availability	
System failures Virus and worm attacks Denial of service attacks by hackers	Business continuity planning, backup data and systems Firewall, encryption, vulnerability assessment, intrusion detection, penetration testing

when they access the system or records. The use of user IDs, passwords, and authority tables are intended to limit access to authorized users and to limit authorized users to only those files or records they must access to perform their assigned duties. Computer logs help management monitor user access and to discover unauthorized access and any resulting security breaches. Firewalls and encryption of data can limit unauthorized access by hackers or other outsiders.

Vulnerability testing and penetration testing allow the company to regularly test the vulnerability of the network connections used for e-business or EDI. **Vulnerability testing** is examining the system to determine the adequacy of security measures and to identify security deficiencies. **Penetration testing** is intentionally attempting to circumvent IT system access controls to determine whether there are weaknesses in any controls. This testing can help uncover vulnerabilities so that these problems can be fixed before they are exploited by outsiders or hackers. **Intrusion detection** software alerts the organization to hacking or other unauthorized use of the system or network.

Strong authentication controls that validate users and computer logs that record transactions can also help prevent repudiation of transactions by the seller. For example, a seller could claim that the electronic payment for a purchase was not received. Authentication of users and computer logs allow the organization to maintain an electronic audit trail that confirms that the electronic check was sent to the valid and authorized vendor and can help avoid repudiation of this payment transaction.

PROCESSING INTEGRITY

In e-business or EDI purchase transactions, vendors may be accessing files and records on the buyer's computer system and may be entering or transmitting data. Therefore, there are risks that the vendor's IT system can introduce erroneous or incomplete data. Data entered or transmitted by the vendor should be subject to input validation controls to ensure the accuracy and completeness of the data. These input validation checks include field checks, validity checks, limit checks, and reasonableness checks. In addition, the data entered into EDI translation software, or e-business web forms must be integrated into the backoffice systems such as the receiving and accounts payable systems. These same input validation checks can assist in reducing errors as data are integrated into other systems within the organization. Finally, computer logs of all transactions conducted with sellers can serve as part of the audit trail to help trace or re-create transactions.

AVAILABILITY

Interruptions to the system can cause critical problems for companies that purchase and pay electronically. System slowdowns or failures can cause the company to be unable to purchase or pay as needed, which can cause the flow of products to be interrupted and thereby slow or stop manufacturing or sales. Anytime the web systems or EDI connections are unavailable, there may be resulting interruptions in manufacturing and thus the ability to have products to sell. Therefore, the company should put controls in place that minimize service disruptions, such as redundant systems, disaster recovery plans, testing of software changes, and capacity planning and testing.

Redundancy is needed for servers, data, and networks. A redundant server system requires maintaining one or more computers as extra, back-up web servers that can operate as the server if the main server goes down. Redundant data as a control is usually accomplished by having data stored in redundant array of inexpensive disks (RAID). A RAID storage maintains one or more disk drives that mirror each other. In this manner, one or more exact duplicates of the data are maintained. A backup network structure should be in place if communication is lost through the regular network.

Disaster recovery plans must be in place to ensure uninterrupted access to EDI or e-business processing even through natural disasters such as fire, flood, or earthquake. The company must have plans to continue service when disasters occur.

As changes are made to the purchasing website or the underlying software to process e-business or EDI purchases, it is important that the changes be tested before they are implemented. If such changes are not tested, they may fail and disrupt operations.

Managers must properly plan for sufficient capacity in the e-business or EDI system and servers to ensure that the system is not overwhelmed by the number of users accessing it or the number of transactions conducted. Managers should ensure that there are regular steps to monitor, test, and adjust the capacity of the system to meet its needs.

Controls that prevent or detect viruses or system intrusion must be in place. These controls are necessary because hackers, intruders, or viruses can slow or interrupt system operations. Intrusion detection and vulnerability testing can help prevent or detect possible intrusions by outsiders or hackers.

E-PAYABLES (STUDY OBJECTIVE 9)

Accounting managers within organizations are usually interested in new systems and software that reduce costs or increase the efficiency of payables processing. The newest technologies related to invoicing and payables are generally referred to as **e-payables**. However, a more specific name for these electronic invoicing and payment systems is **electronic invoice presentment and payment,** or **EIPP.** Most EIPP systems take advantage of the connectivity of the Internet to electronically send invoices or payments. This means that an accounts payable process in an organization could receive invoices electronically via the Internet and make payment via the Internet. Such systems usually utilize web browsers as the interface for accounts payable employees to receive and view invoices and make payments.

Although these systems are newer in technology and software, they have the same advantages and risks as those already described. That is, they improve the efficiency of invoice and payment processing, but they pose security, confidentiality, processing integrity, and availability risks. The Real World Example in the opening of this chapter describes some advantages that General Electric experienced by using EIPP.

PROCUREMENT CARDS (STUDY OBJECTIVE 10)

Within the past couple of decades, many companies have instituted procurement cards as a method to eliminate or reduce the time-consuming steps in purchase and payment transactions. **Procurement cards,** often called p-cards, are credit cards that the organization gives to certain employees to make designated purchases. Procurement cards are normally not used to purchase raw materials or products, but are used for small-dollar-amount purchases such as supplies or maintenance, and to pay for travel and entertainment expenses.

THE REAL WORLD

General Electric Co. (GE) uses a procurement card for all purchases under $2500. GE switched to procurement cards after an investigation of its accounts payable processing revealed that 82% of its invoices were for less than $2500 and that it took 25 to 40 days to process an invoice. This caused GE to miss 77% of early payment discounts. This is typical for many large companies. They have a relatively small number of large-dollar-amount invoices from the purchase of raw materials or products for resale and a huge volume of low-dollar-amount invoices for other purchases. This means that the accounts payable staff spends about 70% to 80% of its time processing and matching invoices for small-dollar purchases.

Using a procurement card can eliminate much time and cost associated with this processing of small-dollar purchases. The procurement card accomplishes the following improvements:

- Employees have more control over their purchases than when things are purchased by a centralized purchasing department.
- Many activities are reduced or eliminated, such as soliciting bids, negotiating with suppliers, keying or entering purchase order and invoice data, matching documents, managing orders that do not match, and writing checks for small-dollar purchases.
- The company can receive one large, consolidated bill from the credit card issuer.
- The information from the credit card issuer can be sorted or examined by employee name, purchase type, or other key needs.
- Managers can place limits on credit cards to control purchasing activity.
- Credit cards can be restricted to certain types of vendors, thereby reducing the chance that the card could be used at an amusement park or strip club, or for some other fraudulent purpose.

ETHICAL ISSUES RELATED TO EXPENDITURES PROCESSES (STUDY OBJECTIVE 11)

In the absence of a strong ethical "tone at the top," encouragement of ethical behavior by all employees, and strong internal controls, there are many opportunities for ethical lapses or fraud to occur in the expenditures processes. Ethical lapses may occur at the upper levels of management when corporate funds are used for personal purchases, as well as at the lowest employee levels when fake travel and entertainment expenses are submitted for reimbursement. While it is not likely that all such ethical problems will be completely eliminated, management can reduce the chances of expenditure fraud or ethics violations by maintaining good internal controls and enforcing ethical conduct.

THE REAL WORLD

There are many examples of frauds related to the expenditures process committed by upper level managers. In addition to the fraud committed at Phar-Mor as described in Chapter 3, Michael Monus, as President and Chief Operating Officer of Phar-Mor, made fraudulent payments on typewritten checks drawn on a special Phar-Mor checking account. The checks supported the World Basketball League (WBL) that Monus founded. The use of a special checking account allowed Monus to bypass the normal purchase order controls, invoice matching system, and computer check writing policies that accompanied Phar-Mor's main operating account, so that he could use Phar-Mor funds to keep the financially troubled WBL afloat. By most accounts, his fraud diverted nearly 10 million dollars to the WBL in a period of three years.

Mr. Monus specifically established a separate checking account that avoided the internal control structure. Since top management is above the level of internal control, proper internal control systems may not prevent expenditure fraud conducted by the top officials. However, the board of directors and upper level management should ensure that the corporate managers adhere to a code of ethical conduct. Ethics codes are not guarantees of fraud prevention either, but when ethical conduct is expected and rewarded, an environment is created in which such management fraud is more difficult to conceal.

THE REAL WORLD

Lower level employees or managers may conduct expenditure related fraud by submitting fictitious invoices or creating fictitious vendors. As an example of fraud in accounts payable, consider the case of Paul Pigeon. Pigeon worked for a Canadian company of about 3000 employees.[4] As the manager of employee training, he regularly hired consultants to conduct training programs for employees. These consultants were paid through a traditional accounts payable system after submitting an invoice. When one of the consultants informed Pigeon that he was retiring, Pigeon used the opportunity to begin a fraud scheme. He began submitting fictitious, handwritten invoices, using plain paper and a rubber stamp for the consultant's name. Since Pigeon was in a position of expenditures authority, he approved the invoices and they were paid through the accounts payable system. Over a two year period, he submitted false invoices totaling $490,000.

Interestingly, Paul Pigeon was apparently not satisfied with just one fraud scheme, as he was perpetrating another fraud at the same time: He was submitting his own travel expenses in duplicate. For the first submission he used his original receipts, and for the second submission he used his credit card receipts. On the second submission, he always added a very small invoice at the bottom so that the amount would be different from his previous submission. He also changed dates to lessen possible suspicion about duplicate payments. He defrauded his employer of $32,923 by this duplicate travel-expense fraud.

Many internal control policies should have been in place to help prevent such frauds. Even simple policies such as accepting only valid original receipts for travel would have helped prevent the duplicate travel-expense fraud. In the case of the fictitious invoice fraud, controls such as periodic verification of the existence of vendors, examining expenditures over budget (variances), and training accounts payable personnel to look for suspicious documentation may have prevented this fraud. This company's example again illustrates that when the tone at the top is not focused on good internal controls and high ethical standards, fraud and ethical lapses are much more likely to occur.

[4] Alan M. Langley, "Phantom Vendors," *Internal Auditor,* August 2001, pp. 91–93.

The board of directors and management of an organization have an ethical obligation to establish the proper tone at the top, strong internal controls, and high ethical standards. If they do not, owners of the organization are harmed when the company is defrauded. In addition, employees and those who conduct business with the organization are also harmed when changes (such as failure to grant pay raises and increased sales prices) are implemented in efforts to recover losses from fraud. It is important to establish internal control policies and IT controls to help prevent or detect such fraud, ethical lapses, or errors. By establishing controls and a code of ethics, the board and management are protecting the assets entrusted to them by owners and shareholders.

THE REAL WORLD

Wal-Mart has an extensive "Statement of Ethics" policy available on its website at investor.walmartstores. com. The policy addresses many areas within the organization, including purchasing. Part of the ethics policy is directed to those who conduct purchasing for Wal-Mart. A portion of that policy prohibits employees from accepting gifts or gratuities from suppliers, including free merchandise, meals, tickets to entertainment events, tips, kickbacks, and personal favors.[5] This is an example of how management can help prevent purchasing agents from favoring certain suppliers and benefiting personally from doing so.

CORPORATE GOVERNANCE IN EXPENDITURE PROCESSES (STUDY OBJECTIVE 12)

Recall that Chapter 5 identified four primary functions of the corporate governance process: management oversight, internal controls and compliance, financial stewardship, and ethical conduct. While corporate governance is important for all business processes, it is particularly necessary in the expenditures processes. Funds expended by an organization do not belong to managers. Managers are stewards, or temporary managers, of those funds. Corporate governance policies and procedures must be in place to ensure that funds are expended only to benefit the organization and its owners, not to benefit the managers or employees personally. For example, corporate governance policies should prevent managers and employees from using company funds to purchase items for their personal use. In other words, strong corporate governance should help prevent fraud, theft, and mismanagement within expenditure processes.

The systems, processes, and internal controls described in this chapter are part of the corporate governance structure. When management designs and implements processes for purchases, purchase returns, and cash disbursements, it assigns responsibility for executing those functions to various managers and employees. As management assigns and oversees these expenditure processes, it is carrying out the corporate governance function of proper management oversight.

Management should also establish appropriate internal controls for expenditures processes, such as those controls described in this chapter, which accomplish the objectives of safeguarding assets within expenditures processes and ensuring accuracy and completeness of expenditures processes data. These internal controls are also part of the corporate governance structure.

[5] http://media.corporate-ir.net/media_files/IROL/11/112761/corpgov/Ethics%20_Current.pdf, p. 9.

When management has designed, implemented, and continually manages processes and internal controls, it is helping to ensure proper stewardship of the company's assets. Corporate governance requires proper financial stewardship. The processes, internal controls, and feedback data from these systems help management report to owners and other stakeholders about proper stewardship of assets within the expenditures processes. These assets would include inventory, raw materials, supplies, cash, and operating assets.

Finally, good corporate governance requires ethical conduct. This chapter described some of the ethical issues that management should consider and address within the expenditures processes. When top management acts ethically and encourages ethical behavior throughout the organization, stronger corporate governance is the result. There are usually fewer cases of frauds, errors, and ethical problems in an organization when top management behaves ethically and encourages ethical behavior.

Perhaps it would be easier to understand the way this chapter's topics fit into corporate governance if you think of it from a negative perspective. For example, if management of a particular organization did not establish sound processes, good internal controls, and ethical policies, it would lack good corporate governance. In that organization, expenditures processes would be poorly executed and poorly controlled. Management would not be exercising proper financial stewardship. Therefore, stakeholders such as investors, creditors, and owners would have little or no trust that funds were expended in a manner that would benefit the organization and its owners. The organization would not represent the type of organization in which we would wish to invest our own money. On the other hand, when an organization has good corporate governance, the stakeholders can properly have more confidence that proper stewardship is occurring. Establishing proper processes, internal controls, and ethical guidelines leads to better corporate governance and, therefore, to good financial stewardship.

SUMMARY OF STUDY OBJECTIVES

An introduction to expenditure processes. There are five typical types of processes related to expenditures. The three that are covered in this chapter are purchasing processes, purchase return processes, and cash disbursement processes.

Purchasing processes and the related risks and controls. Purchasing processes include obtaining a purchase requisition; comparison of the requisition with stock levels; authorizing the purchase request; selecting the vendor; preparing a purchase order; receiving goods at the receiving department; counting, inspecting, and preparing a receiving order for goods received; and updating accounts payable, inventory, and general ledger records. Purchasing process controls can be categorized into authorization, segregation, adequate records, security of assets and records, and independent checks.

Purchase return processes and the related risks and controls. Purchase return processes include rejecting goods already received; matching goods to be returned to the original purchase order; preparing a debit memorandum; receiving credit and/or check from the vendor; and updating accounts payable, inventory, and general ledger records. Purchase return process controls can be categorized into authorization, segregation, adequate records, security of assets and records, and independent checks.

Cash disbursement processes and the related risks and controls. Cash disbursement processes include determining which invoices are due; matching purchase order, invoice, and receiving report; preparing payment; signing and mailing the check; and updating cash, accounts payable, and general ledger records.

An overview of IT systems of expenditure and cash disbursement processes that enhance the efficiency of expenditures processes. Manual tasks of entering and matching documents are extremely time consuming and expensive. Purchasing and payments can become complex because a vendor may occasionally substitute items, ship a different quantity (undership or overship), notify the buyer of back orders, or partially fill an order. Thus, matching takes a large amount of human time to reconcile and approve for payment. IT systems can be used to reduce or eliminate these manual, time-consuming tasks. IT systems for purchasing related processes are computer-based matching, evaluated receipt settlement (ERS), e-business and electronic data interchange (EDI), and e-payables or electronic invoice presentment and payment (EIPP).

Computer-based matching of purchasing documents and the related risks and controls. A computer software system can match an invoice to its related purchase order and receiving report to approve payment of an invoice. To institute an automated matching system, all of the purchasing and receiving files must be online and constantly ready for processing. The system can then access the online purchase order and receiving files and check the match of items, quantities, and prices. The system will not approve an invoice for payment unless the items and quantities match with the packing slip and the prices match the purchase order prices. This ensures that the vendor has billed for the correct items, quantities, and prices. An automated matching system exposes several risks that a company must manage, including security, availability, processing integrity, and confidentiality risks.

Evaluated receipt settlement systems and the related risks and controls. An ERS system conducts a comparison by matching the purchase order to the goods received. If the PO matches the goods, payment is made to the vendor. This eliminates the need for the vendor to send an invoice, since payment is approved as soon goods are received (when they match a purchase order). Thus, it is an invoiceless system. An ERS system poses several risks that a company must manage, including security, availability, processing integrity, and confidentiality risks.

E-business and electronic data interchange (EDI) systems and the related risks and controls. E-business and EDI systems were covered in Chapter 8 from the seller's perspective. This chapter describes only the difference from the buyer's perspective. The buyer receives goods and pays cash in the exchange, while the seller receives the cash and ships the goods. When these exchanges are viewed from the buyer's perspective as opposed to the seller's, the processes, risks, and controls are very similar. E-business and EDI systems carry with them several risks that a company must manage, including security, availability, processing integrity, and confidentiality risks.

E-payables systems. EIPP systems take advantage of the connectivity of the Internet to electronically send invoices or payments. This means that an accounts payable process in an organization could receive invoices electronically via the Internet and make payment via the Internet. These systems typically utilize web browsers as the interface across which accounts payable employees receive and view invoices and make payments.

Procurement cards. Procurement cards are essentially credit cards that the organization gives to certain employees to make designated purchases. These cards are normally not used to purchase raw materials or products, but are used for small-dollar-amount purchases such as supplies or maintenance, and to pay for travel and entertainment expenses.

Ethical issues related to expenditure processes. The board of directors and management of an organization have an ethical obligation to establish the proper tone at the top, strong internal controls, and high ethical standards. If they do not, owners of the organization are harmed when the company is defrauded through management fraud, fictitious vendor payments, and expense reimbursement fraud. It is important to establish internal control policies and IT controls to help prevent or detect such fraud, ethical lapses, or errors.

Corporate governance in expenditure processes. Corporate governance policies are critically important within expenditure processes, as they help to ensure that funds are expended only in an approved manner. Corporate governance policies should incorporate the four areas of management oversight, internal controls, financial stewardship, and ethical behavior. A strong form of corporate governance should help prevent fraud, theft, and misuse of corporate assets.

KEY TERMS

Accounts payable subsidiary ledger
Automated matching
Bill of lading
Blind purchase order
Business process reengineering (BPR)
Cash disbursements journal (or check register)
Cash management
Common carrier
Cutoff
Debit memo
Dual signature requirement
e-payables
Electronic invoice presentment and payment (EIPP)
ERS
Evaluated Receipt Settlement (ERS)
Intrusion detection software (ERS)
Intrusion detection software
Packing Slip
Penetration testing
Procurement card
Purchase order (PO)
Purchase invoice
Purchase requisition
Receiving log
Receiving report
Remittance advice
Three-way match
Transaction processing systems
Vendor
Vulnerability testing

END OF CHAPTER MATERIAL

CONCEPT CHECK

1. Within the purchasing processes, which of the following is the first document prepared and thereby the one that triggers the remaining purchasing processes?
   a. The invoice
   b. The receiving report

c. The purchase order
d. The purchase requisition

2. Personnel who work in the receiving area should complete all of the following processes except
   a. counting the goods received.
   b. inspecting goods received for damage.
   c. preparing a receiving report.
   d. preparing an invoice.
3. Which of the given departments will immediately adjust the vendor account for each purchase transaction so that the company will know the correct amount owed to the vendor?
   a. Purchasing
   b. Receiving
   c. Accounts payable
   d. Shipping
4. One of the most critical controls to prevent theft of inventory purchased is to
   a. require authorization of the purchase requisition.
   b. segregate inventory custody from inventory record keeping.
   c. compare the purchase order, receiving report, and invoice.
   d. segregate the authorization of purchases from the inventory record keeping.
5. Internal control is strengthened by the use of a blind purchase order, upon which the quantity of goods ordered is intentionally left blank. This blind copy is used in which department?
   a. The department that initiated the purchase request
   b. The receiving department
   c. The purchasing department
   d. The accounts payable department
6. Which of the following questions would most likely be included in an internal control questionnaire concerning the completeness of purchase transactions?
   a. Is an authorized purchase order required before the receiving department can accept a shipment or the accounts payable department can record a voucher?
   b. Are prenumbered purchase requisitions used and are they subsequently matched with vendor invoices?
   c. Is there a regular reconciliation of the inventory records with the file of unpaid vouchers?
   d. Are prenumbered purchase orders, receiving reports, and vouchers used, and are the entire sequences accounted for?
7. Which of the following controls is not normally performed in the accounts payable department?
   a. The vendor's invoice is matched with the related receiving report.
   b. Vendor invoices are selected for payment.
   c. Asset and expense accounts to be recorded are assigned.
   d. Unused purchase orders and receiving reports are accounted for.

8. In a system of proper internal controls, the same employee should not be allowed to
   a. sign checks and cancel the supporting voucher package.
   b. receive goods and prepare the related receiving report.
   c. prepare voucher packages and sign checks.
   d. initiate purchase requisitions and inspect goods received.
9. The document prepared when purchased items are returned is a(n)
   a. debit memo.
   b. invoice.
   c. receiving report.
   d. sales journal.
10. Within cash disbursements, all of the following should be true before a check is prepared, except that
    a. The purchase order, receiving report, and invoice have been matched.
    b. The purchased goods have been used.
    c. Sufficient cash is available.
    d. The invoice discount date or due date is imminent.
11. A manager suspects that certain employees are ordering merchandise for themselves over the Internet without recording the purchase or receipt of the merchandise. When vendors' invoices arrive, one of the employees approves the invoices for payment. After the invoices are paid, the employee destroys the invoices and related vouchers. To trace whether this is actually happening, it would be best to begin tracing from the
    a. cash disbursements.
    b. approved vouchers.
    c. receiving reports.
    d. vendors' invoices.
12. Within accounts payable, to ensure that each voucher is submitted and paid only once, each invoice approved to be paid should be
    a. supported by a receiving report.
    b. stamped "paid" by the check signer.
    c. prenumbered and accounted for.
    d. approved for authorized purchases.
13. For proper segregation of duties in cash disbursements, the person who signs checks also
    a. reviews the monthly bank reconciliation.
    b. returns the checks to accounts payable.
    c. is denied access to the supporting documents.
    d. is responsible for mailing the checks.
14. Which of the following internal controls would help prevent overpayment to a vendor or duplicate payment to a vendor?
    a. Review and cancellation of supporting documents after issuing payment
    b. Requiring the check signer to mail the payment directly to the vendor

c. Review of the accounts where the expenditure transaction has been recorded
d. Approving the purchase before the goods are ordered from the vendor

15. Which of the following is not an independent verification related to cash disbursements?
    a. The cash disbursements journal is reconciled to the general ledger.
    b. The stock of unused checks should be adequately secured and controlled.
    c. The bank statement is reconciled on a monthly basis.
    d. The accounts payable subsidiary ledger is reconciled to the general ledger.
16. Which of the following IT systems is designed to avoid the document matching process and is an "invoiceless" system?
    a. Computer-based matching system
    b. Electronic data interchange
    c. Evaluated receipt settlement
    d. Microsoft Dynamics GP®
17. Input controls such as field check, validity check, limit check, and reasonableness check are useful in IT systems of purchasing processes to lessen which of the following risks?
    a. Unauthorized access
    b. Invalid data entered by vendors
    c. Repudiation of purchase transactions
    d. Virus and worm attacks
18. Which of the following is most likely to be effective in deterring fraud by upper level managers?
    a. Internal controls
    b. An enforced code of ethics
    c. Matching documents prior to payment
    d. Segregating custody of inventory from inventory record keeping

DISCUSSION QUESTIONS

19. (SO 2) Name the first document that should be prepared when a production employee recognizes that the quantity of goods on hand is insufficient to meet customer demand.
20. (SO 2) How does the maintenance of a receiving log enhance internal controls?
21. (SO 2) Why should a receiving clerk be denied access to information on a purchase order?
22. (SO 2) Under what circumstances would it be necessary to manually update accounts payable prior to the receipt of a vendor's invoice?
23. (SO 4) Which department is responsible for making sure that payments are made in time to take advantage of vendor discounts?
24. (SO 4) Why would some checks need to include two signatures?
25. (SO 4) During the process of reconciling the bank account, why is it necessary to review the dates, payees, and signatures on the canceled checks?

26. (SO 4, 6) What specifically does a cash disbursements clerk do when he or she "cancels" an invoice? How does this compare with the procedures followed when computer-based matching in the system is utilized?
27. (SO 4) Why should accountants periodically review the sequence of checks issued?
28. (SO 2, 4) What accounting records are used by accounts payable personnel to keep track of amounts owed to each vendor?
29. (SO 5) Identify some inefficiencies inherent in a manual expenditures processing system.
30. (SO 5) What are the advantages of BPR?
31. (SO 5, 6, 7, 8) List three examples of BPR used in the expenditures processes.
32. (SO 6) Explain how system logic errors could cause cash management problems.
33. (SO 6) Explain how system availability problems could cause cash management problems.
34. (SO 8) How is an audit trail maintained in an IT system where no paper documents are generated?
35. (SO 6) What can a company do to protect itself from business interruptions due to power outages?
36. (SO 7) What paper document is eliminated when ERS is used?
37. (SO 7) Identify compensating controls needed for an effective ERS system.
38. (SO 5) What is typically the most time-consuming aspect of the expenditures process?
39. (SO 8) Identify each category of risk that can be reduced by using authority tables, computer logs, passwords, and firewalls.
40. (SO 6) Explain why the availability of computer systems in the receiving department is such an important component of an automated expenditures process.
41. (SO 5, 8) Identify three ways that buyers and sellers may be linked electronically.
42. (SO 8) What techniques can a company use to reveal problems concerning potential exposure to unauthorized access to its systems?
43. (SO 9) How are web browsers used in e-payables systems?
44. (SO 10) Explain how procurement cards provide for increased efficiencies in the accounts payable department.

BRIEF EXERCISES

45. (SO 2, 4) Describe what is likely to occur if company personnel erroneously recorded a purchase transaction for the wrong vendor. What if a cash disbursement were posted to the wrong vendor? Identify internal controls that would detect or prevent this from occurring.
46. (SO 4) Debate the logic used in the following statement: "The person responsible for approving cash disbursements should also prepare the bank reconciliation because he is most familiar with the checks that have been written on that bank account."

47. (SO 8) Expenditures systems are crucial in the automobile manufacturing industry, where hundreds or thousands of parts must be purchased to manufacture cars. Briefly describe how EDI would be beneficial in this industry.
48. (SO 2, 4) Describe how the matching of key information on supporting documents can help a company determine whether purchase transactions have been properly executed.
49. (SO 2, 3) Describe how the use of prenumbered forms for debit memos can help a company ascertain that purchase return transactions have not been omitted from the accounting records.
50. (SO 5, 7) Describe how an ERS system could improve the efficiency of expenditures processes.
51. (SO 10) Describe how a procurement card improves the efficiency of purchasing supplies.

PROBLEMS

52. (SO 2, 3, 4) Identify an internal control procedure that would reduce the following risks in a manual system:
    a. The purchasing department may not be notified when goods need to be purchased.
    b. Accounts payable may not be updated for items received.
    c. Purchase orders may be prepared on the basis of unauthorized requisitions.
    d. Receiving clerks may steal purchased goods.
    e. Payments may be made for items not received.
    f. Amounts paid may be applied to the wrong vendor account.
    g. Payments may be made for items previously returned.
    h. Receiving clerks may accept delivery of goods in excess of quantities ordered.
    i. Duplicate payments may be issued for a single purchase transaction.
53. (SO 1, SO 10) Chris Smith started a new business, a coffee and pastry cart located at the local library. Chris hired her brother, Pat, as her assistant. Chris and Pat personally make all the purchases of items needed to stock the cart, using procurement cards issued in the name of the company. Because Chris is personally liable for payments made on the procurement cards, she recognizes the need to establish policies for her brother to follow for the use of this card. Suggest some controls that should be in place. Identify some resources that need to be purchased for this business.
54. (SO 1, 5) AZQ Company is considering a business process reengineering (BPR) project whereby its current (mostly manual) expenditures processing would be converted to an automated system. Brainstorm ideas for this project. Specifically, what processes could be redesigned? What current IT developments should AZQ consider implementing? You may find it helpful to use the Internet to locate information on BPR related to the expenditures process.
55. (SO 2, 4) The following list presents statements regarding the expenditures processes. Each statement is separate and should be considered to be from

a separate company. Determine whether each statement is an internal control strength or weakness; then describe why it is a strength or weakness. If it is an internal control weakness, provide a method or methods to improve the internal control.

a. A purchasing agent updates the inventory subsidiary ledger when an order is placed.

b. An employee in accounts payable maintains the accounts payable subsidiary ledger.

c. Purchasing agents purchase items only if they have received an approved purchase requisition.

d. The receiving dock employee counts and inspects goods and prepares a receiving document that is forwarded to accounts payable.

e. The receiving dock employee compares the packing list with the goods received and if they match, forwards the packing list to accounts payable.

f. An employee in accounts payable matches an invoice to a receiving report before approving a payment of the invoice.

g. A check is prepared in the accounts payable department when the invoice is received.

56. (SO 2) The following figure shows a packing list received by Hitchins, Inc. When a packing slip arrives at the receiving dock with a shipment, a worker prepares a receiving report. The receiving report triggers the process for payment in accounts payable.

Frazier Stamping Corporation **Packing Slip**
10493 North Oak Street
Gainesville, FL
Phone (625) 555-9988
Fax (625) 555-9989

Order Date:	September 25, 2007	**Date:**	September 30, 2007
Order Number:	75489	**Customer Contact:**	Erin Smithers
Purchase Order:	PO549364	**Customer Account:**	5404
Ship To:	Hitchins, Inc. Attn: Research Department 5242 Main Street Haverhill, FL 33422	**Bill To:**	Hitchins, Inc. Attn: Accounts Payable 5242 Main Street Haverhill, FL 33422

Part #	Description	Unit Type	Order Quantity	Ship Quantity	Backorder Quantity
918-0142	Pulley end, 5/8"–18 splined	Each	50	50	0
725–1396	Solenoid	Each	80	80	0
725–0267	Starter switch	Each	50	40	10

Required:

Assume that Hitchins, Inc., is preparing to computerize the manual input processes such as completing a receiving report. Use Microsoft Excel to design an appropriate format for a data entry screen that could be used at the receiving dock to enter information from the packing slip in the company's expenditures system.

57. (SO 4) Since the accounts payable system of matching purchase orders, invoices, and receiving reports can often be complex, organizations must routinely check to ensure that they are not making a duplicate payment. The textbook website contains a spreadsheet titled "invoices.xls." Using your knowledge of spreadsheets and the characteristics of duplicate payments, identify any payments within the spreadsheet that appear to be duplicate or problem payments.

58. (SO 8) Fracho Manufacturing Company operates two plants that manufacture shelves and display units for retail stores. To manufacture these items, the purchasing agents purchase raw materials such as steel, aluminum, plastic, lexan, and miscellaneous screws, rubber end caps, bolts, and nuts. Two purchasing agents work at the first, and original, plant location. They do all the purchasing for both plants, which are located in Milwaukee, Wisconsin. Each purchasing agent has a PC that is connected to a company network consisting of a server at the first plant and PCs in both plants. The company has always used mailed purchase orders to purchase items, but they are now considering the installation of an internet EDI system to place purchases.

Required:

Describe the IT controls that Fracho should include when it implements an internet EDI system. For each control you suggest, describe the intended purpose of the control.

59. (SO 2, 3, 4) Wikkam, Inc. is a small company with three people working in the expenditures processes. One of the three employees is the supervisor of the other two. Some tasks that must be accomplished within the expenditures processes are the following:

a. Accounts payable record keeping
b. Authorization of new vendors
c. Authorization of purchase returns
d. Authorization of purchases
e. Cash disbursements record keeping
f. Check-signing authority
g. Custody of inventory in the receiving area
h. Maintaining custody of cash
i. Preparation of a debit memo for a purchase return

Required:

Consider the duties you would assign to each of the three employees (supervisor, employee 1, and employee 2). No employee should have more than three tasks, and there should be a proper separation of duties to achieve appropriate internal control. List the three people, the duties you assigned to each, and a description of why those assignments should achieve proper separation of duties.

60. (SO 7) Using a search engine, search the Internet for information about evaluated receipt settlement, or ERS. You may have more success searching for the terms "ERS" and "invoices" together in one search. From what you read about ERS on the web, what do you think appear to be the difficulties encountered when a company chooses to implement ERS?

61. (SO 9) Using a search engine, search the Internet for information about electronic invoice presentment and payment. You may have more success searching for the terms "EIPP" and "invoices" together in one search. From what you read about EIPP on the web, what would you say are the advantages and disadvantages of EIPP? One of the concepts about EIPP is that it should benefit both the buying company and the selling company. What do you think the benefits are to the buyer and to the seller?

62. (SO 9) Visit the e-commerce website for Jupitermedia Corporation at www.ecommerce-guide.com and search for EIPP under the News and Trends tab. Identify the company that introduced an EIPP product in 2002 as part of its Financial Management Solutions Package. What does this company call its EIPP application?

63. (SO 11) Suppose you are an accounts payable clerk for a small home-improvements contractor. This morning one of the site supervisors submitted an invoice requesting immediate payment to a new vendor for items he claims were delivered directly to a work site. The supervisor attached a note to the invoice asking that the check be returned to him upon issuance so that he could personally deliver it to the vendor. This would ensure the timeliness of future deliveries. He claims that, unless the payment is made immediately, there will be delivery delays on items needed to complete this job, as well as delays on items for another contract in progress. Although you are suspicious of this unusual request, you are tempted to accommodate it. You know that timely completion and collection on these contracts is critical to the company's production scheduling and cash management. Moreover, the company president is on vacation and therefore not available to grant special authorization for this payment. Speculate on the type of fraud that could be in process here. What (if anything) could you do to ascertain the propriety of the transaction and still make the payment today?

64. (SO 11) Two of the most common ways that employees commit fraud against their employers is the misstatement of reimbursable expense accounts and the misuse of office supplies for personal purposes. Although these schemes are usually not individually significant, their magnitude can be damaging if these practices are widespread. Develop suggestions for internal controls that could curb the occurrence of such fraudulent activities.

CASES

65. Breston Incorporated has the following processes related to purchasing: When it is determined that an item should be ordered, the purchasing department prepares a three-copy invoice. The first copy is mailed to the vendor, the second copy is filed by PO number in the purchasing department, and the third copy is forwarded to inventory control. Inventory con-

trol updates the inventory ledger with the quantities that were ordered and files the purchase order copy by date.

When ordered items arrive at the receiving dock, the packing slip is inspected and a two-copy receiving report is prepared. The first copy is forwarded to the purchasing department, where it is filed with the purchase order. The second copy is filed in the receiving department by date. The packing slip is forwarded to the accounts payable department.

Vendors mail invoices directly to the accounts payable department. The accounts payable department reviews the invoice and related packing slip, prepares a cash disbursement voucher, updates the accounts payable ledger, and files the invoice by date. The cash disbursement voucher is forwarded to the cash disbursements department. The packing slip is returned to the receiving department. The cash disbursements department prepares a two-copy check, mails the first copy to the vendor, and forwards the second copy to the general ledger department. The cash disbursement voucher is forwarded to the accounts payable department where it is filed with the invoice.

The general ledger department updates the general ledger accounts, using the second copy of the check, and then forwards the check copy to cash disbursements to be filed by check number.

Required:

1. Draw a document flowchart of the purchase processes of Breston.
2. Identify any weaknesses in internal controls within the purchase processes and indicate the improvements you would suggest.

66. Mershay Enterprises is a wholesaler that purchases consumer merchandise from many different suppliers. Mershay then sells this merchandise to many different retail chain stores. The following paragraphs describe the expenditures processes at Mershay:

Warehouse employees constantly monitor the level of each merchandise item by assessing how many remaining boxes of items are on warehouse shelves. When a warehouse worker sees the need to order a particular product, he fills out a postcard-size order requisition form with the product name and item number. The number is Mershay's item number.

When the purchasing department receives a requisition from the warehouse employee, a buyer looks up the last purchase of that item and completes a purchase order to buy the item from that vendor. The manager of the purchasing department approves the purchase order before it is mailed to the vendor. One copy of the purchase order is mailed to the vendor, one copy is filed in the purchasing department, one copy is forwarded to the receiving department, and one copy is forwarded to the accounts payable department.

When the receiving department receives an order, it compares the packing slip with the purchase order. If no purchase order exists, the item is returned to the vendor. A receiving report is prepared for the number of items indicated on the packing slip. One copy of the receiving report is filed in the receiving department, one copy is forwarded to the purchasing department, and one copy is forwarded to the accounts payable department. Items received are then transported to the warehouse.

When the accounts payable department receives an invoice from the vendor, an employee in the accounts payable department compares the purchase order, receiving report, and invoice. If the three documents match correctly, a cash disbursement voucher is prepared. If it does not match, the employee contacts the vendor to try to reconcile the differences. The cash disbursement voucher is reviewed by the manager of the accounts payable department. If it appears correct to her, she writes a check and forwards the check to the treasurer to be signed and mailed to the vendor.

Required:

1. List any strengths and weaknesses in the internal control procedures of Mershay Enterprises.
2. Draw a document flowchart of the expenditure processes.
3. Describe any benefits that Mershay may receive by installing a newer, IT system to process purchases, goods received, accounts payable, and checks. Be specific as to how IT systems could benefit each of the processes described.

67. Hamburg Metals, Inc. is a manufacturer of aluminum cans for the beverage industry. Hamburg purchases aluminum and other raw materials from several vendors. The purchasing process at Hamburg occurs as follows:

When inventory of any raw material seems low, a purchasing agent examines the records to determine the vendor who supplied the last purchase of that raw material. The purchasing agent prepares a three-copy purchase order and mails the top copy to the vendor. One copy is filed in the purchasing department, and one copy is forwarded to the inventory control department (inventory record keeping). Inventory control personnel update the inventory subsidiary ledger and file the purchase order by number in the inventory control files.

When the goods arrive at the receiving dock, a receiving report is prepared from information on the packing slip. One copy of the receiving report is filed in the receiving department, and one copy is forwarded to purchasing so that the purchasing department is informed of the receipt of goods.

The vendor mails an invoice for the raw materials directly to the accounts payable department. When the invoice is received, accounts payable personnel prepare a cash disbursement voucher to approve payment. The voucher is forwarded to the cash disbursements department. The accounts payable department also updates the accounts payable subsidiary ledger and files the invoice by invoice number.

Upon receiving the cash disbursement voucher, an employee in the cash disbursements department prepares a two-copy check. The top copy of the check is mailed to the vendor, and the second copy is forwarded to the general ledger department. The cash disbursement voucher is stamped "paid" and returned to the accounts payable department. The voucher is filed with the invoice in the accounts payable department.

The general ledger department records the check in the general ledger and returns the check copy to the cash disbursements department, where it is filed.

Required:

a. Draw two process maps to reflect the business processes at Hamburg. One process map should depict the purchasing processes, and the second process map should depict the cash disbursements processes.
b. Draw two document flowcharts to reflect the records and reports used by these processes at Hamburg. One flowchart should depict the

purchasing processes, and the second flowchart should depict the cash disbursements processes.

c. Describe any weaknesses in these processes or internal controls. As you identify weaknesses, also describe your suggested improvements.

d. Draw two new process maps that include your suggested improvements. One process map should depict the purchasing processes, and the second process map should depict the cash disbursement processes.

68. The United States General Accounting Office (GAO) Office of Special Investigations was responsible for investigating a potential purchase fraud case. The man who allegedly committed the fraud was Mark J. Krenik, a former civilian employee of the U.S. Air Force.

Mr. Krenik was the Air Force's technical representative on contracts with Hughes STX. Hughes STX provided hardware, software maintenance, technical support, and training to the Air Force. Part of Mr. Krenik's alleged fraud included opening accounts under his control at banks in Maryland. The accounts were opened under the names Hughes STX and ST Systems Corporation. A section of the GAO report on this fraud investigation reads as follows:[6]

> On December 15, 1992, Mr. Krenik opened post office box 215 in Vienna, Virginia, in his own name. On December 24, 1992, Mr. Krenik delivered to the Air Force Finance Office 11 bogus invoices totaling $504,941.19. Accompanying the invoices were the respective DD-250s, on which Mr. Krenik had falsely certified that work had been performed and deliveries made. Special instructions on the invoices directed that payments be remitted to ST Systems Corporation at the Vienna, Virginia post office box.

Mr. Krenik deposited the checks in the accounts he controlled at the Maryland banks. His fraud was unsuccessful because bank employees became suspicious when he tried to withdraw large sums from the accounts.

Required:

Describe internal controls that should be in place at the Air Force to help prevent such fraud.

69. The document flowchart given next shows part of the purchasing and cash disbursement processes for Jidd, Inc., a small manufacturer of gadgets and widgets. Some of the flowchart symbols are labeled to indicate operations, controls, and records.

Required:

For each of the symbols in the flowchart (numbered 1. through 12.), select one response (lettered A. through T.) from the answer lists. Each response may be selected once or not at all.

1. _____	5. _____	9. _____
2. _____	6. _____	10. _____
3. _____	7. _____	11. _____
4. _____	8. _____	12. _____

[6]Report to the Chairman, Subcommittee on Administrative Oversight and the Courts, Committee on the Judiciary, U.S. Senate. General Accounting Office, September 1998, p. 10.

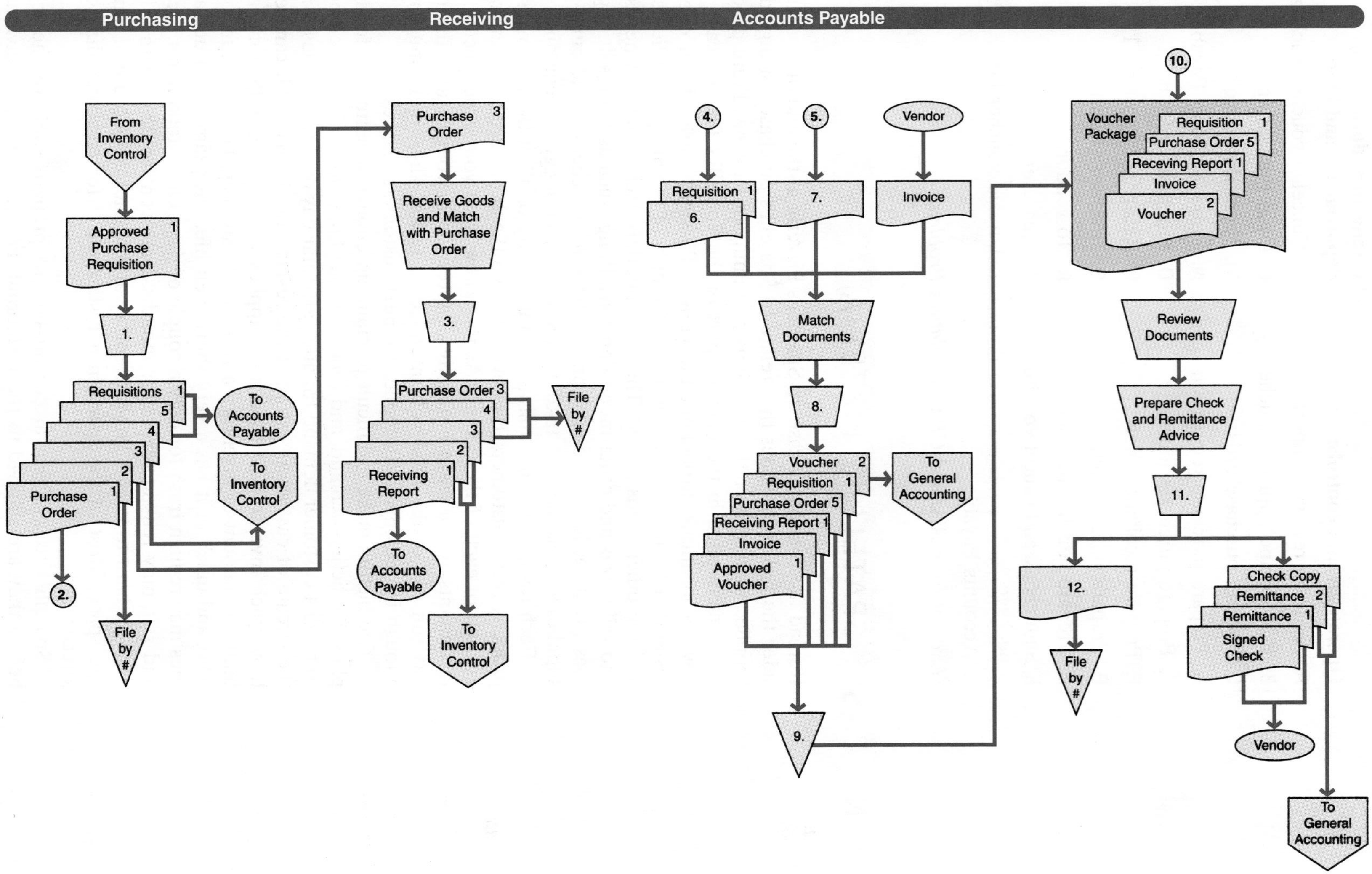

Purchasing
Receiving
Accounts Payable
From Inventory Control
Approved Purchase Requisition 1
1.
Requisitions 1
5
4
3
2
Purchase Order 1
To Accounts Payable
To Inventory Control
2.
File by #
Purchase Order 3
Receive Goods and Match with Purchase Order
3.
Purchase Order 3
4
3
2
Receiving Report 1
File by #
To Accounts Payable
To Inventory Control
4.
5.
Vendor
Requisition 1
6.
7.
Invoice
Match Documents
8.
Voucher 2
Requisition 1
Purchase Order 5
Receiving Report 1
Invoice
Approved Voucher 1
To General Accounting
9.
10.
Voucher Package
Requisition 1
Purchase Order 5
Receving Report 1
Invoice
Voucher 2
Review Documents
Prepare Check and Remittance Advice
11.
12.
File by #
Check Copy
Remittance 2
Remittance 1
Signed Check
Vendor
To General Accounting

Operations and controls:

A. Approve receiving report
B. Prepare and approve voucher
C. Prepare purchase order
D. Prepare purchase requisition
E. Prepare purchases journal
F. Prepare receiving report
G. Prepare sales journal
H. Prepare voucher package
I. Sign check and cancel voucher package
J. Accounts Payable

Connectors, documents, departments, and files:

K. Canceled voucher package
L. From Purchasing
M. From Receiving
N. From Accounts Payable
O. Purchase order no. 5
P. Receiving report no. 1
Q. Inventory Control
R. To vendor
S. Treasurer
T. Unpaid voucher file

(Excerpt from Adapted CPA Simulation Problem)

CONTINUING CASE: SPATELLI'S PIZZERIA

Reread the continuing case on Spatelli's Pizzeria at the end of Chapter 1. Consider the following issues that relate to Spatelli's purchases of ingredients and supplies, then answer the questions pertaining to its expenditure processes.

As mentioned in the opening part of the Spatelli's Pizzeria case, there are now 49 locations throughout the greater Pittsburgh area. Each one of those restaurant locations needs an ongoing supply of the many ingredients of pizzas and the other foods served. The raw materials each restaurant needs to make and sell pizzas and other menu items are things such as flour, salt, sugar, tomatoes, potatoes, lettuce, tomato paste, spices, meats, cheeses, and buns, as well as supplies such as napkins, take-out packages and doggy-bag containers.

Each restaurant must maintain an inventory of all of these items in order to properly serve customers. However, it is a difficult balance to maintain the right amount of each of these items. As you know from your experience in eating at restaurants, it can leave a negative impression in your mind if the restaurant has run out of the food you intended to order. Thus, there must always be enough ingredients and supplies to meet customers' desires.

Two factors make it difficult to maintain enough inventory of food and supplies: predicting demand, and time or space limitations. First, it can be difficult to predict customer demand for any particular day or week. The less predictable the stream of customers eating at the restaurant, the harder it can be to know how much inventory of food and supplies to keep. Secondly, time and space limit the amount of inventory a restaurant can keep. Food inventory is perishable, and much of it has a very short shelf life. For example, lettuce and tomatoes may remain fresh for only a couple of days. Other food items, such as flour and salt, may remain usable for months. But even for items with a long shelf life, it is hard to keep a large inventory at a restaurant because of limited storage space. Most of the space in a restaurant is for customer dining and the kitchen.

Spatelli's uses a central commissary to prepare some of the ingredients before they are shipped to the restaurant. For example, the individual restaurant locations do not make dough on the premises. The flour, salt, yeast, and other ingredients are maintained, mixed, and prepared at the commissary, and this premade dough is then shipped by truck to restaurants daily. The pizza sauce and many ingredients for sandwiches and salads are also premade at the commissary.

All of these factors taken together mean that Spatelli's must continually be purchasing the ingredients for pizzas and other foods, and supplies. These inventory items must be delivered to the commissary and then to each of the 49 Spatelli's locations to ensure that they never run out of the items needed to serve customers. Since there is a short shelf life for much of the inventory, the purchasing takes place on a daily basis to keep the commissary and each restaurant location properly stocked.

Required:

a. Describe how you believe an efficient and effective purchasing system should be organized at Spatelli's. Consider details such as the following:
   1. How many purchasing agents should be employed?
   2. Where will these purchasing agents be located?
   3. How will the necessary information for purchasing flow between restaurants and these purchasing agents?
   4. How will IT systems be used in purchasing?
   5. How and when will purchased items be delivered to the restaurants? (Remember that all 49 locations are within the Pittsburgh area and none would be more than a one-hour drive from the corporate Headquarters.)

b. Draw a process map of your proposed purchasing system.

c. Describe any IT controls that would be necessary or desirable in your purchasing system.

SOLUTIONS TO CONCEPT CHECK

1. (SO 2) Within the purchasing processes, the first document prepared, and thereby the one that triggers the remaining purchasing processes, is **d. the purchase requisition.** When a determination has been made that more supplies or inventory must be purchased, a purchase requisition is prepared and then forwarded to other departments to begin the purchasing processes.
2. (SO 2) Personnel who work in the receiving area should complete all of the following processes except **d. preparing an invoice.** When goods arrive at the receiving department, workers should inspect the goods for damage, count the goods, and prepare a receiving report. The invoice is prepared by the vendor.
3. (SO 2) The department that will immediately adjust the vendor account for each purchase transaction so that the company will know the correct amount owed to the vendor is **c. accounts payable.** Accounts payable maintains records of the amounts owed to vendors, in the form of an accounts payable subsidiary ledger. When purchase transactions occur, accounts payable should update the accounts payable subsidiary ledger to show the new amount owed to the vendor.

4. (SO 2) One of the most critical controls to prevent theft of inventory purchased is to **b. segregate inventory custody from inventory record keeping.** Each of the remaining options are good internal controls, but not all of them help deter theft of inventory. The best control to prevent theft of inventory is to segregate custody from record keeping. Segregating these makes it much more difficult for a person to steal inventory AND alter inventory records.
5. (CPA Adapted) (SO 2) Internal control is strengthened by the use of a blind purchase order, upon which the quantity of goods ordered is intentionally left blank. This blind copy is used in **b. the receiving department.** This control allows the goods to be independently inspected and counted upon receipt. Receiving department employees must actually count the goods rather than just check off an amount. Each of the other options are for departments that need to know the quantity of goods in order to complete their responsibilities.
6. (CPA Adapted) (SO 2) The following question would most likely be included in an internal control questionnaire concerning the completeness of purchasing transactions: **d. Are prenumbered purchase orders, receiving reports, and vouchers used, and are the entire sequences accounted for?** Accounting for an entire sequence of prenumbered documents provides preventive control against record omissions. In other words, it helps ensure the completeness of the records. Option a. is incorrect because it is concerned with the assertion regarding authorization. Although options b. and c. each have some relevance to the completeness assertion, b. is not the best response because purchase requisitions may not always result in a purchase transactions (rather, purchase orders and receiving reports are better indicators that a purchase transaction occurred) and c. is incorrect because vouchers represent purchase transactions that should have already been recorded; accordingly, this control would be more likely to address completeness of the inventory records.
7. (CPA Adapted) (SO 2, 4) The following control is not normally performed in the accounts payable department: **d. Unused purchase orders and receiving reports are accounted for.** In order to enhance the effectiveness of internal controls via segregation of duties, this task is normally performed by an employee who does not have access to the accounts payable records. This prevents the opportunity to create a fictitious purchase transaction and record it in the company's accounting records. Each of the other options represent accounts payable department tasks.
8. (CPA Adapted) (SO 2, 4) In a system of proper internal controls, the same employee should not be allowed to **c. prepare voucher packages and sign checks.** This violates the segregation of duties principles in that it would permit record keeping (preparation of voucher packages) and custody (check-signing authority) functions to be carried out by the same employee. Each of the other options represents tasks that ARE typically performed by the same employee or within the same department.
9. (SO 3) The document prepared when purchased items are returned is the **a. debit memo.** When purchased items are to be returned, a debit memo is prepared. An invoice is prepared by the vendor. A receiving report is prepared when purchased goods are received. A sales journal is part of the revenue processes, not the purchasing processes.

10. (SO 4) Within cash disbursements, all of the given statements should be true before a check is prepared, except for **b. The purchased goods have been used.** Prior to approving payment for purchased goods, the processes in the company should ensure that the purchase order, receiving report, and invoice have been matched; sufficient cash is available; and either the invoice due date or discount date warrants payment. A company could not wait until the goods are used to pay, since vendors want payment upon the due date.
11. (CPA Adapted) (SO 4) A manger suspects that certain employees are ordering merchandise for themselves over the Internet without recording the purchase or receipt of the merchandise. When vendor's invoices arrive, one of the employees approves the invoices for payment. After the invoices are paid, the employee destroys the invoices and related vouchers. To trace whether this is actually happening, it would be best to begin tracing from the **a. cash disbursements.** The record of payment would be the only option for possibly uncovering this scheme. Since these fraudsters are not recording the receipt of merchandise and they are destroying invoices and vouchers, options b., c., and d. would each be incorrect.
12. (CPA Adapted) (SO 4) Within accounts payable, to provide assurance that each voucher is submitted and paid only once, each invoice approved to be paid should be **b. stamped "paid" by the check signer.** This represents the cancellation of the invoice, which should prevent a duplicate payment. Although each of the other options represents an internal control, they are not effective at preventing duplicate payments.
13. (CPA Adapted) (SO 4) For proper segregation of duties in cash disbursements, the person who signs checks also **b. returns the checks to accounts payable.** This allows for the recording of the payments (separate from the custody and authorization functions). Option c. is incorrect because check signers typically review supporting documentation to determine the propriety of the payment. Options a. and d. are incorrect because they would represent violations of proper segregation of duties.
14. (CIA Adapted) (SO 4) The internal control that would help prevent overpayment to a vendor or duplicate payments to a vendor is **a. review and cancellation of supporting documents when a check is issued.** Option b. is incorrect because it represents a violation of segregation of duties and would not necessarily prevent a duplicate payment. Although options c. and d. are internal controls, neither is effective in the prevention of duplicate payments.
15. (SO 4) The following is not an independent verification related to cash disbursements: **b. The stock of unused checks should be adequately secured and controlled.** This is a security control, not an independent verification. Independent verifications are independent checks on accuracy and completeness, such as reconciliations.
16. (SO 5, 7) The IT system designed to avoid the document-matching process and that is an "invoiceless" system is **c. evaluated receipt settlement (ERS).** In an ERS system, there is an invoiceless match that takes place by matching the purchase order to the goods received. If the PO matches the goods, payment is made to the vendor. This eliminates the need for the vendor to send an invoice, since payment is approved as soon goods are received (when they match a purchase order). Thus, it is an invoiceless system.

17. (SO 5, 8) Input controls such as field check, validity check, limit check, and reasonableness check are useful in IT systems of purchasing processes to lessen the risk of **b. invalid data entered by vendors.** IT controls such as field check, validity check, limit check, and reasonableness check are input validation controls. They are intended to prevent or detect the invalid input of data. These controls are of little or no value in preventing unauthorized access, repudiation of transactions, or virus and worm attacks.
18. (SO 11) The option most likely to be effective in deterring fraud by upper level managers is **b. an enforced code of ethics.** Upper level managers are above the level of internal controls; therefore, internal control systems, matching documents, or segregating duties have little impact on the prevention of fraud by upper level management. Having and enforcing a code of ethics sets the proper "tone at the top" and makes it more difficult for upper level managers to conduct fraud.

CHAPTER 10

Expenditures Processes and Controls–Payroll and Fixed Assets

Study Objectives

This chapter will help you gain an understanding of the following concepts:

1. An introduction to payroll and fixed asset processes
2. Payroll processes
3. Risks and controls in payroll processes
4. IT systems of payroll processes
5. Fixed asset processes
6. Risks and controls in fixed asset processes
7. IT Systems of fixed asset processes
8. Ethical issues related to payroll and fixed assets processes
9. Corporate governance in payroll and fixed assets processes

THE REAL WORLD

Photodisc/Getty Images

Soon after implementing a new ERP system, the Prince George's County, Maryland, school district processed the regular payroll for its 19,000 teachers, administrators, school bus drivers, and other employees. Of those 19,000 paychecks, 1400 were incorrect. In some cases, teachers were paid only 50% of what they were owed. In other cases, teachers were paid more than they were owed, and had to return the overage. This is an extremely high number of errors for payroll, and employees get very upset with such errors. The school district had just implemented a new $9.5 million integrated accounting software system from Oracle®. However, after an investigation, it was determined that the payroll errors were not hardware or software problems, but problems with people and processes.[1]

The problems were related to the steps that employees used to submit time cards for payroll—in other words, payroll processes. The processes in this case that were faulty included a time-consuming policy of assigning timekeepers at each school, who had to personally review each time card before submission. Prince George's County also had payroll employees who were inadequately trained in the use of the new payroll module.

Regardless of the degree of sophistication in a company's hardware and software systems, there are still underlying processes involving people that affect whether the system succeeds. If those underlying processes are not well understood or well executed, errors and problems occur. This chapter will describe two types of processes: the expenditures processes for payroll and fixed asset purchases. Both manual and computerized processes are discussed.

INTRODUCTION TO PAYROLL AND FIXED ASSET PROCESSES (STUDY OBJECTIVE 1)

This chapter is an extension of Chapter 9, as it continues to present the vital processes of acquiring the resources needed to run the business, recording the resulting liabilities, and making the related payments at a later date. The distinction here is the types of resources involved and the frequency of the record keeping and payments.

The most frequent types of revenues and expenditure transactions were discussed in Chapters 8 and 9. The processes related to buying goods from vendors and selling goods to customers presented in those chapters are so common that they are typically encountered every day. These processes are sometimes called routine business processes because they involve the transactions that a business encounters on a regular, recurring basis. The volume of those transactions tends to be so large that the transactions and the related accounting activities become routine, almost like second nature, to the employees responsible for handling them. Therefore, specific authorization for each individual routine transaction is not necessary. For example, it would be an overwhelming task to specifically authorize every sale or purchase before it could be processed. On the other hand, there are many different types of transactions that do not occur

[1]"Don't Let 'Peopleware' Tank a New Automated Payroll System," *Human Resources Department Management Report,* vol. 4 issue 1, Jan 2004, pp. 6–7.

regularly. They are sometimes called nonroutine transactions due to their limited occurrence and their requirement for specific authorization.

This chapter presents two categories of expenditures that do not occur nearly as often as the inventory purchases discussed in Chapter 9, namely, human resources and capital resources. The processes that comprise acquiring and maintaining these valuable business resources specifically involve (1) paying wages and salaries to employees (payroll); and (2) accounting for property, plant, and equipment (fixed assets).

Although the processes surrounding payroll and fixed assets transactions are by no means unusual, they do not typically occur every day. Rather, they are triggered by events that tend to occur irregularly, such as the hiring or firing of an employee and the purchase or disposal of a machine. Also, these processes typically involve a relatively small number of transactions. Therefore, they have characteristics of nonroutine transactions. However, during the life of these resources, these transactions (namely, the related paychecks or depreciation) need to be accounted for on a regular, recurring basis—typically, weekly, biweekly, monthly, or quarterly. This means that they have features of both routine and nonroutine processes. Some components have similarities to those discussed in Chapters 8 and 9, such as the cash disbursements activities common to all of these processes; but the differences are significant enough to warrant their presentation in a separate chapter. Additional topics with unique characteristics, including the conversion process and various treasury and administrative processes, will be addressed in Chapters 11 and 12, respectively.

Exhibit 10-1 highlights the portions of the expenditure processes addressed in this chapter, as they relate to the overall accounting system. A company must have systems in place to capture, record, summarize, and report activities for both routine and nonroutine processes. **Payroll processes** include the policies and procedures that employees follow in acquiring and maintaining human resources, capturing and maintaining employee data, paying the employees for their time worked, and recording the related cash and payroll liabilities and expenses. **Fixed asset processes** include the policies and procedures involved in purchasing property; capturing and maintaining relevant data about the assets; paying for and recording the related assets; recording depreciation and other expenses; and accounting for gains or losses.

Various risks that may affect these types of expenditure transactions are also addressed in this chapter, including the following:

- Recorded expenditures may not be valid; that is, they may involve a fictitious employee or vendor, or they may have been prepared in duplicate.
- Expenditure transactions may be recorded in the wrong amount.
- Valid expenditure transactions may have been omitted from the accounting records.
- Expenditure transactions may have been recorded in the wrong employee or vendor account.
- Transactions may not have been recorded in a timely manner.
- Transactions may not have been accumulated or transferred to the accounting records correctly.

The first part of this chapter presents the payroll processes, beginning with features of a typical traditional system and the related controls and followed by trends

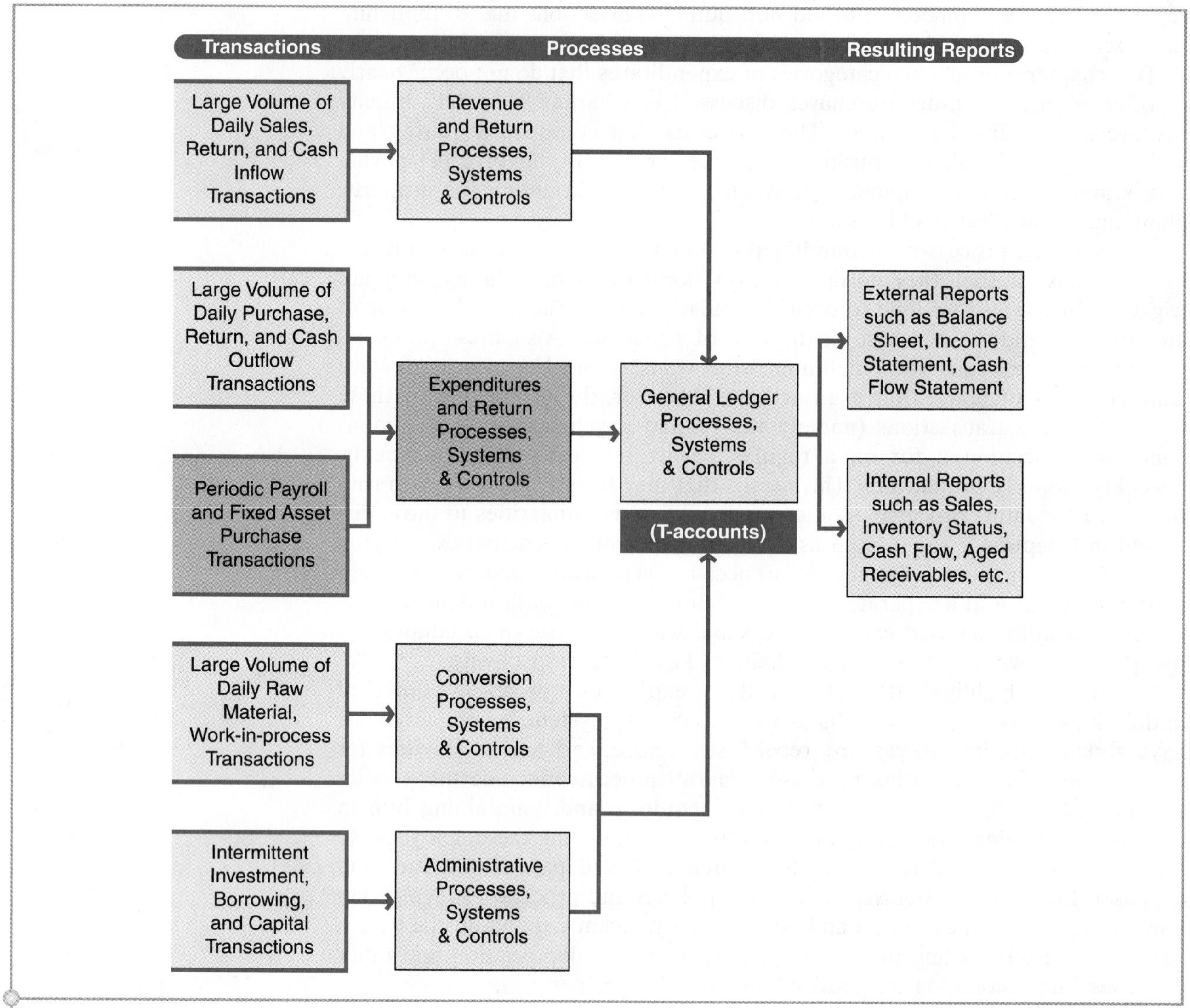

Exhibit 10–1
Expenditure Processes within the Overall System

in computer-based systems. The latter part of the chapter gives a similar presentation of fixed asset systems. The internal controls procedures that help reduce the risks are presented following the discussion of each process category. Finally, ethics issues related to these expenditure processes are covered.

Keep in mind that individual companies may have differences in their payroll and fixed assets practices. This chapter provides common, simple methods of conducting these business processes. The sections on these methods should help you understand most accounting systems involving these expenditure processes, even if they are not exactly like the ones you may have seen in your personal experience.

PAYROLL PROCESSES (STUDY OBJECTIVE 2)

The payroll process is initiated when employees are hired by the company. Different companies may have very diverse hiring processes. For example, some companies may have an employment office or placement department to handle their recruiting and hiring, while in others (especially smaller companies) personnel in the various departments that have job vacancies may conduct these activities. Regardless of the manner in which it is handled, the hiring of employees is typically considered a nonroutine process. Accordingly, members of management are required to specifically approve all employees hired by the company, even if they are initially screened by an employment office. A hiring decision usually happens as a result of an interview or interviews and is documented on a signed letter and/or signed employment contract.

Since companies need human resources in order to conduct business operations, the hiring process must occur before other business transactions can take place. Although this may be true initially, the payroll process is also an ongoing organizational process. A company may need to hire new employees at various times throughout its life cycle in order to accommodate growth and replace employees who have left the company, have retired, or have been relocated, reassigned, or terminated.

Information for all employees must be retained and updated regularly. The **human resources department** is responsible for maintaining records for each job and each employee within the organization, as well as tracking job vacancies and supporting the company's recruitment efforts. Most companies maintain an **organization chart** to map out the jobs and reporting relationships. Exhibit 10-2 presents an example of an organization chart for a generic business.

This organization chart presents only the top branches of the organization's structure. A complete organization chart would include a box or cell for each position within the company. The organization charts of different companies may look different, and the numbers of layers and boxes depend on the complexity of the organizational structure and the number of middle management positions. For example, the sales department may include several sales territories, and each territory may have a manager and several employees making up its sales force. The human resources department typically maintains job profiles or job descriptions that explain the qualifications and responsibilities of each position shown on the chart. These job profiles are further supported by policies and procedures manuals that outline specific activities performed by each position.

In addition to maintaining job records, the human resources department also keeps personnel files; thus, it is often referred to as the personnel department. Personnel files include the information that the company needs, relevant to the people who work there. Personnel records typically include documentation related to the initial hiring, such as an employment application and contract, resume, recommendation letters, interview reports, wage or salary authorization, and results from a background investigation. Personal information must also be maintained, such as the employee's address, Social Security number, employment history, etc. Important information related to payroll processing is also contained in each employee's personnel file, such as overtime and commission rates, applicable tax withholdings, and authorization for payroll deductions.

In addition to the necessary tax withholdings, most companies have employee payroll deductions for such things as contributions to employee benefits programs, unions, savings plans, retirement plans, and charities. Employees must authorize which of these options they choose to be deducted from their pay. In addition, employees may have wage attachments for items such as child support, loans, or bankruptcies. Written records authorizing each of these amounts must be included in the personnel file. Also included in a personnel file is documentation regarding vacation and sick time, as well as records of attendance, performance

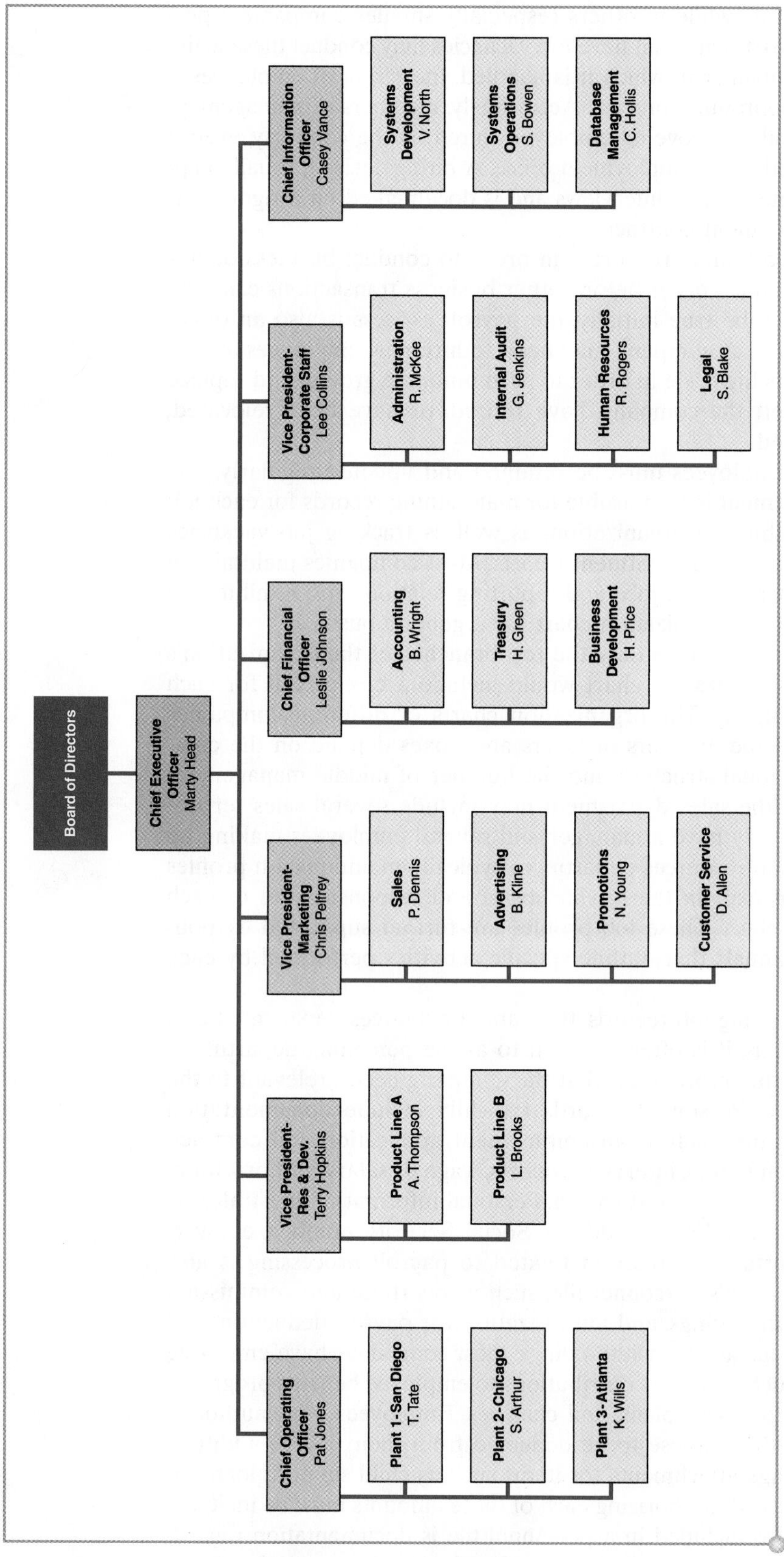

Exhibit 10-2
Generic Organization Chart

evaluations, work schedule, promotion, and termination. Although a detailed examination of these types of employee processes and records is beyond the scope of this chapter, they are mentioned here as examples of the diverse and specialized nature of these records. Each employee's personnel file is as individual as the person it represents, so there are significant differences in the processes required to keep the records up to date. The record-keeping responsibilities of employees in the human resources department must be thorough in order to take into consideration all the different possibilities for an employee's pay status.

One unique feature of the information contained in an individual personnel file is that it is accessed frequently, but changed relatively infrequently. After all the information is established in an employee's file, it needs to be accessed each time payroll is processed in order for net pay to be accurately computed. It is important that the supporting information be kept up to date. Although payroll information may change periodically due to such things as tax rate changes and pay raises, the frequency of these kinds of changes is slight in comparison with the number of times the information is accessed for payroll purposes.

Depending upon the amount of computerization of the company's system, personnel records may be retained in hard copy or they may be entered into the system and retained electronically. Given the varying extent of information collected from employees, most modern companies have implemented some level of automation of their personnel records and payroll applications. After we examine the basic features of a manual payroll system, the related IT processes will be discussed.

Once an employee's personnel file is complete and the term of employment has begun, routine activities take place regarding payroll processing. Exhibit 10-3 is a business process map depicting these activities. Exhibit 10-4 shows a document flowchart for payroll processing and Exhibit 10-5 presents a data flow diagram of these processes. This is undoubtedly the most important process from the perspective of the company's employees, because it is the source of employees' paychecks. The payroll process is also unique because of its widespread nature; it affects everyone within the company. It requires the involvement of each individual within each department or location. Accordingly, personnel-related expenses are usually among the largest expenses reported on the company's income statement. For these reasons, it is important that the company has a reliable system in place to handle its payroll activities. Without paychecks, few employees would remain with the company. And without human resources, few companies would be able to survive.

As employees perform their jobs, they earn their pay and the company accrues a corresponding liability for the wages and salaries. Determining the correct amount of pay depends on the employees keeping adequate records of their hours and projects. A **time sheet** is the record of hours worked by an employee for a specific payroll period. A time sheet covers a specified time (ranging from one week to one month, depending on the frequency with which paychecks are prepared). In order to ensure that the time sheets include the most accurate and up-to-date information, they need to be updated by each employee on a daily basis. Salaried employees sometimes are not required to report their hours worked on a daily basis, but are often required to report the activities performed within the period. Employees in the production area are often required to prepare very detailed (to-the-minute) time reports, identifying the types of projects they worked on and the exact lengths of time spent, so that the company can determine the precise cost of its products. Additional information on the conversion processes is discussed in Chapter 11.

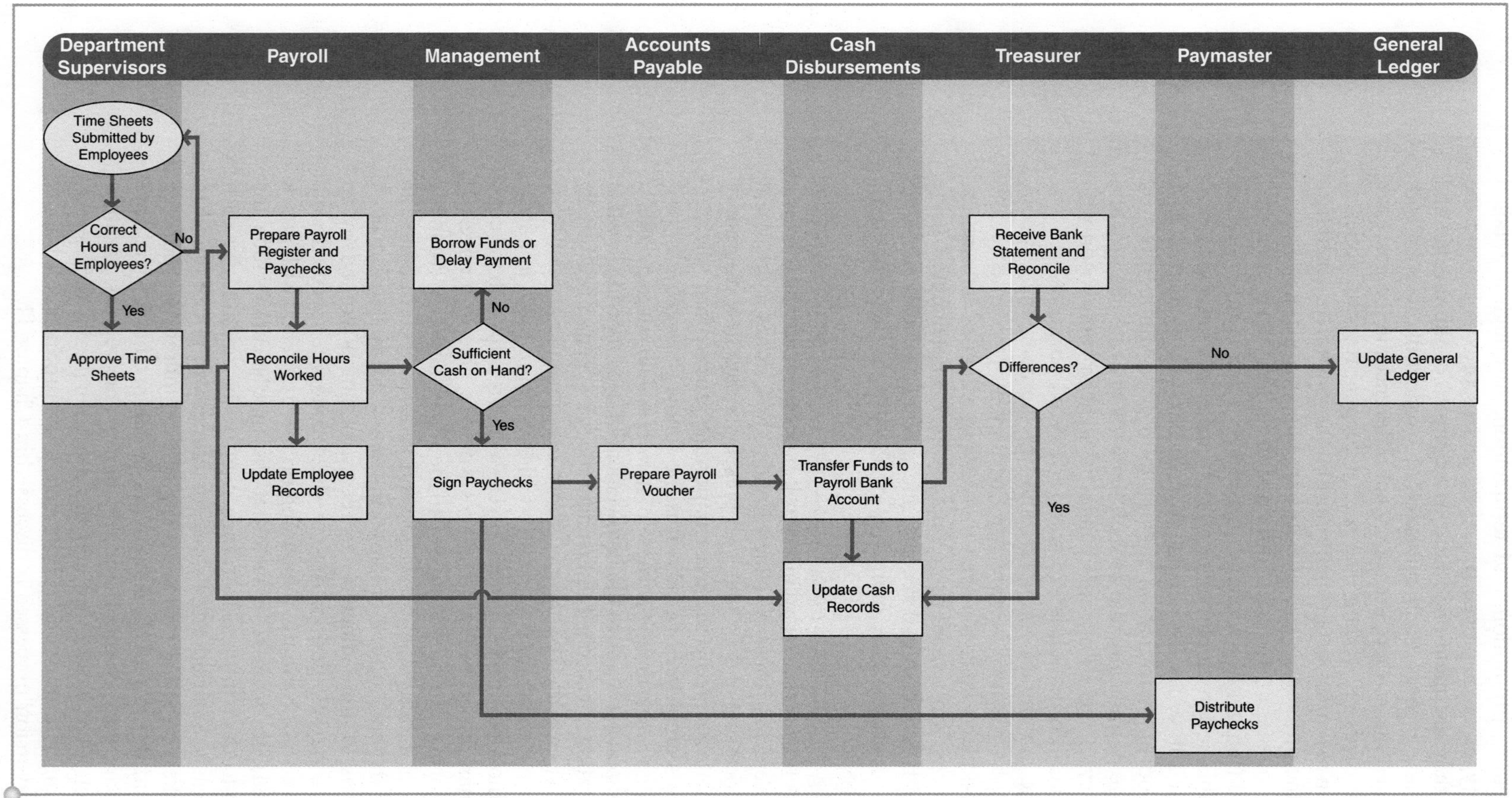

Exhibit 10-3
Payroll Process Map

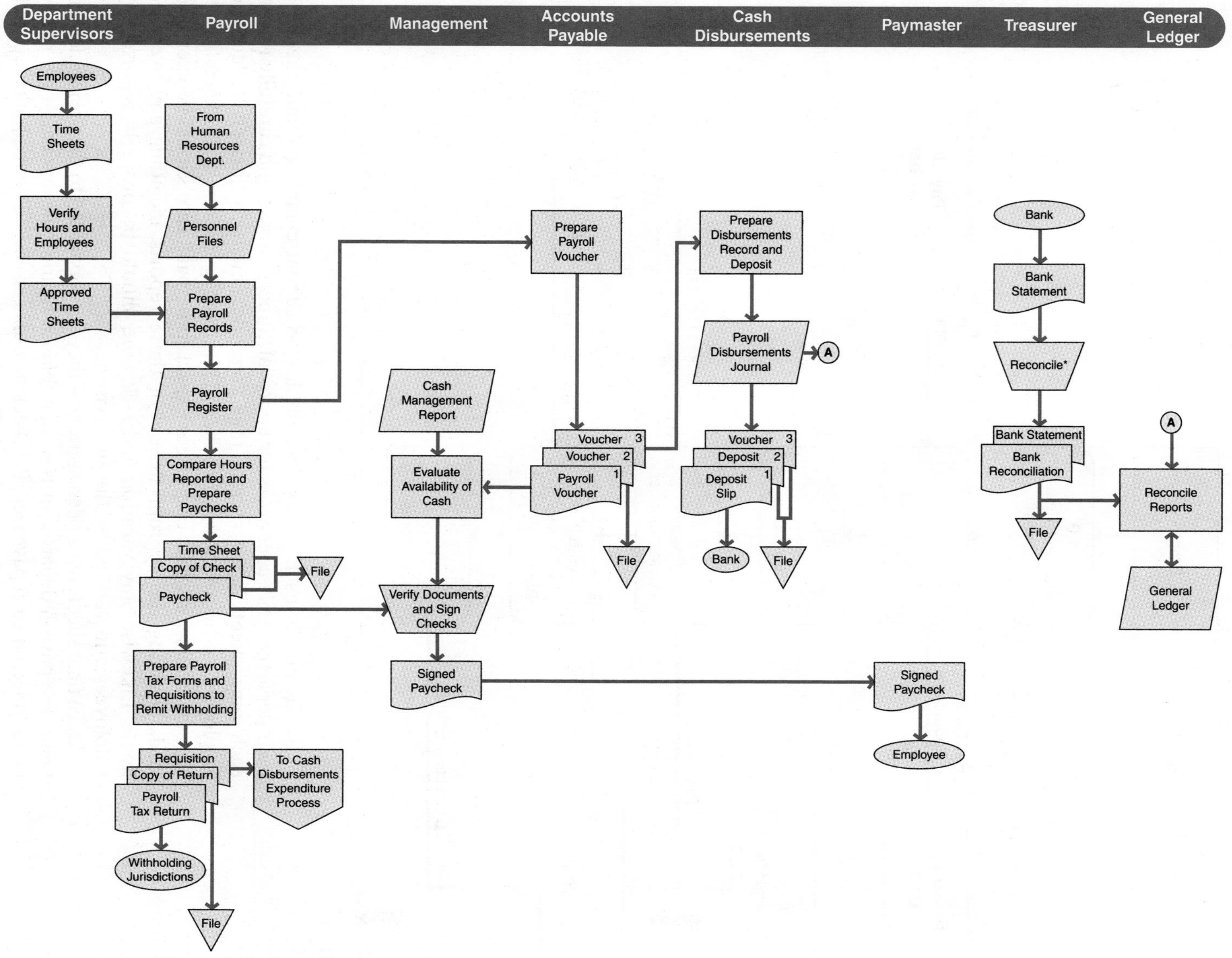

* Involves comparisons of payroll register, voucher and deposits.

Exhibit 10-4
Document Flowchart of the Payroll Processes

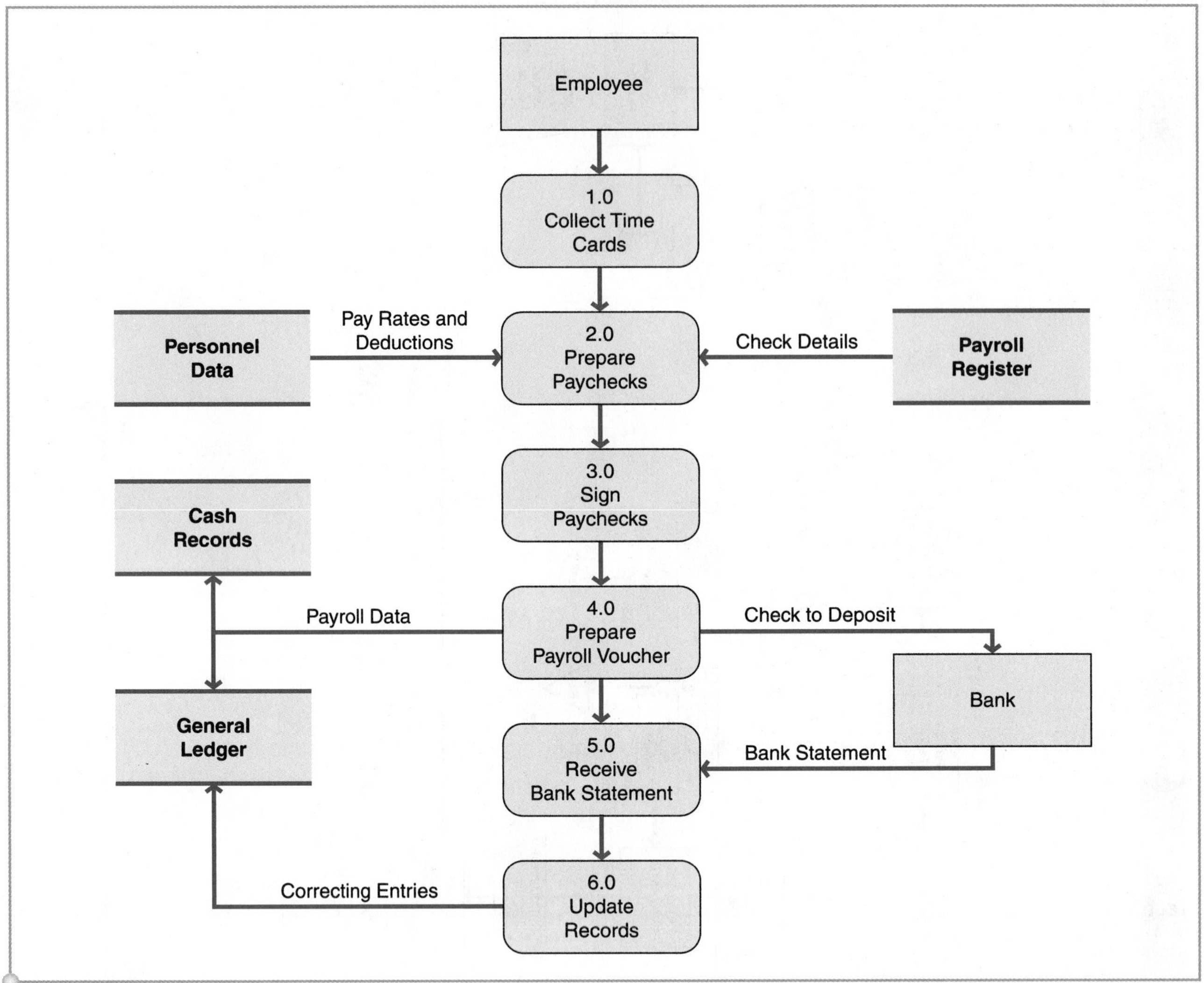

Exhibit 10-5
Payroll Processes Data Flow Diagram

At the end of each pay period, employees submit completed time sheets to their departmental supervisors for approval. Supervisors should carefully review each time sheet, being certain that these documents accurately reflect the employees and hours worked in their departments. Because time sheets represent the hours for which employees expect to be paid, care should be exercised in determining the appropriateness of these reports, including any overtime hours. Likewise, any vacation and sick time should be properly reported by employees and verified by the supervisors.

Once time sheets have been approved, they are forwarded to the payroll department. The payroll department is responsible for figuring the amount of net pay to be included on each paycheck. Paycheck amounts are based on the hours reported on time sheets and pay rates and deductions authorized in the respective personnel files. The computations required to support the paychecks are as follows:

$$\text{Gross Pay} = \text{Hours Reported} \times \text{Authorized Pay Rate}$$
$$\text{Net Pay, i.e., Paycheck Amount} = \text{Gross Pay} - \text{Authorized Deductions}$$

Although these are relatively simple formulas that may be considered part of a routine process, it may actually be challenging to figure the amount of deductions applicable to an employee's pay. This is because each employee's deductions are likely to be different. In addition, the payroll formulas must be applied to every employee in the company, one at a time. The process is further complicated by the fact that the inputs tend to change constantly. Each payroll period will include some changes in the number of hours worked, pay rates or withholdings. An accounting software program is a very efficient tool to assist the payroll department in managing this abundance of information. On the other hand, when done manually, the process of extracting all these inputs from the records and performing the mathematical computations is extremely time-consuming.

The payroll department prepares a payroll register to accumulate all paycheck data. A **payroll register** is a complete listing of salary or wage detail for all employees for a given time. Exhibit 10-6 shows a payroll register entry as it would be established in Microsoft Dynamics GP® accounting software. Note that this entry is for a single employee, but because this employee worked overtime hours, distinct entries are needed for the standard hours and overtime hours. Since overtime is paid at a higher rate (usually, one and one-half times

Exhibit 10-6
Preparing a Payroll Register in Microsoft Dynamics GP®

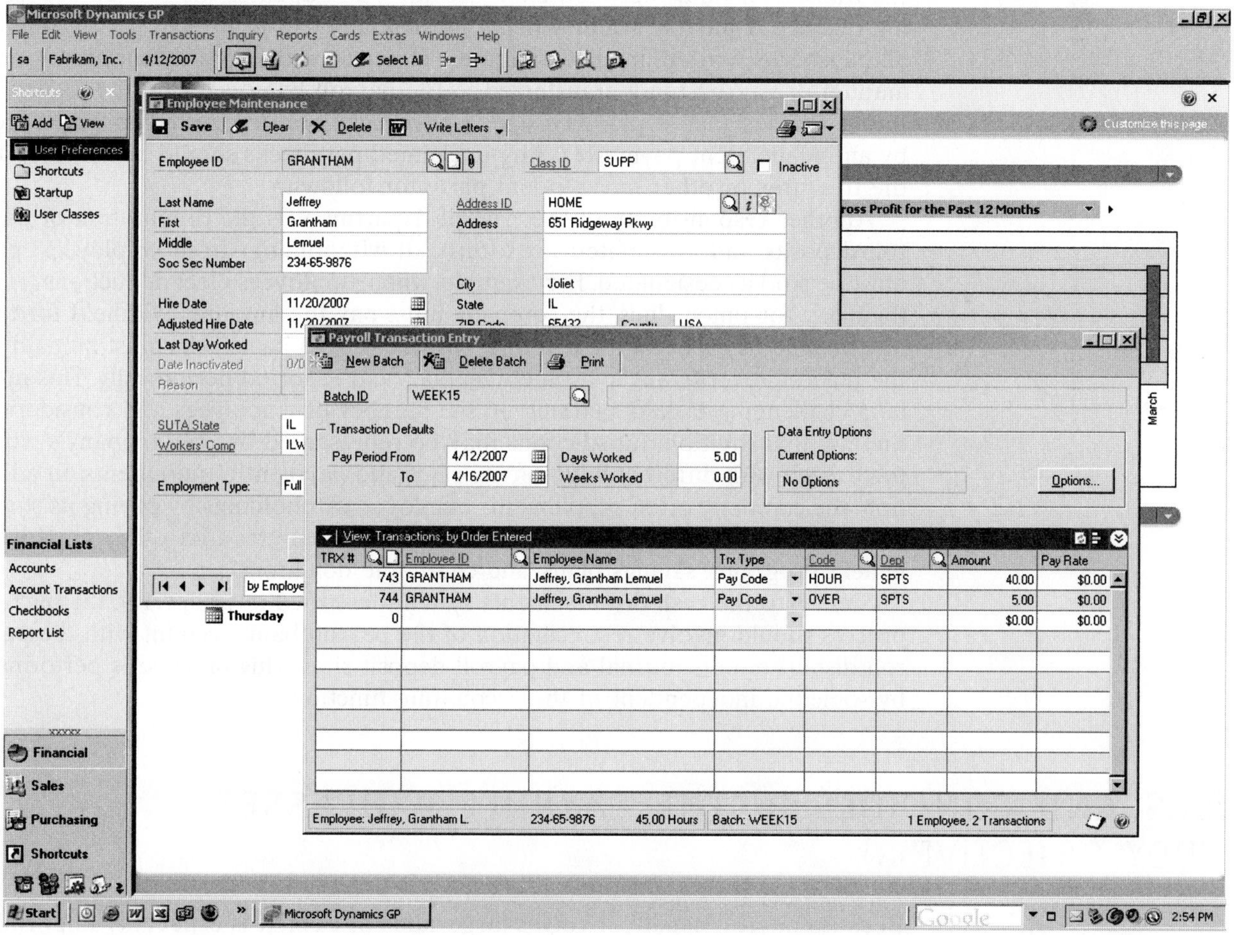

the standard rate), it must be shown separately. Also note that inputs to this software application include the employee's identification number, hours worked, and applicable dates. All other information needed for the preparation of the payroll register and paycheck is retained in the system so that the payroll department personnel do not have to look it up each pay period.

The payroll department should compare the hours reported on time sheets with the hours accumulated in the payroll register before the paychecks are sent to management for authorization. Authorization is typically indicated by a manager's signature on the paychecks.

Before signed paychecks can be given to employees, the company must be sure that it has sufficient cash on hand to cover the total amount of the payroll. In addition, the cash must be deposited in the payroll cash account. Since employees usually do not hesitate to cash their paychecks, the timing of these activities is important. The accounts payable department determines the total amount of the net payroll from the payroll register and prepares a payroll voucher. A payroll voucher authorizes the transfer of cash from the company's main operating account into the payroll cash account. Most companies maintain a separate bank account to handle payroll transactions. This makes it easier to account for payroll transactions and to distinguish them from cash disbursements for other business purposes.

The cash disbursements department receives the payroll voucher, carries out the transfer of funds between bank accounts, and updates the related accounting records. A **payroll disbursements journal** is prepared to provide a listing of all paychecks written, in check-number sequence, with the total supporting the amount of payroll funds transferred to the payroll bank account.

On the designated pay day, signed paychecks are distributed to employees by an independent paymaster. Any unclaimed paychecks should be returned to the treasurer or other independent party for followup.

Another responsibility of the payroll department is the preparation of payroll deposits and the related tax forms. All withholdings from employees' pay must be paid as designated. For example, when employees elect deductions from their pay for union dues, the company must pay the amounts withheld for the union. Similarly, federal income taxes withheld from paychecks must be paid to the federal government in a timely manner and reported periodically. This may be a challenging task, depending on the number of employees and considering the fact that multiple jurisdictions may be represented by the company's work force, each with different withholding rates and payment requirements. In addition, the company often supplements employee withholdings by paying its share of contributions for such things as insurance premiums and other employee benefit programs, savings plans, and charitable donations.

Similar to the cash disbursements system described in Chapter 9, the payroll process should involve reconciliation of the payroll bank account with the payroll disbursements journal and payroll deposit slips. This practice is performed by someone independent of the accounting function.

RISKS AND CONTROLS IN THE PAYROLL PROCESSES (STUDY OBJECTIVE 3)

Because payroll usually involves large sums of cash, it is especially important that sufficient internal controls are included in the related business processes. In terms of the five internal control activities introduced in Chapter 3, following are some procedures to be considered for implementation in this process.

AUTHORIZATION OF TRANSACTIONS

Management plays an especially important role in carrying out payroll transactions correctly. If management takes its responsibilities seriously by carefully reviewing the payroll documents, then most employee errors and fraud should be prevented. Departmental supervisors must be certain that all time sheets represent actual time worked by currently active employees. The supervisors are expected to be familiar enough with their respective departments that they will recognize unusual data. In particular, they should be on the lookout for fraud schemes such as overstated hours (including unapproved overtime) and time sheets or paychecks of former employees who are no longer entitled to receive compensation.

In addition to the authorization procedures covering time reports, employee personnel files should contain evidence of proper authorization for various payroll amounts. Included in the files should be approval for pay-rate adjustments, hiring, promotion, and termination (authorized by management), as well as approval for all deductions (authorized by individual employees).

Like the cash disbursements discussed in Chapter 9, payroll disbursements should be authorized by the accounts payable department on the basis of the company's need to satisfy its obligation to its employees. In addition, designated members of management should be given authority for the approval of the paychecks, noted by their signatures on the faces of the checks. The bank will keep records of those members of management with authority to sign checks drawn on the payroll account, and it should not pay a check that does not include such a designated signature.

SEGREGATION OF DUTIES

The goal of segregation of duties within the payroll process is to prevent the preparation and payment of a fraudulent or erroneous paycheck. In order to accomplish this, certain payroll accounting functions such as authorizing, timekeeping, record keeping, and custody of the paychecks should all be separated. Namely, the human resources department, which is responsible for authorizing new employee hiring and maintaining personnel files, should be separate from the payroll time-reporting and record-keeping functions, performed primarily by the payroll, cash disbursements, and general ledger departments. In addition, employees in each of these departments should not have check-signing authority and should not have access to the signed checks or cash account. The person who distributes paychecks to employees, often referred to as a **paymaster**, should not have responsibility for any of the related payroll accounting functions and should not have custody of cash. The paymaster should also be independent of the departmental supervision responsibilities, so that a determination can be made that paychecks are being distributed to active employees. Finally, information systems operations and programming related to the payroll processing should be separate from custody of payroll cash and record keeping for these processes.

ADEQUATE RECORDS AND DOCUMENTS

Personnel files and the payroll register are the fundamental records in the payroll process. In addition, there are numerous forms and reports that are required to be filed at designated times throughout the year. These documents must be filed with various taxing authorities and other organizations to summarize and remit amounts withheld from employees' paychecks. Due to the number of inputs required for accurate payroll processing and reporting, the care with which these records are prepared and maintained is crucial to the internal control environment.

The practice of issuing paychecks on prenumbered checks from a separate bank account is another control that helps to create clear records of the payroll transactions. When checks are issued numerically, a sequence can be checked to determine whether all payroll transactions have been recorded. A separate bank account clarifies the accounting process by isolating the payroll transactions in their own account. This makes it easier and quicker to reconcile the account and to identify any unusual transactions that may require investigation.

SECURITY OF ASSETS AND DOCUMENTS

Payroll information is very sensitive. Because it includes personal information about employees, their pay, and their performance, it must be kept confidential. Accordingly, access to personnel files and payroll records should be limited to designated persons within the human resource and payroll departments. Electronic controls and physical controls should be in place to ensure the confidentiality of payroll information.

Similarly, access to payroll cash should be limited to the authorized paycheck signers. Blank payroll checks should be protected by the use of physical controls so that no one has an opportunity to create a fake paycheck. Similarly, any unclaimed paychecks should not be maintained by employees working in human resources or payroll functions, so that they do not have an opportunity to alter the records and cash the checks for their personal use.

INDEPENDENT CHECKS AND RECONCILIATION

There are several payroll-related reconciliation procedures that should be performed regularly. For example, the number of hours reported on time sheets should be reconciled to the payroll register, and time sheets may be reconciled with production reports. Each of these reconciliations should be performed before paychecks are signed in order to ensure the accuracy of the underlying payroll information. In addition, the payroll register should be reconciled to the general ledger on a regular basis. Moreover, someone separate from the payroll processing functions should reconcile the bank statement for the payroll cash account on a monthly basis. This bank reconciliation should follow the same procedures as required for the company's general checking account, as discussed in the cash disbursements section of Chapter 9.

COST–BENEFIT CONSIDERATIONS

The more employees a company has and the more frequently it pays its employees, the more important it becomes to implement strong internal controls surrounding these processes. Other conditions that may warrant the need for strong controls include the existence of irregular pay schedules, complex withholding arrangements, frequent changes in pay rates, and a decentralized payroll function. Many companies implement thorough controls covering the payroll processes because of the confidential nature of the underlying data. In order to protect the privacy of its employees and promote high morale, a company may choose to incur significant costs related to its efforts to protect the accuracy and security of payroll records.

Exhibit 10-7 summarizes examples of internal controls in the payroll process and the related business risks that are minimized as a result of the

Control:	Minimizes the Related Risk of:
Authorization:	
Supervisor approves time sheets prior to preparation of payroll documents.	Invalid paycheck or fictitious employees, inaccurate paychecks
Manager approves payroll prior to signing paycheck.	Invalid paycheck or fictitious employees
Segregation of Duties:	
Separation of the custody of payroll cash from the responsibility for reconciling the bank account	Invalid payroll transactions, incorrect amounts, omitted transactions
Separation of duties related to payroll register preparation, authorization of new hiring and pay rates, information systems, and general accounting	Invalid payroll transactions, incorrect amounts or accounts, omitted transactions
Independent paymaster	Fictitious employees
Records and Documents:	
Paychecks are prepared on prenumbered checks.	Omitted paychecks
The payroll register is checked for mathematical accuracy and agreement with authorized pay rates and deductions.	Incorrect amounts
Security:	
Physical controls in areas where cash and paychecks are held	Lost or stolen cash or paychecks, invalid paychecks, omitted paychecks
IT controls over computer records and physical controls in records storage areas	Invalid payroll transactions, incorrect amounts or accounts, timing issues, duplicate transactions
Independent Checks and Reconciliations:	
Time sheets are reconciled with the payroll register.	Omitted or inaccurate paychecks
The payroll register is reconciled with the general ledger.	Omitted or duplicate payroll transactions, incorrect amounts or accounts, timing issues, incorrect accumulations
Time sheets are reconciled with production reports.	Omitted or duplicate payroll transactions, incorrect amounts or accounts, timing issues
Preparation of a bank reconciliation	Invalid or omitted paychecks, incorrect amounts or accounts, timing issues, lost or stolen cash

Exhibit 10-7
Payroll Controls and Risks

implementation of these controls. This exhibit does not include all the possible controls and risks that may be encountered in the payroll process, but provides some common situations.

IT SYSTEMS OF PAYROLL PROCESSES (STUDY OBJECTIVE 4)

The preceding presentation demonstrates the importance of information technology in the payroll processes. Without computerized records, the human resources and payroll departments would be forced to search all personnel files in order to obtain the data used to generate a payroll register. Numerous mathematical computations would also need to be performed in order to figure the amount of net pay for each employee. This manual process would be nearly impossible for medium- and large-size companies that disburse hundreds, or thousands of employee paychecks each period. It is clear that computer technology can be a necessary ally of the payroll process. Because of the modern pressures to cut costs and competitive nature of the business world, many companies require their human resources and payroll departments to process massive amounts of employee data in extremely short periods. Therefore, even the smallest companies may find it worthwhile to enhance their payroll processing with computerized systems.

Routine payroll processing occurs at specified time intervals, namely, the weekly, biweekly, or monthly pay dates. Because of this infrequency and the sequential nature of the payroll process, many companies find that batch processing is well-suited for payroll activities. With batch processing, the human resources department is responsible for keying employee information into a personnel master file, and the timekeeper can accumulate all time sheets and enter them in the computer system in batches. The timekeeper should prepare control totals and hash totals in order to check the system before paychecks are generated. An alternative to manual batch accumulations is the use of electronic timekeeping devices, such as time clocks or badge readers. Electronic time clocks collect time and attendance data when employees insert their time sheets into the clock. The time clocks read bar codes on the employees' time sheets. Similarly, badge readers collect data when employee identification badges are swiped through an electronic reader. These systems accumulate data throughout the period and automatically calculate batch totals. The data batches are then used to prepare paychecks and the payroll register.

THE REAL WORLD

Scott Paper Company, a manufacturer and marketer of paper tissue products, implemented an automated payroll system a few years ago. Traditional time clocks and manual time sheets were replaced with bar code readers that collect time and attendance data. Before its new system was implemented, Scott management collected time sheets by hand from thousands of employees, and personnel manually keyed the numbers into a payroll system. Now the payroll figures are electronically calculated and automatically fed into the payroll system. Many different work schedules and complex pay and deduction arrangements are accommodated. In terms of increased efficiency, Scott's new approach paid for itself within its first year of implementation.

In order to smooth out the process and avoid the heavy workload that falls at the end of the payroll period, many companies use online software systems that integrate their human resources and payroll functions. With integrated systems, real-time personnel data are available, and the general ledger and production system can be automatically updated at the end of the payroll period. As with any online system, though, care must be exercised in restricting access to the payroll programs. Passwords and access logs should be used, and reviewed for the possibility of unauthorized access.

The Internet and company intranets are also increasingly important tools for circulating payroll information. As more employees have offsite work arrangements, the Internet allows them to send relevant information to their supervisors for timely updating of time and attendance records. In some cases, employees may even make changes to their payroll deductions via the Internet or intranets, and their pay stubs can be sent to them via e-mail. This makes it possible for payroll operations to remain centralized. The World Wide Web also provides many resources for employees in the human resources and payroll departments, such as access to current legislative changes that may affect payroll deductions.

Another popular use of the Internet involves the outsourcing of payroll services. Many companies use independent, Internet-based service providers to handle their payroll processing. These payroll providers specialize in offering solutions and constant access to payroll information. With outsourced payroll processing, enrolled companies are given secure access information so that a designated individual can log on and transfer payroll information via the Internet. This information can be viewed, edited, and approved before processing occurs. The company's payroll administrator will receive an e-mail message as notification that the paychecks and payroll reports have been prepared. Payroll outsourcing has become prevalent because it offers increased convenience, confidentiality, and protection from the risk of liability for failure to submit tax withholdings and the related reports.

Automation is also commonly used to enhance controls via the electronic transfer of payroll funds. Many employees elect to have their paychecks directly deposited into their personal bank accounts. This ensures the timely deposit of the funds and eliminates the need for an independent paymaster. It also simplifies the process of reconciling the bank statement, as there are fewer outstanding checks. Employees who take advantage of direct deposit realize savings of time and check-cashing fees, as well as increased confidentiality. When the automatic deposit feature is used, the company should have procedures in place to be sure that multiple paychecks are not being deposited in a single bank account. Since each employee should receive only one paycheck at a time, the transfer of multiple paychecks into a single account could mean that a paycheck was created for a fictitious employee.

In addition to the electronic transfer of paychecks, companies can use electronic transfers to make payments of tax deposits and other payroll withholdings. Many companies have become part of governmental electronic funds transfer programs, wherein the federal and state income taxes withheld from employee paychecks are transferred online to the appropriate taxing authorities. Another efficient use of electronic transfers is for the disbursement of wage attachments. Although it may be time consuming to implement these programs due to the many different rules which apply to the various jurisdictions and agencies that receive payroll withholdings, the up-front investment tends to pay off in the long run. These programs promote savings in terms of time, expense, and increased accuracy.

FIXED ASSETS PROCESSES (STUDY OBJECTIVE 5)

There may be many kinds of fixed assets owned by a company. The fixed assets pool may include the following categories: vehicles, office equipment and computers, machinery and production equipment, furniture, and real estate (such as land and buildings). These assets are all necessary for the company to conduct business. They are considered long-term assets because they were purchased with the intention of benefiting the company for a long time. For many companies, the investment in fixed assets is often the largest asset reported on the balance sheet.

Even though fixed assets are classified as long-term assets, they are constantly changing. Companies continually add to or replace items in their fixed assets pool as the old items become used, worn, or outdated. Due to this frequency of change, it is important that clear accounting records exist so that the status of fixed assets accounts can be determined at any point during their useful life.

This section presents three phases of fixed assets processes: acquisition, continuance, and disposal. These three phases span the entire useful life of the fixed assets.

FIXED ASSET ACQUISITIONS

Acquisitions of fixed assets are carried out in much the same way as inventory purchases described in Chapter 9. Exhibit 10-8 presents a business process map of the fixed assets acquisition process. You can see the similarities in these processes by comparing this exhibit with Exhibit 9-3 in Chapter 9. Two notable differences here are the placement of the acquired assets in the user department (rather than a warehouse) and the inclusion of a fixed assets department (instead of the inventory control department). Exhibit 10-9 presents a document flowchart of the records used in a fixed asset acquisition process, and Exhibit 10-10 is a data flow diagram of that process.

Fixed assets acquisitions are generally initiated when a user department identifies a need for a new asset, either to replace an existing asset or to enhance its current pool. If the need is for an asset whose cost is below a preestablished dollar amount, the process will be carried out in a routine manner, as illustrated in Exhibit 10-8. That is, a member of management will authorize the purchase of the asset, and the purchasing department will select a vendor and prepare the purchase order.

Sometimes, large cash outlays are required for fixed asset purchases. The company should have a policy in place requiring special processing for purchases of fixed assets that exceed a preestablished dollar limit. Accordingly, large fixed asset acquisitions would be regarded as non-routine transactions that require specific authorization. This may delay the process significantly, as it may take weeks or months for management or the board of directors to approve large fixed asset purchase requests. Some companies require that large cash outlays for fixed assets be included in the capital budget. A **capital budget** is a

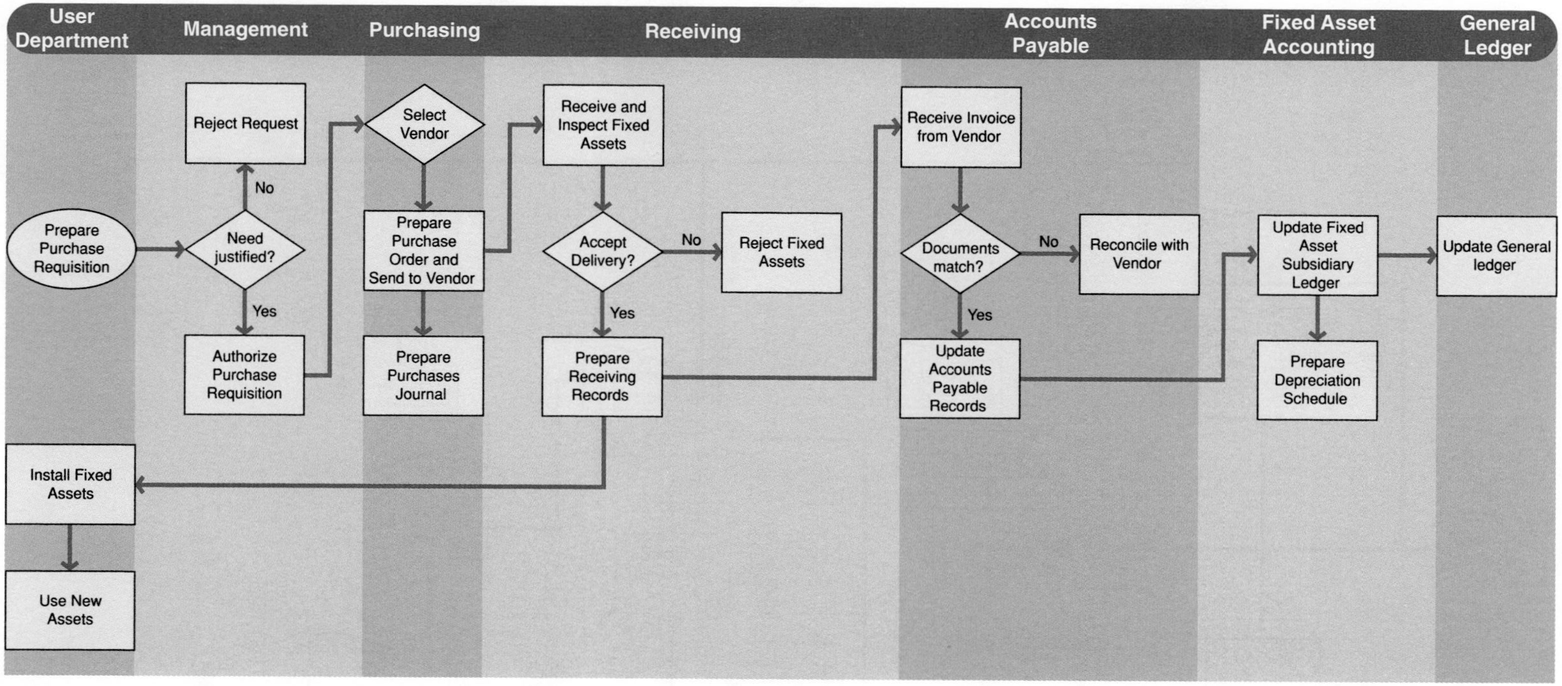

Exhibit 10-8
Fixed Assets Acquisitions Process Map

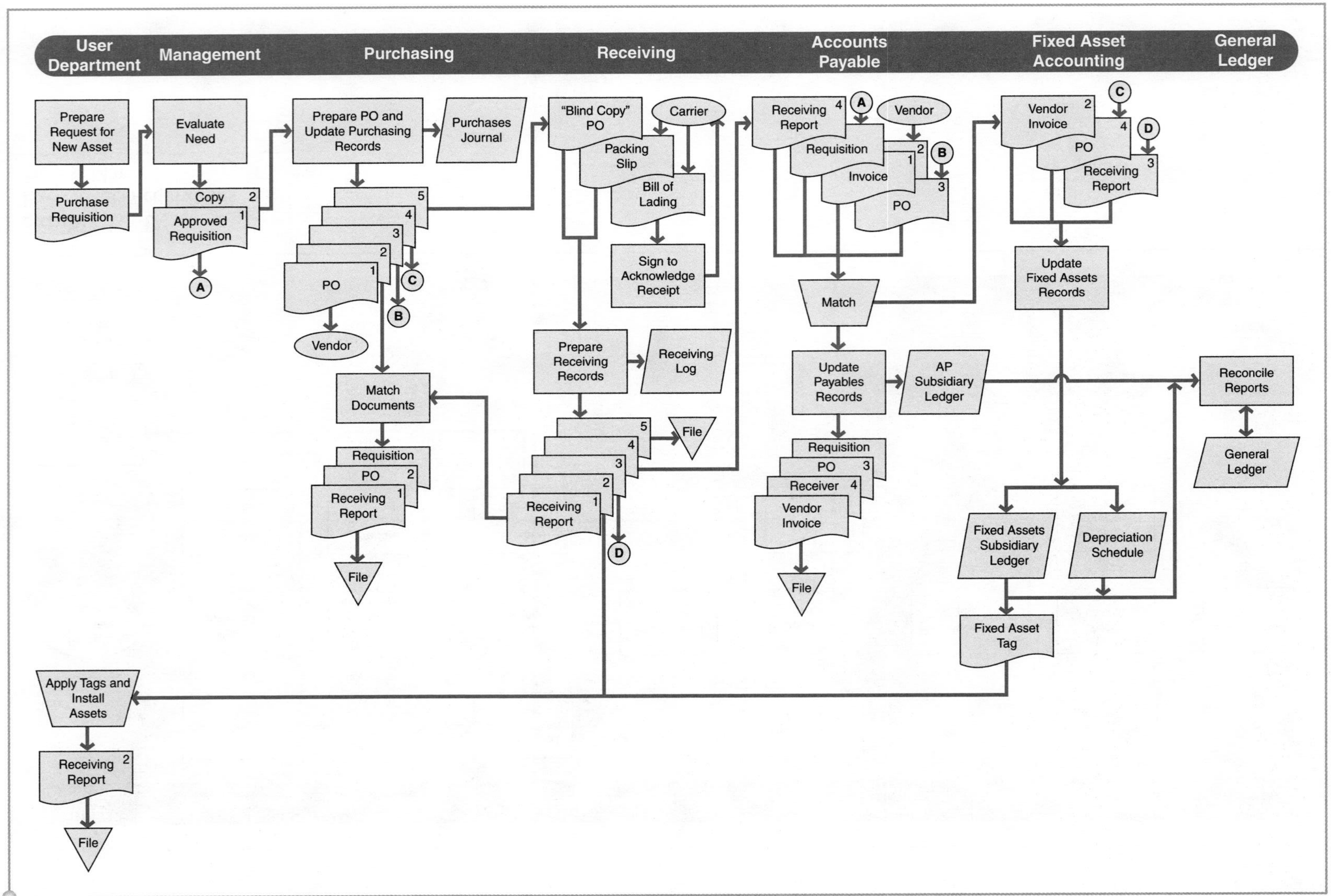

Exhibit 10-9
Document Flowchart for Fixed Asset Acquisition Processes

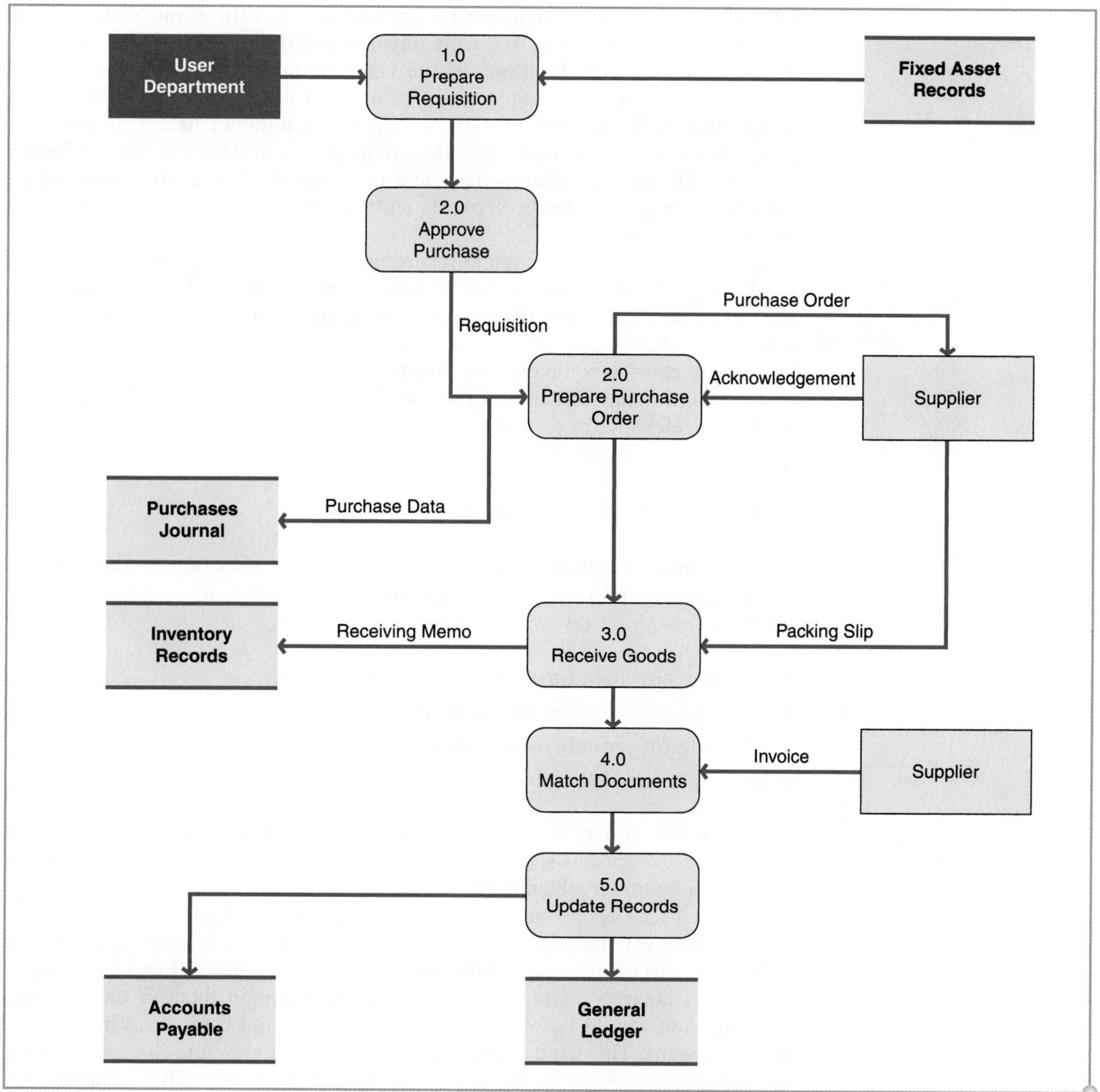

Exhibit 10-10
Fixed Asset Acquisitions Processes Data Flow Diagram

financial plan detailing all of the company's investments in fixed assets and other investments. In addition, the company may require that an investment analysis or feasibility study be conducted in order to assess the merit of the purchase request in terms of the relative costs and benefits. Accordingly, these purchases need to be planned well in advance of their desired implementation time.

Upon receipt, new fixed assets are inspected by the receiving department. A receiving report is prepared, and the items are sent to the user department for installation and use. Many companies apply a fixed asset tag, number, or label to the item so that it can be tracked in the future and distinguished from other, similar assets. Accounts payable and cash disbursement activities are also initiated at this time, in the same manner as for the expenditure processes described in Chapter 9. In addition, a fixed asset subsidiary ledger is updated. A **fixed asset subsidiary ledger** is a detailed listing of the company's fixed assets, divided into categories consistent with the general ledger accounts. Historically, companies have maintained all the subsidiary ledger details within spreadsheets. Separate spreadsheets may be prepared for each category of fixed assets.

Extreme care must be taken in recording all the necessary information in the fixed asset subsidiary ledger. All relevant information should be documented, such as acquisition dates, costs, tag numbers, and estimates of useful lives and salvage values.

In some cases, a company may construct its own fixed assets instead of purchasing them. When this occurs, the conversion processes as described in Chapter 11 are relevant.

FIXED ASSETS CONTINUANCE

The **fixed assets continuance** phase refers to the processes required to maintain accurate and up-to-date records regarding all fixed assets throughout their useful lives. This phase involves the following activities:

- updating cost data for improvements to the assets
- updating estimated figures as needed
- adjusting for periodic depreciation
- keeping track of the physical location of assets

Cost information may need to be updated when new costs are incurred related to an asset. Companies should have written procedures in place describing the circumstances under which these costs are capitalized to the fixed asset account or recorded as a repair and maintenance expense. New costs should be capitalized whenever the expenditure causes the fixed asset to become enhanced, either in terms of increased efficiency or an extended useful life. On the other hand, costs incurred to repair the assets or to maintain them in their current working state should be recorded as expenses, and not capitalized in the fixed assets account. The fixed asset accountant must make sure the appropriate adjustments are made in the fixed asset subsidiary ledger. This facilitates the accuracy of depreciation calculations.

Fixed asset accounting depends on the use of estimates. Each asset must be assigned an estimated useful life and an estimated salvage value. The judgmental nature of fixed asset accounting makes it different than the other expenditure processes discussed in Chapter 9 and earlier in this chapter. The use of estimates also means that recorded amounts may need to be changed as time passes and new information is discovered that renders the original estimates misleading. The fixed assets subsidiary ledger may need to be adjusted from time to time as the company makes changes in the estimates that feed its depreciation calculations. For instance, it may be discovered that the asset's useful life will be shortened because of heavy usage of the asset, or lengthened due to a capital improvement. Similarly, an asset's estimated salvage value may be reduced because a new product will make the asset obsolete, or increased when the outlook for an after-market sale becomes more favorable. Regardless of the type of change, the fixed asset accountant must again exercise care in recording these changes in order to ensure the accuracy of depreciation calculations.

The periodic depreciation schedule is the most important part of the asset continuation phase. A **depreciation schedule** is the record detailing the amounts and timing of depreciation for all fixed asset categories except land. The information recorded in the fixed asset subsidiary ledger is used as the basis for computing periodic depreciation. In turn, accumulated depreciation is used to determine the book value of an asset at any point in its life. These activities recognize the fact that fixed assets diminish in value throughout their lives. Therefore, the accounting records need to gradually reduce a portion of the asset's cost in order to reflect the asset's proper book value. The related computations may be relatively straightforward when performed for one individual asset at a time, but the process tends to be complicated by the large number of fixed assets the company maintains. There may be many different categories of fixed assets, and the useful lives of the company's fixed assets may range from two years to several decades. Different methods of depreciation may also be used. In addition, because of the staggered timing of fixed assets purchases, depreciation may not even be computed consistently within a particular category. Moreover, there may be multiple sets of records required by the company for financial statement and tax purposes. Because of all these varying inputs, the accounting for fixed assets may become quite complex. This is certainly an area where strong internal controls are warranted.

FIXED ASSETS DISPOSALS

When an asset becomes old, outdated, inefficient, or damaged, the company should dispose of it and adjust its records accordingly. Disposing of an asset may include selling or exchanging it, discarding it (throwing it away), or donating it to another party who may be able to use it. The activities and documents that make up the fixed assets disposal process are depicted in Exhibits 10-11 and Exhibit 10-12, respectively.

Because fixed asset disposals involve the flow of assets out of the company, there are many similarities between these processes and those related to the revenue processes discussed in Chapter 8. The most significant difference between these activities is the role of the company's fixed asset accountant. This employee or department must carry out four basic steps in accounting for the disposal of fixed assets:

1. The date of disposal is noted, and depreciation computations are updated through this date.
2. The disposed assets are removed from the fixed asset subsidiary ledger.
3. The depreciation accounts related to disposed assets are removed from the depreciation schedule and the fixed asset subsidiary ledger.
4. Gains or losses resulting from the disposal are computed.

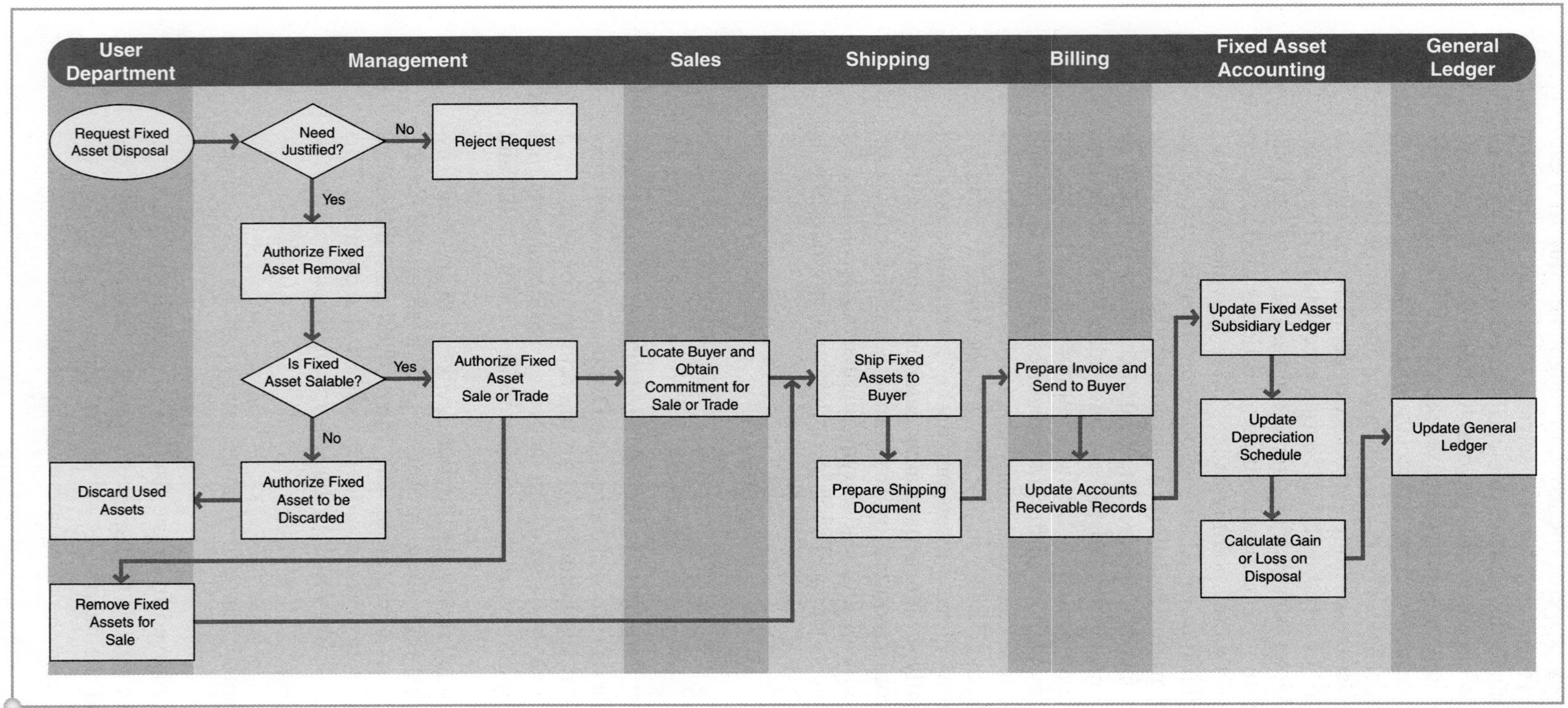

Exhibit 10-11
Fixed Assets Disposal Process Map

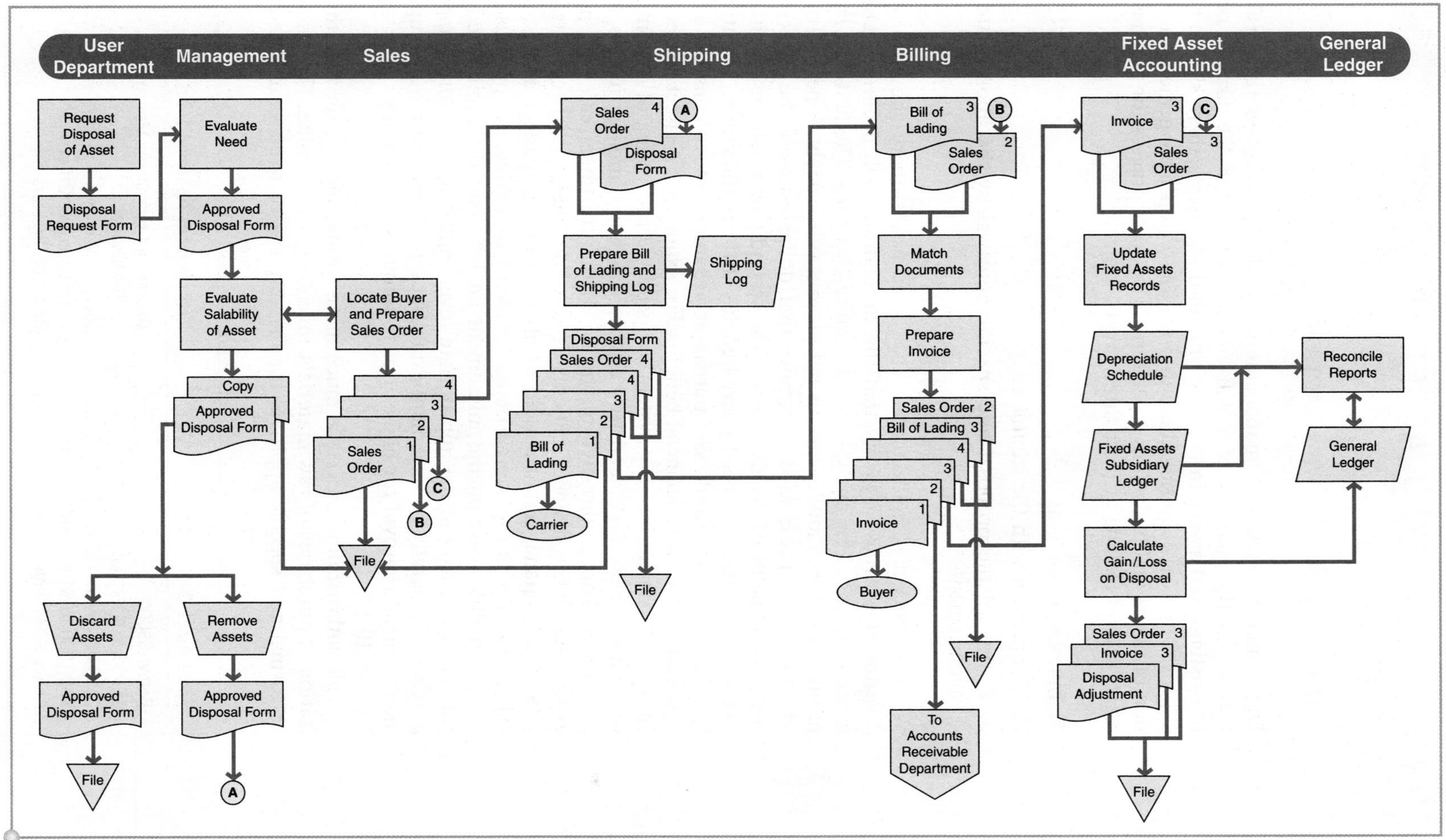

Exhibit 10-12
Document Flowchart for Fixed Asset Disposals

RISKS AND CONTROLS IN FIXED ASSETS PROCESSES (STUDY OBJECTIVE 6)

AUTHORIZATION OF TRANSACTIONS

Designated members of management should be assigned responsibility for authorizing the purchase of new fixed assets, as well as the disposal or transfer of existing fixed assets. In the case of high-dollar items, there should be a strict approval process requiring the authorization of top management or the initiation of the capital budgeting procedures. This strict process for purchasing fixed assets should include at least three formal steps:

1. Investment analysis
2. Comparison with the capital budget
3. Review of the proposal and specific approval by the appropriate level of management

When a request is made to purchase fixed assets, there should be a formal investment analysis to justify that the expenditure will generate benefits that exceed the cost. This analysis could require two parts. The first part is financial justification with a model such as net present value, payback period, or internal rate of return. These models require that dollar estimates be determined for costs and benefits of the fixed asset. The second part would be a written narrative of the benefits, especially any benefits that are difficult to quantify in dollars. In many cases fixed asset purchases are important to consider even when financial costs exceed financial benefits. For example, if a direct competitor purchases a document imaging system to speed the processing of customer paperwork, a company may need to purchase similar technology just to stay competitive. A written narrative of the need for investment can help justify the expenditure when financial benefits do not immediately surpass costs.

Secondly, management should establish a capital budget and compare all expenditures with the capital budget prior to approving any purchase of fixed assets. Finally, based on the investment analysis and the capital budget comparison, a manager at the appropriate level should approve or disapprove the purchase. Generally, management establishes a system that requires upper level management approval for higher dollar amounts of fixed asset purchases, as in Exhibit 10-13.

This authorization process is much more formal and specific than the authorization of purchases of raw materials, inventory, and supplies. There should also be formal and specific approval for the disposal of fixed assets. Requests for

Exhibit 10-13
An Example of Fixed Asset Approval Levels

Fixed Asset Cost	Management Approval Level
Below $5000	Operating Department Manager
$5000 to $100,000	Plant Manager
$100,000 to $500,000	Division Manager
$500,000 to $1 Million	Chief Executive Officer
Above $1 Million	Board of Directors

these purchase and disposal transactions, and the related authorizations, should be written and retained.

Companies should also require management approval for the selection of a depreciation method and assignment of useful lives and estimated salvage values. Likewise, a designated manager should handle asset quality specifications, vendor selection, and negotiation of payment terms for fixed asset purchases.

SEGREGATION OF DUTIES

Custody of fixed assets needs to be separate from the related record keeping. Adequate segregation of duties reduces the risk of undetected errors or fraud by requiring separate employees to handle the different transactions that occur in each phase of the asset's life. Ideally, those with custody of fixed assets should not perform any duties in the purchasing, receiving, or fixed asset accounting departments. In addition, key IT functions such as programming, operations, data input, and security should be segregated from each other and from the related accounting duties.

ADEQUATE RECORDS AND DOCUMENTS

Fixed asset subsidiary ledgers are used to control the physical custody, cost, and accumulated depreciation of the fixed assets. Just like the expenditures process for inventory purchases, fixed asset purchases should be supported by a purchase requisition, PO, receiving report, and vendor invoice. These documents need to be matched in order to establish the validity of the acquisition and to determine whether any items have been omitted from the records. Fixed asset tags may also be used to account for the numerical sequence of items acquired. In addition, management should prepare and follow a capital budget.

SECURITY OF ASSETS AND DOCUMENTS

Adequate supervision is an important control concerning the security of fixed assets, because fixed assets tend to be located throughout the company where many employees could have access to them. Supervisors need to make certain that the assets are being used for their intended purposes. Physical controls should also be in place to protect fixed assets from unauthorized use, and electronic controls are needed to control access to automated records. The appropriate security features depend on the nature and value of the property.

A company should also protect its investment in fixed assets by maintaining adequate insurance coverage and conducting regular preventative maintenance procedures such as tune-ups for machinery and vehicles.

INDEPENDENT CHECKS AND RECONCILIATIONS

Actual fixed asset expenditures should be compared with the capital budget, and additional approval should be required if budgets are exceeded. In addition, periodic counts of fixed assets should be made by someone not otherwise responsible for fixed-asset-related activities. Those physical counts should be reconciled with the accounting records. Also, performing independent verifications to match key purchasing documents and the related accounts payable reports may uncover errors or fraud within these records.

The value of fixed assets should be appraised periodically for insurance purposes. This procedure may also uncover the possibility of impairment issues on these assets. Exhibit 10-14 summarizes the fixed asset controls and risks.

Control:	Minimizes the Related Risk of:
Authorization:	
Requirement for specific approval for acquisitions of large-dollar items or inclusion in the capital budget.	Invalid or fraudulent acquisitions, invalid vendors, unapproved pricing, timing issues, inaccurate records
Management approval of fixed asset changes prior to recording the transaction.	Invalid or fraudulent transfers, disposals or estimate adjustments, timing issues, duplicate transactions
Segregation of Duties:	
Separation of duties related to fixed asset ordering, receiving, subsidiary ledger preparation, authorization of new acquisitions and fixed asset changes, cash disbursements, information systems, and general accounting	Invalid fixed asset transactions, incorrect amounts or accounts, omitted transactions
Records and Documents:	
Updating of the fixed assets subsidiary ledger for all acquisition, disposal, and change transactions.	Fictitious transactions, omitted transactions, timing issues
Updating of depreciation schedules for periodic depreciation on all depreciable assets, using the appropriate bases, dates, useful lives, and methods.	Omitted transactions, incorrect amounts, timing issues
Computation and recording of gains and losses for all disposals of fixed assets (if applicable).	Omitted transactions, incorrect amounts or accounts
Review of the fixed asset subsidiary ledger and depreciation schedule for mathematical accuracy and agreement with authorized documentation.	Incorrect amounts
Security:	
Physical controls in areas where fixed assets are held	Lost or stolen fixed assets
IT controls over computer records and physical controls in records storage areas	Invalid fixed asset transactions, incorrect amounts or accounts, timing issues, duplicate transactions
Independent Checks and Reconciliations:	
Performance of physical counts of fixed assets and reconciliation with the fixed asset subsidiary ledger	Stolen or fraudulent fixed assets, omitted transactions, duplicate purchases, timing issues
Reconciliation of the fixed asset subsidiary ledger with the general ledger	Omitted or duplicate fixed asset transactions, incorrect amounts or accounts, timing issues, incorrect accumulations or postings
Review of the fixed asset subsidiary ledger to ensure that repair and maintenance expenses are not capitalized	Incorrect amounts or accounts
Reconciliation of fixed asset acquisitions and related expenses with budgeted amounts	Invalid or omitted transactions, duplicate transactions, incorrect amounts or accounts, timing issues

Exhibit 10-14:
Fixed Assets Controls and Risks

COST–BENEFIT CONSIDERATIONS

The general nature of fixed assets makes them susceptible to theft, since they are distributed throughout the business and are therefore in the hands of so many different employees. Some additional factors that indicate the need for internal controls over fixed asset processes include large quantities of fixed assets, large quantities of fixed asset changes (such as additions, transfers, and disposals), high likelihood of obsolescence due to technological changes, the existence of assets under capital leasing arrangements, and widely dispersed fixed asset locations.

Companies tend to implement internal controls when they can justify the expense in terms of increased benefits. Accordingly, companies should assess their risk from factors such as those mentioned previously, and decide on the appropriate mix of internal controls. The examples presented in Exhibit 10-14 identify internal controls used in the fixed assets processes and the related risks that are minimized through their implementation. Although this exhibit does not represent a comprehensive list, it includes many reasonable combinations of items that affect fixed asset processes. In addition, the purchasing process maps in Chapter 9 show some purchases and cash disbursements processes that are also relevant to fixed asset systems.

IT SYSTEMS OF FIXED ASSETS PROCESSES (STUDY OBJECTIVE 7)

The complexities of the fixed asset processes described earlier indicate the obvious fact that information technology is a friend of the fixed asset processes. More and more companies are using specialized asset management software programs instead of spreadsheets or traditional manual systems. Due to the abundance of fixed asset data, the time-consuming and tedious requirements for tracking changes, and the intricacy of the tax laws, most companies can justify the investment in computerized systems dedicated to fixed asset accounting. IT systems have evolved into simple, customized applications that may be integrated with other accounting software. These fixed assets applications automate the processes of creating and maintaining the financial records and tax documents required for adequate fixed assets management.

The benefits of automated fixed asset systems are numerous. Most companies would find it much more expensive and time consuming to manage their fixed assets by manual procedures or spreadsheets than by purchasing and implementing fixed asset software. The shortcomings of a spreadsheet-based system are as follows:

- The design of spreadsheets is very time consuming. In addition, most companies have complex structures that are nearly impossible to replicate in spreadsheets. For example, the multiple categories and locations of fixed assets require detailed design and linkages that are very difficult to maintain in a spreadsheet system.
- Spreadsheets are not flexible enough to accommodate changes efficiently. When assets are relocated or disposed of, or changes are made to the underlying cost basis or estimates, updating the spreadsheet is time consuming and prone to error. Add to this the complexity when such changes are implemented to entire categories or departments of fixed assets, and the benefits of automated systems become even more obvious.

- It is difficult to apply varying depreciation policies within spreadsheets. Since many companies use varying rates of depreciation, especially for financial and tax purposes, they need a flexible record-keeping system.
- Spreadsheets are not well-suited for handling the nonfinancial data (locations and descriptions) that are necessary for maintaining physical control of the company's assets.
- It is difficult to establish an audit trail through spreadsheets, so tracking fixed assets changes is difficult.
- Manual processes are typically required to link the spreadsheets with the general ledger and other accounting programs.
- There are limited opportunities to customized reporting. In particular, spreadsheets do not meet the needs of companies to project depreciation information and prepare specialized management reports.

Computer-based fixed asset systems can handle all of the listed items that spreadsheets cannot. It is therefore clear why most companies have replaced their spreadsheet systems with automated ones.

With automated fixed asset management systems, information related to fixed asset acquisitions and changes to existing assets are input into the software by an employee in the fixed asset accounting department. This can be done in real time or in batches, depending upon the company's reporting needs and the volume of transactions. For most companies, fixed asset acquisitions are considered nonroutine processes because they require specific authorization and are carried out infrequently. Thus, the on-line approach is most reasonable. On the other hand, for large companies that have numerous acquisitions, a batch process may be a better match.

All of the relevant information regarding depreciation policies must also be input in the computer so that the system can automatically prepare the depreciation schedule and update the fixed asset control accounts in the general ledger. Similarly, when asset disposal information is input, the system can instantly remove the related asset records and record any resulting gain or loss. Regardless of the type of information entered in the fixed asset system, the company should implement controls to ensure that unauthorized access does not occur. The control environment may be enhanced through the implementation of various access controls, including passwords, limits on the number of employees who have access to the system, and limits on the number of computer workstations where information may be entered.

Fixed asset management systems are easiest to implement at the beginning of the company's fiscal year. By timing the conversion for after the prior-year numbers are finalized and before any current-year depreciation is recorded, the need for midyear adjustments is eliminated.

ETHICAL ISSUES RELATED TO PAYROLL AND FIXED ASSETS PROCESSES (STUDY OBJECTIVE 8)

Chapter 9 presented ethics issues related to expenditure processes, such as those involving the traditional systems of purchasing and cash disbursements. This chapter examines additional issues specific to the payroll and fixed assets processes.

Although there is no direct benefit (in terms of immediate cash received) to a fraudster who engages in earnings management, it is nonetheless unethical because it results in the falsification of the company's financial statements. Many investment and credit decisions are made on the basis of assumptions that the financial statements are a fair representation of the company's financial situation, so many parties stand to benefit or lose from the information contained therein. Fraudsters would realize indirect benefits if the company were able to continue to operate with favorable financial results reported. For instance, they may have increased job security, or they may receive a year-end bonus. However, the people who make business decisions on the basis of misstated information may suffer financial losses if they rely on the accuracy of falsified information when making their decisions.

CORPORATE GOVERNANCE IN PAYROLL AND FIXED ASSETS PROCESSES (STUDY OBJECTIVE 9)

Recall that Chapter 5 identified four primary functions of the corporate governance process: management oversight, internal controls and compliance, financial stewardship, and ethical conduct. While corporate governance is essential for all business processes, it is especially important in the areas of payroll and fixed assets, where historically there has been a large number of cases of fraud, theft, manipulation, and misuse of funds.

Without good corporate governance, time sheets may be more easily altered, payroll funds can be readily stolen, and fixed assets are more likely to be misused or stolen.

Payroll funds and fixed assets do not belong to the managers of the organization; rather, the managers are stewards, or temporary managers, of those assets. Corporate governance policies and procedures must be in place to ensure that expenditures occur only to benefit the organization and its owners, not to benefit the managers or employees personally. In addition, corporate governance policies should prevent a manager or employee from taking fixed assets for personal use.

THE REAL WORLD

Adelphia Business Solutions, Inc. provides an example of poor corporate governance leading to misuse of corporate funds earmarked for fixed asset purchases. In the late 1990s, Adelphia was the sixth largest cable television company in the United States. The corporation was majority-owned and managed by members of the Rigas family. John Rigas was the founder and chairman, and three of his sons occupied top management positions and served as directors. When the Rigas's fraud schemes were discovered in 2001, it was apparent that many millions of dollars in corporate funds had directly benefited Rigas family members.

The Rigas family manipulated and commingled corporate funds with family funds and caused the corporation to buy fixed assets that benefited only the family. These purchases included land and several luxury Manhattan condominiums, as well as the construction of a $12.8 million private golf course. The board of directors, which included Rigas family members, was not an independent board that exercised good corporate governance. Good corporate governance should begin with a strong and independent board of directors, and effective policies, procedures, and systems must be in place throughout the entire organization.

The systems, processes, and internal controls described in this chapter are part of the corporate governance structure. When management designs and implements processes for payroll and fixed assets, it assigns responsibility for executing those functions to various managers and employees. As management assigns and oversees these expenditure processes, it carries out the corporate governance function of proper management oversight.

Management should also establish appropriate internal controls for payroll and fixed assets, such as those internal controls described in this chapter. These controls accomplish the objectives of safeguarding assets within expenditure processes and ensuring the accuracy and completeness of expenditure processes data. These controls are also part of the corporate governance structure.

When management has designed and implemented, and continually manages, processes and internal controls, it is helping to ensure proper stewardship of the company's assets. Corporate governance requires proper financial stewardship. The processes, internal controls, and feedback data from its systems help management report to owners and other stakeholders about proper stewardship of assets within the expenditure processes. These assets include funds for payroll and fixed assets.

Finally, good corporate governance requires ethical conduct. This chapter described some of the ethical issues that management must consider and address within the payroll and fixed assets processes. When top management acts ethically and encourages ethical behavior throughout the organization, stronger corporate governance is the result. There are usually fewer cases of fraud, error, or ethical problems in an organization when top management behaves ethically and encourages ethical behavior.

Perhaps it would be easier to understand the way this chapter's topics fit into corporate governance if you think of it from a negative perspective. For example, if management of a particular organization did not establish sound business processes, good internal controls, and ethical policies, it would lack good corporate governance. In such an organization, expenditure processes would be poorly executed and poorly controlled. Management would not be exercising proper financial stewardship. Therefore, stakeholders such as investors, creditors, and owners would have little or no trust in management's ability to use funds in a manner that would benefit the organization and its owners. The organization would not represent the type of enterprise in which we would wish to invest our own money. On the other hand, when an organization has good corporate governance, the stakeholders can properly have confidence that proper stewardship is occurring. Establishing and executing proper processes, internal controls, and ethical guidelines leads to better corporate governance and, therefore, good financial stewardship.

SUMMARY OF STUDY OBJECTIVES

An introduction to payroll and fixed asset processes. Payroll and fixed asset processes are different from other expenditures in two ways. First, they tend to have fewer transactions than the process of purchasing raw materials. Second, each of these processes has both routine and nonroutine aspects. Payroll has routine processes for weekly, biweekly, or monthly payroll activities, but there are also nonroutine processes for hiring, terminating, or changing the status of employees. Fixed asset processes are routine for depreciating fixed assets, but nonroutine for approving the purchase and disposal of fixed assets.

Payroll processes. Employees must first be hired through the human resources department. The routine accounting processes for maintaining valid employees is the collection, review, and approval of time cards; the calculation of payroll based on pay rates, hours, and deductions; the preparation, approval, and signing of paychecks; a transfer of sufficient funds to the payroll account; distribution of paychecks; and updating payroll and general ledger records.

Risks and controls in payroll processes. Payroll processes involve large sums of cash and the potential for erroneous or inflated timekeeping. Proper controls are necessary to protect the cash and to ensure accurate and complete payroll records. These internal controls can be categorized into authorization, segregation, adequate records and documents, security of assets and documents, and independent checks.

IT systems of payroll processes. Payroll requires routine mathematical calculations and the storing of a large volume of data regarding employees, deductions, vacation days, sick days, and other data. These characteristics of payroll make it a good fit for IT systems. IT systems can include payroll and human resources software, automated timekeeping through bar codes or ID badges, Internet-based timekeeping, and electronic transfer of funds. Some organizations outsource payroll to a payroll processing firm that uses IT systems to provide efficient and cost-effective payroll services.

Fixed asset processes. Many of the processes to purchase fixed assets are similar to those processes to purchase raw materials. The differences in processes occur in the authorization of the purchase, the continuance of the fixed asset after purchase, and the disposal of fixed assets. Authorization is usually specific and based on investment analysis and comparison with the capital budget. Fixed asset continuance requires maintenance of a fixed asset subsidiary ledger for changes in location of fixed assets, ongoing costs to enhance or maintain the assets, and updating of depreciation records. Disposal of fixed assets requires specific approval and record keeping to remove fixed assets from the records and to recognize any gain or loss.

Risks and controls in fixed asset processes. Some of the risks and controls of fixed assets are similar to risks and controls for raw materials purchases. The major differences are that the authorization is more formal and specific for fixed asset acquisitions and the physical security of fixed assets requires more widespread supervision. Segregation of duties, records and documents, and independent checks are very similar to those for raw materials purchases.

IT systems of fixed asset processes. The efficiency and effectiveness of accounting for fixed assets can be greatly improved through the use of specialized asset management software. Such software simplifies the record keeping regarding location and description of fixed assets, depreciation and maintenance records, audit trail, and linkages to the general ledger.

Ethical issues related to payroll and fixed assets processes. Payroll is subject to much unethical employee manipulation such as inflation of hours worked, falsification of overtime or commission records, overstatement of job-related expenses, and creation of ghost employees. Fixed asset information is more likely to be manipulated by management to unethically enhance the financial statements. Often, this occurs when management misclassifies expenses as fixed asset purchases.

Corporate governance in payroll and fixed assets processes. Because payroll funds and fixed assets are particularly susceptible to theft, business organizations must be careful to maintain effective corporate governance systems with respect to these processes. In addition to the need for strong management oversight, internal controls, and ethical practices, corporate managers must recognize their responsibility to be good stewards of the assets underlying the payroll and fixed assets processes.

KEY TERMS

Capital budget
Depreciation schedule
Fixed asset continuance
Fixed asset processes
Fixed asset subsidiary ledger
Ghost employee
Human resources department
Organization chart
Paymaster
Payroll disbursements journal
Payroll processes
Payroll register
Time sheet

END OF CHAPTER MATERIAL

CONCEPT CHECK

1. Which of the following statements about payroll and fixed asset processes is true?
   a. Both have only routine processes.
   b. Both have only nonroutine processes.
   c. Both have routine and nonroutine processes.
   d. Payroll has only routine processes, while fixed asset has only nonroutine processes
2. For a given pay period, the complete listing of paychecks for the pay period is a
   a. payroll register.
   b. payroll ledger.
   c. payroll journal.
   d. paymaster.
3. A payroll voucher
   a. authorizes an employee paycheck to be written.
   b. authorizes the transfer of cash from a main operating account to a payroll account.
   c. authorizes the transfer of cash from a payroll account to a main operating account.
   d. authorizes the paymaster to distribute paychecks.
4. For proper segregation of duties, the department that should authorize new employees for payroll would be
   a. payroll.
   b. human resources.
   c. cash disbursement.
   d. general ledger.
5. Which of the following is not an independent check within payroll processes?
   a. Time sheets are reconciled with production records.
   b. Time sheets are reconciled with the payroll register.

c. Paychecks are prepared on prenumbered checks.

d. The payroll register is reconciled with the general ledger.

6. An integrated IT system of payroll and human resources may have extra risks above those of a manual system. Passwords and access logs are controls that should be used in these integrated systems to lessen the risk of

a. hardware failures.

b. erroneous data input.

c. payroll data that does not reconcile to time cards.

d. unauthorized access to payroll data.

7. Internal control problems would be likely to result if a company's payroll department supervisor was also responsible for

a. reviewing authorization forms for new employees.

b. comparing the payroll register with the batch transmittal data.

c. authorizing changes in employee pay rates.

d. hiring subordinates to work in the payroll department.

8. Which of the following procedures would be most useful in determining the effectiveness of a company's internal controls regarding the existence or occurrence of payroll transactions?

a. Observe the segregation of duties concerning personnel responsibilities and payroll disbursement.

b. Inspect evidence of accounting for prenumbered payroll checks.

c. Recompute the payroll deductions for employee fringe benefits.

d. Verify the preparation of the monthly payroll account bank reconciliation.

9. In meeting the control objective of the safeguarding of assets, which departments should be responsible for distribution of paychecks and custody of unclaimed paychecks, respectively?

	Distribution of paychecks	Custody of unclaimed paychecks
a.	Treasurer	Treasurer
b.	Payroll	Treasurer
c.	Treasurer	Payroll
d.	Payroll	Payroll

10. A company's internal controls policies may mandate the distribution of paychecks by an independent paymaster in order to determine that

a. payroll deductions are properly authorized and computed.

b. pay rates are properly authorized and separate from the operating function.

c. each employee's paycheck is supported by an approved time sheet.

d. employees included in the period's payroll register actually exist and are currently employed.

11. The purpose of segregating the duties of hiring personnel and distributing payroll checks is to separate the

a. authorization of transactions from the custody of related assets.

b. operational responsibility from the recordkeeping responsibility.

12. Which of the following departments or positions most likely would approve changes in pay rates and deductions from employee salaries?
    a. Human resources
    b. Treasurer
    c. Controller
    d. Payroll
13. The purchase of fixed assets is likely to require different authorization processes than the purchase of inventory. Which of the following is not likely to be part of the authorization of fixed assets?
    a. Specific authorization
    b. Inclusion in the capital budget
    c. An investment analysis or feasibility analysis of the purchase
    d. Approval of the depreciation schedule
14. Which of the following is not a part of "adequate documents and records" for fixed assets?
    a. Fixed asset journal
    b. Fixed asset subsidiary ledger
    c. Purchase order
    d. Fixed asset tags
15. Which of the following questions would be least likely to appear on an internal control questionnaire regarding the initiation and execution of new property, plant, and equipment purchases?
    a. Are requests for repairs approved by someone higher than the department initiating the request?
    b. Are prenumbered purchase orders used and accounted for?
    c. Are purchase requisitions reviewed for consideration of soliciting competitive bids?
    d. Is access to the assets restricted and monitored?
16. Which of the following reviews would be most likely to indicate that a company's property, plant, and equipment accounts are not understated?
    a. Review of the company's repairs and maintenance expense accounts.
    b. Review of supporting documentation for recent equipment purchases.
    c. Review and recomputation of the company's depreciation expense accounts.
    d. Review of the company's miscellaneous revenue account.
17. Which of the following is not an advantage of fixed asset software systems when compared with spreadsheets?
    a. Better ability to handle nonfinancial data such as asset location
    b. Easier to apply different depreciation policies to different assets
    c. Manual processes to link to the general ledger
    d. Expanded opportunities for customized reporting
18. The term "ghost employee" means that
    a. hours worked has been exaggerated by an employee.
    b. false sales have been claimed to boost commission earned.

18. The term "ghost employee" means that
    a. hours worked has been exaggerated by an employee.
    b. false sales have been claimed to boost commission earned.
    c. overtime hours have been inflated.
    d. someone who does not work for the company receives a paycheck.

DISCUSSION QUESTIONS

19. (SO 1) Sales and inventory purchases are routine processes that occur nearly every day in a business. How are these routine processes different from payroll or fixed asset processes?
20. (SO 1) Even though payroll and fixed asset processes may not be as routine as revenue processes, why are they just as important?
21. (SO 2) Why do you think management should specifically approve all employees hired?
22. (SO 2) Why is it important that the human resources department maintain records authorizing the various deductions from an employee's paycheck?
23. (SO 2) Explain why an employee's individual record is accessed frequently, but changed relatively infrequently.
24. (SO 2) Explain two things that should occur to ensure that hours worked on a time card are accurate and complete.
25. (SO 2) Explain the reasons for an organization having a separate bank account established for payroll.
26. (SO 3) What is the purpose of supervisory review of employee time cards?
27. (SO 3) Why is it important to use an independent paymaster to distribute paychecks?
28. (SO 3) Why do payroll processes result in sensitive information, and what is the sensitive information?
29. (SO 4) Why is batch processing well suited to payroll processes?
30. (SO 4) What are the advantages of automated time keeping such as bar code readers, or ID badges that are swiped through a reader?
31. (SO 4) What are the advantages of outsourcing payroll?
32. (SO 5) Fixed assets are purchased and retired frequently. Given this frequent change, why are clear accounting records of fixed assets necessary?
33. (SO 5) Why is it important to conduct an investment analysis prior to the purchase of fixed assets?
34. (SO 5) Explain why categorizing fixed asset expenditures as expenses or capital assets is important.
35. (SO 5) What are some of the practical characteristics of fixed assets that complicate the calculation of depreciation?
36. (SO 6) What is different about the nature of fixed asset purchasing that makes authorization controls important?
37. (SO 6) Explain the necessity of supervision over fixed assets.
38. (SO 6) Why are some fixed assets susceptible to theft?

39. (SO 7) Explain why a real-time update of fixed asset records might be preferable to batch processing of fixed asset changes.
40. (SO 7) Why is the beginning of a fiscal year the best time to implement a fixed asset software system?
41. (SO 7) What negative things might occur if fixed asset software systems lacked appropriate access controls?
42. (SO 8) Why might a supervisor collude with an employee to falsify time cards?
43. (SO 8) How does the misclassification of fixed asset expenditures result in misstatement of financial statements?

BRIEF EXERCISES

44. (SO 2) Describe the type of information that a human resources department should maintain for each employee.
45. (SO 2) The calculation of gross and net pay can be a complicated process. Explain the items that complicate payroll calculations.
46. (SO 3) Explain how duties are segregated in payroll. Specifically, who or which departments conduct the authorization, timekeeping, recording, and custody functions?
47. (SO 3) Explain the various reconciliation procedures that should occur in payroll.
48. (SO 4) Explain the ways in which electronic transfer of funds can improve payroll processes.
49. (SO 5) Explain the kinds of information that must be maintained in fixed asset records during the asset continuance phase.
50. (SO 6) The authorization to purchase fixed assets should include investment analysis. Explain the two parts of investment analysis.
51. (SO 8) Explain the types of unethical behavior that may occur in the fixed assets area.

PROBLEMS

52. (SO 2) Following is a time sheet completed by an hourly wage earner at Halfrid, Inc.:

Name: Janice Ketteler

Pay Period Ending: 05/02/07

SS# 222-55-6666 Approval: KTB

Mon.	IN	08:02	M
	OUT	11:40	M
	IN	12:34	M
	OUT	17:02	M
Tue.	IN	08:00	T
	OUT	11:45	T
	IN	12:44	T
	OUT	17:01	T

Wed.	IN	08:11	W
	OUT	11:30	W
	IN	12:15	W
	OUT	17:00	W
Thur.	IN	07:57	Th
	OUT	11:44	Th
	IN	12:52	Th
	OUT	17:16	Th
Fri.	IN	12:01	F
	OUT	16:15	F
	IN	17:10	F
	OUT	21:05	F
Sat.	IN	09:00	Sa
	OUT	12:04	Sa
	IN		
	OUT		
Sun.	IN		
	OUT		
	IN		
	OUT		

Use Microsoft Excel to perform the following tasks:

a. Design an appropriate format for a data entry screen that could be used in the payroll department to enter information from this time sheet in the company's payroll software program.

b. Prepare a payroll journal with the column headings shown in the next table. Enter the relevant information from the preceding time sheet onto this journal and calculate gross pay, federal withholdings, and net pay. Use two lines for this employee, and assume that the pay rate is $19.75 per hour, with time-and-a-half for overtime. (Overtime applies to any time worked over 40 hours within one week.) Use the following withholding rates: FICA (Social Security)—6.2% of gross pay; Medicare—1.45% of gross pay; federal income taxes—20%. Assume no additional withholdings.

Date	**Employee /SS#**	**Hours: Regular/ Overtime**	**Pay Rate: Regular/ Overtime**	**Gross Pay**	**FICA Withheld**	**Medicare Withheld**	**Federal Inc. Tax Withheld**	**Net Pay**

53. (SO 2) The textbook website has a Microsoft Excel spreadsheet titled payroll_problem.xls. This spreadsheet is used by Naltner Company to calculate its biweekly payroll. Using the information in that spreadsheet, calculate all details for the February 22, 2008 payroll. Hours worked by each employee are contained in the first worksheet. The following four worksheets contain details for each of the three employees and a total for the three employees. The sixth and last worksheet contains federal tax withholding tables to calculate federal tax to withhold. Calculate the gross pay and deductions for all three employees.

54. (SO 5) The textbook website has a Microsoft Excel spreadsheet titled fixed_asset.xls. The spreadsheet represents a fixed asset subsidiary ledger for Brozzos Corporation. On July 3, 2008, Brozzos purchased for the office a multifunction printer/fax/copier from Brereton Office Supplies for $2000. The machine has no salvage value and a four-year life. Add a new ledger record for this machine and calculate and record the 2008 depreciation expense for all fixed assets. Brozzos uses straight-line depreciation with a half-year convention.

55. (SO 6) Explain the process of approval of purchases for fixed assets. How does this process differ from that of purchasing raw materials?

56. (SO 3) Using an Internet search engine, search for the phrase "biometric time recording." (Be sure to include the quotation marks.) From your search results, describe a biometric time recording system and its advantages.

57. (SO 7) Using an Internet search engine, search for the phrase "fixed asset software." (Be sure to include the quotation marks.) Examine the results to find companies that sell fixed asset software. List and explain some of the features of fixed asset software that these companies offer as selling points for their software.

58. (SO 8) Read the article at this link: http://www.fixedassetinfo.com/articles/adventures1.asp. Describe why the scenario described is unethical. Also, list controls or other steps that management could have taken to prevent or detect this situation.

59. (SO 8) Using an Internet search engine, search for the terms "Patti Dale" and "theft." (Be sure to include the quotation marks around the name.) Explain the unethical behavior that occurred. Also, explain any internal controls that you believe were missing or not followed in this case.

CASES

60. Zammer Company is a small manufacturing firm with 60 employees in seven departments. When the need arises for new workers in the plant, the departmental manager interviews applicants and hires on the basis of those interviews. The manager has each new employee complete a withholding form. The manager then writes the rate of pay on the W-4 and forwards it to payroll.

When workers arrive for their shift, they pull their time cards from a holder near the door and keep the time card with them during the day to complete the start and end times of their work day. On Friday, the time cards are removed from the holder and taken to payroll by any employee who is not busy that morning. If there were any pay rate changes for the payroll period due to raises or promotions, the manager calls the payroll department to inform payroll of these rate changes.

Using the rate changes and the time cards, the payroll department prepares the checks from the regular bank account of the Zammer Company. The manager of the payroll department signs the checks, and the checks are then forwarded to each department manager for distribution to employees.

Required:

Describe any improvements you would suggest to strengthen the payroll internal controls at Zammer.

61. Wegstram Industries has payroll processes as described in the following paragraphs:

When a new employee is hired, the human resources department completes a personnel action form and forwards it to the payroll department. The form contains information such as pay rate, number of exemptions for tax purposes, and the type and amount of payroll deductions. When an employee is terminated or voluntarily separates from Wegstram, the human resources department completes a personnel action form to indicate separation and forwards it to the payroll department.

Each employee in the production department maintains his own time card weekly. Employees fill out their time cards in ink each day, and at the end of the week, the time cards are forwarded to the payroll department. Employees in the payroll department use the time cards and employee records to prepare a weekly paycheck for each employee who has turned in a time card. A copy of the payroll checks is forwarded to the accounts payable department, and the original payroll checks are forwarded to the cash disbursements department to be signed. The payroll department updates the payroll subsidiary ledger. After the paychecks are signed, they are given to department supervisors to distribute. Any unclaimed checks are returned to the payroll department.

Required:

a. Prepare a process map of the payroll processes at Wegstram.

b. Identify both internal control strengths and internal control weaknesses of the payroll processes.

c. For any internal control weaknesses, describe suggested improvements.

62. Brahaman Enterprises is a midsize manufacturing company with 120 employees and approximately 45 million dollars in sales. Management has established a set of processes to purchase fixed assets, described in the following paragraphs:

When a user department determines that it may be necessary to purchase a new fixed asset, the departmental manager prepares an asset request form. When completing the form, the manager must describe the fixed asset, the advantages or efficiencies offered by the asset, and estimates of costs and benefits. The asset request form is forwarded to the director of finance. Personnel in the finance department review estimates of costs and benefits and revise these if necessary. A discounted cash flow analysis is prepared and forwarded to the vice president of operations, who reviews the asset request forms and the discounted cash flow analysis, and then interviews user department managers if she feels it is warranted. After this review, she selects assets to purchase until she has exhausted the funds in the capital budget.

When an asset purchase has been approved by the VP of operations, a buyer looks up prices and completes a purchase order. The purchase order is mailed to the vendor, and a copy is forwarded to accounts payable. The fixed asset is delivered directly to the user department so that it can be installed and used as quickly as possible. The user department completes a receiving report and forwards a copy to accounts payable. If the invoice, purchase order, and receiving report match, payment is approved and cash disbursements prepares and mails a check.

The accounts payable department updates the accounts payable subsidiary ledger and the fixed asset spreadsheet file.

Required:

a. Identify any internal control strengths and weaknesses in the fixed asset processes at Brahaman. Explain why each is a strength or weakness.

b. For each internal control weakness, describe improvement(s) in the processes that you would recommend to address the weakness.

63. The Rampert Company has the following processes related to fixed assets: When a department manager determines a need for a new fixed asset, he prepares a purchase requisition, which is forwarded to the chief financial officer. If the requested fixed asset purchase will not exceed remaining funds in the capital budget, the CFO approves the purchase and forwards the requisition to the purchasing department.

The purchasing agent assigned to purchase the fixed assets begins phoning vendors until she finds a vendor selling the requested asset. The purchase order is prepared and mailed to the vendor. Vendors are instructed to deliver the fixed asset to the requesting department.

A copy of the invoice is forwarded to the fixed asset department to record the asset details. Personnel determine the estimated life and salvage value by looking up the last similar asset purchase and using the previous estimated life and salvage value.

Required:

Describe any improvements you would suggest to strengthen the fixed asset internal controls at Rampert.

64. (CMA Adapted) Bellott Co. makes automobile parts for sale to major automobile manufacturers in the United States. The following information is available regarding internal controls over machinery and equipment:

When a departmental supervisor needs a new item of machinery or equipment, he or she must initiate a purchase request. The acquisition proposal must be presented to the plant manager. If the plant manager agrees with the need, he must review the corporate budget allocation for his plant to determine the availability of funds to cover the acquisition. If the allocation is sufficient, the departmental supervisor is notified of the approval and a purchase requisition is prepared and forwarded to the purchasing department.

Upon receipt of a purchase requisition for machinery and equipment, the purchasing department researches the company records in order to locate an appropriate vendor. A purchase order is then completed and mailed to the vendor.

As soon as new machinery or equipment is received from the vendor, it is immediately sent to the department for installation. Bellott's policy is to place new assets into service as soon as possible so that the company may immediately begin to realize the economic benefits from the acquisition.

The property accounting department is responsible for maintaining property, plant, and equipment ledger control accounts. The ledger is supported by lapsing schedules that are used to compute depreciation. These lapsing schedules are organized by year of acquisition so that depreciation computations can be prepared in units that combine all assets of the same type that were acquired the same year. Standard depreciation methods, rates, and salvage values were determined ten years ago and have been used consistently since that time.

When machinery or equipment is retired or replaced, the plant manager notifies the property accounting department so that the proper adjustments can be made to the ledger and lapsing schedules. No regular reconciliation between the physical assets on hand and the accounting records has been performed.

Required:

Identify any internal control weaknesses and suggest improvements to strengthen the internal controls over machinery and equipment at Bellott.

CONTINUING CASE: SPATELLI'S PIZZERIA

Reread the continuing case on Spatelli's Pizzeria at the end of Chapter 1. Consider the following issues that relate to Spatelli's payroll and fixed assets systems, then answer the questions pertaining to these expenditure processes:

As mentioned in the opening part of the Spatelli's Pizzeria case, there are now 49 locations throughout the greater Pittsburgh area. Each one of those restaurant locations employs a full-time store manager and varying numbers of kitchen staff, servers, and delivery staff. The kitchen staff, servers, and delivery staff vary between full-time and part-time status. There tend to be high rates of turnover, especially among the part-time staff.

Spatelli's pays its employees on a weekly basis each Friday for the week ending on the previous Saturday. Employee paychecks include withholdings for federal taxes as well as state and local taxes applicable for the employee's residence. Employees may live in one of three states and over twenty-five municipalities that are included in the greater Pittsburgh regional area. All payroll accounting is handled by Spatelli's at its home office.

Each restaurant must also maintain various fixed assets in order to operate. Following is a general list of fixed assets for each store:

- Furniture and store fixtures, including tables, chairs, and built-in items such as shelving, counters, and booths
- Kitchen equipment, such as refrigerators, stoves, ovens, and dishwashing machines
- Computers

Note that the number of each of these fixed assets maintained at each location varies, depending upon the size of the store. Also note that each member of the delivery staff uses his or her personal automobile (rather than a company-owned car) for customer deliveries.

In addition, the home office maintains the following types of fixed assets:

- Land and the office building
- Office furniture and fixtures
- Computers and other office equipment
- Telephone systems

Finally, fixed assets maintained at the commissary include the following:

- Fixtures, such as built-in cabinets and shelving
- Kitchen equipment
- Computers
- Delivery trucks

All fixed asset accounting is handled by Spatelli's at its home office.

Required:

A. Describe how you believe an efficient and effective payroll system should be organized at Spatelli's. Include details such as the answers to these questions:
   a. What types of payroll documentation should be prepared at the restaurant locations?
   b. How will the necessary information for payroll flow between restaurants and the home office?
   c. How should IT systems be used in the payroll processes?

B. How could Spatelli's prevent the occurrence of a ghost employee at one of its restaurant locations?

C. From a cost–benefit perspective, what risks factors exist in Spatelli's payroll processes that make it worthwhile to implement thorough internal controls? Describe the related internal control that could help detect or prevent each risk.

D. If Spatelli's wished to reduce the payroll risks you identified previously, it could consider outsourcing much of the payroll processing. (ADP is an example of a payroll processing company.) Search the website of a payroll processing firm to determine the benefits to Spatelli's of outsourcing a substantial portion of its payroll processing. Describe these benefits, the risks avoided by outsourcing, and the risks still borne by Spatelli's after outsourcing. Also, describe the payroll record keeping functions that Spatelli's must still maintain even if it outsources a substantial portion of its payroll processing.

E. Describe how you believe an efficient and effective system of fixed assets accounting should be organized at Spatelli's. Be sure to include the following issues in your response:
   a. How should the fixed assets accounting department maintain control over fixed assets in the various restaurant locations?
   b. How should IT systems be used in the fixed assets process?

SOLUTIONS TO CONCEPT CHECK

1. (SO 1) Which of the statements about payroll and fixed asset processes is true? **c. Both have routine and nonroutine processes.** Examples of routine processes are regular payroll runs and recording depreciation. Nonroutine processes are hiring employees and purchasing fixed assets.
2. (SO 2) For a given pay period, the complete listing of paychecks for the pay period is a **a. payroll register.**
3. (SO 2) A payroll voucher **b. authorizes the transfer of cash from a main operating account to a payroll account.** After reviewing the payroll register, accounts payable prepares a payroll voucher to transfer an amount of cash necessary to cover the payroll checks written.
4. (SO 3) For proper segregation of duties, the department that should authorize new employees for payroll would be **b. human resources.** This segregates the authorization from the timekeeping and payroll record keeping.
5. (SO 3) Which of the statements is not an independent check within payroll processes? **c. Paychecks are prepared on prenumbered checks.** This is an important control concerning completeness, but it is not part of the independent check control procedures.
6. (SO 4) An integrated IT system of payroll and human resources may have extra risks above those of a manual system. Passwords and access logs are controls that should be used in these integrated systems to lessen the risk of **d. unauthorized access to payroll data.** Passwords and logs are both examples of access controls, whereas the other options are related to equipment controls and data controls.
7. (CPA Adapted) (SO 3) Internal control problems would be likely to result if a company's payroll department supervisor was also responsible for **c. authorizing changes in employee pay rates.** This would be a violation of the principle of segregation of duties, as the same employee would have both record keeping and authority functions.
8. (CPA Adapted) (SO 3) The procedure most useful in determining the effectiveness of a company's internal controls regarding the existence or occurrence of payroll transactions would be **a. to observe the segregation of duties concerning personnel responsibilities and payroll disbursement.** Option b. is concerned with the completeness assertion, option c. related to accuracy, and option d. is an independent check.
9. (CPA Adapted) (SO 3) In meeting the control objective of safeguarding assets, the **a. treasurer** should be responsible for distribution of paychecks and the **treasurer** should have custody of unclaimed paychecks. The payroll department should not have responsibility for either of these payroll custody functions, because it is responsible for payroll record keeping.
10. (CPA Adapted) (SO 3) A company's internal control policies may mandate the distribution of paychecks by an independent paymaster in order to determine that **d. employees included in the period's payroll register actually exist and are currently employed.** Each of the other options is related to authorization for payroll transactions.
11. (CPA Adapted) (SO 3) The purpose of segregating the duties of hiring personnel and distributing payroll checks is to separate the **a. authorization of**

transactions from the custody of related assets. The human resources department has authorization responsibility with regard to payroll transactions, whereas the distribution of paychecks involves custody of payroll cash.

12. (CPA Adapted) (SO 3) The **a. personnel** department most likely would approve changes in pay rates and deductions from employee salaries. This is another name for human resources. None of the other responses is appropriate, because they each include record keeping or custody functions.
13. (SO 5) The purchase of fixed assets is likely to require different authorization processes than the purchase of inventory. **d. Approval of the depreciation schedule** is not likely to be part of the authorization of fixed assets. This is generally categorized as an independent check rather than an authorization function.
14. (SO 6) **a. A fixed asset journal** is not a part of "adequate documents and records" for fixed assets. While there should be either a manual or computerized fixed asset subsidiary ledger, a fixed asset journal is nonexistent.
15. (CPA Adapted) (SO 6) The question least likely to appear on an internal control questionnaire regarding the initiation and execution of new property, plant, and equipment purchases would be **d., Is access to the assets restricted and monitored?** This question is concerned with safeguarding of the asset after it is placed in service. Each of the other responses relates to acquisitions.
16. (CPA Adapted) (SO 6) **a. Review of the company's repairs and maintenance expense accounts** is most likely to be an indication that a company's property, plant, and equipment accounts are not understated. Fixed asset additions are sometime misclassified as repairs or maintenance expenses, so it is wise to monitor this account for the nature of the underlying expenditures.
17. (SO 7) **c. Manual processes to link to the general ledger** are not an advantage of fixed asset software systems compared with spreadsheets. Fixed asset system software usually has linkages to the general ledger. Spreadsheets do not have linkages to the general ledger and require manual processes to enter data into the general ledger.
18. (SO 8) The term "ghost employee" means that **d. someone who does not work for the company receives a paycheck.**

CHAPTER 11

Conversion Processes and Controls

Study Objectives

This chapter will help you gain an understanding of the following concepts:

1. Basic features of conversion processes
2. The components of the logistics function
3. Cost accounting reports generated by conversion processes
4. Risks and controls in conversion processes
5. IT systems of conversion processes
6. Ethical issues related to conversion processes
7. Corporate governance in conversion processes

THE REAL WORLD

Digital Vision

Nissan Motor Company's automobile plant near Jackson, Mississippi has cutting-edge technology and robotic assemblers.

"Assembly lines are powered by enormous robots; at one stop in the line, a bay of over 25 robots each make 12 welds per second. Suppliers are tied into the line by computers; parts actually arrive in the order they'll be used."[1]

The complex technology allows Nissan to handle four different models in random order and to finish a vehicle in 13 hours. The plant can produce 400,000 vehicles in a five-day period with two shifts operating.

Manufacturing has changed dramatically over the last few years due to robotics, computers, and global competition. Manufacturers must have more flexible activities, as in the Nissan example. They must also have processes and accounting systems that help them predict, order, and track the various raw materials and parts they use in manufacturing. This chapter examines the activities and information flows in the manufacturing process.

The first part of the chapter examines the basic features of the conversion processes, beginning with a typical traditional system and the related controls, followed by trends in computer-based systems. The latter part of the chapter examines ethical issues and corporate governance related to the conversion processes.

As was true in the previous three chapters, individual companies may have differences in their conversion processes. This chapter explains common, simple methods of conducting these business activities, and these explanations should help you understand many accounting systems involving these conversion processes, even if they are not exactly like the ones you may have seen in your personal experience, or will see in the future.

BASIC FEATURES OF CONVERSION PROCESSES (STUDY OBJECTIVE 1)

A company's conversion processes involve the activities related to the transformation of resources into goods or services. These resources include the following:

- Materials, including raw materials inventory
- Labor, namely, the human resources required for operations
- Overhead, including fixed assets, indirect materials, indirect labor, and various other expenses necessary to run the operating facility

Exhibit 11-1 highlights the portions of the conversion processes addressed in this chapter, as they relate to the overall accounting system.

A company must have systems in place to capture, record, summarize, and report all of its conversion activities. The major activities within this process include operational planning that supports the company's strategies, optimizing

[1]G. Pascal Zachary, "Dream Factory," *Business 2.0*, vol. 6, no. 5, June 2005, p. 99.

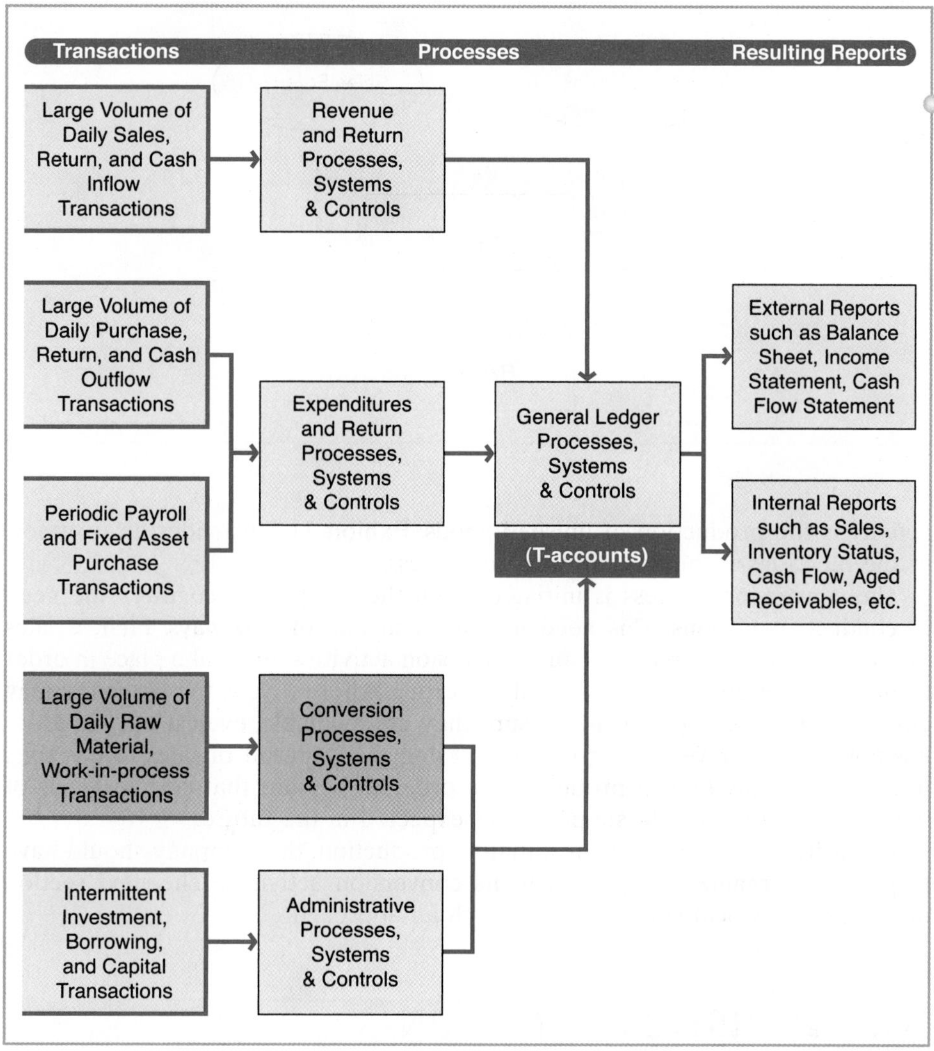

Exhibit 11-1
Conversion Processes within the Overall System

the use of the employees, property, and inventories that are needed in operations, controlling production flows, ensuring product quality, and preparing the related cost accounting and financial accounting records. These are considered routine processes in most companies because of the large number of transactions encountered on a daily basis.

Although many companies are not considered manufacturing firms—that is, their principal functions are not manufacturing operations—most companies do conduct some sort of productive activity. For example, even in service organizations such as professional firms and health care organizations, the processes of converting resources into outputs (services) are considered conversion activities. Therefore, whether the company is in business to manufacture automobiles, build houses, treat patients in a medical facility, or provide consulting services, there is some sort of productive activity that drives its business. Thus, the contents of this chapter are relevant to most companies, even nonmanufacturing companies. However, the discussion in the remainder of this chapter is set in the context of a manufacturing environment where the principal business

Exhibit 11-2
Overview of the Conversion Process

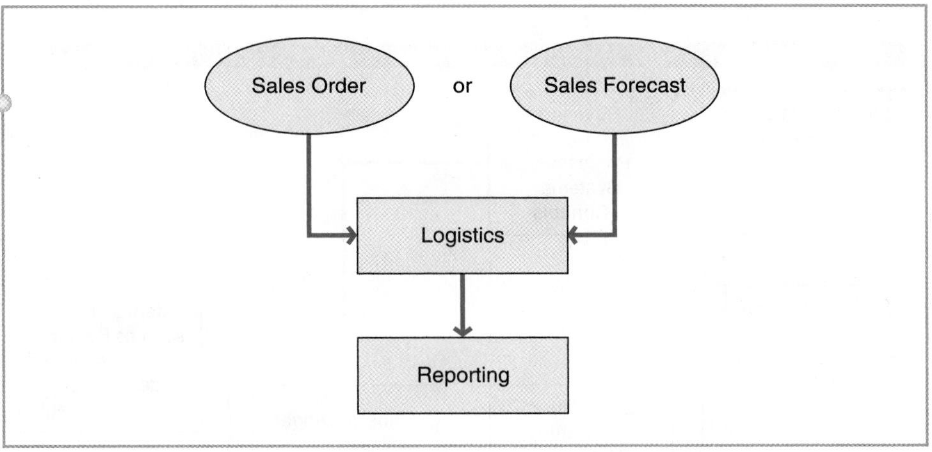

activity is the production of finished goods. Exhibit 11-2 provides an overview of the functions within the conversion process.

The conversion process is initiated when the company recognizes the need to conduct operations. This need may arise in one of two ways. First, a sales order may have been received and conversion activities must take place in order to produce the goods needed to fill the order. Alternatively, the company may desire to produce goods to make sure they are available, even if a sales order has not yet been received for the related items. As a result of sales forecasting, management may launch production in order to be sure that certain levels of inventory are on hand to support sales expected in the future.

Regardless of the reason for initiating production, the company should have in place an organized approach to its conversion activities. The next section describes the typical components of such an approach.

COMPONENTS OF THE LOGISTICS FUNCTION (STUDY OBJECTIVE 2)

The major function within the conversion process is the logistics function. **Logistics** is the logical, systematic flow of resources throughout the organization. It involves the well-planned and coordinated efforts of many departments. Its goal is to make the most efficient use of the resources available in order to support the organization.

The logistics function has three primary components: planning, resource management, and operations. Exhibit 11-3 presents these components and their subcomponents.

PLANNING

The **planning** component of the logistics function directs the focus of operations. It is concerned with determining what products should be produced, how many products should be produced, what resources should be available, and what timing is needed. It is supported by the efforts of research and development, capital budgeting, engineering, and scheduling.

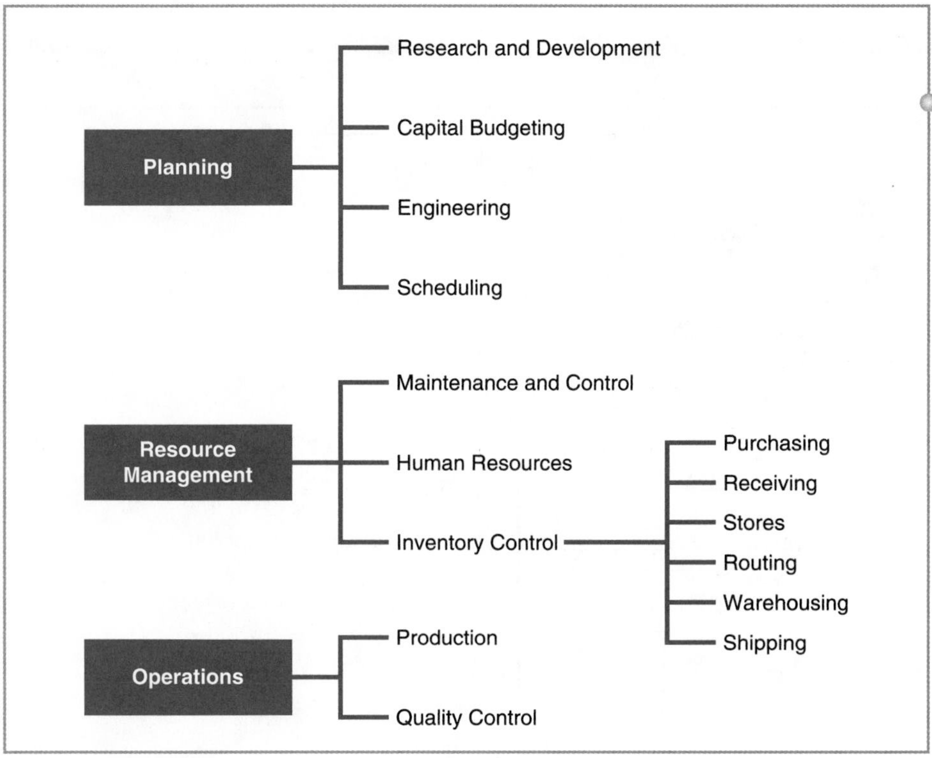

Exhibit 11-3
Components of the Logistics Function

Research and development focuses on product improvement. Its efforts involve investigating and developing new, innovative products and methods of producing those products. The research and development department may also conduct studies to determine which parts should be manufactured and which will be purchased, considering the most efficient manner of conducting operations. This department is also responsible for researching and testing new or improved products and processes before they are put into practice.

Capital budgeting plans the capital resources needed to support production. It is concerned primarily with fixed assets, including the facilities and equipment needed to conduct operations as planned. Since capital resources typically involve the outlay of large sums of cash, it is essential that they be planned in advance so that securing the necessary approvals and financing arrangements does not delay their implementation. The fixed assets acquisition processes were discussed in Chapter 10.

Engineering is responsible for planning the specifications for products that will be manufactured. This department prepares the detailed design of each product, identifying the component parts and methods of production. Engineers also prepare the following two important documents used in the conversion process:

1. A **bill of materials** is the form that specifies the components of a product, including descriptions and quantities of materials and parts needed.
2. An **operations list** describes the chain of events that constitute a product's production. It includes all the necessary operations to be performed, identifying the locations, resources used, and standard timing for each phase.

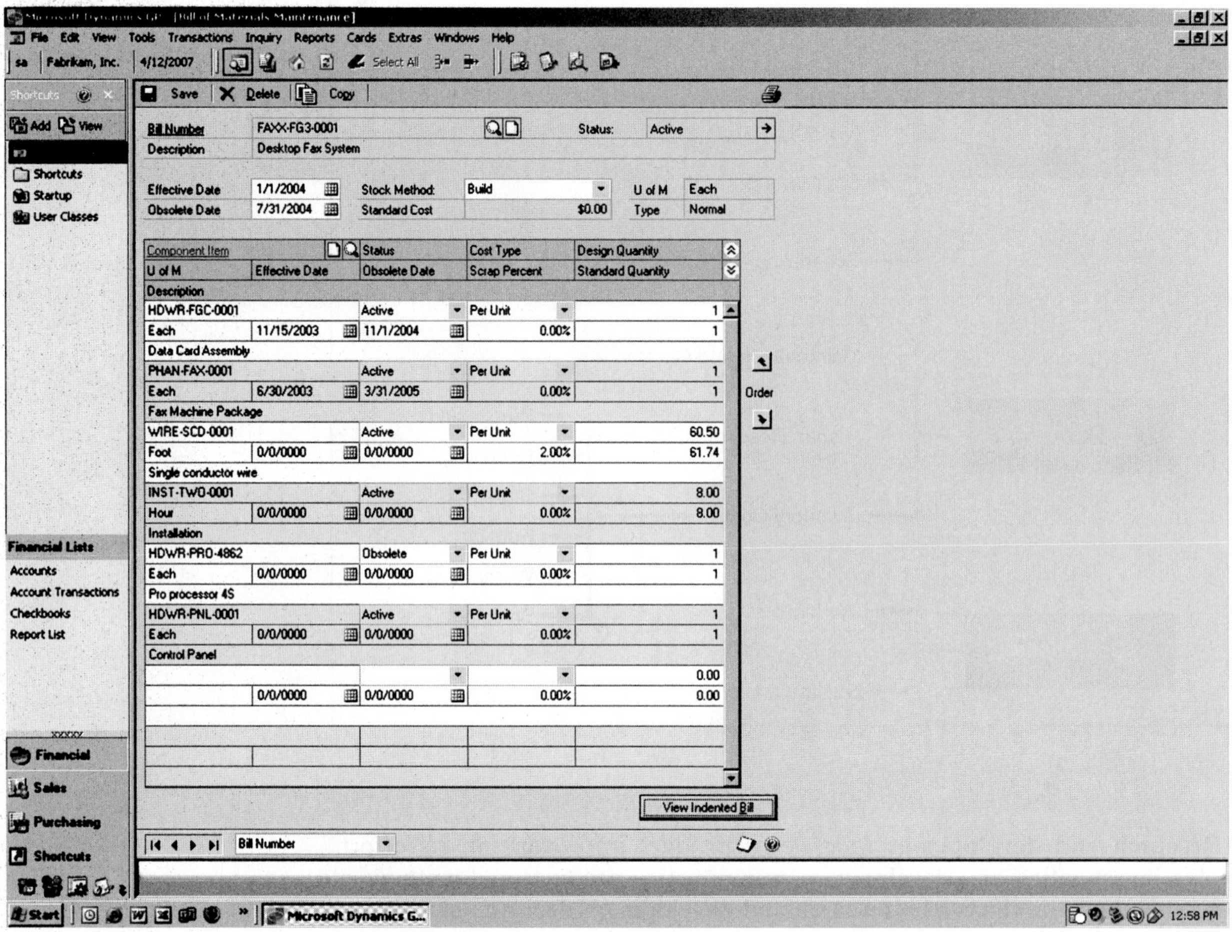

Exhibit 11-4
Preparing a Bill of Materials in Microsoft Dynamics GP®

Engineering's role in the planning process is essentially similar to writing a recipe for a product. The bill of materials details all the required ingredients and amounts, and the operations list provides the instructions for preparation. Exhibit 11-4 is a screen shot of the bill of materials form prepared in Microsoft Dynamics GP® accounting software. The bill of materials shown relates to a desktop fax system that includes six component parts: a data card, fax machine package, and various hardware.

Scheduling plans the timing for production activities, taking into consideration all the open sales orders, inventory needs, and the resources available. It uses the operations lists to determine how the timing for particular products will fit in with other demands on production resources. Its dual goal is to meet the customer's needs while making the most efficient use of the company's resources. Accordingly, the scheduling department must plan the production process so that idle time is minimized, since idle time is unproductive time. Although idle time may be the result of factors (such as machine breakdowns or power failures) that are beyond the control of those in a planning role, its impact may be minimized by the use of proper planning and control.

Scheduling personnel prepare important documentation used in the conversion process. **Production orders** authorize production activities for a particular sales order or forecasted need. A **production schedule** outlines the specific timing required for a sales order, including the dates and times designated for the production run. These documents combine information from the sales order (or forecast), bill of materials, and operations list. The goal is to plan the production schedule in such a manner that there is no idle time between production activities.

RESOURCE MANAGEMENT

There are many resources that feed the conversion process. Although the specific resources vary greatly from company to company, they tend to fall into three broad categories: maintenance and control, human resources, and inventory control.

In a manufacturing environment, it is important to designate responsibility for maintenance and control to a person or department that can devote sufficient attention to these matters. **Maintenance and control** is concerned with maintaining the capital resources used to support production, including production facilities and other fixed assets such as machinery, equipment, computers, and vehicles. The maintenance of these fixed assets includes all of the activities necessary to keep them in good working condition, such as scheduling tune-ups and other preventative maintenance procedures. It also requires timely repair in the case of breakdowns or other interruptions. Control of fixed assets includes the ongoing monitoring necessary to support production in the most effective and efficient manner. In this role, employees in the maintenance and control department often work closely with those in the various planning functions. For example, they may interact with personnel responsible for capital budgeting in order to determine asset replacement schedules or additions to production facilities. Or they may work with engineers and schedulers to consider product design specifications, the layout of the production stations, and other potential enhancements to the production processes.

The **human resources** department is responsible for managing the placement and development of sufficient qualified personnel. This includes hiring and training workers, as well as maintaining records of their performance. Chapter 10 discussed this function in more detail, but the focus here is the optimal use of human resources to support production. Plant managers and supervisors must be placed in order to oversee production in the various work stations, plants, or locations. Line workers must be placed effectively to handle production in these various areas. Human resources personnel must often work with those responsible for scheduling to ensure that adequate human resources are available to sustain the company's planned course of action. Care must also be taken to prepare and accumulate job time tickets or time sheets for all production employees so that these actual labor costs can be included in the cost of products.

The **inventory control** department is responsible for managing and recording the movement of inventory in the many different directions that it may go throughout the conversion process. Exhibit 11-3 lists the many departments or groups within the company that are involved with these functions. Several of these functions have been introduced in previous chapters. For instance, the purchasing and receiving functions are discussed in Chapter 9, and the shipping function is discussed in Chapter 8. This chapter will focus on the activities comprising the Stores, Routing, and Warehousing functions, as they are not discussed elsewhere in this text.

One inventory control function that is important to the conversion process is the determination of **economic order quantities (EOQ)**, or the most efficient quantity of products to purchase. This determination is based on the relative costs of maintaining inventory and ordering materials. Many companies rely on their inventory managers to notify the purchasing function about the number of units that are needed to replenish inventories to their desired levels. This activity is closely related to the purchasing function. Although details of the purchasing function are presented in Chapter 9, there is no previous coverage of EOQ.

The EOQ can be calculated by the following formula:

$$\mathrm{EOQ} = \sqrt{\frac{2RS}{A}},$$

where

R = the number of units of this item required for the year;

S = the cost of placing an order to purchase this item; and

A = the cost of holding a unit of this item in inventory for the year.

The inventory **stores** function concerns the control of raw materials inventory held in storage or in holding areas, waiting for processing. **Raw materials** include the basic components of the company's products, including anything from wood, metal, and nails to finished parts purchased as subassemblies. The storage of these materials is necessary when they are purchased in large quantities or in order to maintain designated levels of stock in anticipation of future sales. After the items are received, they are usually moved to a storeroom. The storeroom should be organized in a manner that makes it easy to locate the items when they are needed in production.

Routing is the issuance and movement of materials into the various production phases. When items are removed from the storeroom and taken into production, a routing slip is prepared to document the movement of inventory. A **routing slip** documents the descriptions and quantities of materials taken into production for a specified sale or other authorized production activity. It should also be prepared whenever purchased materials are taken directly into production from the receiving area. The routing slip is also sometimes called a materials issuance form, or move ticket. It is important in tracking the physical movement of inventory items. Accordingly, it should be updated when the items are subsequently moved from one production station to another. Some companies use routing slips with multiple removable stubs so that a record of the materials movement can be retained in each production station.

When inventory is routed out of the shipping or storage area, it is no longer considered raw materials inventory; rather, it becomes **work-in-process inventory**. Likewise, when production is completed and inventory is prepared for disposition to the warehouse or to the customer, it becomes **finished goods inventory**. These three classifications of inventory—raw materials, work-in-process, and finished goods—are important in the accounting processes.

Inventory status reports are prepared at various stages of the production process in order to document the extent of work completed and the resulting level of inventory. Inventory status reports provide detail on the resources used in production to-date, as well as the resources available to complete production of the goods. These reports should be monitored regularly so that the scheduling department can be notified if changes need to be made.

Inventory **warehousing** involves managing the holding area for finished goods awaiting sale. Companies maintain inventories of finished goods when they produce fairly homogeneous products or when it is important for them to be able to fill sales orders quickly. Accordingly, an inventory warehouse should be well organized so that the items can be located and moved into the shipping department as quickly as possible. Likewise, it should be controlled in order to prevent theft, loss, or damage.

The goal of inventory control is to minimize the cost of maintaining inventories. Whether inventory is maintained in the form of raw materials, work-in-process, or finished goods, most companies weigh the costs and benefits of carrying inventories. The costs are generally incurred in the areas of stores and warehousing, whereas the benefits tend to be more difficult to measure because they relate to keeping customers satisfied. Ideally, the elimination of inventories is desirable, except in cases where inventory is needed to meet immediate needs due to sales that may result from unexpected changes in production scheduling or increased demand for the company's products.

OPERATIONS

Operations is the term commonly used to refer to the major business activity in which a company engages. It is often synonymous with the terms "production" and "manufacturing." This function involves the day-to-day performance of production activities, including monitoring the related costs, time, and quality.

Depending on the size of the company and the diversity of its product offerings, operations may be performed by a variety of methods, including the following:

- Continuous processing of homogeneous products
- Batch processing, where each batch contains homogeneous products, but each batch is not necessarily the same type of product
- Custom, made-to-order processing, where each order may be unique

A company's production process may be conducted in a single operating facility or multiple locations and stations. Regardless of its production complexity as determined by the method of production and the number of locations, each scheduled production order follows a designated physical flow through the production process. The production process generally involves a systematic flow similar to that described in Exhibit 11-5. The documents used in this process are presented in a document flow chart in Exhibit 11-6. Exhibit 11-7 shows a data flow diagram of the conversion process.

Except for the preparation of the documents that initiate the production planning process and the general ledger accounting that finalizes this process, all of the other processes depicted in Exhibit 11-5 are components of the logistics function. These activities and the related documentation were described earlier in this chapter.

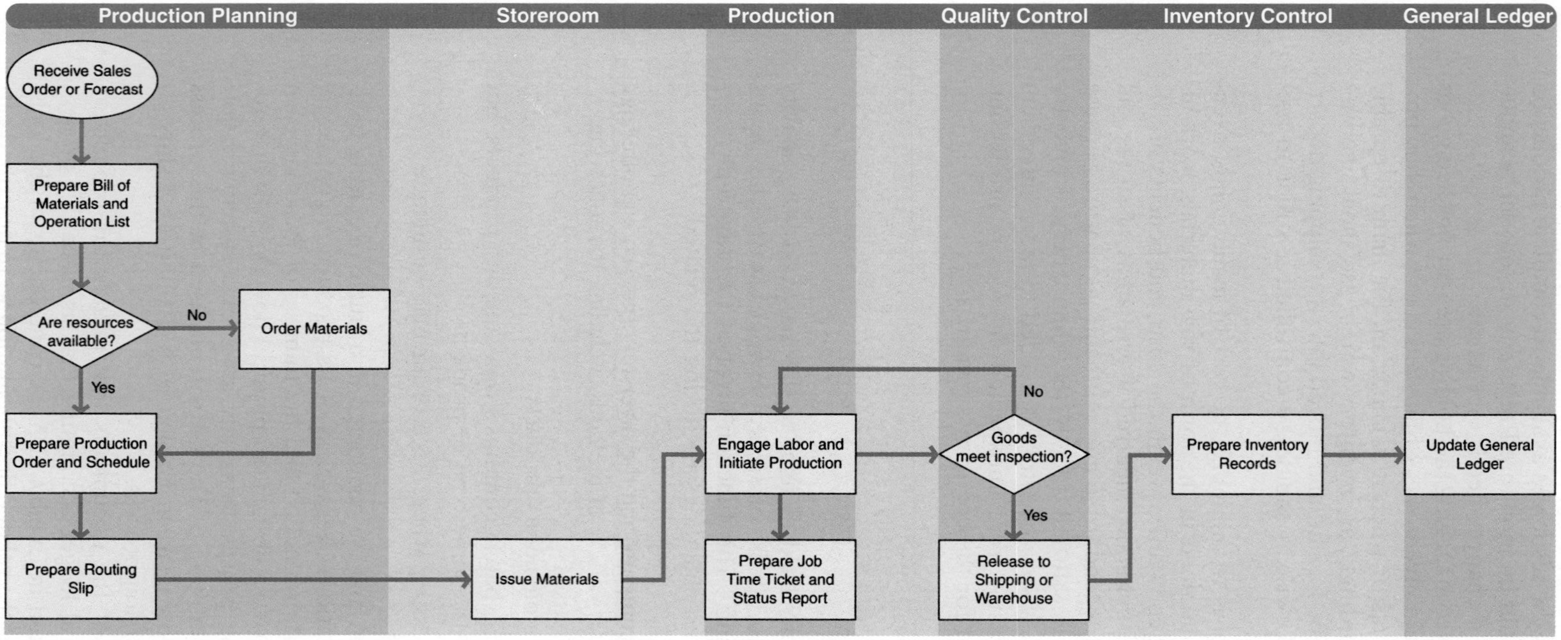

Exhibit 11-5
Production Process Map

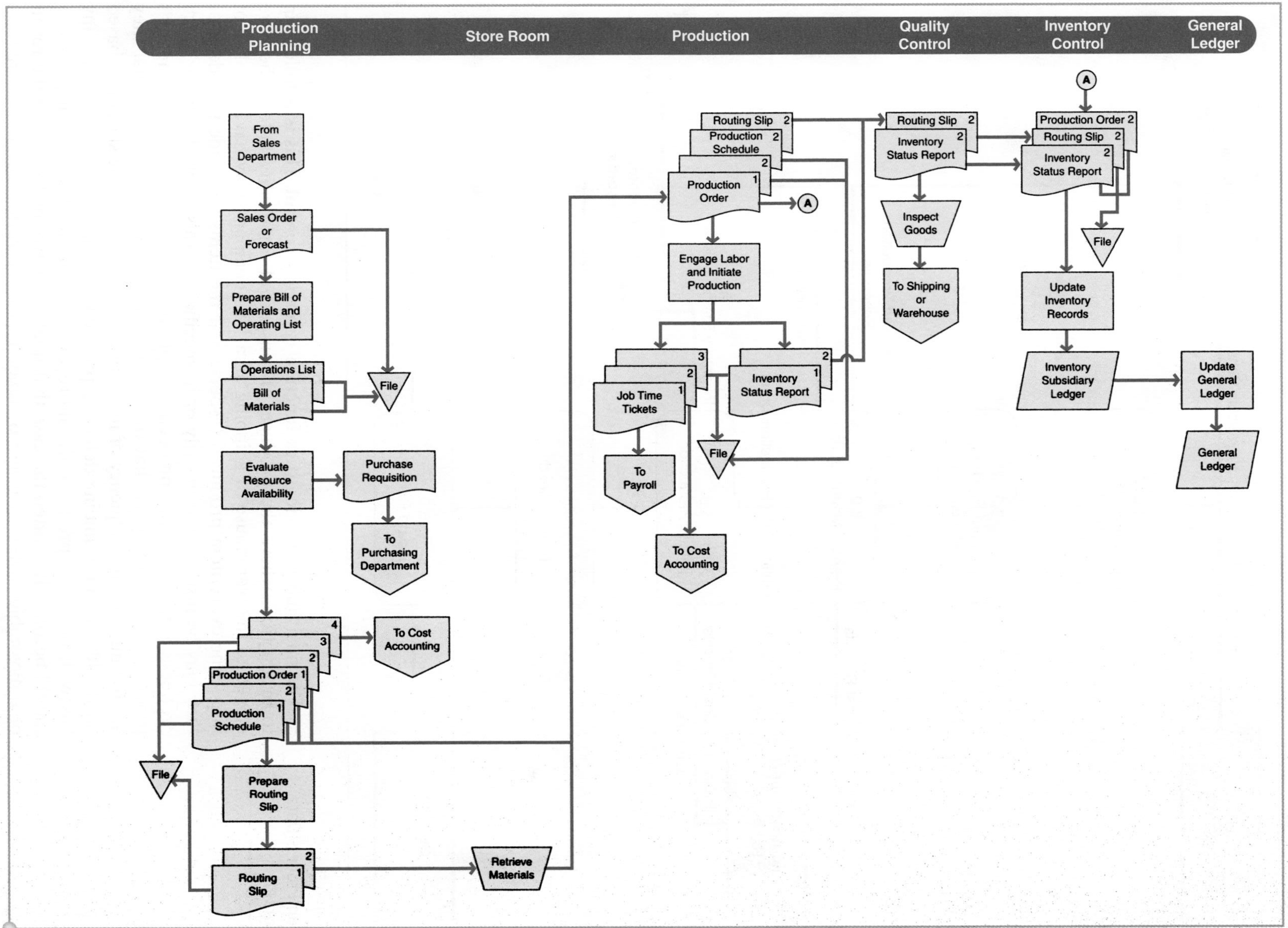

Exhibit 11-6
Document Flowchart of the Production Process

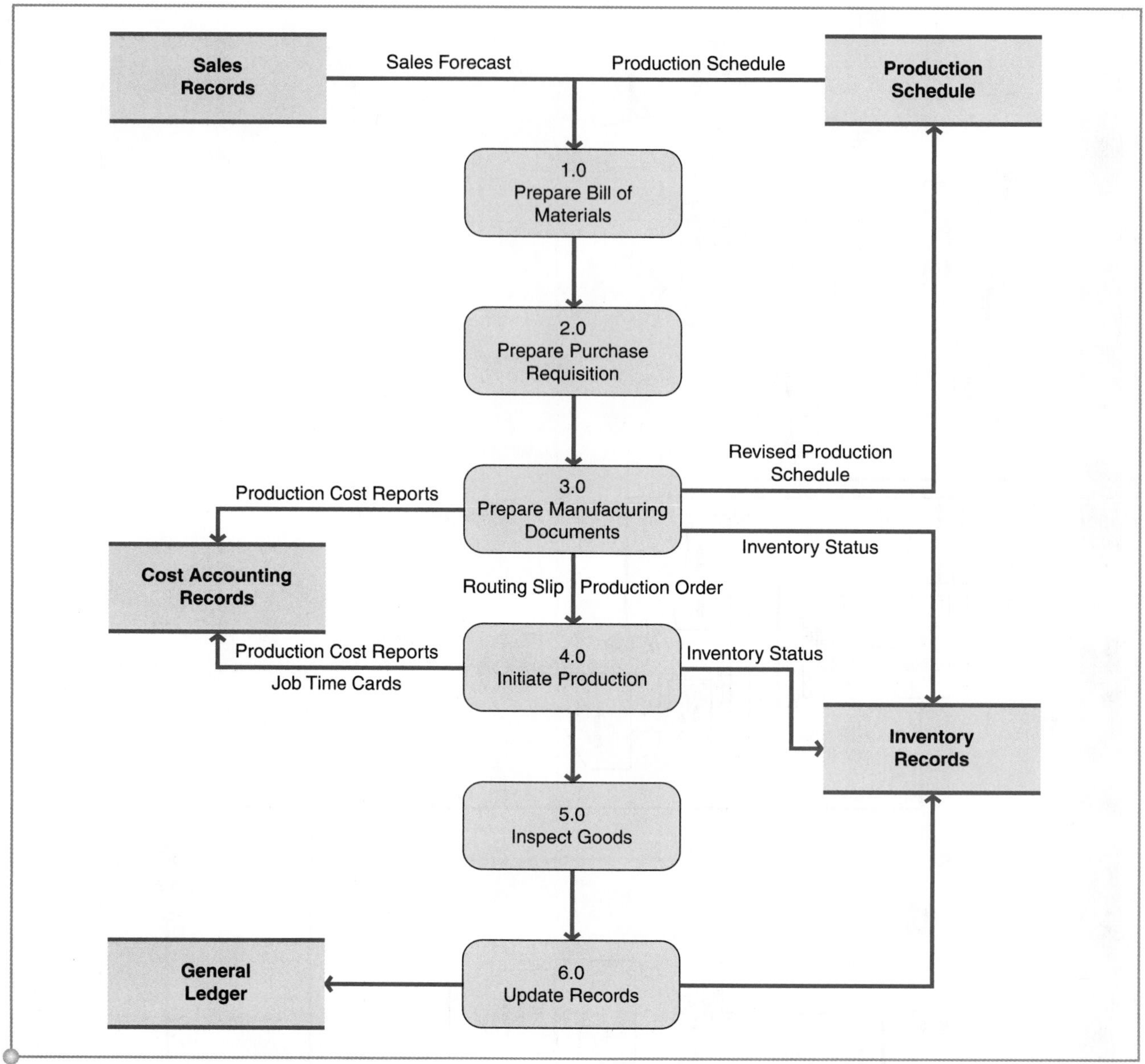

Exhibit 11-7
Conversion Process Data Flow Diagram

The final hub in the logistics function is **quality control**. This is a follow-up to production, where the products are inspected for quality before they are moved to the warehouse or shipping area. The company may have a policy of inspecting every item produced (especially if the items are made to order), or they may be inspected arbitrarily or in specific intervals (more likely for batch production runs or with homogeneous products). The nature of a company's products may also require that they be tested in order to determine that they are top quality. The frequency of inspections or product testing should be based on the likelihood of finding defective products. The more problems a company has with defective products, the more extensive its quality control processes should become. It is often the case that quality control problems are the result of unfavorable materials usage or labor efficiency variances. For this reason, quality control personnel often work closely with cost accountants and resource managers to solve production problems.

Defective products may be returned to the production floor for rework. **Rework** refers to the additional procedures necessary to bring a product up to its required specifications. In some cases, the extent of a product's defect may be so great that it is not cost effective for it to be reworked. When this occurs, the product may be scrapped or discarded. The costs of rework and scrap must be taken into account when accounting for the production process.

COST ACCOUNTING REPORTS GENERATED BY CONVERSION PROCESSES (STUDY OBJECTIVE 3)

Production accounting and the related financial reporting are performed by the various accounting departments. Many of these accounting applications were discussed in previous chapters. Cost accounting, however, relates specifically to the conversion process and is therefore discussed further in this section. Cost accountants prepare production cost analyses, inventory records, and standard costing information. This information is critical in helping managers make business decisions concerning the conversion processes.

Once the bill of materials and operations list have been established for a particular product, cost accountants can begin the process of determining standard costs. **Standard costs** are expected costs based on projections of a product's required resources. Standard costs include direct materials, direct labor, and overhead. Overhead consists of indirect materials (such as nails, glue, and other supplies), indirect labor (attributed to production management and maintenance personnel), and costs of maintaining the production facility (such as rent, utilities, insurance, and depreciation of production equipment). Standard costs are helpful tools in controlling costs and monitoring the quality of the production process. Developing standard overhead rates is also important in the process of applying overhead to products.

During the period, cost accountants accumulate the costs of actual materials and labor for the company's products. Materials costs are based on review of the routing slips and inventory status reports, and journal entries are prepared for the transfer of items from the raw materials inventory account to work-in-process. Labor costs are derived from time sheets and are added to work-in-process. Overhead costs must be applied to work-in-process, with the standard overhead rate applied to actual activity (hours or units), as documented in the inventory status report.

After work-in-process costs have been determined, cost accountants review completed production transactions for items transferred to the warehouse or shipping area. Care must be taken to ensure that production orders are canceled when the items are completed. The work-in-process and finished goods inventory accounts should be updated to reflect the completion of products and their movement out of production.

Most manufacturing companies prepare perpetual inventory records to record the flow of inventories. **Perpetual inventory systems** involve recording purchases as raw materials inventory, recording all the components of work-in-process for inventories in various stages of production, and recording the total cost of sales for products completed and sold. While perpetual inventory records are the generally preferred way of controlling inventory quantities, they are not always used in practice. Some small companies with relatively simple inventories may be able to control their inventories with periodic systems. **Periodic inventory systems** involve updating the inventory and cost of sales accounts only at the end of the period. When periodic systems are in place, close management supervision and ongoing monitoring of key operating statistics are necessary to achieve adequate control.

After costs have been recorded for materials, labor, and overhead in the respective inventory accounts, cost accountants compute variances for these three cost components. **Variances** represent the differences between actual costs and the standard costs applied. Other types of analyses often prepared by cost accountants include comparisons of actual costs with budgets and/or prior periods and computations of ratios for financial analysis. Comparisons of actual costs with amounts reported by other production stations are also helpful in pinpointing problem areas. The differences noted from these analyses should be discussed among various employees within the logistics function. Unfavorable differences should be investigated to determine whether logistics changes are needed to improve the conversion processes.

RISKS AND CONTROLS IN CONVERSION PROCESSES (STUDY OBJECTIVE 4)

Because conversion processes involve the physical movement of inventory throughout the operating facility and may be spread among multiple locations, departments, and employees, it is important that sufficient internal controls be included in the related business processes. In terms of the five internal control activities introduced in Chapter 3, following are some procedures to be considered for implementation in conversion processes:

AUTHORIZATION OF TRANSACTIONS

Designated employees in the company should be given responsibility for purchasing raw materials, including specifying the quality of the items needed, selecting of vendor, and determining the appropriate quantities to order.

The following activities in the conversion process require express authorization:

- Initiation of production orders
- Issuance of materials into the production process
- Transfer of finished goods to the warehouse or shipping areas

These responsibilities require continuous monitoring of the production activities, and should therefore be conducted by an experienced member of management.

SEGREGATION OF DUTIES

Custody of inventories and the accounting for inventories and cost of sales need to be separate in order for internal control objectives to be met. Adequate segregation of duties reduces the risk of errors or fraud by requiring separate processing by different employees at the various stages of the conversion process. This feature is enhanced by the performance of independent reviews and reconciliations, discussed later.

Ideally, those responsible for handling inventories in the materials storeroom and warehouse and issuing the movement of inventories into and out of these areas should be separate from the production stations and from the cost accounting function. Similarly, the inventory control functions should not be performed by those responsible for production or by those performing cost accounting functions. With respect to IT processing, companies should strive to separate the duties of systems development, computer operators, and users. The IT functions should also be separate from the accounting and custody functions.

ADEQUATE RECORDS AND DOCUMENTS

Complete, up-to-date, and accurate documentation on production orders, inventory and cost of sales records, and inventory status reporting is needed to support the conversion process. The practice of issuing documents on prenumbered forms is a control that helps to create clear records of the conversion transactions. When production orders and routing slips are issued numerically, a sequence can be accounted for to determine whether all conversion transactions have been recorded.

The creation and monitoring of variance reports is another control that is especially important in the conversion process. Its importance lies in the ongoing analysis of the information as it relates to production activities. The usefulness of variance data depends upon the integrity of the underlying system and the timeliness of its preparation. These variance reports are useful only if they contain reliable and accurate information. Likewise, they must be provided in a timely manner so that management can use them to make decisions in time to make a difference in the process.

SECURITY OF ASSETS AND DOCUMENTS

Physical controls should be in place in the company's storerooms, warehouses, and production facilities in order to safeguard the inventories held therein. These physical controls may include fences and alarm systems, security guards, or other, high-tech security tools such as retina scanners. In addition, water sprinkler systems, fire prevention devices, and adequate insurance coverage should be maintained in inventory storage areas. There should be policies in place to ensure that only authorized employees handle the inventories in each of these locations.

Likewise, only authorized employees should access the inventory records. In order to control this, companies should assign passwords to employees who access the files. These employees should be required to log all transactions in the logistics function. Timely backup of production files is also important in protecting the information and guaranteeing continued processing, even in the event of destruction of the original files.

INDEPENDENT CHECKS AND RECONCILIATION

There are many recommended procedures for overseeing the conversion process through the performance of various supervision and review activities.

Probably the most typical control is the requirement for conducting periodic physical inventory counts and comparing the results with recorded inventory quantities. A **physical inventory count** determines the quantity of inventory on hand by actually counting all items on the premises and in other areas of the company's responsibility. This should be performed for all three categories of inventory (raw materials, work-in-process, and finished goods), regardless of whether perpetual or periodic systems are in place. Companies using periodic inventory systems rely upon the physical inventory counts as a basis for determining the end-of-period inventory and cost of sales amounts. However, even companies that maintain perpetual records tend to conduct physical counts as a means of determining the accuracy of their records and the related general ledger control accounts. In perpetual systems, the quantity determined via the physical inventory count must be compared with the perpetual records. This activity is referred to as the **physical inventory reconciliation**.

In addition to the physical inventory reconciliation, someone independent of the record keeping and custody functions should review the materials, labor, and overhead reports that support the inventory amounts. Specifically, production orders should be reconciled with records of work-in-process and finished goods inventory. Labor reports should also be reconciled with employee time sheets. In addition, routing slips should be reconciled with records of inventories transferred to the warehouse or shipping areas.

The records and documentation section just presented describes the importance of the cost variance reports as control features. These reports need to be monitored and reconciled in order to determine the source of problems within the conversion process. These review procedures typically involve members of management who can overview the process and authorize improvements.

COST–BENEFIT CONSIDERATIONS

The more products a company has and the more complex its conversion process is, the more internal controls should be in place to monitor and safeguard its assets. There are other factors that influence the level of risk inherent in a business that may warrant the implementation of strong controls. Namely, if the goods are extremely valuable, they may be especially susceptible to theft. For instance, if a company's inventory consists of fine jewelry, its inventory storage facility is likely to be controlled much differently than the warehouses of a company whose inventory consists of construction materials such as lumber and cement mix. In addition, if a company's inventory items are difficult to differentiate or to inspect, strong controls may be needed in order to properly identify the items. Other conditions within the production facility may warrant the need for additional controls, such as inconsistent or high levels of inventory movement, which can make it difficult for supervisors to review the reasonableness of conversion transactions without additional information. Finally, there are factors about the organization of the company that affect the design of operation of its internal controls. If the inventory is held at various locations or the process of valuing inventories is particularly complex, additional controls may also be recommended.

Exhibit 11-8 summarizes examples of internal controls in the conversion process and the related business risks that are minimized as a result of the

Control:	Minimizes the Related Risk of:
Authorization:	
Approval of production order prior to commencing production	Invalid order or fictitious transactions, inaccurate cost accounting reports
Management approval of routing slip before issuing materials into production	Invalid inventory transactions or incorrect amounts
Segregation of Duties:	
Separation of the custody of inventory from those responsible for maintaining inventory cost of sales records	Invalid inventory transactions, incorrect amounts, omitted transactions
Separation of duties related to cost accounting, authorization of new production orders, issuance of resources into production, information systems, and general accounting	Invalid inventory transactions, incorrect amounts or accounts, omitted transactions
Records and Documents:	
Preparation of production orders and routing slips on prenumbered forms	Omitted transactions
Review of the inventory report for mathematical accuracy and agreement with physical quantities and established product costs	Incorrect amounts
Security:	
Physical controls in areas where inventory is held	Lost or stolen inventory, invalid or omitted inventory records
IT controls over computer records and physical controls in records storage areas	Invalid inventory transactions, incorrect amounts or accounts, timing issues, duplicate transactions
Independent Checks and Reconciliations:	
Reconciliation of time sheets with production reports for work-in-process and finished inventories	Omitted or duplicate payroll transactions, incorrect amounts or accounts, timing issues
Reconciliation of inventory records with the general ledger	Omitted or duplicate payroll transactions, incorrect amounts or accounts, timing issues, incorrect accumulations
Investigation and reconciliation of variances	Invalid or omitted transactions, incorrect amounts or accounts, timing issues
Reconciliation of physical inventory quantities with the inventory records	Invalid or omitted transactions, incorrect amounts or accounts, timing issues, lost or stolen inventory

Exhibit 11-8
Conversion Controls and Risks

implementation of these controls. This exhibit does not include all the possible controls and risks that may be encountered in the payroll process, but provides some common situations.

IT SYSTEMS OF CONVERSION PROCESSES (STUDY OBJECTIVE 5)

Because of the potentially large number of inventory items maintained by a company and the variety of processing flows that may affect them throughout the conversion process, it is often difficult to keep current inventory and production records with manual systems. IT systems can be a true friend of the conversion process. Recent technological developments have resulted in significant changes in the way that many companies conduct their conversion processes. Computerized systems may provide the following benefits in this process, which result in huge savings in terms of productivity, quality, flexibility, and time:

- Automatic computation of materials requirements based on sales orders and sales forecasts
- Systematic scheduling that allows for greater flexibility and increased efficiencies
- Timely transfer of inventories throughout the process, due to the automatic notification features
- Validation of data entries that detect errors before they are recorded
- Automatic updating of inventory status reports that saves time and increases accuracy
- Automatic preparation of financial accounting entries and cost accounting reports

In addition to these advantages, integration of all or part of the company's processing applications, planning, resource management, operations functions, and cost accounting system will yield even greater benefits in terms of workforce efficiency, paperwork reduction, and other cost reductions.

A computer-based conversion process needs to have a significant amount of data input into the system. All of the information supporting the bill of materials, operations lists, production orders and schedules, routing slips, time sheets, and inventory status reports must be entered into the computer applications. There are many options for inputting this data. It can be keyed in from terminals or preformatted touch screens, scanned in from bar codes or magnetic strips on the inventory items or employee identification cards, or received automatically from integrated systems in the production process. Once the supporting data are entered, the system can automatically generate the documents listed. It can also identify inventory shortages, calculate economic order quantities, dispatch inventory items to be issued into production, and accumulate information to be used for the periodic posting of conversion activities to the general ledger.

A database containing conversion process information must include files for each category of inventory (raw materials, work-in-process, and finished goods) as well as for key transactions that occur, such as the initiation of productions orders, materials issuance, labor application, and the accumulation of other costs incurred in the production progress. The inventory files include both standard and actual data. In addition, both inventory and transaction files need to be maintained for each production station at each operating facility.

Computerized systems can have programmed constraints that enhance internal controls over the conversion process. For example, the system may be programmed to issue error reports whenever a work-in-process record is not generated for an existing production order, or when the same operation is performed at multiple production stations, or when a single employee performs incompatible operations. These situations indicate that an error has occurred in the production process. The timely notification can allow for corrections to be made with minimal cost and disruption.

Additional trends in computer systems that enhance the conversion process are described in the following paragraphs.

Computer-aided design (CAD) techniques may be used to enhance the engineering function. CAD software allows engineers to work with advanced graphics at electronic work stations to create 3-D models that depict the production environment.

THE REAL WORLD

Jean Larrivée Guitars designs and manufactures steel string guitars known to produce a distinctively clear sound because of their great structural integrity due to the company's symmetrical bracing system. There are nearly six dozen models manufactured; however, before any of them can be made into an actual product, its design is worked out in CAD drawings. The digitized data from the CAD process is then brought to the factory to be replicated.

Larrivée uses CAD to design many pieces of its instruments, including the neck, bridge, fingerboard, kurfing, rosette, and inlays. For the neck alone, approximately 450 hours of programming time were required to precisely design the piece that would appease both professional guitarists and beginners. Even this considerable investment of time is merely a fraction of what would have been required to achieve such precision without computerization. In addition, through CAD, the cost of drawing blueprints is greatly reduced.[2]

Computer-aided manufacturing (**CAM**) involves the complete automation of the production process, including the full replacement of human resources with computers. Industrial robots may also be used in a CAM environment. **Industrial robots** are computers that are programmed to perform repetitive procedures.

THE REAL WORLD

Wild West Motor Company, a custom motorcycle manufacturer, has recently partnered with Autodesk Inc. for its CAD and CAM software needs. In the process, the company has been able to increase sales and production of its motorcycles.

Wild West uses CAD software to prepare digital models of motorcycle tanks and seats. These models are imported into the CAM system to create solid models of the actual parts or as a starting point for a mold or die. The integration of the two systems allows for easy back-and-forth transfers for making refinements. Paul Seiter, Wild West's founder, estimates that the company saves $75,000, plus weeks—or months—of engineering and production time, for each project now being designed and tooled in-house (compared with its previous method of outsourcing).[3]

Materials resource planning (**MRP**) involves the automated scheduling of production orders and movement of materials in the production process.

Manufacturing resource planning (**MRP-II**) considers all manufacturing resources, rather than focusing on materials. MRP-II systems are an expansion of MRP. MRP-II adds features that provide for the forecasting of capacity requirements and for developing schedules for future production processing.

Enterprise-wide resource planning (**ERP**) systems have evolved from MRP-II. ERP systems integrate all of the conversion processes into a single software program while still meeting the needs of each functional area. In addition to the manufacturing applications included in MRP-II systems, ERP offers additional functions such as purchasing, accounts payable, human resources, and payroll.

Computer-integrated manufacturing systems (**CIMs**) integrate all of the conversion processes to allow for minimal disruptions due to reporting requirements or inventory movement issues. They are similar to ERP systems in that they integrate all of the functional areas of the conversion process. However, CIMs are unique because they also integrate the financial and cost accounting

[2]Matthew Larrivée, "What is CAD/CAM, www.larrivee.com.

[3]Al Dean, "Wild Times," http://www.mcadonline.com/index.php?option=content&task=view&id=410.

applications. In the modern business environment, more and more companies are turning to CIMs to gain competitive advantages. CIMs are built upon a network of production equipment that is integrated with the company's computers and recordkeeping systems.

Just-in-time (JIT) production systems are concerned with minimizing or eliminating inventory levels and the related costs of maintaining those inventories. This is accomplished by carefully controlling each stage of the production process so that products are completed just in time to sell them. These systems are feasible only when the company has good relationships with reliable vendors (in order to eliminate the need to maintain stock of raw materials) and there are few quality control problems. JIT also requires extensive computer systems to monitor and record the many transactions and data in a JIT system.

THE REAL WORLD

In the mid-1960s, most retailers were not yet focused on computerized operations. Although there were only 20 Wal-Mart stores at that time, Sam Walton was already focused on the need to computerize merchandise controls in order to outpace new competitors like Kmart, Target, and Woolworth. Sam Walton recruited the top student from IBM's New York training school to come to Bentonville, Arkansas, to lead Wal-Mart's computerization efforts.

Sam Walton's foresight brought unprecedented success. Today, Wal-Mart is known for its sophisticated logistics and just-in-time inventory system. Its computer database is one of the largest in existence, second only to the database system at the U.S. Pentagon.[4]

ETHICAL ISSUES RELATED TO CONVERSION PROCESSES (STUDY OBJECTIVE 6)

Previous chapters examined ethical misconduct related to the purchasing, cash disbursement, payroll, and fixed assets processes. Many of those issues are also pertinent to the conversion system, as the relevant business activities also correspond to processes in the conversion system.

In addition, the conversion system is the target of many types of fraud schemes. Most of these involve the falsification of inventory quantities, hiding of inventory costs, or manipulation of the gross profit figure. These types of fraud schemes are generally perpetrated by management in an attempt to meet or beat earnings targets. **Earnings management** is the act of misstating financial information in order to improve financial statement results.

One method used by managers to increase the gross profit is to offer price discounts to customers. Although many companies offer price discounts, there may be a problem with this scenario if the intention of management is to artificially boost earnings. Sales discounts become problematic when they are offered as a temporary incentive aimed at increasing sales. This is a coercive tactic that lures customers into making a purchase earlier than normal. Although it may be an effective way to increase sales, there are ethical implications to this practice. Customers will expect the discounted prices to be offered in the future, and the temporary increase in cash flow for the company may affect projections that are not likely to be realized.

[4]John Huey, "Builders & Titans," www.time.com/time/time100/builder/profile/walton.html

Another earnings management technique exists whereby managers authorize the production of excessive inventories. This is a method of "gaming" the system by manipulating inventory amounts through the use of absorption costing techniques. **Absorption costing** involves the inclusion of both variable and fixed costs in the determination of unit costs for ending inventories and cost of goods sold. Thus, absorption costing provides for the transfer of fixed manufacturing costs to the balance sheet (via the inventory accounts) in the period when the inventory is sold. Accountants can take advantage of this system by over-producing inventories. When the amount of inventory produced exceeds the company's requirements to support sales orders, the level of finished goods inventories increases. The more inventory units that are on hand, the greater is the proportion of fixed costs that will be allocated to the balance sheet. If normal inventory levels had been maintained, a greater proportion of fixed costs would have been allocated to cost of goods sold and reported on the income statement as a deduction from sales.

THE REAL WORLD

In the early 1990s, an inventory fraud scheme was discovered at F&C International, Inc. F&C is a manufacturer of flavors and fragrances, with operations in New York and Cincinnati. Its founder and majority owner, Jon Fries, engaged in a series of frauds, all of which involved the conversion process. Fries mislabeled inventory items in order to overstate their value, recorded fictitious production and shipping activities, and falsified sales figures in an attempt to meet projections. He even appointed a task force of employees who were ordered to carry out these plans. The task force was also instructed to alter reports and destroy certain supporting documentation. His motive for committing these crimes was threefold: He desired to increase profits in order to improve the reputation of the company, improve his relationship with the company's debtors in order to expand his borrowing potential, and increase his own compensation. Fries was convicted of fraud and served a prison sentence.

Another ethics issue related to the conversion process involves the ethical decisions encountered as the processes become more automated. Management should consider the moral implications of replacing human resources with electronic resources. To the extent possible, management should take an active role in the reassignment (rather than termination) of personnel when production jobs are eliminated as a result of automation.

CORPORATE GOVERNANCE IN CONVERSION PROCESSES (STUDY OBJECTIVE 7)

Recall that Chapter 5 presented the four primary functions of the corporate governance process: management oversight, internal controls and compliance, financial stewardship, and ethical conduct. Each of these functions is applicable to the conversion processes, which must include a proper corporate governance structure in order to properly discourage fraud, theft, and misuse or manipulation of conversion-related resources.

The systems, processes, and internal controls described in this chapter are part of a corporate governance structure. When management designs and implements conversion processes, it assigns responsibility for executing the related logistics and reporting functions to various managers and employees. It must be mindful of the risks of stolen or misused inventories and fixed assets, alteration of documents or reports, and other frauds in this process. Accordingly, it must also implement and monitor internal controls to minimize these risks. As management considers these assignments and subsequently monitors the underlying processes and controls, it is carrying out its corporate governance functions of proper management oversight and internal controls and compliance.

When management has designed, implemented, and continually manages processes and internal controls, it is helping to ensure proper stewardship of the company's assets. Corporate governance requires proper financial stewardship, and since inventories and fixed assets are frequently the largest assets reported on a company's balance sheet, financial stewardship in these areas is especially important. It is also especially challenging, due to the ever-changing nature of the company's inventory items throughout the various stages of the conversion process.

Finally, good corporate governance depends upon the ethical conduct of management. When management sets an appropriate tone at the top by consistently demonstrating and encouraging ethical conduct, it is more likely that a stronger system of corporate governance will result. Improved effectiveness and efficiency and reduced risks of fraud tend to accompany workplace environments marked by effective corporate governance.

SUMMARY OF STUDY OBJECTIVES

Basic features of conversion processes. A company's conversion processes involve the activities related to transforming materials, labor, and overhead into goods or services. The primary functions within the conversion process are logistics and reporting.

Components of the logistics function. The logistics functions includes three components: planning, resource management, and operations. Planning involves research and development, capital budgeting, engineering, and scheduling. Resource management involves maintenance and control, human resources, and inventory control (including the determination of the economic order quantity as well as the purchasing, receiving, stores, routing, warehousing, and shipping activities). Finally, operations involves production and quality control.

Cost accounting reports generated by conversion processes. Cost accountants prepare production cost analyses, inventory records, and standard costing information on the basis of conversion activities. Variance reports may be prepared to explain differences between actual and standard costs. The types of reports prepared may vary greatly from company to company, and may depend upon whether a perpetual or periodic inventory system is in place.

Risks and controls in conversion processes. Conversion activities should be well monitored and controlled. Consideration should be given to establishing proper controls related to the authorization of transactions, segregation of duties, adequate documents and records, security, independent checks and reconciliation, and the related cost–benefit factors.

IT systems of conversion processes. Integration of a company's conversion processing applications and cost accounting systems yields significant benefits in terms of workforce efficiency, paperwork reduction, and other cost savings. Popular computerized systems in the conversion process include computer-aided design (CAD), computer-aided manufacturing (CAM), materials resource planning (MRP), manufacturing resource planning (MRP-II), enterprise-wide resource planning (ERP), computer-integrated manufacturing (CIM), and just-in-time (JIT) production systems.

Ethical issues related to conversion processes. The conversion process is the target of many types of fraud schemes, most of which involve falsification of inventory, manipulation of gross profits, or other earnings management techniques.

Corporate governance in conversion processes. The conversion processes described in this chapter are part of the management oversight of corporate governance. The internal controls and ethical tone and procedures within the conversion process are also part of the corporate governance structure. Establishing and maintaining reliable inventory management processes, internal controls, and ethical practices help ensure proper financial stewardship.

KEY TERMS

Absorption costing
Bill of materials
Capital budgeting
Computer-aided design (CAD)
Computer-aided manufacturing (CAM)
Computer integrated manufacturing (CIM)
Earnings management
Economic order quantity (EOQ)
Engineering
Enterprise-wide resource planning (ERP)
Finished goods
Human resources
Industrial robots
Inventory control
Inventory status report
Just-in-time (JIT) production
Logistics
Maintenance and control
Manufacturing resource planning (MRP-II)
Materials resource planning (MRP)
Operations
Operations list
Periodic inventory systems
Perpetual inventory systems
Physical inventory counts
Physical inventory reconciliation
Production order
Production schedule
Quality control
Raw materials
Research and development
Rework
Routing
Routing slip
Scheduling
Standard costs
Stores
Variances
Warehousing
Work-in-process

END OF CHAPTER MATERIAL

CONCEPT CHECK

1. Manufacturing has changed in recent years as a result of each of the following factors except:
   a. globalization
   b. technological advances
   c. increased competition
   d. lack of economic prosperity
2. The term *conversion processes* is often used synonymously with
   a. operations.
   b. production.
   c. manufacturing.
   d. all of the above.
3. Which of the following activities is not part of the planning component of the logistics function?
   a. Research and development
   b. Capital budgeting
   c. Human resource management
   d. Scheduling
4. Which of the following activities is an inventory control activity?
   a. Engineering
   b. Maintenance
   c. Routing
   d. Quality control
5. Which of the following statements concerning an operations list is true?
   a. It is an engineering document that describes the chain of events within a company's conversion process.
   b. It is an engineering document that specifies the descriptions and quantities of component parts within a product.
   c. It is a capital budgeting document that describes the chain of events within a company's conversion process.
   d. It is a capital budgeting document that specifies the descriptions and quantities of component parts within a product.
6. Which of the following terms relates to the control of materials being held for future production?
   a. Routing
   b. Work-in-process
   c. Stores
   d. Warehousing

7. Which of the following questions is most likely to be found on an internal control questionnaire concerning a company's conversion processes?
   a. Are vendor invoices for materials purchases approved for payment by someone who is independent of the cash disbursements function?
   b. Are signed checks for materials purchased mailed promptly without being returned to the department responsible for processing the disbursement?
   c. Are approved requisitions required when materials are released from the company's warehouse into production?
   d. Are details of payments for materials balanced to the total posted to the general ledger?
8. When additional procedures are necessary to bring a defective product up to its required specifications, this is referred to as
   a. rework.
   b. scrap.
   c. work-in-process.
   d. variance reporting.
9. A firm expects to sell 1000 units of its best-selling product in the coming year. Ordering costs for this product are $100 per order, and carrying costs are $2 per unit. Compute the optimum order size, using the EOQ model.
   a. 10 units
   b. 224 units
   c. 317 units
   d. 448 units
10. Which of the following internal controls is typically associated with the maintenance of accurate inventory records?
    a. Performing regular comparisons of perpetual records with recent costs of inventory items
    b. Using a just-in-time system to keep inventory levels at a minimum
    c. Performing a match of the purchase request, receiving report, and purchase order before payment is approved
    d. Using physical inventory counts as a basis for adjusting the perpetual records
11. If a manufacturing company's inventory of supplies consists of a large number of small items, which of the following would be considered a weakness in internal controls?
    a. Supplies of relatively low value are expensed when acquired.
    b. Supplies are physically counted on a cycle basis, whereby limited counts occur quarterly and each item is counted at least once annually.
    c. The stores function is responsible for updating perpetual records whenever inventory items are moved.
    d. Perpetual records are maintained for inventory items only if they are significant in value.
12. The goal of a physical inventory reconciliation is to
    a. determine the quantity of inventory sold.
    b. compare the physical count with the perpetual records.

c. compare the physical count with the periodic records.
d. determine the quantity of inventory in process.

13. Which of the following is not considered a benefit of using computerized conversion systems?
    a. Automatic computation of materials requirements
    b. Increased sales and cost of sales
    c. Increased efficiency and flexibility
    d. Early error detection and increased accuracy
14. Which of the following represents a method of managing inventory designed to minimize a company's investment in inventories by scheduling materials to arrive at the time they are needed for production?
    a. The economic order quantity (EOQ)
    b. Material resource planning (MRP)
    c. First-in, first-out (FIFO)
    d. Just-in-time (JIT)
15. For which of the following computerized conversion systems is Wal-Mart well known?
    a. CAD/CAM
    b. MRP-II
    c. CIMs
    d. JIT

DISCUSSION QUESTIONS

16. (SO 1) What are the three resources that an organization must have to conduct a conversion (or transformation) process?
17. (SO 1) Do conversion processes occur in manufacturing companies only? Why or why not?
18. (SO 1) Why are conversion activities typically considered routine data processes?
19. (SO 2) Differentiate between a bill of materials and an operations list.
20. (SO 2) Differentiate between the roles of the engineering and the research and development departments.
21. (SO 2) What are the two types of documents or reports are likely to trigger the conversion process?
22. (SO 2) What are the three primary components of logistics?
23. (SO 2) What types of information must be taken into consideration when scheduling production?
24. (SO 2) Differentiate between a routing slip and an inventory status report.
25. (SO 2) What are the conversion responsibilities of the maintenance and control, inventory control, inventory stores, and human resources departments?
26. (SO 2) What is the purpose of an inventory status report?
27. (SO 2) What is the overall goal of the inventory control department?
28. (SO 2) What is the purpose of the quality control department?
29. (SO 3) What is the purpose of determining standard costs?

30. (SO 3) What should be done when unfavorable variances are discovered?
31. (SO 3) Why would perpetual inventory records be preferable to periodic inventory records in a manufacturing company?
32. (SO 4) Which three activities in the conversion process should require specific authorization before they are begun?
33. (SO 4) Why is it important to separate the functions of inventory control and the production stations? What could go wrong if these functions were not separated?
34. (SO 4) Why is it so important that variance reports be prepared in a timely manner?
35. (SO 4) Explain how a physical inventory count would differ in a company using a perpetual inventory system versus one using a period inventory system.
36. (SO 5) When IT systems are used in conversion processes, what are some of the resulting advantages to the organization?
37. (SO 5) How can programmed controls within the IT system for conversion processes enhance internal controls?
38. (SO 5) What is the difference between CAD, CAM, and CIM?
39. (SO 5) What is the difference between MRP, MRP-II, and ERP?
40. (SO 6) How can conversion processes be manipulated to show higher earnings?

BRIEF EXERCISES

41. (SO 1) Consider a company that is in the business of producing canned fruits for grocery stores. (It is not in the business of growing the fruit.) List the items that would likely be included as this company's direct materials, direct labor, indirect materials, and other overhead.
42. (SO 2) Give some examples of manufacturing processes that would fit into each of the three different types of production processes: continuous processing, batch processing, and custom made-to-order.
43. (SO 2) List and describe each activity within the planning component of the logistics function.
44. (SO 2) Some companies use the same facility for both inventory stores and warehousing. Describe the difference between these two inventory control activities, and how the respective areas might be distinguished within the facility.
45. (SO 2) For the following activities within the conversion process, place them in sequence that indicates the order in which they would normally be performed:
    - Inspection of goods
    - Materials issuance
    - Preparation of time sheets
    - Preparation of a bill of materials
    - Preparation of an inventory status report
    - Preparation of a production schedule

46. (SO 2, 3) Describe the purpose of each of the following cost accounting records or reports:
    - Work-in-process and finished goods inventory accounts
    - Bill of materials
    - Variance reports
    - Routing slips
47. (SO 3) Describe how a cost accountant would cancel a production order upon completion of the related product. Why is this important?
48. (SO 4) When taking a physical inventory count at a typical manufacturing facility, which category of inventory (raw materials, work-in-process, or finished goods) is likely to be the most time consuming to count and determine the relevant costs for? Why?
49. (SO 4) Identify several factors that indicate the need for more extensive internal controls covering conversion processes.
50. (SO 5) Match the IT systems on the left with their definitions on the right:

CAD	a. A network including production equipment, computer terminals, and accounting systems
CAM	b. Electronic workstation including advanced graphics and 3-D modeling of production processes
MRP	c. Automated scheduling of manufacturing resources, including scheduling, capacity, and forecasting functions
MRP-II	d. The minimization of inventory levels by the control of production so that products are produced on a tight schedule in time for their sale
ERP	e. A single software system that includes all manufacturing and related accounting applications
CIMs	f. Automated scheduling of production orders and materials movement
JIT	g. Production automation, including use of computers and robotics

PROBLEMS

51. (SO 2) Suppose a company has 1000 units of a raw material part on hand. If 750 of these units are routed into production, should the company place an order to stock up on more of these parts? In order to answer this question, determine the economic order quantity (EOQ) for this part, assuming that the following are true:
    - The company plans to use 10,000 units during the coming year.
    - The company orders this part in lots of 1000 units, and each order placed carries a processing cost of $2.50.
    - Each unit of inventory carries an annual holding cost of $6.40.

52. (SO 4) Suppose a company is experiencing problems with omitted transactions in the conversion process; i.e., inventory transactions are not always being recorded as they occur. Refer to Exhibit 7-7 to describe at least three internal controls that should be in place to help alleviate such problems.

53. (SO 5) Using an Internet search engine, search for the terms "CAD" + "industrial robots." Identify a company (name and location) that provides manufacturing automation by using robotics. Describe some of the robotic operations that are featured on the company's website.

54. (SO 5) Using an Internet search engine, search for the terms "just in time" + "automotive." From the results you find, explain why just-in-time inventory systems are such an important factor in the competitive automotive industry.

55. (SO 6) Explain how the over-production of inventories can be seen as unethical in an absorption costing environment.

56. (SO 6) Price discounts are commonly used in the business world as incentives for customers. How may this practice (or its misuse) be deemed unethical?

57. (SO 3) Texas Bar Supply manufactures equipment for bars and lounges. While the company manufactures several different products, one is a blender that bartenders use to make certain kinds of drinks. From the textbook website at http://www.wiley.com/college/turner, download the spreadsheet template named requisition.xls. Using information in the spreadsheet template, complete the requisition form to calculate the quantity and cost of the parts needed to manufacture a batch of 500 bar blenders. To look up the cost from the price list sheet, you will use a spreadsheet function called VLOOKUP. Be sure to design your formulas in a way that will incorporate changes in the batch size or changes to costs of individual parts.

CASES

58. Bellamy Toy Enterprises is a manufacturer of model trains that sell under the name Bellamy Toy Trains in toy stores and hobby shops throughout the United States and Europe. The company employs 160 people in its home office and sole manufacturing and storage facility, which are both located in Bellamy, Indiana.

The inventory storeroom is called the stores department, and it is managed by Henry Cauff. Both materials and finished goods are maintained in this area, as well as the supporting inventory records. Henry performs a daily review of the items on hand by monitoring the inventory subsidiary ledger and determining whether additional materials are needed. If they are, Henry prepares a materials requisition form to submit to the production planning department.

The production planning department is led by Alberta "Berta" Hennig. Upon receipt of a materials requisition form from Henry, Berta files the form. Berta's files contain not only the materials requisition forms received from Henry, but also sales forecasts received from the sales department. These files are monitored on a daily basis; if there is a match between the needs identified by both stores and sales, a bill of materials and a routing slip are prepared and forwarded to the production room. If inventory quantities for supporting materials are sufficient, a production schedule is prepared and forwarded to the production room. If materials are needed to support production of the items, a purchase requisition is prepared and forwarded to the purchasing and stores department.

Berta Hennig is also the supervisor of the production room. Once new documents are obtained from the production planning department, the bill of materials and routing slip are sent to stores, where Henry retrieves the necessary materials. He makes a copy of the bill of materials and routing slips and then returns these documents to the production room, along with the requested materials. At the end of the day, Henry updates the inventory subsidiary ledger and prepares a journal voucher summarizing the day's use of materials.

In the production room, the leaders of each production line collect employee time cards at the end of each week and send them to the payroll and cost accounting departments. They also prepare weekly job cost reports for the cost accounting department, itemizing the various costs that have been incurred.

Dennis McQuele heads the cost accounting department. Dennis uses the job cost reports and time cards to create journal vouchers that update the work-in-process and finished goods inventory accounts. As new cost data are obtained, the cost accountants are continually accumulating actual cost data to be compared with standard costs. Variances are calculated and compared, and the information is used to evaluate the line workers in the production room, as well as the managers and supervisors of each department.

Edwin Smythers is responsible for updating the general ledger on a weekly basis. The information from the journal vouchers is entered in the general ledger program, which automatically updates the respective accounts. All journal vouchers are filed in Edwin's office.

Required:

a. Draw a process map of the conversion processes at Bellamy Toy Enterprises.
b. Draw a document flowchart showing the records used in Bellamy's conversion processes.
c. List any strengths and weaknesses in Bellamy's internal control procedures. For each weakness, suggest an improvement.
d. Describe any benefits that Bellamy may receive by installing newer IT systems within its conversion processes. Be specific as to how IT systems could benefit each of the processes described, or how they could eliminate any weakness identified per item c.

59. Dennan Ski Line, Inc. is a manufacturer of equipment used for snow skiing and water skiing. The company's products are sold under two brand names, one comprising its top-of-the-line equipment and the other comprising its line of moderately priced equipment and ski attire. Dennan's sole location

near Rochester, New York, is home to both its offices and manufacturing facility. Dennan's products are sold worldwide, and current year sales are expected to reach $180 million.

Dennan's conversion process begins in the storekeeping department, where inventories and the related records are maintained. Thom Ells manages the storekeeping function by reviewing the files on a daily basis to determine the inventory needs. He prepares an inventory status report and forwards it to the production planning and control department.

Production planning and control is lead by Ted Drescoll. Every day Ted prepares bills of materials, routing slips, productions orders, and production schedules. Copies of each of these documents are forwarded to the production floor. Ted concurrently determines inventory needs by reviewing the following documents:

- inventory status reports received from the storekeeping department
- sales forecasts from the marketing division

If additional quantities of materials inventory are needed, Ted prepares a purchase requisition and forwards copies to the storekeeping and purchasing departments. If inventory quantities are adequate, no further action is taken.

Ted Drescoll also manages the production processes. Production supervisors on each of the company's six production lines report to Ted. When these supervisors receive production orders and supporting documentation from the production planning and control department, copies of the bill of materials and routing slips are forwarded to Thom Ells. In return, Thom sends the requested materials to the production line. Thom then updates the inventory ledger and sends the bill of materials and routing slips to the cost accounting department. He then prepares a journal voucher for the change in inventories and forwards it to Helene Steines, who is responsible for the general ledger.

At the production lines, the supervisors prepare job tickets to accumulate costs associated with their activities; these tickets are forwarded to cost accounting. They also collect employee time sheets and send them to cost accounting on a weekly basis. The time sheets are prepared in duplicate, and the second copy is sent to the personnel department.

In Dennan's cost accounting department, Brett Hollyster collects all of the documents to determine the actual costs of the products. Actual costs are compared with standards, and variances are computed. Total variances are used to evaluate managers and supervisors. Next, Brett Hollyster updates the work-in-process and finished goods inventory files; then he prepares a journal voucher and forwards it to Helene Steines.

In the general ledger department, Helene updates the general ledger by entering the journal vouchers into the general ledger computer software program. Journal vouchers are filed by date.

Required:

a. Draw a process map of the conversion processes at Dennan.

b. Draw a document flowchart showing the records used in Dennan's conversion processes.

c. List any strengths and weaknesses in Dennan's internal control procedures. For each weakness, suggest an improvement.

60. Crick Footwear, Inc. is a manufacturer of a popular line of casual shoes and sandals that has experienced significant growth within the past 18 months. The unique design of its product line has always been the key to the company's success. It is currently still using a system consisting of manual job costing sheets and inventory cards. Although this system was satisfactory in the past, the company's recent growth has resulted in various problems with operations and inventory control. The biggest problem is with meeting the production and delivery schedules. Many products are delivered late because the products are not completed on time. In addition, some products are delayed in the production process because the required materials are out of stock; it sometimes takes a week or more to restock back-ordered materials. To make matters worse, the company has been unable to control waste of its raw materials. There are significant quantities of materials left over after the production runs. These excess materials are eventually written off because no known scrap market exists.

Job costing sheets and inventory cards are updated at the end of each week. It takes nearly a week for the production clerks to update the accounting records from these documents. When customers inquire about the status of their orders, the production clerks use the job costing sheets to estimate delivery dates. Because of the back-orders problems, though, these estimates are often overly optimistic. This inability to provide accurate delivery dates has been a serious source of customer dissatisfaction.

The production and inventory managers have recognized the need for the company to improve its system of tracking customer orders and maintaining raw materials inventory. They have tried to convince top management of the need to improve the timeliness of information flow between the production, inventory, and accounting departments. However, top management believes that customers will be willing to wait for their orders because the products are in high demand. Furthermore, top management is reluctant to spend money on automation.

Recently, competitors have started to imitate Crick's footwear designs, and some customers have hinted that they are tempted to place future orders with these competitor companies. Crick's production and inventory managers are making another plea to top management for a new computerized inventory information system.

Required:

a. List the problems with the existing system at Crick.

b. Identify the relevant information that the production and inventory managers need to accumulate in order to support the decision to automate the conversion process.

c. List specific items that could be provided by an automated system, and describe how this could be essential to the company's continued success.

61. (CMA Adapted) Errod Dynamics Inc., produces computer chips for personal electronic devices used to record music. The chips are sold primarily to large manufacturers; however, occasional production overruns may be discounted and sold to small manufacturers. Since Errod's operating budget assigns all fixed production expenses to its predictable market—large manufacturers—there are no fixed expenses allocated to products sold to

small manufacturers. This results in significant profits in the small manufacturer market segment, even though the products are discounted.

All of Errod's products are tested for quality standards, and rejected chips are reworked to acceptable levels. The projected failure rate of reworked chips is determined to be 10%. Recently, however, customer feedback has suggested that the rework process is not always bringing the chips up to quality standards. Marty Cambiss, cost accountant, and Jamie Trogg, quality control engineer, have determined that a failure to maintain precise temperature levels during chip production results in a product defect that has a 50% failure rate. Unfortunately, current testing techniques do not detect this defect, so the company has no way to identify which chips will fail. Enhancements to the rework process would alleviate the defects problem; however, the additional cost is believed to be excessive, considering that half of the products would not benefit from the enhancement. Marty Cambiss and Jamie Trogg discussed this issue with Errod's marketing manager, Wynn Elliston, who has indicated that the defect problem will have a significant negative impact on the company's reputation.

Marty Cambiss has documented the problem in her report, which will be presented at the meeting of the board of directors next week. She is convinced that the problem will have a serious impact on the company's profitability.

Upon reviewing the cost accounting report to be presented to the board of directors, the plant manager became enraged and stormed into the office of the controller, demanding that the report be revised to downplay the rework issue. The controller agreed that the report's current presentation would draw too much attention to the problem and would likely be alarming to the board members. He instructed Marty Cambiss to revise the report and tone down the issue so as to avoid upsetting the board members.

Marty Cambiss is convinced that the board members would be misinformed if the serious nature of this problem were not highlighted in her report. She went back to Jamie Trogg and Wynn Elliston to try to solicit their support in pressing this issue; however, both of them were unwilling to get further involved in a matter that appears controversial.

Required:

a. What should Marty Cambiss do? Explain your answer and discuss the ethical considerations that she should recognize in this situation.
b. What corporate governance functions are missing at Errod? Be specific and describe the facts of the case and their relevance to corporate governance.

CONTINUING CASE: SPATELLI'S PIZZERIA

Reread the continuing case on Spatelli's Pizzeria at the end of Chapter 1. Consider any issues related to Spatelli's conversion processes, and then answer the following questions:

a. Briefly describe Spatelli's conversion processes; that is, *what* gets converted, *how* is it done, and *where* are the underlying processes performed [at which Spatelli's location(s)]?
b. What procedures and internal controls would you recommend to Spatelli's to minimize the risk of lost sales due to stock-outs (i.e., running

out of ingredients) and the resulting idle time that may be incurred while employees are awaiting delivery from the commissary?

c. Revise the accompanying example of the structure of a bill of materials to show specific details of the subassembly of the dough and the various components (sauce, toppings, and cheese) and underlying materials (ingredients) that would likely be included on Spatelli's bill of materials for a large deluxe pizza.

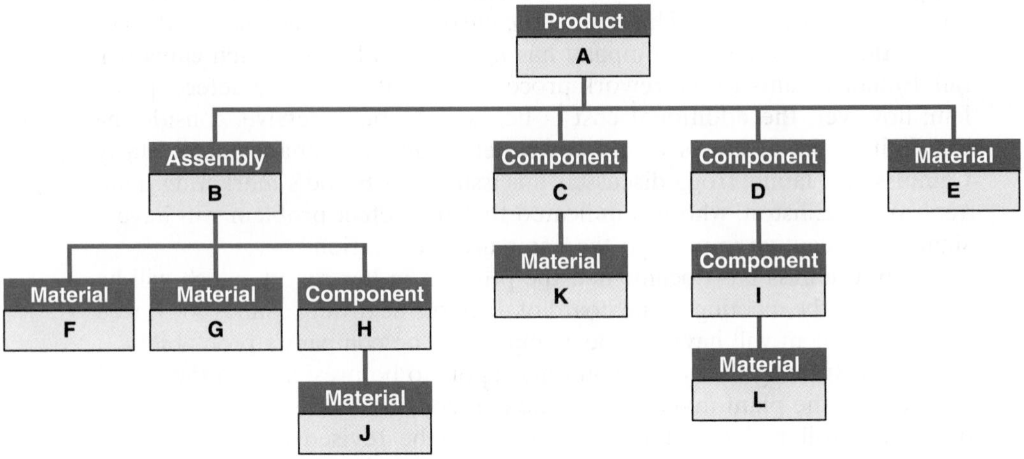

SOLUTIONS TO CONCEPT CHECK

1. Manufacturing has changed in recent years as a result of each of the factors except **d. lack of economic prosperity**.
2. (SO 2) The term conversion processes is used synonymously with **d. all of the above**. Operations, production, and manufacturing are all synonyms for the conversion process.
3. (SO 2) **c. Human Resource Management** is part of the resource management component, not part of the planning component of the logistics function.
4. (SO 2) **c. Routing** is an inventory control activity. Answer a. is part of the planning component; b. is part of the resource management component; d. is part of the operations component.
5. (SO 2) The following statement concerning an operations list is true: **a. It is an engineering document that describes the chain of events within a company's conversion process**. Answer b. is incorrect because an operations list does not describe a product's components. Answers c. and d. are incorrect because an operations list is not a capital budgeting document.
6. (SO 2) **c. Stores**. relate to the control of materials being held for future production. Answers a. and b. relate to current production and answer d. relates to finished goods (past production).
7. (CPA Adapted) (SO 2) The following question is most likely to be found on an internal control questionnaire concerning a company's conversion processes: **c. Are approved requisitions required when materials are**

released from the company's warehouse into production? This is the only response that pertains specifically to the conversion process. Responses a. and b. concern the expenditures and cash disbursements functions, and response d. pertains to general accounting.

8. (SO 2) When additional procedures are necessary to bring a defective product up to its required specifications, this is referred to as **a. rework**. Answer b. relates to defective products for which no additional procedures are deemed worthwhile; answer c. relates to the original production (rather than additional procedures); answer d. relates to quantification of production differences.
9. (CIA Adapted) (SO 2) A firm expects to sell 1000 units of its best-selling product in the coming year. Ordering costs for this product are $100 per order, and carrying costs are $2 per unit. Compute the optimum order size, using the EOQ model. The answer is **c. 317 units**. This is the square root of (2 × 1,000 × $100) / $2, or the square root of 100,000. Answer a. is incorrect because total carrying costs are used rather than unit carrying costs. Answer b. is incorrect because it failed to multiply by the constant 2. Answer d. is incorrect because it failed to divide by carrying costs.
10. (CPA Adapted) (SO 4) The following internal control is typically associated with the maintenance of accurate inventory records: **d. using physical inventory counts as a basis for adjusting the perpetual records**. Answer a. is incorrect because the most recent costs do not necessarily reflect the carrying cost of inventories. Answer b. is incorrect because it relates to cost savings rather than to an internal control improvement. Answer c. is incorrect because it relates to the existence of inventory rather than its accurate reporting.
11. (CPA Adapted) (SO 4) If a manufacturing company's inventory of supplies consists of a large number of small items, the following would be considered a weakness in internal controls: **c. The stores function is responsible for updating perpetual records whenever inventory items are moved.** Since the stores function is responsible for movement of inventory (a custody function), a violation of the principles of segregation of duties exists if this function is also responsible for recordkeeping. Each of the other responses represents common practices that are not considered control weaknesses.
12. (SO4) The goal of a physical inventory reconciliation is to **b. compare the physical count with the perpetual records.**
13. (SO 5) **b. Increased sales and cost of sales** is not considered a benefit of using computerized conversion systems. Each of the other answers relates to improvements in terms of cost savings, efficiencies, and/or improved controls.
14. (CMA Adapted) (SO 5) **d. JIT** represents a method of managing inventory designed to minimize a company's investment in inventories by scheduling materials to arrive at the time they are needed for production. Answer a. relates to optimum order quantites. Answer b. relates to manufacturing systems. Answer c. is an inventory costing method.
15. (SO 5) Wal-Mart is well known for the computerized conversion system **d. JIT**. Each of the other answers relates to manufacturing systems and therefore would not likely be used by a retail business.

CHAPTER 12

Administrative Processes and Controls

Study Objectives

This chapter will help you gain an understanding of the following concepts:

1. An introduction to administrative processes
2. Source of capital processes
3. Investment processes
4. Risks and controls in capital and investment processes
5. General ledger processes
6. Risks and controls and risks in general ledger processes
7. Reporting as an output of the general ledger processes
8. Ethical issues related to administrative processes and reporting
9. Corporate governance in administrative processes and reporting

THE REAL WORLD

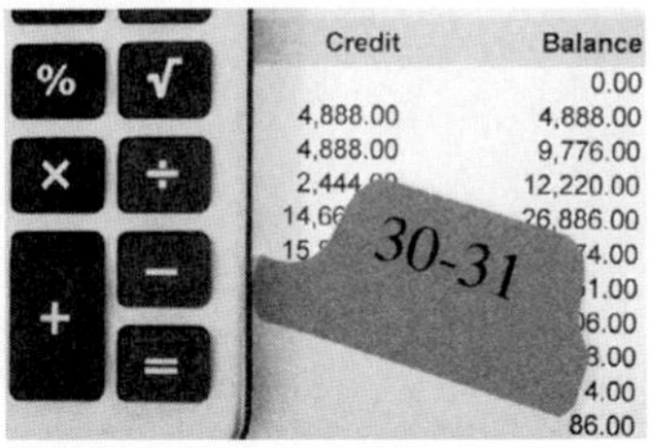

Linda and Colin McKle/ iStockphoto

All but the smallest organizations do a monthly closing of the general ledger and provide feedback reports to management after the closing process. The closing process is necessary to ensure that all expenses are accrued and posted to the proper accounts prior to reports being prepared. The closing process entails posting all monthly transaction summaries not yet posted and correcting any errors that are detected. This closing process can be very time consuming, especially in situations where one department must wait on another department. For example, the general ledger cannot be closed until the payroll department receives and processes all month-end time cards. A typical timing of the closing process is shown in Exhibit 12-1.[1]

Notice that in this typical process, the total time required is 12 working days and management does not receive financial reports until eight days after month end. Many managers believe eight days is too long to wait to receive financial feedback reports. The modern, integrated IT systems in use today can help to drastically reduce the time of the monthly closing. However, many companies still have long closing processes because of a lack of system integration and the time-consuming nature of the human steps in the process (such as error correction and rekeying of data). Even in the largest corporations with modern IT systems, there are still human processes in the general ledger closing because systems are not always integrated.

Accrue payroll					X	X						
Close accounts payable						X	X					
Close manufacturing							X	X				
Book depreciation	X	X										
Monthly reporting									X	X	X	X
Day of close	−3	−2	−1	0	1	2	3	4	5	6	7	8

Month End (↑ at day 0)

Exhibit 12-1
Map of a Traditional Closing

THE REAL WORLD

At its North American headquarters in Erlanger, Kentucky, Toyota Motor Company uses a real-time purchasing process called WARP, which stands for Worldwide Automotive Real-Time Purchasing. Toyota uses WARP to generate purchase orders for its 350 parts and components suppliers in Canada and the United States However, this real-time purchasing system is not automatically integrated with the general ledger. This means that some purchase order data must be rekeyed into the PeopleSoft accounting system at Toyota so that purchase orders can be processed and posted to the general ledger.

This rekeying of data dramatically increases the total time of the monthly close because general ledger closing may have to wait until the relevant purchase orders are rekeyed.

By working to integrate systems with the general ledger, reducing or eliminate rekeying and error correction, and streamlining processes, many companies are moving toward an instant close. An instant close can deliver reports to management only hours after the month-end date. The interesting fact is that the IT systems can support an instant close—it is the human processes that must be streamlined to achieve an instant close.

[1]Adapted from Buzz Adams, "Creating Value with an Instant Close," *Strategic Finance*, September 2002, p. 49.

The posting and closing process of the general ledger is one of the administrative processes described in this chapter. Also described here are source of capital processes, investing processes, and reporting. Therefore, there are three administrative processes described in this chapter:

1. Source of capital processes
2. Investment processes
3. General ledger processes

INTRODUCTION TO ADMINISTRATIVE PROCESSES (STUDY OBJECTIVE 1)

The previous chapters described many processes that occur within an organization, including sales of products and services, cash collections, purchases of materials and fixed assets, payroll, cash disbursements, and conversion processes. While these are all different processes, they do have several things in common. Each of these processes involves a regular, recurring transaction process that occurs daily or weekly. These processes usually generate a large number of transactions that must be recorded in the accounting system. In addition, top management has usually established procedures and controls that allow these processes to occur without intervention or specific authorization by management. For example, a salesperson does not have to wait for specific approval for each sale she negotiates.

The previous chapters described the processes that collect data within these business processes, record the transaction data, and trigger subsequent events to occur. This chapter will focus on two different sets of remaining processes. Both are administrative processes and are depicted in Exhibit 12-2.

The first set of processes presented in this chapter is shown in the lower left-hand box of Exhibit 12-2. These processes are unlike those described in the previous chapters they are not regular, recurring, or high-volume processes. Examples of such processes are the sale of stocks or bonds, the initiation of loans, bonds or notes payable, and the investment of funds in marketable securities. These types of processes can be categorized as either source of capital processes or investment processes. They are not regular, but occur only when the need arises. Moreover, the nature of these processes usually dictates that specific authorization for each transaction would be necessary. For example, a company would initiate the sale of common stock only upon approval of the top management or board of directors. Even though these processes are not regular, recurring events, there must be established processes, procedures, and controls to conduct, record, and report the results of the processes. Without established procedures and internal controls, the processes might not be properly authorized, recorded, or reported.

The second type of administrative processes is shown in the middle and right-hand boxes of Exhibit 12-2. Each of the transactions and processes on the left-hand side boxes of Exhibit 12-2 must result in financial information being recorded in general ledger accounts. That is, any sale, cash collection, expense, or payment must eventually affect general ledger accounts such as revenue

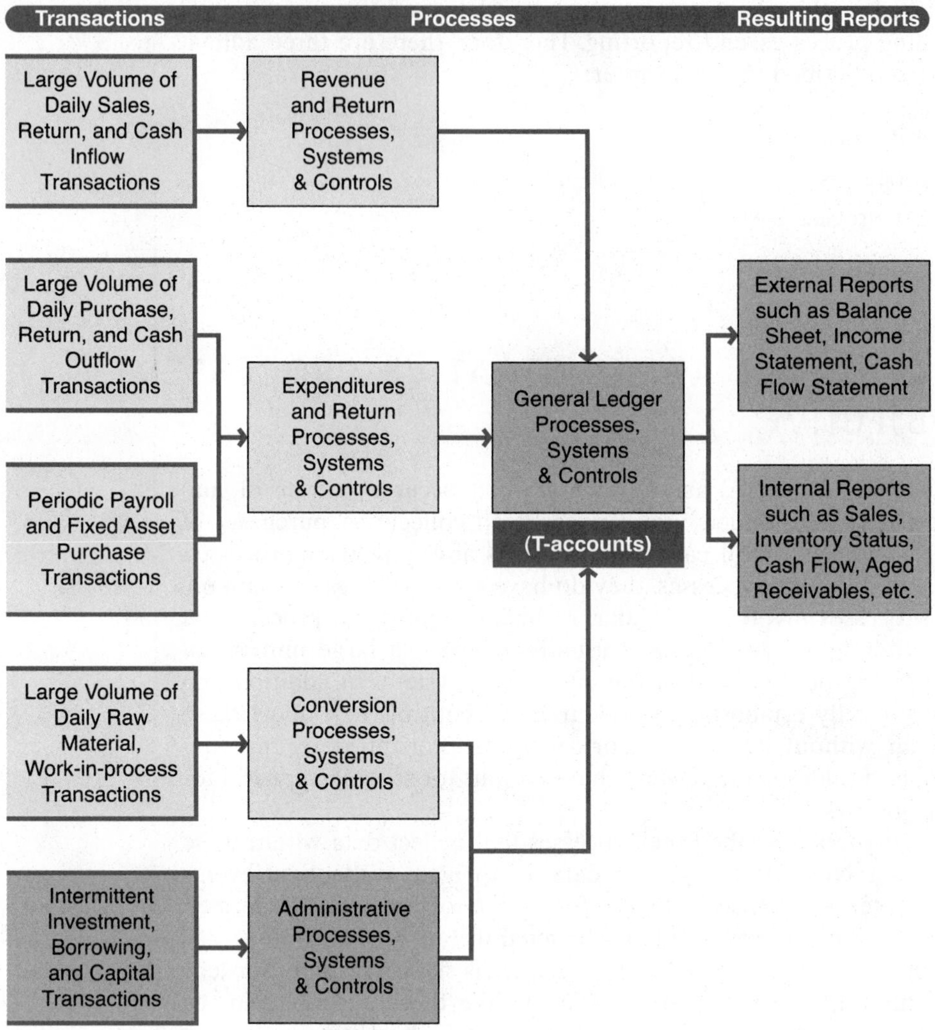

Exhibit 12-2
Overall View of Transactions, Processes, and Resulting Reports

accounts, expense accounts, and cash accounts. Therefore, there must be processes within the organization that funnel all of the transaction information from each of these processes into general ledger accounts. The general ledger account balance information and other information are then used to prepare reports for both internal and external users.

Each of the processes just described is an administrative process. **Administrative processes** are transactions and activities that either are specifically authorized by top managers or are used by managers to perform administrative functions. Investment of excess funds and raising capital funds are nonroutine processes that occur when specifically authorized. On the other hand, the general ledger and reporting processes provide feedback to owners and managers and assist these groups in the administration of the organization. These administrative processes are further described in the following sections period instead of colon.

SOURCE OF CAPITAL PROCESSES (STUDY OBJECTIVE 2)

The operation of any organization requires long-term, capital assets such as land, buildings, and equipment. To purchase these capital assets, top management must have capital available. **Capital** is the funds used to acquire the long-term, capital assets of an organization. Capital usually comes from long-term debt or equity. Long-term debt is typically loans or bonds payable, and equity is common or preferred stock. These financial instruments enable top management to raise the capital necessary to acquire long-term, capital assets. **Source of capital processes** are those processes to authorize the raising of capital, the execution of raising capital, and the proper accounting of that capital. Because of the magnitude and importance of these methods of raising capital, it is important that these financial instruments are used only when necessary.

The transactions and resulting processes related to loans, bonds payable, and stock should be executed only when top management or the board of directors authorizes them, and use of the resulting capital must be properly controlled. These processes are administrative processes because top managers, the administrators of the organization, are responsible for the authorization, control, and use of the capital. Exhibit 12-3 shows the processes related to raising capital

Exhibit 12-3
Source of Capital Process Map

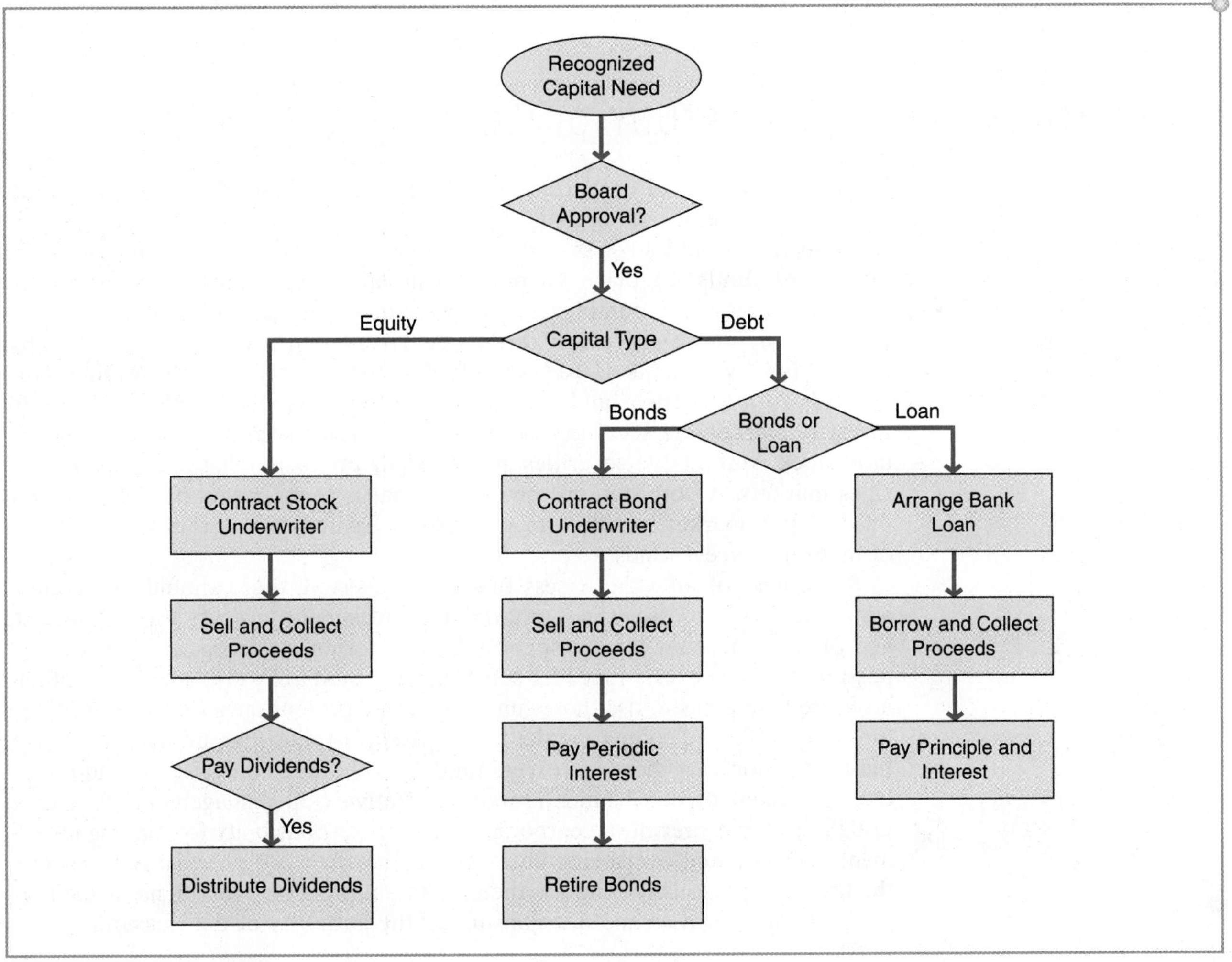

and retiring debt. The processes related to expenditures of capital (purchases of fixed assets) were described in Chapter 10.

Occasionally, top management may recognize the need to raise capital. This need might arise from the desire to accomplish organizational goals that require substantial funds. Some examples of these organizational goals would be to expand the organization, to replace a substantial amount of plant, property, and equipment, or to acquire other businesses. To accomplish any of these goals, management would need access to a substantially large amount of capital. Top management would then investigate the most appropriate method of raising the needed capital.

The board of directors must decide between the two general sources of capital funds: debt or equity. If the board chooses to use equity as the source of capital, the corporation will need to sell common or preferred stock. Corporations are usually unable to access the stock market directly and must conduct a sale of stock through an underwriter. An **underwriter** is a third party that contracts with a corporation to bring a new issue of securities to the public market.

Since top management authorizes and controls these capital transaction processes, there is inherent control. The fact that these processes cannot occur without specific authorization and oversight by top management is a strong internal control.

INVESTMENT PROCESSES (STUDY OBJECTIVE 3)

In many instances, an organization finds that it has more funds on hand than necessary to operate the organization. The proper performance of the stewardship function would suggest that management should "park," or invest, these excess cash funds in a place where they can earn a return. Management should properly manage, or administer, the investment of excess funds. **Investment processes** are those processes which authorize, execute, manage, and properly account for investments of excess funds. While there are several ways for a corporation to invest such funds, the most frequently used methods would be to invest in marketable securities or repurchase the company's outstanding common stock. Marketable securities are stocks or bonds purchased on open securities markets. A corporation's own stock that is repurchased by the company on the open market is called treasury stock. Exhibit 12-4 shows the processes of investing excess funds.

Regardless of how the excess funds are invested, there should be a set of administrative processes that authorize the investment, execute the investment, and properly account for investments. It is important to recognize that it is not possible to invest excess funds for some future period unless top management has no immediate plans to use those funds. Top management must be monitoring the funds available and comparing the future need for funds that are available. Thus, the recognition that there are excess funds and the related decision to authorize the investment of those funds are administrative (top management) functions. Usually, the treasurer of the corporation has the responsibility for making investment decisions and overseeing investments. This does not necessarily mean that the treasurer personally conducts the investment processes; rather, he or she may delegate the processes and decisions under the authority of the treasurer.

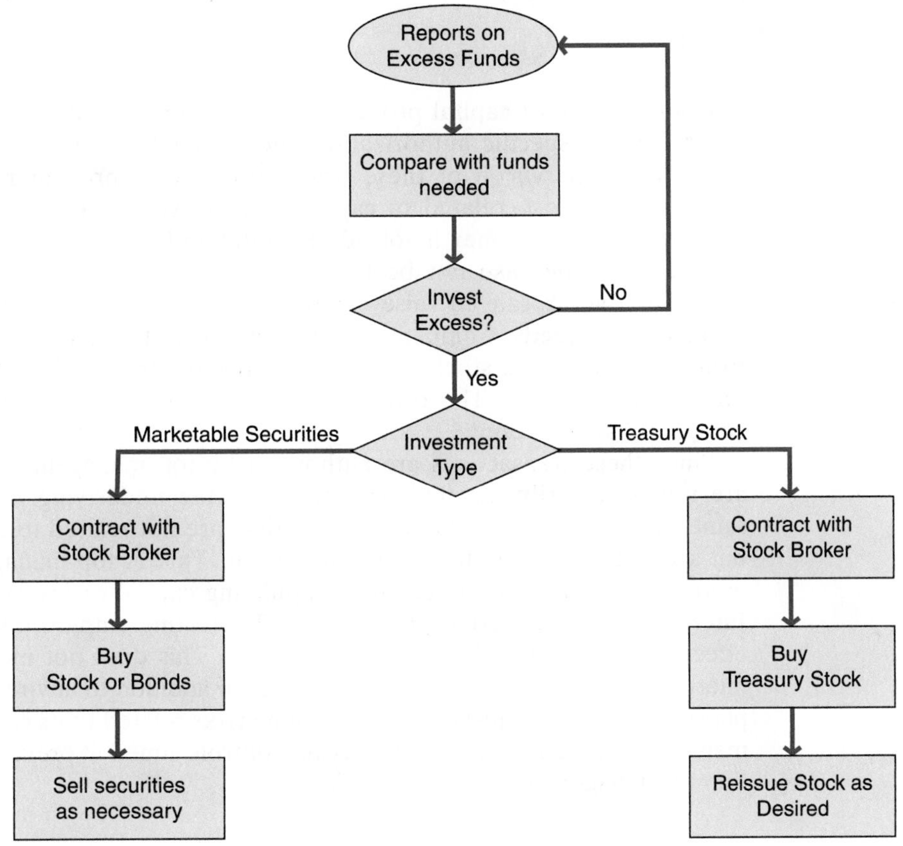

Exhibit 12-4
Investment Process Map

The exact nature of the parties that make up top management depends upon the type of organization. For a corporation, the board of directors is the top management level that authorizes and controls source of capital processes. For partnerships or proprietorships, the owners are the top managers. For the purpose of explaining the processes in Exhibit 12-4, a corporation with a board of directors is the type of organization and management depicted.

Securities and treasury stock often are not purchased directly on the market; rather, a brokerage firm is used to execute the purchase. After purchase of securities or treasury stock, the treasurer of the company often maintains custody of the securities and the record of those securities. In some companies, a trustee is used to maintain custody of the securities or records of the securities. At some point in the future, management will determine that there are more important or profitable uses for invested funds. The securities or treasury stock can then be resold through a broker.

Since most large corporations have complex IT accounting systems, the accounting system can automate much of the investment processes, including notifying management when excess funds exist. That is, the IT system can forecast future cash needs and future cash inflows by examining the timing of future accounts payable due dates and future collections of accounts receivable. The system can continually compare current cash balances with forecasted needs and sources and provide feedback to top management about potential excess funds.

RISKS AND CONTROLS IN CAPITALS AND INVESTMENT PROCESSES (STUDY OBJECTIVE 4)

For both source of capital processes and investment processes, the important control is the specific authorization and oversight by top management. The very close supervision of these transactions helps prevent risks of theft or misuse of the cash related to capital and investment processes. In addition, the large sums of money involved in capital and investment decisions usually dictates that the cash not be handled by regular company employees. For example, a stock sale to raise capital might result in millions or billions of dollars in proceeds. Company employees are not likely to handle any cash from the result of a stock sale. Instead, the funds would probably be transferred electronically. The broker would electronically transfer funds to the company bank account.

Since these transactions are authorized by top management and the funds are not necessarily handled by employees, the underlying risks are not the same as other processes. Generally, the risks are not related to employee fraud, but are instead related to management fraud. That is, top management is much more likely to conduct fraud by manipulating capital or investment processes. Internal controls aimed at preventing and detecting employee fraud are not as effective in capital and investment decisions. This does not mean that regular internal controls should be ignored, but that in addition to any regular controls in place, the company must carefully examine risks related to its capital and investment processes and implement relevant controls aimed at prevention and detection of management fraud.

THE REAL WORLD

An example of management fraud in stock transactions is a case filed by the Securities and Exchange Commission in June 2003 against Nathan A. Chapman, Jr. and three of his companies. In 2000, Chapman's company, echapman.com, was scheduled to sell stock through an initial public offering (IPO). In an IPO, the company offering stock must explain to potential investors the manner in which funds from the IPO will be used. An SEC press release said the following regarding Chapman:

> The defendants concealed their fraud with false and misleading statements regarding the use of the IPO proceeds in quarterly and annual reports filed with the Commission, prepared and signed by Chapman . . .[2]

Chapman was using proceeds from the sale of new stock to buy more of his own stock. These purchases were only intended to show a larger volume of sales of the stock, thereby making it look like a more attractive stock. He was attempting to artificially pump up the price of the stock through these purchases of his own stock. To conceal this fraud, his company created fraudulent financial statements.

This example illustrates that typical internal controls such as segregation of duties and reconciliations may not prevent or detect management frauds that can occur in capital and investment processes. The more important controls are the specific authorization by top management and close scrutiny by the internal and external auditors.

[2]SEC Press Release, June 26, 2003.

GENERAL LEDGER PROCESSES (STUDY OBJECTIVE 5)

Reexamine Exhibit 12-2 and notice that each of the processes described in this chapter and previous chapters feed data into the general ledger. The general ledger is the set of accounts within the chart of accounts. From the perspective of your accounting courses, recall that the general ledger is the entire set of T-accounts for the organization. Each set of processes described affects general ledger accounts. For example, sales and sales return processes affect the accounts receivable, sales, inventory, and cost of goods sold accounts. For manual accounting systems, the process in which transactions are posted to the general ledger is called the accounting cycle. Exhibit 12-5 is a summary of the processes in the accounting cycle.

Exhibit 12-5
Accounting Cycle Process Map

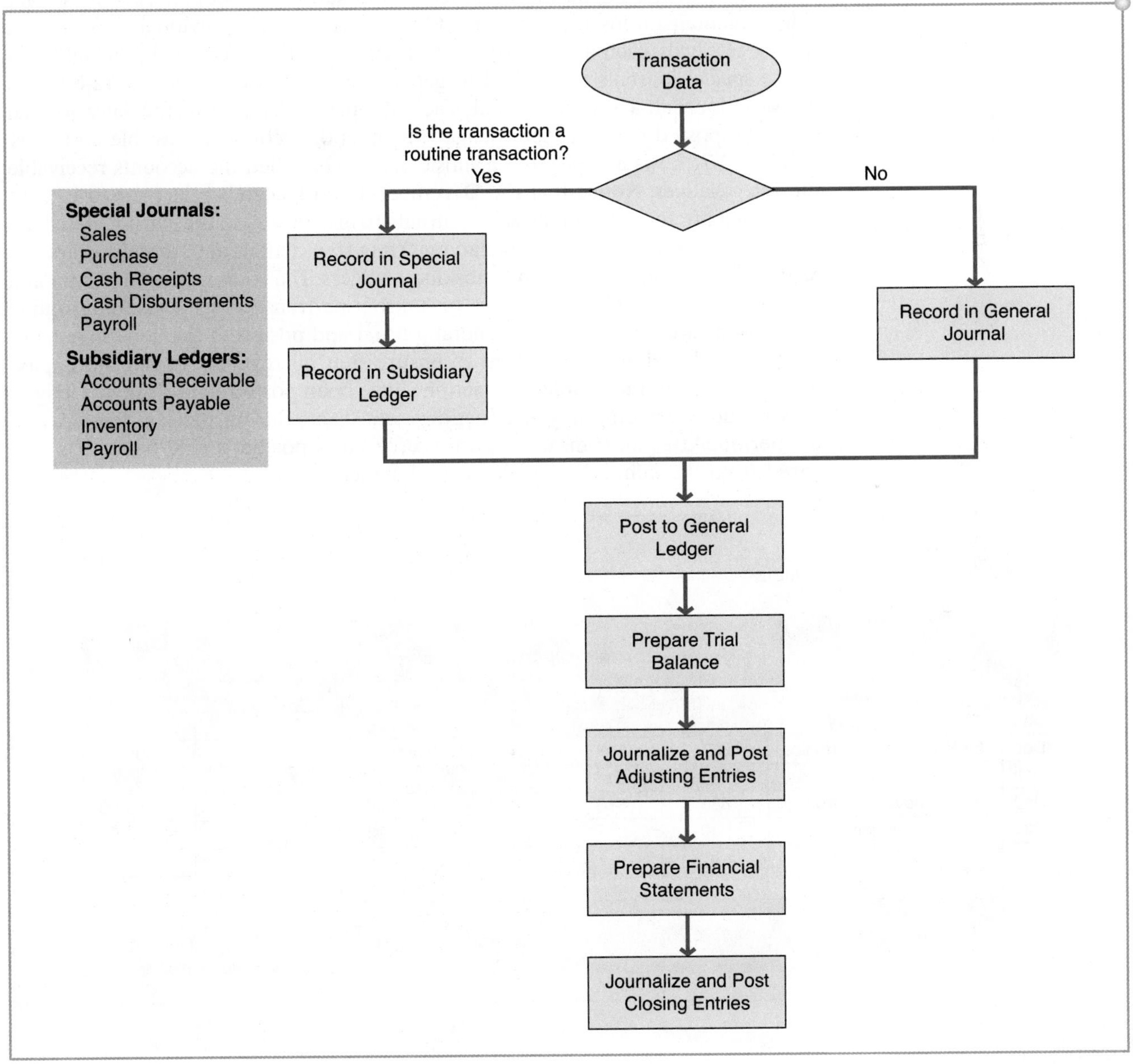

Business processes in an organization include events that are accounting transactions. When such an event occurs, the accountant keeping manual records must decide whether the transaction is a regular, recurring transaction. If the transaction is regular and recurring, it would be recorded in a special journal. **Special journals** are journals that are established to record specific types of transactions. For example, a sale to a customer would be recorded in a special journal called the sales journal. The sales journal would be the appropriate place to record all credit sales. The sales journal is designed to have columns to record the amount of the sale and the corresponding receivable. That is, one column exists for sales dollar amounts (a credit), and one column for accounts receivable amounts (a debit). In addition, regular, recurring transactions are posted to subsidiary ledgers. **Subsidiary ledgers** maintain the detail information regarding routine transactions, with an account established for each entity. For example, a credit sale to a customer must be recorded in the accounts receivable subsidiary ledger. This subsidiary ledger maintains transaction details and balances for each individual customer. At regular intervals, such as the end of each day or end of each week, the subtotals of the special journals are posted to general ledger accounts. Exhibit 12-6 shows the sales journal, a special journal. The subtotals of $41,100 in the sales journal would be posted to the general ledger accounts of accounts receivable and sales. Exhibit 12-7 shows a page from a subsidiary ledger called the accounts receivable subsidiary ledger. Notice that the December 4 and December 11 sales to Electro World that are recorded in the sales journal are also posted to the subsidiary ledger.

Some transactions are not regular, recurring transactions and, therefore, are not recorded in special journals and subsidiary ledgers. The transactions in capital and investment processes are examples of nonroutine transactions. These nonroutine transactions are entered in the general journal and posted to the general ledger.

At period end, it is important to ensure that all revenue, expenditure, payroll, payable, and receivable transactions have been posted to the general ledger. This includes accruing any transactions that occur during the last few days of the period. After all transactions are accrued and posted, a trial balance is prepared from the general ledger account balances.

SALES JOURNAL DECEMBER

Date		Customer	Invoice or Cr. Memo Number	Subsid. Acct. No.	Subsid. Post	Debit: Acct. Rec. G/L 10200	Debit: Sales Returns G/L 30200	Credit: Sales G/L 31000
Dec.	4	ABW-Electro World	836	516	X	15,000.00		15,000.00
Dec.	5	Windover Electronics	837	518	X	5,600.00		5,600.00
Dec.	11	ABW-Electro World	838	516	X	7,580.00		7,580.00
Dec.	13	Windover Electronics	839	518	X	1,820.00		1,820.00
Dec.	18	Clean Imagery, Inc.	840	517	X	11,100.00		11,100.00
					Monthly Totals	41,100.00	–	41,100.00

Exhibit 12-6
A Special Journal

516 ElectroWorld
675 Main Street
Covington, KY 41011

Credit Limit: $ 20,000.00

Date		Description	Debit	Credit	Balance
Oct.	1	Balance Forward			–
Nov.	2	Invoice #832	19,400.00		19,400.00
Nov.	13	Partial payment #832		16,000.00	3,400.00
Dec.	4	Invoice #836	15,000.00		18,400.00
Dec.	9	Payment #836		15,000.00	3,400.00
Dec.	11	Invoice #838	7,580.00		10,980.00
Dec.	23	Invoice #838		3,400.00	7,580.00
					7,580.00
					7,580.00

Exhibit 12-7
A Subsidiary Ledger

After correction of any recording or posting errors, the adjusting entries are recorded in the general journal and posted to the general ledger. The financial statements are prepared from the adjusted balances in the general ledger. To prepare the general ledger for the next accounting period, and to transfer earnings to retained earnings, closing entries are recorded in the general journal and posted to the general ledger. This ends the accounting cycle for the current fiscal period, and the cycle begins anew in the next fiscal period.

These examples of accounting records focus only on sales and receivables. There are similar special journals and subsidiary ledgers for other regular, recurring transactions. There can be special journals for purchases, cash receipts, cash disbursements, and payroll. Also, there are other subsidiary ledgers such as accounts payable, inventory, payroll, and fixed assets. When a transaction occurs, the accountant must choose the correct set of special journals and subsidiary ledgers in which to record the transaction.

While very few organizations use manual accounting systems, much of the accounting software in use today is built on the concepts underlying the manual accounting cycle processes. For example, when entering transactions in Microsoft Dynamics GP® accounting software, one must choose the correct module from the menu. This module selection is similar to choosing the correct special journal. Exhibit 12-8 has a screen capture of the module selection menu from Microsoft Dynamics GP®. As examples, if a payroll transaction is to be processed in the software, the user would choose "Payroll," and for sales transactions the user would choose "Sales."

Therefore, whether the accounting system is manual or computerized, we must understand the processes and the special journals, subsidiary ledgers, and general ledger accounts in an accounting system.

Transaction recording in special journals and subsidiary ledgers takes place at the time the transaction occurs. Thus, the special journals and subsidiary ledgers are updated as the processes for that journal occur. The revenue transactions, such as those described in Chapter 8, would be recorded in the correct special journal as the related shipping transaction takes place. Only the posting to the general ledger occurs at a later time. This chapter focuses only on the general ledger process. In other words, the discussion of the general ledger processes

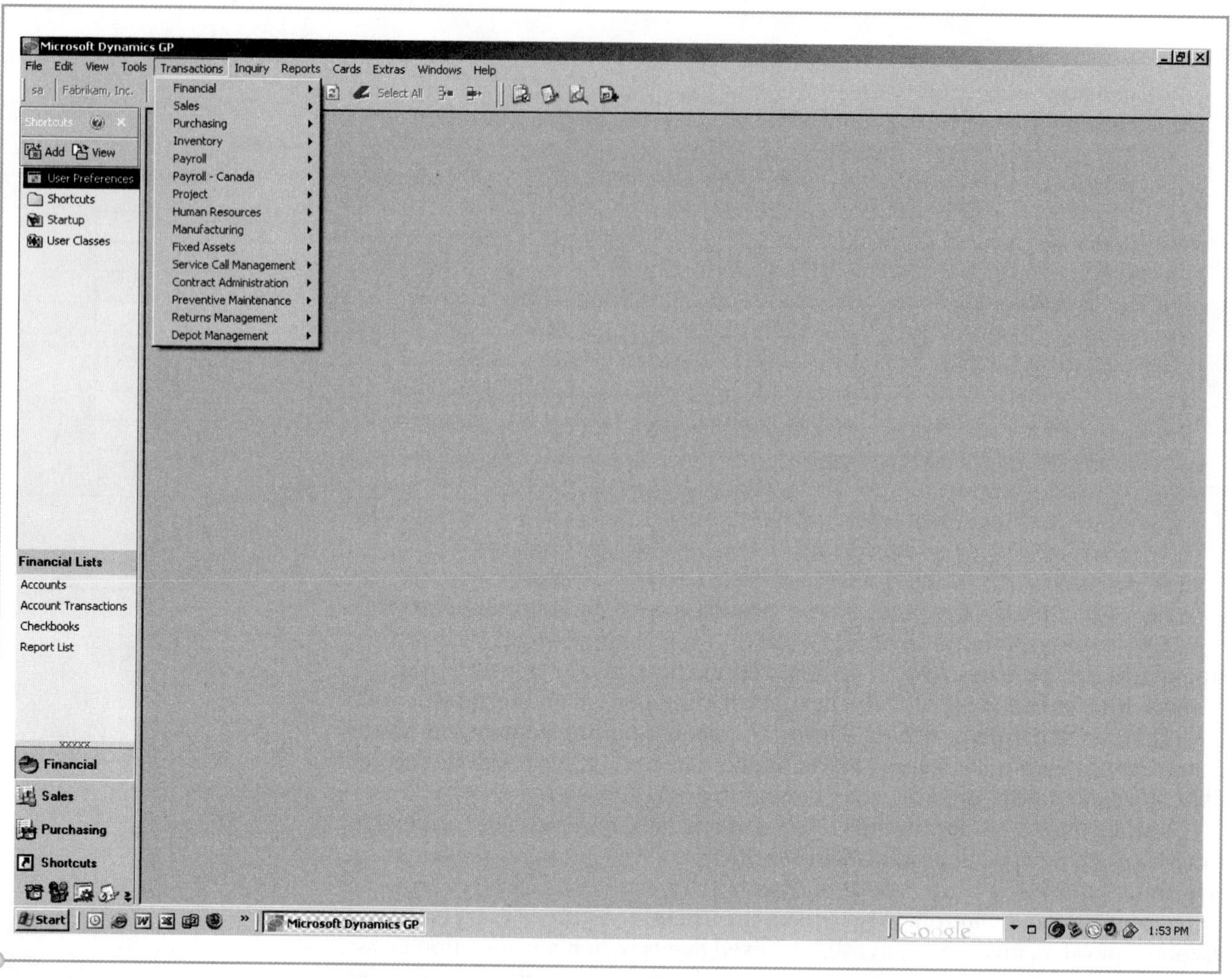

Exhibit 12-8
Transaction Modules in Microsoft Dynamics GP®

assumes that transactions have already been recorded in special journals and subsidiary ledgers as the transactions occurred.

RISKS AND CONTROLS IN GENERAL LEDGER PROCESSES (STUDY OBJECTIVE 6)

In terms of the five internal control activities described in Chapter 3, following are common procedures associated with the general ledger:

AUTHORIZATION OF TRANSACTIONS

The general ledger accumulates subtotal data from the previous processes within the company. For example, sales subtotals are posted to the general ledger sales account. Each of those individual sales was authorized when the sale occurred. Chapter 8 describes the authorization of sales. However, there must also be proper authorization to begin the process of posting from the sales journal to the general ledger.

In the case of a manual accounting system, a journal voucher is prepared by a manager in the sales department, and that approved journal voucher is forwarded to the general ledger department. The journal voucher includes the dollar subtotals, the accounts affected, and an authorized signature. Posting subtotals to the general ledger should not occur without a signed, authorized journal voucher from the other department that accounted for other process. For example, a payroll subtotal of wages and deductions is not posted to the general ledger until the payroll department forwards a signed journal voucher. The signed journal voucher serves as authorization to post the payroll data to the general ledger.

In a computerized accounting system, paper journal voucher documents may not exist. In these systems, individual transactions may be entered into special modules, but not posted to the general ledger until the batch of transactions is completely entered and errors are corrected. For example, sales for an entire day may be entered in the "Sales" module, but not posted to the general ledger until the end of the day.

Approvals for each journal voucher are general authorizations rather than a specific authorization. Through the assignment of limited access to the general ledger module, management can limit the capability of general ledger posting to selected employees. When an employee with the appropriate access level logs into the accounting system, he can process the general ledger posting. Employees who have not been given access to general ledger posting will be unable to post to the general ledger. One set of employees would have log-in access that would allow them to enter individual sales in the "Sales" module. Another employee or set of employees has a user ID and password that allows her or them the access to post to the general ledger. This assignment of separate duties enables management to give authority to general ledger employees to post to the general ledger.

Computerized accounting systems have different levels of automation. As the computerized accounting systems become more complex and integrated, there are usually fewer manual processes. With more automation and fewer manual steps, responsibility for authorization gets moved to lower and lower levels of employees. For example, if a computerized accounting system automatically updates the general ledger as individual transactions are entered, there is no need for a separate posting step. Thus, the employee who enters the details of the sale has, in effect, authorized the general ledger posting. In many IT systems today, the accounting systems are extremely complex, automated, and integrated, and they place the authorization at the lower level employees.

THE REAL WORLD

Consider the checkout lanes at a department store such as Wal-Mart. Around the world, there are employees working checkout lanes who are scanning products by passing them over the bar code scanner and accepting payment. In a large company such as Wal-Mart, it would be tremendously inefficient for the system to be set up such that these sales are not posted into the general ledger until a specific employee logs in to conduct the posting. Rather, when the checkout lane employee "authorizes" a sale by accepting payment and printing a sales receipt, he or she has authorized an event that will automatically update sales, inventory, and cash balances.

Many large corporations that sell to other companies have even more complex IT accounting systems, often connected to vendor and customer IT systems. In these systems, a sale might actually be authorized by the customer. Therefore, these systems require preexisting and negotiated relationships between buyer and seller companies. Both parties must have already approved these processes and established IT systems that execute the processes.

THE REAL WORLD

Wal-Mart and Procter & Gamble (P&G) have interconnected IT systems. P&G sells consumer products such as soap, shampoo, and diapers to Wal-Mart. A sale by P&G to Wal-Mart is actually triggered by the Wal-Mart IT inventory system. As Wal-Mart inventory levels of certain products fall below established reorder points, the systems interact and authorize a transfer of products from P&G to Wal-Mart. This means that P&G's sale and the subsequent update of its sales and receivable accounts are triggered by its customer's computer system.

Whether the system is manual or computerized, posting to general ledger accounts should occur only when proper authorization exists. In manual systems and less complex computerized systems, the authorization to post is vested in the journal voucher. In more complex accounting systems, certain employees are authorized to record specific events. A certain employee or employees may have the access that allows him or her to post transaction subtotals to the general ledger. This access is controlled by user IDs and passwords. In very complex systems, the authority to record things may exist for low-level employees, or even in other IT systems. In all cases, management must establish the method of authorization it desires in its accounting system.

SEGREGATION OF DUTIES

In manual accounting systems, segregation of duties is possible and desirable as an internal control. Employees who post journal vouchers have responsibility for record keeping. For proper segregation, those employees should never have authorization or custody functions. General ledger employees should only record journal vouchers from other operational departments that have been authorized by managers in those departments. The general ledger employees should never be given responsibility for authorizing any journal vouchers. Also, general ledger employees should never have custody of any assets that they record in the general ledger. If these employees have both custody and record keeping functions, they have a capability to steal assets and alter the records.

A third segregation in a manual general ledger system is that general ledger functions should be segregated from special journal and subsidiary ledger tasks. The special journals, subsidiary ledgers, and general ledger serve important, but separate, record keeping and control functions Special journals and subsidiary ledgers have details of many subaccounts, such as sales revenues and an account balance for each customer in the accounts receivable subsidiary ledger. The general ledger sales and accounts receivable accounts maintain overall increases, decreases, and a balance in those accounts. At all times and for each special journal and subsidiary ledger, total balances should equal the balance in the corresponding general ledger account. As examples, the total of the sales in the sales journal should equal the balance of sales in the general ledger, and the total of the accounts in the inventory subsidiary ledger should equal the balance of inventory in the general ledger. By separating the record keeping function for these two types of records, control is enhanced. Two separate parties are keeping independent, but related records. If there are problems with the reconciliation of the two records, it may be the case that errors or fraudulent acts have occurred. Separating general ledger from subsidiary ledger functions increases the likelihood that errors or fraud will be prevented or detected.

In summary, three important segregations should be in place in a manual general ledger system. General ledger employees should record journal vouchers, but they should not

1. authorize journal vouchers,
2. have custody of assets, or
3. have recording responsibility for any special journals or subsidiary ledgers.

Computerized accounting systems may not have the same types of segregation. Segregation of functions may not be possible in IT systems if manual functions have been computerized. Whether segregation of functions is possible depends on the complexity of the IT accounting system. Simple accounting systems may still have some segregation of functions for general ledger record keeping, while more complex systems will not. Microsoft Dynamics GP® software is an example of a relatively less complex accounting software system for small and midsize businesses. In such an accounting system, segregation is achieved by allowing different levels of access for different employees. This concept was described in the previous section on authorization. Essentially, general ledger functions and posting can be assigned to certain employees by the limiting of access to the general ledger functions on the basis of log-in IDs. Exhibit 12-9 shows a general ledger posting window in Microsoft Dynamics GP® accounting software. User IDs and passwords can limit access to this window to only selected employees. The employee who is given access to this window would choose which batch entries to post, place a checkmark in the box next to the batch, and select the Post option.

More complex accounting software may post to the general ledger system automatically as transactions are processed. In this case, segregation of general ledger functions is not likely, because there are no employee functions within the general ledger system. However, incompatible duties in processes that eventually post to the general ledger can still be segregated.

THE REAL WORLD

In an ERP system with potentially thousands of users and processes that automatically trigger other processes, how is segregation of duties managed? A typical ERP system has many automated triggering processes. Lightle and Vallario offer the following example of automatic triggering and the effect on segregation of duties:

> Customer orders for goods may automatically trigger production runs, which in turn trigger inventory purchases communicated by electronic data interchange to specified suppliers. When the warehouse clerk receives inventory from the supplier, he or she makes an entry to the system from the receiving dock, changing the status of the purchase order from "open" to "received." When accounts payable receives the invoice, which may occur electronically, the system matches goods received to invoices received, automatically creating a payable and scheduling payment.[3]

[3]S.S. Lightle, and C.W. Vallario, "Segregation of Duties in ERP," *Internal Auditor,* October 2003, p. 28.

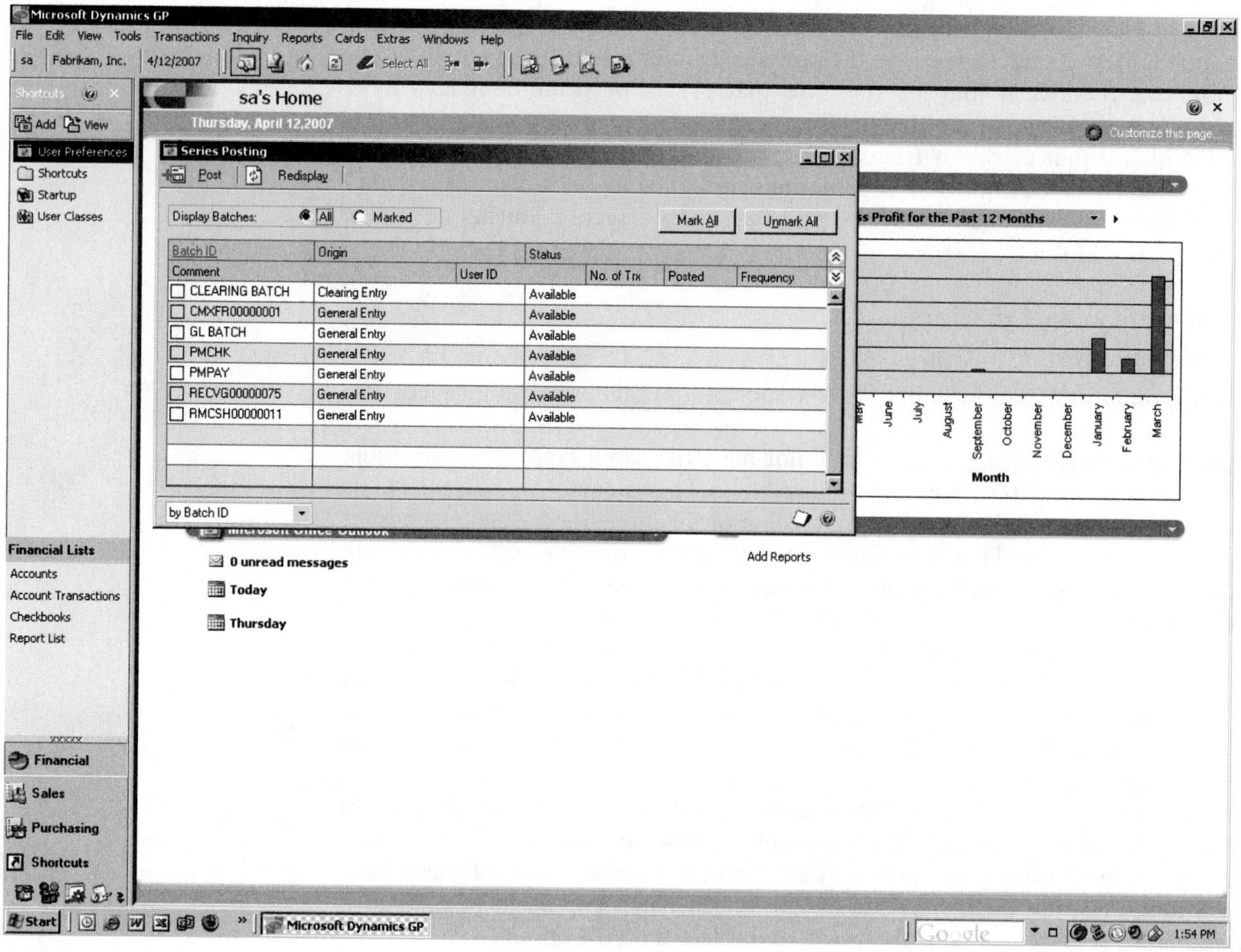

Exhibit 12-9
General Ledger Posting in Microsoft Dynamics GP®

Notice in this ERP example that if one person's user ID and password allowed the authority to both trigger the purchase and make the receiving entry, he or she could execute processes that automatically match goods to invoices and prepare a payment. Therefore, as user IDs and passwords are assigned, proper segregation must be built into user profiles. A user should not be able to process incompatible duties, such as those cited in the foregoing purchase and receiving example. In addition, an ERP system should segregate authorizing a transaction from updating the related master file. As an example, a user's profile should not allow the initiation of a purchase and the maintenance of the approved vendor list (the master file). Since incompatible duties may allow one person to process potentially fictitious or fraudulent transactions that would eventually be posted to the general ledger, these transactions would automatically be included in the company's financial statements. Therefore, in order to promote accurate financial reporting, ERP systems must control access so that incompatible duties cannot be performed by any employee.

ADEQUATE RECORDS AND DOCUMENTS

To maintain adequate records and documents in a manual general ledger system, there are two important requirements. First, the organization must have a well-defined chart of accounts. To reduce the chance of misclassified transactions that are posted to an incorrect account, the chart of accounts must be designed in a way that minimizes confusion about the types of transactions that belong in each individual account. The chart of accounts should have a sufficient number and type of accounts that facilitate the accurate classification of transactions. For example, if there is no "Rent Expense" ledger account, users will be uncertain where to post a payment for rent. Different users could post it to different accounts. This would make the balances in those accounts less useful, since no one could easily tell whether rent is included.

Second, there must be an adequate audit trail to allow tracing transactions back to the source. All transactions of the organization should have an audit trail that allows the transaction to be traced from its initiation through its recording in the general ledger. In a manual system, the source documents, special journals, subsidiary ledgers, journal vouchers, and general ledger make up the audit trail. Using this documentation, a transaction can be traced from the source document to the general ledger. Transaction tracing can also occur in the opposite direction. Amounts in the general ledger accounts can be traced back to the original source documents.

In computerized IT accounting systems, the audit trail may be made up of electronic images in files, with no supporting paper documents or records. Thus, the audit trail could be either of these extremes—paper documents or computer files—or the audit trail could be partially paper based and partially electronic images. For example, the audit trail would be made up of paper source documents, transaction logs, transaction files, and master files.

SECURITY OF THE GENERAL LEDGER AND DOCUMENTS

In manual systems, the general ledger and supporting documents must be protected from unauthorized access. Unauthorized access can allow records to be fraudulently altered. The paper documents and records of manual systems can be protected by a limitation on the number of people who have access to these documents.

IT accounting systems protect record access in a different way. For electronic file images, access can be limited through the proper use of user IDs, passwords, and resource authority tables. These general controls establish which employees have access to specific records or files.

INDEPENDENT CHECKS AND RECONCILIATION

In a manual general ledger system, the reconciliation of special journals and subsidiary accounts to the general ledger control accounts is an independent check on the accuracy of recording regular, recurring transactions. In addition, appropriate managers should regularly review general ledger reports for accuracy and completeness. In an IT system, these reports are also checked for correctness. Various reports in the IT system are printed and cross-checked against each

Exhibit 12-10
General Ledger Controls and Risks

Control	Minimizes the Related Risk of:
Authorization:	
Manual systems and simple IT systems: Signed journal vouchers	Fraudulent posting to cover theft; errors caused by posting batches before errors are corrected in the batch
More complex IT systems: Log-in procedures such as user ID and password limit authority to designated employees	Fraudulent entries or transactions
Segregation of Duties:	
Manual systems and simple IT systems: Segregate 1) authorization from general ledger recording; 2) asset custody from general ledger recording; 3) special journal and subsidiary ledger recording from general ledger recording	Theft and fraud; undetected errors that cause accounts, special journals, or subsidiary ledgers to be out of balance
More complex IT systems: Not as much segregation is possible because the system prepares and posts entries. Separate custody from general ledger access	Theft and fraud
Records and Documents:	
Well-defined and complete chart of accounts	Amounts posted to wrong accounts
Audit trail of paper documents and records, electronic file images in an IT system, or a combination of paper and electronic audit trail	Transactions not recorded or recorded incorrectly
Security:	
IT controls over computer records and physical controls in general ledger record storage areas	Invalid general ledger postings
Independent Checks and Reconciliations:	
In manual and simple IT systems, subsidiary ledgers reconciled to general ledger control accounts	Fraud and errors
Regular, periodic general ledger reports reviewed by appropriate managers	Fraud and errors

other to ensure their accuracy. Exhibit 12-10 summarizes the controls and risks and general ledger processes.

REPORTING AS AN OUTPUT OF THE GENERAL LEDGER PROCESSES (STUDY OBJECTIVE 7)

The information in the general ledger accounts provides important feedback for both internal and external parties. External parties such as investors and creditors use general purpose financial statements to evaluate business performance. Investors and creditors use periodic financial reports that summarize the business.

Internal managers need financial and nonfinancial feedback for proper planning and control of operations. Internal managers need much more frequent and detailed reports than external users. The sections that follow describe the external and internal reporting concepts.

EXTERNAL REPORTING

The four general purpose financial statements—balance sheet, income statement, statement of cash flows, and statement of retained earnings—are created from general ledger account balances. These financial statements are generated at the end of the accounting cycle. The dollar amounts reported are all derived from general ledger account balances. Usually, accounts are combined and summarized when reported in general purpose financial statements. External users do not need detailed balance information on every existing account in the general ledger. For example, a large company may have several general ledger accounts for various types of cash and cash equivalents. These individual cash accounts are combined, or "rolled up," into one cash dollar amount on the balance sheet. This same summary process occurs for all of the line items on the general purpose financial statements. Sales revenue as reported on the income statement is a combination of many revenue accounts in the general ledger. There may be a revenue account for each product or product line so that managers can track sales of individual products. However, external users would be overwhelmed by the detail in several revenue accounts. Therefore, the revenue accounts are rolled up into only one or a few lines on the income statement.[4]

The IT accounting systems are programmed to combine, or roll up, accounts when the system processes the financial statements. The reports that are the financial statements are designed and programmed into the IT system when the system is designed and implemented. When these financial statement reports are needed at the end of the period, they may be printed by the IT system. Prior to the printing and distribution of these reports, the CFO and the accounting staff oversee the closing process to ensure that the dollar amounts are correct and complete, usually by printing various reports in the IT system and cross-checking them against each other to ensure their accuracy.

INTERNAL REPORTING

The internal reports to be provided to managers vary, greatly depending on several factors. Internal reports are usually not general purpose financial statements, but reports that are tailored to the specific needs of each management level and function. The many factors that affect the type of report provided to internal users can be summarized so that they fall into three categories: the type of organization, the underlying function managed, and the time horizon.

Type of Organization

Although this may be obvious, the type of organization affects the type of reports that are needed to manage the organization. For example, manufacturing

[4]While the details are beyond the scope of this chapter, the FASB has issued guidelines for segment reporting that direct a company how to report revenue and expense items by major segments.

firms need different reports than retail firms or service firms. Manufacturing firms must manage the flow of raw materials, work in process, and manufacturing labor. Retail firms do not have these processes. Therefore, a manufacturing firm must provide and use many reports about raw materials, labor, and work in process. Retail and manufacturing firms manage inventories, while service firms do not. Therefore, service firm internal reports are more likely to focus on sales and the status of projects. Certainly, all three types of firms use revenue and profitability related reports. Some organizations, such as governmental or charitable foundations, are not profit oriented. Reports in these types of organizations are focused on cash flows, funding sources, and expenditures.

Function Managed

The type of function that a manager oversees also affects the type of reports needed. An operations manager needs reports about operations. Therefore, a production line supervisor needs reports about machine hours, down-time of machines, units produced, defective units, and material usage. These types of operational reports may not be prepared from data in the general ledger. However, as transactions are recorded in the accounting processes, financial as well as nonfinancial data are accumulated. Therefore, the accounting system often records both financial and operational data that can be used in reports.

Managers who direct financial aspects of a business need financial data in reports. For example, an accounts receivable manager needs reports that show aged accounts receivable. Higher-level managers examine financial reports regularly to properly manage sales, expenditures, cash flows, inventories, and many other financial aspects. These financial reports are prepared directly from ledgers, journals, and other accounting records.

Time Horizon

A large study of the information that managers use was conducted by Bruns and McKinnon in the 1990s. In summarizing their findings, they said:

> Unit data is the metric in which day-to-day management takes place, and financial information increases in importance and use as the management horizon lengthens.[5]

Their results indicate that in day-to-day management, managers are more likely to use unit measures and physical counts. For management, time horizons of one month or longer are likely to involve financial measures. As an example, Bruns and McKinnon suggest that the day-to-day management of purchasing is likely to focus on physical counts such as quantities ordered. However, as the time horizon lengthens to a month, financial data such as purchase price variances were more useful to managers. This general finding about time horizons applies to most management situations. Therefore, for time horizons of one month or longer, reports generated by information in the general ledger are likely to be very important.

[5]W.J. Bruns, Jr. and S.M. McKinnon, "Information and Managers: A Field Study," *Journal of Management Accounting Research,* Fall 1993, vol. 5, p. 94.

ETHICAL ISSUES RELATED TO ADMINISTRATIVE PROCESSES AND REPORTING (STUDY OBJECTIVE 7)

Unethical or fraudulent behavior can occur in administrative processing and the reporting functions of an organization. However, unethical and fraudulent behaviors are much more likely to be initiated by management, not employees. Employee fraud is more prevalent in the routine processes of sales, purchases, payroll, and other processes described in previous chapters. Management fraud is more prevalent in administrative processes and reporting. There are several reasons that unethical and fraudulent behavior would tend to be management- rather than employee-initiated.

First, in a properly controlled system of administrative and reporting functions, employees do not have access to related assets or source documents. A review of the previous chapters reveals processes where employees have daily access to assets, source documents, and records. In processes such as sales, sales returns, cash receipts, purchasing, and payroll, employees have access to assets such as inventory and cash. In addition, employees have access to source documents or records that can be fraudulently used. As examples, employees can inflate hours in their time card, steal cash or checks if they work in the mail room, steal inventory if they work in the warehouse, or process fictitious vendor payments if they work in accounts payable.

Second, administrative processes are tightly controlled and supervised by top management, as they require specific authorization. Employees do not have the authority to authorize or initiate processes such as capital sources and investing. However, in processes such as sales, purchasing, cash receipts, and cash disbursements, employees are given general authorization to initiate and process transactions. This general authority can allow employees to initiate fraudulent transactions. Many relevant examples have been described in previous chapters, but another example may illustrate employee fraud when general authorization exists: If an accounts receivable employee is given general authorization to write off uncollectible accounts, that employee might write off the account of a friend or relative even when it could be collected.

Finally, the routine nature of processes such as sales, purchasing, payroll, and conversion generates a huge volume of transactions. The routine nature and huge volumes of these processes make it easier for employees to hide fraudulent transactions or unethical behavior within the masses of transactions. As an analogy, think about the differences in very large classes and very small classes. The large classes with hundreds of students create an atmosphere that makes it easier for an individual student to remain anonymous, to not read material for class, to sleep in class, or to cheat on exams or assignments. However, the intimacy of smaller classes makes it much harder to hide such behaviors. Likewise, the huge volume of transactions in routine processes makes it easier to hide fraudulent or unethical behavior. Administrative processes are nonroutine, and the number of transactions varies. Thus, unethical or fraudulent behavior is harder to conduct or hide.

UNETHICAL MANAGEMENT BEHAVIOR IN CAPITAL SOURCES AND INVESTING

Source of capital processes and investment processes, described in the early part of this chapter, present important sources and uses of capital in an organization.

These processes should be undertaken for the overall good of the organization and in an ethically responsible manner. They must be undertaken ethically, and financial reports and other disclosures must be complete and accurate. Unfortunately, such processes can be misused or abused by management. For example, when raising capital, it is imperative that the investors or creditors be fully informed of all relevant information while making investment or credit decisions. Often, management tries to hide negative information when borrowing funds or selling stock. Such a lack of full and complete disclosure is unethical. If management is selling stock, it should not try to mislead potential investors.

THE REAL WORLD

The following excerpted paragraphs describe a July 2004 lawsuit filed against Krispy Kreme Doughnuts, Inc., alleging that the company misled investors in the sale of its stock:

> The Complaint alleges that Krispy Kreme, along with certain of its officers and directors, violated the federal securities laws by issuing a series of materially false and misleading statements to the market. These misstatements have had the effect of artificially inflating the market price of Krispy Kreme's securities.
>
> Specifically, the Complaint alleges that the Company failed to disclose and misrepresented the following material adverse facts which were known to defendants or recklessly disregarded by them: (1) that the Company used aggressive bookkeeping to boost its earnings when it acquired its Michigan franchise in 2003; (2) that Krispy Kreme's core businesses were actually underperforming; (3) that the Company expanded too quickly, and would now be forced to shut down six factory stores and three Doughnut and Coffee shops in an effort to improve productivity. . . .[6]

Notice that in this Real World example, the Krispy Kreme lawsuit alleges not only that financial statements have been misstated, but that other information in the annual report is misleading. This suit may or may not have merit, but it illustrates the fact that management can mislead investors. To conduct stock sales ethically, management should fully and honestly disclose relevant information to investors.

The lawsuit against Krispy Kreme also illustrates that investors depend on data over and above the numbers in financial statements. Certainly, the financial statements should be accurate and complete. But in addition, all footnote disclosures and other disclosures in the annual report should be complete and honest. Likewise, when borrowing funds from a bank or through bonds payable, management should fully disclose any relevant information to creditors. Management should be completely honest in the financial statements presented, footnote disclosures, and any related disclosures. Management should not try to mislead creditors about the financial status of the company or its ability to repay any borrowing.

INTERNAL REPORTING ETHICAL ISSUES

To manage ongoing operations, management must review many reports. In addition, proper management of operations requires that reports be disseminated

[6]Press release of July 12, 2004, by Much, Shelist, Freed, Denenberg, Ament, & Rubenstein, P.C. Carol V. Gilden, Esq.

to lower level managers. These reports to lower level managers are usually used for two purposes. First, the reports are feedback to lower level managers who monitor and control the processes in which they are engaged. Second, these reports are used by upper management to evaluate and reward the performance of lower level managers.

Top management has an ethical obligation to use financial and other reports to encourage beneficial and ethical behavior. Perhaps it is easier to understand this ethical obligation by looking at how the use of these reports can encourage unethical behavior. There is an old saying: "What gets measured gets done." So, if top management uses a report such as a division income statement to evaluate and reward division managers, then division managers are motivated to increase profit in their division. A problem may arise when top management places too much emphasis on division profit and does not measure and reward other facets of performance. A heavy emphasis on profitability can lead to unethical behavior such as manipulating numbers and transactions in order to show a higher profit. The manner in which top management uses interim reports can set either a proper ethical tone or an improper one.

To set a proper ethical tone, top managements should measure several factors of managerial performance without over-emphasizing profitability or cost cutting. Many firms have adopted or are considering a balanced scorecard approach to internal reporting. A balanced scorecard measures several factors balanced among measures focused on four areas: financial, customer, internal processes, and learning and growth. When a firm uses several measures and includes nonfinancial measures, there is less pressure on lower level managers to focus only on the financial numbers. Such an environment is less likely to encourage unethical behavior.

CORPORATE GOVERNANCE IN ADMINISTRATIVE PROCESSES AND REPORTING (STUDY OBJECTIVE 8)

The four primary functions of the corporate governance process—management oversight, internal controls and compliance, financial stewardship, and ethical conduct—were introduced in Chapter 5. Each of these functions is applicable to the administrative and reporting processes, as these processes must include a proper corporate governance structure in order to properly deter instances of fraud, theft, and misuse or manipulation of administrative resources and reports.

The systems, processes, and internal controls described in this chapter are part of a corporate governance structure. When management designs and implements administrative processes, it assigns responsibility for executing the related capital, investment, and general ledger functions to various employees. It must be mindful of the risks of stolen or misused capital, alteration of documents or reports, and other frauds in this process. Accordingly, it must also implement and monitor internal controls to minimize these risks. As management considers these assignments and subsequently monitors the underlying processes and controls, it is carrying out its corporate governance functions of proper management oversight and internal controls and compliance.

When management has designed, implemented, and continually manages processes and internal controls, it is helping to insure proper stewardship of the company's assets. Corporate governance requires proper financial stewardship, and since financing and investing transactions that are included in the administrative processes are concerned with proper use of cash—the asset on a company's balance sheet that is most susceptible to theft—financial stewardship is especially important.

One method of exercising corporate governance over administrative processes and financial reporting is through the company's budgeting process. If management is involved in the establishment and monitoring of measurable goals, it can be confident that it is addressing its financial stewardship obligation. Budget information can be monitored to help managers identify problem areas, as well as to establish responsibility for various functions and evaluate employee performance.

Finally, good corporate governance depends upon the ethical conduct of management. When management sets an appropriate tone at the top by consistently demonstrating and encouraging ethical conduct, it is more likely that a stronger system of corporate governance will result. Improved effectiveness and efficiency and reduced risks of fraud tend to accompany workplace environments marked by effective corporate governance.

SUMMARY OF STUDY OBJECTIVES

An overview of administrative processes. There are three types of administrative processes: source of capital processes, investment processes, and general ledger processes. Source of capital and investment processes are nonroutine, low-transaction-volume processes that occur only as needed. The general ledger processes record data from all other business processes into the general ledger, and involve monthly closing and reporting.

Source of capital processes. Organizations undertake processes to raise capital only when necessary. These processes require specific approval by upper management, a determination of the type of capital source, executing the issuance of debt or equity, collecting the proceeds, and properly accounting for these processes.

Investment processes. Organizations undertake investment processes when there are excess funds that are not immediately needed in operations. Upper management must determine when to invest excess funds, decide whether to invest in marketable securities or treasury stock, execute the investment, and properly account for the investment processes.

Risks and controls in capital and investment processes. Raising capital is specifically authorized by upper management and closely supervised by management. In addition, employees do not usually handle cash or assets in these processes. Therefore, the most important controls are the proper management authorization and supervision of capital and investment processes.

General ledger processes. General ledger processes include recording all financial transactions in the appropriate ledger and journal, posting to the general ledger, and period-end processes such as adjusting entries and closing entries. In manual systems, the general ledger processes involve special journals, subsidiary ledgers, a general journal, and a general ledger. In IT systems for general ledger processes, there may be few or no paper documents or records. Accounting software modules accomplish functions similar to special journals and subsidiary ledgers. The posting to the general ledger may occur automatically in more complex IT systems.

Risks and controls in general ledger processes. Two of the more important internal controls in the general ledger processes are the authorization to record transactions and segregation of duties. In manual systems, the authorization is through a journal voucher and the segregation is accomplished by preventing general ledger employees from authorizing journal vouchers, maintaining custody of assets, and recording special journals or subsidiary ledgers. In IT systems, the authorization of recording transactions may be pushed to lower level employees or even trading partners. Adequate documents and records, security, and independent checks are also internal controls necessary in the general ledger.

Reporting as an output of the general ledger processes. Both external and internal reports are prepared from general ledger information. The external reports are usually general purpose financial statements. Internal reports are numerous and varied. The nature of an internal report can vary with the type of organization, the function managed, and the time horizon.

Ethical issues related to administrative processes and reporting. Unethical or fraudulent behavior in administrative processes is more likely to be undertaken by upper level mangers than by employees. In capital and investment processes, full and complete disclosure is a very important ethical obligation. Managers should also use internal reports in a manner that encourages ethical behavior.

Corporate governance in administrative processes and reporting. The administrative processes described in this chapter are part of the management oversight of corporate governance. The internal controls and ethical tone and procedures within the administrative and reporting processes are also part of the corporate governance structure. Setting and monitoring financial goals, and establishing and maintaining reliable accounting journals and ledgers so that performance can be properly reported, are important to effective corporate governance. In addition, internal controls and ethical practices within the administrative processes help ensure proper financial stewardship of a company's administrative resources.

KEY TERMS

Administrative processes
Capital
Capital processes
Investment processes
Special journal
Subsidiary ledger
Underwriter

END OF CHAPTER MATERIAL

CONCEPT CHECK

1. Which of the following is not part of an administrative process?
   a. The sale of stock
   b. The sale of bonds

c. The write-off of bad debts

d. The purchase of marketable securities

2. Which of the following statements is not true regarding source of capital transactions?

   a. These processes should not be initiated unless there is specific authorization by management at a top level.

   b. Source of capital processes will result in potential dividend or interest payments.

   c. Retirement of debt is a source of capital process.

   d. The fact that these transactions and processes cannot occur without oversight by top management means other controls are not necessary.

3. The officer within a corporation that usually has oversight responsibility for investment processes is the

   a. controller.

   b. treasurer.

   c. chief executive officer (CEO).

   d. chief accounting officer (CAO).

4. Which of the following statements is not true regarding internal controls of capital and investment processes?

   a. Internal controls aimed at preventing and detecting employee fraud in capital and investment processes are not as effective.

   b. Top management fraud, rather than employee fraud, is more likely to occur.

   c. Any fraud is likely to involve manipulating capital and investment processes.

   d. Because of top management oversight, the auditor need not review these processes.

5. Which of the following statements is true?

   a. Routine transactions are recorded in the general journal.

   b. Nonroutine transactions are entered in the general journal.

   c. Nonroutine transactions are recorded in a subsidiary ledger.

   d. Nonroutine transactions are recorded in a special journal.

6. Regarding subsidiary ledgers and general ledger control accounts, which of the following is not true?

   a. Total balances in a subsidiary ledger should always equal the balance in the corresponding general ledger account.

   b. The general ledger maintains details of subaccounts.

   c. Control is enhanced by separating the subsidiary ledger from the general ledger.

   d. Reconciling a subsidiary ledger to the general ledger can help to detect errors or fraud.

7. Which of the following statements regarding the authorization of general ledger posting is not true?

   a. Posting to the general ledger always requires specific authorization.

   b. User IDs and passwords can serve as authorization to post transactions to the general ledger.

c. A journal voucher serves as authorization for manual systems.

d. As IT systems become more automated, the authorization of general ledger posting is moved to lower levels of employees.

8. In a manual system with proper segregation of duties, an employee in the general ledger department should only
   a. authorize posting to the general ledger.
   b. post transactions to the general ledger.
   c. reconcile the subsidiary ledger to the general ledger.
   d. post transactions to the subsidiary ledger.
9. Which of the following statements about reporting is true?
   a. External users need detailed, rather than summarized, information.
   b. All reports, internal and external, are derived only from general ledger data.
   c. All organizations need similar internal reports.
   d. Internal reports are tailored to the specific needs of each management level and function.
10. Which of the following is not an area of measure in a balanced scorecard?
    a. Vendor
    b. Customer
    c. Financial
    d. Learning and growth

DISCUSSION QUESTIONS

11. (SO 1) What characteristics of administrative processes are different from the characteristics of revenue, expenditures, or conversion processes?
12. (SO 1) How do other processes (revenue, expenditures, conversion) affect the general ledger?
13. (SO 2) How would you describe capital?
14. (SO 2) Describe the nature of the authorization of source of capital processes.
15. (SO 2) How does the specific authorization and management oversight of source of capital processes affect internal controls?
16. (SO 3) Describe when an organization would have a need to undertake investment processes.
17. (SO 3) Why is the monitoring of funds flow an important underlying part of investment processes?
18. (SO 3) How are IT systems potentially useful in monitoring funds flow?
19. (SO 4) Explain how cash resulting from source of capital processes may be handled differently than cash in revenue processes.
20. (SO 4) What advantages would motivate management to conduct fraud related to source of capital processes?

21. (SO 4) Why are internal controls less effective in capital and investment processes?
22. (SO 5) How is a special journal different from a general journal?
23. (SO 5) How is a subsidiary ledger different from a general ledger?
24. (SO 5) In what way are subsidiary ledgers and special journals replicated in accounting software?
25. (SO 6) Within accounting software systems, what is the purpose of limiting the number of employees authorized to post to the general ledger?
26. (SO 6) In a complex IT system, how may a customer actually "authorize" a sale?
27. (SO 6) To properly segregate duties, what are the three functions that general ledger employees should not do?
28. (SO 6) In an IT accounting system, which IT controls ensure the security of the general ledger?
29. (SO 7) Describe the nature of reports for external users.
30. (SO 7) Does the general ledger provide all information necessary for internal reports?
31. (SO 7) How would operational internal reports differ from financial internal reports?
32. (SO 7) How does time horizon affect the type of information in internal reports?
33. (SO 8) Why are managers, rather than employees, more likely to engage in unethical behavior in capital and investment processes?
34. (SO 8) How do processes with large volumes of transactions make fraudulent behavior easier?
35. (SO 8) Explain the importance of full disclosure in source of capital processes.

BRIEF EXERCISES

36. (SO 2) Describe the steps in source of capital processes and explain how top management is involved.
37. (SO 3) Describe the steps in investment processes and explain how top management is involved.
38. (SO 4) Explain the internal control environment of source of capital and investment processes.
39. (SO 5) Describe the steps in a manual accounting cycle.
40. (SO 6) Describe why it is true that there may be two authorizations related to revenue, expenditures, and conversion processes before they are posted to the general ledger.
41. (SO 7) For each report shown, indicate in the appropriate column whether the report is likely to be for internal or external users (some reports may be both), and whether data would come exclusively from the general ledger.

Report Name	Internal or External	Exclusively G/L Data?
Income statement		
Aged accounts receivable		
Inventory stock status		
Open purchase orders		
Machine down-time		
Cash flow statement		
Production units produced		

PROBLEMS

42. (SO 1, 2) Compare source of capital processes with sales processes in terms of
    a. the frequency of transactions;
    b. the volume of transactions;
    c. the magnitude in dollars of a single transaction; and
    d. the manner of authorization.
43. (SO 1, 3) Compare investment processes with sales processes in terms of
    a. the frequency of transactions;
    b. the volume of transactions;
    c. the magnitude in dollars of a single transaction; and
    d. the manner of authorization.
44. (SO 5) Exhibit 12-9 shows a screen capture from Dynamics GP® accounting software. The following modules in Dynamics GP® are shown:
    - Financial
    - Sales
    - Purchasing
    - Inventory
    - Payroll
    - Manufacturing
    - Fixed Assets
45. For each of the following transactions listed, explain which module you would choose and why:
    a. Entering an invoice received from a supplier
    b. Entering the receiving of materials at the shipping dock
    c. Entering a check received in payment of an account receivable
    d. Posting a batch of sales invoices to the general ledger
    e. Entering hours worked by employees
    f. Printing checks for suppliers

CASE

46. (SO 6) Ebbicott Industries is a manufacturer of stereo speaker systems. The company prepares special journals and subsidiary ledgers for its revenue, expenditures, payroll, and conversion processes. For administrative processes, however, journal vouchers are created for the related general ledger entries. Cam Emilio is the accounting clerk who has responsibility for preparing journal vouchers.

    Journal vouchers are prepared on preprinted forms; however, these forms are not prenumbered. Cam records a sequential journal voucher number on each form that is prepared. This procedure is in place because of the large number of journal vouchers that are typically voided each period at Ebbicott Industries. Because of the nonrouting nature of the underlying processes, it is not unusual for a journal entry to be revised once or twice before it is actually recorded.

    Journal vouchers are posted to the general ledger on a biweekly basis. Once a journal voucher has been posted, Cam records it in a voucher log. This log is simply a chronological listing of all journal vouchers written that allows Cam to account for the numerical sequence of vouchers.

    On a bimonthly basis, Cam reconciles the subsidiary accounts to their control accounts in the general ledger and verifies that the general ledger is in balance.

Required:

Describe the internal control strengths and weaknesses of Ebbicott's general ledger accounting processes. For any weaknesses, suggest an improvement.

CONTINUING CASE: SPATELLI'S PIZZERIA

Reread the continuing case on Spatelli's Pizzeria at the end of Chapter 1. Consider any issues related to Spatelli's administrative and general ledger processes, and then answer the following questions:

a. Refer to the process map showing accounting cycle processes in Exhibit 12-5. Which typical special journals and subsidiary ledgers would be needed at Spatelli's? Which ones would not be needed and why?
b. How do the daily close procedures and summarizations that are the responsibility of Spatelli's restaurant managers fit into the company's overall accounting cycle process? Use information from this chapter to describe Spatelli's general ledger processes.

SOLUTIONS TO CONCEPT CHECK

1. (SO 1) The following is not part of an administrative process: **c. The write-off of bad debts**. The write-off of bad debts occurs within revenue processes.
2. (SO 2) The following statement is not true regarding source of capital transactions: **d. The fact that these transactions and processes cannot occur without oversight by top management means other controls are not necessary**.

Management oversight is an important internal control, but it does not negate the need for other controls.

3. (SO 3) The officer within a corporation that usually has oversight responsibility for investment processes is the **b. treasurer**. The treasurer is normally the officer with oversight and decision authority for investment processes.
4. (SO 4) The following statement is not true regarding internal controls of capital and investment processes: **b. Because of top management oversight, the auditor need not review these processes**. Even with top management oversight, it is still important for auditors to review these transactions.
5. (SO 5) The following statement is true: **b. Nonroutine transactions are entered in the general journal**. Routine transactions are initially posted to special journals and subsidiary ledgers. Nonroutine transactions are initially recorded in the general journal.
6. (SO 5) Regarding subsidiary ledgers and general ledger control accounts, the following is not true: **b. The general ledger maintains details of subaccounts**. Subsidiary ledgers maintain details of accounts, such as accounts for each customer in the accounts receivable subsidiary ledger.
7. (SO 6) The following statement regarding the authorization of general ledger posting is not true: **a. Posting to the general ledger always requires specific authorization**. Especially in IT systems, general authorization is given to certain employees to post to the general ledger. The employees with this general authorization are given this authority through user ID and password.
8. (SO 6) In a manual system with proper segregation of duties, an employee in the general ledger department should only **b. post transactions to the general ledger**. These employees should never authorize general ledger posting, post to subsidiary ledgers, or reconcile subsidiary ledgers to general ledger accounts.
9. (SO 7) The following statement about reporting is true: **d. Internal reports are tailored to the specific needs of each management level and function**. Internal reports do vary greatly and are tailored specifically to the management level and function.
10. (SO 8) **a. Vendor**. is not an area of measure in a balanced scorecard. The four areas of measure in a balanced scorecard are financial, customer, internal processes, and learning and growth.

CHAPTER 13

Data and Databases

STUDY OBJECTIVES

This chapter will help you gain an understanding of the following concepts:

1. The need for data collection and storage
2. Methods of storing data and the interrelationship between storage and processing
3. The differences between batch processing and real-time processing
4. The importance of databases and the historical progression from flat-file databases to relational databases
5. The need for normalization of data in a relational database
6. Data warehouse and the use of a data warehouse to analyze data
7. The use of OLAP and data mining as analysis tools
8. Distributed databases and advantages of the use of distributed data
9. Controls for data and databases
10. Ethical issues related to data collection and storage, and their use in IT systems

THE REAL WORLD

Suprijono Suharjoto/ iStockphoto

Think about the volume of sales transactions that occur on the websites of large Internet retailers such as L.L. Bean, Lands' End, and J.Crew. These companies each process an average of approximately 120,000 transactions each day on their websites. For each of these transactions, important data must be collected about the customer, location, payment, and the items sold.

Even more overwhelming is the volume of sales transactions that are processed by Wal-Mart on any given day. In addition to its web-based sales, consider Wal-Mart's thousands of retail centers with several check-out lines at each location and long hours of operation. Think about the number of accountants and computers that might be required to manage all of the related records. It is no wonder that Wal-Mart has the largest database of any business organization in the world. In fact, its computer database is one of the largest in existence, second only to the database system at the U.S. Pentagon.[1]

THE NEED FOR DATA COLLECTION AND STORAGE (STUDY OBJECTIVE 1)

Each day that a business operates, it may have hundreds or thousands of transactions with customers and vendors. Every one of these transactions generates data that must be processed to fill customer orders and purchase inventory and supplies. **Data** are the set of facts collected from transactions, whereas **information** is the interpretation of data that have been processed. For example, to process a sale to a customer, the business must collect many data items from the customer such as name, address, credit card number, items ordered, and shipping address. These data collected from all transactions that occur represent a large amount of data. This may be more obvious when you think of the volume of sales that occur at large companies such as L.L. Bean, Lands' End, J.Crew, and Wal-Mart, as presented in The Real World example above. Similarly, each purchase of inventory or supplies involves collecting and processing a large amount of data. It is necessary to collect and process these data so that they can be translated into information that is useful to the business. Previous chapters described the accounting information systems that capture and process this large volume of data. However, those chapters did not describe the detail regarding the storage, retrieval, and use of these data.

The data collected in any transaction must be stored for many reasons. First, to complete a transaction such as a sale, detailed data must be collected and stored. For example, the warehouse employees would not know which items to pull from warehouse shelves and ship to customers if they could not see a record of items ordered. Second, the data must be stored for future transactions or followup. For example, if you create an account on the J.Crew website to order clothes, you want your customer information to be stored so that you can place your next order without reentering your name, address, and other basic information. Third, the data collected from a transaction must be incorporated into the accounting system so that regular financial statements can be prepared. Without the underlying data for each transaction, it would be impossible for the system to provide information about assets, liabilities, revenues, and expenses for any accounting period. Fourth, management needs to examine and analyze

[1]John Huey, "Builders & Titans": www.time.com/time/time100/builder/profile/walton.html

data from transactions to operate the organization in an efficient and effective manner. While there may be other reasons, this short list summarizes the main reasons to store transaction data:

1. To complete transactions from beginning to end. For a sale, this may involve taking the order, pulling items from the warehouse, shipping items, billing the customer, collecting the cash, and crediting the customer account for payment.
2. To follow up with customers or vendors and to expedite future transactions. For example, if the company stores name, address, and other details about a customer, it need not reenter that data when the customer places future orders.
3. To create accounting reports and financial statements.
4. To provide feedback to management so they can effectively and efficiently manage.

This chapter describes the typical storage and processing techniques used in organizations to manage the mountain of data resulting from their transactions. The topics described in this chapter include the following:

1. The storage media types for data: sequential and random access
2. Methods of processing data: batch and real time
3. Databases and relational databases
4. Data warehouses, data mining, and OLAP
5. Distributed data processing and distributed databases

After studying this chapter, you should have an understanding of how data are processed and stored, how they are used for processing and inquiries, and what considerations pertain to physical location of the processing and storage of data. There are many details and concepts in each of these areas, and this chapter provides only an overview of each of these. However, it should give you, an accountant, the general understanding you need to use, audit, and assist in the design of IT systems. In addition, ethical concerns related to data and the controls over data are discussed in this chapter.

STORING AND ACCESSING DATA (STUDY OBJECTIVE 2)

The storage of data and the way in which data are used are strongly interrelated. To understand this concept, it may be helpful to think of how you store and use things in your personal life. Things that you need to find and use frequently, you put in places where you can easily grab them and go. For example, you frequently need your car keys, and you usually don't have time to search for them. So, you probably have a habit of keeping your keys in a handy spot at home to make them easy to get and use. In other words, the need to quickly access and use your keys has led you to store them in a fashion that makes it easy to find them and use them. On the other hand, you have items that you need less frequently. For example, you may have kept an accounting book from a previous class in case you ever needed it for reference. Since you probably will not refer to it often, your book can be put in a less accessible location, such as on a closet shelf. As you know, there is a limit to how much you can store in easy-to-access locations. Therefore, some items, such as your old accounting book, have to be put in less accessible places.

This personal-life example leads us to an important concept about storing and using data. Data that will be needed quickly and frequently must be stored in a manner that allows frequent and quick access. The reverse of this is true also. Data that are stored in a manner that allows frequent and quick access are easy to access and use. By contrast, data that are needed less frequently or less quickly can be stored in a manner that does not allow frequent or quick access. This general principle of the relationship between intended data usage and method of storage is key to the underlying the concepts within this chapter.

DATA STORAGE TERMINOLOGY

The terminology used in data storage must first be mastered for you to properly understand the storage and usage of data in an IT system. The typical hierarchy of data is character, field, record, file, and database. A **character** is a single letter, number, or symbol. A **field** is a set of characters that fill a space reserved for a particular kind of data. For example, last name, address, and hire date are all fields within a payroll data set. A field can be thought of as a column of data in a table. A set of related fields make a record. A **record** is the entire set of fields for a specific entity. For example, each employee must have a record in the payroll system. Each employee record includes fields such as last name, address, and hire date. The entire set of related records is a **file**. Exhibit 13-1 shows the concepts of field, record, and file.

An entire set of files is a **database**. For example, the payroll file, the accounts receivable file, the inventory file, and all other files in the IT system make up the database.

Field →

EmpID	Last Name	First Name	Title	Hire Date	Address	City	State	Zip Code
101	Labbe	John	Sales Representative	02/28/99	9065 Arlington Road	Cincinnati	OH	45238
102	Grissom	Andrew	Accountant	03/05/98	312 Production Dr	Dayton	OH	45239
103	Laver	Mitchell	Finance Manager	04/08/01	1062 Whirlway Dr	Aurora	IN	45226
104	Prosser	Margaret	Accountant Staff 1	02/21/97	919 New Haven Road	Cincinnati	OH	45248
105	Buckhalter	Nancy	Maintenance Specialist	09/07/98	8595 Stonebridge Dr	Florence	KY	41042–3563
106	Singh	Ravi	Accountant Staff 2	10/27/01	677 Ridge Ave	Cincinnati	OH	45241
107	Klinger	Robert	Accountant Staff 2	09/30/01	1605 Deercroft Court	Harrison	OH	45030–2009
108	Courdell	Anne	HR Coordinator	07/21/02	8425 North Bend Rd	Cincinnati	OH	45242–3706
109	Sampson	Jessica	Sales Representative	09/06/99	617 Sheppherd Dr	Villa Hills	KY	41017

Record → (row 103)

File (all rows)

Exhibit 13-1
Data Hierarchy

DATA STORAGE MEDIA

The media on which data are stored has evolved and improved over the years, in the same way that the speed and power of computers have evolved and improved. In the early days of mainframe computers, data were stored on magnetic tape. **Magnetic tape** is a storage medium that allows only a sequential access type of storage. **Sequential access** means that data are stored in sequential or chronological order. This sequential storage can be thought of in the same way that music is stored on cassette tapes in a particular order. If music is on cassette tape, it must be played in the order it was recorded. Using tape makes it more difficult to listen to songs in any order other than the sequence on the tape. Likewise, data on magnetic tape stores data in sequential order, and the data must be read in that sequence. To read record 10, the system must first read records 1 through 9. This is a very limiting type of storage because it is more difficult and time consuming to access, read, or modify any specific record. The entire tape must be read in sequence to find that single record.

A magnetic tape of data storage media would not work well in modern IT systems. As described in the previous section of this chapter, the process and storage methods are interrelated. Storing records in sequential order prevents the quick and easy access of a single record. Within organizations today, much of the data must be stored in a way that allows a single record to be accessed quickly. For example, to process a customer order, it is important to access that particular customer record without necessarily accessing all customer records. When a single record must be easily and quickly accessed from a file, random access rather than sequential access is needed. **Random access** means that any data item on the storage media can be directly accessed without reading in sequence. Therefore, random access is often referred to as direct access. Random, or direct, access is similar to the manner in which music is stored on a CD. While there appears to be some order in which songs are stored, they can in fact be played in any order. If you choose to play only one song from a CD, your CD player can quickly find, access, and play that song. Likewise, random access media will allow a single data item to be accessed or modified without reading the data in sequence. Disk storage is an example of random access media. The large majority of IT systems use disk storage. This direct access storage is much more flexible because data can be accessed in sequence or directly. Much as you can choose to play songs on a CD in order or in any way you choose, data on disk can be accessed in sequence or in any other order.

DATA PROCESSING TECHNIQUES (STUDY OBJECTIVE 3)

In transaction processing systems, transactions are processed either in batches or one at a time. **Batch processing** occurs when similar transactions are grouped into a batch and that batch is processed as a group. A familiar example of batch processing is processing payroll checks. All time cards for the pay period are collected, and the resulting pay checks are processed and printed in a group, or batch. Accounts payable and accounts receivable transactions are often processed in batches. For example, payments to vendors are often processed in batches. The alternative to batch processing is real-time processing. **Real-time processing** occurs when transactions are processed as soon as they are entered.

This processing is interactive because the transaction is processed when it is entered.

When determining whether batch or real-time processing is appropriate, system professionals must consider response time, efficiency, complexity, control, and storage media. Batch systems have slow response times because the transactions are not processed until the whole group is ready to be processed. Real-time systems have fast response times because transactions are processed as entered. Batch processing is more efficient for a large volume of similar transactions. This is true for several reasons. First, persons who focus on gathering and processing like transactions become efficient at handling those transactions. That is, they become more specialized. There are also efficiencies of scale. Much as an assembly line is efficient, moving many like transactions through a system at the same time is efficient in terms of optimizing the use of personnel and computer resources. Real-time processing is less efficient for large volumes of transactions, since there is duplication of effort involved in processing all transactions individually. Batch systems are much simpler than real-time systems. They are simpler because the hardware, the processes, and the audit trail are less complex. Batch systems have a very definable and obvious audit trail, since there are well-defined begin and end dates and a defined set of transactions between those dates. Payroll is, again, a good example of this. If payroll is processed every two weeks, then there is a well-defined beginning date, ending date, and transaction group that belong in this batch.

Real-time systems are more complex because of the interactive nature of processing. If transactions are processed as they occur, it is more difficult to maintain an audit trail of changes to files. In addition, control is easier to maintain in batch systems. Since there are well-defined dates and transaction sets, control totals can be used to ensure accuracy and completeness. For example, the total number of hours on all time cards can be manually added, and this total can be compared with the computer-processed hours to ensure that the batch was accurately and completely entered and processed. Within real-time systems, control totals are difficult to use because there are no groups of transactions for which totals can be derived. Finally, if real-time processing is to occur, records must be stored on random access media. To process a single record at a time, it is necessary to access that single record. Batch processing systems can use either sequential or random access storage media. Exhibit 13-2 summarizes the characteristics of batch and real-time processing.

Characteristic	Batch Processing	Real Time Processing
Response Time	Slow	Rapid
Efficiency	Very efficient for large volumes of transactions	Less efficient for large volumes of transactions
Complexity	Simple	Complex
Control	Easier to control and to maintain an audit trail	More difficult to control and to maintain an audit trail
Storage	Data can be stored sequentially	Data must be random access

Exhibit 13-2
Comparison of Batch and Real-Time Processing

Since batch and real-time processing are opposite in each characteristic, as shown in Exhibit 13-2, system designers must weigh the trade-offs in deciding which is more appropriate. For example, if rapid response time is critical, system designers will choose real-time processing, even though it may mean less processing efficiency, more complexity, and more difficult control. Sales order systems are often designed as real-time processing systems to provide better customer service because the customer may need a rapid response. On the other hand, there is no immediate need for rapid response in a payroll system, since workers expect to wait until the end of the pay period to receive their paychecks. Therefore, batch processing is often used in payroll.

DATABASES (STUDY OBJECTIVE 4)

A **database** is a collection of data stored on the computer in a form that allows the data to be easily accessed, retrieved, manipulated, and stored. The term "database" usually implies a shared database within the organization. Rather than each computer application having its own file, a database implies a single set of data that is shared by each application that uses the data. Exhibit 13-3 illustrates this data sharing concept.

The top half of the exhibit shows the traditional file-oriented approach to data storage. Each application owns the data file that it uses, and there is no sharing of data. This is true even though inventory and purchasing do in fact use the same type of data such as inventory part numbers and descriptions. This lack of sharing leads to data redundancy. **Data redundancy** occurs when the same data are stored in more than one file. In this case, inventory part numbers and descriptions may exist in all three files. Data redundancy causes concurrency problems. **Concurrency** means that all of the multiple instances of the same data are exactly alike. If the same records are stored in many different locations, it is difficult to make sure that they all are updated at the same time (concurrently). For example, changing the address of a customer may mean changing it in three different places. In such cases of data redundancy, errors in updating the data are much more likely to occur. Thus, the data are more likely to have errors. Due to this data redundancy, adding records, deleting records, and editing or changing records are more likely to cause errors in the data.

The lower half of Exhibit 13-3 illustrates a shared database approach. All data are stored once in a shared database, and those data are available to all applications that use the data. Notice that this eliminates data redundancy and concurrency problems. Since the data are stored only once, any and all changes to a record are immediately available to those who share the data. Adding records, deleting records, and editing records are less likely to cause erroneous data when those data are stored only once.

The DBMS symbol in Exhibit 13-3 represents the database management system. The **database management system (DBMS)** is software that manages the database and controls the access and use of data by individual users and applications. The DBMS determines which parts of the database can be read or modified by individuals or processes. Before beginning the technical discussion of databases, it is useful to define database terms and to examine a brief history of databases. This history is useful in understanding the current environment and database use in organizations.

Exhibit 13-3
Traditional File-Oriented Approach and the Database Approach

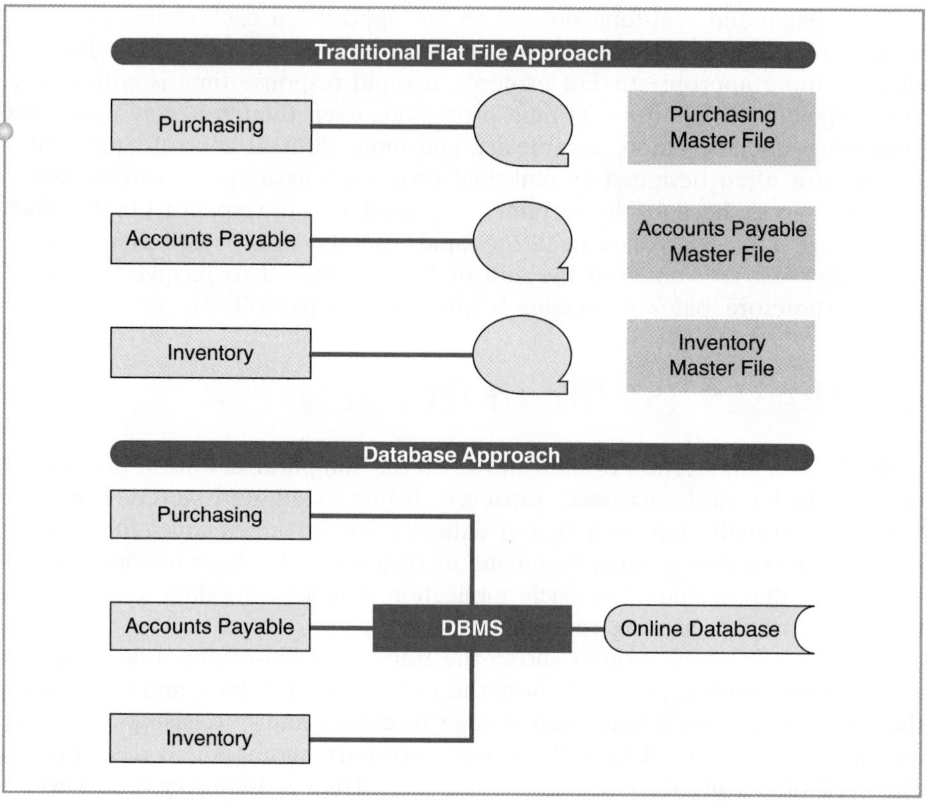

Data reveal relationships between records. These relationships can be thought of as parent–child relationships. One parent can be related to one or more children. The types of relationships in data are one-to-one, one-to-many, and many-to-many. **One-to-one relationships** are those where one entity in the data is related to only one other entity. An example of one-to-one would be employees and Social Security numbers. Each employee has only one Social Security number, and each Social Security number belongs to only one person. **One-to-many relationships** are those where one entity in the data is related to more than one other entity. Each individual employee can have several time cards in a given year. Notice, however, that this one-to-many relationship is in one direction only. That is, while an employee is related to several time cards, each time card belongs to only one employee. Most data in accounting transactions exhibit one-to-many relationships. Examples are a vendor to many invoices, a customer to many orders, a customer to many payments, and an order to many items in the order. **Many-to-many relationships** are those in which one entity is related to many other entities, and the reverse is also true. An example of a many-to-many relationship is vendors to items and items to vendors. That is, a single vendor can supply several items, and any single item can be supplied by many vendors.

THE HISTORY OF DATABASES

Flat File Database Model

The earliest databases, from the period of the 1950s and 1960s, are called **flat file databases**. The term "flat file" comes from the idea that data are stored in

EmpID	Last Name	First Name	Title	Hire Date	Address	City	State	Zip Code
101	Labbe	John	Sales Representative	02/28/99	9065 Arlington Road	Cincinnati	OH	45238
102	Grissom	Andrew	Accountant	03/05/98	312 Production Dr	Dayton	OH	45239
103	Laver	Mitchell	Finance Manager	04/08/01	1062 Whirlway Dr	Aurora	IN	45226
104	Prosser	Margaret	Accountant Staff 1	02/21/97	919 New Haven Road	Cincinnati	OH	45248
105	Buckhalter	Nancy	Maintenance Specialist	09/07/98	8595 Stonebridge Dr	Florence	KY	41042-3563
106	Singh	Ravi	Accountant Staff 2	10/27/01	677 Ridge Ave	Cincinnati	OH	45241
107	Klinger	Robert	Accountant Staff 2	09/30/01	1605 Deercroft Court	Harrison	OH	45030-2009
108	Courdell	Anne	HR Coordinator	07/21/02	8425 North Bend Rd	Cincinnati	OH	45242-3706
109	Sampson	Jessica	Sales Representative	09/06/99	617 Sheppherd Dr	Villa Hills	KY	41017

Exhibit 13-4
Database Table

two-dimensional tables with rows and columns. In a flat file table, each row is a record and each column is a characteristic related to the records. For example, each employee has the characteristic of a certain hire date. In database terminology, columns are called attributes. Therefore, **attributes** are characteristics of a related record. Exhibit 13-4 illustrates such a table.

Flat file records are stored in text format in sequential order, and all processing must occur sequentially. No relationships are defined between records. These systems must use batch processing only, and batches must be processed in sequence. The system makes the processing of large volumes of similar transactions very efficient. However, it does not allow a single record to be quickly and easily retrieved or stored. Therefore, interactive, real-time processing is not possible with sequential, flat file databases.

Each table in a database must meet the following conditions:

1. Items in a column must all be of the same type of data. The column in Exhibit 13-4 titled "LastName" must have only last names from each record.
2. Each column must be uniquely named.
3. Each row must be unique in at least one attribute (one column). If there were no differences in any column, the rows would be identical and one row could be deleted since it is a duplicate of another row.
4. Each cell at the intersection of a row and column must contain only one data item. In this example, each employee can have only one hire date.

The flat file database and each database model described next are based on tables with the four characteristics just listed.

Hierarchical Database Model As computer processing power increased, databases evolved into the hierarchical model. **Hierarchical databases** define relationships between records by an inverted tree structure. These relationships are called parent–child, and they represent one-to-many relationships. Therefore, the hierarchical model of a database could incorporate one-to-one and one-to-many relationships in the data. These relationships are permanently and explicitly defined in the database by data linkages. The data are linked by these explicit relationships in a record linkage structure such as record pointers. A **record pointer** is a column value in the table that points to the next address with the linked attribute. This linkage allows quick retrieval of records in that linkage chain. For example, a payroll database could have linkages from plant

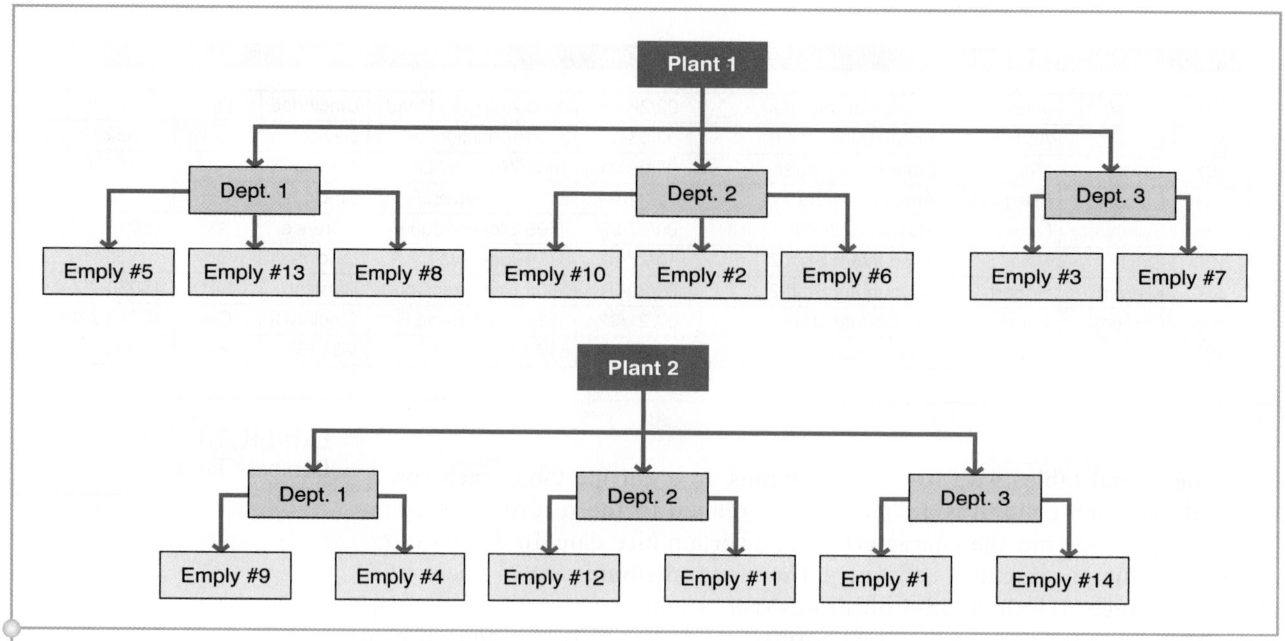

Exhibit 13-5
Linkages in a Hierarchical Database

location to department to employee. Exhibit 13-5 illustrates a hierarchical relationship linkage.

If the desire is to quickly retrieve records for employees in Plant 1, the record access can be quick because of the built-in linkage. However, if we desired to retrieve only records of all employees who work in Department 1, there is no single set of linkages that make the retrieval easy. Each record would be read in sequence to see whether that employee worked in Department 1. Hierarchical databases are efficient in processing large volumes of transactions, but they do not allow for easy retrieval of records except for those within an explicit linkage. This means that hierarchical databases are not flexible enough to allow various kinds of inquiries of the data.

Network Database Model

To slightly improve the recognition of relationships in databases, the network model of databases was developed next. **Network databases** are also built on the inverted tree structure, but they allow more complex relationship linkages by the use of shared branches. This essentially means that there is more than one set of inverted tree branches into the data. However, the network model has not been very popular, and it is rarely used today. Both the hierarchical and network models have many disadvantages. In both models it is impossible to add new data unless all related information is known. A new vendor cannot be added to a database until it is known which items will be purchased from that vendor. In addition, deleting any parent record will also delete all child records.

Relational Database Model

In 1969, a mathematician named E.F. Codd developed a new model of databases to allow the inclusion of more complex data relationships. He termed this model the relational database. A **relational database** stores data in two-dimensional tables that are joined in many ways to represent many different kinds of relationships in the data. Although it took many years for the computing technology to be available to implement his ideas broadly, the relational database structure is the most widely used database structure today. IBM DB2, Oracle Database, and Microsoft Access® are all examples of relational databases.

THE NEED FOR NORMALIZED DATA (STUDY OBJECTIVE 5)

Relational databases consist of several small tables, rather than one large table as in the flat file database. The small tables in a relational database can be joined together in ways that represent relationships among the data.

For example, examine the tables and relationships of a Microsoft Access® database in Exhibit 13-6. Each box is a table, and the field names are listed in each box. The bolded field is the primary key. The **primary key,** the unique identifier for each record in each table, is used to sort, index, and access records from that table. The lines between boxes indicate the relationships between the tables. The relationships indicated in these tables are one to many. For example, one customer (CustomerID), can have many orders listed in the Orders table. Note that the Customers table and the Orders table are linked by CustomerID. In the Orders table, the CustomerID field is a foreign key field. In other words, CustomerID is in a different (foreign) table, but is needed in the Orders table to establish the link between Customers and Orders.

These separate tables and the relationships between the tables are what establish the advantage of a relational database. The advantage is that a relational database has flexibility in retrieving data from queries. The developer of the relational database envisioned an English-like query language that could be used to directly access data from the relational database. The query language that has become the industry standard is **structured query language**, or **SQL**. By using SQL and joining these tables together in certain ways, nearly any query about customer orders can be answered. If a manager wished to know which customers had placed orders that have been shipped, the Customers and Orders tables can be joined to extract the columns (fields) for CustomerID, CompanyName, OrderID, and ShippedDate. The view of this query and the SQL to extract the data are shown in Exhibit 13-7.

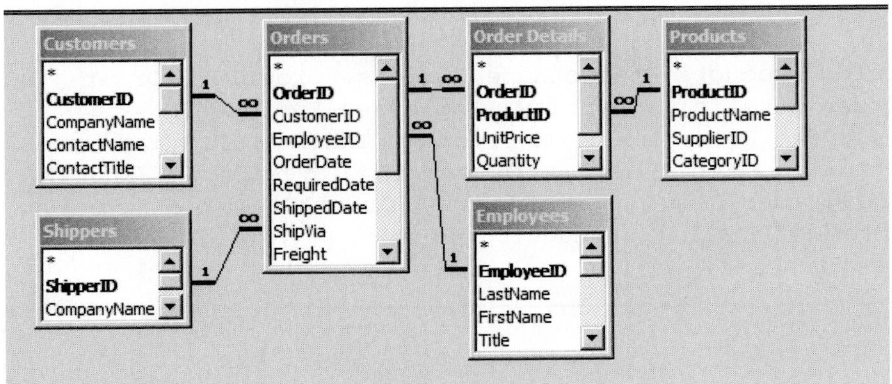

Exhibit 13-6
A Relational Database in Microsoft Access®

Exhibit 13-7
Design View and SQL of a Simple Query

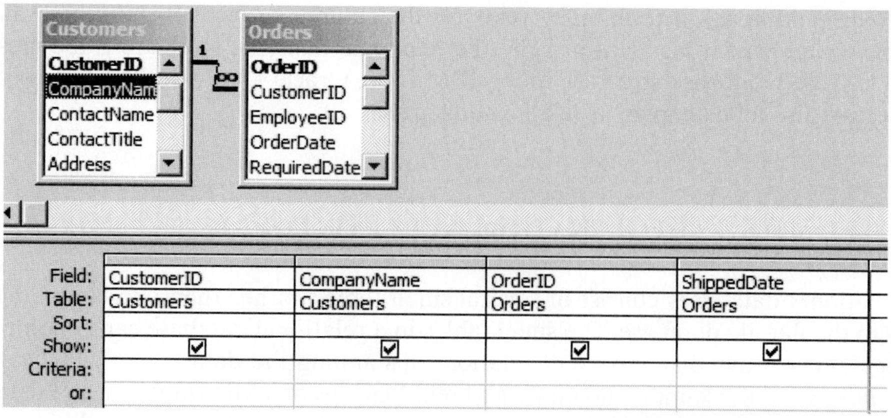

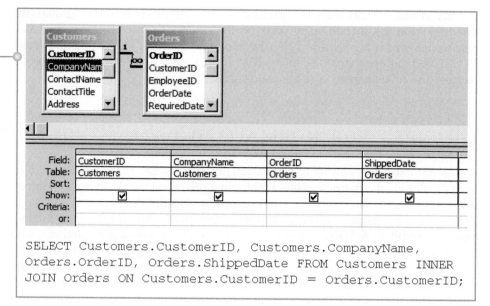

```
SELECT Customers.CustomerID, Customers.CompanyName,
Orders.OrderID, Orders.ShippedDate FROM Customers INNER
JOIN Orders ON Customers.CustomerID = Orders.CustomerID;
```

Notice that the SQL query language is relatively English-like. It identifies which fields are selected from which tables and how the tables are to be joined. The tables are joined by OrderID. That relationship is a one-to-many relationship. Any customer may have more than one order.

A more complex example involves a manager who needs to know which employees have sold product 52371. By using SQL, the manager can join the Orders, Employees, Order Details, and Products tables to retrieve these data. Exhibit 13-8 shows the Access design view of this query.

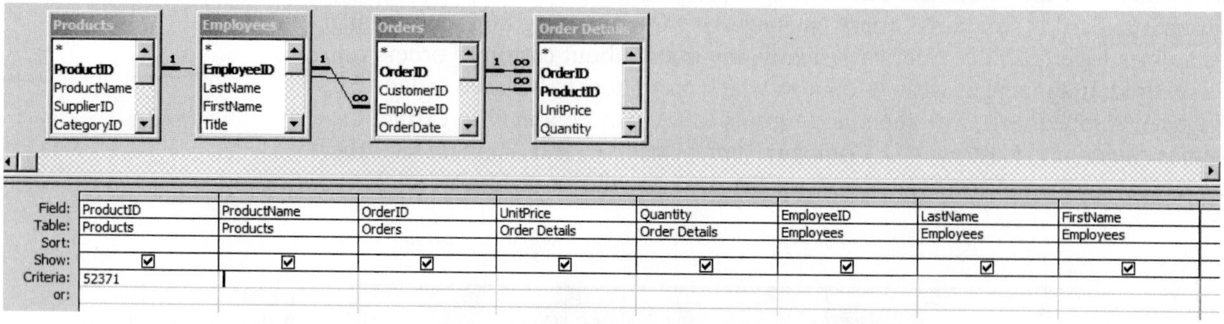


```
SELECT Products.ProductID, Products.ProductName, Orders. OrderID, [Order
Details].UnitPrice, [Order Details]. Quantity, Employees.EmployeeID,
Employees.LastName, Employees.FirstName FROM Products INNER JOIN ((Employees
INNER JOIN Orders ON Employees.EmployeeID = Orders. EmployeeID) INNER JOIN
[Order Details] ON Orders.OrderID = [Order Details].OrderID) ON
Products.ProductID = [Order Details].ProductID WHERE
(((Products.ProductID)=52371));
```

Exhibit 13-8
Design View and SQL of a Complex Query

Notice that this query has a "WHERE" condition. The extracted data are filtered in the sense that the ProductID must be equal to 52371. These queries show the flexibility of the relational database that is constructed with many tables. The relational database is flexible because any number of different queries can be answered by joining tables in various ways. Some examples of queries that could be answered from the tables in Exhibit 13-6 are as follows:

1. Quantity and price of orders by customer
2. Customers who purchased from a specific employee
3. Orders shipped by a specific shipping method
4. Number of products sold between certain dates

There are only a small set of the queries that could not be answered by joining these tables in various ways. The tables are flexible enough to answer an unlimited number of queries. To obtain this flexibility, the tables within a relational database must be designed according to specific rules. The process of converting data into tables that meet the definition of a relational database is called **data normalization**. There are seven rules of data normalization, and these rules are additive. The additive characteristic means that if a table meets the third rule, it has also met rules one and two. Most relational databases are in third normal form, which means they met the first three rules of data normalization. The first three rules of data normalization are as follows:

1. *Eliminate repeating groups.* This rule requires that any related attributes (columns) that would be repeated in several rows must be put in a separate table. An example of the application of this rule can be seen in the tables in Exhibit 13-6. There is an order table and an order details table. If these were not separate tables, basic information about the order, such as customer ID and ship date, would have to be repeated for each item ordered.
2. *Eliminate redundant data.*
3. *Eliminate columns not dependent on the primary key.*

The flexible querying within relational databases is possible only when the tables are constructed to achieve third normal form.

TRADE-OFFS IN DATABASE STORAGE

As discussed in the beginning of this chapter, the method of storage affects the usage of the data. While the relational database is very flexible for queries, it is not the most efficient way to store data that will be used in other ways. The quickest way to access and process records from a database when their intended use is the processing of a large volume of transactions is the hierarchical model. But, the hierarchical model is not flexible for querying. Thus, there is a trade-off of transaction processing efficiency for flexibility. If the major use of the data is for processing transactions and not for answering queries, the hierarchical model is a more efficient storage choice. If the major usage of the data is to answer queries, the relational model is superior.

Obviously, a large number of the data from transactions require both operations: processing transactions and querying. In today's IT environment, most organizations are willing to accept less transaction processing efficiency for better query opportunities. Therefore, most organizations use relational databases. The transaction processing efficiency loss is not a great loss because computing power has tremendously increased as the cost has also decreased.

The relational database has become very widely used in organizations because of this flexibility. Using relational databases and SQL, managers are able to query and extract data from the database on their own. They do not need to make requests to the IT department to design certain reports. This gives managers much more timely and flexible feedback information about operations. This improved access to information can help managers better manage.

USE OF A DATA WAREHOUSE TO ANALYZE DATA (STUDY OBJECTIVE 6)

In many instances, the data that managers need are much broader than that set of data currently used in day-to-day operations. Management often needs data from several fiscal periods from across the whole organization. A data warehouse can serve as this source of broader information for management. A **data warehouse** is an integrated collection of enterprise-wide data that includes five to ten years of nonvolatile data used to support management in decision making and planning. The data warehouse can be better understood if we compare it with the operational database. The **operational database** is the data that are continually updated as transactions are processed. Usually, the operational database includes data for the current fiscal year and supports day-to-day operations and record keeping for the transaction processing systems. Each time a new transaction is completed, parts of the operational data must be updated. For example, recording a sale means that sales, inventory, and receivables balances must be updated. This type of update does not occur in a data warehouse. Exhibit 13-9 shows the data warehouse and operational data layout.

The data are enterprise-wide because the data are pulled from each of the operational databases, and these data are maintained in the data warehouse for many fiscal periods. Ideally, the data warehouse should contain five to ten years of data. The data in the data warehouse are pulled from sales order processing, inventory systems, receivables, and many other transaction processing systems

Exhibit 13-9
The Data Warehouse and Operational Databases

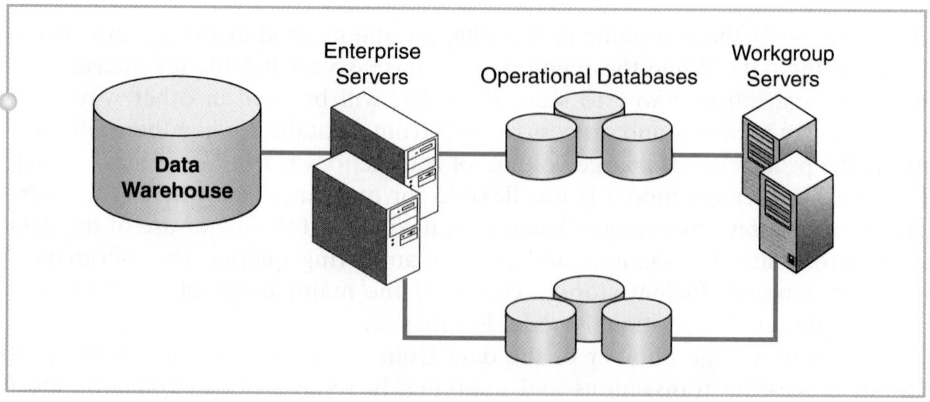

with the organization. The data in a data warehouse are called nonvolatile because they do not change rapidly in the same way that operational data change. Periodically, new data are uploaded to the data warehouse from the operational data, but other than through this updating process, the data in the data warehouse do not change.

BUILD THE DATA WAREHOUSE

To ensure the usefulness of a data warehouse, it is important to ensure that it is built correctly. The data in the data warehouse must support users' needs and must be standardized across the enterprise. Rather than collect and incorporate all of the available data into the data warehouse, it is important to include only data that meet user needs. Management, accounting, finance, production, and distribution functions will be using this data warehouse to budget, plan, forecast, and analyze profitability.

IDENTIFY THE DATA

The data in the data warehouse must provide the right kind of information to these user groups. To determine data that should be in a data warehouse, it is important to examine user needs and **high-impact processes (HIPs)**. HIPs are the critically important processes that must be executed correctly if the organization is to survive and thrive. The identification of HIPs must take into account the long-term strategic objectives of the organization.

THE REAL WORLD

Anheuser-Busch Companies Inc. must make sure that it keeps convenience stores and liquor stores stocked with the right amount and type of beer. If too little is stocked, Anheuser-Busch will lose sales; if too much is stocked, excessive stocking costs may be incurred and freshness concerns may arise. Therefore, the company's distribution system is a high-impact process. Warranty repairs are not important at all to Anheuser-Busch. On the other hand, warranty repair processes are likely to be critical to a company such as Hewlett-Packard Co. HP sells computer products that typically carry warranties of 90 days to one year. Without customer responsive warranty repair systems, HP would very likely lose sales.

An organization must set up cross-functional teams to identify the HIPs and the data that flow in and out of those processes. Each team must consider which critical processes will help the company achieve its long-term strategic objectives. The cross-functional teams also must ask users what kind of data they need and the kind of business problems they face. By identifying and examining both HIPs and user data needs, the set of data needed in the data warehouse can be determined.

STANDARDIZE THE DATA

The data in the data warehouse will come from many different processes and subunits across the enterprise. Different applications within the enterprise might use the same information, but in a different manner. For example, both sales order processing and marketing functions may use a field called "customer number." The marketing system may have a customer account number that is five digits with three leading zeros. So, a customer account number might be 00053425. Sales order processing systems may use a customer field with five digits and two leading zeros. Therefore, the same customer in the sales order application would be 0053425. To incorporate all information about this customer from both the marketing and sales order systems, the account number must be standardized within the data warehouse. One could fairly ask, Why not change the underlying marketing or sales order systems so that they agree? Most companies do not feel that they can afford the time or effort to rewrite source code in the older, legacy systems. Rather than change existing systems, it is easier to standardize data in the data warehouse.

CLEANSE, OR SCRUB, THE DATA

Since the data in a data warehouse are likely to come from many different sources within the enterprise, there will probably be errors and inconsistencies in the data. To the extent possible, the data should be cleansed, or "scrubbed," to remove or fix errors and problems in the data.

UPLOAD THE DATA

Data from each of the HIP systems must be uploaded to the data warehouse. Also, on a regular basis, new data should be uploaded to the data warehouse. Between the dates that data are uploaded, the data warehouse is static—it does not change. As an example, if data are uploaded at the end of every month, there are no changes in the data warehouse up until the last day of the month.

DATA ANALYSIS TOOLS (STUDY OBJECTIVE 7)

The purpose of a data warehouse is to give managers a rich source of data that they can query and examine for trends and patterns. The data warehouse allows managers to examine important patterns or trends so that they can better plan and control the business. The data warehouse can help managers examine trends such as sales by product, region, or model over a long time frame. Data in the data warehouse are analyzed by data mining and analytical processing.

Various techniques and tools have been developed to analyze data in a data warehouse, and this analysis enhances the ability of the business to meet customer needs, improve strategic planning, and increase performance. While there are many data analysis tools and techniques, this section will describe one important category of techniques and tools. The general technique is called data mining. The tools used in data mining are generally called online analytical processing (OLAP). There are special variations of OLAP called relational online analytical processing (ROLAP), and multidimensional analytical processing (MOLAP; also called data cubes). But these special types of OLAP are much more technical topics that are beyond the scope of this chapter. The descriptions here will focus on the general characteristics of data mining and OLAP.

DATA MINING

Data mining is the process of searching for identifiable patterns in data that can be used to predict future behavior. Although there are many purposes to predict future behavior, the most popular use of data mining is to predict future buying behavior of customers. If businesses are able to more accurately predict customer buying behavior, they can plan appropriately to produce, distribute, and sell the right products to customers at the right time. Data mining techniques have considerable potential in a variety of areas. In the 1998 book *Discovering Data Mining,*[2] the following are offered as examples of the questions that data mining can answer:

- What kind of behavior pattern does your customer emulate?
- How can the organization make more sales to existing customers?
- In the sales databases, are there hidden patterns of buying?
- Who are the better customers, and who are the high-risk customers?
- How can you maintain loyalty from current customers?
- How can you identify unknown buying habits and specifically market to those habits?
- What are customer perceptions of company products?
- How do you improve operational and strategic business plans based on data mining results?

THE REAL WORLD

Anheuser-Busch uses data mining to track and predict beer buying behavior. Using a combination of its own data, market data, and data from a third party, Anheuser-Busch can track its own sales and competitors' sales, revise marketing strategies, and design promotions targeted to ethnic groups. Anheuser-Busch has a name for its database and the process of using it: BudNet. The company attributes its market share growth from 48.9% to 50.1% to BudNet. Anheuser-Busch even maintains a website for sales reps and distributors to use in accessing and analyzing data. The website, www.budnet.com, is protected to allow use only by authorized parties.

Anheuser-Busch collects its own sales data by providing each of its salespeople with a handheld computer to use when they visit stores that stock Anheuser-Busch beer brands. Salespeople enter data such as new orders, shelf space devoted to Anheuser-Busch and competitor brands, and marketing promotions in use by competitors. The data are transmitted daily to regional Anheuser-Busch distributors and from the distributors to corporate headquarters. Brand managers then examine the data and provide sales and demand information and new promotion campaigns to distributors. Anheuser-Busch uses this data and computer technology to model and predict retail outlet buying patterns for the next 14–28 days. The model uses information such as sales history, price-to-consumer, holidays, special events, daily temperature, and forecasted data such as anticipated temperature, to create forecasts of sales by store and by product. Data are used by salespeople and distributors to rearrange displays, rotate stock, and inform stores of promotion campaigns.

In addition to using the internal data, Anheuser-Busch contracts with Information Resources Inc. (IRI) to collect market sales data. IRI tracks every bar-coded purchase of beer at convenience stores and liquor stores. IRI also conducts consumer surveys of beer buyers. Using these buying trends, Anheuser-Busch creates promotional campaigns, new products, and local or ethnic targeting of markets. For example, more beer is sold by the can in blue-collar neighborhoods, whereas more bottles are sold in white-collar neighborhoods.[3]

[2]Peter Cabena et al., *Discovering Data Mining: From Concept to Implementation*, Upper Saddle River, N.J., Prentice Hall PTR, c1998.

[3]www.cnn.com/2004/TECH/ptech/02/25/bus2.feat.beer.network

Although it is difficult to describe the exact size of a data warehouse such as that used by Anheuser-Busch, certainly it must be very large, since it incorporates historical sales, shelf space information, and competitor information on a store-by-store basis. A data warehouse that large would require specific software tools to examine and analyze trends or patterns in the data. This is also true for any organization that maintains a large data warehouse. Software must be used to search for trends and patterns in the data. The general term for these software tools is **online analytical processing**, or **OLAP**, described in the following section:

OLAP

OLAP is a set of software tools that allow online analysis of the data within a data warehouse. The analytical methods in OLAP usually include the following:

1. **Drill down** is the successive expansion of data into more detail, going from high-level data to successively lower levels of data. For example, if a person is examining sales, drill down would involve examining sales for the year, then by month, then by week or day. This examination of successive levels of detail is drill down.
2. **Consolidation,** or roll-up, is the aggregation or collection of similar data. It is the opposite of drill down in that consolidation takes detailed data and summarizes it into larger groups.
3. **Pivoting,** or rotating, data is examining data from different perspectives. As an example, sales of beer can be examined by time (months), by store type (convenience store or liquor store), by container type (cans or bottles), etc.
4. **Time series analysis** to identify trends is the comparison of figures such as sales over several successive time periods.
5. **Exception reports** present variances from expectations.
6. **What-if simulations** present potential variations in conditions that are used to understand interactions between different parts of the business.

OLAP is the software tool that allows managers to access and analyze the data in the data warehouse. OLAP finds and highlights trends or patterns in the data.

DISTRIBUTED DATA PROCESSING (STUDY OBJECTIVE 8)

Many small companies house all of their operations in a single building. For these companies there is usually no need to consider the physical location of their database. A small company with only a single building would obviously store its data on a computer within that building. However, most midsized or large organizations have multiple locations, sometimes located throughout the world. Large and midsized organizations must decide where their data should be physically stored and in which locations they should be processed. For a fast-food franchise like McDonalds Corp., for example, management could decide to maintain one database of prices for the food products that it sells. Should that price data be in one location and all restaurant computer systems access that one database, or should prices be stored in regions or localities so that each location can charge different prices? This is only an example of the problems of physical data storage facing large organizations. The location of the data storage and the location of the processing of the data can have tremendous impact upon the efficiency and effectiveness of the company.

THE REAL WORLD

McDonald's has restaurants, warehouses, and offices located throughout the world; yet its corporate headquarters is in Oakbrook, Illinois. If McDonald's management decided that all data, including prices, must be stored in a database at corporate headquarters, what would have to happen when you order a cheeseburger at a McDonald's in Los Angeles? The cash register system would have to read pricing data from the database in Oakbrook, Illinois. This would be inefficient for several reasons. First, each McDonald's restaurant would be trying to read the same database simultaneously in order to fill customer orders all around the world. Each of the McDonald's restaurants would need to be networked to that data in Illinois and would need to be able to read price data quickly in order to process the sale. This would generate so much network traffic that it would very likely overwhelm the network and computer system. In addition, if prices are stored only at corporate headquarters, it would become more difficult for each location to set its own prices. Certainly, it would be much more efficient for McDonald's to maintain pricing data at the local restaurants or in regional centers.

Like McDonald's, all large organizations must make decisions about the data they maintain—decisions involving where data is physically stored and which locations process various data.

This question of locations for data storage and processing is usually considered in the context of choosing from two general approaches: centralized or distributed. Data can be stored in a central location, or it can be distributed across various locations. Similarly, the processing of data and transactions can occur only in a central location, or distributed across the various locations. In the early days of computing, data processing and databases were stored and maintained in a central location. These are called **centralized processing** and **centralized databases**. However, in today's IT environment, most processing and databases are distributed. In **distributed data processing (DDP)** and **distributed databases (DDB)**, the processing and the databases are dispersed to different locations of the organization. A distributed database is actually a collection of smaller databases dispersed across several computers on a computer network. The data are stored on different computers within the network, and the application programs access data from these different sites.

DDP AND DDB

Current IT systems use networks such as LANs and WANs extensively, enabling the easy distribution of processing and databases. Distributing the processing and data offers the following advantages:

1. **Reduced hardware cost.** Distributed systems use networks of smaller computers rather than a single mainframe computer. This configuration is much less costly to purchase and maintain.
2. **Improved responsiveness.** Access is faster, since data can be located at the site of the greatest demand for that data. Processing speed is improved, since the processing workload is spread over several computers.

3. **Easier incremental growth.** As the organization grows or requires additional computing resources, new sites can be added quickly and easily. Adding smaller, networked computers is easier and less costly than adding a new mainframe computer.
4. **Increased user control and user involvement.** If data and processing are distributed locally, the local users have more control over the data. This control also allows users to be more involved in the maintenance of the data, and users are therefore more satisfied.
5. **Automatic integrated backup.** When data and processing are distributed across several computers, the failure of any single site is not as harmful. Other computers within the network can take on extra processing or data storage to make up for the loss of any single site.

However, it is important to recognize that there are also disadvantages to the use of DDP and DDB, namely, increased difficulty of managing, controlling, and maintaining integrity of the data. A large database that is stored, maintained, and accessed at a central location is much easier to manage and control. To consider why this is true, think of a large building with only a single door. Controlling access to items stored in the building can be controlled by having security at that single door. However, every door that is added to the building affords another opportunity for someone to gain unauthorized access. Every door that is added to the building increases the points at which security must be enhanced. The same is true of distributed systems, wherein several sites within the organization can access the databases. The increased number of sites accessing the data causes a greater need for security and control of the database.

In addition, when data are located at several sites, concurrency control is a problem. Think about the McDonald's pricing situation presented earlier in this section. If McDonald's decides to increase the price of cheeseburgers by 10%, that pricing change has to be made at every locality which maintains pricing data. Notice that this price change would be much easier to implement if there were only one centralized price database. The price could be changed in this single centralized database, and the price change would immediately be seen by all those who use that database. These disadvantages do not cause organizations to avoid the use of DDP and DDB, but they do cause greater attention to be paid to security and control issues. Organizations that use DDP and DDB must have better controls in place to ensure the security and concurrency of the data.

There are also management issues that are more difficult to control in DDP and DDB. If local users have more control over the systems, there is a greater chance that local sites will have incompatible hardware, systems, or data. For example, a local site may buy hardware that is incompatible with the larger network system of the organization. Management can lessen these problems by enforcing policies regarding the purchase and use of hardware and software, and through tighter management of the databases.

CLIENT/SERVER SYSTEMS

The most popular type of distributed system is a client/server system. In a **client/server system**, each computer or process on the network is either a *client* or a *server*. Servers are computers or processes that manage files and databases, printers or networks. Clients are usually PCs or workstations that run the applications. Clients rely on servers for resources, such as files, printers, and even processing power. The client has its own operating system, keyboard, mouse, and screen and can process local data without the server. The larger database is held on a dedicated database server, which processes requests for data from the client and passes the results to the client. The server's role is to manage the database and to wait passively for a client to request a service or data.

This distribution of processing allows the client to offer the more user-friendly environment of a PC and leads to less complex and expensive systems than traditional mainframe systems. *Client/server* computing differs from the use of a shared network file *server* in that the powerful database *server* does all the database searching and filtering and transmits the result to the *client* PC. Thus, tasks are distributed to the computer that best matches its capabilities. The server manages the larger database and sends subsets of data to the client, while the client processes this subset of data in a user-friendly PC. This system makes much more efficient use of local area networks. Much of the accounting software in use is based on this architecture of LANs, WANs, and client/server systems.

IT CONTROLS FOR DATA AND DATABASES (STUDY OBJECTIVE 9)

The database of an organization is a critically important component of the organization. The data are a valuable resource that must be protected with good internal controls. Chapter 4 described many of the IT internal controls that should be used to protect the security and integrity of the database. You might find it useful to review the IT control section of Chapter 4. A brief summary of some of the IT controls is offered here. Three of the major control concerns related to databases are unauthorized access, adequate backup of the data, and data integrity.

IT general controls assist in preventing unauthorized access and in ensuring adequate backup. To help prevent unauthorized users from accessing, altering, or destroying data in the database, it is important to use authentication and hacking controls such as log-in procedures, passwords, security tokens, biometric controls, firewalls, encryption, intrusion detection, and vulnerability assessment. In addition to these control procedures, the database management system (DBMS) must be set up so that each authorized user has a limited view (schema) of the database. That is, an employee who logs in as an accounts receivable processor should not have access to payroll data. Each user's schema of the data limits the user's view to only a subset of the data. Controls such as these are intended to keep unauthorized users from accessing or using data in the database. Business continuity planning, data backup procedures, and disaster recovery planning can help ensure adequate backup of databases.

To ensure integrity (completeness and accuracy) of data in the database, IT application controls should be used. These controls are input, processing, and output controls such as data validation, control totals and reconciliation, and reports that are analyzed by managers.

ETHICAL ISSUES RELATED TO DATA COLLECTION AND STORAGE (STUDY OBJECTIVE 10)

There are many ethical issues related to the collection, storage, and protection of data in databases. Companies collect and store a wealth of information about customers in their databases. These ethical issues related to such data in databases can be examined from three perspectives:

1. Ethical responsibilities of a company to its customers
2. Ethical responsibilities of employees to the company and its customers
3. Ethical responsibilities of customers to the company

The ethical responsibilities that companies have to customers revolve around collecting only necessary data from customers, properly protecting customer data, limiting the sharing of customer data, and correcting errors in customer data. The ethical responsibilities of employees is to avoid browsing through data or customer records unless necessity dictates, not selling customer data to competitors, and not disclosing customer data to related parties. Customers also have ethical responsibilities related to their providing data to companies that they deal with. These would include providing accurate and complete data when those data are necessary, and upholding the obligation not to disclose or use company data that they may have access to. Each of these types of responsibilities is discussed in detail in the sections that follow. This discussion of ethical issues is intended not to list and describe all ethical issues related to databases, but to describe many of the important ethical considerations.

ETHICAL RESPONSIBILITIES OF THE COMPANY

The data collected and stored in databases in many instances consist of information that is private between the company and its customer. For example, your bank has your Social Security number in customer records, as well as the Social Security numbers of all its customers. This is an example of nonpublic data that your bank should not share with anyone else. The bank has an ethical obligation to maintain the privacy of your data such as Social Security number, account balance, and telephone number. All companies collect at least some private data from customers. The sensitivity and privacy of that data depend on the nature of the business and the type of services or products sold. For example, a medical office has very private and confidential files on each patient. The medical office has an extremely high level of responsibility to protect the privacy of client information. On the other hand, a bookstore has very few pieces of private or confidential information from customers. However, a bookstore may have some data that are private, such as credit card numbers and data on buying habits and types of books purchased. Even companies that do not sell to end consumers collect and store private data. For example, Anheuser-Busch sells beer to convenience store chains and grocery store chains. Each chain it sells to has data that it wishes to keep from competitors, such as data on credit limits, prices paid, and quantities purchased.

Online companies that sell via websites have an even higher duty to maintain customer privacy and confidentiality. In fact, the AICPA Trust Services Principles (described in Chapter 4) have an entire section devoted to online privacy. Within the Trust Services Principles, the privacy framework lists ten privacy practices that should be adhered to by online companies:

1. **Management.** The organization should assign a specific person or persons, the responsibility of privacy practices for the organization. That responsible person should insure that the organization has defined and documented its privacy practices. That person should also insure that privacy practices have been communicated to both employees and customers. Management would also include the responsibility to insure that privacy practices are followed by employees.
2. **Notice.** The organization should have policies and practices to maintain privacy of customer data. Notice implies that the company provides the privacy practices to customers in some form. At the time that data is to be collected, a notice should be available to the customer that describes the privacy policies and practices. Many e-commerce organizations accomplish this by providing a link on their website to privacy policies. Notice should include information regarding the purpose of collecting the information, and how that information will be used.
3. **Choice and consent.** The organization should provide choice to its customers regarding the collection of data, and also should ask for consent to collect, retain, and use the data. The customer should be informed of any choices that the customer may have to opt out of providing information. The customer should have access to descriptions about the choices available. The customer should also be able to read policies about how the data will be used. As in "notice" above, these descriptions usually are in the form of a link to privacy policies.
4. **Collection.** The organization should collect only the data that is necessary for the purpose of conducting the transaction. In addition, the customer should have provided implicit or explicit consent before data is collected. Explicit consent might be in the form of placing a check mark by a box indicating consent. Implicit consent occurs when the customer provides data that is clearly marked as voluntary, or when the customer has provided data and has not clearly stated that it can not be used.
5. **Use and retention.** The organization uses customers' personal data only in the manner described in "notice" from part a. above. The use of this data occurs only after the customer has given implicit or explicit consent to use the data. Such personal data is retained only as long as necessary.
6. **Access.** Every customer should have access to the data provided so that the customer can view, change, delete, or block further use of the data provided.
7. **Disclosure to third parties.** In some cases, e-commerce organizations forward customer information to third parties. Before this forwarding of data occurs, the organization should receive explicit or implicit consent of the customer. Personal data should only be forwarded to third parties that have equivalent privacy protections.
8. **Security for privacy.** The organization has necessary protections to try to insure that customer data is not lost, destroyed, altered, or subject to unauthorized access. The organization should put internal controls in place that prevent hackers and unauthorized employees from accessing customer data.

9. **Quality.** The organization should institute procedures to insure that all customer data collected retains quality. Data quality means that the data remains "accurate, complete, current, relevant, and reliable".
10. **Monitoring and enforcement.** The organization should continually monitor to insure that its privacy practices are followed. The organization should have procedures to address privacy related inquiries or disputes.

In addition to these ethical obligations to customers, companies have an ethical obligation to shareholders to ensure that company data are properly protected. For example, competitors may try to gain access to company data through what is generally called **industrial espionage**. Data are a valuable commodity, and the company value to shareholders can be harmed if sensitive data fall into the hands of competitors.

To properly protect data, companies should have appropriate internal controls as described in Chapter 4. These controls help prevent unauthorized access and browsing of data. Controls, including log-in procedures, passwords, smart cards, biometric controls, encryption of data, and firewalls, can provide some protection from unauthorized access to data.

ETHICAL RESPONSIBILITIES OF EMPLOYEES

Within organizations, many employees must have access to private data about clients and customers. These employees have an ethical obligation to avoid misuse of any private or personal data about customers. Three examples may help illustrate this ethical responsibility. Internal Revenue Service (IRS) employees regularly must see and work with tax returns. However, they should never browse through, disclose, or improperly use tax return data. This is a legal duty, as well as an ethical duty, in the case of the IRS. Medical offices also maintain very private data about personal medical histories. The protection of those data from improper use is both an ethical and a legal responsibility. In the third case, the duty to avoid misuse of customer data is an ethical duty, but not necessarily a legal obligation. For example, a payroll clerk in a company may have access to employee pay rates. While it is not illegal for the clerk to disclose these pay rates to others, it is certainly unethical to do so.

In addition, some employees have access to proprietary data that would be harmful to the company if disclosed. An example would be sales information by product. Competitors such as Pepsico, Inc. and Coca Cola, Co. could gain competitive advantage if one of them acquired detailed knowledge about the other's sales data. Employees should never disclose proprietary or confidential data about their company to outsiders.

There are no specific IT controls that would always prevent authorized employees from disclosing private information, but having and enforcing a code of ethics within the organization can reduce the chances of such disclosure. Proper IT controls, such as log-in procedures, passwords, smart cards, biometric controls, encryption of data, and firewalls, can help reduce unauthorized access by employees.

ETHICAL RESPONSIBILITIES OF CUSTOMERS

Certainly, customers have an obligation to provide accurate and complete information to companies that they deal with when the requests for such data are legitimate business needs. For example, when you apply for a new credit card, the issuing company deserves full and complete disclosure of your credit history. In addition to this obligation, customers in some cases may have access to company data that should be kept confidential. Customers have an ethical obligation to avoid the improper use of data that they gain from accessing a database as a customer.

THE REAL WORLD

Near Lexington, Kentucky, the breeding and racing of thoroughbred horses is a significant industry. Tracking the bloodlines of the thoroughbreds used as studs in breeding is important information to those who breed and race these horses. During the 1970s, a company named Bloodstock began maintaining a database of stud horse and mare bloodlines and race handicapping data. Breeders and others could establish an account with Bloodstock and access this computer database in choosing a stud horse to use for breeding or for handicapping races. Eventually, this database became a web-based resource called BRISNET.

In 1997, someone began establishing and using fictitious customer accounts to access the BRISNET database. Over a period of months, this person accessed and downloaded BRISNET data. He then posted these data to his own database and website and began selling the data at prices below those charged by Bloodstock. Upon discovery of this unethical act, the United States Attorney of the district, surprisingly, declined to charge the violator with federal crimes. However, Bloodstock settled out of court with the violator for an undisclosed dollar amount.[4]

SUMMARY OF STUDY OBJECTIVES

The need for data collection and storage. Businesses need to collect and store data so that they can properly record and complete transactions in their day-to-day operations. This enables the company to carry out transactions in a manner that will satisfy customers and suppliers. It also allows the company to maintain detailed records that facilitate followup, feedback for future decision making, and preparation of financial statements.

Methods of storing data and the interrelationship between storage and processing. Data may be stored in characters, fields, records, files, and databases. The media on which data are stored may be sequential access or random access. The choice of data storage media may depend on the use of the data. Data that are accessed sequentially may be stored on magnetic tape, whereas disk storage is used for data that need to be accessed randomly or directly.

The differences between batch processing and real-time processing. Batch processing involves the grouping of similar transactions into a batch and processing all of these items together. On the other hand, real-time processing involves continuous processing, where transactions are processed as soon as they occur or as soon as they are entered into the system. Although real-time processing is preferred because of the timely response, batch systems are still used for processing large volumes of data due to their lower cost and ease of control.

The importance of databases and the historical progression from flat-file databases to relational databases. A database makes it possible for an organization to

[4] "The Bluegrass Conspiracy," *AIPLA Quarterly Journal*, Summer 2001, vol. 29, no. 3, pp. 319–322.

share data, often across widely distributed users. Flat-file databases store data in two-dimensional tables in text format. Hierarchical databases use an inverted tree structure to define relationships among data. Network databases are an advanced version of a hierarchical database because they use the inverted tree structure; however, networks share branches. Relational databases are used in practice today more than the other types of databases. A relational database stores data in two-dimensional tables that are joined in many ways to represent many different kinds of relationships in the data.

The need for normalization of data in a relational database. The two-dimensional tables used in a relational database must be flexible enough to handle an unlimited number of queries. To obtain this flexibility, the database tables must be designed according to precise specifications. Data must be translated, or normalized, in order to meet these specifications.

Data warehouse and the use of a data warehouse to analyze data. A data warehouse is an integrated set of data that spans a long period (up to 10 years). The data are nonvolatile; however, they are used to support the company's strategic planning and the ongoing decision making of its managers. In order to build a data warehouse, the data must be identified, standardized, and cleansed before they are uploaded. An operational database, on the other hand, contains current-period data that are continually updated to support current operations and reporting.

The use of OLAP and data mining as analysis tools. Data mining involves analyzing data for patterns that can be used to predict future behavior. Data mining techniques are used in business organizations to predict customers' buying behaviors. OLAP is also used to find trends or patterns in data. OLAP is the software tool that allows managers to access and analyze the data in a data warehouse.

Distributed databases and the advantages of the use of distributed data. Distributed data processing is very important in companies where operations are dispersed among multiple locations. A distributed database is a dispersed system of networked databases. The most popular type of distributed database is a client/server system, whereby local area networks are used to distribute tasks to the area that is best able to handle the related data processing. Centralized data processing, on the other hand, requires that the database is maintained at one centralized location, usually the company's headquarters.

Controls for data and databases. Business organizations must exercise care in ensuring the protection and security of its data. The most crucial controls for data protection include unauthorized access, adequate back-up of the data, and data integrity. These topics were discussed in detail in Chapter 4.

Ethical issues related to data collection and storage Companies have ethical obligations to their customers and employees, while customers and employees have ethical obligations to each other and to the companies with whom they do business. Each of these parties must be discreet in their business dealings so that privileged information is not divulged to outsiders. Employees also have an ethical duty to protect information obtained in the course of their jobs; such information should not be shared with others. Finally, customers have an obligation to provide complete and accurate information to the companies with whom they are doing business.

KEY TERMS

Attributes
Batch Processing
Centralized processing
Character
Client/server systems
Concurrency
Consolidation
Data
Data mining
Data normalization
Data redundancy
Data warehouse
Database
Database management systems
Direct storage access
Disk storage
Distributed processing
Drill down
Exception reports
Field
File
Flat file database
Hierarchical database
High-impact processes
Industrial espionage
Information
Magnetic tape
Many-to-many relationships
Network databases
OLAP
One-to-many relationships
One-to-one relationships
Pivoting
Primary key
Random access
Real-time processing
Record
Record pointer
Relational database
Sequential access
Structured query language
Time series analysis
What-if simulations

END OF CHAPTER MATERIAL

CONCEPT CHECK

1. Which of the following best describes the relationship between data and information?
   a. Data is interpreted information.
   b. Information is interpreted data.
   c. Data is more useful than information in decision making.
   d. Data and information are not related.
2. A *character* is to a field as
   a. water is to a pool.
   b. a pool is to a swimmer.
   c. a pool is to water.
   d. a glass is to water.
3. Magnetic tape is a form of
   a. direct access media.
   b. random access media.
   c. sequential access media.
   d. alphabetical access media.

4. Which of the following is not an advantage of using real-time data processing?
   a. Quick response time to support timely record keeping and customer satisfaction
   b. Efficiency for use with large volumes of data
   c. Provides for random access of data
   d. Improved accuracy due to the immediate recording of transactions
5. If a company stores data in separate files in its different departmental locations and is able to update all files simultaneously, it would not have problems with
   a. attributes.
   b. data redundancy.
   c. industrial espionage.
   d. concurrency.
6. When the data contained in a database are stored in large, two-dimensional tables, the database is referred to as a
   a. flat file database.
   b. hierarchical database.
   c. network database.
   d. relational database.
7. Database management systems are categorized by the data structures they support. In which type of database management system is the data arranged in a series of tables?
   a. Network
   b. Hierarchical
   c. Relational
   d. Sequential
8. A company's database contains three types of records: vendors, parts, and purchasing. The vendor records include the vendor number, name, address, and terms. The parts records include part numbers, name, description, and warehouse location. Purchasing records include purchase numbers, vendor numbers (which reference the vendor record), part numbers (which reference the parts record), and quantity. What structure of database is being used?
   a. Network
   b. Hierarchical
   c. Relational
   d. Sequential
9. Which of the following statements is not true with regard to a relational database?
   a. It is flexible and useful for unplanned, ad hoc queries.
   b. It stores data in tables.
   c. It stores data in a tree formation.
   d. It is maintained on direct access devices.

10. A collection of several years' nonvolatile data used to support strategic decision-making is a(n)
    a. operational database.
    b. data warehouse.
    c. data mine.
    d. what-if simulation.
11. Data mining would be useful in all of the following situations except
    a. identifying hidden patterns in customers' buying habits.
    b. assessing customer reactions to new products.
    c. determining customers' behavior patterns.
    d. accessing customers' payment histories.
12. A set of small databases where data are collected, processed, and stored on multiple computers within a network is a
    a. centralized database.
    b. distributed database.
    c. flat file database.
    d. high-impact process.
13. Each of the following is an online privacy practice recommended by the AICPA Trust Services Principles Privacy Framework except:
    a. Redundant data should be eliminated from the database.
    b. Notification of privacy policies should be given to customers.
    c. Private information should not be given to third parties without the customer's consent.
    d. All of the above.

DISCUSSION QUESTIONS

14. (SO 1) How does data differ from information?
15. (SO 1) Why is it important for companies to store transaction data?
16. (SO 2) Which type of data storage medium is most appropriate when a single record of data must be accessed frequently and quickly?
17. (SO 3) Identify one type of business that would likely use real-time data processing rather than batch processing. Describe the advantages of real-time processing to this type of business.
18. (SO 4) Differentiate between data redundancy and concurrency.
19. (SO 4) What is the term for the software program(s) that monitors and organizes the database and controls access and use of data? Describe how this software controls shared access.
20. (SO 4) Describe the trade-offs of using the hierarchical model of database storage.
21. (SO 4) Describe the organization of a flat file database.
22. (SO 4) What four conditions are required for all types of databases?

23. (SO 4) Within a hierarchical database, what is the name for the built-in linkages in data tables? Which data relationships can be contained in a hierarchical database?
24. (SO 4) Which database models are built on the inverted tree structure? What are the disadvantages of using the inverted tree structure for a database?
25. (SO 4) Which database model is used most frequently in the modern business world? Why do you believe it is frequently used?
26. (SO 5) How is the primary key used in a relational database?
27. (SO 5) What language is used to access data from a relational database? Why is the language advantageous when accessing data?
28. (SO 5) Which type of database model has the most flexibility for querying? How does this flexibility assist management?
29. (SO 5) What are the first three rules of normalization? What is meant by the statement that the rules of normalization are additive?
30. (SO 6) Differentiate between a data warehouse and an operational database.
31. (SO 7) How is data mining different than data warehousing?
32. (SO 7) How has Anheuser-Busch used data warehousing and data mining successfully?
33. (SO 7) Identify and describe the analytical tools in OLAP.
34. (SO 8) Differentiate between centralized data processing and distributed data processing.
35. (SO 8) What are the "clients" and "servers" in a client/server distributed database system?
36. (SO 9) Why is control over unauthorized access so important in a database environment?
37. (SO 9) What are some internal control measures that could prevent a hacker from altering data in your company's database?
38. (SO 9) Why are data considered a valuable resource that is worthy of extensive protection?

BRIEF EXERCISES

39. (SO 2) Arrange the following data storage concepts in order from smallest to largest, in terms of their size: file, record, database, character, and field.
40. (SO 2) Think of a telephone book as a database. Identify the fields likely to be used in this database. If you were constructing this database, how many spaces would you allow for each field?
41. (SO 3) Suppose that a large company uses batch processing for recording its inventory purchases. Other than its slow response time, what would be the most significant problem with using a batch processing system for recording inventory purchases?
42. (SO 4) Arrange the following database models in order from earliest development to most recent: network databases, hierarchical databases, flat file databases, and relational databases.

43. (SO 4) Categorize each of the following as one-to-one, one-to-many, or many-to-many.
    - Subsidiary ledgers and general ledgers
    - Transactions and special journal
    - General ledgers and trial balances
44. (SO 6) How might a company use both an operational database and a data warehouse in the preparation of its annual report?
45. (SO 7) Using Anheuser-Busch's BudNet example presented in this chapter, think about the queries that might be valuable if a company like Gap Inc. used data mining to monitor its customers' buying behavior.

PROBLEMS

46. (SO 3) Differentiate between batch processing and real-time processing. What are the advantages and disadvantages of each form of data processing? Which form is more likely to be used by a doctor's office in preparing the monthly patient bills?
47. (SO 4) Allibyr Company does not use a database system; rather, it maintains separate data files in each of its departments. Accordingly, when a sale occurs, the transaction is initially recorded in the sales department. Next, documentation is forwarded from the sales department to the accounting department so that the transaction can be recorded there. Finally, the customer service group is notified so that its records can be updated. Describe the data redundancy and concurrency issues that are likely to arise under this scenario at Allibyr.
48. (SO 6) List and describe the steps involved in building a data warehouse.
49. (SO 8) Describe the advantages and disadvantages of using a distributed database and distributed data processing. Do you think the advantages are worthwhile? Explain your answer.
50. (SO 8) Read an online article from CIO magazine at http://www.cio.com/article/30522/IT_Organization_Management_Revisiting_Centralization. Summarize the points discussed in this article about centralization versus distributed systems.
51. (SO 10) Describe the ethical obligations of companies to their online customers.
52. (SO 6) Using an Internet search engine search for the terms "data warehouse" + Amazon.com Inc. + Neteeza Corporation. Neteeza assisted Amazon in implementing new data warehouse systems in mid-2005. Describe some feature of this new data warehouse and why it is so important to Amazon.com's business.
53. (SO 8) Oracle Corp. is the world's largest enterprise software company. Its business is based on information—helping people use it, share it, manage it, and protect it. Using a Internet search engine, search using the terms Google and "distributed database." Describe how and why Google uses a

distributed database. What problems is Google encountering related to its distributed database?

54. (SO 10) List and describe the ten privacy practices recommended by the AICPA Trust Services Principles Privacy Framework. If you have ever made a purchase online, you have likely seen these practices in use. Provide any examples from your own personal experience.

CASES

55. The screen capture that follows shows the relationships in a Microsoft Access database. For each relationship, explain the following:
    a. The type of parent-child relationship it represents.
    b. Which attributes in the table are used to link the relationship.
    c. The purpose of the relationship.
56. Shuttle-Eze operates airport shuttle vans in 12 large cities: Los Angeles, San Diego, San Francisco, Phoenix, Las Vegas, Houston, Dallas, Chicago, New York City, Washington DC, Miami, and Orlando. Shuttle-Eze operates passenger vans to shuttle travelers to and from the airports for a $25 fee per person.

Required:

a. Design the tables that the company would need in its database to operate these shuttles. Remember that they must collect, record, and track information about customers, payments, flights, gates, vans, drivers, and pick-up and delivery addresses. You may wish to add other types of data. The tables you design should have attributes (columns) for each critical piece of data. See Exhibit 13-4 for the concept of the table layouts. Your tables should meet the first three rules of data normalization.

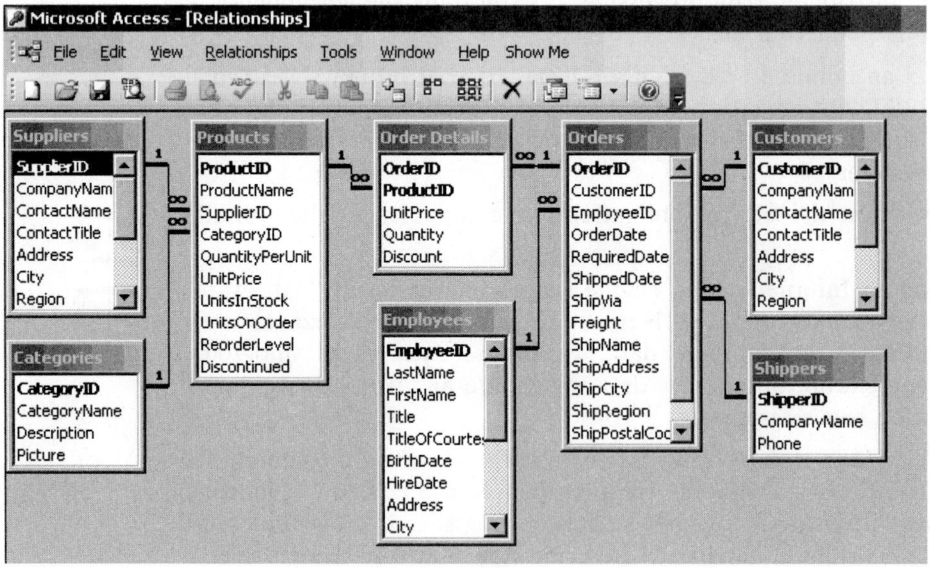

b. Describe the advantages and disadvantages for Shuttle-Eze of using a centralized database as opposed to a separate database for each location.

57. Kroger Co., a large, nationwide grocery chain, maintains a customer reward system titled the "Kroger Plus Shopper's Card." Customers who enroll in this system are entitled to discounts on products at Kroger stores and on Kroger gasoline. To earn discounts and other rewards, the shopper must use the "Kroger Plus" card at the time of checkout. The card has a bar code that identifies the customer. For Kroger, the system allows the opportunity to determine customer buying patterns and to use these data for data mining.

Required:

Using a web search engine, search for "data mining" and "grocery." Describe what types of information grocery stores collect that they can use for data mining purposes. Also, describe how grocery chains use data mining to improve performance.

CONTINUING CASE: SPATELLI'S PIZZERIA

Refer to the Spatelli's Pizzeria case at the end of Chapter 1. In addition, read the article Peter Greyton mentioned regarding Anheuser-Busch at http://www.cnn.com/2004/TECH/ptech/02/25/bus2.feat.beer.network/index.html. Use this article regarding the sales and inventory management systems in place at Anheuser-Busch, and

a. Describe the purpose of a data warehouse and describe how Anheuser-Busch uses data warehousing.

b. Describe the purpose and use of data mining and describe how Anheuser-Busch uses data mining.

c. Describe how data warehousing and data mining can facilitate reporting and analysis at Spatelli's.

SOLUTIONS TO CONCEPT CHECK

1. (SO 1) The following statement best describes the relationship between data and information: **b. Information is interpreted data.** Information is useful for decision making, whereas data typically require processing before they become practical for use in a decision-making process.
2. (SO 2) A *character* is to a *field* as **a. water is to a pool.** In data storage terminology, characters are contained within a field.
3. (SO 2) Magnetic tape is a form of **c. sequential access media.** Magnetic tape must be accessed in the order it was recorded.
4. (SO 3) The following is not an advantage of using real-time data processing: **b. efficiency for use with large volumes of data.** This is a characteristic of batch processing rather than real-time processing.
5. (SO 4) If a company stores data in separate files in its different departmental locations and is able to update all files simultaneously, it would not have problems with **d. concurrency**. Concurrency problems arise when a company has difficulty updating data at its various locations at the same time.

6. (SO 4) When the data contained in a database are stored in large, two-dimensional tables, the database is referred to as a **a. flat file database.** The two dimensions for a flat file database are rows and columns.
7. (CIA Adapted) (SO 4) Database management systems are categorized by the data structures they support. In a **c. relational** database management system, the data are arranged in a series of tables.
8. (CIA Adapted) (SO 4) A company's database contains three types of records: vendors, parts, and purchasing. The vendor records include the vendor number, name, address, and terms. The parts records include part numbers, name, description, and warehouse location. Purchasing records include purchase numbers, vendor numbers (which reference the vendor record), part numbers (which reference the parts record), and quantity. The structure of the database being used is **c. relational,** since the links are contained within the data records themselves. Answers a. and b. are incorrect because these structures would have directional pointers or trees, respectively, rather than explicit data values. Answer d. is incorrect because it is an access method rather than a database structure.
9. (CIA Adapted) (SO 4, 5) The following statement is not true with regard to a relational database: **c. It stores data in a tree formation.** This response is characteristic of a hierarchical database.
10. (SO 6) A collection of several years' nonvolatile data used to support strategic decision making is a **b. data warehouse.** The data in a data warehouse do not change except for the occasional upload of new data.
11. (SO 7) Data mining would be useful in all of the following situations except **c. assessing customers' payment histories.** Assessing customers' payment history would likely require a data warehouse, whereas data mining is focused on behavioral patterns.
12. (SO 8) A set of small databases where data are collected, processed, and stored on multiple computers within a network is a **b. distributed database.**
13. (SO 10) Each of the given statements is an online privacy practice recommended by the AICPA Trust Services Principles Privacy Framework except the following: **a. Redundant data should be eliminated from the database.** Redundancy is addressed in the rules of data normalization, but not in the AICPA's Privacy Framework.

CHAPTER 14

E-Commerce and E-Business

STUDY OBJECTIVES

This chapter will help you gain an understanding of the following concepts:

1. An introduction to e-commerce and e-business
2. The history of the Internet
3. The physical structure and standards of the Internet
4. E-commerce and its benefits
5. Privacy expectations in e-commerce
6. E-business and IT enablement
7. E-business enablement examples
8. Intranets and extranets to enable e-business
9. Internal controls for the Internet, intranets, and extranets
10. XML and XBRL as e-business tools
11. Ethical issues related to e-business and e-commerce

INTRODUCTION TO E-COMMERCE AND E-BUSINESS (STUDY OBJECTIVE 1)

THE REAL WORLD

Jose Luis Gutierrez/iStockphoto

Recently, Wal-Mart announced to its 10,000 small and midsize suppliers that they had one year to begin using Internet EDI (EDIINT AS2). This was a change in method for Wal-Mart's suppliers. For many years, Wal-Mart had used traditional EDI and value added networks. This change by Wal-Mart was expected to have a dramatic impact not only on the suppliers, but also on the companies who serve as value added networks (VANs).

Shawn Willett, a principal analyst for application infrastructure with Current Analysis said, "The balance is tipping slowly towards the Internet side. Everyone thought it would happen right away, but there's been a gradual uptake."[1]

Pete Abell of AMR Research said, "VANs realize that their days are numbered." He predicts that VANs will try to transition to providing Internet EDI.[2]

Organizations use information technology to improve efficiency and effectiveness of their operations. Wal-Mart transitioned to Internet EDI to save costs and to take advantage of the new EDI technology. In many cases this IT enablement causes major changes for not only that organization, but also for its trading partners and other aspects of the economy. The Wal-Mart decision caused 10,000 Wal-Mart suppliers to invest in new IT systems and resulted in major changes in the demand for value added network services.

The Wal-Mart transition is an example of e-business. **E-business** is the use of electronic means to enhance business processes. E-business encompasses all forms of on-line electronic trading, consumer-based e-commerce, and business-to-business electronic trading and process integration, as well as the internal use of IT and related technologies for process integration inside organizations.

"E-business" is a term used widely in business and in the mass media. However, there are sometimes misunderstandings about e-business and e-commerce, and any differences between the two. In addition, the sheer number of acronyms in use in e-business and the technological nature of some of the acronyms can make it difficult to understand e-business. The first purpose of this chapter is to define and clarify many of the terms and concepts related to e-business and e-commerce. In addition, this chapter describes the advantages, disadvantages, security issues, and controls related to e-business.

There is some overlap between e-commerce and e-business, and this leads some to confuse the two concepts. **E-commerce** is electronically enabled transactions between a business and its customers. E-business is a broader concept that includes not only electronic trade with customers, but also servicing customers and vendors, trading information with customers and vendors, and electronic recording and control of internal processes. These internal processes include electronic internal employee services such as access to personnel records, access to fringe benefit information, travel and expense reporting, and

[1]Demir Barlas, "Wal-Mart Upgrades EDI Model," LINE56, October 10, 2002.

[2]*Ibid.*

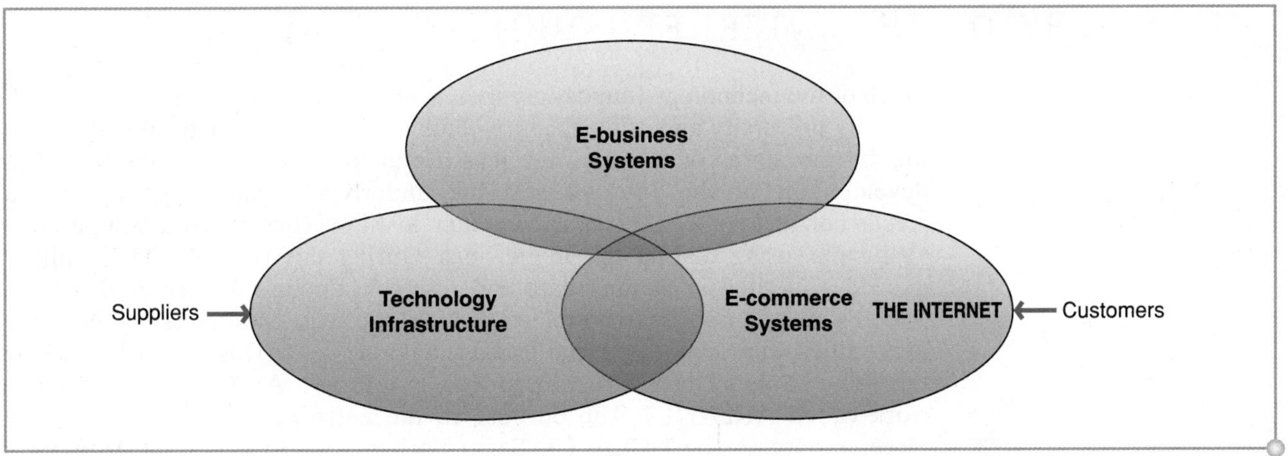

Exhibit 14-1
E-business and E-commerce

purchase of items such as office supplies. Exhibit 14-1 shows the differences and the overlap between the two concepts.

E-commerce is the sale of goods or services from a business to an end-user consumer. Since E-commerce involves selling to consumers, the usual sale will be a relatively small dollar amount when only a few items are sold. The company making the sale will strive for high volume sales to many consumers to generate a profit. Its customers will use a user-friendly interface, such as a web browser, to place the order and pay with a credit card. Amazon.com, Inc. is a well-known example of an e-commerce enterprise. The sales between Amazon.com and its customers are sales between a company and end-user customers.

On the other hand, E-business is a broader concept that encompasses many business processes, using IT systems to enhance or streamline these processes. A part of E-business includes company-to-company sales. E-business includes the sale of goods, services, or raw materials between companies in a supply chain. An example of a supply chain sale is a manufacturer that buys raw materials from a vendor, using the Internet as the electronic network. These e-business sales tend to be much larger in dollar value, and there are likely to be many items on each order. The buyer and seller will use common business documents such as purchase orders and invoices, but in electronic form. The software interface between buyer and seller will usually involve more than just a web browser. The vendor's and buyer's computer systems may be linked, and the vendor may actually be able to access and monitor the buyer's inventory systems.

For a large majority of e-business enabled companies, the infrastructure that supports e-business and e-commerce includes software systems such as ERP, CRM, and SCM. The details of this infrastructure cannot be covered in this chapter, however will be described in the following chapter.

The most common method of conducting e-commerce and e-business is to use the Internet to electronically exchange data. However, there are other forms of conducting business electronically. These other methods, such as EDI and EFT, may use private lines or value-added networks (VANs) to connect companies together electronically. These other forms will be described briefly near the end of this chapter. Internet-based forms of e-business and e-commerce are the focus of this chapter.

THE HISTORY OF THE INTERNET (STUDY OBJECTIVE 2)

Much of the technology foundation upon which the Internet is based was developed by university and military researchers nearly 40 years ago. To understand the current status of the Internet, it is useful to briefly review the historical development of the Internet and the underlying technology. In 1965, a researcher at MIT connected a computer in Massachusetts to a computer in California, using dial-up telephone lines. During this time, the U.S. military needed a method of sharing data and research among universities that were working on defense research projects. In 1969, the large computers at four major universities were connected via leased telephone lines. This network, used by the United States Defense Advanced Research Project Agency, grew into a network called ARPANET. The purpose of the network was to share military research data among UCLA, UC Santa Barbara, Stanford, and the University of Utah. Over the next few months, many other universities, NASA, and the Rand Corporation were connected to this network.

Two of the technologies developed for ARPANET form the basic foundation of the Internet of today. Packet switching and routers are necessary to send data over the network. **Packet switching** is the method used to send data over a computer network. Computer data are divided into packets (small packages of data). Each packet is sent individually over the network, with each packet possibly transmitted via a different route. When the packets arrive at the destination, they are reassembled into the correct order to recreate the original data. When data are sent packet switched, small parts of the data are transmitted, they are verified for correctness, and then more information is sent toward the destination.

A **router** is an electronic hardware device that is located at the gateway between two or more networks. The router forwards the packets of data along the best route so that the data reach their destination. The ARPANET used both of these technologies, which have continued to be used in the Internet of today.

The ARPANET was developed during the height of the Cold War and nuclear weapon proliferation. Thus, the network was designed so that if some of the sites were destroyed by a nuclear attack, the other sites could still function and share the military research data. Therefore, routers were designed to route the network traffic via many possible alternative routes.

E-mail, which is simply another form of data that can be transmitted over a network, was adapted to ARPANET in 1972. Ray Tomlinson of BBN Technologies developed the idea of using the @ symbol to separate the user name from the address. BBN Technologies has been involved in much of the development of the Internet. BBN Technologies also developed a communication protocol for ARPANET that is still used today. Since there were several different brands, or types, of computers in the network ARPANET, a common communication protocol was necessary to allow different types of computers to communicate. A **protocol** is a standard data communication format that allows computers to exchange data. Computers must have a common communication method to be linked together in a network. As an analogy, think about what would happen if a foreign exchange student from Japan met a foreign exchange student from Spain in the hallway of the business building at your college. They would be completely unable to communicate in their native languages. However, if both were accompanied by an English translator, their native languages could be translated into English, communicated between the translators (the network), and then translated into the language of either student. Likewise, a common and standard communication protocol allows computers with different operating systems to communicate on a network. Thus, a UNIX® computer, or Digital Equipment Company's (DEC) OpenVMS can communicate with a Windows XP or Apple Mac OS computer.

In the 1970s, BBN Technologies helped develop the TCP/IP protocol that continues in use in the Internet today. **TCP/IP** is an abbreviation for transmission control protocol/Internet protocol.

Through the 1970s and 1980s, the ARPANET continued to add universities, research organizations, and libraries to its network. However, other than universities, libraries, and research organizations, there were no other users of ARPANET. In 1986, the National Science Foundation (NSF) funded and began to develop a backbone set of servers, gateways, and networks that eventually became what we now call the Internet. The NSF also set rules for the use of the Internet by government, university, and research users. Throughout its history of development, and until the early 1990s, the Internet was not user friendly and was not used by the general public. The **Internet** is the global computer network, or "information super-highway." The term "Internet" comes from the concept of *inter*connected *net*works. Thus, the Internet evolved from a variety of university- and government-sponsored computer networks built largely for research. That network became the Internet and is now made up of millions upon millions of computers and subnetworks throughout the world. The Internet serves as the backbone for the World Wide Web (WWW).

In 1993, Marc Andreessen developed the first graphical user interface (GUI) browser, which he named Mosaic. Using the ideas and concepts in the Mosaic browser, Andreessen developed the Netscape® Navigator web browser. Netscape became a phenomenon and fueled the use of the Internet by the general public. A GUI browser made the use of the Internet user friendly so that the Internet could be used by the general public. During this period, more commercial enterprises became involved in adding to the network backbone of servers, routers, and gateways. In 1992, commercial enterprises such as Delphi Corporation and America Online (AOL) began offering Internet access to subscribers. This was the first time that the general public could access the Internet by buying a monthly subscription account with an Internet service provider. In 1994, the first business transaction occurred on the Internet.

In 1995, the NSF relinquished control of the Internet backbone to commercial enterprises, and the NSF funded backbone was separated from the Internet and returned to a research network. Since that time, all Internet traffic has been routed through commercial networks. The latter half of the decade of the 1990s saw the explosive growth of the Internet. Retailers and other corporations began to conduct business via the Internet, and many new Internet based companies were formed. Companies such as Amazon.com, eBay, Webvan, and Pets.com were started during this time. These are only a few examples of the so-called dot-com firms of the 1990s, some of which did not survive beyond the beginning of the next decade.

As the Internet grew, the backbone was continually updated and improved to build in additional servers, routers, and networks that transmit data much faster. The speed and the amount of network traffic grew very rapidly as the technology allowed improvements. The exponential growth of the Internet during the late 1990s can be seen in Exhibit 14-2.

Exhibit 14-2
Chart of the Number of Web Servers

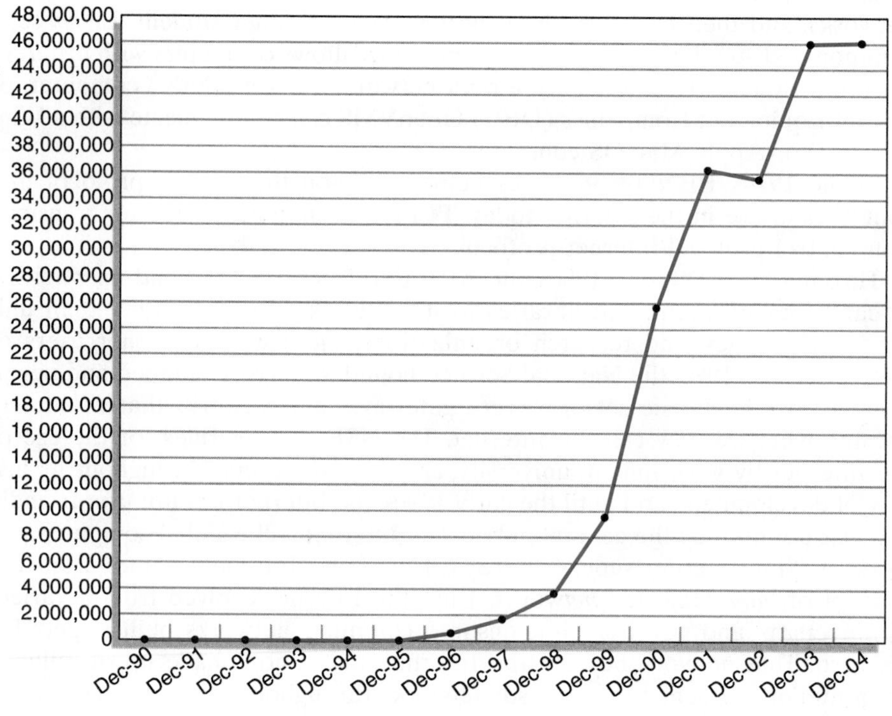

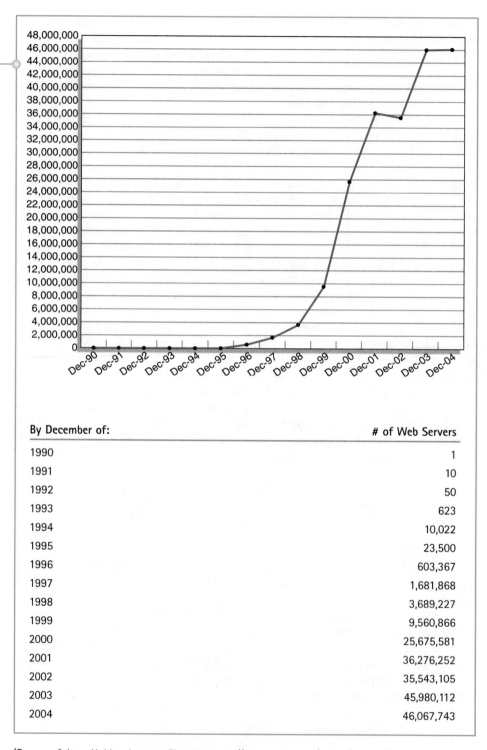

By December of:	# of Web Servers
1990	1
1991	10
1992	50
1993	623
1994	10,022
1995	23,500
1996	603,367
1997	1,681,868
1998	3,689,227
1999	9,560,866
2000	25,675,581
2001	36,276,252
2002	35,543,105
2003	45,980,112
2004	46,067,743

(Source of data: Hobbes Internet Timeline, http://www.zakon.org/robert/Internet/timeline)

As you will note by looking at Exhibit 14-2, the tremendous growth in web servers occurred between 1995 and 2001. During 2001 in the United States, the economic downturn and other factors led to what many call the dot-com bust, a time when many of the dot-com firms begun in the previous three to four years either failed or were purchased by other companies.

THE PHYSICAL STRUCTURE AND STANDARDS OF THE INTERNET (STUDY OBJECTIVE 3)

THE NETWORK

Exhibit 14-3 shows the types of organizations that make up the inter-connected networks of the Internet. The Internet includes backbone providers, network access points, regional Internet service providers (ISPs), local ISPs, and Internet subscribers. The Internet is a hierarchical arrangement: There are a few large backbone providers, many more regional and local ISPs, and millions of Internet subscribers. Internet subscribers are the individual users of the Internet.

A **backbone provider** is an organization which supplies access to high-speed transmission lines that make up the main network lines of the Internet. Much like the way that your spinal bones, or backbone, support all the skeletal systems of your body, the Internet **backbone** is the main trunk line of the Internet. The backbone has extremely high capacity and high-speed network lines. The actual speed and capacity of the backbone lines continually increase as the technology is upgraded, and the speed of the U.S. backbone is one trillion bytes per second. This means that one trillion bits of data could be transmitted over the network lines in one second. The backbone providers connect to each other either directly through private lines or through network access points (NAPs). Major backbone providers in the United States are companies such as MCI, Sprint, Qwest, UUNET, AGIS, and BBN.

Regional ISPs connect to the backbone through lines that have less speed and capacity than the backbone. Examples of regional ISPs would be Earth-Link, America Online, and BellSouth. The network lines used to connect

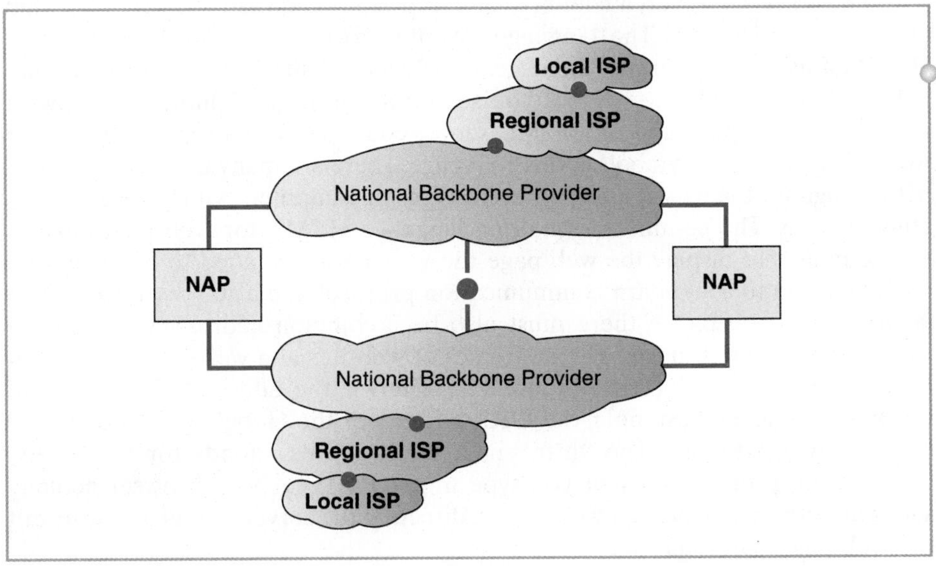

Exhibit 14-3
Architecture of the Internet

regional ISPs to the backbone are usually T3 lines. A T3 line carries data at 44.476 megabits per second (44 million bits per second). Local ISPs connect to regional ISPs by either T3 or T1 lines. A T1 line carries data at a speed of 1.544 megabits per second (Mbps). Regional and local ISPs usually use several T3 or T1 lines simultaneously. You might envision how this works by thinking about water hoses. If you squirt one water hose at a house fire, only a small volume of water reaches the fire. The use of four water hoses, all aimed at the same fire, will send four times the volume of water. Examples of local ISPs are local telephone companies and local cable companies.

Local ISPs connect individual users to the Internet. These Internet subscribers are connected to local ISPs using either dial-up modems, digital subscriber lines (DSL), or cable TV lines. Dial-up modem speeds are typically 56 kilobytes per second, while DSL speed is usually approximately 5 mbps and cable broadband speeds are approximately 5 to 10 mbps.

At each of these organizations and gateways, there are computers that function as web servers. A **web server** is a computer and hard drive space that stores web pages and data. These web servers respond to requests for web pages or data, and transmit the web pages or data over the network. Through these interconnected networks and web servers, any computer connected to the Internet can communicate with any other computer on the Internet. This system enables e-business, e-commerce, and e-mail to function as we know it today.

THE COMMON STANDARDS OF THE INTERNET

Since any computer can theoretically link to any other computer on the Internet, there must be common and standard methods to display and communicate the data transmitted via the Internet. Each computer on the Internet uses the TCP/IP protocol to communicate with the network. While every computer connected to the Internet could possibly be part of the World Wide Web, every such computer is not necessarily part of the web. The World Wide Web is an information-sharing network that uses the Internet as the network to share data.

Web pages that are part of the World Wide Web are available to anyone using a web browser. However, a common way to present and read the data on a web page is also necessary. The language invented to present data on websites is **HTML,** a hypertext markup language. Nearly all websites use HTML to format the words, data, and pictures that you see on a web page. Exhibit 14-4 shows a very simple web page and the HTML source code that formats and presents the words and the arrow symbol on this web page. There are many users of the Internet throughout the world, using different types of computers with different operating systems. The common formatting language HTML for web pages allows any computer to display the web page the way it was intended to be displayed.

In addition to a standard communication protocol and a standard formatting language for web pages, there must also be a common addressing method to store and locate web pages. The addresses of websites and web pages use a uniform resource locater (URL) address. A **URL** is the address you type in to reach a website. For example, the URL address of the Google search engine is http://www.google.com. The "http" in a URL address stands for "hypertext transmission protocol." When you type in a URL, your web browser actually sends an http command to a web server, directing the server to find and transmit the web page you requested.

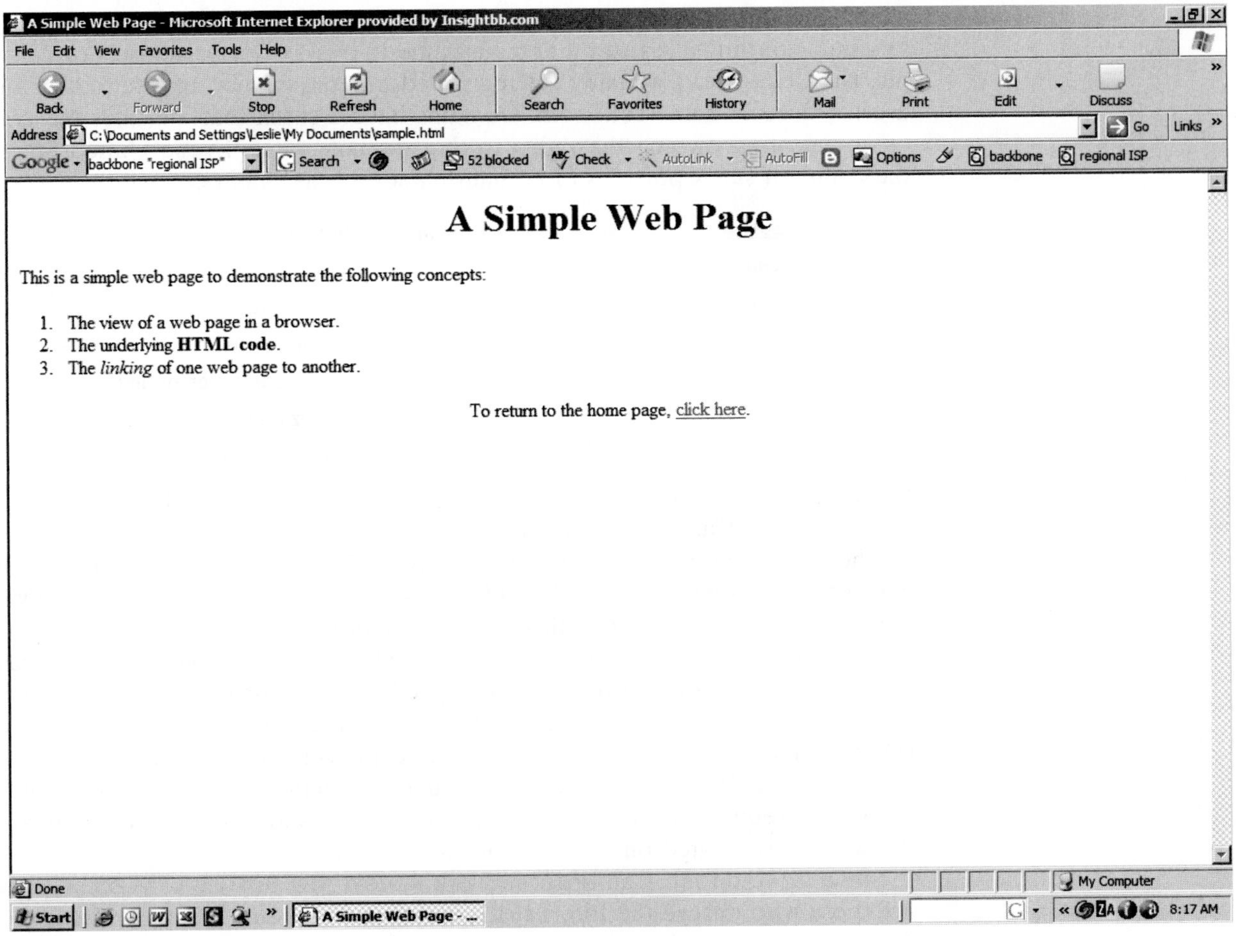

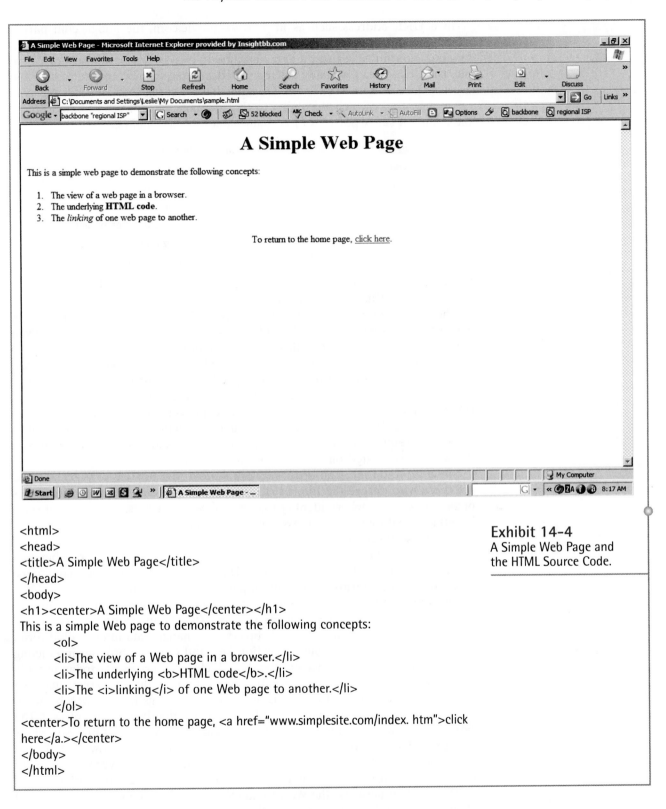

```
<html>
<head>
<title>A Simple Web Page</title>
</head>
<body>
<h1><center>A Simple Web Page</center></h1>
This is a simple Web page to demonstrate the following concepts:
        <ol>
        <li>The view of a Web page in a browser.</li>
        <li>The underlying <b>HTML code</b>.</li>
        <li>The <i>linking</i> of one Web page to another.</li>
        </ol>
<center>To return to the home page, <a href="www.simplesite.com/index. htm">click
here</a.></center>
</body>
</html>
```

Exhibit 14-4
A Simple Web Page and the HTML Source Code.

In a URL address such as http://www.google.com, the google.com part is called the **domain name**—the unique name that identifies the Internet site. Organizations must register a domain name to own its exclusive use. For example, The Coca-Cola Company has registered, and pays a monthly fee to own and use the domain name coke.com. Domains have a suffix that indicates the type of organization owning the rights to that domain name. In the United States, the common suffix portions of domain names are as follows:

Suffix	Organization Type
.com	commercial business
.edu	educational institution
.org	nonprofit organization
.gov	governmental organization or unit
.mil	military organization
.net	network or commercial business

For domains outside the United States, the suffix indicates the country. For example, .ca is Canada and .au is Australia.

The URL addressing system actually uses IP addresses rather than domain names that are spelled out. An IP address is an Internet protocol address. A given domain name is associated with a single IP address. In the same way that your postal address allows your mail carrier to locate your exact home, an IP address is the unique information that allows a specific website or server to be located.

There are specialized servers on the Internet called domain name servers (DNS), which function to store, index, and provide the IP address for each domain name. When a domain name such as coke.com is typed into a web browser, a request is sent to a DNS to find the IP address of the domain, and the website is located on the basis of the IP address.

Since the Internet is an open network system that anyone can access, there are those who misuse the Internet for illegal and fraudulent activity. Examples of such risks are hackers, identity thieves, password sniffers, and denial of service attacks. Without an extra layer of protection, any data exchange between a user and a web server is open for anyone to read. This means if you enter your credit card number on an e-commerce website, your credit card number and other data can possibly be intercepted. Therefore, the majority of e-commerce sites use common forms of encryption and data protection.

The standard form of encryption embedded in e-commerce sites and in web browser software is **secure sockets layering (SSL)**, an encryption system in which the web server and the user's browser exchange data in encrypted form. The web server uses a public encryption key, and only the browser interacting with that web server can decode the data. Web browsers in use today use 128 bit encryption. Persons using a web browser will know they are connected to a secure encrypted site that uses SSL by seeing two things in their web browser. First, a website using SSL will have a URL address that begins with https://. The extra "s" at the end of the http denotes a secure site. Also, most browsers show a picture of a locked padlock in the lower bar of the web browser. SSL and encryption allow the general public to conduct e-commerce over websites with less fear of exposure regarding credit card or other private information.

The Internet network, the World Wide Web, and the common standards used allow the general public to browse the web, share data, send e-mail, and conduct e-commerce. The next section describes e-commerce.

E-COMMERCE AND ITS BENEFITS (STUDY OBJECTIVE 4)

There has never been complete agreement on an exact definition of e-commerce. However, most would agree that e-commerce is a transaction between a business and customer, in which the transaction information is exchanged electronically. Under such a broad definition, there are many forms of exchange that could be called e-commerce. The use of a credit card at a department store, ATM transactions with a bank, EDI transactions between vendor and buyer, and web-based transactions all fit into this definition of e-commerce. With the explosive growth of "web based" commerce in the last decade, e-commerce has widely come to be thought of as web-based. That is, the average person thinks that e-commerce is web-based commerce. Since web-based commerce is the most common form of e-commerce, this section will focus on the web-based form of e-commerce.

Hereafter, the references to e-commerce will be to web-based e-commerce. Also, e-commerce will refer to business-to-consumer sales. The common term for business-to-consumer e-commerce is **B2C**. Conversely, the term e-business will include business-to-business electronic transactions. The common term for business-to-business electronic sales is **B2B**.

B2C sales are transactions between a business and a consumer, which usually involve a retail or service company whose customers are end-user consumers. While there are literally thousands of different types of B2C transactions, some examples are as follows:

1. Buying a book on Amazon.com
2. Downloading a song purchased from Musicmatch.com
3. Buying an airline ticket on Expedia.com
4. Buying a computer at Dell.com

The common aspect in these transactions in that the consumer interacts with the business via the business's website.

There are many advantages of B2C sales to the business and to the customer. Both parties benefit from the increased access to the market, the speed and convenience of e-commerce, and the ability to share information.

BENEFITS AND DISADVANTAGES OF E-COMMERCE FOR THE CUSTOMER

The major benefits to the customer of buying products or services relate to the increased access, speed, convenience, and information sharing mentioned previously. More specifically, the benefits to the customer are the following:

1. E-commerce provides access to a much broader market for goods and services. By using e-commerce, the customer is not constrained by geography or geographic boundaries. If a customer wishes to buy a shirt, he can access any number of websites selling shirts, some of which may be in other states or countries. The customer need not physically visit a store to buy.
2. E-commerce also provides more convenient times for shopping. Orders can be placed 24 hours a day, 7 days a week. As mentioned in item 1, the

customer does not need to go to a store to buy the product or service and is not limited by location or hours of operation of the website, as he would be when shopping at a store.

3. The wider access to the marketplace also provides more choices to the customer. This may enable the customer to more easily find the same product at a less expensive price. In addition, the wider market access may allow the customer to find a product with better features at a more competitive price.
4. E-commerce is likely to provide lower prices, for many reasons. Businesses that sell via e-commerce can reduce many costs, and these cost savings can be passed on to the customer. The details of the cost savings will be discussed later in the section on the benefits to businesses of e-commerce. In addition, the customer may not be required to pay sales taxes for e-commerce purchases. However, in many cases, the tax savings may be offset by shipping or delivery costs.
5. The information-sharing aspect of the Internet and World Wide Web allows the customer to exchange information with businesses before, during, and after the purchase. Some e-commerce websites have live chat sessions with product or service specialists to answer questions.
6. E-commerce can allow quicker delivery of the product, enabled by the faster processing time of e-commerce. To fill an order, the business does not have to undertake steps such as entering order information into the computer system. As soon as the customer enters the order via the website, order processing can begin.
7. Customers can receive targeted marketing from businesses that they frequently purchase from. For example, Amazon.com analyzes customer buying patterns and can recommend specific books that may be of interest to the customer.

While there are significant advantages to e-commerce to the customer, there are also disadvantages. The free and open nature the World Wide Web allows the opportunity for fraud, theft of assets, or theft of data. Customers have concerns about the privacy and security of personal information shared with businesses during e-commerce transactions. Hackers and identity thefts can potentially steal credit card information, banking information, and private data. Because such concerns may prevent some customers from purchasing via e-commerce, businesses must respond by trying to ensure the security and privacy of customer data. The details of privacy principles are covered later in this chapter.

The other disadvantage for the customer is the inability to handle or try out the product. Compared with a store shopping experience, the customer does not have the same ability to see and handle the product.

BENEFITS AND DISADVANTAGES OF E-COMMERCE FOR THE BUSINESS

Advantages to the business are as follows:

1. E-commerce provides access to a much broader market, including the potential of a global market for even small businesses. Traditional geographic boundaries are no longer a constraint if the business uses e-commerce.
2. Dramatically reduced marketing costs are a typical result of the expanded market. While a business may still spend for advertising, such as for web-based

ads, the cost per customer reached is usually substantially less than that for traditional forms of marketing. For example, suppose that an electronics store can place a local television advertisement at a cost $10,000 to reach 10,000 customers. That same amount spent on a web-based ad has the potential to reach millions of potential customers.

3. E-commerce provides the potential for much richer marketing concepts that include video, audio, product comparisons, and product testimonials or product tests. On its website, the business can provide links to these marketing tools.
4. The company can quickly react to changes in market conditions. For example, if market changes require price drops, the business can quickly change prices on the website, and all customers will see the new price immediately. If a company uses mail-order catalogs instead of e-commerce, price changes can occur only when a new catalog is printed. If a chain store such as Wal-Mart wished to change prices in all of its stores in a specific region or state, it would be somewhat time-consuming to update the signs and systems in order to institute the price changes.
5. The business using e-commerce is likely to experience reduced order-processing and distribution costs. Order-processing costs are reduced because e-commerce automates all or most of the order processing. Rather than business employees taking sales orders by phone or mail and keying them into the IT system, the customer enters all order information. Distribution costs are reduced simply because e-commerce uses a much different model than traditional retail businesses. Many e-commerce businesses do not maintain stocks of inventory in stores or warehouses. The business may instead order only when the customer orders and have the product drop-shipped directly from the supplier to the customer.
6. The customer convenience aspect of e-commerce means that the business is likely to experience higher sales.
7. Higher sales coupled with reduced marketing, order processing, and distribution costs can lead to much higher profits.

There are also some disadvantages to e-commerce, for businesses. The IT systems necessary to conduct e-commerce are usually much more complex and costly. The e-commerce software and systems must also be implemented in a way that integrates the existing general ledger, inventory, and payment IT systems. (The IT software and hardware infrastructure that supports e-commerce and e-business is discussed in the next chapter.) In addition, the free and open nature of the World Wide Web opens a business to greater chances for fraud, hackers, and compromised customer privacy.

THE COMBINATION OF E-COMMERCE AND TRADITIONAL COMMERCE

Much of the preceding discussion focused on the comparison of e-commerce with traditional forms of commerce, namely, catalog and store commerce. However, in the retail environment of today, most retailers or service businesses use a combination of traditional commerce and e-commerce. For example, Wal-Mart, Target, and Kmart are traditional store-based retailers that now also offer to customers web-based shopping. Local, regional, and national banks all used to depend on customers' walking, riding, or driving to a bank branch office. Today, banks also offer web-based banking. So, traditional forms of commerce have changed to incorporate e-commerce. However, the converse is true also. Many e-commerce retailers that began purely as e-commerce forms of business have found that they must add the traditional customer interaction in the form of stores or offices. For example, E*TRADE Financial Corp., a web-based brokerage firm, found that to better service customers, it needed some physical office locations. E*TRADE opened offices around the country and placed a link on its website, called "Physical Locations." The web page that customers access by clicking on that link presents the addresses of regional offices of E*TRADE in large cities.

This merging and melding of forms of commerce has led to new terminology in the world of commerce. Companies that work from purely traditional stores, are called **bricks and mortar** retailers in e-commerce. At one point in the evolution of e-commerce, businesses that were purely web-based were called **e-tailers**. As businesses merged the two, the resulting combined forms are referred to as **clicks and mortar** businesses. Alternatively, some call this form of business **bricks and clicks**.

PRIVACY EXPECTATIONS IN E-COMMERCE (STUDY OBJECTIVE 5)

Chapter 4 described the relationship between IT risks and controls, using the AICPA's Trust Services Principles and criteria as the framework to examine risks and controls. That section of Chapter 4 provided details regarding four (items 1, 2, 3, and 5) of the five risk areas identified in the Trust Services Principles. The fourth risk area of IT systems described in the AICPA Trust Services Principles is "online privacy." Regarding this risk area, the Trust Services Principles states that the "online privacy principle focuses on protecting the personal information an organization may collect from its customers, employees, and other individuals"[3] through its e-commerce systems. This personal information consists of many different kinds of data. The Trust Services Principles provide the following partial list of personal information to be protected:

- Name, address, Social Security number, or other government ID numbers
- Employment history
- Personal or family health conditions
- Personal or family financial information
- History of purchases or other transactions
- Credit records

In the course of conducting business with customers, an organization may have legitimate reasons to collect and keep these customer data. However, to conduct e-commerce, the organization must provide to customers a level of confidence in the privacy and security of this kind of personal information shared. To engender such confidence, the organization must demonstrate to customers that it has taken appropriate steps to ensure privacy. The Trust Services Principles

[3] "Trust Services Principles, Criteria and Illustrations for Security, Availability, Processing Integrity Confidentiality, and Privacy," American Institute of Certified Public Accountants, 2006, pp. 50–53.

explain ten privacy practices that an organization should follow to ensure adequate customer confidence regarding privacy of information, as follows:[4]

1. **Management.** The organization should assign a specific person or persons, the responsibility of privacy practices for the organization. That responsible person should insure that the organization has defined and documented its privacy practices. That person should also insure that privacy practices have been communicated to both employees and customers. Management would also include the responsibility to insure that privacy practices are followed by employees.
2. **Notice.** The organization should have policies and practices to maintain privacy of customer data. Notice implies that the company provides the privacy practices to customers in some form. At the time that data is to be collected, a notice should be available to the customer that describes the privacy policies and practices. Many e-commerce organizations accomplish this by providing a link on their website to privacy policies. Notice should include information regarding the purpose of collecting the information, and how that information will be used.
3. **Choice and consent.** The organization should provide choice to its customers regarding the collection of data, and also should ask for consent to collect, retain, and use the data. The customer should be informed of any choices that the customer may have to opt out of providing information. The customer should have access to descriptions about the choices available. The customer should also be able to read policies about how the data will be used. As in "notice" above, these descriptions usually are in the form of a link to privacy policies.
4. **Collection.** The organization should collect only the data that is necessary for the purpose of conducting the transaction. In addition, the customer should have provided implicit or explicit consent before data is collected. Explicit consent might be in the form of placing a check mark by a box indicating consent. Implicit consent occurs when the customer provides data that is clearly marked as voluntary, or when the customer has provided data and has not clearly stated that it can not be used.
5. **Use and retention.** The organization uses customers' personal data only in the manner described in "notice" from part a. above. The use of this data occurs only after the customer has given implicit or explicit consent to use the data. Such personal data is retained only as long as necessary.
6. **Access.** Every customer should have access to the data provided so that the customer can view, change, delete, or block further use of the data provided.
7. **Disclosure to third parties.** In some cases, e-commerce organizations forward customer information to third parties. Before this forwarding of data occurs, the organization should receive explicit or implicit consent of the customer. Personal data should only be forwarded to third parties that have equivalent privacy protections.
8. **Security for privacy.** The organization has necessary protections to try to insure that customer data is not lost, destroyed, altered, or subject to unauthorized access. The organization should put internal controls in place that prevent hackers and unauthorized employees from accessing customer data.

[4] Ibid.

9. **Quality.** The organization should institute procedures to insure that all customer data collected retains quality. Data quality means that the data remains "accurate, complete, current, relevant, and reliable".
10. **Monitoring and enforcement.** The organization should continually monitor to insure that its privacy practices are followed. The organization should have procedures to address privacy related inquiries or disputes.

In summary, these practices require that a company establish, enforce, monitor, and update policies and practices that protect the privacy and security of customer information. The company should consider not only its own privacy practices and policies, but also the practices and policies of any third parties who will share information. Companies that fail to establish good policies or that fail to enforce policies have violated the ethical standards that customers expect when conducting e-commerce. The ethics-related aspects of privacy are addressed at the end of this chapter.

E-BUSINESS AND IT ENABLEMENT (STUDY OBJECTIVE 6)

As discussed previously, e-business is a very broad, encompassing term for the electronic enabling of business processes. The business processes enabled by IT systems can be internal and external. Examples of internal processes are the movement of raw materials within a company, the timekeeping and labor management of workers, the dissemination of employee information such as health and retirement benefits, and the sharing of data files among workers. These types of internal processes can be streamlined and enhanced by incorporating electronic forms of these processes through the use of IT systems. Likewise, there are many external business processes that can be streamlined and enhanced through the use of IT systems. For example, the processes that involve suppliers and distributors can be streamlined, enhanced, and improved by the use of IT systems.

The **supply chain** is the set of linked processes that take place from the acquisition and delivery of raw materials, through the manufacturing, distribution, wholesale, and delivery of the product to the customer. The supply chain includes vendors; manufacturing facilities; logistics providers; internal distribution centers such as warehouses, distributors, and wholesalers; and any other entities that are involved, up to the final customer. In some cases, the supply is larger at both ends because it can include secondary suppliers to the company's suppliers and the customers of the company's immediate customers. Exhibit 14-5 illustrates the entities in a sample supply chain for a manufacturer and the relationships between those entities. Service firms have a less complex supply chain.

To gain an understanding of the supply chain, it may be helpful to begin in the middle of the exhibit. A manufacturer makes products. Upon completion of the manufacturing, the finished products are sent to and stored in warehouses. As those products are needed, they are shipped to distributors or wholesalers. The distributors or wholesalers eventually ship the products to retail companies, and the retail companies sell the products to end-user consumers.

However, before a manufacturing company can produce products, it must buy the raw materials that are the ingredients of the products. For example, a wine maker must buy grapes. In some instances, a manufacturing company's supply chain may include secondary suppliers. For example, a company that manufactures personal computers (PCs) may buy components such as graphics cards

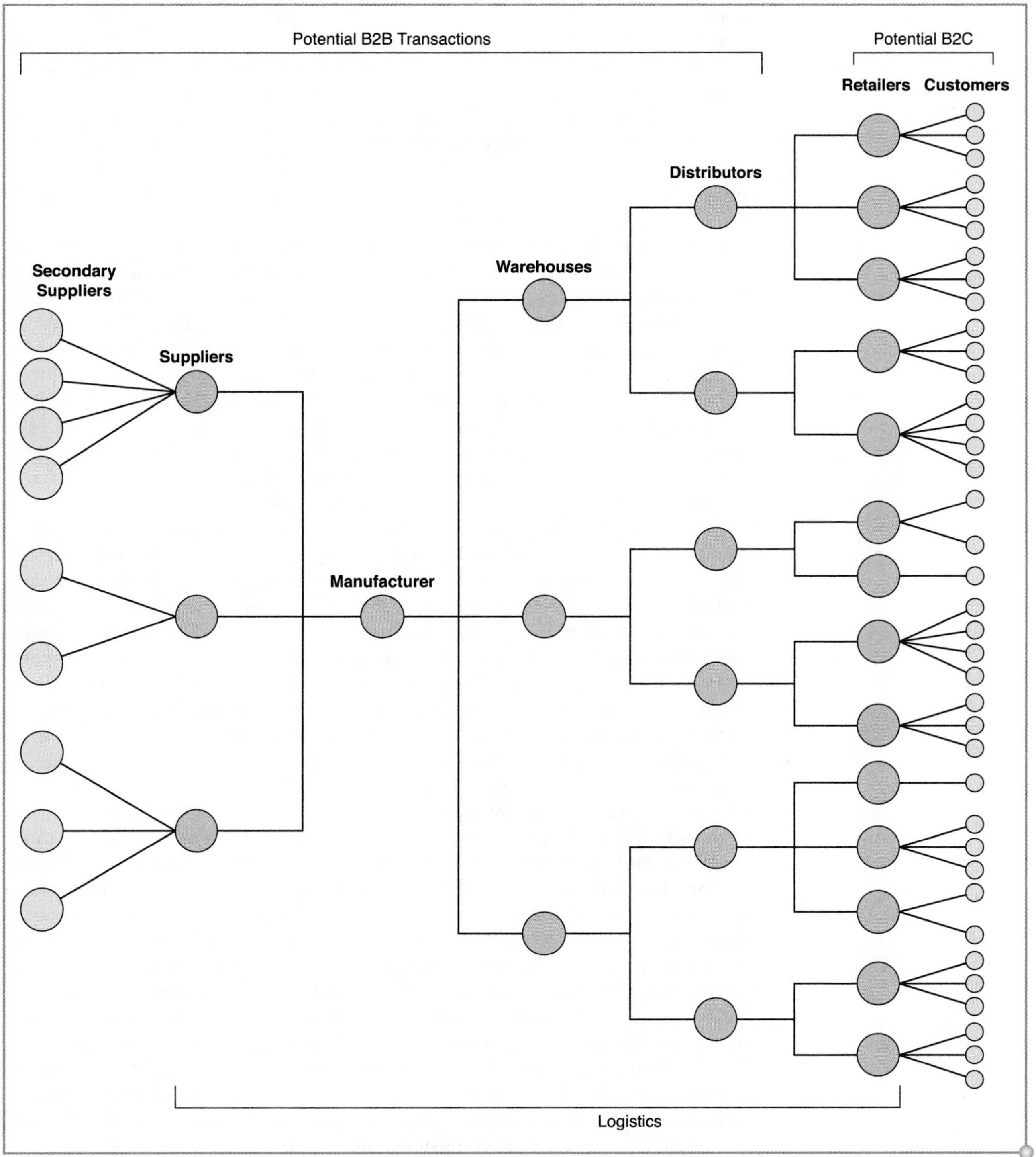

Exhibit 14-5
The Supply Chain for a Manufacturing Company

from a supplier. The supplier, however, makes the graphics cards after buying chips and circuit boards from secondary suppliers. While there may not be direct exchanges between the manufacturer (maker of the PC) and the secondary supplier's (the chip maker), the secondary supplier's performance and product quality have a dramatic effect on the manufacturer. For example, if the chip maker runs out of chips, the graphics card maker is prevented from making graphics cards on time, which thereby makes the PC maker unable to make and ship PCs. Similarly, poor quality chip production by the chip maker affects the quality of the graphics board, and therefore the quality of the PC.

This interdependency of entities in the supply chain means that companies should be interested in enhancing and streamlining the processes and exchanges that occur throughout the supply chain. Poor quality, slow performance, or a process bottleneck anywhere in the supply chain affects other parts of the supply chain. There is an old saying that a chain is only as strong as the weakest link. Similarly, a supply chain is only as efficient as its weakest, or most inefficient, link.

Many interactions between entities and many business processes must occur to complete the steps that result in raw materials being converted into products and eventually sold to the customer. Any of these processes or linkages between entities can be enabled or enhanced by the use of IT systems. Any that are enabled by IT become a part of e-business. This view of the supply chain shows how broad the scope of e-business is in comparison with e-commerce. E-commerce, or B2C sales, includes only the extreme right-hand part of the diagram in Exhibit 14-5, when the sale is between a company and the end-user customer. E-business includes the entire supply chain, and there is overlap between e-business and e-commerce. E-commerce is a subset of e-business.

Some companies may choose to be involved in many parts of their supply chain. For example, a vertically integrated company may have its own related subsidiaries so that each of the interactions within the supply chain is owned or controlled by the larger corporate entity. Vertical integration occurs when a single company owns all of the entities that make up the supply chain, from the movement of raw materials to the delivery of the finished product to the customer.

Other companies may choose to focus on only a small part of the supply chain. For example, a company could choose to do only the manufacturing portion of the supply chain; all other entities within the supply chain, such as suppliers, distributors, wholesalers, and retailers, are separate companies. These differing levels of integration within the supply chain mean that the processes which occur within a supply chain may be internal to a company or may involve exchanges with external companies. In either case, internal or external, those processes and exchanges can be streamlined or enhanced through e-business.

The "Logistics" label in Exhibit 14-5 illustrates that there are entities within the supply chain whose function is to provide the physical support that moves materials and goods between parts of the supply chain. For example, a manufacturer must have a means of moving raw materials from the supplier to the plant and of moving finished goods from the plant to the warehouse and distributor. Logistics are the types of services provided by entities such as trucking companies, air and rail freight companies, and freight expediting companies.

Any of the interactions between the entities within the supply chain can be a point at which e-business can be applied to streamline or reduce costs. The next section describes a smaller subset of e-business interactions within the supply chain: B2B, or business-to-business electronic transactions.

B2B: A PART OF E-BUSINESS

B2B is the sale of products or services between a business buyer and a business seller that is electronically enabled by the Internet. In B2B sales, neither buyer nor seller is an end-user consumer. Although there are many ways to

Exhibit 14-6
E-commerce B2C vs. E-Business B2B[5]

Differences between E-Commerce and E-Business

E-COMMERCE, or B2C	B2B form of E-BUSINESS
• business to consumer	• business to business
• few line items per order	• many line items per order
• large order volume	• very specific shipping data
• geared to consumer's ease of use	• user-selected information content and interaction tools, deeper functionality
• use of credit card purchasing	• use of purchase orders • sophisticated transaction protocols
• no necessity of a preexisting relationship between buyer and seller	• buyer and seller usually have a pre-existing relationship and negotiated prices and delivery details

conduct business electronically between businesses, this chapter focuses on Internet based e-business. As in the case of e-commerce, both parties benefit from the increased access to the market, the speed and convenience of e-business, and ability to share information. There are also many differences between B2C and B2B transactions, as illustrated in Exhibit 14-6. When comparing B2B with B2C, B2B has the following differing characteristics:

- The transaction or exchange is between businesses.
- The order would have many line items, and the dollar amount of each sale is usually large.
- While a B2C sale might be a single book purchased from Amazon, a B2B sale might be tons of raw materials, as in the case of grapes to make wine.
- The B2B sale will have specific shipping details such as type of carrier used, delivery dates, and locations of delivery to different plants within the company.
- The B2B transaction can involve electronic forms of standard business documents such as purchase order and invoice.
- The B2C transaction is between the company and any potential customer on the Internet. There need not be any preexisting relationship. The B2B transaction is between buyer and supplier, and the parties usually have a preexisting relationship. The buyer knows which suppliers it will use, and the supplier knows that the buyer will be buying raw materials or services. The buyer and supplier would have already negotiated many of the details of the transaction, such as prices, discounts, payment terms, credit limits, delivery dates, and locations of delivery.

When conducted via the Internet, B2B transactions between supplier and buyer offer many advantages to both parties. Many of the advantages are similar to those described in the e-commerce section of this chapter. Internet based transactions offer a wider potential market, reduced transaction cost, and higher profits. B2B will also result in faster cycle times for the purchases from suppliers. The cycle time is the time from the placement of an order for goods to the receipt of, and payment for, the goods. The faster cycle time results from the

[5]Adapted from Janet Gould, "What's the Difference between E-Commerce and E-Business? And Why Should you Care?" *ID Systems,* Vol. 19 Issue II, November 1999.

increased efficiency of processing transactions via the Internet. In B2B transactions between suppliers and buyers, the two IT systems exchange data through the Internet network. The Internet allows companies to reduce or eliminate manually keying the order into the computer system, mailing documents to initiate the order, entering receipt of goods, and keying in documents to initiate payment. The fact that the two IT systems communicate eliminates data errors, since data may no longer be manually keyed into the system.

E-BUSINESS ENABLEMENT EXAMPLES (STUDY OBJECTIVE 7)

There is much more to e-business than just B2B transactions. The Internet can be used in so many different ways to streamline business processes, reduce operational costs, and enhance efficiency that it is difficult to describe the entire range of e-business possibilities. The summaries that follow are real business examples of the ways in which businesses adopt e-business strategies.

THE REAL WORLD

General Electric Company (GE)

On April 26, 2000, Jack Welch, the well-known CEO of General Electric Company, spoke at the GE annual meeting of shareholders and described how e-business affects four aspects of business at GE. He called these four areas "buy, make, sell, and strategic." Regarding these four areas, he said the following:[6]

> On our "buy" side, we now measure the number of auctions on line, the percentage of the total buy on line and the dollars saved.
>
> On the "make" portion, the Internet is all about getting information from its source to the user without intermediaries. The new measurement is how fast information gets from its origin to users and how much unproductive data gathering, expediting, tracking orders and the like can be eliminated. This tedious work in a typical big company is the last bastion—the Alamo—of functionalism and bureaucracy. Taking it out improves both productivity and employee morale.
>
> On the "sell" side, the new measurements are number of visitors, sales on line, percentage of sales on line, new customers, share, span and the like.
>
> Strategically, the breadth of our business portfolio exposes us to a very wide range of emerging companies, many of them Internet based. This intimate knowledge has enabled us to make successful strategic investments in over 250 companies.

Mr. Welch was indicating that GE uses e-business to improve how it buys, makes, sells, and strategically positions the company. The buy and sell concepts of e-business are somewhat evident and have been described here. However, notice that Mr. Welch indicates that e-business can be used within the company in internal processes such as manufacturing. GE uses Internet communication within the company to expedite and track orders, reducing manual processes.

General Motors Corporation (GM)

Ecommerce indicated the following about a new GM e-business initiative called eGM.[7]

[6] "GE and the Internet: An Executive Speech Reprint" http://callcentres.com.au/GE2_Jack_Welch.htm

[7] "GM Launches E-com Drive," Ecommerce, August 10, 1999, http://www.internetnews.com/ec-news/article.php/179701.

eGM has been charged with the task of transitioning GM's traditional automotive operations into a global e-business enterprise. Under the plan, GM expects to improve upon customer service, efficiency and slash costs via eGM's integration of business development, strategic e-marketing, e-sales, e-product management and technology and operations units to one central unit.

Again, notice that GM's e-business strategy included much more than sales. GM expected to apply Internet and IT systems to reduce costs through e-business based marketing and e-business management of products and parts. Mark Hogan, the division president in charge of eGM, expected that this e-business initiative would reduce internal costs by 10 percent.[8] To achieve this goal, GM planned to "webify"[9] the design, engineering, and manufacture of vehicles. The internal processes of tracking parts and the manufacture of cars was to be enhanced by the use of internal websites to reduce or eliminate the manual processes and paper processing the company previously used to track and order parts, to move those parts between warehouses to plants, and to more efficiently track the manufacturing process. In addition, GM intended to use e-business to reduce the cost and improve the effectiveness of marketing efforts. Two examples of this were e-mail newsletters sent to customers and web-based advertisements that potential buyers could click on as they surfed the Internet.

Komatsu LTD.

Komatsu is one of the world's largest manufacturers of construction, mining, and utility equipment such as dump trucks, bulldozers, skid loaders, and backhoe loaders. Komatsu sells this equipment through distributors. To assist distributors, Komatsu recently established an application utilizing e-business that allows distributors online access to price quotations for warranties.[10] This enables distributors to answer customer inquiries about warranties more quickly than ever before.

Kenworth Truck Company

Kenworth Truck Company is a leading manufacturer of heavy- and medium-duty trucks. Kenworth has established an e-business application, which they have named PremierCare® Connect, that allows Kenworth dealers to provide better service to customers who buy Kenworth trucks. This Internet link between the customer, dealer, and Kenworth enables the customer to generate part inventory orders automatically when the parts need to be reordered. F.L. Moore & Sons, a trucking company with 65 trucks, was able to cut its parts inventory costs by $25,000 by using PremierCare® Connect.[11]

These examples illustrate the broad nature of e-business, even though they do not encompass all the ways that e-business is used to streamline processes, reduce costs, and improve relationships with suppliers, distributors, wholesalers, retailers, and customers. To gain the advantages available in e-business, organizations must utilize various levels of networks within and attached to the Internet. Companies must use the Internet network to interact electronically with the entities in the

[8]"eGM head pursues broad e-commerce plan," *Infoworld*, March 6, 2000, p.18.

[9]*Ibid.*

[10]Walt Moore, "E-business catches on: High hopes for buying and selling electronically haven't materialized, but the equipment industry is finding practical value online," Special Report, *Construction Equipment*, March 2002.

[11]Sean Kilcarr, "Buying Parts Online," July, 2000 <http://driversmag.com/ar/f lett_buying_parts_online/>.

supply chain. The levels of the Internet network structure that enable e-business are the Internet, extranets, and intranets. These levels of the network serve as the platform to connect parties throughout the supply chain.

INTRANETS AND EXTRANETS TO ENABLE E-BUSINESS (STUDY OBJECTIVE 8)

In many cases, interaction between entities within the supply chain occurs between entities that are part of the same company. As an example, in the eGM vignette, GM was using e-business to enhance the engineering and manufacturing of vehicles. Therefore, engineers and plant personnel have interaction electronically. This interaction within the same company would use an intranet. Exhibit 14-7 depicts the three levels of network platforms—intranets, extranets, and the Internet—that are used in e-business.

An **intranet** is a private network accessible only to the employees of a company. The intranet uses the same common standards and protocols of the Internet. An intranet uses TCP/IP protocol and the same type of html web pages as the Internet. However, the computer servers of the intranet are accessible only from internal computers within the company. The purposes of an intranet are to distribute data or information to employees, to make shared data or files available, and to manage projects within the company. For example, GM engineers located in several different offices across the United States may collaborate on the design of a new car. Those engineers can share project files and information by the use of the internal network, the intranet.

To engage in B2C e-commerce, a company must access the Internet, since it is the network platform that gives a wide range of customers access to B2C sales. For example, Amazon.com could not exist as it currently does if it were not able to reach customers anywhere and any time over the Internet. However, when an organization engages in B2B e-business and e-business throughout the supply chain, it is not interested in reaching the general public. Instead, e-business activities require network access to entities such as suppliers, distributors, logistics providers, and wholesalers. When communicating with these

Exhibit 14-7
Internet, Extranet, and Intranet

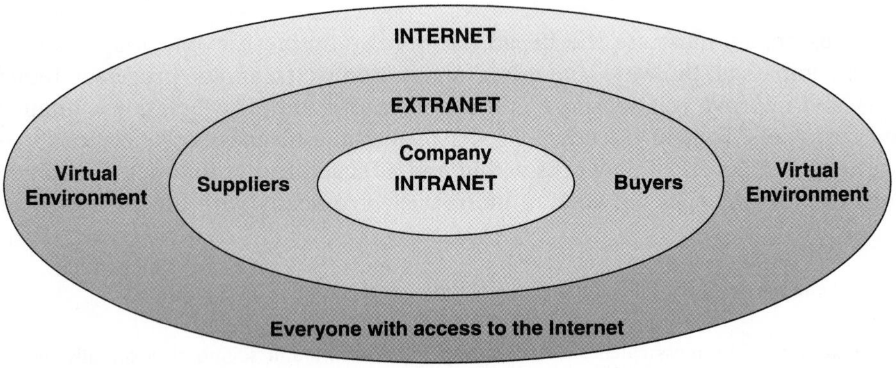

Figure adapted from "Strategic Issues of B2B E-Business," Christoph Wenna, White paper of March 2002, Johannes Kepler University.

entities, the company in fact needs to exclude access by the general public. For example, if Dell Inc. is buying computer hard drives from a supplier, Western Digital Corporation, it would be more appropriate for these two businesses to use a network that does not allow the general public to have access. Rather than using the Internet, this type of exchange may use an extranet.

An **extranet** is similar to an intranet except that it offers access to selected outsiders—buyers, suppliers, distributors, or wholesalers in the supply chain. Extranets are the networks that allow business partners to exchange information through limited access to company servers and data. The external parties have access only to the data necessary to conduct supply chain exchanges with the company. For example, suppliers would need access to raw material inventory levels of the company they sell to, but they would not need access to finished product inventory levels. Conversely, a wholesaler within the value chain may need access to the manufacturer's finished product inventory, but would not need access to raw material inventory levels.

THE REAL WORLD

An Extranet Example of B2B

Staples, Inc., the office supply company, provides a good example of an organization using an extranet to link to large companies to facilitate purchases of office supplies. StaplesLink (www.stapleslink.com) is the extranet available only to established customers of Staples who have 50 or more employees. With a proper company ID, user ID, and password, an employee of a company can log into StaplesLink to purchase office supplies. This e-business arrangement offers advantages to both the company buying supplies and to Staples. The company will have negotiated prices, acceptable products that employees can order, and payment terms. These agreements give company employees convenience and control over their office supply purchases, yet at the same time allow the company to restrict the type and amount of office supplies purchased. Employees of a company using StaplesLink can order supplies online at any time and at a pricing structure that is advantageous to the StaplesLink customer. The StaplesLink customer can also block its employees from purchasing certain items. For example, a company may block the purchase of furniture, printers, or fax machines.

Through such an agreement, Staples has assured itself of an ongoing customer as long as it continues to satisfy the agreement terms. Therefore, Staples increases its volume of sales but accepting a slightly smaller profit margin on each sale. The extranet provides benefits to both Staples and the companies that use StaplesLink.

INTERNAL CONTROLS FOR THE INTERNET, INTRANETS, AND EXTRANETS (STUDY OBJECTIVE 9)

The Internet, intranets, and extranets are all networks that are intended for the sharing of information and the conducting of transactions. In all three networks, controls must be in place to limit access and prevent hackers and other network break-ins. As illustrated in Exhibit 14-7, extranets must have more limited access than the Internet, and intranets must limit access to those inside the company. For all three network levels, a company must establish the correct level of controlled access. In the case of intranets, only internal employees are given access to the network and information. Extranet access should be limited to those parties in the supply chain who will be sharing information or engaging in exchanges with the company. The general public must be prevented from gaining access to these intranet and extranet networks. The Internet connections of a company must also be controlled. When a company uses the Internet for exchanges such as B2C transactions, it must by default give access to all potential customers. However, controls must still exist to limit those customers' access. For example, a potential customer of Amazon.com would need to know whether a particular book was in stock and available for immediate shipment, but would not need to know the number of units in stock of that book. On the other hand, a supplier in the supply chain of Amazon.com would probably need access to inventory levels by virtue of being a part of the extranet of Amazon.com. The point of this illustration is that a company must establish and maintain controls that limit access to the appropriate level for related parties. Customers, suppliers, and employees need different levels of access, as well as access to different types of data. Therefore, a company must carefully implement and maintain proper controls over Internet, extranet, and intranet network connections.

Access is limited by establishing appropriate internal controls such as firewalls and user authentication. The establishment and use of user authentication is intended to prevent log-in to the intranet or extranet by unauthorized users. Firewalls prevent external users from accessing the network and data on the extranet or intranet. Chapter 4 described in detail risks and controls for IT systems. Two of the categories of risks and controls that can limit access to intranets and extranets are reproduced in Exhibit 14-8.

Exhibit 14-8
Controls to Limit Access to Intranets and Extranets

Authentication of users

- User ID
- Password
- Security token or smart card
- Biometric devices
- Login procedures
- Access levels
- Computer logs
- Authority tables

Hacking and other network break-ins

- Firewall
- Encryption
- Security policies
- Security breach resolution
- Secure socket layers (SSL)
- Virtual private network (VPN)
- Wired equivalency privacy (WEP)
- Service set identifier (SSID)
- Antivirus software
- Vulnerability assessment
- Penetration testing
- Intrusion detection

XML AND XBRL AS TOOLS TO ENABLE E-BUSINESS (STUDY OBJECTIVE 10)

Within the environment of the Internet, intranets, and extranets, two languages have emerged as important tools to enable e-business: XML and XBRL. Both languages have important uses.

XML, short for eXtensible Markup Language, is designed specifically for web documents. Using XML, designers create customized tags for data that enable the definition, transmission, validation, and interpretation of data between applications and between organizations. XML is a rich language that facilitates the exchange of data between organizations via web pages.

XBRL, short for eXtensible Business Reporting Language, is an XML-based markup language developed for financial reporting. XBRL provides a standards-based method to prepare, publish, reliably extract, and automatically exchange financial statements. In XBRL, dynamic financial statements can be published and manipulated on websites. The next sections explain the uses of XML and XBRL.

XML IN INTERNET EDI

Chapter 9 described EDI (electronic data interchange) as a method to conduct purchase transactions electronically. Traditional EDI is a technology that companies began to implement in the late 1960s. EDI was especially popular in industries such as rail and road transportation, auto manufacturing, and health care. Over the years, EDI came to be the form of conducting electronic business for large companies. However, two limiting factors have made it difficult for small to medium-size businesses to implement EDI. First, traditional EDI requires establishing very expensive networks such as private leased lines or value added networks (VANs), and small and medium-sized companies in many cases could not justify the cost. Usually, small to medium-sized businesses adopted EDI only when forced to by a large company that they dealt with. For example, if a small company were a supplier to Ford Motor Company, it would have no choice but to implement an EDI system, since Ford conducts purchases only via EDI. The second limiting factor is that traditional EDI in the United States is based on an old document standard (ANSI X.12) that limits the kind of data that can be exchanged via EDI. The ANSI X.12 standard for EDI defines standards for common business documents such as purchase orders and invoices. However, the standard was never intended to cover the more extensive and complex exchange of information, such as shared files or databases, that occurs when two companies collaborate on a project. Given these two limitations, traditional EDI was never widely adopted by small to medium-sized businesses.

The growth of the Internet over the last decade has provided a powerful and inexpensive alternative to traditional EDI. **Internet EDI** uses the Internet to transmit business information between companies. Internet EDI is also referred to as EDIINT. There are several advantages to using the Internet or extranets to transmit EDI, compared with private leased lines or VANs. By far the biggest advantage is that the Internet or extranets allow cost-free exchange of data. The companies using the Internet or extranets avoid the cost of leasing private lines and paying fees to VANs. This allows any business, including small and medium-sized businesses, to employ EDI at a relatively low cost.

Exhibit 14-9
Traditional EDI using VAN versus Internet EDI

VAN	Internet EDI
Expensive	Low-cost
Transaction fees	Zero transaction fees
Complicated	Easy to use
Heavy infrastructure	Minimal infrastructure
Proprietary	Industry standard
Batch-related Store & forward	Real-time
Limited usage	Entire supply chain
Limited data transport	All data transport
Limited access	Web browser

The Internet EDI method of transmission is a relatively new development, but some companies have implemented it throughout their supply chain. A partial list of companies using Internet EDI extensively would include General Electric, Procter & Gamble, Wal-Mart, Kohl's, and Meijer. Exhibit 14-9 summarizes the advantages of Internet EDI in comparison with traditional EDI employing value added networks.

A value added network is expensive because a company must pay monthly fees or transaction fees to use the VAN. Internet EDI is much less costly because the Internet network can be used without fees. In addition, the hardware and IT systems necessary to support traditional EDI via a VAN are very complex and expensive. Much computer hardware and software must be dedicated to providing traditional EDI. Internet EDI is much less complex and requires only minimal computer hardware and software. Internet EDI can be operated with only a PC or network of PCs that are Internet connected. This allows the easy adoption of Internet EDI by small and medium-sized businesses.

Traditional EDI is a batch-oriented system that processes transactions in batches. This means there is some delay while transactions are batched, temporarily stored, and then finally transmitted when the batch is complete. Internet EDI operates in a real-time environment, just as B2C commerce is in real time. Because of these problems with EDI, traditional EDI is limited to larger organizations and to the type of data included in standard business documents. The low cost and communication capabilities of the Internet remove those limitations for Internet EDI. All companies in the supply chain are more likely to be able to afford Internet EDI, and they will be able to transmit more types of data than simply standard business documents. The Wal-Mart example at the beginning of this chapter is an example of a company changing from traditional EDI to Internet EDI.

The network of computers connected to the Internet does allow for more types of data to be communicated between business partners. However, the traditional EDI data format of ANSI X.12 would not accommodate more rich data types such as graphics or spreadsheets. Therefore, Internet EDI can be more flexible if a different data format is used to transmit data. The format used in Internet EDI is eXtensible Markup Language, or XML.

Traditional EDI is capable of transmitting many standard business documents between companies, such as purchase orders, invoices, and even payments by electronic funds transfer (EFT). However, given the capabilities of the Internet and extranets for sharing information, this traditional EDI data format is too limited. In addition to business documents, companies may need to transmit or share product descriptions, pictures of products, or even databases of information. Traditional EDI cannot accomplish such sharing of data. Internet EDI does provide the capability of sharing much richer forms of data through the use of XML. XML is a metalanguage, which means that it is a computer language that defines a language. XML is a tagged data format in which each data piece is preceded by a tag that defines the data piece. The same tag then marks the end of that piece of data. Thus, a tag surrounds each piece of data. XML is the standard markup language utilized in Internet EDI.

XML allows businesses to exchange transaction data over the Internet in a rich format. As XML becomes the accepted standard in Internet EDI, it will enable companies to exchange more than standard business documents. Spreadsheets, graphs, and databases could all be exchanged between businesses by the use of XML documents to tag the data and the manner in which the data should be presented. Those who predict the future of the IT environment predict that XML will revolutionize the way in which businesses share data with each other and with customers.

XBRL FOR FINANCIAL STATEMENT REPORTING

A special variant of XML called eXtensible Business Reporting Language, or XBRL, is predicted to revolutionize business reporting to creditors, stockholders, and government agencies. XBRL is predicted to become the standard format that will be used to provide annual reports and financial statements to creditors, customers, and the Securities and Exchange Commission (SEC). The idea behind XBRL is that financial data are tagged in a computer readable format that allows the users to readily obtain, analyze, exchange, and display the information.

XBRL financial statements have two major advantages over paper-based financial statements. Financial statements that are coded in XBRL can easily be used in several formats. They can be printed in paper format, displayed as an HTML web page, sent electronically to the SEC, and transmitted to banks or regulatory agencies as an XML file. When a financial statement is prepared in XBRL, a computer program such as a web browser can extract pieces of information from the XBRL file. This is not possible with an HTML file. For example, while a financial statement in HTML format can be viewed on a website, the computer cannot extract sales. However, a XBRL financial statement would tag the dollar amount of sales with the tag that names that number sales. The computer can then extract specific pieces of data. This capability allows investors and creditors to more easily analyze financial statements, which should result in better investment and credit decisions.

For XBRL to be implemented widely, common standards regarding the tags that identify data must be developed and accounting software vendors must use these tags within the software. The SEC strongly encourages public companies to use XBRL for financial statement reporting. In February 2005, the SEC announced a voluntary program to allow companies to furnish XBRL financial statement filings to the SEC. The SEC Chairman, William H. Donaldson, said the following regarding this voluntary program:

"As I mentioned when the Commission first announced this initiative, this initiative is part of the Commission's broader effort to improve the quality of information available to investors and the marketplace. By working to enhance the Commission's filing and disclosure process through the use of new data formats, including tagged data, the Commission can improve how content is organized and analyzed—improvements that will benefit everyone who utilizes the SEC's public disclosure process."[12]

ETHICAL ISSUES RELATED TO E-BUSINESS AND E-COMMERCE (STUDY OBJECTIVE 11)

Companies that engage in e-commerce, B2C sales with consumers have the same kind of obligations to conduct their business ethically as companies transacting business any other way. However, the lack of geographic boundaries and the potential anonymity of web-based commerce suggest that B2C companies have an even greater necessity to act ethically. A customer who orders merchandise or services on a website may not be able to easily assess the ethics or trustworthiness of a company who sells online. For example, if you buy a defective or spoiled product from your local grocery store, you can simply return it quickly. Your grocery store has a local presence, and you buy there because you know the company is real and trustworthy. However, anyone can establish a website that looks like a bona fide company, but may be just a false storefront used to defraud customers. In B2C e-commerce, customers do not have the same capability to visit and become familiar with the company as they do when they are buying from a local store.

In a previous section of this chapter, the "Online Privacy" section of the AICPA Trust Services Principles was described. For the most part, these types of practices are an ethical obligation, but not necessarily a legal requirement. For example, there is no legal requirement to disclose privacy policies on a company's website. However, ethical obligations would suggest that customers should be so informed regarding customer privacy. The practices described in the Trust Services Principles are more than good business practices. The online privacy policies represent ethical obligations to customers. As a reminder, the privacy practices include the following concepts:

a. management
b. notice
c. choice and consent
d. collection
e. use and retention
f. access
g. onward transfer and disclosure
h. security
i. quality
j. monitoring and enforcement

These principles can be distilled into the ethical concept that management has an obligation to treat customer information with due care. Companies

[12]Securities Exchange Commission Press Release, 2005-12.

should honestly and fully disclose to customers the information they will collect and how they will protect it, use it, and share it. Management has an ethical obligation to create and enforce policies and practices which ensure that private customer data are not misused. Unfortunately, the profit motive sometimes leads management to focus too much on potential revenue and not enough on customer privacy.

When a customer engages in e-commerce, she is sharing data such as name, address, e-mail address, credit card number, and buying habits. These data have potential value to many other companies and are sometimes sold to other companies. You may have even received a mail or e-mail solicitation and wondered how that company ever came to know your name and address. This might mean that your name and address have been sold to another company or shared with a related company or subsidiary. There are many, many examples of companies who have compromised customer privacy to earn revenue. Customer lists or other private data about customers are a valuable resource. Too often, companies are willing to sell or share customer lists or customer data. In some cases, companies have no policies about the privacy of customer data and are thus willing to sell or share the data. In other cases, companies with policies regarding the privacy of customer data have violated their own policies.

THE REAL WORLD

Gateway Learning Corporation, the company behind Hooked on Phonics®, was charged by the Federal Trade Commission with deceptive and unfair practices. Starting in the year 2000, Gateway disclosed a privacy policy on its www.hop.com website stating that it would not share customers' personal information with any third parties without explicit consent from the customer.

In April 2003, Gateway allegedly began violating this policy by renting to telemarketers customer information such as name, address, phone number, age, and gender of children. A retroactive change was posted to the company's privacy statement on its website.

To settle this charge out of court, Gateway was required to pay a fine, was restricted from using deceptive claims regarding its privacy policy, and cannot materially change its privacy policy without customers' consent.[13]

While there is no requirement to disclose a privacy policy on a website, it is an ethical obligation to disclose and follow the policy. Moreover, when a policy is disclosed, the Federal Trade Commission holds companies to a legal standard of following their stated policy.

There are also regulations passed by the U.S. Government regarding the privacy of medical information. The Health Insurance Portability and Accountability Act of 1996 (HIPAA) includes a section on the security of health care information. The Act requires health care providers, health plans, hospitals, health insurers, and health clearinghouses to follow regulations that protect the privacy of medical-related information.

As the issue of consumer privacy continues to become more important, there may be new regulations and requirements affecting companies. Even if there were no new regulations, ethical obligations would dictate that companies take adequate care to guard the security and privacy of data collected through e-commerce.

[13]Parry Aftab, "Hooked on Phonics Gets Hooked," Information Week, August 2, 2004 <http://www.informationweek.com/story/showArticle.jhtml?articleID=26100417>

SUMMARY OF STUDY OBJECTIVES

An introduction to e-commerce and e-business. E-business is the use of electronic means to enhance business processes. E-business encompasses all forms of online electronic trading, consumer-based e-commerce, business-to-business electronic trading and process integration, as well as the internal use of IT and related technologies for process integration inside organizations. There is an overlap between e-commerce and e-business, which leads some to confuse the two concepts. E-commerce is electronically enabled transactions between a business and its customers. E-business is a broader concept that includes e-commerce, as well as all forms of electronic means of servicing customers and vendors, trading information with customers and vendors, and recording and control of internal processes.

The history of the Internet. The Internet of today evolved from an early government research network called ARPANET. Many of the network standards were developed in the period of ARPANET. Routers, TCP/IP, and e-mail all came about during this time. ARPANET gradually evolved into a fully commercial network called the Internet. After the Internet became available for commercial transactions in 1994, it experienced tremendous and rapid growth.

The physical structure and standards of the Internet. Backbone providers, regional Internet service providers, and local Internet service providers make up the physical structure of the Internet that connects global users. The common standards that allow computers to communicate with each other over the Internet are TCP/IP, HTML, domain names, addresses based on uniform resource locater (URL), and SSL encryption.

E-commerce and its benefits. The most well-known form of e-commerce is business-to-consumer (B2C) transactions using the World Wide Web. B2C sales transactions offer many benefits to both the consumer and the business.

Privacy expectations in e-commerce. Businesses have an ethical obligation to establish systems and procedures to protect the privacy of customers. The AICPA Trust Services Principles establish nine privacy practices that companies should follow: notice, choice and consent, collection, use and retention, access, onward transfer and disclosure, security, integrity, and management and enforcement.

E-business and IT enablement. E-business is the use of IT to enable processes within the supply chain. The supply chain is the set of linked processes that take place from the acquisition and delivery of raw materials through the manufacturing, distribution, wholesale, and delivery of the product to the customer. There are many benefits to the IT enablement of processes within the supply chain. E-business includes business-to-business (B2B) electronic transactions.

E-business enabling examples. There are many forms of e-business. This section provides examples of ways that businesses streamline business processes, reduce operational costs, and enhance efficiency through e-business.

Intranets and extranets to enable e-business. An intranet is a private network accessible only to the employees of that company. The intranet uses the same common standards and protocols of the Internet. An intranet uses TCP/IP protocol and the same type of html web pages as the Internet. However, the computer servers of the intranet are accessible only from internal computers within the company. An extranet is similar to an intranet, except that it offers access to selected outsiders, such as buyers, suppliers, distributors, or wholesalers in the supply chain. Extranets are the networks that allow business partners to exchange information. These business partners will be given limited access to company servers and data.

Internal controls for the Internet, intranets, and extranets. The Internet, intranets, and extranets are all networks that are intended to share information and conduct transactions. In all three networks, controls must be in place to allow the intended users access, but also limit access to unauthorized users. Therefore, proper user authentication and hacking controls must be implemented in these networks.

XML and XBRL as e-business tools. XML and XBRL are markup languages that allow designers to create customized tags for data that enable the definition, transmission, validation, and interpretation of data between applications and between organizations. XML is a rich language that facilitates the exchange of data between organizations via web pages. XML is used in Internet EDI. XBRL is a business reporting language that will allow businesses to provide dynamic financial statements to users over the World Wide Web.

Ethical issues related to e-business and e-commerce. The online privacy policies of the AICPA Trust Services Principles represent ethical obligations to customers. These are ethical, but not necessarily legal, obligations. However, if a company does choose to disclose privacy practices on its website, it is then legally obligated to follow those practices.

KEY TERMS

B2B
B2C
Backbone
Backbone provider
Bricks and mortar
Bricks and clicks
Clicks and mortar
Domain name
E-business
E-commerce
E-tailer
Extranet
HTML
Internet
Internet EDI
Intranet
Local ISP
Packet switching
Protocol
Regional ISP
Router
Secure sockets layering
Supply chain
TCP/IP
URL
Web server
XBRL
XML

END OF CHAPTER MATERIAL

CONCEPT CHECK

1. Which of the following statements is true?
   a. E-business is a subset of e-commerce.
   b. E-commerce is a subset of e-business.
   c. E-business and e-commerce are exactly the same thing.
   d. E-business and e-commerce are not related.
2. An electronic hardware device that is located at the gateway between two or more networks is a
   a. packet switch.
   b. URL.
   c. router.
   d. protocol.
3. The type of organization that serves as the main trunk line of the Internet is called a
   a. local ISP.
   b. regional ISP.
   c. global ISP.
   d. backbone provider.
4. Which of the following is not a direct advantage for the consumer from e-commerce?
   a. Access to a broader market
   b. More shopping convenience
   c. Reduced order-processing cost
   d. Information sharing from the company
5. Each of the following represents a characteristic of B2B commerce except
   a. electronic data interchange.
   b. electronic retailing.
   c. data exchanges.
   d. preexisting business relationships.
6. Each of the following represents an application of B2C commerce except
   a. software sales.
   b. electronic retailing.
   c. data exchanges.
   d. stock trading.
7. Before forwarding customer data, an organization should receive explicit or implicit consent of the customer. This describes which of the AICPA Trust Services Principles online privacy practices?
   a. Consent
   b. Use and retention
   c. Access
   d. Onward transfer and disclosure
8. Which of the following processes within a supply chain can benefit from IT enablement?
   a. All processes throughout the supply chain
   b. Only internal processes within the supply chain

c. Only external processes within the supply chain

d. Exchange processes between a company and its suppliers

9. When a company has an e-business transaction with a supplier, it could be using

a. the Internet.

b. an intranet.

c. an extranet.

d. either the Internet or an extranet.

10. Intranets are used for each of the following except

a. communication and collaboration.

b. business operations and managerial monitoring.

c. web publishing.

d. customer self-service.

11. When there is no necessity for a preexisting relationship between buyer and seller, that transaction is more likely to be classified as

a. B2B.

b. B2C.

c. B2E.

d. either B2B or B2C.

12. Which of the following IT controls would not be important in an extranet?

a. Encryption

b. Password

c. Antivirus software

d. Penetration testing

e. All of the above are important IT controls.

13. A company's computer network uses web servers, HTML, and XML to serve various user groups. Which type of network best serves each of the following users?

Employees	*Suppliers*
a. Intranet	Extranet
b. Intranet	Internet
c. Internet	Extranet
d. Internet	Internet

14. An extensible markup language designed specifically for financial reporting is

a. Internet EDI

b. XML

c. XBRL

d. XFRL

DISCUSSION QUESTIONS

15. (SO 1) How do e-commerce and e-business differ?

16. (SO 2) What was the original purpose of the network of computers that eventually became the Internet?

17. (SO 2) Why was ARPANET designed with many different alternative routes for network traffic?
18. (SO 2) Why is a standard protocol necessary in computer networks?
19. (SO 2) How quickly did Internet usage by the public grow after the Internet was opened to business transactions in 1994?
20. (SO 3) Describe the relationship between national backbone providers, regional ISPs, and local ISPs.
21. (SO 3) What is the importance of a standard formatting language for web pages and a standard addressing system?
22. (SO 4) Which types of costs can be reduced when a company decides to engage in B2C e-commerce on the Internet?
23. (SO 4) What are the differences between bricks-and-mortar retailers and clicks-and-mortar retailers?
24. (SO 5) According to the Online Privacy section of the AICPA Trust Services Principles, what types of personal information should be protected?
25. (SO 5) If you could condense the ten areas of Online Privacy in the AICPA Trust Services Principles, into a shorter list (three, four, or five point list), how would you word that list?
26. (SO 5) What is meant by "monitoring and enforcement" regarding online privacy practices?
27. (SO 6) How is e-business a broader concept than e-commerce?
28. (SO 6) Describe the concept of a supply chain.
29. (SO 6) Why is it important to ensure an efficient flow of goods throughout the supply chain?
30. (SO 6) Which functions within the supply chain can be enhanced through the use of e-business?
31. (SO 6) How are activities in the supply chain interdependent?
32. (SO 6) In what ways are the characteristics of e-business different from those of e-commerce?
33. (SO 8) What are the three levels of network platforms that are utilized in e-business, and which groups use each level?
34. (SO 8) Which type of users should have access to an intranet?
35. (SO 8) Which type of users should have access to an extranet?
36. (SO 9) What types of controls should be used to properly limit access in intranets and extranets?
37. (SO 10) Why is the use of XML advantageous in Internet EDI?
38. (SO 10) In what ways are XBRL financial statements advantageous compared with traditional paper financial statements?
39. (SO 11) What are some of the ethical obligations of companies related to e-commerce?
40. (SO 11) Is there a difference between ethical obligations and legal obligations with regard to online privacy?

BRIEF EXERCISES

41. (SO 1) Much of the e-business and e-commerce conducted by companies uses the Internet as the form of electronic communication. Describe other electronic means to conduct e-business or e-commerce.

42. (SO 3) How does the use of HTML, URLs, domain names, and SSL contribute to an Internet that can be used worldwide?
43. (SO 4) Describe the benefits to the **consumer** of B2C sales.
44. (SO 4) Describe the benefits to the **company** of B2C sales.
45. (SO 6) Describe the benefits to a company that engages in B2B transactions via the Internet.
46. (SO 5) What are the ten areas of privacy practices described in the Online Privacy section of the AICPA Trust Services Principles?
47. (SO 6) Describe the activities that take place in the supply chain of a manufacturing firm.
48. (SO 6) Describe the differences between B2C and B2B.
49. (SO 9) Explain the importance of user authentication and network break-in controls in extranets.
50. (SO 10) What are the advantages of Internet EDI over traditional EDI?

PROBLEMS

51. (SO 2) Explain the hardware and technology standards that were developed during the ARPANET that were an important foundation for the Internet of today.
52. (SO 4) The Pizza Pie Pit is a local chain of pizza restaurants in Dallas, Texas. The chain has 30 locations throughout the city and its suburbs. The management is considering opening a website to conduct e-commerce with customers. Describe any benefits that might be derived from this move.
53. (SO 5) Using your favorite search website, enter the term "privacy seal" and search. Answer the following questions:
    a. What is the purpose of a web privacy seal?
    b. Which organizations provide web privacy seals to web-based companies?
    c. What are the advantages to a company that maintains a web privacy seal?
    d. What are the benefits to a consumer of shopping from a website that has a privacy seal?
54. (SO 5) Visit the website www.cpawebtrust.org and answer the following questions:
    a. What is a WebTrust seal?
    b. Which organization sanctions the WebTrust seal?
    c. What kind of professional can provide a WebTrust seal to a company?
    d. What must this professional do before providing a WebTrust seal?
55. (SO 5) Enter the website of a popular retail company that sells a large volume of goods or services on the Internet. Search for the company's "Privacy Policies" on that website. If you do not find any privacy policies, continue visiting other company websites until you do find privacy policies. Once you have found a company with privacy policies, describe how the company policies do or do not meet the privacy practices in the AICPA Trust Services Principles.

56. (SO 10) Using an Internet search engine, search for the terms "Internet EDI" and "kateandashley." Explain how Cody applies Internet EDI.

57. (SO 10) Visit the www.xbrl.org website. Click on the "Latest News" link, and then the "articles" link. After reading three or four of the most recent articles about XBRL, briefly describe what those articles say about XBRL.

58. (SO 5) List and describe the nine privacy practices recommended by the AICPA Trust Services Principles Privacy Framework. If you have ever made a purchase online, you have likely seen these practices in use. Provide any examples from your own personal experience.

59. (SO 5) Describe the ethical obligations of companies to their online customers.

CASES

60. Beach Beauties Corporation (BBC), is a regional wholesaler of women's swimwear and beach attire. The company is located in Jacksonville, Florida, and it sells to retail stores in resort communities in Florida, Georgia, and the Carolinas. BBC employs six salespeople, with each one having responsibility for collecting sales orders from one of the following territories: Southern Florida, Florida Gulf Coast, Eastern Florida, Georgia, South Carolina, and North Carolina.

    Each sale representative mails seasonal catalogs to the customers in his or her territory. Online catalogs are also provided via the company's website. Sales orders are obtained directly by the sales representatives via e-mail. On a daily basis, the sales representatives submit orders to the corporate office via the Internet; a web browser client is used to enter the e-mail orders into a dedicated web server. The sales representatives maintain files consisting of each customer's e-mail orders, accompanied by a printout of the sales orders entered in the computer. All deliveries are sent via common carrier from the Jacksonville headquarters to each of the customer locations.

    Recently, BBC has experienced delivery problems. Namely, a few retail stores located on the eastern Georgia seaboard have claimed that they never received their deliveries. Ellen Hainett, BBC's controller, has been investigating these problems along with Alex Ruminez, the Georgia sales representative. Through her review of the shipping records, Ellen discovered that each of the problem scenarios involved shipment to a warehouse rather than to the customer's retail store. Interestingly, the sales order files maintained by Alex indicate that shipment should have been set up for delivery to the respective retail store locations.

    Upon further investigation, Ellen reviewed the company's access log and verified that Alex's and the other sales representatives' authorized passwords were the only ones used to access the company's web server.

    Required:

    a. Speculate as to potential causes of this problem.
    b. What additional information would be needed to determine the actual cause of this problem?
    c. What controls could be implemented to avoid repeated instances of this problem?

61. Caseline Analytics is a financial services consulting firm that assists its clients with financial analyses surrounding proposed business ventures. John Y. Case is the firm's founder and project director. As such, he is responsible for preparing most of each client firm's financial analyses and reports, as well as presenting the results to each client's management. Due to the varying numbers of managers who may make up a client's top management, Case always prepares at least a dozen report copies so that there are plenty to distribute to all persons in attendance at the presentation.

    Data for financial analyses are obtained directly from the accounting and production databases of the firm's clients. Direct queries are prepared by Case's staff accountants, and the resulting presentation reports are prepared by the staff and reviewed by Case. This is a time-consuming process, and many of Case's clients have demanded more current information. This problem recently led Case to investigate the possibility of developing a software package that could produce the financial analyses and reports automatically.

    As Case considers the significant investment that would be required to program a new system, he is concerned about the loss of control that may be inherent in an automated system. For instance, he worries about the accuracy and completeness of analyses and reports prepared automatically.

    Required:

    Perform an online research of XBRL at www.xbrl.org and determine whether or not XBRL would be appropriate for Case's business. Would XBRL be more effective and reliable? Why or why not? Your response should focus on the existence of any enhancements or concerns that are likely to result in terms of the timeliness of information, internal controls, and security.

CONTINUING CASE: SPATELLI'S PIZZERIA

Consider the case of Spatelli's Pizzeria as presented at the end of Chapter 1. In particular, reread the sections on ordering and Internet orders.

Required:

Answer the following questions regarding Spatelli's:

a. Discuss whether Spatelli's Internet order activities can be termed e-commerce.

b. Given the privacy practices described in the AICPA Trust Services Principles, describe the kind of customer data that Spatelli's could reasonably collect and store, and also describe some data that Spatelli's should not collect and store. Explain the reasons for these differences.

c. Describe the internal controls related to Internet orders that Spatelli's should have in place.

SOLUTIONS TO CONCEPT CHECK

1. (SO 1) The following statement is true: **b. E-commerce is a subset of e-business.** E-business is a broader concept that includes e-commerce, as depicted in Exhibit 14-1.

2. (SO 2) An electronic hardware device that is located at the gateway between two or more networks is a **c. router**. A router is a hardware device that connects networks at a network gateway.
3. (SO 3) The type of organization that serves as the main trunk line of the Internet is called a **d. backbone provider**. Backbone providers provide and maintain the main trunk lines of the Internet, as shown in Exhibit 14-3.
4. (SO 4) **c. Reduced order-processing costs** is not a direct advantage for the consumer from e-commerce. Reduced order processing cost is a direct benefit to the seller, not the consumer. Lower cost may lead to lower prices for the consumer also, but this would be an indirect advantage to the consumer. The other answers are direct benefits to the consumer.
5. (CIA Adapted) (SO 4) Each of the options represents a characteristic of B2B commerce except **b. electronic retailing**, which is a characteristic of B2C.
6. (CIA Adapted) (SO 4) Each of the options represents an application of B2C commerce except **c. data exchanges**, which are a characteristic of B2B.
7. (SO 5) Before forwarding customer data, an organization should receive explicit or implicit consent of the customer. This describes **d. onward transfer and disclosure** of the AICPA Trust Services Principles online privacy practices. When an organization will be forwarding customer data to third parties, it should provide a policy to consumers to disclose the onward transfer.
8. (SO 6) **a. All processes throughout the supply chain** can benefit from IT enablement. Any process throughout the supply chain is a potential process that could benefit from IT enablement.
9. (SO 8) When a company has an e-business transaction with a supplier, it could be using **d. either the Internet or an extranet.** Two companies could transact business using either the Internet or an extranet. An intranet is usually limited to those inside a company, therefore excluding other trading partners.
10. (CMA Adapted) (SO 8) Intranets are used for each of the options except **a. customer self-service**. Customers would not access the intranet, as it is for internal use.
11. (SO 4) When there is no necessity for a preexisting relationship between buyer and seller, that transaction is more likely to be classified as **b. B2C**. This is a characteristic of business to consumer. Business-to-business transactions presume a preexisting relationship.
12. (SO 8) Of the given IT controls in an extranet, **e. all are important IT controls**. Each option is either a user authentication or hacking IT control that should be implemented to protect an extranet.
13. (CIA Adapted) (SO 8) A company's computer network uses web servers, HTML, and XML to serve various user groups. The following type of network best serves the following user:

Employees	*Suppliers*
a. Intranet	**Extranet**

An intranet and extranet are similar; however, an intranet aids in internal communication, whereas an extranet facilitates communication (and trading) externally with the company's business partners.

14. (SO 10) An extensible markup language designed specifically for financial reporting is **c. XBRL**. XBRL stands for eXtensible Business Reporting Language.

CHAPTER 15

IT Infrastructure for E-Business

STUDY OBJECTIVES

This chapter will help you gain an understanding of the following concepts:

1. An overview of an ERP system
2. The history of ERP systems
3. Current ERP system characteristics
4. The modules of an ERP system
5. The market segments of ERP software systems
6. Implementation issues of ERP systems
7. The benefits and risks of ERP systems
8. ERP systems and the Sarbanes–Oxley Act

OVERVIEW OF ERP SYSTEMS (STUDY OBJECTIVE 1)

As you studied the chapters in this book that described business processes and the resulting data, you saw that there are processes which deal with a very high volume of transactions. For example, sales and purchase processes are recurring, high-volume transaction processes in which much data are generated, processed, and stored. These processes also result in data that must be entered and summarized in the general ledger through general ledger processes. Earlier chapters also examined how IT systems can improve the efficiency and cost of those processes. Ideally, all of an organization's business processes would be controlled by one software system that incorporates all business processes. That is, one software system would collect, process, store, and report the data resulting from all revenue, expenditures, conversion, and administrative processes. This is the intention of an enterprise resource planning (ERP) system. The ERP system is the IT infrastructure that has enhanced and enabled e-commerce and e-business. ERP systems and e-business are mutually supporting parts of the organization. ERP systems enhance e-business, and e-business has enhanced the process efficiency of ERP systems.

THE REAL WORLD

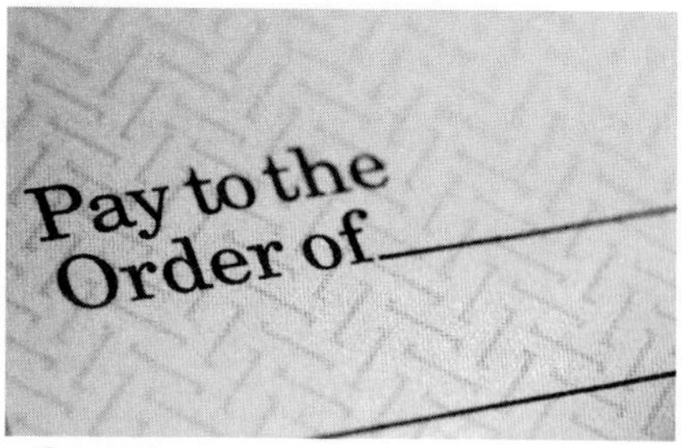

iStockphoto

Agri-Beef Co. is a privately-held, Idaho firm with annual sales in excess of $500 million. Believing that its old accounting systems were antiquated, the management at Agri-Beef recently switched to an ERP system. They experienced a very successful implementation that took only six weeks and they began experiencing benefits immediately. The treasurer of the company, while describing the benefits with regard to the preparation and handling of intracompany transactions, said the following:

> "With the old method, we had to walk each transaction through. Now we can post transactions straight through to another division's general ledger account."

The improved efficiency resulted in two check runs instead of 22 runs, and a 200 man hour savings per month.[1]

An **enterprise resource planning (ERP)** system is a multimodule software system that integrates all business processes and functions of the entire organization into a single software system, using a single database. Each module is intended to collect, process, and store data of a functional area of the organization and to integrate with related processes. For example, a module may be designed to process purchasing transactions and record all data about purchase orders. This module must integrate with accounts payable and inventory, since the vendor must be paid and inventory increased as the purchased goods arrive. Each of the software modules of an ERP system automates business activities of a functional area within an organization. Information is updated in real time in the ERP database so that employees in all business units are using the same information and all information is up to date. Since the data are stored in a single database, each functional area can easily share information with other areas of

[1]Bartholomew, Doug "The ABC's of ERP," *CFO*, Fall 2004, vol. 20, issue 12, p. 19.

the organization. For example, when a customer order is entered into an ERP system, a customer representative can have access to information such as the customer's order and credit history and account balance details, inventory levels, production schedules, and shipping schedules. Therefore, the employee can answer any questions that the customer may ask, such as the following:

1. Is the product in stock?
2. If not, when will it be produced or restocked?
3. How soon can it be shipped?
4. When did we place the last order for this item?

To answer these questions, the customer service representative must have access to inventory information, production planning and scheduling information, shipping scheduling information, and customer history information. All of these functional areas have data stored in a single, shared database to enable the necessary integration.

You may think it obvious that an ERP system that integrates all business functions and shares data across functions would be most efficient. However, ERP systems did not become popular until the 1990s. Prior to that time, hardware and software systems to accomplish the functions of an ERP system were not available or were not cost effective. ERP systems were not possible until computer hardware and software capabilities evolved to a certain point. In the 1980s and 1990s, the increasing power of computers and the decreasing cost made it much more realistic for companies to have enough computing power to accomplish the functions of an ERP system. The very first ERP systems were modified MRP II systems. Software companies such as SAP® evolved their MRP II software into products that became known as ERP systems. An **MRP II** software system is a **manufacturing resource planning** software system—a system that focuses on the movement and use of resources needed by a manufacturing company. ERP systems expanded upon the MRP system, adding functions across the entire spectrum of processes in the enterprise. For example, marketing, distribution, human resources, and other enterprise processes became part of the ERP system.

ERP software operates on a relational database such as Oracle, Microsoft SQL Server, or IBM's DB2. An ERP system includes the following modules:

1. Financials
2. Human resources
3. Procurement and logistics
4. Product development and manufacturing
5. Sales and services
6. Analytics

Data within the ERP system are stored in a(n)

1. Operational database
2. Data warehouse

These components are tightly integrated and affect each other. For example, the manufacturing modules and data are integrated so that sales personnel can

Exhibit 15-1
An ERP System

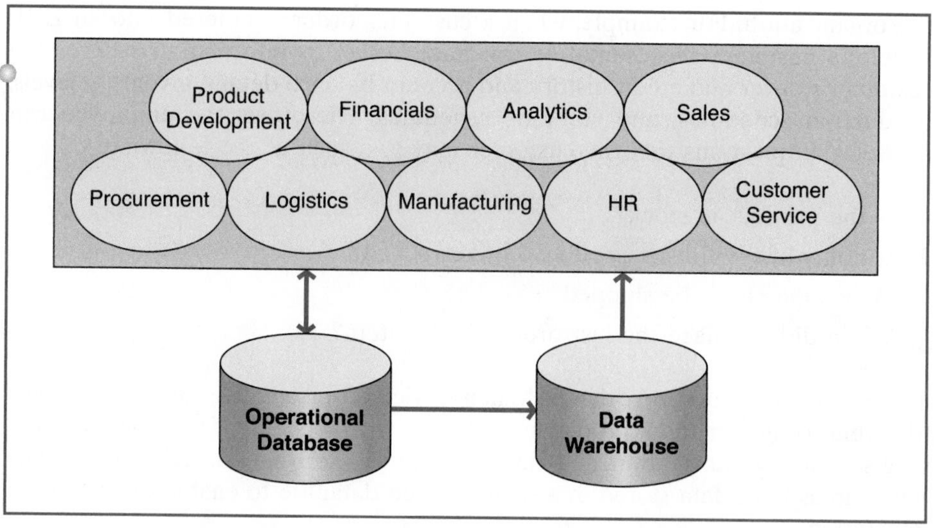

immediately see production schedule information and therefore, give customers more accurate information about product delivery dates. Exhibit 15-1 is a depiction of an ERP system.

The ERP system often utilizes two different databases: the operational database and the data warehouse. The **operational database** contains the data necessary to conduct day-to-day operations and produce management reports used to oversee day-to-day operations. The operational database contains the data that are continually updated as transactions are processed. Each time a new transaction is completed, parts of the operational data must be updated. For example, recording a sale means that sales, inventory, and accounts receivable balances must be updated.

The **data warehouse** is an integrated collection of enterprise-wide data that ideally should include 5 to 10 years of nonvolatile data. It is used to support management in decision making and planning. The data are enterprise-wide because they are pulled from the operational databases and they are maintained in the data warehouse for many fiscal periods. The data in the data warehouse are pulled from sales order processing, inventory systems, receivables, and many other transaction-processing systems within the organization. The information in a data warehouse is called nonvolatile because it does not change rapidly in the same way that operational data change. Periodically, new data are uploaded to the data warehouse from the operational data, but other than this updating process, the data in the data warehouse represent historical data that will not change.

Notice the direction of the arrows touching the two databases in Exhibit 15-1. The arrow between the ERP modules and the operational database shows data flow in both directions. This indicates that the modules store data in the database as transactions are processed, and those data are read by modules to process transactions and to prepare operational reports. The arrow between the operational database and the data warehouse shows data flow in one direction only. This arrow depicts the periodic update of data in the data warehouse by the uploading of data from the operational database. Notice that data for the data warehouse are never used to update data in the operational database.

The arrow between the data warehouse and the ERP module also depicts data flow in one direction only. The data in the data warehouse are only read, manipulated, and reported. Those data are not updated as transactions are processed.

The various interactions between the modules are difficult to capture in a two-dimensional drawing. Each of the modules may have some interaction with the other modules. For example, to plan and execute the manufacturing process, the manufacturing module must interface with sales, logistics, materials management, human resources, finance, and reporting. This interface is necessary because the manufacturing process must have these resources:

1. Feedback regarding expected sales of products from the sales module
2. Status information about raw materials in stock and on order from the materials management module
3. Information about how and when materials, subassemblies, and finished goods are moved through the plant and warehouses from the logistics module
4. Staffing and payroll information from the human resources module
5. Posting to and cost tracking in the general ledger and subledgers within the finance module
6. Various operations reports to monitor and control the manufacturing process

This list provides examples of some of the interactions between modules as a process occurs. This type of interaction between modules would be necessary for most of the business processes within an organization. In order for this interaction to occur and for the necessary reports to be available, the data must be in the operational database that is shared by all modules. In addition, some processes require more information than the current fiscal-year data. Therefore, the data warehouse is an important component to provide the full range of reports required to manage all business processes.

HISTORY OF ERP SYSTEMS (STUDY OBJECTIVE 2)

ERP systems can be traced back to software that was developed during the 1960s and 1970s to track inventory in manufacturing companies. The first generation of this software was called **materials requirements planning (MRP)** software. MRP software of the 1970s allowed plant managers to coordinate the planning of production and raw material requirements. MRP software determined order size and timing of raw materials on the basis of sales forecasts, factoring in lead times for order and delivery of materials.

The typical computer hardware and software of the 1970s that were used to enable an MRP system were mainframe computers, sequential file processing, and electronic data interchange (EDI). The EDI allowed up-to-date information about inventories and status of orders to be processed quickly. As mainframe computers improved in speed and power during the 1980s, MRP software evolved into manufacturing resource planning (MRP II) systems. MRP II was much broader and more encompassing than MRP software. MRP software was intended to provide for the purchase of raw materials to support manufacturing needs. The purpose of MRP II was to integrate manufacturing, engineering, marketing, and finance units to run on the same information system and to use a single database for all of these functions.

As MRP and MRP II systems became more popular in large manufacturing companies, early pioneers of ERP systems were working on a broader concept of information system software. Five former IBM systems analysts began work on an early version of ERP software in 1972. These five innovators formed a company that was to become Systems, Applications and Products in Data Processing (SAP). SAP designed the first true ERP system, also called SAP®. SAP was intended to integrate all business processes, not just manufacturing, and to make data available in real time. To the financial accounting system, they added modules for materials management, purchasing, inventory management, and invoice verification. SAP release 2, or SAP R/2®, was introduced in 1978. The new version took full advantage of the current mainframe computer technology, allowing for interactivity between modules and additional capabilities like order tracking.

However, ERP software did not become popular in the large corporation software market until the 1990s. In 1992, SAP released its third version of SAP, called SAP R/3®. Two important features led to a tremendous growth in the demand for SAP R/3. First, it used client–server hardware architecture. This setup allowed the system to run on a variety of computer platforms such as Unix® and Windows NT®. This meant that large corporations could use Windows NT based PCs as the client systems. R/3 was also designed with an open-architecture approach, allowing third-party companies to develop software that would integrate with SAP R/3. The success of SAP R/3 led other software developers to create competing products. Companies such as Oracle Corporation, PeopleSoft, J.D. Edwards, and Baan produced competing ERP systems.

During the last half of the 1990s, there was a very rapid growth in the sales of ERP software to Fortune 500 companies. Two major factors contributed to this growth. One was the explosion of e-commerce and the dot-com boom that occurred in the late 1990s. To enable e-commerce and the business process acceleration necessary to meet the demands of e-commerce sales, companies needed integrated systems such as ERP.

A second factor was the valid concern about Y2K compatibility of existing software systems in companies. Many companies were facing a large amount of uncertainty as to whether their legacy software would work after 1999, or would be **Y2K compatible.** The concern arose because of an artifact from the early days of programming. The amount of useable memory in the early computers was extremely small compared with computers today. To save memory space, programmers always used only two digits to store the year when storing dates. For example, 1999 was stored as "99." However, when the calendar rolled to 2000, the two digits would not have been sufficient to express the new century dates. Systems professionals were concerned that older legacy systems would process the year "00" as 1900 rather than 2000, or that the system could not even handle "00," "01," "02," and so forth. There was genuine concern that the actual programming logic in those older systems would "blow up" when faced with a 2000 or later date. For example, consider the potential problem if an older computer software system was used to calculate interest due on a note payable. It would calculate this by subtracting dates to determine the number of days and then multiply number of days times interest rate. If the note were issued on December 1, 1999, and due on January 30, 2000, the number of days outstanding should be 60 days. However, an older software system would probably calculate this as December 1, 1999 minus January 30, 1900, and return a negative number of days.

Therefore, many companies were rapidly trying to replace legacy software in the late 1990s before the year 2000 changeover occurred. Many large companies purchased and implemented ERP systems such as SAP R/3, PeopleSoft, Oracle, and J.D. Edwards. Sales of ERP system software soared and continued to grow until the dot-com bust of 2001. Immediately after the Y2K rush to implement ERP systems, there was a dramatic slowdown in the sale and implementation of ERP systems. At the same time, however, there were many changes occurring in business related to the Internet and e-commerce.

To increase the marketability of their ERP software, ERP providers began modifying their ERP software to include e-commerce capability. During this period, Gartner Inc. a leading provider of research in, and analysis of, the global information technology industry, coined a new name for these evolving ERP systems: ERP II. A major addition to ERP II systems was the ability to support e-commerce. However, the evolution to ERP II included more than simply e-commerce. A whole range of modules to improve the processes between a company and its trading partners is part of an ERP II system. These modules include **customer relationship management (CRM)** and **supply chain management (SCM)** modules. These modules will be described in more detail in a later section of this chapter. The evolution of ERP systems into ERP II systems changed the focus of ERP systems from an internal management perspective to an interactive, internal, and external perspective of business processes.

CURRENT ERP SYSTEM CHARACTERISTICS (STUDY OBJECTIVE 3)

The evolution of ERP II systems has resulted in most large businesses implementing ERP systems that are connected to the IT systems of their trading partners. EDI, Internet EDI, or extranets are used to connect a company's ERP system to the IT systems of its suppliers and customers. For example, suppliers may monitor their customers' inventory levels and electronically trigger a shipment when items they supply reach pre-arranged reorder levels. Another example of this trading partner connection of ERP systems is that a customer could access a supplier's production schedule to assess when its order may be filled. Exhibit 15-2 depicts a view of an ERP II system. The term "ERP II" has not yet been widely adopted, and the software systems are still generally referred to as ERP systems, even though they have expanded modules and functions compared with the original ERP systems of the 1990s.

Exhibit 15-2
An ERP II System

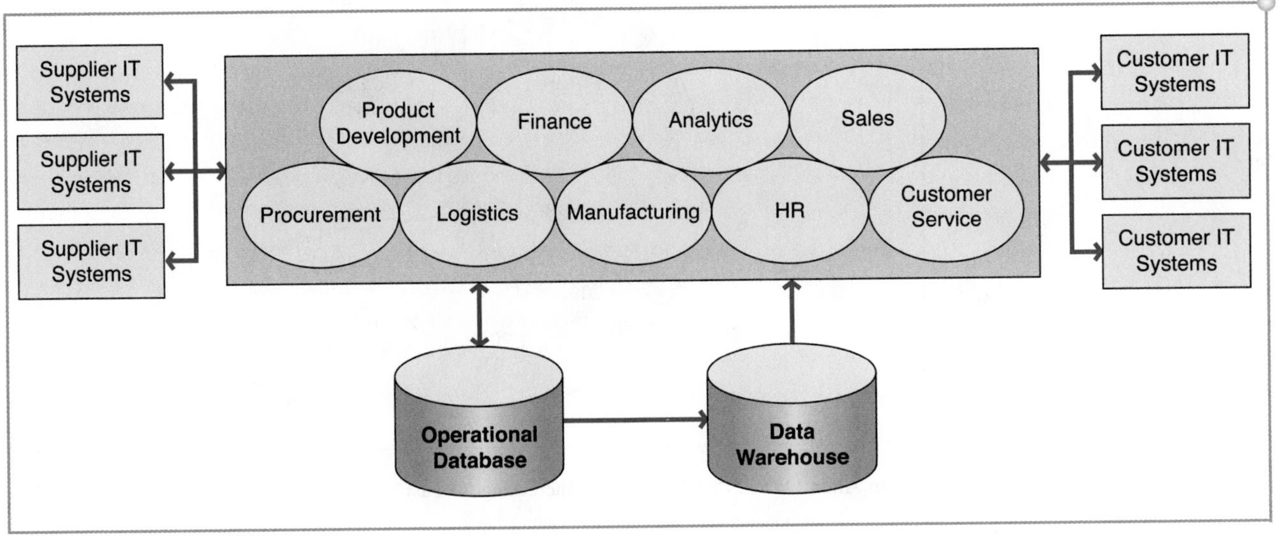

Because of the decline in the U.S. stock market following and the tragic events of September 11, 2001, nearly all companies made drastic reductions in expenditures on IT systems and software around that time. IT spending on ERP systems was flat between 2001 and 2003. Beginning in 2004, IT spending on ERP systems began to rise again. In 2005, spending on ERP systems increased above the level of 2004. According to a 2005 survey by CIO Insight, many companies increased the amount they spent on ERP systems. ERP is so important to daily operations that companies cannot allow their ERP systems to become outdated. The survey found the ERP spending in 2005 was up 16% over 2004. Some of the reasons for this increased ERP spending are as follows:[2]

1. The need to improve customer service through standardizing and combining business processes requires ERP software that can support standardized and combined processes.
2. Global companies that operate in several countries may have separate ERP systems in the different countries. Many of these companies decide to replace these various ERP systems with one centrally managed ERP system for the entire company.
3. Aging ERP systems that were installed prior to Y2K need replacement to meet competitive demands faced by companies today.
4. Bigger IT budgets in 2005 replaced leaner budgets between 2001 and 2004. Companies began increasing overall IT spending, including spending on ERP systems.
5. Many companies needed upgraded systems to enhance compliance with the Sarbanes–Oxley Act.

Exhibit 15-3 highlights the relative frequency of ERP implementations in recent years.

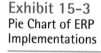

Exhibit 15-3
Pie Chart of ERP Implementations

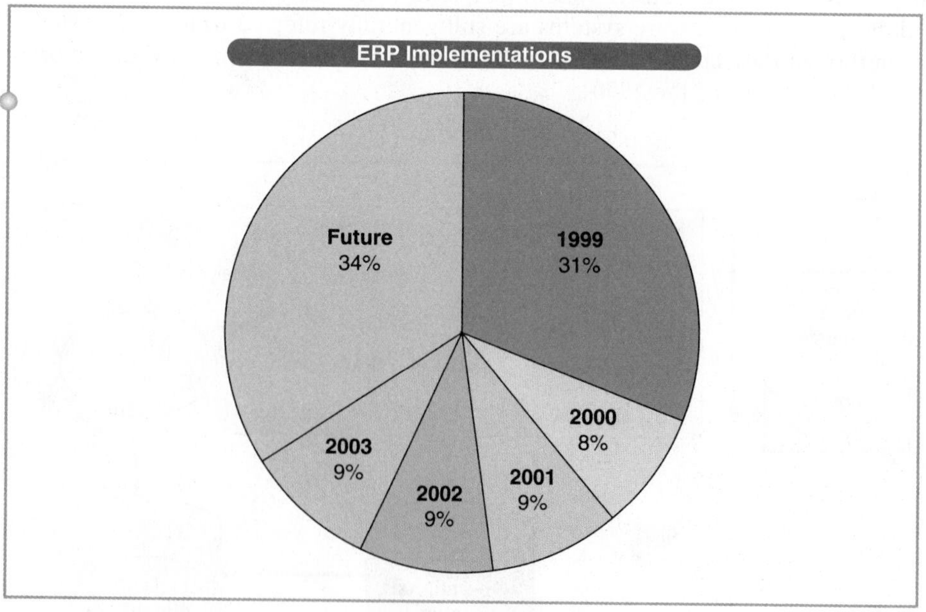

[2]Allan Alter, "Why is ERP Spending Increasing So Fast?" *CIO Insight,* Feb. 2005, Issue 50, p. 75.

THE REAL WORLD

Viper Motorcycle Company, a Minneapolis-based manufacturer and seller of luxury motorcycles, began business in 2002. In the fall of 2003, Viper was looking for an accounting software system that "would tie together the company's accounting with manufacturing, order processing, and other business functions, while complying with Sarbanes–Oxley."[3] Viper had been using Quickbooks Premier®, but found it did not fully meet its needs. Viper then selected SAP Business One® as its ERP software system.

This section has provided a brief overview of the ERP modules, the databases, and the interactive connection between the ERP system and trading partners. The next section will describe selected ERP modules in more detail.

ERP MODULES (STUDY OBJECTIVE 4)

Exhibits 15-1 and 15-2 depicted simple overviews of ERP systems. The ERP systems used by today's large organizations are actually more complex and encompass more of the enterprise than the systems depicted in Exhibits 15-1 and 15-2. The top-selling ERP system for large corporations and organizations is SAP. SAP describes its current ERP system as having many modules. Exhibit 15-4 is adapted from information provided on the SAP website.

This section will not describe each of these modules in detail, but will focus on those modules most closely tied to accounting.

FINANCIALS

The financials module contains what is normally considered the components of an accounting system. This includes the general ledger, special journals, and

Exhibit 15-4
SAP® View of ERP Modules

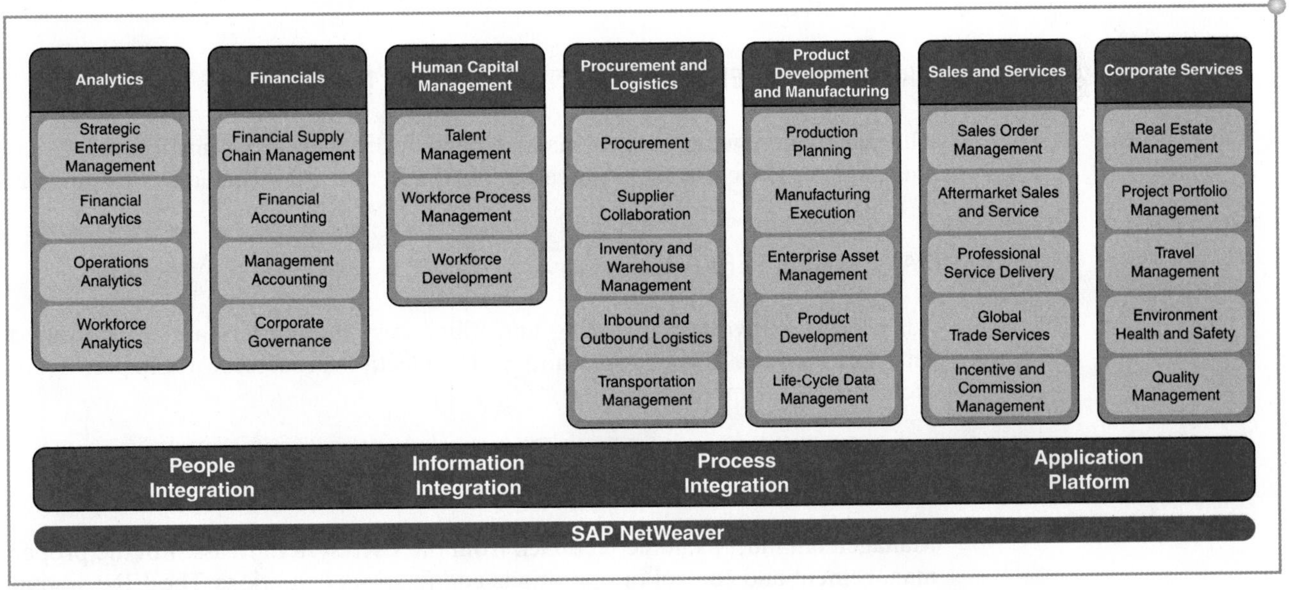

[3] Gary Lowenthal, "SAP Customer Success Story," CFO Viper Motorcycle Company, http://www.sap.com/

subsidiary ledgers for processes such as sales, cash receipts, purchasing, cash disbursements, and the remaining processes discussed in earlier parts of this book.

The difference between a typical accounting software system and the financials module of an ERP system is that the financials module is tightly integrated to the other modules on a real-time basis. This means that as events occur in the organizations, the data are updated in records that can be considered the subsidiary ledgers, special journals, and the general ledger, in real time. In other words, management can see the financial effects of those events immediately. As soon as a transaction is entered at the source by an employee, the financial posting occurs in all related data files that are akin to subsidiary ledgers, special journals, and general ledger accounts. This real-time availability of financial data allows managers to have immediate feedback useful for making operating decisions and managing operating events.

This type of real-time integration did not exist in accounting systems before ERP systems were developed. With the type of real-time feedback available to management in an ERP system, management is in a better position to make strategic and operational decisions necessary to make the organization successful.

HUMAN RESOURCES

This module in an ERP system incorporates all human resource and payroll processes and data. This would include all employee information on processes such as performance review, raises, and current wage and deductions.

PROCUREMENT AND LOGISTICS

Included in this ERP module are all processes and data related to the purchase and movement of materials and finished goods. This module incorporates the purchasing processes described in Chapter 9.

PRODUCT DEVELOPMENT AND MANUFACTURING

The planning, scheduling, and management of production are incorporated into this module. The conversion processes of Chapter 12 are included in this module.

SALES AND SERVICES

All processes involved in taking and filling customer orders are incorporated into this module. The revenue and cash collection processes of Chapter 8 are included in this module.

ANALYTICS

Management must examine feedback from the ERP system to assist in the proper management and control of operations and financial conditions. The ERP system is designed to incorporate all enterprise processes into a single database that can be uploaded to a data warehouse. As described in Chapter 13, data mining and analytical techniques can be employed for managers to gain decision-making insights. The Analytics module in the ERP system incorporates the appropriate data mining and analytical tools to provide reports to management.

SUPPLY CHAIN MANAGEMENT (SCM)

Supply chain management has become a critical aspect of many businesses. SCM is described as follows:

> Supply Chain Management encompasses the planning and management of all activities involved in sourcing and procurement, conversion, and all Logistics Management activities. Importantly, it also includes coordination and collaboration with channel partners, which can be suppliers, intermediaries, third party service providers, and customers. In essence, Supply Chain Management integrates supply and demand management within and across companies.[4]

SCM is the management and control of all materials, funds, and related information in the logistics process, from the acquisition of raw materials to the delivery of finished products to the end user (customer). Processes in the supply chain involve trading processes from a supplier to a business, as well as trading processes between the business and its customers and other intermediaries. Similar to internal processes, the efficiency of trading processes can be improved by the use of ERP systems to initiate, record, store, and report these processes.

ERP systems now include SCM modules. An SCM module represents a module that can assist an organization in supply chain management.

CUSTOMER RELATIONSHIP MANAGEMENT (CRM)

CRM is a term for software solutions that help businesses manage customer relationships in an organized way. An example of a CRM would be a database of detailed customer information that management and salespeople can reference. This database generally includes information regarding customers' purchases, which can be used to do things such as match customer needs with products, inform customers of service requirements, and analyze customer buying behavior.

A successful CRM strategy does not depend only on installing and integrating a software package designed to support CRM processes. The organization must also train employees, modify business processes to match customers' needs, and implement relevant IT systems such as a CRM module in an ERP system.

MARKET SEGMENTS OF ERP SYSTEMS (STUDY OBJECTIVE 5)

There are at least two tiers of ERP systems within the market for ERP software. **Tier one** includes software often used by large, multinational corporations. **Tier two** describes software used by midsize businesses and organizations. As discussed in an earlier chapter, software vendors attempt to expand the market for their software products by appealing to a market segment outside their normal market. For example, tier one vendors attempt to make changes in their

[4]The definition of Supply Chain Management as adopted by The Council of Supply Chain Management Professionals. http://www.cscmp.org.

software that make it appealing to smaller companies in the tier two market. Likewise, tier two vendors attempt to scale up their products so that they appeal to larger companies that may be tier one companies. The typical tier market ERP systems are explained next.

TIER ONE SOFTWARE

Tier one software is usually implemented in very large organizations and is extremely expensive. A minimum cost to purchase tier one ERP software is approximately $350,000. Often, the cost of the software with all desired modules exceeds $1 million, and consulting fees to implement the software can add an extra $1 million or more. The three most popular ERP systems in tier one are SAP, Oracle, and Peoplesoft.

SAP

A brief history of SAP was given earlier in this chapter. The company called **SAP** was formed in 1972 by five former IBM employees. Their intent was to develop and sell application software for real-time processing of business processes. In 1973, they released version 1 of their software, called SAP R/1. The "R" stood for real-time processing. In the 1980s, SAP incorporated multinational currency capability and other enhancements into the software release entitled SAP R/2.

In the early 1990s, SAP modified its ERP software system to be based on client–server architecture. This version, SAP R/3, became the top selling ERP system in that decade and into the early 2000s. SAP R/3 was a true ERP system that included modules for financials, human resources, logistics, sales and distribution, and other typical ERP process modules.

After 2000, the company evolved the ERP system into a software system that was web-centric. This ERP version, entitled mySAP®, incorporates web-based functionality to fully support e-business and e-commerce. Through 2005, SAP continues to be the top-selling tier one ERP system in the United States.

Oracle

Oracle was founded in 1979 as a database software provider. In 1992, Oracle began offering an ERP software system for business application processing. Oracle moved this software to client–server architecture software in 1993. In 1998, Oracle incorporated a CRM module into its ERP software. Oracle ERP software is the second best selling tier one ERP software system.

The current ERP system, Oracle Applications®, offers a fully Internet-enabled application. Oracle advertises this release as a version that fully integrates back office and front office applications. The **back office** modules are the ERP modules such as financials, manufacturing, supply chain management, procurement and logistics, and human resources applications. The **front office** modules, such as customer relationship management (CRM), include customer interfacing applications for sales, marketing, service, and call-center functions. Oracle suggests that the Internet business solutions aspect integrates the back office and front office processes of a company's business.

Peoplesoft

Peoplesoft, founded in 1987, developed a client–server based human resource application system. Peoplesoft continued adding other modules around this HR application to build it into an ERP system. In 2000, Peoplesoft introduced the first "pure Internet" architecture, with no programming code residing on the client computer.

In 2003, Peoplesoft acquired another ERP software system called JD Edwards. Part of the purpose of this acquisition was to make Peoplesoft a larger company and, therefore, a more difficult acquisition target. However, Oracle began working on its acquisition of Peoplesoft in late 2003. That acquisition was completed, and Peoplesoft is now part of Oracle. For the foreseeable future, Oracle plans to continue upgrading and supporting Peoplesoft ERP software.

TIER TWO SOFTWARE

Tier two ERP software is intended for organizations in the range of approximately \$25 to \$250 million in sales. There are many ERP software systems in the tier two market. Some of the popular ERP systems are Axapta, Epicor, MAS 500 ERP, Microsoft Dynamics®, and Macola ERP. ERP software systems such as these have a price range between \$30,000 and \$100,000.

IMPLEMENTATION OF ERP SYSTEMS (STUDY OBJECTIVE 6)

There are many important factors and issues to bear in mind when an organization considers implementation of an ERP system. The management of an organization must consider each of these issues either before or during the ERP implementation. These issues include the following:

1. Hiring a consulting firm
2. The best fit ERP system
3. Which modules to implement
4. Best of breed versus ERP modules
5. Business process reengineering
6. Customization of the ERP system
7. The costs of hardware and software
8. Testing the ERP system
9. Data conversion
10. Training of employees
11. Method of conversion, or "go live"

Many of these issues are interrelated, but the following discussion will address these issues one at a time.

HIRING A CONSULTING FIRM

Very frequently, organizations considering an ERP implementation hire a consulting firm to assist with all or part of the implementation. If a consultant is hired to assist in the entire process, the consulting firm will help with the remaining factors 2. through 11. described in the next subsections. For example, the consulting firm is likely to assist the organization in evaluating and selecting an ERP system, implementing the software, and training employees to use the new system. Alternatively, an organization might choose to use a consulting firm for only selected parts of the ERP implementation process.

THE BEST FIT ERP SYSTEM

An organization must choose the ERP system that best suits its needs. Chapter 6 described some of the factors involved in software selection. Those concepts apply also in selecting an ERP system; however, there are additional factors unique to ERP systems that must be considered. One such factor is the area of specialization of the ERP system. While ERP systems encompass all business processes, each vendor's software has special areas of strengths. For example, SAP's ERP system evolved from manufacturing resources planning (MRP II) software and therefore has been considered particularly strong in its manufacturing related modules. Thus, a manufacturing firm might prefer SAP to Peoplesoft. Peoplesoft evolved from a human resources software system and therefore has been known for its particularly strong HR modules.

The organization must consider its business processes and how well each ERP system operates for those processes. Consulting firms are often used to assist in selecting an ERP system.

WHICH MODULES TO IMPLEMENT

ERP systems have modules available for all typical processes and functions of an organization. However, each additional module that an organization chooses to purchase and implement adds cost, implementation time, and implementation difficulties. For some processes, a company may choose to keep a legacy system rather than purchase an ERP module. For example, a company may have an existing legacy system that records and reports fixed asset processes. Rather than purchase a fixed asset module of an ERP system, the organization may choose to continue using the legacy system.

When determining whether to purchase a particular module, the organization must also recognize that there are many problems inherent in integrating a legacy system into an ERP system. Either approach—purchasing an ERP module or keeping a legacy system—has costs and benefits that must be weighed.

BEST OF BREED VERSUS ERP MODULES

While ERP systems usually are intended to fit all business processes of an organization, some experts believe that ERP systems do not necessarily offer the best solution for all processes. It is difficult for any single software system to offer the best possible modules in all areas of business processes. This is especially true since ERP systems are designed to have a very broad appeal across many different kinds of organizations. This broad appeal is accomplished by building ERP modules around standard, generic business processes. Therefore, some experts believe that an organization is better served by using one brand of ERP system for many processes, but to select some modules from other vendors that are "best of breed." **Best of breed** means the best software on the market for a particular type of business process for this size of an organization.

A best of breed approach is usually applied when an organization has some processes that may be different from the generic processes. Those processes that may be unique or a little more specialized might be better handled by a best of breed rather than the ERP module.

Similar to the factors in decision making regarding legacy systems or ERP modules are the costs and benefits of using either the ERP module or the best of breed system. The ERP module is likely to be easier to integrate into the whole system, but might not offer as much functionality as the best of breed. The organization must evaluate this trade-off and determine which approach best suits the many modules it wishes to implement.

BUSINESS PROCESS REENGINEERING

Chapter 1 introduced the concept of business process reengineering. Recall that **business process reengineering (BPR)** is the purposeful and organized changing of business processes to make them more efficient. BPR not only aligns business processes with the IT systems used to record processes, but it also improves the efficiency and effectiveness of these processes. Thus, the use of sophisticated IT systems usually leads to two kinds of efficiency improvements. First, the underlying processes are reengineered so as to be conducted more efficiently. Second, the IT systems improve the efficiency of the underlying processes through automation. By rethinking and redesigning processes, the organization may be able to improve, and thereby enhance, the process. Rethinking and redesign are especially aided by the use of IT. When computerized technology is introduced into processes, the processes can be radically redesigned to take advantage of the speed and efficiency of computers to improve processing efficiency. IT and BPR have a mutually enhancing relationship. IT capabilities should support the business processes, and any business process should be designed to match the capabilities that the IT system can provide. BPR should leverage the capabilities of IT to improve the efficiency of processes.

BPR is an important aspect of ERP system implementation. Since most organizations' processes do not match the processes in the ERP system for any individual module, BPR is usually undertaken to make the business processes more compatible with the ERP modules. For example, an organization's sales and delivery processes may not currently be done in the same manner as the ERP system module that was written to handle such processes. Since ERP systems have been developed through many years of working experience with many organizations, the ERP systems are usually built around effective and efficient process steps. This means that organizations are usually best served by BPR to change their processes to match those in the ERP system. As described in the preceding paragraph, BPR not only makes the individual process more efficient, but it allows the organization to improve process efficiency overall by capturing the extra efficiencies of the advanced IT processes in the ERP system.

CUSTOMIZATION OF THE ERP SYSTEM

As often as possible, organizations should attempt to undertake BPR to match their processes to the ERP system. However, there are cases in which it may be necessary to customize the ERP system rather than change the business processes. Most consultants and experts would recommend that the number of customizations be limited to the least amount necessary. The two primary reasons for limiting customization is cost and upgrading of the system. Any customizations may require changing or writing new programming code, which can be a very expensive and time-consuming task. The cost of customization can easily exceed the cost of packaged ERP software. Second, customizations cannot be automatically incorporated when the ERP vendor provides an upgraded version of the ERP system. Therefore, upgrading to the next version may mean losing any customization.

In practice, many organizations do wish to have some customization. However, customization should be limited, and the organization should fully understand the extra costs and problems inherent in customization.

THE COSTS OF HARDWARE AND SOFTWARE

Implementation of ERP systems usually requires the purchase of new computer hardware, systems software, network equipment, and security software. The cost of hardware is dependent on the size of the organization, its current hardware and software, and the scope of implementation of the ERP system. For ERP implementation in large organizations, hardware costs often exceed one million dollars; while in midsized organizations, hardware typically costs about half a million dollars.

The cost of an ERP software system varies depending on the size of the organization, the number of modules to implement, and whether any best of breed modules are to be purchased. As discussed earlier, a minimum cost of tier one ERP systems is approximately one million dollars, and in the largest corporations, the total cost can be as much as $100 to $200 million.

TESTING OF THE ERP SYSTEM

As you consider the previous paragraphs, notice the potential complexity of an ERP system implementation. It can involve integrating ERP modules, legacy systems, and best of breed modules. The primary measure of success for ERP implementation is ERP integration. Because an ERP implementation may involve much integration of various modules, legacy systems, and modules from other vendors, it is imperative that these systems be tested extensively prior to implementation.

DATA CONVERSION

The implementation of an ERP system will involve converting data from legacy systems. Second generation ERP systems use relational database management systems (RDBMS) to store enterprise data. Conversion from data in legacy systems to RDBMS can be error prone and time consuming. Often, the data must be cleansed and errors must be corrected prior to conversion. An ERP system is intended to bring many data sources into a single database. The various operational databases of the legacy systems might have incompatible data in several different formats. An appropriate amount of time, effort, and dollars must be devoted to the proper cleansing and conversion of data.

TRAINING OF EMPLOYEES

Since ERP system implementation usually requires BPR, many processes that employees are involved with will change. Thus, training is necessary because workers will often have to learn a new set of processes. As is true of data conversion, it is expensive and time-consuming to train employees. However, this is a step that organizations should not take lightly. Poorly trained employees may prevent the organization from fully realizing the benefits of the ERP system and can cause errors and problems in the processes. Such errors can disrupt business processes and introduce incorrect data into the system.

THE METHODS OF CONVERSION TO THE ERP SYSTEM

Near the end of the implementation process, the organization must "go live" with the new ERP system. That is, after data conversion, training, software installation, and related tasks, there must be a switch over to the new ERP system. There are several methods of making this switch-over. The usual approaches are big bang, location-wise, and modular implementation. These approaches are described in the sections that follow.

Big Bang

In the **big bang** approach to implementation, the company implements all modules and all functional areas of the ERP system at once. There is a particular date established as the "go live" date, and the ERP system is turned on fully on that date. Therefore, the installation of ERP systems of all modules happens across the entire company (including any subsidiaries) at once. The big bang approach requires that all functional areas of the company are ready to "go live" at the same time. This approach demands a tremendous amount of planning and coordination across the entire company. If well-planned and executed, the big bang approach has the potential to reduce the time and cost of implementation. However, it is extremely difficult to execute a big bang conversion well. Such a tremendous effort in planning and coordination is needed that most companies are not able to pull it off.

The underlying premise of a big bang method is that the ERP implementation is simply the implementation of a big information system, which typically follows an SDLC (systems development life cycle) model. But ERP implementation requires a great deal of business process reengineering and is not like IT system changes from years ago. As processes are changed through BPR, implementation becomes more difficult and time consuming. Some have said that an ERP implementation is 60% about changing attitudes and only 40% about changing systems. Although the big bang method dominated early ERP implementations, it partially contributed the higher rate of failure in ERP implementation. Today, not many companies dare to attempt it anymore.

THE REAL WORLD

The City of Tacoma, Washington, attempted a $50 million dollar implementation of SAP R/3 to handle all aspects of business processes within the city. The software was intended to incorporate the city's budgeting, accounting, human resources and payroll, police, fire, and city utilities. The city decided to implement the software in a big bang fashion with the assistance of a consulting firm. The communications supervisor of the city said of the implementation that "they threw the switch at one time, and a lot of failures happened." These failures included problems with payroll checks, utility bills to city residents, and the budget module. An industry expert indicated that the city "tried to do too much at one time." These failures in implementation caused the city to spend much more money to fix the problems. For example, the new system workflow required customer service representatives to examine five different screens of customer data to access customer data and answer inquiries. The city had to spend an extra $405,000 to have the consulting firm modify the ERP system so that important customer data were collapsed into one screen. The problems that occurred in this implementation are examples of the type of problems encountered in implementing an ERP system by a big bang approach.[5]

More than half of the ERP implementations by the big bang approach experienced significant failures or problems in the 1990s, with nearly one-third of these implementations abandoned in progress. However, there have also been successful big bang implementations of ERP systems.

THE REAL WORLD

Marathon®, is a $41 billion energy company with over 28,000 employees worldwide (2003 statistics). Marathon began a big bang implementation of SAP R/3® in late 2000. Since Marathon is in a specialized industry, many of its business processes are different from most companies and have unique information needs. Despite the size and uniqueness of Marathon, it was able to fully implement the ERP system and "go live" after 13 months on January 2, 2002. The team at Marathon undertook several steps to ensure a successful implementation. First, Marathon selected a cross-functional team to manage the implementation. The company also studied the ERP market and selected the ERP software that best suited its needs. The team also studied the reasons for the failures in implementation that other companies had experienced. ERP systems often require underlying changes to business processes. Marathon had an effective plan to manage change in the organization. All of these factors contributed to the success of the implementation at Marathon.[6]

If a company plans a big bang approach to implementation, it must consider the many risks and potential problems. To avoid the risk inherent in a big bang approach, other approaches can be used for the implementation of an ERP system, described in the sections that follow.

[5]Marc L. Songini, "$50 Million SAP Rollout Runs Into Trouble in Tacoma," *Computerworld*, November 22, 2004, vol. 38, no. 47, p. 52.

[6]Gregg Stapleton and Catherine J. Rezak, "Change Management Underpins A Successful ERP Implementation at Marathon Oil," *Journal of Organizational Excellence*, Autumn 2004, pp. 15–22.

Location-Wise Implementation

In a **location-wise** implementation of an ERP system, the organization chooses a specific location or subunit of the organization and implements the ERP system in that place only. This approach can be considered a "pilot" approach in which the ERP is first carried out in a subunit of the larger organization. This means that any resulting problems will be isolated within the pilot unit so that the entire organization is not impacted. This location-wise approach allows the implementation team to work out many of the implementation and operational issues of the ERP system while its impact is minimized within a single location. Once the pilot implementation has been completed and any related issues have been addressed, the ERP implementation can be continued across the entire organization.

Modular Implementation

In a **modular implementation,** the ERP system is implemented one module at a time. The implementation team will normally focus on the most critical module first and complete the implementation of modules in descending order. This allows the organization to take advantage of the new features of the module in the ERP system without affecting all processes in the organization.

A modular implementation normally limits the scope of implementation to one functional department. The implementation team can choose to implement the module in a single location, or organization-wide. A modular implementation reduces the risks associated with installation and operation of ERP systems because it reduces the scope of the implementation. A modular approach will mean that the organization cannot take advantage of all modules in the ERP system until all intended modules have been phased in. This means that the interaction of many of the ERP modules cannot be fully realized until all selected modules are implemented.

BENEFITS AND RISKS OF ERP SYSTEMS (STUDY OBJECTIVE 7)

As is true of any IT system, there are both benefits and disadvantages to ERP systems. The next several sections describe some of the benefits and disadvantages.

BENEFITS OF ERP SYSTEMS

ERP systems have characteristics that allow an organization to experience many benefits. However, to gain any benefits from an ERP system, the organization must successfully implement and operate the ERP system. The characteristics that allow organizations to benefit are the following:

1. The interactive nature of the modules allows processes to interact with each other. For example, the ordering and receiving processes can automatically trigger payment processes.
2. The real-time nature of processing decreases the total processing time and allows more immediate feedback to management.
3. The "best practices" nature of the processes in ERP systems—ERP systems have evolved from many years of software experience with various companies, and the software reflects tried and true practices.
4. The single database enhances sharing of information between the business's functional areas and between processes.

5. There is the capability to analyze large amounts of data in a single database. Analytical tools that enable detailed analysis of the data are incorporated into ERP systems.
6. The capability to enhance e-commerce and e-business—the ERP systems of today incorporate modules to fully incorporate e-commerce and e-business.
7. ERP systems have the capability to interact in real-time with trading partners. ERP systems are built to interact with the IT systems of trading partners such as customers and suppliers.
8. ERP systems are **scalable**, which means that the system can grow with the business.

These characteristics can allow more efficient processes, better information flow between processes and to management, and therefore increased organization efficiency, effectiveness, and cost control.

Two researchers named Shari Shang and Peter Seddon undertook an extremely detailed study of business cases in which companies had implemented ERP systems. They examined the websites of the top software sellers of ERP systems. Each of these websites contained the success stories of customers who had implemented ERP systems. Shang and Seddon studied 233 of these business cases and developed a list of benefits that can be gained by implementing ERP systems. Exhibit 15-5 is a summary of the five dimensions of benefits that Shang and Seddon identified as a result of their study.[7]

Exhibit 15-5
Five Dimensions of ERP Benefits

Operational
- Reduction of cost and cycle time
- Improvement of productivity, quality, and customer service

Managerial
- Improved performance, decision making, and resource management

Strategic
- Support for business growth and business alliance
- Building cost leadership and business innovations
- Generating product differentiation
- Building external linkages
- Generating or sustaining competitiveness
- Enabling e-commerce and increasing web integration

IT infrastructure
- Building business flexibility for current and future changes
- IT cost reduction
- Increased IT infrastructure capability

Organizational
- Changing work patterns and work focus
- Facilitating organizational learning
- Empowerment
- Building common vision
- Increased employee morale and satisfaction

[7]Shari Shang and Peter B. Seddon "Assessing and Managing the Benefits of Enterprise Systems: The Business Manager's Perspective" *Information Systems Journal*, October 2002, vol. 12, Issue 4, pp. 271–299.

RISKS OF ERP SYSTEMS

The risks inherent in ERP systems can be categorized into the two primary risk areas: implementation and operation.

Implementation Risks

The risks inherent in an ERP implementation are very similar to risks of implementing any IT system. However, the scope, size, and complexity of an ERP system increase many of these risks. Since the intent of ERP is to implement the system across the entire enterprise and to incorporate all business processes into the ERP system, the scope, size, and complexity increase tremendously. This causes the implementation of an ERP system to be very costly, time consuming, and potentially disruptive to current operations.

ERP implementation cost and the time required have been briefly discussed in other parts of this chapter. In summary, large organizations may spend in excess of $100 million dollars and one to two years to implement an ERP system. Upgrading ERP systems to new versions of the same ERP system are also expensive and time consuming, but not as expensive or time consuming as the original implementation.

The complexity of an ERP system is due to the enterprise-wide scope and integrated nature of an ERP system. All business processes are incorporated into the ERP system, but the system is also integrated in the sense that each process affects other processes. For example, the sale of goods in an ERP system may automatically trigger more production, which in turn would trigger the purchase of raw materials. The need to ensure that these integrated processes are triggered at the correct time and in the correct amounts is a very complex implementation issue.

Operation Risks

As was true for implementation risks, the operation risks inherent in ERP systems are similar to those for other IT systems. The extent of the risks may be larger, since the ERP system is enterprise-wide and processes are integrated. For example, a risk of any IT system is availability. An IT system failure can stop or disrupt operations. The failure of a legacy system that is not enterprise-wide may stop or disrupt only part of the organization's processes. For example, if a separate legacy system for payroll fails, it would not necessarily disrupt sales or purchase processes. However, an ERP system would normally incorporate all business processes. Therefore, if the ERP system fails, it has the potential to stop or disrupt all processes across the entire enterprise.

The full scope of operation risks are those identified in the AICPA Trust Services Principles as described in Chapter 4. Those risks are as follows:

1. **Security**. The system is protected against unauthorized (physical and logical) access.
2. **Availability**. The system is available for operation and use as committed or agreed.
3. **Processing integrity**. System processing is complete, accurate, timely, and authorized.

4. **Online privacy**. Personal information obtained as a result of e-commerce is collected, used, disclosed, and retained as committed or agreed.
5. **Confidentiality**. Information designated as confidential is protected as committed or agreed.

Each of these risks becomes magnified when the IT system is an ERP system. Security becomes a greater risk because the processes are integrated and, often, automatically triggered in ERP systems. Therefore, any unauthorized user can affect more processes than in an older, legacy system. For example, unauthorized access to a purchase module in an ERP system could allow an unauthorized user to trigger not only purchase activities, but also the related payment within accounts payable.

Processing integrity risks are also magnified in ERP systems due to the integrated nature of the processes. Incorrect data generated in a given process can automatically trigger other processes and post flawed data to other processes. Processes may be triggered at the wrong time, and incorrect data can be spread over several processes and ERP modules. It is important to understand that such processing integrity problems are possible in any IT system. But they have the potential to be more damaging in an ERP system.

Online privacy and confidentiality risks are also magnified in ERP systems. ERP systems often have sales and customer relationship management modules in an e-commerce mode. This means that sales and customer data are exchanged via the web or EDI. In ERP systems, these front-office systems of e-commerce and sales are automatically integrated into the back-office systems of an ERP system. The back-office modules include the financials, supply chain management, and human resources modules. Therefore, in an ERP system, the e-commerce activity of customers often automatically integrates into the general ledger and related processes. This interconnectivity causes more areas for private and confidential information to be available.

ERP SYSTEMS AND THE SARBANES–OXLEY ACT (STUDY OBJECTIVE 8)

Referring back to Exhibit 15-4, you will notice that within the financials module, there is a section entitled "Corporate Governance." Since the passage of the Sarbanes–Oxley Act of 2002, ERP systems have been enhanced to include functions that assist management in complying with sections of the Act. For example, Section 404 of the Act requires assessment of internal controls. An internal control report is required to accompany each financial statement filing. The internal control report must establish management's responsibility for the company's internal controls and related financial reporting systems. It must also include an assessment of the effectiveness of the company's internal controls and related financial reporting systems. If there are any weaknesses in internal controls, they must be disclosed in this report.

Enhanced ERP systems provide feedback information to management regarding internal controls. For processes tracked by the ERP software, a report can be generated that identifies which employees are authorized to initiate and conduct processes. Based on each employee's ID and password, audit trails can be constructed and reports generated to identify the employees who initiated or conducted specific transactions or tasks. This module within the ERP system can map processes to assist management in understanding whether duties are appropriately segregated within each process. Segregation of duties is an important part of internal control that can help prevent errors and fraud.

ERP systems can be used to properly segregate duties. The ERP system can incorporate a matrix of tasks that are incompatible. For each employee ID and password, the system can check the employee's access to various tasks to ensure that no employee can initiate or conduct any incompatible tasks. The ERP system electronically segregates duties by limiting the types of tasks each employee can perform. For example, a single employee should not have system access to initiate a purchase and record it as received. In a ERP system in which integrated modules often automatically trigger events, recording the receipt can automatically initiate a check for payment. Thus, it is important that a single employee not have authorization in the ERP system to initiate a purchase and also record the receipt.

In addition to the preventative nature of attempting to restrict incompatible duties, an ERP system also allows real-time monitoring and reporting of exceptions. As processes and transactions occur that may be exceptions to what was expected, they can be reported to management in real time. Therefore, an ERP system can assist management in monitoring internal control, monitoring errors and problems, and monitoring exceptions to internal controls.

SUMMARY OF STUDY OBJECTIVES

The overview of an ERP system. An enterprise resource planning (ERP) system is a multimodule software system that can integrate all business processes and functions of the entire organization into a single software system using a single database. Each module is intended to collect, process, and store data of a functional area of the organization and to integrate with related processes. The ERP system is the IT infrastructure that has enhanced and enabled e-commerce and e-business. ERP systems and e-business are mutually supporting parts of the organization. ERP systems enhance e-business, and e-business has enhanced the process efficiency of ERP systems. ERP systems contain modules and use an operational database and a data warehouse.

The history of ERP systems. ERP systems can be traced back to software that was developed during the 1960s and 1970s to track inventory in manufacturing companies. The first generation of this software was called materials requirements planning (MRP) software. MRP software evolved into manufacturing resource planning (MRP II) systems. MRP II was much broader and more encompassing than MRP software. MRP software was intended to support the purchase of raw materials for manufacturing needs. The purpose of MRP II was to integrate manufacturing, engineering, marketing, and finance units to run on the same information system and to use a single database for these functions. As MRP and MRP II systems were becoming popular in large manufacturing companies, early pioneers of ERP systems were working on a broader concept of information system software. However, ERP software did not become popular in the large corporation software market until the 1990s. During the last half of 1990s, there was very rapid growth in the sales of ERP software to Fortune 500 companies.

Current ERP system characteristics. Most large businesses have implemented ERP systems that are connected to the IT systems of trading partners. EDI, Internet EDI, or extranets are used to connect a company's ERP system to the IT systems of its suppliers and customers. For example, suppliers may monitor their customers' inventory levels and electronically trigger a shipment when items they supply reach pre-arranged reorder levels. IT spending on ERP systems was flat between 2001 and 2003. In 2004 and 2005, however, the amount of IT spending on ERP systems began to rise. ERP has become so important to daily operations that companies cannot allow their ERP systems to become outdated.

The modules of an ERP system. The ERP systems used by large organizations are actually more complex and encompass more of the enterprise than depicted in Exhibit 15-1. There are many modules in modern ERP systems that encompass the entire organization. This chapter does not describe each of these modules in detail, but focuses on those modules most closely tied to accounting: financials, human resources, procurement and logistics, product development and manufacturing, sales and services, analytics, supply chain management (SCM), and customer relationship management (CRM).

The market segments of ERP software systems. There are at least two tiers of ERP systems within the market for ERP software. Tier one includes software often used by large, multinational corporations. The three most popular tier one ERP systems are SAP, Oracle, and Peoplesoft. Tier two describes software used by midsized businesses and organizations.

Implementation issues of ERP systems. There are many important factors and issues to bear in mind when an organization considers implementation of an ERP system. The management of an organization must consider each of these issues before or during the ERP implementation. These issues include hiring a consulting firm, the best fit ERP system, which modules to implement, whether to use the best of breed or the entire package of brand-provided ERP modules, business process reengineering, customization of the ERP system, the costs of hardware and software, testing the ERP system, data conversion, training of employees, and the choice from the various methods of conversion or "go live."

The benefits and risks of ERP systems. There are many benefits to ERP systems. The characteristics of an ERP system allow more efficient processes, better information flow between processes and to management, and the consequent increased organization efficiency, effectiveness, and cost control. There are also implementation and operation risks of ERP systems. The inherent implementation risks are very similar to risks of implementing any IT system. However, the scope, size, and complexity of an ERP system increase many of these risks.

ERP systems and the Sarbanes–Oxley Act. Since the passage of the Sarbanes–Oxley Act of 2002, ERP systems have been enhanced to include functions that assist management in complying with sections of the Act. These enhanced ERP systems provide feedback information to management regarding internal controls. By tracking each employee's ID and password, audit trails can be constructed and reports generated that identify which employees initiated or conducted specific transactions or tasks. ERP systems can also be used to properly segregate duties. The ERP system can incorporate a matrix of tasks that are incompatible. For each employee ID and password, the system can limit employee's access to ensure that no employee can initiate or conduct incompatible tasks. In addition to the preventative nature of attempting to restrict incompatible duties, an ERP system also allows real-time monitoring and reporting of exceptions.

KEY TERMS

Availability
Back office modules
Best of breed
Big bang implementation
Business process reengineering (BPR)
Customer relationship management (CRM)
Data warehouse
Enterprise resource planning (ERP)
Front office modules
Location-wise implementation
Manufacturing resource planning (MRP II)
Materials requirements planning (MRP)
Modular implementation
Operational database
Oracle
Peoplesoft
Processing integrity
SAP
scalable
Security
Supply chain management (SCM)
Tier one
Tier two
Y2K compatability

END OF CHAPTER MATERIAL

CONCEPT CHECK

1. Which of the following advantages is least likely to be experienced by a company implementing an enterprise resource planning (ERP) system?
   a. Reduced cost
   b. Improved efficiency
   c. Broader access to information
   d. Reduced errors
2. An ERP system is a software system that provides each of the following except
   a. collection, processing, storage, and reporting of transactional data.
   b. enhancement of e-commerce and e-business.
   c. coordination of multiple business processes.
   d. physical controls for the prevention of inventory theft.
3. Which of the following is not a feature of an ERP system's database?
   a. Increased efficiency
   b. Increased need for data storage within functional areas
   c. Increased customer service capability
   d. Increased data sharing across functional areas

4. Manufacturing companies implement ERP systems for the primary purpose of
   a. increasing productivity.
   b. reducing inventory quantities.
   c. sharing information.
   d. reducing investments.
5. What company developed the first true ERP systems?
   a. Microsoft
   b. Peoplesoft
   c. SAP
   d. IBM
6. In the late 1990s, the Y2K compatability issue was concerned primarily with computer systems'
   a. file retrieval capability.
   b. data storage.
   c. human resource comparisons.
   d. capital budgeting.
7. The primary difference between ERP and ERP II systems is that ERP II may include
   a. Internet EDI.
   b. logistics modules.
   c. reporting modules.
   d. a data warehouse.
8. Which of the following is not one of the reasons for increased spending on ERP systems in recent years?
   a. The need for Sarbanes-Oxley compliance
   b. Globalization and increased competitive pressures
   c. The need for earnings management
   d. The need for customer service enhancements
9. Supply chain management (SCM) is a critical business activity that connects a company more closely with its
   a. customers.
   b. suppliers.
   c. subsidiaries.
   d. customers and suppliers.
10. The type of ERP system used by large, multinational corporations is known as
    a. big bang implementation.
    b. modular implementation.
    c. Tier one software.
    d. Tier two software.
11. Which of the following ERP approaches accomplishes the ERP implementation beginning with one department?
    a. the pilot method
    b. the modular implementation approach

c. the big bang approach

d. the location-wise implementation method

12. Which of the following statements best describes the risks of ERP systems?

a. The risks of implementing and operating ERP systems are nearly identical to the risks of implementing and operating IT systems.

b. The risks of operating and implementing ERP systems are greater than the risks of implementing and operating IT systems, due to the scope, size, and complexity of ERP systems.

c. The risks of implementing ERP systems are greater than the risks of implementing IT systems, but the operating risks are nearly identical.

d. The risks of operating ERP systems are greater than the risks of operating IT systems, but the implementation risks are nearly identical.

DISCUSSION QUESTIONS

13. (SO 1) Describe how ERP systems enhance efficiency in a business organization.
14. (SO 1) Why is real-time processing essential in an ERP system?
15. (SO 1) How has ERP increased the responsibilities of customer service representatives?
16. (SO 1) What is an MRP II system and how is it different from the ERP systems in use today?
17. (SO 1) What are the two databases used by ERP systems?
18. (SO 1) Differentiate between the enterprise-wide and nonvolatile features of a company's data warehouse.
19. (SO 2) What was unique about SAP's first ERP system?
20. (SO 2, 5) Differentiate between the features of SAP's R/1, R/2, and R/3. What does the "R" stand for in this name?
21. (SO 3) How do ERP II systems allow businesses to improve efficiencies with respect to sharing information with trading partners?
22. (SO 3) How did the tragic events of September 11, 2001 affect the market for ERP systems?
23. (SO 4) What are some of the activities included in an ERP module for supply chain management?
24. (SO 4) What are some of the features of an ERP module for customer relationship management?
25. (SO 5) Which company is today's top-seller of ERP systems in the United States?
26. (SO 5) Differentiate between Oracle's back office and front office modules.
27. (SO 5) Which tier one company introduced the first ERP system that was "pure Internet," requiring no programming code to reside on the client computer?
28. (SO 5, 6) Which of the tier one ERP companies is likely to provide the "best fit" for a manufacturing firm? for a human resources placement company?
29. (SO 6) Why is business process reengineering an important aspect of ERP implementation?

30. (SO 6) Why should customization of an ERP system be limited?
31. (SO 6) Differentiate between location-wise and modular implementation approaches to the conversion to an ERP system.
32. (SO 7) Which method of conversion to an ERP system is sometimes referred to as a "pilot" method? Why is this name appropriate?
33. (SO 8) How can an ERP system assist a company in its efforts to comply with the Sarbanes–Oxley Act of 2002?

BRIEF EXERCISES

34. (SO 2) Why was there so much growth in the sales of ERP systems in the late 1990s?
35. (SO 3) What are the five most common reasons for increased spending on ERP systems in the early 2000s? Which of these reasons was the impetus for Viper's ERP implementation in 2003?
36. (SO 4) Match the ERP modules on the left with their purpose of the related processes on the right:

Financials	a. Taking customer orders and preparing for the impending revenue and cash collection
Human Resources	b. Maintaining of the general ledger and supporting journals and subledgers
Procurement and Logistics	c. Keeping track of purchasing and movement of goods and materials
Product Development and Manufacturing	d. Accounting for personnel and payroll activities
Sales and Services	e. Data mining and other processes for obtaining feedback and supporting managerial decision making
Analytics	f. Planning and scheduling of conversion activities

37. (SO 6) Discuss the potential advantages and disadvantages that exist with respect to engaging a consultant for an ERP implementation.
38. (SO 7) What are the primary benefits of an ERP system? What are the primary risks?
39. (SO 7) What are Shang and Seddon's five dimensions of ERP benefits?
40. (SO 7) Name the AICPA Trust Services Principles' five operations risks. Why are these risks greater for ERP systems than for other IT systems?
41. (SO 8) Explain how an ERP system can enhance internal controls. Specifically, how can it facilitate the separation of duties?

PROBLEMS

42. (SO 1) Describe the ERP's modular interface that is necessary in a typical manufacturing environment.
43. (SO 2) Identify and describe the first generation of ERP systems used in the 1970s and the second generation of ERP systems used in the 1980s.

44. (SO 4) Compare and contrast the functionality of the logistics module and supply chain management activities.

45. (SO 7, 8) Suppose a company is experiencing problems with omitted transactions in the conversion processes; that is, inventory transactions are not always being recorded as they occur. How can an ERP system help to alleviate such a problem?

46. (SO 6) Using an Internet search engine search for the terms "best of breed" + ERP. Locate information that addresses the debate and dilemma faced by many companies regarding the implementation choice between best of breed technology versus new applications from an ERP vendor. Write a brief memo to discuss this issue.

47. (SO 6) Using an Internet search engine search for the terms "big bang" + ERP. Identify at least one company that represents a success story with regard to this ERP implementation method (other than Marathon, as described in this chapter's Real World example). Also identify at least one company that experienced problems with this approach (other than the city of Tacoma, as described in this chapter's Real World example).

48. (SO 6, 7) Access the web site at www.big4guy.com and find an article titled *Why Implement an ERP Enterprise Resource System SAP Oracle.* Briefly describe the reasons for an ERP implementation. Discuss whether the points in this article match with concepts in this chapter.

CASES

49. Hupman Industries is a manufacturer of warehouse and inventory tracking systems. Hupman has four U.S. plants and three warehouses. The company employees 3500 workers at these facilities and the corporate headquarters. Hupman is using legacy systems for its accounting, materials requirement planning, receivables, payables, inventory, and payroll processes. These various legacy systems were developed at different times and do not necessarily have common data formats or programming. Often, Hupman must export data from one legacy system to incorporarte into a second legacy system. The president has decided that the company must switch to an ERP system to bring the company's systems up to date and to enable the company to remain competitive.

Required:

a. Describe how an ERP system could improve performance at Hupman.

b. Describe the relative advantages and disadvantages of a big bang versus a modular implementation.

c. If Hupman chooses a modular implementation, how might it choose the order in which to implement modules?

50. Chacon University is a Midwestern university with 16,000 students, using various legacy systems for student records, financial systems, human resources, and financial aid. The president of Chacon heard a presentation about ERP systems at a seminar for university administrators. Required:

Read the article at http://www.cio.com/article/107706/, then summarize the problems with using an ERP system at a university.

CONTINUING CASE: SPATELLI'S PIZZERIA

Consider the case of Spatelli's Pizzeria as presented at the end of Chapter 1. Assume that Spatelli's management wishes to upgrade its accounting software to an ERP system. To answer some of the questions here, you may have to do research about ERP systems on the Internet. One example of a website with information about accounting software is www.accountingsoftware411.com or www.2020software.com

Required:

Answer the following questions regarding Spatelli's:

a. What advantages could Spatelli's expect by upgrading to an ERP system?

b. As Spatelli's considers modules to purchase, which four or five modules do you believe would be most critical? Why?

c. Which method of implementation of an ERP system do you suggest for Spatelli's? Why?

d. Recommend two or three ERP systems that would be appropriate for Spatelli's. Be specific with respect to the name of the ERP software system and the provider company. When making these recommendations, consider the size of Spatelli's and, therefore, what it might be able to afford.

SOLUTIONS TO CONCEPT CHECK

1. (CIA, CMA Adapted) (SO 1) **a. Reduced cost** is the advantage least likely to be experienced by a company implementing an ERP system. Although ERP systems can lead to significant benefits, many companies experience increases in IT equipment costs and related staffing costs. This is because multiple additional computer systems are needed to link the ERP systems and facilitate their smooth functioning.
2. (SO 1) An enterprise resource planning (ERP) system is a software system that provides each of the given options except **d. physical controls for the prevention of inventory theft**.
3. (SO 1) **b. Increased need for data storage within functional areas** is not a feature of an ERP system's database. ERPs operate on an operational database, which allows for the centralized storage of data.
4. (CIA Adapted) (SO 1) Manufacturing companies implement ERP systems for the primary purpose of **c. sharing information**. To compete globally, companies must be able to share information quickly and effectively across the organization.
5. (SO 2) **b. SAP** developed the first true ERP systems.
6. (SO 2) In the late 1990s, the Y2K compatibility issue was concerned primarily with computer systems' **b. date storage**. The concern was that older legacy systems would "blow up" when faced with a date of 2000 or later, as they might interpret the year "00" as 1900 instead of 2000.

7. (SO 2) The primary difference between ERP and ERP II systems is that ERP II may include **a. Internet EDI**. EDI, Internet EDI, or extranets are used to connect a company's ERP systems with the IT systems of its trading partners.
8. (SO 3) **c. The need for earnings management** is not a reason for increased spending on ERP systems in recent years.
9. (SO 4) Supply chain management is a critical business activity that connects a company more closely with its **d. customers and suppliers**.
10. (SO 5) The type of ERP system used by large, multinational corporations is known as **c. tier one software**. Answers a. and b. are implementation methods rather than types of systems.
11. (SO 6) **b. The modular implementation approach** accomplishes the ERP implementation one department at a time. This approach normally limits the scope of implementation to one functional department, gradually phasing in each module.
12. (SO 7) The following statement best describes the risks of ERP systems: **a. The risks of operating and implementing ERP systems are greater than the risks of implementing and operating IT systems, due to the scope, size, and complexity of ERP systems.**

Index

A

Absorption costing, 477
Access logs, reviewing, 255
Accountants
  in design/implementation team, 22
  role in AIS, 22
  unethical behaviors and, 23–24, 65
Accounting cycle, 501
Accounting data
  classifying, 5
  collection, 41
  consolidating, 5
  processing, 5, 52–54, 66
  recording, 5
  summarizing, 5
Accounting information systems (AIS), 4–6
  accountant's role in, 22
  auditor of, 22
  components, 4–5
  defined, 4
  ethics and, 22–24, 25, 65
  foundational concepts, 39–76
  function, 2, 5
  importance to accountants, 25
  input methods, 50–52
  integrated, 47
  internal controls, 6
  interrelationships, 41–42, 66
  legacy, 44–46
  manual, 43–44
  new technology adaptation, 40
  objectives, 99
  outputs, 55, 66
  overview, 24
  overview illustration, 6
  REA in, 67–69
  types of, 43–47, 66
  users of, 22
Accounting software
  in-house development, 47
  market segments, 48–49, 66
  popular programs, 49
  purchasing, 47
Accounts payable
  fraud, 84
  invoice copies, 371
  records, 370
  subsidiary ledger, 356
Accuracy, 177
Acknowledgments, 318
Adequate records and documents
  cash collection process, 306
  cash disbursement process, 373
  conversion process, 471
  fixed asset process, 435
  general ledger process, 509
  importance, 96–98
  payroll process, 422
  purchasing process, 358
  purchase return process, 365
  sales process, 293–294
  sales return process, 299–300
Administrative processes
  control, 504–510
  corporate governance in, 515–516, 517
  defined, 496
  ethics in, 513–515, 517
  general ledger, 501–512, 516–517
  introduction to, 495–496
  investment, 498–501, 516
  overall view of, 496
  overview, 516
  process maps, 497, 499, 501
  risks, 510
  sources of capital, 497–498, 500–501, 516
  supervision, 513
  types of, 3, 495
Adverse opinion reports, 263
AICPA Code of Professional Conduct, 266–267
Analytics module (ERP), 606–607
ANSI X.12 standards, 315, 584
Antivirus software, 127
Application controls
  defined, 20, 122, 146, 256
  input, 146–152
  in IT systems, 121
  output, 146, 153–154
  overview, 156
  processing, 146, 152–153
  test of, 256–260
  types of, 146
  validity check, 122
Application software
  defined, 145
  operating system software versus, 140
ARPANET, 562
Asset security. *See also* Security
  cash collection process, 306–307
  cash disbursement process, 373
  conversion process, 471
  defined, 98
  fixed asset process, 435
  payroll process, 422
  purchasing process, 358
  purchase return process, 365
  sales process, 294
  sales return process, 300
Assets
  comparison with records, 98
  internal controls as protection, 91
  misappropriation of, 80
  overstating, 83

Assurance services, 242
Attributes, 62, 533
Audit committee, 173
Audit evidence, 248
Audit programs, 247, 248
Audit trail
  defined, 97
  loss of visibility, 244
  source documents in, 150
  tests, 260
Auditing
  around the computer, 252
  authoritative literature, 245–246, 270
  with the computer, 252
  concentration of, 269
  considerations, 263–266
  continuous, 261
  ethical issues, 266–269, 271
  forensic, 269
  introduction to IT processes, 242
  management assertions in, 246–247, 270
  overview, 270
  through the computer, 252
Auditing Standards Board (ASB), 245
Auditors
  AIS, 22
  authenticity tests, 255
  external, 174
  government, 243
  internal, 173, 243
  IT, 243
  materiality determination, 249
  professional skepticism, 268
  responsibilities, 268
  types of, 242–244, 270
Audits
  completion/reporting phase, 262–263
  compliance, 242–243
  computer use in, 251–252, 270
  external, 243
  financial statement, 243
  objectives, 247
  operational, 243
  phases, 248–251, 270
  planning phase, 249–251
  types of, 242–244, 270
  vendor, 86
Authentication
  controls, 154
  EDI, 317–318
  two factor, 124
  of users, 123–125
Authenticity tests, 255
Authority tables
  defined, 124
  illustrated, 125
Authorization
  defined, 95
  delegation of, 96
  general, 95
  specific, 95, 96
Authorization of transactions
  cash collection process, 302–305
  cash disbursement process, 372–373
  conversion process, 470
  fixed asset process, 434–435
  general ledger process, 504–506
  payroll process, 421
  purchasing process, 357
  purchase return process, 365
  sales process, 293
  sales return process, 296
Automated fixed asset systems, 437–438
Automated matching
  availability risks, 380
  benefits, 378–379
  defined, 16, 377
  process, 378
  processing integrity risks, 379
  requirements, 16
  risks, 379
  security and confidentiality risks, 379
  summary, 390
Availability
  EDI, 317
  ERP system, 617
  Trust Services Principles, 102–103, 132
Availability risks
  automated matching, 380
  defined, 135
  e-business (expenditures), 384–385
  e-business (revenue), 314–315
  evaluated receipt settlement, 382
  hacking, 136
  physical access, 137

B

Back office modules, 608
Backbone, Internet, 565
Backups, off-site, 132
Balancing tests, 260–262
  defined, 257
  overview, 270
Bar codes
  defined, 50
  scanners, 51
  uses, 51
Basel II regulations, 180
Batch processing. *See also* Processing
  advantages, 53, 530
  characteristics, 530
  defined, 12, 529
  determining, 530
  disadvantages, 53–54, 530
  legacy systems, 53
  payroll use, 54, 424
  preprocessing, 53
  real-time processing versus, 549
  requirements, 53
  sequential access files, 13
Batch totals
  defined, 99, 152
  review of, 99
Best of breed, 611
Big bang implementation (ERP system). *See also* ERP implementation
  defined, 613
  examples, 614
  underlying premise, 613
Bills, 291
Bills of lading, 291, 355
Bills of materials
  defined, 461
  preparing, 462
Biometric devices, 124
Bits (binary digits), 11
Blind purchase orders, 354
Board of directors
  capital funds decision, 498
  IT governance functions, 204
  role, 172–173
Bricks and mortar companies, 572
Bricks and clicks, 572
Business continuity planning (BCP), 131

Business process reengineering (BPR)
in business process alignment, 311
defined, 9, 11, 215, 611
in ERP system implementation, 611
fixed asset, 410–412, 426–438
IT enablement, 10
IT relationship, 216
payroll, 410–426
in purchasing and payments, 377
in SDLC, 216
Business processes
accounting effects, 41
administrative, 3, 493–517
cash collection, 302–308
cash disbursement, 367–375
conversion, 3
defined, 2, 41
example, 3–4
expenditure, 3, 348–391
financial status effects, 3
general ledger, 501–512
initiation, 2
input methods, 50–52, 66
interrelationships, 41–42, 66
introduction to, 2–4
investment, 498–501
IT support, 9
new technology adaptation, 40
overview, 24
production, 465–469
purchasing, 351–360
purchase return, 360–367
revenue, 3, 284–287
sales, 287–325
sales returns, 296–301
sources of capital, 497–498, 500–501
in supply chain, 6–8
types of, 3
work steps within, 4–5, 41
Business to business (B2B) sales. *See also* E-business; E-commerce
advantages, 312
B2C versus, 577
characteristics, 312
controls, 312–313
defined, 311, 576
as part of e-business, 576–578
risks, 313–315
strategic issues, 580
transactions, 577–578
Business to consumer (B2C) sales. *See also* E-business; E-commerce
advantages, 312, 569
B2B versus, 577
characteristics, 312
controls, 312–313
defined, 311
engaging in, 580–581
risks, 313–315
transaction examples, 569

C
Capital
budgets, 426–429, 461
defined, 497
raising, 498
Cardinality, 63
Cases, this book
administrative processes/controls, 522
auditing IT-based processes, 278–279
conversion processes/controls, 485–489
corporate governance, 198
data and databases, 555–556
e-commerce and e-business, 594–595
ERP systems, 625–626
expenditure processes, 399–404
foundation concepts, 74
fraud, ethics, and internal control, 113–116
internal controls/risks in IT systems, 163–164
introduction to AIS, 31–32
IT governance, 238–239
payroll and fixed asset processes, 450–453
sales and cash collection processes, 337–343
Cash collection processes
adequate records/documents, 306
authorization of transactions, 302–305
cash receipts journal, 302
controls, 308
cost-benefit considerations, 307–308
data flow diagrams (DFDs), 305
document flowchart, 304
EDI with, 315–316
independent checks and reconciliation, 307
IT-enabled systems, 309–311, 324–325
process map, 303
remittance advice, 302
risks, 308
security of assets/documents, 306–307
segregation of duties, 305–306
summary, 324
Cash collections, 286
Cash disbursement processes
adequate records/documents, 373
authorization of transactions, 372–373
cash disbursements journal, 371–372
cash management, 367–370
controls, 374–375
cost-benefit considerations, 374
data flow diagram (DFD), 370
document flowchart, 369
independent checks and reconciliation, 374
IT systems of, 375–377, 390
process map, 368
remittance advice, 371
risks, 374–375
security of assets/documents, 373
segregation of duties, 373
summary, 390
voucher system, 370
Cash disbursements
department, 371
journal, 371–372
types of, 367
Cash management, 367–370
Cash receipts
journal, 302
theft, 84
Cash registers, 4
Centralized databases, 543
Centralized processing, 543
Certified fraud examiners (CFEs), 269
Certified Information Systems Auditors (CISAs), 267
Certified Internal Auditors (CIAs), 267
Certified public accountants (CPAs)
defined, 243
designation, 267
Sarbanes–Oxley Act restrictions, 267–268
Channel stuffing, 321
Characters, 528
Checks
dual signature, 373
fraud, 86
writing, 367
Clicks and mortar businesses, 572
Clients, 545

Client-server computing
characteristics, 64
clients, 545
defined, 64, 544–545
distributed applications, 65
distributed presentation, 65
example, 64
servers, 545
summary, 67
task assignment, 64
web-based model, 65
Code of ethics. *See also* Ethics
company development/adherence, 20
concepts, 90
defined, 266
as documented guidelines, 80, 90
due care, 267
for financial officers, 185
maintaining, 89–90, 104
need for, 78–80, 103
objectivity and independence, 266
public interest, 266
responsibilities, 266
scope and nature of services, 267
Collusion, 84–85
Committee of Sponsoring Organizations (COSO). *See also* COSO report
accounting internal control structure, 20, 79, 180
defined, 18
Common carriers, 350
Communication, effective, 19
Communities, as stakeholders, 174
Compensating control, 96
Completeness check, 151
Compliance
as corporate governance function, 176–178
internal control, 176–178
Sarbanes–Oxley Act impact, 186–187
Compliance audits, 242–243
Computer fraud. *See also* Fraud
characteristics, 86
DoS attacks, 88
external sources, 87–88
hacking, 88
internal sources, 87
nature of, 104
spoofing, 89
Computer logs, 124, 153
Computer-aided design (CAD), 474
Computer-aided manufacturing (CAM), 475
Computer-assisted audit techniques (CAATs)
defined, 252, 258
embedded audit modules, 258, 259
integrated test facility (ITF), 258, 259
list of, 258
parallel simulation, 258, 259
program tracing, 258–259
test data method, 258
Computer-based conversion process, 473–476
CAD, 474
CAM, 475
CIMs, 475–476
data input, 474
ERP, 475
JIT, 476
MRP, 475
MRP-II, 475
savings, 474
Computer-based fixed asset systems, 437–438
Computer-based matching
availability risks, 380
benefits, 378–379
defined, 377
process, 378
processing integrity risks, 379
risks, 379
security and confidentiality risks, 379
summary, 390
Computer-integrated manufacturing systems (CIMs), 475–476
Computerized accounting systems. *See also* Real-time processing
automation, 505
segregation, 507
Computers
in audits, 251–252, 270
data structures, 11–12
files, 12
networks, 14
processing modes, 12–13
unethical behaviors and, 155
Concept checks, this book
administrative processes/controls, 517–519
AIS foundation concepts, 69–71
auditing IT processes, 272–275
conversion processes/controls, 480–482
corporate governance, 194–195
data and databases, 551–553
e-commerce and e-business, 590–591
ERP systems, 621–623
expenditure processes, 391–394
fraud, ethics, and internal control, 108–110
internal controls and risks, 157–159
introduction to AIS, 26–27
IT governance, 234–236
payroll and fixed asset processes, 444–447
revenue processes, 326–328
Conceptual design. *See also* Systems design
defined, 208, 219
EIPP system, 219
feasibility assessments, 220
Concurrency, 531
Confidentiality
e-business, 312
EDI, 317
ERP system, 618
Trust Services Principles, 103, 132
Confidentiality risks
automated matching, 379
defined, 135
e-business (expenditures), 383–384
e-business (revenue), 313
evaluated receipt settlement, 382
physical access, 137
Configuration tables, 125
Conflict of interest, 190
Consolidation, 542
Consultants, ethical considerations, 231–232
Continuous auditing, 261
Control activities
adequate records and documents, 96–98
authorization of transactions, 95–96
categories, 95
defined, 19, 95
independent checks and reconciliation, 98–99
security of assets and documents, 98
segregation of duties, 96
Control environment
defined, 93
factors, 93
operating style, 93–94
Control Objectives for Information Technology (COBIT)
defined, 102
domains, 107
framework, 106
information criteria, 107

IT resources, 107
processes, 107
Control structures, 17–21
management-generated, 18
overview, 25
Control totals
defined, 153
EDI, 318
run-to-run, 153
Controls
application, 20, 122, 145–154, 156, 256–260
authentication, 154
cash collection process, 308
cash disbursement process, 374–375
categories, 102–103
conversion process, 473, 478–479
data and database, 545, 550
e-business (expenditures), 383
e-business (revenue), 312–313
evaluated receipt settlement, 381–382
fixed asset process, 436, 443
general, 20, 121–137, 155, 253–256
general ledger process, 510, 517
input, 146–152
internal, 90–101, 104
IT, 20, 101–103, 120–156, 140
IT administration, 253–254
output, 146, 153–154
payroll process, 423, 443
processing, 146, 152–153
purchasing process, 359–360
purchase return process, 366–367
sales process, 295
sales return process, 301
security, 254–256
source document, 147–150
tests of, 252–260, 270
Conversion processes
adequate records and documents, 471
authorization of transactions, 470
basic features, 458–460, 478
controls, 473, 478–479
corporate governance, 477–478, 479
cost accounting reports, 469–470, 478
cost-benefit considerations, 472–473
data flow diagram (DFD), 468
database, 474
document flowchart, 467
ethics and, 476–477, 479
independent checks and reconciliation, 471–472
initiation, 460
IT systems with, 473–476, 479
logistics function, 460–469, 478
overview, 460
process map, 466
resources, 458
risks, 473, 478–479
security of assets and documents, 471
segregation of duties, 470–471
types of, 3
within overall system, 459
Corporate governance
in administrative processes, 517
business diversity, 171
conflict of interest, 190
conversion processes, 477–478, 479
defined, 20–21, 171
earnings management, 179
in environment of honesty, 191
ethical conduct, 179
ethics and, 190–192, 193
expenditure process, 388–389, 391
fiduciary duty, 178
financial stewardship, 178–179
fixed asset processes, 441–442
functions, 175–179, 192
history, 179–180, 192
impact on corporate governance, 186–189
importance, 189–190, 193
independence concept, 191–192
internal controls and compliance, 176–178
management oversight, 175–176
overview, 170–171, 192
participants, 171–175, 192
payroll processes, 441–442
in reporting, 517
revenue processes, 323–324, 325
Sarbanes–Oxley Act impact on, 21, 186–189, 193
stakeholders (participants), 171–175
tone at the top, 171
Corrective controls, 92
COSO report. *See also* Committee of Sponsoring Organizations (COSO)
control activities, 95–99
control environment, 93–94
defined, 93, 206
information and communication, 99–100
risk assessment, 94
Cost accounting reports, 469–470
Cost-benefit considerations
cash collection process, 307–308
cash disbursement process, 374
conversion process, 472–473
fixed asset process, 437
payroll process, 423
purchasing process, 358–359
purchase return process, 366
sales process, 294–295
sales return process, 300–301
Costs
actual, 470
ERP hardware/software, 612
standard, 469, 470
variances, 470
Credit card fraud, 86
Credit limit, 287
Credit memoranda, 296
Creditors, as stakeholders, 174
Customer fraud, 86, 104
Customer relationship management (CRM) module, 603
Customers
e-commerce advantages/disadvantages, 569–570
ethical responsibilities with data, 548
as stakeholders, 175
Cutoff
defined, 355
issues, 355–356

D
Data
collection, 526–527, 549
defined, 526
hierarchy, 528
identifying, 539
IT controls for, 545, 550
normalized, 535–538
proprietary, 548
scrubbing, 540
standardizing, 539–540
uploading, 540
Data analysis software (DAS), 262
Data analysis tools
data mining, 541–542
OLAP, 542
Data conversion, 226–227

Data ethics
company responsibilities, 546–547
customer responsibilities, 548
defined, 546
employee responsibilities, 547–548
overview, 550
Data flow diagrams (DFDs). *See also* Documenting systems
cash collection process, 305
cash disbursement process, 370
conversion process, 468
defined, 60
fixed asset acquisition, 429
illustrated, 61
payroll process, 418
purchasing process, 354
purchase return process, 363
sales process, 290
sales return process, 299
symbols, 61
Data mining
defined, 13, 541
software, 190
uses, 13–14, 550
Data normalization
defined, 537
need for, 549
rules, 537
Data preparation procedures, 150
Data redundancy, 531
Data segments, 315
Data storage
media, 529
methods, 549
need for, 549
processing relationships, 549
terminology, 528
tradeoffs, 537–538
Data warehouses
to analyze data, 538–540
building, 539
data identification, 539
data scrubbing, 540
data standardization, 539–540
data upload, 540
defined, 13
enterprise-wide data, 13
ERP system, 600
operational databases and, 538
overview, 549
purpose, 540
Database administrators, 129
Database management system (DBMS)
defined, 142, 531
exposure, 142
illustrated, 142
Databases
approach illustration, 532
centralized, 543
conversion process information, 474
defined, 11, 528, 531
distributed (DDBs), 543–544, 550
exposure, 141–142
flat file, 532–533
hierarchical, 533–534
history of, 532–535, 549
importance of, 549
IT controls for, 545, 550
network, 534
operational, 13, 538, 600
relational, 11, 534–535
storage tradeoffs, 537–538
tables, 533
Debit memos, 363
Defalcation, 80
Denial of service (DoS) attacks, 88
Depreciation, 431
Detail information, 42
Detailed design. *See also* Systems design
defined, 209, 222
inputs, 222–223
internal controls, 223
outputs, 222
processes, 223
Detective controls, 92
Direct access. *See* Random access
Direct cutover conversion, 226
Disaster recovery plans (DRP), 132, 314
Disclaimer reports, 263
Disclosures
in period reports, 184
real-time, 185
Discussion questions, this book
administrative processes/controls, 519–520
AIS foundation concepts, 71–73
auditing IT processes, 275–276
conversion processes/controls, 482–483
corporate governance, 196–197
data and databases, 553–554
e-commerce and e-business, 592–593
ERP systems, 623–624
expenditure processes, 394–395
internal controls and risks, 159–160
introduction to AIS, 27–28
payroll and fixed asset processes, 447–448
revenue processes, 329
Distributed applications, 65
Distributed data processing (DDP), 542–545
advantages, 543–544
client/server, 544–545
defined, 543
disadvantages, 544
management issues, 544
overview, 550
Distributed databases (DDBs)
advantages, 543–544
defined, 543
disadvantages, 544
management issues, 544
Distributed presentation, 65
Document flowcharts. *See also* Documenting systems
cash collection process, 304
cash disbursement process, 369
defined, 58
fixed asset acquisition, 428
fixed asset disposal, 433
illustrated, 60
payroll process, 417
production process, 467
purchasing processes, 353
purchase return process, 362
sales process, 289
sales return process, 298
uses, 58
Document matching
for approve and pay for purchases, 376
problems, 377
tasks, 375–376
three-way matching, 375
Document security. *See also* Security
cash collection process, 306–307
cash disbursement process, 373
conversion process, 471
defined, 98
fixed asset process, 435

general ledger process, 509
payroll process, 422
purchasing process, 358
purchasing return process, 365
sales process, 294
sales return process, 300
Documentation
computerized, 98
paper, 97
policies and procedures, 98
review, 214
supporting, 97
system, 225–226
understanding, 55
Documenting systems
data flow diagrams, 60–61
document flowcharts, 58–60
entity relationship diagrams, 62–64
process maps, 56–57
summary, 66–67
system flowcharts, 57–58
types of, 56
Documents
alteration penalties, 185
internal, 55
source, 43, 147
trading partner, 55
turnaround, 43
Documents, adequate, 96–98
cash collection process, 306
cash disbursement process, 373
conversion process, 471
fixed asset process, 435
general ledger process, 509
payroll process, 422
purchasing process, 358
purchase return process, 365
sales process, 293–294
sales return process, 299–300
Domain names, 568
Drill down, 542
Dual signature checks, 373

E

Earnings management
defined, 80, 179, 440, 476
techniques, 440, 476–477
E-business, 15, 52, 325, 390, 588
availability, 313
availability risks (expenditures), 384–385
availability risks (revenue), 314–315
B2B, 311–312, 569, 576–578
B2C, 311–312, 569
controls (expenditures), 383
controls (revenue), 312–313
defined, 15, 560
e-commerce versus, 561
enablement examples, 578–580, 588
enablement tools, 583–586
ethical considerations, 586–587, 589
introduction to, 560–561, 588
IT enablement and, 574–580
IT infrastructure, 597–621
processing integrity, 312
processing integrity risks (expenditures), 384
processing integrity risks (revenue), 313–314
risks (expenditures), 383–385
risks (revenue), 313–315
security and confidentiality, 312
security and confidentiality risks (expenditures), 383–384
security and confidentiality risks (revenue), 313
term usage, 560
eBusiness Transitionary Working Group (eBTWG), 69
E-commerce, 52, 325
B2B, 311–312, 569
B2C, 311–312, 569
benefits for business, 570–571
benefits for the customer, 569–570
defined, 311, 560
disadvantages for business, 571
disadvantages for the customer, 570
e-business versus, 561
ethical considerations, 586–587, 589
introduction to, 560–561, 588
privacy expectations, 572–574, 588
traditional commerce combined with, 571–572
Economic feasibility, 211, 221
Electronic data interchange (EDI), 15, 390
acknowledgment, 318
advantages, 315–316
authentication, 317–318
availability (expenditure), 384–385
availability (revenue), 317
with cash collection processes, 315–316
control totals, 318
controls, 317–318
data segments, 315
defined, 15, 145, 315
encryption, 318
example use, 52
exposure, 145
header data, 315
as input method, 52
Internet, 583–585
labeling interchanges, 315
process integrity, 317
processing integrity (expenditure), 384
with revenue processes, 315–316
risks, 317
security and confidentiality (expenditure), 383–384
security and confidentiality (revenue), 317
standard business format, 315
summary, 325
systems, 311
with third party network, 315, 316
trailer data, 315
transaction logging, 318
Electronic funds transfer (EFT), 584
Electronic invoice presentment and payment (EIPP)
defined, 16, 385
Internet connectivity, 385
as matchless system, 219
requirements, 219
Electronic time clocks, 424
Electronic transfer, 425
Embedded audit module, 258, 259
Embezzlement, 85
Emergency power supply (EPS), 130
Employee fraud. *See also* Fraud
collusion, 84–85
defined, 84
ethical responsibilities with data, 547–548
kickbacks, 84
larceny, 84
nature of, 104
skimming, 84
types, 84
Employees
ethical considerations, 230–231
ghost, 439–440
hiring, 413
personnel records, 413
protection for, 185
salaried, 415

Employees (*continued*)
as stakeholders, 173
time sheets, 415, 418
training, 224
training (ERP systems), 613
Encryption. *See also* Security
defined, 126
EDI, 318
public key, 126
symmetric, 126
wireless network, 126
Engineering
documents, 461
responsibilities, 461
role in planning process, 462
Enterprise application integration (EAI), 46
Enterprise resource planning (ERP) systems, 16–17, 475. *See also* ERP implementation; ERP modules
as a process, 19
availability, 617
benefits, 615–616, 620
characteristics, 603–605, 620
complexity, 617
confidentiality, 618
customization, 612
data warehouse, 600
defined, 16, 598
ERP II, 603
example use, 599
feedback information, 618
five dimensions, 616
history, 601–603, 619
illustrated, 600
implementation risks, 617
market segments, 607–609, 620
marketability, 603
MRP II software system, 599, 601
online privacy, 618
operation risks, 617–618
operational database, 600
overview, 598–601, 619
processing integrity, 617
real-time interaction, 616
risks, 617–618, 620
Sarbanes–Oxley and, 618–619, 620–621
scalability, 616
security, 617
segregation of duties, 619
software operations, 599
software popularity, 602
software systems, 17
spending, 604
testing, 612
tier one software, 48, 607, 608–609
tier two software, 607, 609
Enterprise risk management (ERM)
defined, 18
management policies and procedures, 19
as management responsibility, 19
Entities, 62
Entity relationship (ER) diagrams. *See also* Documenting systems
attributes, 62
cardinality, 63
defined, 62
entities, 62
illustrated, 63
symbols, 62
uses, 64
E-payables
defined, 16, 385
summary, 390–391
ERP II system, 603
ERP implementation, 604. *See also* Enterprise resource planning (ERP)
best fit ERP system, 610
best of breed, 610–611
big bang approach, 613
BPR, 611
conversion methods, 613–615
customization, 612
data conversion, 612–613
employee training, 613
hardware/software costs, 612
hiring a consulting firm, 609–610
issues, 609
location-wise, 615
modular, 615
module selection, 610
overview, 620
risks, 617
testing, 612
ERP modules, 16–17, 598. *See also* Enterprise resource planning (ERP)
analytics, 606–607
back office, 608
CRM, 603, 607
financial, 605–606
front office, 608
human resources, 606
interactions, 601
overview, 620
procurement and logistics, 606
product development and manufacturing, 606
sales and services, 606
SAP view of, 605
SCM, 603, 607
Errors
avoidance policies, 89, 104
discovery, 150
handling, 150
E-tailers, 572
Ethical conduct, as corporate governance function, 179
Ethics
administrative processes, 517
AIS and, 22–24, 25, 65
auditing, 266–269, 271
capital sources and investing, 513–514
code of, 20, 78–80, 89–90, 104
consultants, 231–232
conversion process, 476–477, 479
data, 546–548, 550
e-business and e-commerce, 586–587, 589
employee, 230–231
expenditures processes, 386–388, 391
fixed asset process, 438–441, 443
internal reporting, 514–515
IT governance, 230–232, 233
IT issues, 154–155, 156
payroll process, 438–441, 443
reporting, 517
revenue processes, 320–323, 325
Sarbanes–Oxley Act impact, 188–189, 193
unethical behaviors and, 23–24, 65
Evaluated receipt settlement (ERS)
availability, 382
BPR and, 377
defined, 16, 380
processing integrity, 302
receipt of goods, 16
risks, 382
security and confidentiality, 382
summary, 390
Evaluation and selection, 208, 220
Event identification, 19
Exception reports, 542

Exercises, this book
administrative processes/controls, 520–521
AIS foundation concepts, 72
auditing IT processes, 276–278
conversion processes/controls, 483–484, 485
corporate governance, 197
data and databases, 554
e-business and e-commerce, 593–594
ERP systems, 624, 625
expenditure processes, 395–396, 399
fraud, ethics, and internal control, 111
internal controls and risks, 160–161
introduction to AIS, 28–29, 29–30
IT governance, 236–237
payroll and fixed asset processes, 448
revenue processes, 329–330
Expenditure processes
cash disbursements, 367–374, 390
categories, 350
computer-based matching, 377–381, 390
corporate governance, 388, 391
e-business, 382–385
EDI, 382–385
e-payables, 385, 390–391
ethical issues, 386–388, 391
evaluated receipt settlement, 380–382, 390
fixed asset, 410–412, 426–438
illustrated, 349
internal controls, 388
IT systems, 375–377, 390
overview, 389
payroll, 410–426
procurement cards, 386, 391
purchasing, 351–357, 389
purchase returns, 360–367, 389–390
revenue processes comparison, 350
types of, 3, 350
Expense account fraud, 84
Expenses, understating, 83
Exposure areas, 137–145
database, 141–142
DBMS, 142
EDI, 145
Internet, 144
LANs, 143
operating system, 139–141
overview, 155–156
telecommuting workers, 144–145
WANs, 143
wireless networks, 143–144
External auditors, as stakeholders, 174
External audits, 243
External reports. *See also* Reports
defined, 55
generation, 511
types of, 511
Extranets. *See also* Internet; Intranets
defined, 14, 581
in e-business enablement, 581, 589
internal controls, 581–582, 589

F

Feasibility study
assessments, 211, 220
defined, 211
economic feasibility, 211, 221
operational feasibility, 211, 221
purpose, 220
schedule feasibility, 211, 221
technical feasibility, 211, 220–221
Fiduciary duty, 178
Field check, 151
Fields, 11, 528
Files
defined, 11, 528
ISAM, 12
master, 11
random access, 12
sequential access, 12
transaction, 11–12
Financial Accounting Standards Board (FASB), 174
Financial module (ERP), 605–606
Financial officers, code of ethics for, 185
Financial statement audits, 243
Financial stewardship
characteristics, 178–179
defined, 178
earnings management and, 179
Sarbanes–Oxley Act impact, 188
Finished goods inventory, 464
Firewalls, 125
Fixed asset acquisitions
capital budget, 426–429
data flow diagram (DFD), 429
defined, 426
document flowchart, 428
initiation, 426
inspection, 429
process map, 427
Fixed asset disposals
accounting for, 431
defined, 431
document flowchart, 433
process map, 432
Fixed asset processes
acquisitions, 426–430
adequate records/documents, 435
approval levels, 434
authorization of transactions, 434–435
automated systems, 437–438
complexities, 437
continuance, 430–431
controls, 436, 443
corporate governance, 441–442
cost-benefit considerations, 437
defined, 411
disposals, 431–433
ethical considerations, 438–441, 443
fixed asset subsidiary ledger, 430
independent checks and reconciliation, 435–436
introduction to, 410–412
IT systems of, 437–438, 443
overview, 443
risks, 411, 436, 443
security of assets/documents, 435
segregation of duties, 435
Fixed asset subsidiary ledger, 430
Fixed assets continuance
activities, 430
cost information updating, 430
defined, 430
estimates, updating, 430–431
periodic depreciation adjustment, 431
Flat file databases. *See also* Databases
attributes, 533
defined, 532–533
tables, 533
Flowcharts. *See* Document flowcharts; System flowcharts
Foreign Corrupt Practices Act (FCPA), 105–106
Forensic auditing, 269
Forms
authorization and control, 149–150
design, 147–149

Forms (*continued*)
example, 148
input screens, 149
Fraud
accounting-related categories, 82
accounts payable, 84
avoidance policies, 89, 104
check, 86
computer, 86–89, 104
credit card, 86
customer, 86, 104
defined, 80
employee, 84–85, 104
expense account, 84, 85
expense report, 84, 85
ghost employee, 439–440
incentive and, 80
management, 82–84, 104
misappropriation of assets, 80
misstatement of financial records, 80
opportunity and, 81
payroll, 84, 439–440
prevention, 81
rationalization and, 81
refund, 86
time sheet, 43
triangle, 80–81
vendor, 86, 104
Fraudulent financial reporting, 80
Front office modules, 608

G
General authorization, 95
General controls. *See also* Controls
AICPA Trust Services Principles perspective, 132–137, 155
authentication of users, 123–125
business continuity planning (BCP), 131–132
defined, 20, 121
hacking/network break-ins, 125–128
IT administration, 253–254
IT systems, 121, 122–132
organizational structure, 128–129
overview, 155
physical environment/security, 129–131
security, 129–131, 254–256
test of, 253–256
General journals, 44
General ledger processes. *See also* Administrative processes
adequate records and documents, 509
authorization of transactions, 504–506
controls, 510, 517
corporate governance, 517
independent checks and reconciliation, 509–510
output, 510–512
overview, 516–517
risks, 510, 517
security of ledger and documents, 509
segregation of duties, 506–508
special journals, 502
subsidiary ledgers, 502, 503
General ledgers
computerized system, 505–506, 507–508
defined, 44
manual systems, 506
posting in Microsoft Dynamics GP, 508
preparation, 503
security, 509
Generalized audit software (GAS), 262
Generally accepted auditing standards (GAAS), 245
Ghost employees. *See also* Fraud
clues, 439–440
defined, 439
fraud, 439–440
Governing bodies, as stakeholders, 174
Government auditors, 243
Graphical user interface (GUI) browsers, 563

H
Hacking
defined, 88
general controls, 125–128
risks from, 136
Hardware exposures, 137–145, 155–156
Hash totals, 152
Header data, 315
Health Insurance Portability and Accountability Act (HIPAA), 587
Hierarchical databases. *See also* Databases
defined, 533
linkages, 534
record pointers, 533
High-impact processes (HIPs), 539
HTML (hypertext markup language)
defined, 566
source code, 567
Human resources department, 413, 463
Human resources module (ERP), 606

I
Independent checks
analysis of reports, 98
cash collection process, 307
cash disbursement process, 374
comparison of physical assets with records, 98–99
conversion process, 471–472
defined, 98
example procedures, 98
fixed asset process, 435–436
general ledger process, 509–510
payroll process, 422
purchasing process, 358
purchase return process, 365–366
recalculation of amounts, 99
reconciliation, 98
review of batch totals, 99
sales process, 294
sales return process, 300
Indexed sequential access method (ISAM), 12
Industrial espionage, 86, 547
Industrial robots, 475
Information
criteria, 107
defined, 526
Information risk
causes, 244
defined, 244
summary, 270
Information Systems Audit and Control Association (ISACA), 102, 203, 246
Information technology (IT). *See also* IT controls; IT enablement; IT systems
BPR relationship, 9, 216
business processes support, 9
defined, 9
ethical issues, 154–155, 156
performance reports, 227
resources, 107
Information Technology Infrastructure Library (ITIL), 203
In-house design. *See also* Systems design
process map, 219
software purchase versus, 218

Input controls. *See also* Application controls
control totals and reconciliation, 152
data input procedures, 150
defined, 146
programmed input validation checks, 150–152
source document, 147–150
test of, 256, 257
types, 146
validation checks, 150–152
Input manipulation, computer fraud, 87
Input methods
bar codes, 50–51
e-business/e-commerce, 52
EDI, 52
POS systems, 51–52
source document and keying, 50
summary, 66
Input validation checks
completeness check, 151
defined, 150
field check, 151
limit check, 151
range check, 151
reasonableness check, 151
self-checking digit, 152
sequence check, 152
sign check, 151
types of, 151
validity check, 151
Integrated systems, 47
Integrated test facility (ITF), 258, 259
Internal auditors
defined, 243
as stakeholders, 173
Internal controls. *See also* Controls
accounting system, 6, 90–101
benefits, 101
cash disbursements, 374–375
cash receipts, 308
compliance, 176–178
conversion, 473
as corporate governance function, 176–178
corrective, 92
COSO report, 79
cost-benefit comparison of, 98
defined, 4
detailed design, 223
detective, 92
e-business and EDI, 318, 383
effectiveness of, 295
evaluating, 251
expenditure processes, 388
for extranets, 581–582, 589
fixed assets, 436
general ledger, 510
for Internet, 581–582, 589
for intranets, 581–582, 589
limit to effectiveness, 101
maintaining, 90–101, 104
management assessment, 184–185
monitoring, 100
need for, 78–80
objectives, 90
overview, 155
payroll, 423
preventative, 92
processes and procedures, 79
purchase returns, 366–367
purchasing, 359–360
reasonable assurance of, 100–101
sales, 295
sales returns, 301
Sarbanes–Oxley Act impact, 186–187
SDLC as, 228–229
as shields to protect assets and records, 91
six-step process, 177–178
standards, 105–106
system, maintaining, 101–102
work steps, 5
Internal documents, 55
Internal environment, 19
Internal reports. *See also* Reports
characteristics of, 511
defined, 55
ethical issues, 514–515
function managed and, 512
organization type and, 511–512
time horizon and, 512
Internal Revenue Service (IRS), 79
Internal theft, 80
International Accounting Standards Board (IASB), 174
International Audit Practices Committee (IAPC), 245
International Organization for Standardization (ISO), 203
Internet. *See also* Extranets; Intranets
architecture, 565
ARPANET and, 562
backbone, 565
in circulating payroll information, 425
defined, 14, 563
exposure, 144
history, 562–565, 588
HTML, 566
internal controls, 581–582, 589
local ISPs, 566
network access points (NAPs), 565
in payroll outsourcing, 425
physical structure, 565–566, 588
regional ISPs, 565–566
standards, 566–568, 588
URL, 566–567
as WWW backbone, 563
Internet EDI. *See also* Electronic data interchange (EDI)
defined, 583
internal controls, 318, 383
traditional EDI versus, 584
VAN versus, 584
XML in, 583–585
Interviews, 215
Intranets
in circulating payroll information, 425
defined, 14, 580
in e-business enablement, 580–581, 589
internal controls, 581–582, 589
Intrusion detection, 128, 384
Inventory
control function, 463–465
finished goods, 464
items, 356
periodic systems, 470
perpetual systems, 469–470
physical count, 472
physical reconciliation, 472
raw materials, 464
status reports, 464–465
stores function, 464
theft, 84
warehousing, 465
work-in-process, 464
Investment processes. *See also* Administrative processes
defined, 498
internal controls, 516
overview, 516
process map, 499
unethical behaviors, 513–514

Investors, as stakeholders, 174
Invoices, filing of, 371
IT administration controls, testing, 253–254
IT auditors, 243
IT controls. *See also* Controls
  application, 20, 122, 146–152
  availability, 102–103
  confidentiality, 103
  data and database, 545, 550
  defined, 20
  general, 121, 122–137, 155
  introduction to, 120–122
  maintaining, 101–103, 104
  online privacy, 103
  processing integrity, 103
  security, 102
  term reference list, 167
  Trust Principles, 102
IT enablement
  BPR with, 10
  business process types, 9
  defined, 8
  e-business and, 574–580
  examples, 15–17, 25
  overview, 24
IT environments
  changes in, 265–266
  types of, 263–265
  unique characteristics, 271
IT governance, 21, 201–233
  board functions, 204
  defined, 203
  ethical considerations, 230–232, 233
  framework models, 103
  importance, 204, 228–229, 233
  introduction to, 202–206
  objectives, 230–232
  operation and maintenance, 207, 227–233, 233
  overview, 232
  SDLC, 129, 205, 206–209
  systems analysis, 207, 212–216
  systems design, 216–224
  systems implementation, 224–227
  systems planning, 207, 209–212, 232
IT governance committee
  defined, 205
  feasibility evaluation, 211–212
  proposed changes evaluations, 210
  proposed changes planning/oversight, 212
  software product selection, 218
IT outsourcing, 265
IT systems
  business process alignment with, 311
  control and risk matrix, 134
  with conversion processes, 473–476, 479
  critical nature, 120
  e-commerce, 310
  EDI, 311
  exposure areas, 138
  fixed asset processes, 437–438, 443
  hardware and software exposures, 137–145, 155–156
  knowledge about, 120
  matching to strategic objectives, 210
  payroll processes, 424–426, 443
  POS, 311

J
Journals
  cash disbursements, 371–372
  cash receipts, 302
  general, 44
  payroll disbursement, 420
  purchases, 351
  sales, 292, 502
  special, 44, 502
  voucher approval, 505
Just-in-time (JIT) production systems, 476

K
Keying
  hours worked, 511
  as input method, 50
Kickbacks, 84, 85

L
Labeling interchanges, 315
LANs, 14
Larceny, 84
"Leaving sales open," 321
Legacy systems
  advantages, 45
  batch processing, 53
  defined, 44–45
  disadvantages, 45
  enterprise application integration (EAI), 46
  replacement, 46
  screen scrapers, 46
  technology, 45
Letters of representation, 262
Liabilities
  for goods received, 356
  recording, 355–356
  understating, 83
Liability and inventory receipt, 356
Limit check, 151
Local area networks (LANs)
  auditor understanding, 264
  defined, 143
  exposure, 143
Local ISPs, 566
Location-wise implementation (ERP system), 615
Log-in, 123
Logistics function. *See also* Conversion processes
  capital budgeting, 461
  components, 460–469, 478
  components illustration, 461
  defined, 460
  engineering, 461–462
  human resources, 463
  inventory control, 463–464
  inventory status reports, 464–465
  maintenance and control, 463
  operations, 465–469
  planning, 460–463
  production orders, 463
  production schedule, 463
  quality control, 468–469
  research and development, 461
  resource management, 463–465
  rework, 469
  routing, 464
  scheduling, 462–463
Loss of audit trail visibility, 244

M
Magnetic tape, 529
Maintenance and control, 463
Management
  earnings, 179
  earnings tactic, 440
  internal controls evaluation, 184–185
  operating style, 93–94
  privacy practices, 573
  in raising capital, 498

risk assessment and, 94
as stakeholders, 173
stewardship, 79
strategic, 203
unethical, 78
Management assertions
defined, 246
list of, 247
summary, 270
Management fraud. *See also* Fraud
characteristics, 83
defined, 82
examples, 83–84
nature of, 104
types of, 83
Management override, 83
Management oversight. *See also* Corporate governance
accounting information systems Sarbanes–Oxley Act impact, 186
defined, 175
examples, 176
Manual systems
data processing, 52
general journal, 44
general ledger, 44, 505
source documents, 43
special journals, 44
subsidiary ledgers, 44
turnaround documents, 43
Manufacturing resource planning (MRP-II)
defined, 475, 599
purpose, 601
Many-to-many relationships, 532
Master files, 11
Matching
automated, 377–380
document, 375–377
invoiceless system, 380
Materiality, 249
Materials resource planning (MRP), 475, 601
Mathematical accuracy tests, 257
Microsoft Dynamics GP®
bill of materials preparation, 462
credit limit, 292
general ledger posting, 508
list price of inventory items, 291
payments, 372
payroll register preparation, 419
purchase orders in, 355
purchase receipts in, 356
purchase returns in, 364
transaction modules, 504
MiniScribe, 321, 322
Misappropriation of assets, 80
Misstatement of financial records, 80
Modular implementation (ERP system), 615
Monitoring, 19, 100
Multidimensional online analytical processing (MOLAP), 540

N

Network access points (NAPs), 565
Network break-ins
general controls, 125–128
risks, 136
Network databases, 534
Networks
defined, 14
LANs, 143, 264
VANs, 315, 561, 583, 584
VPNs, 127, 136
WANs, 143, 264
wireless, 126, 143–144
Nonaudit services, 182
Nonrepudiation, 124
Normalized data
defined, 537
need, 535–538, 549

O

Objectives, setting, 19
Observation, 214
Off-site backup, 132
One-to-many relationships, 532
One-to-one relationships, 532
Online analytical processing (OLAP)
analytical methods, 542
defined, 542
multidimensional (MOLAP), 540
relational (ROLAP), 540
use of, 550
Online privacy
application, 133
ERP system, 618
Trust Services Principles, 103, 132
Online privacy practices, 547
Online processing. *See also* Processing
defined, 12
random access files, 13
uses, 54
Operating system
access, 139–140
application software versus, 140
defined, 139
risks, 141
Operation and maintenance. *See also* System development life cycle (SDLC)
defined, 207
elements of, 233
IT performance reports, 227
Operational audits, 243
Operational databases
defined, 13, 538
ERP system, 600
Operational feasibility, 211, 221
Operations
defined, 465
lists, 461
performance methods, 465
personnel, 129
quality control, 468–469
rework, 469
Oracle, 608
Organization charts
defined, 413
illustrated, 414
Organizational structure, 128–129, 413
Organizations
code of ethics, 20
control environment, 17–21
corporate governance, 20–21
types of, 41
Output controls. *See also* Application controls
authentication, 154
defined, 146
test of, 260
Outputs. *See also* Reports
categories, 55
detailed design, 222
general ledger processes, 510–512
manipulation, computer fraud, 87
screen, 153–154
summary, 66
types of, 55

P
Packet switching, 562
Packing slips, 291, 355
Paper documents, 42
Parallel conversion, 226
Parallel simulation, 258, 259
Passwords
  defined, 123
  SSID, 127
Paymaster, 421
Payments
  BPR in, 377
  electronic forms, 377
  evaluated receipt settlement, 381
  invoice, 371
  Microsoft Dynamics GP®, 372
Payroll
  batch processing, 54, 424
  department, 420
  electronic transfer of funds, 425
  fraud, 84, 439
  outsourcing, 425
  tax deposits, 425
  voucher, 420
Payroll disbursements journals, 420
Payroll processes
  adequate records/documents, 422
  authorization of transactions, 421
  controls, 423, 443
  corporate governance, 441–442
  cost-benefit considerations, 423
  data flow diagram (DFD), 418
  defined, 411
  document flowchart, 417
  ethical issues, 438–441, 443
  independent checks and reconciliation, 422
  initiation, 412
  introduction to, 410–412
  IT systems of, 424–426, 443
  overview, 443
  paycheck computation, 418
  payroll disbursements journal, 420
  payroll register, 419–420
  personnel file, 415
  process map, 416
  risks, 411, 424, 443
  security of assets/documents, 422
  segregation of duties, 421
  time sheet, 415, 418
Payroll registers
  defined, 419
  in Microsoft Dynamics GP®, 419
  preparation, 419–420
  reconciliation, 422
Penetration testing, 128, 255, 384
Peoplesoft, 608–609
Periodic depreciation schedules, 431
Periodic inventory system, 470
Perpetual inventory system, 469–470
Personal computers (PCs), 263–264
Personnel files, 415
Phase-in conversion, 226
Physical environment, general controls, 129–131
Physical inventory count, 472
Physical inventory reconciliation, 472
Pick lists, 291
Pilot conversion, 226–227
Pivoting, 542
Planning (logistics function)
  capital budgeting, 461
  defined, 460
  engineering, 461–462
  production orders, 463
  production schedule, 463
  research and development, 461
  scheduling, 462–463
Point of sale (POS) systems, 15–16
  defined, 15, 51, 311, 319
  examples, 320
  features, 319
  as input method, 51–52
  risks, 319–320
  uses, 52
Post-implementation review, 227
Preliminary investigation, 212–213
Preventative controls, 92
Price lists, 287
Primary keys, 535
Privacy protection. *See also* E-commerce
  overview, 588
  practices, 573
  Trust Services Principles, 572
Problems, this book
  administrative processes/controls, 521
  auditing IT-based processes, 277–278
  conversion processes/controls, 484–485
  corporate governance, 197–198
  data and databases, 554–555
  e-business and e-commerce, 593
  ERP systems, 624–625
  expenditure processes/controls, 396–398
  foundation concepts, 73–74
  fraud, ethics, and internal control, 111–113
  internal controls/risks in IT systems, 161–163
  introduction to AIS, 29
  IT governance, 237–238
  payroll and fixed asset processes/controls, 448–450
  revenue and cash collection processes/controls, 330–336
Process maps. *See also* Documenting systems
  accounting cycle, 501
  cash collection process, 303
  cash disbursement process, 368
  defined, 56
  fixed asset acquisition, 427
  fixed asset disposal, 432
  illustrated, 57, 59
  investment process, 499
  payroll process, 416
  production process, 466
  purchase return process, 361
  purchasing process, 352
  sales process, 288
  sales return process, 297
  source of capital process, 497
  symbols, 56
Processing
  automated, 52–54
  batch, 12–13, 53–54
  in manual systems, 52
  methods, 52–54
  online, 12–13, 54
  real-time, 12–13, 54
Processing controls. *See also* Application controls
  computer logs, 153
  defined, 146, 152
  run-to-run control totals, 153
  test of, 256–259
Processing integrity
  e-business, 312
  EDI, 317
  ERP system, 617
  Trust Services Principles, 103, 132

Processing integrity risks
automated matching, 379
business continuity, 137
defined, 135
e-business (expenditures), 384
e-business (revenue), 313–314
environmental factors, 136
evaluated receipt settlement, 382
Procurement and logistics module (ERP), 606
Procurement cards (p-cards)
defined, 386
summary, 391
Product development and manufacturing module (ERP), 606
Production orders, 463
Production process
conducting, 465
data flow diagram (DFD), 468
document flowchart, 467
planning, 465
process map, 466
quality control, 468–469
rework, 469
Production schedules, 463
Professional skepticism, 268
Program manipulation, computer fraud, 87
Program tracing, 258, 259
Programmers, 129
Proprietary data, 548
Protocols
defined, 562
TCP/IP, 563
Public Company Accounting Oversight Board (PCAOB), 245
Public key encryption, 126
Purchase orders (POs)
blind, 354
defined, 287, 351
in Microsoft Dynamics GP®, 355
Purchase receipts, 356
Purchases
electronic forms, 377
journals, 351
requisitions, 351
returns, 364
Purchasing processes
accounts payable subsidiary ledger, 356
adequate records/documents, 358
authorization of transactions, 357
bill of lading, 355
blind purchase orders, 354
controls, 359–360
cost-benefit considerations, 358–359
data flow diagram (DFD), 354
defined, 349
document flowchart, 353
independent checks and reconciliation, 358
initiation, 380
packing slip, 355
process map, 352
purchase order (PO), 351
purchase requisition, 351
purchases journal, 351
receiving log, 355
receiving report, 355
risks, 359–360
security of assets/documents, 358
segregation of duties, 357–358
summary, 389
Purchasing return process
adequate records and documents, 365
authorization of transactions, 365
controls, 366–367
cost-benefit considerations, 366
data flow diagram (DFD), 363
debit memo, 363
document flowchart, 362
independent checks and reconciliation, 365–366
process map, 361
reasons for, 360
risks, 366–367
segregation of duties, 365
summary, 389–390
unacceptable goods, 360

Q
Qualified opinion reports, 263
Quality control, 468
Questionnaires, 215

R
Random access, 529
Random access files
defined, 12
online processing, 13
Range check, 151
Raw materials, 464
Real-time processing. *See also* Processing
advantages, 54, 530
batch processing versus, 549
defined, 12–13, 529–530
determining, 530
disadvantages, 54, 530
requirements, 54
Reasonable assurance, 98
defined, 101
of internal controls, 100–101
Reasonableness check, 151
Reasonableness tests, 260
Recalculation of amounts, 99
Receiving logs, 296, 355
Receiving reports, 296, 355
Reconciliation
as business process, 4
cash collection process, 307
cash disbursement process, 374
conversion process, 471–472
defined, 98
fixed asset process, 435–436
general ledger process, 509–510
payroll process, 422
physical inventory, 472
purchasing process, 358
purchase return process, 365–366
sales process, 294
sales return process, 300
Record counts, 152
Record pointers, 533
Records
accounts payable, 370
attributes, 533
defined, 11, 528
internal controls as protection, 91
many-to-many relationships, 532
one-to-many relationships, 532
one-to-one relationships, 532
physical asset comparison with, 98
tampering with, 185
Records, adequate
cash collection process, 306
cash disbursement process, 373
conversion process, 471
fixed asset process, 435
general ledger process, 509
importance, 96–98
payroll process, 422

Records, adequate (*continued*)
  purchasing process, 358
  purchase return process, 365
  sales process, 293–294
  sales return process, 299–300
Redundant arrays of independent disks (RAIDs), 131, 385
Redundant servers, 131, 314
Refund fraud, 86
Regional ISPs, 565–566
Relational database management systems (RDBMS), 612–613
Relational databases. *See also* Databases
  defined, 11, 534–535
  illustrated, 535
  use of, 535
Relational online analytical processing (ROLAP), 540
Remittance advice, 302, 371
Reports
  accounting cycle, 97
  accurate, 321
  adverse opinion, 263
  analysis of, 99
  certification failure, 184
  corporate governance and, 515–516
  corporate responsibility, 183–184
  cost accounting, 469, 478
  disclaimer, 263
  ethics and, 513–515
  exception, 542
  external, 55, 511
  generation work steps, 5
  inputs, 222–223
  internal, 55, 511–512
  inventory status, 464–465
  IT performance, 227
  periodic, disclosures, 184
  qualified opinion, 263
  receiving, 355
  systems analysis, 216
  unqualified opinion, 263
  verification failure, 184
Request for proposals (RFPs), 217–218
Research and development, 461
Resource management
  EOQ, 464
  human resources, 463
  inventory control, 463–464
  inventory status reports, 464–465
  inventory stores function, 464
  inventory warehousing, 465
  maintenance and control, 463
  routing, 464
Resources events agents (REA)
  in AIS, 67–69
  defined, 67–68
  development, 69
  example pattern, 68
  practical application, 69
Revenue processes
  corporate governance, 323–324, 325
  cost-benefit considerations, 294
  EDIT with, 315–316
  ethical issues, 320–333, 325
  independent checks, 294
  IT-enabled systems, 309–311, 324–325
  in overall system, 285
  overview, 324
  purchasing processes comparison, 350
  sales, 287–295, 324
  sales return, 296–301, 324
  system flowchart, 310
  types of, 3, 286
Revenues, overstating, 83, 321
Rework, 469
Risk assessment
  defined, 19, 94
  management and, 94
Risk response, 19
Risks
  automated matching, 379
  availability, 135, 136, 137, 314–315
  business continuity, 137
  cash disbursement process, 374–375
  cash receipts process, 308
  categories, 102–103
  confidentiality, 135, 137, 313
  controls, 317–318
  conversion process, 473, 478–479
  defined, 249
  e-business (expenditures), 383–385
  e-business systems, 313–318
  EDI, 317–318
  from environmental factors, 136
  ERP system, 617–618, 620
  evaluated receipt settlement, 382
  fixed asset process, 411, 436, 443
  general ledger process, 510, 517
  from hacking/network break-ins, 136
  information, 244–245, 270
  in not limiting unauthorized users, 133–135
  operating system, 141
  payroll process, 411, 423, 443
  physical access, 137
  POS systems, 319–320
  processing integrity, 135, 136, 137, 313–314
  purchasing process, 359–360
  purchase return process, 366–367
  reduction categories, 17–18
  sales process, 295
  sales return process, 301
  security, 133, 136, 137, 264–265
Rounding error tests, 260
Routers, 562
Routing, 464
Routing slips, 464
Run-to-run control totals, 153, 257

S

Salami technique, 87
Sales allowance, 300–301
Sales and services module (ERP), 606
Sales invoices, 291
Sales journals
  columns, 502
  defined, 292
Sales orders, 287
Sales processes
  adequate records and documents, 293–294
  authorization of transactions, 293
  bill of lading, 291
  controls, 295
  cost-benefit considerations, 294–295
  credit limit, 287
  data flow diagram, (DFD), 290
  document flowchart, 289
  independent checks and reconciliation, 294
  packing slip, 291
  pick list, 291
  price list, 287
  process map, 288
  purchase order, 287
  risks, 295
  sales invoice, 291
  sales journal, 292
  sales order, 287

security of assets/documents, 294
segregation of duties, 293
shipping log, 291
summary, 324
Sales returns, 286
Sales returns processes
adequate records and documents, 299–300
authorization of transactions, 296
controls, 301
cost-benefit considerations, 300–301
credit memorandum, 296
data flow diagram (DFD), 299
document flowchart, 298
independent checks and reconciliation, 300
process map, 297
receiving log, 296
receiving report, 296
risks, 301
sales allowance, 300–301
security of assets/documents, 300
segregation of duties, 296–299
summary, 324
Sales transactions
daily, 286
processes, 286
recording, 292
Salvage values, 440
Sampling, 266
SAP, 608
Sarbanes–Oxley Act, 89–90, 106
application, 180–181
code of ethics for senior financial officers, 185
corporate responsibility for financial reports, 183–184
CPA restrictions, 267–268
criminal penalties for altering documents, 185
defined, 180
disclosures in periodic reports, 184
ERP systems and, 618–619, 620–621
ethical conduct, 188–189
failure of corporate officers to certify financial reports, 184
financial stewardship, 188
impact on corporate governance, 186–189, 193
internal controls and compliance, 186–187
key provisions summary, 181
management assessment of internal controls, 184–185
management oversight, 186
nonaudit services, 182
overview, 192–193
protection for employees, 185
public company audit committees, 183
real-time disclosures, 185
Section 201, 182–183
Section 301, 183
Section 302, 183–184
Section 401, 184
Section 404, 184–185
Section 406, 185
Section 409, 185
Section 802, 185
Section 806, 185
Section 906, 184
Section 1102, 185
services outside the scope of practice of auditors, 182–183
tampering with records, 185
titles, 181
SAS 94, 251
Schedule feasibility, 211, 221
Scheduling
department, 462
personnel, 463
Screen scrapers, 46
Secure sockets layer (SSL), 127, 136, 568
Securities Act of 1933, 180
Securities and Exchange Commission (SEC), 79, 174
Security
controls, testing, 254–256
e-business, 312
e-commerce privacy practices, 573
EDI, 317
ERP system, 617
general controls, 129–131
general ledger, 509
Trust Services Principles, 102, 132
Security of assets/documents
cash collection process, 306–307
cash disbursement process, 373
conversion process, 471
defined, 98
fixed asset process, 435
payroll process, 422
purchasing process, 358
purchase return process, 365
sales process, 294
sales return process, 300
Security risks
automated matching, 379
backup data access, 137
e-business (expenditures), 383–384
e-business (revenue), 313
e-commerce, 264–265
evaluated receipt settlement, 382
hacking, 136
unauthorized access, 133
Security tokens, 123
Segregation of duties
cash collection process, 305–306
cash disbursement process, 373
conversion process, 470–471
defined, 96
ERP systems for, 619
fixed asset process, 435
general ledger process, 506–508
illustrated, 97
payroll process, 421
purchasing process, 357–358
purchase return process, 365
sales process, 293
sales return process, 296–299
Self-checking digits, 151, 152
Sequence check, 152
Sequential access, 529
Sequential access files
batch processing, 13
defined, 12
Servers
defined, 545
Web, 564
Service set identifiers (SSIDs), 127, 136
Shareholders, 172
Shipping logs, 291
Sign check, 151
Skimming, 84
Smart cards, 123
Software
antivirus, 127
application, 140, 145–154
data mining, 190
exposures, 137–145, 155–156
operating system, 140
piracy, 86
programming, 224
selection, 208–209
testing, 224–225

Software purchase
in-house design versus, 218
input screens, 223
process map, 217
RFPs, 217–218
Source documents
in audit trail, 150
controls, 147–150
defined, 43, 147
form authorization, 149–150
form design, 147–149
keying, 50, 150
Sources of capital processes. *See also* Administrative processes
defined, 497
internal control, 516
overview, 516
process map, 497
unethical behaviors, 513–514
Spatelli's Pizzeria case, 75, 198
administrative processes, 522
auditing, 279
background, 33–34
conversion processes, 489–490
data and databases, 556
ERP system, 626
expenditures processes, 404–405
fixed assets, 453–454
Internet orders, 595
Internet risks/controls, 164
introduction, 32–33
IT governance, 239
multiple systems, functions, uses of information, 34–37
payroll processes, 453
sales and cash collection processes, 343–344
Special journals. *See also* Journals
defined, 44, 502
illustrated, 502
transaction recording in, 503
Specific authorization, 95, 96
Spoofing, 89
Stakeholders
audit committee, 173
board of directors, 172–173
communities, 174
as corporate governance participants, 171, 172
creditors, 175
customers and suppliers, 175
defined, 171
employees, 173
external, 171, 174–175
external auditors, 174
governing bodies, 174
internal, 171, 172–173
internal auditors, 173
investors, 174
management team, 173
shareholders, 172
Standard costs, 469
Statements on Auditing Standards (SAS), 105
Stewardship
characteristics, 178–179
defined, 79, 230
earnings management and, 179
Sarbanes–Oxley Act impact, 188
Strategic management
defined, 203
SDLC in, 228
Structured query language (SQL)
of complex query, 536
defined, 535
Subsidiary ledgers
defined, 44, 502
illustrated, 503
Substantive testing, 260
Summary information, 42
Sunbeam, 322
Suppliers
influencing, 8
as stakeholders, 175
Supply chain
business processes in, 6–8
defined, 7, 574
entity interdependency, 576
example, 7
illustrated, 8, 575
management, 8
overview, 24
understanding, 574
Supply chain management (SCM) module, 603, 607
Symmetric encryption, 126
System conversion
direct cutover, 226
parallel, 226
phase-in, 226
pilot, 226–227
System development life cycle (SDLC). *See also* IT governance
defined, 129, 205, 206
illustrated, 206
as internal control, 228–229
operation and maintenance, 207
overview, 206–209, 232
phases, 206–207, 209
process map, 208
in strategic management, 228
systems analysis, 207, 213–216, 232–233
systems design, 207, 216–224, 233
systems implementation, 207, 224–227, 233
systems planning, 207, 209–212, 232
System flowcharts. *See also* Documenting systems
defined, 57
illustrated, 59
symbols, 58
uses, 57–58
System survey
analysis of, 215–216
data collection, 214
data requirements, 214
defined, 213–214
Systems analysis. *See also* System development life cycle (SDLC)
defined, 207
elements of, 232–233
preliminary investigation, 212–213
process map, 213
report, 216
system survey, 213–214
system survey analysis, 215–216
user requirements determination, 214–215
Systems analysts, 129
Systems design. *See also* System development life cycle (SDLC)
conceptual design, 208, 219
defined, 207
detailed design, 209, 222–224
elements of, 233
evaluation and selection, 208, 220–222
in-house design, 218–219
process map, 208
software purchase, 216–218
software selection, 208–209
steps, 216

Systems implementation. *See also* System development life cycle (SDLC)
data conversion, 226
defined, 207
elements of, 233
employee training, 224
post-implementation review, 227
process map, 225
software programming, 224
software testing, 224–225
system conversion, 226–227
system documentation, 225–226
user acceptance, 227
Systems planning. *See also* System development life cycle (SDLC)
defined, 207
elements of, 232
as managerial function, 209
matching to strategic objectives, 210
process map, 210

T
TCP/IP (transmission control protocol/Internet protocol), 563
Technical feasibility, 211, 220–221
Telecommuting
defined, 144
exposure, 144–145
Test data method, 258
Tests
audit trail, 260
authenticity, 255
of balances, 257, 260–262, 270
DAS, 262
GAS, 262
mathematical accuracy, 257
penetration, 255, 384
reasonableness, 260
rounding error, 260
substantive, 260
of transactions, 260–262, 270
vulnerability, 255, 384
Tests of controls
application controls, 256–260
defined, 252
general controls, 253–256
input controls, 256
IT administration controls, 253–254
output controls, 260
process map, 253
processing controls, 256–259
security controls, 254–256
summary, 270
Three-way matches, 375
Time clocks, 424
Time series analysis, 542
Time sheets
approval, 418
defined, 415
employee submission, 418
fraud, 439
supervisory review, 439
Tone at the top, 171, 386
Totals
batch, 152
control, 152, 318
hash, 152
run-to-run, 153, 257
Trading partner documents, 55
Trailer data, 315
Training employees, 224
Transaction authorization
cash collection process, 302–305
cash disbursement process, 372–373
conversion process, 470
fixed asset process, 434–435
general ledger process, 504–506
payroll process, 421
purchasing process, 357
purchase return process, 365
sales process, 293
sales return process, 296
Transaction logging, 318
Transaction processing systems (TPS), 348
Transactions
B2B, 577–578
fixed assets, 411
interrelationships, 41, 42
irregular, 502
payroll, 411
recording in special journals, 503
recurring, 502
sales, 286, 292
tests of, 260–262, 270
tracing, 509
Transparency, 177
Trap door alteration, 87
Treadway Commission, 174
Trojan horse program, 87
Trust Services Principles
availability, 102–103
confidentiality, 103
defined, 102
e-commerce privacy expectations, 572
general control perspective, 132–137, 155
illustrated, 229
online privacy, 103
online privacy practices, 547
processing integrity, 103
reference list for IT control terms, 167
security, 102
Turnaround documents, 43
Two factor authentication, 124

U
Underwriters, 498
Unethical behaviors
accountant potential, 23–24, 65
in administrative processing, 513
in capital sources, 513–514
computers and, 155
in investing, 513–514
management and, 78
Uninterruptible power supply (UPS), 130
U.S. Patriot Act, 180
Unqualified opinion reports, 263
URL (uniform resource locators)
defined, 566
domain name, 568
IP addresses, 568
USB security tokens, 123
Useful lives, 440
User acceptance, 227
User IDs, 123
User profiles, 124
Users
authentication of, 123–125
requirements determination, 214–215
unauthorized, risks in not limiting, 133

V
Validity check, 122, 151
Value-added networks (VANs)
defined, 315
fees, 583
Internet EDI versus, 584
use of, 561

Variances, 470
Vendor audits, 86
Vendor fraud, 86, 104
Vendors
companies as, 348
defined, 7
multiple invoicing and, 378
perspective, 348–349
purchase returns and, 364
Virtual private networks (VPNs), 127, 136
Viruses, 127
Voucher system, 370
Vulnerability assessments, 128, 255
Vulnerability testing, 384

W
Warehousing, inventory, 465
Web servers
defined, 566
growth chart, 564
What-if simulations, 542
Whistleblowers, 185
Wide area networks (WANs)
auditor understanding, 264
defined, 143
exposure, 143
Wired equivalency privacy (WEP), 126, 136
Wireless networks
encryption, 126
exposure, 143–144
Wireless protected access (WPA), 126, 136
Work-in-process inventory, 464
World Wide Web (WWW). *See also* Internet; Web servers
Internet as backbone, 563

X
XBRL (eXtensible Business Reporting Language)
defined, 583
for financial statement reporting, 585–586
implementation, 585
overview, 589
XML (eXtensible Markup Language)
defined, 583
in Internet EDI, 583–585
as metalanguage, 585
overview, 589
as tagged data format, 585

Y
Y2K compatibility, 602